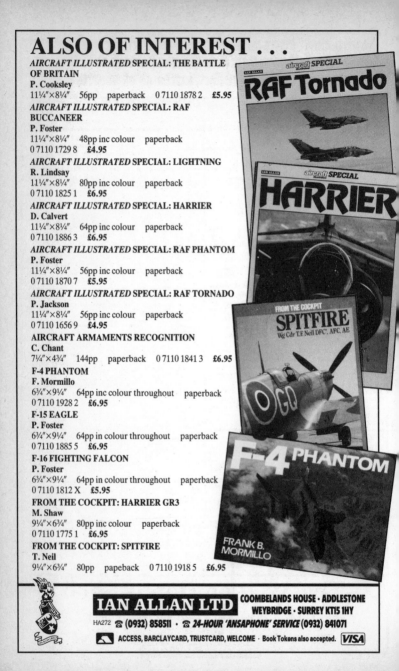

# MILITARY AIRCRAFT MARKINGS 1991

PETER R. MARCH

LONDON

IAN ALLAN LTD

## Contents



*Photographs by Peter R. March (PRM) unless otherwise credited*

This twelfth edition published 1991

ISBN 0 7110 1968 1



Published by Ian Allan Ltd
and phototypeset and printed by Ian Allan Printing Ltd at its works
at Coombelands in Runnymede, England

*Cover:* RAF in the Gulf – a mixed formation of pink Jaguars and Tornado (foreground) photographed during the Gulf War by Mike Rondot.

# Introduction

This twelfth edition of *abc Military Aircraft Markings*, a companion to *abc Civil Aircraft Markings*, again sets out to list in alphabetical and numerical order all the aircraft which carry a United Kingdom military serial, and which are based, or might be seen, in the UK. The term 'aircraft' used here covers powered, manned aeroplanes, helicopters and gliders. Included are all the current Royal Air Force, Royal Navy, Army Air Corps, Ministry of Defence (Procurement Executive), manufacturers' test aircraft and civilian-owned aircraft with military markings, together with gliders of the services' gliding associations.

Aircraft withdrawn from operational use but which are retained in the UK for ground training purposes or otherwise preserved by the Services and in museums and collections are listed. The serials of some incomplete aircraft have been included, such as the cockpit sections of machines displayed by the RAF Exhibition Flight, aircraft used by airfield fire sections and for service battle damage repair training (BDRT), together with significant parts of aircraft held by preservation groups and societies. Many of these aircraft are allocated, and sometimes wear, a secondary identity, such as an RAF Support Command 'M' or a Royal Navy 'A' maintenance number. These numbers are listed against those aircraft to which they have been allocated, and cross-references are included.

A serial 'missing' is either because it was never issued as it formed part of a 'black-out block', or because the aircraft is written off, scrapped, sold, abroad or allocated an alternative marking. Aircraft used as targets on MoD ranges to which access is restricted, and un-manned target drones, are omitted.

In the main, the serials listed are those markings presently displayed on the aircraft. Aircraft which bear a **false** serial are quoted in *italic* type. The manufacturer and aircraft type are given, together with recent alternative, previous, secondary or civil identity shown in *round* brackets. Complete records of multiple previous identities are only included where space permits. The operating unit and its based location, along with any known unit and base code markings in *square* brackets, are given as accurately as possible. The unit markings are normally carried boldly on the sides of the fuselage or on the aircraft's fin. In the case of RAF and AAC machines currently in service, they are usually one or two letters or numbers, while the RN continues to use a well-established system of three-figure codes between 000 and 999 together with a fin letter code denoting the aircraft's operational base. RN squadrons, units and bases are allocated blocks of numbers from which individual aircraft codes are issued. To help identification of RN bases and landing platforms on ships, a list of tail-letter codes with their appropriate name, helicopter code number, ship pennant number and type of vessel is included; as is a helicopter code number/ships' tail-letter code grid cross-reference.

Codes change, for example when aircraft move between units, and therefore the markings currently painted on a particular aircraft might not be those shown in this edition because of subsequent events. At the time of preparing this edition many Tornado GR1s/F3s, Jaguar GR1As, Pumas, Chinooks and Sea Kings are changing bases, units and markings because of their involvement in *Operation Granby* in the Gulf region. Those airframes which may not appear in the next edition because of sale, accident, etc, have their fates, where known, given in italic type in the 'Locations' column.

The guide to the location of operational bases of military aircraft in the UK, compiled by Wal Gandy, includes all RAF, RN, AAC, MoD(PE) and civil airfields at which the military aircraft listed are based or from where they regularly operate.

The Irish Army Air Corps fleet is listed, together with the serials of other overseas air arms whose aircraft might be seen visiting the UK from time to time. The serial numbers are as usually presented on the individual machine or as they are normally identified. Where possible, the aircraft's base and operating unit have been shown.

USAF, US Army and US Navy aircraft based in the UK and in Western Europe, and of types which regularly visit the UK from the USA, are each listed in separate sections by aircraft type. The serial number actually displayed on the aircraft is shown in full, with additional Fiscal Year (FY) or full serial information also provided. Where appropriate, details of the operating wing, squadron allocation and base are added.

Veteran and Vintage aircraft which carry overseas military markings but which are based in the UK have been separately listed showing the identity carried as a principal means of identification.

Information shown is believed to be correct at 31 January 1991, and significant changes can be monitored through the monthly 'Military Markings' column in *Aircraft Illustrated*.

**Acknowledgements**

The compiler wishes to thank the many people who have taken trouble to send comments, criticism and other useful information following the publication of the previous editions of *abc Military Aircraft Markings*. In particular the following correspondents: D. Braithwaite, P. F. Burton, S. Bushell, P. H. Butler, J. R. Cross, D. P. Curtis, P. Moonen, M. C. Powney, L. P. Robinson, P. Robinson, M. K. Thompson, B. Williamson.

This compilation has relied heavily on the publications of the following aviation groups and societies: *Air North, British Aviation Review* (British Aviation Research Group), *Clwyd Air Letter* (Clwyd Aviation Group), *Humberside Air Review* (Humberside Aviation Society), *Norfolk Air Review* (Norfolk Aviation Group), *North-West Air News* (Air Britain, Merseyside), *Osprey* (Solent Aviation Society), *Prestwick Airport Letter* (Prestwick Airport Aviation Group), *Scotland Scanned* & *Scottish Air News* (Central Scotland Aviation Group), *Stansted Aviation Newsletter* (The Stansted Aviation Society), *Strobe* (The East of England Aviation Group), *Ulster Airmail* (Ulster Aviation Society), together with *Wrecks and Relics XII* (Midland Counties Publications).

The new edition of *abc Military Aircraft Markings* would not have been possible without considerable research and checking by Howard Curtis, Wal Gandy, Alison March and Brian Strickland to whom I am indebted.

**PRM**

# Abbreviations

**AAC** Army Air Corps
**A&AEE** Aeroplane & Armament Experimental Establishment
**AAS** Aeromedical Airlift Squadron
**ABS** Air Base Squadron
**ABW** Air Base Wing
**ACCGS** Air Cadets Central Gliding School
**ACCS** } Airborne Command and Control
**ACCW** } Squadron/Wing
**ACR** Armoured Cavalry Regiment
**AEF** Air Experience Flight
**AES** Air Engineering School
**AEW** Airborne Early Warning
**AFRES** Air Force Reserve
**AFSC** Air Force System Command
**AHB** Attack Helicopter Battalion
**AIU** Accident Investigation Unit
**AKG** Aufklarüngs Geschwader (Reconnaissance Wing)
**AMD-BA** Avions Marcel Dassault-Breguet Aviation
**AMG** Aircraft Maintenance Group
**AMS** Air Movements School
**ANG** Air National Guard
**APS** Aircraft Preservation Society
**ARF** Aircraft Restoration Flight
**ARG** Air Refuelling Group
**ARRS** } Aerospace Rescue and Recovery
**ARRW** } Squadron/Wing
**ARS** Air Refuelling Squadron
**ARW** Air Refuelling Wing
**ARWS** Advanced Rotary Wing Squadron
**AS** Aggressor Squadron
**ASF** Aircraft Servicing Flight
**AS&RU** Aircraft Salvage and Repair Unit
**ATC** Air Training Corps
**ATCC** Air Traffic Control Centre
**ATS** Aircrewman Training Squadron
**AvCo** Aviation Company
**AW** Armstrong Whitworth Aircraft/ Aircraft Workshops
**AW&CS** } Airborne Warning & Control Squadron/
**AW&CW** } Wing
**BAC** British Aircraft Corporation
**BAe** British Aerospace Company
**BAOR** British Army of the Rhine
**BAPC** British Aircraft Preservation Council
**BATUS** British Army Training Unit Support
**BBMF** Battle of Britain Memorial Flight
**BDRF** Battle Damage Repair Flight
**BDRT** Battle Damage Repair Training
**BDRTF** Battle Damage Repair Training Flight
**Be** Beech
**Bf** Bayerische Flugzeugwerke
**BFME** British Forces Middle East
**BFWF** Basic Fixed Wing Flight
**BGA** British Gliding & Soaring Association
**BHC** British Hovercraft Corporation
**BNFL** British Nuclear Fuels Ltd
**BP** Boulton & Paul
**B-V** Boeing-Vertol
**BW** Bomber Wing
**CARG** Cotswold Aircraft Restoration Group
**CASA** Construcciones Aeronautics SA
**CATCS** Central Air Traffic Control School
**CBAS** Commando Brigade Air Squadron
**CC** County Council
**CCF** Combined Cadet Force
**CDE** Chemical Defence Establishment
**CEAM** Centre d'Expériences Aériennes Militaires
**CEV** Centre d'Essais en Vol
**CFS** Central Flying School
**CGMF** Central Glider Maintenance Flight
**CinC** Commander in Chief
**Co** Company
**CSDE** Central Servicing Development Establishment
**CTE** Central Training Establishment
**CTTS** Civilian Technical Training School
**CV** Chance-Vought
**EHI** European Helicopter Industries
**D-BD** Dassault-Breguet Dornier
**Det** Detachment
**DH** de Havilland
**DHC** de Havilland Canada
**DTI** Department of Trade and Industry
**EABDR** Engineering and Battle Damage Repair
**ECS** } Electronic Countermeasures
**ECW** } Squadron/Wing
**EE** English Electric
**EFTS** Elementary Flying Training Squadron/Wing
**EMA** East Midlands Airport
**EoN** Elliot's of Newbury

**ETPS** Empire Test Pilots' School
**ETS** Engineering Training School
**EWAU** Electronics Warfare Avionics Unit
**FAA** Fleet Air Arm/Federal Aviation Administration
**FACF** Forward Air Control Flight
**FBS** Flugbereitschaftstaffel
**FBW** Fly by wire
**FCS** Facility Checking Squadron
**FE** Further Education
**FEWSG** Fleet Electronic Warfare Support Group
**FF&SS** Fire Fighting & Safety School
**FGF** Flying Grading Flight
**FH** Fairchild-Hiller
**FI** Falkland Islands
**FIS** Fighter Interceptor Squadron
**Flt** Flight
**FMA** Fabrica Militar de Aviones
**FOL** Forward Operating Location
**FONA** Flag Officer Aviation
**FRADU** Fleet Requirements and Air Direction Unit
**FRL** Flight Refuelling Ltd
**FRSB** Fleet Reserve Storage Base
**FSCTE** Fire School Central Training Establishment
**FTS** Flying Training School
**FW** Foster Wikner
**FY** Fiscal Year
**GAL** General Aircraft Ltd
**GD** General Dynamics
**HFR** Heeresfliegerregiment (Corps transport regiment)
**HFWS** Heeresflieger Waffenschule
**HMS** Her Majesty's Ship
**HP** Handley-Page
**HQ** Headquarters
**HS** Hawker Siddeley
**HSF**
**IAF** Israeli Air Force
**IAM** Institute of Aviation Medicine
**IHM** International Helicopter Museum
**IWM** Imperial War Museum
**IWTU**
**JATE** Joint Air Transport Establishment
**JbG** Jagd Bomber Geschwader (Fighter Bomber Wing)
**JG** Jagd Geschwader (Fighter Wing)
**JMU** Jaguar Maintenance Unit
**JTU** Joint Trials Unit
**LOFTU** Lynx Operational Flying Trials Unit
**LTG** Luft Transport Geschwader (Air Transport Wing)
**LVG** Luftwaffen Versorgungs Geschwader (Air Force Maintenance Wing)
**MAC** Military Airlift Command
**MAG** Military Airlift Group
**MAAG** Military Air Advisory Group
**MAS** Military Airlift Squadron
**MAW** Military Airlift Wing
**McD** McDonnell Douglas
**MFG** Marine Flieger Geschwader (Naval Air Wing)
**MGSP** Mobile Glider Servicing Party
**MH** Max Holste
**MIB** Military Intelligence Battalion
**MIG** Mikoyan — Gurevich
**MoD(PE)** Ministry of Defence (Procurement Executive)
**Mod** Modified
**MR** Maritime Reconnaissance
**MRF** Meteorological Research Flight
**MS** Morane-Saulnier
**MU** Maintenance Unit
**NA** North American
**NACDS** Naval Air Command Driving School
**NAEWF** NATO Airborne Early Warning Force
**NAF** Naval Air Facility
**NASU** Naval Air Support Unit
**NE** North-East
**NHTU** Naval Hovercraft Trials Unit
**NI** Northern Ireland
**NIEF**
**NMSU** Nimrod Major Servicing Unit
**OCU** Operational Conversion Unit
**OEU** Operation Evaluation Unit
**OPITB** Offshore Petroleum Industry Training Board
**OTD** Overseas Training Division
**OTS** Operational Training Squadron
**PAX** Passenger procedural trainer
**PRU** Photographic Reconnaissance Unit
**RAE** Royal Aerospace Establishment
**RAeS** Royal Aeronautical Society
**RAF** Royal Aircraft Factory/Royal Air Force
**RAFC** Royal Air Force College
**RAFGSA** Royal Air Force Gliding and Soaring Association
**RAOC** Royal Army Ordnance Corps
**RCAF** Royal Canadian Air Force
**RE** Royal Engineers
**REME** Royal Electrical & Mechanical Engineers
**RM** Royal Marines
**RMC of S** Royal Military College of Science
**RN** Royal Navy
**RNAS** Royal Naval Air Station
**RNAY** Royal Naval Aircraft Yard
**RNEC** Royal Naval Engineering College
**RNEFTS** Royal Naval Elementary Flying Training School
**RNGSA** Royal Navy Gliding and Soaring Association
**ROC** Royal Observer Corps
**ROF** Royal Ordnance Factory
**R-R** Rolls-Royce
**RS** Reid & Sigrist/Reconnaissance Squadron
**RS&RE** Royal Signals and Radar Establishment
**RSV** Reparto Sperimentale Volo
**RW** Reconnaissance Wing
**SA** Scottish Aviation
**Saab** Svenska Aeroplan Aktieboleg
**SAC** Strategic Air Command
**SAE** School of Aircraft Engineering
**SAH** School of Air Handling
**SAL** Scottish Aviation Limited
**SAOEU** Strike/Attack Operational Evaluation Unit
**SAR** Search and Rescue
**Saro** Saunders-Roe
**SAREW** Search & Rescue Engineering Wing
**SARTU** Search and Rescue Training Unit
**SCF** Scout Conversion Flight
**SEPECAT** Société Européenne de Production de l'avion Ecole de Combat et d'Appui Tactique
**SHAPE** Supreme Headquarters Allied Forces Europe
**SHSU** Sea Harrier Servicing Unit
**SIF** Servicing Instruction Flight
**SKTU** Sea King Training Unit
**SNCAN** Société Nationale de Constructions Aéronautiques du Nord
**SOS** Special Operations Squadron
**SoTT** School of Technical Training
**SPAD** Société Pour les Appareils Deperdussin
**Sqn** Squadron
**SRW** Strategic Reconnaissance Wing
**SSF** Station Servicing Flight
**SSTF** Small Ships Trials Flight
**SW** Strategic Wing
**TAS** Tactical Airlift Squadron
**TASS** Tactical Air Support Squadron
**TAW** Tactical Airlift Wing
**TCW** Tactical Control Wing
**TDCS** Tactical Deployment Control Squadron
**Tech Coll** Technical College

| | | | |
|---|---|---|---|
| **TFS** | Tactical Fighter Squadron | **UNFICYP** | United Nations' Forces in Cyprus |
| **TFW** | Tactical Fighter Wing | **US** | United States |
| **TMTS** | Trade Management Training School | **USAF** | United States Air Force |
| **TOCU** | Tornado Operational Conversion Unit | **USAFE** | United States Air Forces in Europe |
| **TRS** | Tactical Reconnaissance Squadron | **USAREUR** | US Army Europe |
| **TRW** | Tactical Reconnaissance Wing | **USEUCOM** | United States European Command |
| **TSLW** | Technische Schule der Luftwaffe | **USN** | United States Navy |
| **TTTE** | Tri-national Tornado Training Establishment | **VGS** | Volunteer Gliding School |
| **TW** | Test Wing | **VQ** | Air Reconnaissance Squadron |
| **TWCU** | Tornado Weapons Conversion Unit | **VR** | Logistic Support Squadron |
| **TWU** | Tactical Weapons Unit | **VS** | Vickers-Supermarine |
| **UAS** | University Air Squadron | **WLT** | Weapons Loading Training |
| **UK** | United Kingdom | **WRG** | Weather Reconnaissance Group |
| **UKAEA** | United Kingdom Atomic Energy Authority | **WRS** | Weather Reconnaissance Squadron |
| | | **WS** | Westland |
| | | **WW2** | World War II |

# British Military Aircraft Serials

The Committee of Imperial Defence through its Air Committee introduced a standardised system of numbering aircraft in November 1912. The Air Department of the Admiralty was allocated the first batch 1-200 and used these to cover aircraft already in use and those on order. The Army was issued with the next block from 201-800, which included the number 304 which was given to the Cody Biplane now preserved in the Science Museum. By the outbreak of World War 1 the Royal Navy was on its second batch of serials 801-1600 and this system continued with alternating allocations between the Army and Navy until 1916 when number 10000, a Royal Flying Corps BE2C, was reached.

It was decided not to continue with five digit numbers but instead to start again from 1, prefixing RFC aircraft with the letter A and RNAS aircraft with the prefix N. The RFC allocations commenced with A1 an FE2D and before the end of the year had reached A9999 an Armstrong Whitworth FK8. The next group commenced with B1 and continued in logical sequence through the C, D, E and F prefixes. G was used on a limited basis to identify captured German aircraft, while H was the last block of wartime-ordered aircraft. To avoid confusion I was not used, so the new postwar machines were allocated serials in the J range. A further minor change was made in the serial numbering system in August 1929 when it was decided to maintain four numerals after the prefix letter, thus omitting numbers 1 to 999. The new K series therefore commenced at K1000, which was allocated to an AW Atlas.

The Naval N prefix was not used in such a logical way. Blocks of numbers were allocated for specific types of aircraft such as seaplanes or flying-boats. By the late 1920s the sequence had largely been used up and a new series using the prefix S was commenced. In 1930 separate naval allocations were stopped and subsequent serials were issued in the 'military' range which had by this time reached the K series. A further change in the pattern of allocations came in the L range. Commencing with L7272 numbers were issued in blocks with smaller blocks of serials between not used. These were known as blackout blocks. As M had already been used as a suffix for Maintenance Command instructional airframes it was not used as a prefix. Although N had previously been used for naval aircraft it was used again for serials allocated from 1937.

With the build-up to World War 2 the rate of allocations quickly accelerated and the prefix R was being used when war was declared. The letters O and Q were not allotted, and nor was S which had been used up to S1865 for naval aircraft before integration into the RAF series. By 1940 the serial Z9999 had been reached, as part of a blackout block, with the letters U and Y not used to avoid confusion. The option to recommence serial allocation at A1000 was not taken up; instead it was decided to use an alphabetical two-letter prefix with three numerals running from 100 to 999. Thus AA100 was allocated to a Blenheim IV.

This two-letter, three-numeral serial system which started in 1940 continues today with the current issue being in the ZH range. The letters C, I, O, Q, U and Y were, with the exception of NC, not used. For various reasons the following letter combinations were not issued: DA, DB, DH, EA, GA to GZ, HA, HT, JE, JH, JJ, KR to KT, MR, NW, NZ, SA to SK, SV, TN, TR and VE. The first postwar serials issued were in the VP range while the end of the WZs had been reached by the Korean War. At the current rate of issue the Z range should last out the remainder of this century.

**Note:** Whilst every effort has been made to ensure the accuracy of this publication, no part of the contents has been obtained from official sources. The compiler will be pleased to continue to receive comments, corrections and further information for inclusion in subsequent editions of *Military Aircraft Markings.* A monthly up-date of additions and amendments is published in *Aircraft Illustrated.*

# British Military Aircraft Markings

A serial in *italics* denotes that it is not the genuine marking for that airframe.

| Serial | Type (alternative identity) | Owner, Operator or Location | Notes |
|---|---|---|---|
| *164* | Bleriot Type XI (BAPC 106) | RAF Museum, Hendon | |
| *168* | Sopwith Tabloid Scout Replica (G-BFDE) | RAF Museum, Hendon | |
| 304 | Cody Biplane (BAPC 62) | Science Museum, South Kensington | |
| *433* | Bleriot Type XXVII (BAPC 107) | RAF Museum, Hendon | |
| *542* | Sopwith Camel Replica (G-BPOB) | Privately owned, Booker | |
| 687 | RAF BE2b (BAPC 181) | RAF Museum Store, Cardington | |
| *2345* | Vickers FB5 Gunbus Replica (G-ATVP) | RAF Museum, Hendon | |
| 2699 | RAF BE2C | Imperial War Museum, Lambeth | |
| *3066* | Caudron GIII (G-AETA) | RAF Museum, Hendon | |
| *5492* | Sopwith LC-1T Triplane Replica (G-PENY) | Privately owned, Sywell | |
| *5844* | Avro 504K Replica (BAPC 42) | RAF Museum, stored St Athan | |
| *5894* | DH2 Replica (G-BFVH) [FB2] | Privately owned, Duxford | |
| *5964* | DH2 Replica (BAPC 112) | Museum of Army Flying, Middle Wallop | |
| *6232* | RAF BE2C Replica (BAPC 41) | RAF Museum, stored St Athan | |
| *8151* | Sopwith Baby Replica (BAPC 137) | Privately owned | |
| 8359 | Short 184 | FAA Museum, RNAS Yeovilton | |
| A1325 | RAF BE2e | Mosquito Aircraft Museum, London Colney | |
| *A1742* | Scout D Replica (BAPC 38) | RAF St Mawgan, stored | |
| *A4850* | RAF SE5A Replica (BAPC176) | South Yorkshire APS, Firbeck | |
| *A8226* | Sopwith 1½ Strutter Replica (G-BIDW) | RAF Museum, Hendon | |
| B1807 | Sopwith Pup (G-EAVX) [A7] | Privately owned, Keynsham, Avon | |
| *B4863* | Eberhardt SE5 (G-BLXT) [G] | Museum of Army Flying, Middle Wallop | |
| *B4863* | RAF SE5A Replica (BAPC 113) [G] | Privately owned | |
| B6291 | Sopwith Camel F1 (G-ASOP) | Museum of Army Flying, Middle Wallop | |
| *B6401* | Sopwith Camel F1 Replica (G-AWYY/C1701) | FAA Museum, RNAS Yeovilton | |
| *B7270* | Sopwith Camel F1 Replica (G-BFCZ) | Brooklands Aviation Museum | |
| *C1904* | RAF SE5A Replica (G-PFAP) [Z] | Privately owned, Syerston | |
| *C4912* | Bristol M1C Replica (BAPC 135) | Northern Aeroplane Workshops | |
| *C4994* | Bristol M1C Replica (G-BLWM) | RAF Museum Hendon | |
| *D3419* | Sopwith Camel F1 Replica (BAPC 59) | RAF, St Mawgan | |
| D5329 | Sopwith Dolphin | RAF Museum Store, Cardington | |
| D7560 | Avro 504K | Science Museum, South Kensington | |
| *D7889* | Bristol F2b Fighter (G-AANM/BAPC 166) | Privately owned, Sandy | |
| D8096 | Bristol F2B Fighter (G-AEPH) [D] | Shuttleworth Collection, Old Warden | |
| *E373* | Avro 504K Replica (BAPC178) | Privately owned, Eccleston, Lancs | |
| *E449* | Avro 504K (G-EBJE) | RAF Museum, Hendon | |
| *E2466* | Bristol F2b (BAPC165) | RAF Museum, Hendon | |
| E2581 | Bristol F2b Fighter | Imperial War Museum, Duxford | |
| *F141* | RAF SE5A Replica (G-SEVA) [G] | Privately owned, Boscombe Down | |
| *F235* | RAF SE5A Replica (G-BMDB) [B] | Privately owned, Boscombe Down | |
| *F344* | Avro 504K Replica | RAF Museum Store, Henlow | |
| *F760* | SE5A Microlight Replica [A] | Privately owned, Redhill | |
| F904 | RAF SE5A (G-EBIA) | Shuttleworth Collection, Old Warden | |
| F938 | RAF SE5A (G-EBIC) | RAF Museum, Hendon | |
| *F939* | RAF SE5A (G-EBIB/F937) [6] | Science Museum, South Kensington | |
| *F943* | RAF SE5A Replica (G-BIHF) [S] | Privately owned, Booker | |
| *F943* | RAF SE5A Replica (G-BKDT) | Privately owned, Elvington | |
| F1010 | DH9A [19] | RAF Museum, Hendon | |
| F3556 | RAF RE8 | Imperial War Museum, Duxford | |
| *F4013* | Sopwith Camel Replica | Privately owned, Coventry | |
| *F5447* | RAF SE5A Replica (G-BKER) [N] | Privately owned, Cumbernauld | |

| Notes | Reg. | Type | Owner or Operator |
|---|---|---|---|
| | *F5459* | RAF SE5A Replica (BAPC 142) [11-Y] | Cornwall Aero Park, Helston |
| | *F-5459* | RAF SE5A Replica (G-INNY) [Y] | Privately owned, Old Sarum |
| | F6314 | Sopwith Camel F1 [B] | RAF Museum, Hendon |
| | *F8010* | RAF SE5A Replica (G-BDWJ) [Z] | Privately owned, Booker |
| | *F8614* | Vickers Vimy Replica (G-AWAU) | RAF Museum, Hendon |
| | *G1381* | Avro 504K Replica [G] (BAPC 177) | Brooklands Museum, Weybridge |
| | H2311 | Avro 504K (G-ABAA) | Greater Manchester Museum of Science and Industry |
| | *H3426* | Hawker Hurricane Replica (BAPC 68) | Midland Air Museum, Coventry |
| | H5199 | Avro 504N (BK892, 3118M, G-ACNB, G-ADEV) | Shuttleworth Collection, Old Warden |
| | J7326 | DH Humming Bird (G-EBQP) | Privately owned, Hemel Hempstead |
| | J8067 | Pterodactyl 1a | Science Museum, South Kensington |
| | *J9941* | Hawker Hart 2 (G-ABMR) | RAF Museum, Hendon |
| | K1786 | Hawker Tomtit (G-AFTA) | Shuttleworth Collection, Old Warden |
| | *K1930* | Hawker Fury Replica (G-BKBB) | *Sold to Belgium, April 1990* |
| | *K2050* | Hawker Fury Replica (G-ASCM) | Privately owned, Andrewsfield |
| | *K2059* | Isaacs Fury (G-PFAR) | Privately owned, Dunkeswell |
| | *K2060* | Isaacs Fury II (G-BKZM) | *Crashed 14 June 1990, Port Dinorwie* |
| | *K2567* | DH Tiger Moth (G-MOTH) (really DE306/7035M) | Russavia Collection, Duxford |
| | *K2568* | DH Tiger Moth (G-APMM) (really DE419) | Privately owned, Bedford |
| | *K2571* | DH Tiger Moth Replica | Privately owned, RAF Hereford |
| | *K2572* | DH Tiger Moth (G-AOZH) (really NM129) | Privately owned, Shoreham |
| | K3215 | Avro Tutor (G-AHSA) | Shuttleworth Collection, Old Warden |
| | *K3584* | DH 82B Queen Bee (BAPC 186) | Mosquito Aircraft Museum, London Colney |
| | *K3731* | Isaacs Fury Replica (G-RODI) | Privately owned, Dunkeswell |
| | K4232 | Avro Rota I (SE-AZB) | RAF Museum, Hendon |
| | K4235 | Avro Rota I (G-AHMJ) | Shuttleworth Collection, Old Warden |
| | K4972 | Hawker Hart Trainer IIA (1764M) | RAF Museum Restoration Centre, Cardington |
| | *K5054* | Supermarine Spitfire Replica (G-BRDV) | Privately owned, Hullavington |
| | *K5414* | Hawker Hind (G-AENP/ BAPC 78) [XV] | Shuttleworth Collection, Old Warden |
| | *K5682* | Isaacs Fury II (G-BLMU) [6] | Crashed Barton 1989 |
| | K6038 | Westland Wallace II (2365M) | RAF Museum Store, Cardington |
| | *K7271* | Hawker Fury II Replica (BAPC 148) | RAF Cosford Aerospace Museum |
| | K8042 | Gloster Gladiator II (8372M) | RAF Museum, Hendon |
| | *K9926* | VS Spitfire Replica | RAF Bentley Priory, on display |
| | K9942 | VS Spitfire IA (8383M) [SD-V] | RAF Museum, Hendon |
| | *L1070* | VS Spitfire Replica [XT-A] | RAF Turnhouse, on display |
| | *L1096* | VS Spitfire Replica [PR-O] | RAF Church Fenton, on display |
| | L1592 | Hawker Hurricane I [KW-Z] | Science Museum, South Kensington |
| | *L1710* | Hawker Hurricane Replica [AL-D] | RAF Biggin Hill, on display |
| | *L1592* | Hawker Hurricane I Replica (BAPC 63) [KW-Z] | Kent Battle of Britain Museum, Hawkinge |
| | L2301 | VS Walrus I (G-AIZG) | FAA Museum, RNAS Yeovilton |
| | L2940 | Blackburn Skua I | FAA Museum, RNAS Yeovilton |
| | L5343 | Fairey Battle I [VO-S] | RAF Museum, Hendon |
| | *L6906* | Miles Magister I (G-AKKY/T9841) (BAPC 44) | Brooklands Museum, Weybridge |
| | L7775 | Vickers Wellington IA (fuselage) | South Yorkshire Aircraft Museum, Firbeck, Notts |
| | *L8756* | Bristol Bolingbroke IVT (RCAF 10001) [XD-E] | RAF Museum, Hendon |
| | N248 | Supermarine S6A | Southampton Hall of Aviation |
| | N1671 | Boulton Paul Defiant I (8370M) [EW-D] | RAF Museum, Hendon |
| | N1854 | Fairey Fulmar II (G-AIBE) | FAA Museum, RNAS Yeovilton |
| | *N2078* | Sopwith Baby | FAA Museum, RNAS Yeovilton |
| | *N2276* | Gloster Gladiator II (really N5903) [H] | FAA Museum, RNAS Yeovilton |
| | *N2308* | Gloster Gladiator I (G-AMRK) (really L8032) [HP-B] | Shuttleworth Collection, Old Warden |
| | N2980 | Vickers Wellington IA [R] | Brooklands Museum, Weybridge |
| | *N3194* | VS Spitfire I Replica [GR-Z] | RAF Biggin Hill, on display |

| Reg. | Type | Owner or Operator | Notes |
|---|---|---|---|
| *N3289* | VS Spitfire Replica [OW-K] (BAPC65) | Kent Battle of Britain Museum, Hawkinge | |
| N3788 | Miles Magister (G-AKPF) (really G-ANLT) | *Restored as G-AKPF* | |
| *N4389* | Fairey Albacore I [4M] (really N4172) | FAA Museum, RNAS Yeovilton | |
| N4877 | Avro Anson I (G-AMDA) [VX-F] | Skyfame Collection, Duxford | |
| *N5180* | Sopwith Pup (G-EBKY) | Shuttleworth Collection, Old Warden | |
| *N5182* | Sopwith Pup Replica (G-APUP) | RAF Museum, Hendon | |
| N5195 | Sopwith Pup (G-ABOX) | Museum of Army Flying, Middle Wallop | |
| *N5226* | Gloster Sea Gladiator II (really N5903) | Shuttleworth Collection, FAA Museum, RNAS Yeovilton | |
| *N5492* | Sopwith Triplane Replica (BAPC 111) | FAA Museum, RNAS Yeovilton | |
| N5628 | Gloster Gladiator II | RAF Museum, Hendon | |
| N5912 | Sopwith Triplane (8385M) | RAF Museum, Hendon | |
| N6004 | Short Stirling I | RAeS Medway Branch, Rochester | |
| *N6160* | Sopwith Pup Replica (G-BIAT) | Privately owned, Hatch | |
| *N6452* | Sopwith Pup Replica (G-BIAU) | FAA Museum, RNAS Yeovilton | |
| N6466 | DH Tiger Moth (G-ANKZ) | Privately owned, Barton | |
| N6720 | DH Tiger Moth (7014M) [RUO-B] | No 1940 Sqn ATC, Levenshulme | |
| N6812 | Sopwith Camel | Imperial War Museum, Lambeth | |
| N6847 | DH Tiger Moth (G-APAL) | Privately owned, Little Gransden | |
| N6848 | DH Tiger Moth (G-BALX) | Privately owned, Sedlescombe | |
| N6965 | DH Tiger Moth (G-AJTW) | Privately owned, Tibenham | |
| N6985 | DH Tiger Moth (G-AHMN) | Museum of Army Flying, Middle Wallop | |
| N9191 | DH Tiger Moth (G-ALND) | Privately owned, Shipdham | |
| N9389 | DH Tiger Moth (G-ANJA) | Privately owned, Shipmeadow, Suffolk | |
| N9510 | DH Tiger Moth (G-AOEL) | *To G-AOEL* | |
| N9899 | Supermarine Southampton I | RAF Museum Restoration Centre, Cardington | |
| P2617 | Hawker Hurricane I (8373M) [AF-F] | RAF Museum, Hendon | |
| *P3059* | Hawker Hurricane Replica [SD-N] (BAPC64) | Kent Battle of Britain Museum, Hawkinge | |
| P3175 | Hawker Hurricane I (Wreckage) | RAF Museum, Hendon | |
| *P3386* | Hawker Hurricane Replica | RAF Bentley Priory, on display | |
| *P3395* | Hawker Hurricane [JX-B] (really KX829) | Birmingham Museum of Science and Technology | |
| *P4139* | Fairey Swordfish II [5H] (really HS618/A2001) | FAA Museum, RNAS Yeovilton | |
| *P5865* | CCF Harvard 4 (G-BKCK) [LE-W] | Privately owned, North Weald | |
| P6382 | Miles M.14A Hawk Trainer 3 (G-AJRS) | Shuttleworth Collection, Old Warden | |
| P7350 | VS Spitfire IIA (G-AWIJ) [UO-T] | RAF Battle of Britain Memorial Flight, Coningsby | |
| P7540 | VS Spitfire IIA [DU-W] | Dumfries & Galloway Aviation Museum, Tinwald Downs | |
| *P8448* | VS Spitfire IIA Replica [UM-D] | RAF Swanton Morley, on display | |
| *P9390* | VS Spitfire I Replica (BAPC 71) [KL-B] | Norfolk & Suffolk Aviation Museum, Flixton | |
| P9444 | VS Spitfire IA [RN-D] | Science Museum, South Kensington | |
| R1914 | Miles Magister (G-AHUJ) | Privately owned, Strathallan | |
| R3950 | Fairey Battle I (RCAF 1899) [HA-L] | *To Brussels Museum* | |
| R4907 | DH Tiger Moth (G-ANCS) | Privately owned, Felthorpe | |
| R4959 | DH Tiger Moth (G-ARAZ) [59] | Privately owned, Goodwood | |
| R5086 | DH Tiger Moth (G-APIH) | Privately owned, Shobdon | |
| R5250 | DH Tiger Moth (G-AODT) | Privately owned, Swanton Morley | |
| R5868 | Avro Lancaster I (7325M) [PO-S] | RAF Museum, Hendon | |
| R6915 | VS Spitfire I | Imperial War Museum, Lambeth | |
| R9125 | Westland Lysander III (8377M) [LX-L] | RAF Museum, Hendon | |
| *S1287* | Fairey Flycatcher Replica (G-BEYB) [5] | Privately owned, Duxford | |
| *S1579* | Hawker Nimrod Replica [571] (G-BBVO) | Privately owned, Dunkeswell | |
| S1595 | Supermarine S6B | Science Museum, South Kensington | |
| *S1595* | Supermarine S6B Replica (BAPC 156) | *To Planes of Fame Museum, Chino, USA* | |
| *S3398* | SPAD XIII Replica (G-BFYO) [2] | FAA Museum, RNAS Yeovilton | |
| T5424 | DH Tiger Moth (G-AJOA) | Privately owned, Chiseldon | |

| Notes | Reg. | Type | Owner or Operator |
|---|---|---|---|
| | T5493 | DH Tiger Moth (G-ANEF) | Privately owned, Cranwell North |
| | T5672 | DH Tiger Moth (G-ALRI) | Privately owned, Chalmington |
| | T5854 | DH Tiger Moth (G-ANKK) | Privately owned, Halfpenny Green |
| | T5879 | DH Tiger Moth (G-AXBW) | Privately owned, Tongham |
| | T5968 | DH Tiger Moth (G-ANNN) | Privately owned, Kilkerran |
| | T6099 | DH Tiger Moth (G-AOGR/ XL714) | Privately owned, Clacton |
| | T6296 | DH Tiger Moth (8387M) | RAF Museum, Hendon |
| | T6313 | DH Tiger Moth (G-AHVU) | Privately owned, Liphook |
| | T6818 | DH Tiger Moth (G-ANKT) | Shuttleworth Collection, Old Warden |
| | *T7019* | DH Tiger Moth (G-AOIM) (really T7109) | Privately owned, Shobdon |
| | T7281 | DH Tiger Moth (G-ARTL) | Privately owned, Egton, nr Whitby |
| | T7404 | DH Tiger Moth (G-ANMV) | Privately owned, Booker |
| | T7909 | DH Tiger Moth (G-ANON) | Privately owned, Sherburn-in-Elmet |
| | T7997 | DH Tiger Moth (G-AOBH) | Privately owned, Benington |
| | T8191 | DH Tiger Moth | RN Historic Flight, RNAS Yeovilton |
| | *T9707* | Miles Magister (G-AKKR/8378M/T9708) | Greater Manchester Museum of Science and Industry |
| | T9738 | Miles Hawk Trainer III (G-AKAT) | Privately owned, Breighton |
| | V3388 | Airspeed Oxford (G-AHTW) | Skyfame Collection, Duxford |
| | *V6028* | Bristol Bolingbroke IVT (GB-D] (G-MKIV) (Rear fuselage) (really RCAF 10038) | British Aerial Museum, Duxford |
| | V7350 | Hawker Hurricane I | Brenzett Aviation Museum |
| | *V7467* | Hawker Hurricane Replica [LE-D] | RAF Coltishall, on display |
| | *V7767* | Hawker Hurricane Replica (BAPC 72) | Air Museum, North Weald |
| | *V9281* | WS Lysander III (G-BCWL) [RU-M] | Privately owned, Henstridge |
| | V9300 | WS Lysander III (RCAF 1558/ G-LIZY) | British Aerial Museum, Duxford |
| | *V9441* | WS Lysander IIIA (RCAF2355/G-AZWT) [AR-A] | Privately owned, Strathallan |
| | W1048 | HP Halifax II (8465M) [TL-S] | RAF Museum, Hendon |
| | W4041 | Gloster E28/39 [G] | Science Museum, South Kensington |
| | W4050 | DH Mosquito I | Mosquito Aircraft Museum, London Colney |
| | W5856 | Fairey Swordfish II (G-BMGC) | RN Historic Flight, BAe Brough |
| | X4590 | VS Spitfire I (8384M) [PR-F] | RAF Museum, Hendon |
| | *X4277* | VS Spitfire XVIe [XT-M] (really TB382) (7244M) | RAF Exhibition Flight, Abingdon |
| | *X4474* | VS Spitfire SVIe [QV-I] (really TE311) (7241M) | RAF Exhibition Flight, Abingdon |
| | Z2033 | Fairey Firefly I (G-ASTL) | Skyfame Collection, Duxford |
| | Z7015 | Hawker Sea Hurricane IB (G-BKTH) | Shuttleworth Collection, Duxford |
| | Z7197 | Percival Proctor III (G-AKZN/ 8380M) | RAF Museum, Hendon |
| | *Z7258* | DH Dragon Rapide (G-AHGD) | Privately owned, Old Warden (really NR786) |
| | *Z7381* | Hawker Hurricane XII [XR-T] (G-HURI) | The Fighter Collection, Duxford |
| | *AA908* | VS Spitfire Replica [GJ-C] | Privately owned, Farnborough |
| | AB910 | VS Spitfire VB [EB-J] | RAF Battle of Britain Memorial Flight, Coningsby |
| | AE436 | HP Hampden (parts) | RAFM c/o Lincolnshire Aviation Heritage Centre, East Kirkby |
| | AL246 | Grumman Martlet I | FAA Museum, RNAS Yeovilton |
| | AM561 | Lockheed Hudson V (remains) | Cornwall Aero Park, Helston |
| | AP507 | Cierva C30A (G-ACWP) [KX-P] | Science Museum, South Kensington |
| | AR213 | VS Spitfire IA (G-AIST) [PR-O] | Privately owned, Booker |
| | AR501 | VS Spitfire FVC (G-AWII) [NN-A] | Shuttleworth Collection, Old Warden |
| | BB807 | DH Tiger Moth (G-ADWO) | Southampton Hall of Aviation store |
| | BB814 | DH Tiger Moth (G-AFWI) | RN Historic Flight, Yeovilton |
| | *BE421* | Hawker Hurricane IIC Replica [XP-G] | RAF Museum, Hendon |
| | BL614 | VS Spitfire VB (4354M) [ZD-F] | Greater Manchester Museum of Science and Industry |
| | BM597 | VS Spitfire FVB (5718M) [PR-O] (G-MKVB) | Privately owned, Audley End |

| Reg. | Type | Owner or Operator | Notes |
|---|---|---|---|
| *BN230* | Hawker Hurricane IIC (5466M) (really LF751) [FT-A] | RAF Manston, Memorial Pavilion | |
| *BR600* | VS Spitfire LFXIV Replica [SH-V] | RAF Uxbridge, on display | |
| BR601 | VS Spitfire IX (*PV260*) | Warbirds of GB, Thruxton | |
| BW853 | Hawker Sea Hurricane XII A | Privately owned, Milden | |
| BW881 | Hawker Sea Hurricane XII A | Privately owned, Milden | |
| DE208 | DH Tiger Moth (G-AGYU) | Privately owned, Audley End | |
| DE363 | DH Tiger Moth (G-ANFC) | Military Aircraft Preservation Group, Hadfield, Derbyshire | |
| DE373 | DH Tiger Moth T2 (A680/A2127) | Privately owned | |
| DE623 | DH Tiger Moth (G-ANFI) | Privately owned, St Athan | |
| DE638 | DH Tiger Moth (G-ANEJ) | *To R. Malay AF Museum, Kuala Lumpur* | |
| DE673 | DH Tiger Moth (G-ADNZ/ 6948M) | Privately owned, Hampton | |
| DF128 | DH Tiger Moth (G-AOJJ) [RCO-U] | Privately owned, Abingdon | |
| DF155 | DH Tiger Moth (G-ANFV) | Privately owned, Shempston Farm, Scotland | |
| DF198 | DH Tiger Moth (G-BBRB) | Privately owned, Biggin Hill | |
| DG202 | Gloster F9/40 Meteor (5758M) [G] | RAF Cosford Aerospace Museum | |
| DG590 | Miles Hawk Major (G-ADMW/8379M) | Museum of Army Flying, Middle Wallop | |
| DP872 | Fairey Barracuda II | FAA Museum, RNAS Yeovilton | |
| DR613 | FW Wicko GM1 (G-AFJB) | Privately owned, Berkswell | |
| *DR628* | Beech D.17s (N18V) [PB-1] | Privately owned, Duxford | |
| DV372 | Avro Lancaster I (nose only) | Imperial War Museum, Lambeth | |
| EE416 | Gloster Meteor III (nose only) | Science Museum, South Kensington | |
| EE531 | Gloster Meteor F4 (7090M) | Midland Air Museum, Coventry | |
| EE549 | Gloster Meteor F4 (7008M) | RAF Cosford Aerospace Museum | |
| EJ693 | Hawker Tempest V [SA-J] | Privately owned | |
| EM720 | DH Tiger Moth (G-AXAN) | Privately owned, Staverton | |
| EM727 | DH Tiger Moth (G-AOXN) | Privately owned, Yeovil | |
| EM903 | DH Tiger Moth (G-APBI) | Privately owned, Audley End | |
| EN224 | VS Spitfire F XII (G-FXII) | Privately owned, Newport Pagnell | |
| *EN343* | VS Spitfire Replica | RAF Benson, on display | |
| *EN398* | VS Spitfire IX Replica (BAPC184) [JE-J] | Aces High Ltd, North Weald | |
| EP120 | VS Spitfire VB (5377M/8070M) [QV-H] | RAF, stored St Athan | |
| EX280 | NA Harvard IIA (G-TEAC) [G] | Privately owned, North Weald | |
| EX976 | NA Harvard III | FAA Museum, RNAS Yeovilton | |
| EZ259 | NA Harvard III (G-BMJW) | Privately owned, Bracknell | |
| EZ407 | NA Harvard III | RN Historic Flight, Lee-on-Solent | |
| FE905 | NA Harvard IIB (LN-BNM/12392) | RAF Museum Restoration Centre, Cardington | |
| FE992 | NA Harvard IIB (G-BDAM) | Privately owned, North Weald | |
| FH153 | NA Harvard IIB (G-BBHK) [GW-A] | Privately owned, Exeter | |
| *FR870* | Curtiss Kittyhawk III (NL1009N) [GA-S] | The Fighter Collection, Duxford | |
| FS728 | NA Harvard IIB (G-BAFM) | Privately owned, Sandown | |
| FS890 | NA Harvard IIB (7554M) | A&AEE, stored Boscombe Down | |
| *FT239* | NA Harvard IV (G-BIWX) | Privately owned, North Weald | |
| *FT323* | NA Harvard III (really P.AF.1513) | Vintage Aircraft Team, Cranfield | |
| FT375 | NA Harvard IIB | MoD(PE) A&AEE Boscombe Down | |
| FT391 | NA Harvard IIB (G-AZBN) | Old Flying Machine Company, Duxford | |
| *FX301* | NA Harvard III (G-JUDI) (really EX915) | Privately owned, Bryngwyn Bach, Clwyd | |
| FX442 | NA Harvard IIB | Privately owned, Bournemouth | |
| HA457 | Hawker Tempest II | RAF Museum, at Duxford | |
| *HB275* | Beech C-45 Expeditor II (N5063N) | Privately owned, North Weald | |
| HB614 | Fairchild Argus III (G-AJPI) | Privately owned, White Waltham | |
| HB751 | Fairchild Argus III (G-BCBL) | Privately owned, Little Gransden | |
| *HD368* | NA TB-25J Mitchell [VO-A] | *Painted as 44-30861 (N9089Z)* | |
| HH379 | GAL48 Hotspur II (rear fuselage only) | Museum of Army Flying, Middle Wallop | |
| HJ711 | DH Mosquito NFII [VI-C] | Night Fighter Preservation Team, Elvington | |
| HM354 | Percival Proctor III (G-ANPP) | Privately owned, Stansted | |
| HM580 | Cierva C-30A (G-ACUU) | Imperial War Museum, Duxford | |
| HR792 | HP Halifax GR II | Yorkshire Air Museum, Brough | |
| *HS503* | Fairey Swordfish IV (BAPC 108) | RAF Cosford Aerospace Museum, stored | |

| Notes | Reg. | Type | Owner or Operator |
|---|---|---|---|
| | *HX922* | DH Mosquito TT35 (G-AWJV) [EG-F] (really TA634) | Mosquito Aircraft Museum, London Colney |
| | JV482 | Grumman Wildcat V | Ulster Aviation Society, Newtownards |
| | *JV928* | PBY-5A Catalina (G-BLSC) [Y] | Plane Sailing, Duxford |
| | KB889 | Avro Lancaster B10 (G-LANC) | Imperial War Museum, Duxford |
| | KB976 | Avro Lancaster B10 (G-BCOH) [LQ-K] | Privately owned, Cranfield |
| | KB994 | Avro Lancaster B10 (fuselage) | Warbirds of GB, Bournemouth |
| | KD431 | CV Corsair IV [E2-M] | FAA Museum, RNAS Yeovilton |
| | KE209 | Grumman Hellcat II | FAA Museum, RNAS Yeovilton |
| | *KE418* | Hawker Tempest (rear fuselage) | RAF Museum Store, Cardington |
| | KF183 | NA Harvard IIB | MoD(PE) A&AEE Boscombe Down |
| | KF388 | NA Harvard IIB (nose only) | Privately owned, Bournemouth |
| | KF435 | NA Harvard IIB | Booker Aircraft Museum |
| | KF594 | NA Harvard IIB (cockpit section) | Newark Air Museum, Winthorpe |
| | *KG374* | Douglas Dakota C-4 [YS] (really KN645/8355M) | RAF Cosford Aerospace Museum |
| | *KJ351* | HP Horsa II [23] (really TL659) composite (BAPC 80) | Museum of Army Flying, Middle Wallop |
| | KK995 | Sikorsky Hoverfly I [E] | RAF Museum, Hendon |
| | KN448 | Douglas Dakota C4 (nose only) | Science Museum, South Kensington |
| | KN751 | Consolidated Liberator VI [F] | RAF Cosford Aerospace Museum |
| | KP208 | Douglas Dakota C-4 [YS] | Airborne Forces Museum, Aldershot |
| | KX829 | Hawker Hurricane IV [JV-I] | *Repainted as P3395* |
| | KZ321 | Hawker Hurricane IV (G-HURY) [JV-N] | Warbirds of GB, Bournemouth |
| | | | |
| | LA198 | VS Spitfire F21 (7118M) [RAI-G] | RAF, stored St Athan |
| | LA226 | VS Spitfire F21 (7119M) | RAF, Bentley Priory, for display |
| | LA255 | VS Spitfire F21 (6490M) [JX-U] | RAF No 1 Sqn, Wittering |
| | LA564 | VS Seafire F46 | Privately owned, Newport Pagnell |
| | LB294 | Taylorcraft Plus D (G-AHWJ) | Museum of Army Flying, Middle Wallop |
| | LB312 | Taylorcraft Plus D (G-AHXE) | Privately owned, Shoreham |
| | LB375 | Taylorcraft Plus D (G-AHGW) | Privately owned, Coventry |
| | LF363 | Hawker Hurricane IIC [GN-A] | RAF Battle of Britain Memorial Flight, Coningsby |
| | LF738 | Hawker Hurricane IIC (5405M) | RAF, RAeS Medway Branch, Rochester |
| | LF858 | DH Queen Bee (G-BLUZ) | Privately owned, Meppershall |
| | LH208 | Airspeed Horsa I (parts only) (8596M) | Museum of Army Flying, Middle Wallop |
| | LS326 | Fairey Swordfish II (G-AJVH) [L2] | RN Historic Flight, RNAS Yeovilton |
| | LZ551 | DH Sea Vampire I [G] | FAA Museum, RNAS Yeovilton |
| | LZ766 | Percival Proctor III (G-ALCK) | Skyfame Collection, Duxford |
| | | | |
| | *MD497* | WS 51 Widgeon (G-ANLW) [NE-X] | Privately owned, Blackpool |
| | MF628 | Vickers Wellington T10 | RAF Museum, Hendon |
| | MH434 | VS Spitfire HF.IXB (G-ASJV) | Privately owned, Duxford |
| | *MH486* | VS Spitfire IX Replica [FF-A] | RAF Museum, Hendon |
| | *MH777* | VS Spitfire Replica | RAF Northolt, on display |
| | MJ627 | VS Spitfire TIX (G-ASOZ/ G-BMSB) | Privately owned, Kenilworth |
| | MJ730 | VS Spitfire HFIXe (G-HFIX) [HT-W] | Privately owned, East Midlands Airport |
| | MK356 | VS Spitfire IX (5690M) [21-V] | RAF Battle of Britain Memorial Flight, Abingdon |
| | MK912 | VS Spitfire LFIXe (SM-29) (G-BRRA) [MN-P] | Privately owned, Ludham |
| | ML407 | VS Spitfire TIX (G-LFIX) [OU-V] | Privately owned, Goodwood |
| | ML417 | VS Spitfire LFIXE (G-BJSG) [2I-T] | Privately owned, Duxford |
| | ML427 | VS Spitfire IX (6457M) [I-ST] | Birmingham Museum of Science & Industry |
| | ML796 | Short Sunderland V | Imperial War Museum, Duxford |
| | ML814 | Short Sunderland V (G-BJHS) | Privately owned, Calshot |
| | ML824 | Short Sunderland V [NS-Z] | RAF Museum, Hendon |
| | MN235 | Hawker Typhoon IB | RAF Museum, Hendon |
| | MP425 | Airspeed Oxford I (G-AITB) | RAF Museum Restoration Centre, Cardington |
| | MT438 | Auster III (G-AREI) | Privately owned, Chessington |
| | MT719 | VS Spitfire LFVIIIC (G-VIII) [YB-J] | Privately owned, Duxford |
| | MT847 | VS Spitfire FRXIVe (6960M) | RAF Cosford Aerospace Museum |

| Reg. | Type | Owner or Operator | Notes |
|---|---|---|---|
| MV154 | VS Spitfire HF VIII (G-BKMI/ A58-671) | Privately owned, Filton | |
| MV262 | VS Spitfire XIV (G-CCVV) [42-G] | Privately owned, Micheldever | |
| *MV363* | VS Spitfire XIV (G-SPIT/G-BGHB) (really MV293) | Privately owned, Duxford | |
| MV370 | VS Spitfire XIV (G-FXIV) [AV-L] | Aces High Ltd, North Weald | |
| *MW100* | Avro York C1 (G-AGNV/TS798) | RAF Cosford Aerospace Museum | |
| MW401 | Hawker Tempest II (G-PEST) (IAF HA604) | Privately owned, Byfleet | |
| MW763 | Hawker Tempest II (G-TEMT) (IAF HA586) | Privately owned, Byfleet | |
| NF370 | Fairey Swordfish II | Imperial War Museum, Duxford | |
| NF389 | Fairey Swordfish III [5B] | RNAY Fleetlands Museum | |
| NF875 | DH Dragon Rapide 6 (G-AGTM) [603/CH] | Privately owned, Audley End | |
| NH238 | VS Spitfire IX (N238V/ G-MKIX) | Warbirds of GB, Bournemouth | |
| NH799 | VS Spitfire XIV | Privately owned, Duxford | |
| NJ673 | Auster 5D (G-AOCR) | Privately owned, Wyberton | |
| NJ695 | Auster 4 (G-AJXV) | Privately owned, Leicester East | |
| NJ703 | Auster 5 (G-AKPI) | Privately owned, Doncaster | |
| *NJ719* | Auster 5 (G-ANFU) (really TW385) | North-East Aircraft Museum, Usworth | |
| NL879 | DH Tiger Moth (G-AVPJ) | Privately owned, Wellesbourne Mountford | |
| NL985 | DH Tiger Moth (7015M) | Vintage Aircraft Team, Cranfield | |
| NP181 | Percival Proctor IV (G-AOAR) | Privately owned, Biggin Hill | |
| NP184 | Percival Proctor IV (G-ANYP) [K] | Privately owned, Chatteris | |
| NP294 | Percival Proctor IV [TB-M] | Lincolnshire Aviation Museum, East Kirkby | |
| NP303 | Percival Proctor IV (G-ANZJ) | Privately owned, Byfleet, Surrey | |
| NR747 | DH Dragon Rapide (G-AJHO) | Privately owned, Duxford | |
| NV778 | Hawker Tempest V (8386M) | RAF Museum, Hendon | |
| NX611 | Avro Lancaster VII (G-ASXX/ 8375M) [YF-C] | Lincolnshire Aviation Heritage Centre, East Kirkby | |
| PA474 | Avro Lancaster I [PM-M$^2$] | RAF Battle of Britain Memorial Flight, Coningsby | |
| *PF179* | HS Gnat T1 (XR541/8602M) | RAF CTTS, St Athan | |
| PK624 | VS Spitfire F22 (8072M) [RAU-T] | RAF, stored St Athan | |
| PK664 | VS Spitfire F22 (7759M) [V6-B] | RAF, stored St Athan | |
| PK683 | VS Spitfire F24 (7150M) | Southampton Hall of Aviation | |
| PK724 | VS Spitfire F24 (7288M) | RAF Museum, Hendon | |
| PL344 | VS Spitfire IX (G-IXCC) | Privately owned, Micheldever | |
| PL965 | VS Spitfire XI (G-MKIX) [3-W] | Privately owned, Rochester | |
| PL983 | VS Spitfire XI (G-PRXI) | Warbirds of GB, Bournemouth | |
| PM631 | VS Spitfire PR XIX [N] | RAF Battle of Britain Memorial Flight, Coningsby | |
| PM651 | VS Spitfire XIX (7758M) [X] | RAF Museum, Hendon | |
| PN323 | HP Halifax VII (nose only) | Imperial War Museum, Lambeth | |
| PP972 | VS Seafire LIII | Warbirds of GB, Thruxton | |
| PS853 | VS Spitfire XIX [C] | RAF Battle of Britain Memorial Flight, Coningsby | |
| PS915 | VS Spitfire PR XIX (7548M/7711M) | RAF Battle of Britain Memorial Flight, Coningsby | |
| PT462 | VS Spitfire TIX (G-CTIX) | Privately owned, Duxford | |
| PV202 | VS Spitfire TRIX (G-TRIX) [VZ-M] | Privately owned, Denham | |
| PZ865 | Hawker Hurricane IIc (G-AMAU) [RF-U] | RAF Battle of Britain Memorial Flight, Coningsby | |
| RA848 | Slingsby Cadet TX1 | Privately owned, Leeds | |
| RA854 | Slingsby Cadet TX1 | The Aeroplane Collection store, Wigan | |
| RA897 | Slingsby Cadet TX1 | Newark Air Museum store, Hucknall | |
| RD253 | Bristol Beaufighter TF10 (7931M) | RAF Museum, Hendon | |
| RF342 | Avro Lincoln B2 (G-29-1/ G-APRJ) | Warbirds of GB, Bournemouth | |
| RF398 | Avro Lincoln B2 (8376M) | RAF Cosford Aerospace Museum | |
| *RG333* | Miles Messenger IIA (G-AIEK) | Privately owned, Felton, Bristol | |
| *RG333* | Miles Messenger IIA (G-AKEZ) | Privately owned, Chelmsford | |

| Notes | Reg. | Type | Owner or Operator |
|---|---|---|---|
| | RH377 | Miles Messenger 4A (G-ALAH) | Privately owned, Stretton, Cheshire |
| | RH746 | Bristol Brigand TF1 | North-East Aircraft Museum, Usworth |
| | RL962 | DH Dragon Rapide (G-AHED) | RAF Museum Store, Cardington |
| | RM221 | Percival Proctor IV (G-ANXR) | Privately owned, Biggin Hill |
| | RM689 | VS Spitfire XIV (G-ALGT) [MN-E] | Rolls-Royce, Filton |
| | RN201 | VS Spitfire XIV (SG-31 RB AF) (G-BSKP) | Privately owned, Ludham |
| | *RN218* | Isaacs Spitfire Replica (G-BBJI) [N] | Privately owned, Langham |
| | RR232 | VS Spitfire HFIXc(G-BRSF) | Privately owned, Micheldever |
| | RR299 | DH Mosquito T3 (G-ASKH) [HT-E] | British Aerospace, Hawarden |
| | RT486 | Auster AOP5 (G-AJGJ) | Privately owned, Popham |
| | RT520 | Auster 5 (G-ALYB) | South Yorkshire Air Museum, Firbeck |
| | RT610 | Auster 5A (G-AKWS) | Privately owned, Exeter |
| | RW382 | VS Spitfire XVIe (7245M/ 8075M) [NG-C] | Privately owned, Audley End |
| | RW386 | VS Spitfire XVIe (6944M/ G-BXVI) [RAK-A] | Warbirds of GB, Biggin Hill |
| | RW388 | VS Spitfire XVIe (6946M) [U4-U] | Stoke-on-Trent City Museum, Hanley |
| | RW393 | VS Spitfire XVIe (7293M) [XT-A] | RAF, stored St Athan |
| | RX168 | VS Seafire LFIIIc | Privately owned, High Wycombe |
| | SL542 | VS Spitfire XVIe (8390M) [4M-N] | RAF, stored St Athan |
| | SL674 | VS Spitfire XVIe [RAS-H] (8392M) | RAF, stored St Athan |
| | SM832 | VS Spitfire XIV (G-WWII) | Privately owned, Duxford |
| | SM969 | VS Spitfire XVIIIe (G-BRAF) | Warbirds of GB, Bournemouth |
| | SX137 | VS Seafire XVII | FAA Museum, RNAS Yeovilton |
| | SX300 | VS Seafire XVII (A646/A696/ A2054) | Privately owned, Warwick |
| | SX336 | VS Seafire XVII (A2055) (G-BRMG) | Privately owned, Twyford, Berks |
| | TA122 | DH Mosquito FBVI [UP-G] | Mosquito Aircraft Museum, London Colney |
| | TA634 | DH Mosquito B35 (G-AWJV) | Mosquito Aircraft Museum, London Colney |
| | TA639 | DH Mosquito TT35 (7806M) [AZ-E] | RAF Cosford Aerospace Museum |
| | TA719 | DH Mosquito TT35 (G-ASKC) [6T] | Skyfame Collection, Duxford |
| | TB252 | VS Spitfire XVIe (7257M/7281M/ 8073M) [GW-H] | Privately owned, Audley End |
| | TB382 | VS Spitfire LFXVIe (7244M) | *Repainted as X4277* |
| | TB752 | VS Spitfire XVIe (7256M/ 7279M/8086M) [KH-Z] | RAF Manston, Memorial Pavilion |
| | TB885 | VS Spitfire LFXVIe | Shoreham Aircraft Preservation Society |
| | TD248 | VS Spitfire XVIe (7246M) (G-OXVI) | Privately owned, Audley End |
| | TE184 | VS Spitfire LF XVIe (G-MXVI) | Privately owned, East Midlands |
| | TE311 | VS Spitfire XVIe (7241M) | *Repainted as X4474* |
| | TE356 | VS Spitfire XVIe (7001M) (G-SXVI) [D-A] | *Sold in USA as N356EV* |
| | TE392 | VS Spitfire XVIe (7000M/8074M) | Warbirds of GB, Thruxton |
| | TE462 | VS Spitfire XVIe (7243M) | Royal Scottish Museum of Flight, East Fortune |
| | TE476 | VS Spitfire XVIe (7451M/ 8071M) (G-XVIB) | *Sold in USA* |
| | TE517 | VS Spitfire LFIX (2046/G-BIXP/ G-CCIX) | Privately owned, Micheldever |
| | TE566 | VS Spitfire HFIXe (G-BLCK) | Privately owned, Ludham |
| | TG263 | Saro SR.A1 (G-12-1) [P] | Imperial War Museum, Duxford |
| | TG511 | HP Hastings T5 (8554M) | RAF Cosford Aerospace Museum |
| | TG517 | HP Hastings T5 [517] | Newark Air Museum, Winthorpe |
| | TG528 | HP Hastings C1A | Skyfame Collection, Duxford |
| | TG568 | HP Hastings C1A | RAE Bedford Fire Section |
| | TJ118 | DH Mosquito TT35 (nose only) | Mosquito Aircraft Museum store |
| | TJ138 | DH Mosquito B35 (7607M) [VO-L] | RAF St Athan Historic Aircraft Collection |
| | TJ343 | Auster 5 (G-AJXC) | Privately owned, Popham |
| | *TJ398* | Auster AOP5 (BAPC 70) | Aircraft Preservation Society of Scotland, East Fortune |

| Reg. | Type | Owner or Operator | Notes |
|---|---|---|---|
| TJ569 | Auster 5 (G-AKOW) | Museum of Army Flying, Middle Wallop | |
| TJ672 | Auster 5 (G-ANIJ) | Privately owned, RAF Swanton Morley | |
| TJ704 | Auster 5 [JA] (G-ASCD) | Yorkshire Air Museum, Elvington | |
| TK718 | GAL Hamilcar I | Museum of Army Transport, Beverley | |
| TK777 | GAL Hamilcar I | Museum of Army Flying, Middle Wallop | |
| TL615 | Airspeed Horsa II | Mosquito Aircraft Museum, London Colney | |
| *TL659* | Airspeed Horsa II (BAPC 80) | *See KJ351 composite* | |
| TP298 | VS Spitfire XIV (fuselage) | Privately owned, Ludham | |
| TS291 | Slingsby Cadet TX1 (BGA852) | Museum of Flight, East Fortune | |
| TS423 | Douglas Dakota 3 (G-DAKS) | Aces High Ltd, North Weald | |
| TV959 | DH Mosquito T3 [AF-V] | Imperial War Museum, Lambeth | |
| TW117 | DH Mosquito T3 (7805M) | RAF Museum, Hendon | |
| TW439 | Auster 5 (G-ANRP) | Privately owned, Dorchester | |
| TW448 | Auster 5 (G-ANLU) | Privately owned, Chilbolton | |
| TW467 | Auster 5 (G-ANIE) | Privately owned, Cranfield | |
| *TW511* | Auster 5 (G-APAF) | Privately owned, Skegness | |
| TW536 | Auster AOP6 (7704M/G-BNGE) [TS-V] | Privately owned, Middle Wallop | |
| TW591 | Auster 6A (G-ARIH) [N] | Privately owned, Burnaston | |
| TW641 | Auster AOP6 (G-ATDN) | Privately owned, Biggin Hill | |
| TX183 | Avro Anson C19 (G-BSMF) | Privately owned, Arbroath | |
| TX192 | Avro Anson C19 | Guernsey Airport Fire Section | |
| TX213 | Avro Anson C19 (G-AWRS) | North-East Aircraft Museum, Usworth | |
| TX214 | Avro Anson C19 (7817M) | RAF Cosford Aerospace Museum | |
| TX226 | Avro Anson C19 (7865M) | Imperial War Museum, Duxford | |
| TX228 | Avro Anson C19 | City of Norwich Aviation Museum | |
| TX235 | Avro Anson C19 | Snowdon Mountain Aviation Museum, Caernarfon | |
| VD165 | Slingsby T7 Kite | Russavia Collection, Dunstable | |
| VF301 | DH Vampire F1 (7060M) [RAL-B] | Midland Air Museum, Coventry | |
| VF516 | Auster AOP6 (G-ASMZ) [T] | Privately owned, Crediton | |
| VF548 | Beagle Terrier 1 (G-ASEG) | Privately owned, Dunkeswell | |
| VF611 | Beagle A61 Terrier 2 (G-ATBU) | *Reverted to G-ATBU* | |
| VH127 | Fairey Firefly TT4 | RNAY Fleetlands Museum | |
| VL348 | Avro Anson C19 (G-AVVO) | Newark Air Museum, Winthorpe | |
| VL349 | Avro Anson C19 (G-AWSA) | Norfolk & Suffolk Aviation Museum, Flixton | |
| VM325 | Avro Anson C19 | Midland Air Museum, Coventry | |
| VM360 | Avro Anson C19 (G-APHV) | Royal Scottish Museum of Flight, East Fortune | |
| *VM791* | Slingsby Cadet TX3 (really XA312) (8876M) | No 135 Redhill & Reigate Sqn ATC, RAF Kenley | |
| VN148 | Grunau Baby IIb (BAPC 33) (BGA 2400) | Russavia Collection, Duxford | |
| VN485 | VS Spitfire F24 (7326M) | Imperial War Museum, Duxford | |
| VP293 | Avro Shackleton T4 | *Scrapped July 1990 at Strathallan* | |
| VP519 | Avro Anson C19 (nose only) (G-AVVR) | Military Aircraft Preservation Group, Hadfield, Derbyshire | |
| VP952 | DH Devon C2 (8820M) | RAF Cosford Aerospace Museum | |
| VP953 | DH Devon C2 | FSCTE, RAF Manston | |
| VP955 | DH Devon C2 (G-DVON) | Privately owned, Bournemouth | |
| VP956 | DH Devon C2 | FSCTE, RAF Manston | |
| VP957 | DH Devon C2 (8822M) | RAF Bishop's Court NI, BDRT | |
| VP959 | DH Devon C2 [L] | MoD(PE) RAE West Freugh | |
| VP960 | DH Devon C2 | FSCTE, RAF Manston | |
| VP961 | DH Devon C2 | *To G-ALFM, Leavesden* | |
| VP962 | DH Devon C2 (G-BLRB) | *To G-BLRB, Booker* | |
| VP963 | DH Devon C2 | FSCTE, RAF Manston | |
| VP965 | DH Devon C2 [DE] (8823M) | FSCTE, RAF Manston | |
| VP967 | DH Devon C2 (G-KOOL) | East Surrey Technical College, Redhill | |
| VP968 | DH Devon C2 | A&AEE Boscombe Down, derelict | |
| VP975 | DH Devon C2 [M] | Science Museum, Wroughton | |
| VP976 | DH Devon C2 (8784M) | RAF Northolt Fire Section | |
| VP977 | DH Devon C2 (G-ALTS) | RAE West Freugh Fire Section | |
| VP981 | DH Devon C2 | RAF Battle of Britain Flight, Coningsby | |
| VR137 | Westland Wyvern TF1 | FAA Museum, RNAS Yeovilton | |
| VR192 | Pervical Prentice T1 (G-APIT) | Second World War Aircraft Preservation Society, Lasham | |
| VR249 | Percival Prentice T1 (G-APIY) [FA-EL] | Newark Air Museum, Winthorpe | |
| VR259 | Percival Prentice T1 (G-APJB) | Privately owned, Coventry | |

| Notes | Reg. | Type | Owner or Operator |
|---|---|---|---|
| | VR930 | Hawker Sea Fury FB11 (8382M) | RN Historic Flight, RNAS Yeovilton, for spares |
| | VS356 | Percival Prentice T1 (G-AOLU) | Privately owned, Perth |
| | VS562 | Avro Anson T21 (8012M) | Privately owned, RAE Llanbedr |
| | VS610 | Percival Prentice T1 (G-AOKL) [K-L] | Privately owned, Southend |
| | VS623 | Percival Prentice T1 (G-AOKZ) [KQ-F] | Midland Air Museum, Coventry |
| | VT229 | Gloster Meteor F4 (7151M) [60] | Privately owned, Winthorpe |
| | VT260 | Gloster Meteor F4 (8813M) [67] | Imperial War Museum, Duxford |
| | *VT409* | Fairey Firefly AS5 (really WD889) | North-East Aircraft Museum, Usworth |
| | VT812 | DH Vampire F3 (7200M) [N] | RAF Museum, Hendon |
| | VT921 | Grunau Baby | *Scrapped at RAF Honington* |
| | VT935 | Boulton Paul P111A (VT769) | Midland Air Museum, Coventry |
| | VV106 | VS517 (7175M) | FAA Museum, RNAS Yeovilton |
| | VV119 | Supermarine 535 (nose only) (7285M) | Lincolnshire Aviation Museum, East Kirkby |
| | VV217 | DH Vampire FB5 (7323M) | RAF Barnham, on display |
| | VV901 | Avro Anson T21 | Pennine Aviation Museum, Bacup |
| | VV950 | Avro Anson T21 | *Scrapped at RAF Kinloss* |
| | VW453 | Gloster Meteor T7 (8703M) | Cotswold Aircraft Restoration Group, RAF Innsworth |
| | VW985 | Auster AOP6 (G-ASEF) | Privately owned, Upper Arncott, Oxon |
| | VX118 | Auster 6A (G-ASNB) | Privately owned, Shobdon |
| | VX185 | EE Canberra B(I)8 (nose only) (7631M) | Science Museum, South Kensington |
| | VX250 | DH Sea Hornet 21 [48] (rear fuselage) | Mosquito Aircraft Museum, London Colney |
| | VX272 | Hawker P1052 (7174M) | RNAY Fleetlands Museum |
| | VX275 | Slingsby Sedbergh TX1 (8884M) (BGA 572) | RAF Museum, Hendon |
| | VX461 | DH Vampire FB5 (7646M) | RAF Museum Store, Cardington |
| | VX573 | Vickers Valetta C2 (8389M) | RAF Cosford Aerospace Museum |
| | VX577 | Vickers Valetta C2 | North-East Aircraft Museum, Usworth |
| | VX580 | Vickers Valetta C2 | Norfolk & Suffolk Aviation Museum Flixton |
| | VX595 | WS51 Dragonfly HR1 [29] | RNAY Fleetlands Museum |
| | VX653 | Hawker Sea Fury FB11 | RAF Museum, Hendon |
| | VZ304 | DH Vampire FB5 (7630M) | Vintage Aircraft Team, Cranfield |
| | VZ345 | Hawker Sea Fury T20S | A&AEE Boscombe Down |
| | VZ462 | Gloster Meteor F8 | Second World War Aircraft Preservation Society, stored |
| | VZ467 | Gloster Meteor F8 [01] | RAF, stored Scampton |
| | VZ477 | Gloster Meteor F8 (nose only) (7741M) | Kimbolton School CCF, Cambs |
| | VZ608 | Gloster Meteor FR9 | Newark Air Museum, Winthorpe |
| | VZ634 | Gloster Meteor T7 (8657M) | Newark Air Museum, Winthorpe |
| | VZ638 | Gloster Meteor T7 (G-JETM) [HF] | Privately owned, Charlwood, Surrey |
| | VZ728 | RS4 Desford Trainer (G-AGOS) | Royal Scottish Museum of Flight, East Fortune |
| | VZ962 | WS51 Dragonfly HR1 [904] | International Helicopter Museum, Weston-super-Mare |
| | VZ965 | WS51 Dragonfly HR5 | FAA Museum, at RNAS Culdrose |
| | WA473 | VS Attacker F1 [102/J] | FAA Museum, RNAS Yeovilton |
| | WA576 | Bristol Sycamore 3 (G-ALSS/ 7900M) | Dumfries & Galloway Aviation Museum, Tinwald Downs |
| | WA577 | Bristol Sycamore 3 (G-ALST/ 7718M) | North-East Aircraft Museum, Usworth |
| | WA591 | Gloster Meteor T7 (7917M) [W] | RAF Woodvale, on display |
| | WA630 | Gloster Meteor T7 [69] (nose only) | Robertsbridge Aviation Museum |
| | WA634 | Gloster Meteor T7/8 | RAF Cosford Aerospace Museum |
| | WA638 | Gloster Meteor T7 | Martin Baker Aircraft, Chalgrove |
| | WA662 | Gloster Meteor T7 | Martin Baker Aircraft, Chalgrove |
| | WA984 | Gloster Meteor F8 [A] | Tangmere Military Aviation Museum |
| | WB188 | Hawker Hunter F3 (7154M) | RAF Cosford Aerospace Museum |
| | WB271 | Fairey Firefly AS5 [204/R] | RN Historic Flight, RNAS Yeovilton |
| | WB440 | Fairey Firefly AS6 | Greater Manchester Museum of Science and Industry |

| Reg. | Type | Owner or Operator | Notes |
|---|---|---|---|
| WB491 | Avro Ashton 2 (nose only) | Wales Aircraft Museum, Cardiff (TS897/G-AJJW) | |
| WB533 | DH Devon C2 (G-DEVN) | *To Frankfurt, Germany, Aug 90* | |
| WB550 | DH Chipmunk T10 [F] | RAF EFTS, Swinderby | |
| WB556 | DH Chipmunk T10 | RAFGSA, Bicester | |
| WB560 | DH Chipmunk T10 | RAF No 4 AEF, Exeter | |
| WB565 | DH Chipmunk T10 [X] | AAC BFWF, Middle Wallop | |
| WB567 | DH Chipmunk T10 | RAF No 12 AEF, Turnhouse | |
| WB569 | DH Chipmunk T10 [2] | RAF No 1 AEF, Manston | |
| WB575 | DH Chipmunk T10 [907] | RN Flying Grading Flt, Plymouth | |
| WB584 | DH Chipmunk T10 PAX (7706M) | No 327 Sqn ATC, Kilmarnock | |
| WB585 | DH Chipmunk T10 (G-AOSY) [RCU-X] | Privately owned, Blackbushe | |
| WB586 | DH Chipmunk T10 [A] | RAF No 6 AEF, Abingdon | |
| WB588 | DH Chipmunk T10 (G-AOTD) [D] | Shuttleworth Collection, Old Warden | |
| WB615 | DH Chipmunk T10 [E] | AAC BFWF, Middle Wallop | |
| WB624 | DH Chipmunk T10 PAX | The Aeroplane Collection, Long Marston | |
| WB626 | DH Chipmunk T10 PAX | Privately owned, Swanton Morley | |
| WB627 | DH Chipmunk T10 [N] | RAF No 5 AEF, Cambridge | |
| WB647 | DH Chipmunk T10 [R] | AAC BFWF, Middle Wallop | |
| WB652 | DH Chipmunk T10 [V] | RAF No 5 AEF, Cambridge | |
| WB654 | DH Chipmunk T10 [14] | RAF No 10 AEF, Woodvale | |
| WB657 | DH Chipmunk T10 [908] | RN Flying Grading Flt, Plymouth | |
| WB660 | DH Chipmunk T10 (G-ARMB) | Privately owned, Henstridge | |
| WB670 | DH Chipmunk T10 (8361M) | No 1312 Sqn ATC, Southend | |
| WB671 | DH Chipmunk T10 [910] | RN Flying Grading Flt, Plymouth | |
| WB685 | DH Chipmunk T10 PAX | North-East Aircraft Museum, Usworth | |
| WB693 | DH Chipmunk T10 [S] | AAC BFWF, Middle Wallop | |
| WB697 | DH Chipmunk T10 [O] | RAF No 3 AEF, Filton | |
| WB702 | DH Chipmunk T10 (G-AOFE) | Privately owned, Denham | |
| WB703 | DH Chipmunk T10 (G-ARMC) | Privately owned, White Waltham | |
| WB732 | DH Chipmunk T10 (G-AOJZ/ *G-ASTD*) | Air Service Training Ltd, Perth | |
| WB739 | DH Chipmunk T10 [8] | RAF No 8 AEF, Shawbury | |
| WB754 | DH Chipmunk T10 [H] | AAC BFWF, Middle Wallop | |
| WB758 | DH Chipmunk T10 (7729M) [P] | Privately owned, Torbay | |
| WB763 | DH Chipmunk T10 (G-BBMR) [14] | Southall Technical College | |
| | | | |
| WD286 | DH Chipmunk T10 [J] (G-BBND) | Privately owned, Bourn | |
| WD288 | DH Chipmunk T10 (G-AOSO) [38] | Privately owned, Charlton Park | |
| WD289 | DH Chipmunk T10 [N] | RAF EFTS, Swinderby | |
| WD293 | DH Chipmunk T10 PAX (7645M) | No 1367 Sqn ATC, Caerleon | |
| WD305 | DH Chipmunk T10 (G-ARGG) | Privately owned, Coventry | |
| WD310 | DH Chipmunk T10 [H] | RAF EFTS, Swinderby | |
| WD318 | DH Chipmunk T10 PAX (8207M) | No 145 Sqn ATC, Timperley | |
| WD325 | DH Chipmunk T10 [N] | AAC BFWF, Middle Wallop | |
| WD331 | DH Chipmunk T10 [A] [6] | RAF EFTS, Swinderby | |
| WD335 | DH Chipmunk T10 PAX | No 1955 Sqn ATC, Wells, Somerset | |
| WD356 | DH Chipmunk T10 (7625M) | Privately owned, Huntingdon | |
| WD363 | DH Chipmunk T10 (G-BCIH) [5] | Privately owned, Stansted | |
| WD370 | DH Chipmunk T10 PAX | No 176 Sqn ATC, Hove | |
| WD373 | DH Chipmunk T10 [12] | RAF No 2 AEF, Bournemouth | |
| WD374 | DH Chipmunk T10 [903] | RN Flying Grading Flt, Plymouth | |
| *WD379* | DH Chipmunk T10 (really WB696/G-APLO) [K] | Privately owned, Jersey | |
| WD386 | DH Chipmunk T10 PAX | No 1284 Sqn ATC, Tenby | |
| WD390 | DH Chipmunk T10 [68] | RAF No 9 AEF, Finningley | |
| WD413 | Avro Anson C 21 (G-BFIR/ 7881M) | Privately owned, Strathallan | |
| WD646 | Gloster Meteor TT20 (8189M) [R] | No 2030 Sqn ATC, Sheldon | |
| WD686 | Gloster Meteor NF11 | Imperial War Museum, Duxford | |
| WD790 | Gloster Meteor NF11 (8743M) (nose only) | North-East Aircraft Museum, Usworth | |
| WD889 | Fairey Firefly AS6 | North-East Aircraft Museum, Usworth | |
| WD931 | EE Canberra B2 (nose only) | No 425 Sqn ATC, Aldridge, W Midlands | |
| WD935 | EE Canberra B2 (8440M) (cockpit) | Privately owned, Burgess Hill | |

| Notes | Reg. | Type | Owner or Operator |
|---|---|---|---|
| | WD954 | EE Canberra B2 (nose only) | Privately owned, Romford, Essex |
| | WD955 | EE Canberra T17A [EM] | RAF No 360 Sqn, Wyton |
| | WE113 | EE Canberra B2 [BJ] | RAF No 231 OCU, Wyton |
| | WE122 | EE Canberra TT18 [845] | MoD(PE) RAE Llanbedr |
| | WE139 | EE Canberra PR3 (8369M) | RAF Museum, Hendon |
| | WE146 | EE Canberra PR3 (cockpit only) | MoD(PE) RAE Farnborough |
| | WE168 | EE Canberra PR3 (8049M) (nose) | Privately owned, Colchester |
| | WE173 | EE Canberra PR3 (8740M) | RAF Coltishall Fire Section |
| | WE188 | EE Canberra T4 | Solway Aviation Society, Carlisle |
| | WE192 | EE Canberra T4 [92] | Solway Aviation Society, Carlisle |
| | *WE402* | DH Venom FB50 (G-VIDI) | Vintage Aircraft Team, Cranfield |
| | WE569 | Auster T7 (G-ASAJ) | Privately owned, Middle Wallop |
| | WE600 | Auster T7 (mod) (7602M) | RAF Cosford Aerospace Museum |
| | WE925 | Gloster Meteor F8 | Classic Jet Aircraft Collection, Loughborough |
| | WE982 | Slingsby Prefect TX1 (8781M) | RAF Museum, stored Henlow |
| | WE990 | Slingsby Prefect TX1 (BGA 2583) | Privately owned, RAF Swanton Morley |
| | WF122 | Sea Prince T1 (A2673) [575/CU] | Cornwall Aero Park, Helston |
| | WF125 | Sea Prince T1 (A2674) [CU] | RN Predannack Fire School |
| | WF128 | Sea Prince T1 (8611M) [CU] | Norfolk & Suffolk Aviation Museum, Flixton |
| | WF137 | Sea Prince C1 | Second World War Aircraft Preservation Society, Lasham |
| | WF219 | Hawker Sea Hawk F1 (A2439) | FAA Museum, RNAS Yeovilton |
| | WF225 | Hawker Sea Hawk F1 (A2645) [CU] | RNAS Culdrose, at main gate |
| | WF259 | Hawker Sea Hawk F2 (A2483) [171/A] | Royal Scottish Museum of Flight, East Fortune |
| | WF369 | Vickers Varsity T1 [F] | Newark Air Museum, Winthorpe |
| | WF372 | Vickers Varsity T1 [T] | Brooklands Aviation Museum |
| | WF376 | Vickers Varsity T1 | Bristol Airport Fire Section |
| | WF408 | Vickers Varsity T1 (8395M) | RAF Cosford Aerospace Museum |
| | WF410 | Vickers Varsity T1 [F] | Brunel Technical College, Lulsgate |
| | WF413 | Vickers Varsity T1 [V] | FSCTE, RAF Manston |
| | WF425 | Vickers Varsity T1 | Imperial War Museum, Duxford |
| | WF643 | Gloster Meteor F8 [X] | Norfolk & Suffolk Aviation Museum, Flixton |
| | *WF714* | Gloster Meteor F8 (Really WK914) | Privately owned, Duxford |
| | WF784 | Gloster Meteor T7 (7895M) | RAF Quedgeley, at main gate |
| | WF825 | Gloster Meteor T7 (8359M) [A] | Avon Aviation Museum, Yatesbury |
| | WF877 | Gloster Meteor T7 (G-BPOA) | Aces High Ltd, North Weald |
| | WF890 | EE Canberra T17A [EJ] | RAF No 360 Sqn, Wyton |
| | WF911 | EE Canberra B2 (nose only) | Privately owned, Preston |
| | WF916 | EE Canberra T17 [EL] | RAF No 360 Sqn, Wyton |
| | WF922 | EE Canberra PR3 | Midland Air Museum, Coventry |
| | WG300 | DH Chipmunk T10 PAX | RAFGSA, Bicester |
| | WG303 | DH Chipmunk T10 PAX (8208M) | RAFGSA, Bicester |
| | WG307 | DH Chipmunk T10 (G-BCYJ) | Privately owned, Shempston Farm, Scotland |
| | WG308 | DH Chipmunk T10 [71] | RAF No 7 AEF, Newton |
| | WG316 | DH Chipmunk T10 (G-BCAH) | Privately owned, Shoreham |
| | WG321 | DH Chipmunk T10 [G] | AAC BFWF, Middle Wallop |
| | WG323 | DH Chipmunk T10 [F] | AAC BFWF, Middle Wallop |
| | WG348 | DH Chipmunk T10 (G-BBMV) | Privately owned, Moulton St Mary |
| | WG350 | DH Chipmunk T10 (G-BPAL) | Privately owned, Old Sarum |
| | WG362 | DH Chipmunk T10 PAX (8437M/8630M) | RAF EFTS, Swinderby |
| | WG403 | DH Chipmunk T10 [O] | AAC BFWF, Middle Wallop |
| | WG407 | DH Chipmunk T10 [67] | RAF No 9 AEF, Finningley |
| | WG418 | DH Chipmunk T10 PAX (8209M/G-ATDY) | RAF No 10 AEF, Woodvale |
| | WG419 | DH Chipmunk T10 PAX (8206M) | No 1053 Sqn ATC, Armthorpe |
| | WG422 | DH Chipmunk T10 (G-BFAX/8394M) [16] | Privately owned, Biggin Hill |
| | WG430 | DH Chipmunk T10 [3] | RAF No 1 AEF, Manston |
| | WG432 | DH Chipmunk T10 [L] | AAC BFWF, Middle Wallop |
| | WG458 | DH Chipmunk T10 | RAF No 4 AEF, Exeter |

| Reg. | Type | Owner or Operator | Notes |
|---|---|---|---|
| WG463 | DH Chipmunk T10 PAX (8363M/G-ATDX) | No 188 Sqn ATC, Ipswich | |
| WG464 | DH Chipmunk T10 PAX (8364M/G-ATEA) | No 131 Sqn ATC, Jesmond Barracks, Newcastle-on-Tyne | |
| WG465 | DH Chipmunk T10 (G-BCEY) | Privately owned, Southend | |
| WG466 | DH Chipmunk T10 | RAF Gatow Station Flight, Berlin | |
| WG469 | DH Chipmunk T10 [72] | RAF No 7 AEF, Newton | |
| WG471 | DH Chipmunk T10 PAX (8210M) | No 301 Sqn ATC, Bury St Edmunds | |
| WG472 | DH Chipmunk T10 (G-AOTY) | Privately owned, White Waltham | |
| WG477 | DH Chipmunk T10 PAX (8362M/G-ATDI/G-ATDP) | No 281 Sqn ATC, Birkdale | |
| WG478 | DH Chipmunk T10 [L] | RAF EFTS, Swinderby | |
| WG479 | DH Chipmunk T10 [K] | RAF EFTS, Swinderby | |
| WG480 | DH Chipmunk T10 [D] | RAF EFTS, Swinderby | |
| WG486 | DH Chipmunk T10 | RAF Gatow Station Flight, Berlin | |
| WG511 | Avro Shackleton T4 (fuselage only) | Cornwall Aero Park, Helston | |
| WG655 | Hawker Sea Fury T20 [910/GN] | *Written off 14 July 1990, nr Yeovilton* | |
| WG718 | WS51 Dragonfly HR3 (A2531) [934/-] | Wales Aircraft Museum, Cardiff | |
| WG719 | WS51 Dragonfly HR5 (G-BRMA) [902] | International Helicopter Museum, Weston-super-Mare | |
| WG724 | WS51 Dragonfly HR5 [932] | North-East Aircraft Museum, Usworth | |
| WG751 | WS51 Dragonfly HR5 | Privately owned, Ramsgreave, Lancs | |
| WG752 | WS51 Dragonfly HR3 [911/CU] | Imperial War Museum, Duxford | |
| *WG754* | WS51 Dragonfly HR3 (really WG725) (7703M) [912/CU] | Cornwall Aero Park, Helston | |
| WG760 | EE P1A (7755M) | RAF Cosford Aerospace Museum | |
| WG763 | EE P1A (7816M) | Greater Manchester Museum of Science and Industry | |
| WG768 | Short SB5 (8005M) | RAF Cosford Aerospace Museum | |
| WG774 | BAC 221 | Science Museum, RNAS Yeovilton | |
| WG777 | Fairey FD2 (7986M) | RAF Cosford Aerospace Museum | |
| WG789 | EE Canberra B2/6 (cockpit only) | Booker Aircraft Museum | |
| WH132 | Gloster Meteor T7 (7906M) [J] | No 276 Sqn ATC, Chelmsford | |
| WH166 | Gloster Meteor T7 (8052M) | RAF Digby, at main gate | |
| WH291 | Gloster Meteor F8 | Second World War Aircraft Preservation Society, Lasham | |
| WH301 | Gloster Meteor F8 (7930M) [T] | RAF Museum, Hendon | |
| WH364 | Gloster Meteor F8 (8169M) | RAF Kemble, at main gate | |
| WH453 | Gloster Meteor D16 [L] | MoD(PE) RAE Llanbedr | |
| WH646 | EE Canberra T17A [EG] | RAF No 360 Sqn, Wyton | |
| WH657 | EE Canberra B2 | Brenzett Aeronautical Collection | |
| WH664 | EE Canberra T17 [EH] | RAF No 360 Sqn, Wyton | |
| WH665 | EE Canberra T17 (8763M) [J] | BAe Filton, derelict | |
| WH670 | EE Canberra B2 [CB] | RAF No 100 Sqn, Wyton | |
| *WH699* | EE Canberra B2T (8755M) (really WJ637) | RAFC Cranwell, Trenchard Hall on display | |
| WH703 | EE Canberra B2 (8490M) [S] | RAF Abingdon, BDRF | |
| WH718 | EE Canberra TT18 [CW] | RAF No 100 Sqn, Wyton | |
| WH724 | EE Canberra T19 (nose only) | RAF Shawbury Fire Section | |
| WH725 | EE Canberra B2 | Imperial War Museum, Duxford | |
| WH734 | EE Canberra TT18 | MoD(PE) RAE Llanbedr | |
| WH740 | EE Canberra T17 (8762M) [X, K] | RAF No 2 SoTT, Cosford | |
| WH773 | EE Canberra PR7 (8696M) | Privately owned, Charlwood, Surrey | |
| WH774 | EE Canberra PR7 | *Scrapped at RAE Farnborough* | |
| WH775 | EE Canberra PR7 [O] (8128M/8868M) | RAF No 2 SoTT, Cosford | |
| WH779 | EE Canberra PR7 [CK] | RAF No 100 Sqn, Wyton | |
| WH780 | EE Canberra T22 [853] | RN, stored St Athan | |
| WH791 | EE Canberra PR7 (8165M/8176M/8187M) | RAF Cottesmore, at main gate | |
| WH796 | EE Canberra PR7 (nose only) | Bomber County Aviation Museum, Hemswell | |
| WH797 | EE Canberra T22 [851] | RN, stored St Athan | |
| WH798 | EE Canberra PR7 (8130M) | Wales Aircraft Museum, Cardiff | |
| WH801 | EE Canberra T22 [850] | RN, stored St Athan | |
| WH803 | EE Canberra T22 [856] | RN, stored St Athan | |

| Notes | Reg. | Type | Owner or Operator |
|---|---|---|---|
| | WH840 | EE Canberra T4 (8350M) | RAF Locking, at main gate |
| | WH846 | EE Canberra T4 | Yorkshire Air Museum, Elvington |
| | WH848 | EE Canberra T4 [BD] (fuselage only) | RAF Canberra Servicing School, Wyton |
| | WH849 | EE Canberra T4 [BE] | RAF No 231 OCU, Wyton |
| | WH850 | EE Canberra T4 | Macclesfield Historical Aviation Society, Chelford, Cheshire |
| | WH854 | EE Canberra T4 (nose only) | Martin Baker Aircraft, Chalgrove |
| | WH863 | EE Canberra T17 (8693M) (nose only) | Newark Air Museum, Winthorpe |
| | WH869 | EE Canberra B2 (8515M) | RAF Abingdon, BDRF |
| | WH876 | EE Canberra D14 | *Scrapped at Boscombe Down, January 1990* |
| | WH887 | EE Canberra TT18 [847] | RN FRADU, Yeovilton |
| | WH902 | EE Canberra T17A [EK] | RAF No 360 Sqn, Wyton |
| | WH903 | EE Canberra B2 (nose only) | Privately owned, Charlwood, Surrey |
| | WH904 | EE Canberra T19 [04] | Newark Air Museum, Winthorpe |
| | WH911 | EE Canberra B2 | Privately owned, Bournemouth |
| | WH914 | EE Canberra B2 (G-27-373) [U] | Privately owned |
| | WH919 | EE Canberra B2 | RAF, stored St Athan |
| | WH946 | EE Canberra B6 (Mod) (8185M) (nose only) | Privately owned, Tetney, Grimsby |
| | WH952 | EE Canberra B6 | Royal Artillery Museum, Woolwich |
| | WH953 | EE Canberra B6 (Mod) | MoD(PE) RAE Bedford |
| | WH957 | EE Canberra E15 (8869M) [N] | RAF No 2 SoTT, Cosford |
| | WH960 | EE Canberra B15 (8344M) [A] | RAF No 2 SoTT, Cosford |
| | WH964 | EE Canberra E15 (8870M) [CX] | RAF No 2 SoTT, Cosford |
| | WH972 | EE Canberra E15 [CM] | *Crashed 27 June 1990, nr Kinloss* |
| | WH981 | EE Canberra E15 [CN] | RAF No 100 Sqn, Wyton |
| | WH983 | EE Canberra E15 [CP] | RAF No 100 Sqn, Wyton |
| | WH984 | EE Canberra B15 (8101M) (nose only) | RAF CTTS, St Athan |
| | WH984 | EE Canberra B15 (8101M) [E] (fuselage etc) | RAF No 2 SoTT, Cosford |
| | WH991 | WS51 Dragonfly HR3 | Privately owned, Storwood, East Yorks |
| | *WJ231* | Hawker Sea Fury FB11 [115/O] (really WE726) | RNAY Fleetlands Museum |
| | *WJ237* | WAR Sea Fury Replica (G-BLTG) [113/O] | Privately owned, Little Gransden |
| | WJ288 | Hawker Sea Fury FB11 (G-SALY) [029] | *To USA 1990* |
| | WJ350 | Percival Sea Prince C2 | Guernsey Airport Fire Section |
| | WJ358 | Auster AOP6 (G-ARYD) | Museum of Army Flying, Middle Wallop |
| | WJ565 | EE Canberra T17 (8871M) [CL] | RAF No 2 SoTT, Cosford |
| | WJ567 | EE Canberra B2 [CC] | RAF No 100 Sqn, Wyton |
| | WJ574 | EE Canberra TT18 [844] | RN, stored St Athan |
| | WJ576 | EE Canberra T17 | Wales Aircraft Museum, Cardiff |
| | WJ581 | EE Canberra T17 | Wales Aircraft Museum, Cardiff |
| | WJ603 | EE Canberra B2 (8664M) [G] | RAF Wattisham Fire Section |
| | WJ607 | EE Canberra T17A [EB] | RAF No 360 Sqn, Wyton |
| | WJ614 | EE Canberra TT18 [846] | RN FRADU, Yeovilton |
| | WJ629 | EE Canberra TT18 (8747M) [845] | RAF Chivenor, BDRT |
| | WJ630 | EE Canberra T17 [ED] | RAF No 360 Sqn, Wyton |
| | WJ633 | EE Canberra T17A [EF] | RAF No 360 Sqn, Wyton |
| | WJ635 | EE Canberra B2 (nose) | *Burnt, 1989* |
| | WJ636 | EE Canberra TT18 [CX] | RAF No 100 Sqn, Wyton |
| | WJ639 | EE Canberra TT18 [39] | North-East Aircraft Museum, Usworth |
| | WJ640 | EE Canberra B2 (8722M) [L] | RAF No 2 SoTT, Cosford |
| | WJ657 | EE Canberra B2 | Brenzett Aeronautical Collection |
| | WJ676 | EE Canberra B2 (7796M) | Princess Alexandra RAF Hospital, Wroughton |
| | WJ677 | EE Canberra B2 (nose only) | RNAS Yeovilton Fire Section |
| | WJ678 | EE Canberra B2 (8864M) [CF] | RAF Abingdon, BDRF |
| | WJ680 | EE Canberra TT18 [CT] | RAF No 100 Sqn, Wyton |
| | WJ682 | EE Canberra TT18 [CU] | RAF No 100 Sqn, Wyton |
| | WJ715 | EE Canberra TT18 [CV] | RAF No 100 Sqn, Wyton |
| | WJ717 | EE Canberra TT18 [841] | RN, stored St Athan |
| | WJ721 | EE Canberra TT18 [21] | Pennine Aviation Museum, Bacup |
| | WJ728 | EE Canberra B2 | *Scrapped at RAE Farnborough* |
| | WJ731 | EE Canberra B2T [BK] | RAF No 231 OCU, Wyton |

| Reg. | Type | Owner or Operator | Notes |
|---|---|---|---|
| WJ756 | EE Canberra E15 [CL] | RAF No 100 Sqn, Wyton | |
| WJ775 | EE Canberra B6 (8581M) [Z] | CSDE, RAF Swanton Morley | |
| WJ815 | EE Canberra PR7 (8729M) | RAF Coningsby Fire Section | |
| WJ817 | EE Canberra PR7 (8695M) [FU2] | RAF Wyton, Fire Section | |
| WJ821 | EE Canberra PR7 (8668M) | Bassingbourn, on display | |
| WJ857 | EE Canberra T4 (nose only) | BAe Warton Fire Section | |
| WJ861 | EE Canberra T4 [BF] | RAF, stored St Athan | |
| WJ863 | EE Canberra T4 (nose only) | Cambridge Airport Fire Section | |
| WJ865 | EE Canberra T4 | RAE Farnborough, wfu | |
| WJ866 | EE Canberra T4 [BL] | RAF No 231 OCU, Wyton | |
| WJ870 | EE Canberra T4 (8683M) | RAF St Mawgan, BDRT | |
| WJ872 | EE Canberra T4 (8492M) (nose only) | No 327 Sqn ATC, Kilmarnock | |
| WJ874 | EE Canberra T4 [BM] | RAF No 231 OCU, Wyton | |
| WJ876 | EE Canberra T4 (nose only) | RAF Exhibition Flight, Abingdon | |
| WJ877 | EE Canberra T4 [BG] | RAF No 231 OCU, Wyton | |
| WJ879 | EE Canberra T4 [BH] | RAF No 231 OCU, Wyton | |
| WJ880 | EE Canberra T4 (8491M) [39] (nose only) | South Yorkshire Aircraft Preservation Society, Firbeck | |
| WJ893 | Vickers Varsity T1 | RAE Aberporth Fire Section | |
| WJ902 | Vickers Varsity T1 [C] | *Scrapped at RAF Wittering* | |
| WJ903 | Vickers Varsity T1 [C] (nose only) | Dumfries & Galloway Aviation Museum, Tinwald Downs | |
| WJ907 | Vickers Varsity T1 [G] | *Scrapped at Norwich Airport* | |
| WJ944 | Vickers Varsity T1 | Wales Aircraft Museum, Cardiff | |
| WJ945 | Vickers Varsity T1 (G-BEDV) [21] | Duxford Aviation Society | |
| WJ975 | EE Canberra T19 [S] | Bomber County Aviation Museum, Hemswell | |
| WJ981 | EE Canberra T17A [EN] | RAF No 360 Sqn, Wyton | |
| WJ986 | EE Canberra T17 [EP] | RAF No 360 Sqn, Wyton | |
| WJ992 | EE Canberra T4 | MoD(PE) RAE Bedford | |
| WK102 | EE Canberra T17 [EQ] (8780M) | RAF No 2 SoTT, Cosford | |
| WK111 | EE Canberra T17 [EA] | RAF No 360 Sqn, Wyton | |
| WK118 | EE Canberra TT18 [CQ] | RAF No 100 Sqn, Wyton | |
| WK119 | EE Canberra B2 (nose) | RAF Wyton, fire section | |
| WK122 | EE Canberra TT18 [22] | Cornwall Aero Park, Helston | |
| WK123 | EE Canberra TT18 [CY] | RAF No 100 Sqn, Wyton | |
| WK124 | EE Canberra TT18 [CR] | RAF No 100 Sqn, Wyton | |
| WK126 | EE Canberra TT18 [843] | RN St Athan, stored | |
| WK127 | EE Canberra TT18 [FO] (8985M) | RAF Wyton, BDRT | |
| WK128 | EE Canberra B2 | MoD(PE) RAE Llanbedr | |
| WK142 | EE Canberra TT18 [848] | RN FRADU, Yeovilton | |
| WK143 | EE Canberra B2 | RAE Llanbedr Fire Section | |
| WK144 | EE Canberra B2 (8689M) | RAF St Athan Fire Section | |
| WK145 | EE Canberra B2 | RAE Llanbedr Fire Section | |
| WK146 | EE Canberra B2 (nose only) | RAF Exhibition Flight, Abingdon | |
| WK162 | EE Canberra B2 [CA] (8887M) | RAF Wyton Fire Section | |
| WK163 | EE Canberra B6 | MoD(PE) RAE Bedford | |
| WK198 | VS Swift F4 (7428M) | North-East Aircraft Museum, Usworth | |
| WK275 | VS Swift F4 | Privately owned, Upper Hill, nr Leominster | |
| WK277 | VS Swift FR5 (7719M) [N] | Newark Air Museum, Winthorpe | |
| WK281 | VS Swift FR5 (7712M) [S] | RAF Museum, Hendon | |
| WK511 | DH Chipmunk T10 [905] | RN, stored Shawbury | |
| WK512 | DH Chipmunk T10 [A] | AAC BFWF, Middle Wallop | |
| WK517 | DH Chipmunk T10 [84] | RAF No 11 AEF, Topcliffe | |
| WK518 | DH Chipmunk T10 | RAF Battle of Britain Flight, Coningsby | |
| WK522 | DH Chipmunk T10 (G-BCOU) | Privately owned, High Easter | |
| WK549 | DH Chipmunk T10 [Y] | Privately owned, Currock Hill | |
| WK550 | DH Chipmunk T10 [J] | RAF EFTS, Swinderby | |
| WK554 | DH Chipmunk T10 [4] | RAF No 1 AEF, Manston | |
| WK558 | DH Chipmunk T10 (G-ARMG) | Privately owned, Wellesbourne Mountford | |
| WK559 | DH Chipmunk T10 [M] | AAC BFWF, Middle Wallop | |
| WK562 | DH Chipmunk T10 [T] | RAF No 3 AEF, Filton | |
| WK570 | DH Chipmunk T10 PAX (8211M) | No 424 Sqn ATC, Southampton | |
| WK572 | DH Chipmunk T10 [X] | RAF No 3 AEF, Filton | |
| WK574 | DH Chipmunk T10 | RNAS Yeovilton Station Flight | |
| WK575 | DH Chipmunk T10 PAX [F] | *Scrapped April 1989 at Bury St Edmunds* | |

| Notes | Reg. | Type | Owner or Operator |
|---|---|---|---|
| | WK576 | DH Chipmunk T10 PAX (8357M) | No 1206 Sqn ATC, Lichfield |
| | WK585 | DH Chipmunk T10 | RAF No 12 AEF, Turnhouse |
| | WK586 | DH Chipmunk T10 [X] | RAF No 8 Sqn, Lossiemouth |
| | WK587 | DH Chipmunk T10 PAX (8212M) | |
| | WK589 | DH Chipmunk T10 [C] | RAF No 6 AEF, Abingdon |
| | WK590 | DH Chipmunk T10 [69] | RAF No 9 AEF, Finningley |
| | WK608 | DH Chipmunk T10 [906] | RN Flying Grading Flt, Plymouth |
| | WK609 | DH Chipmunk T10 [L] | RAF No 3 AEF, Filton |
| | WK611 | DH Chipmunk T10 (G-ARWB) | Privately owned, Shoreham |
| | WK613 | DH Chipmunk T10 [P] | Pennine Aviation Museum, Bacup |
| | WK620 | DH Chipmunk T10 [T] | AAC BFWF, Middle Wallop |
| | WK622 | DH Chipmunk T10 (G-BCZH) | Privately owned, Norwich |
| | WK624 | DH Chipmunk T10 [12] | RAF No 10 AEF, Woodvale |
| | WK626 | DH Chipmunk T10 PAX (8213M) | No 358 Sqn ATC, Welling, London |
| | WK628 | DH Chipmunk T10 (G-BBMW) | Privately owned, Shoreham |
| | WK630 | DH Chipmunk T10 [11] | RAF No 2 AEF, Bournemouth |
| | WK633 | DH Chipmunk T10 [B] | RAF EFTS, Swinderby |
| | WK634 | DH Chipmunk T10 [902] | RN Flying Grading Flt, Plymouth |
| | WK635 | DH Chipmunk T10 | RNAS Yeovilton Station Flight |
| | WK638 | DH Chipmunk T10 [83] | RAF No 11 AEF, Topcliffe |
| | WK639 | DH Chipmunk T10 [10] | RAF No 10 AEF, Woodvale |
| | WK640 | DH Chipmunk T10 [C] | RAF EFTS, Swinderby |
| | WK642 | DH Chipmunk T10 [M] | RAF No 3 AEF, Filton |
| | WK643 | DH Chipmunk T10 [G] | RAF EFTS, Swinderby |
| | WK654 | Gloster Meteor F8 (8092M) [X] | RAF Neatishead, at main gate |
| | WK800 | Gloster Meteor D16 [Z] | MoD(PE) RAE Llanbedr |
| | *WK864* | Gloster Meteor F8 (really WL168) [C] (7750M) | RAF Finningley on display |
| | WK935 | Gloster Meteor Prone Pilot (7869M) | RAF Cosford Aerospace Museum |
| | WK991 | Gloster Meteor F8 (7825M) | Imperial War Museum, Duxford |
| | WL131 | Gloster Meteor F8 (nose only) (7751M) | 4th Guernsey (Forest) Air Scouts, Guernsey Airport |
| | WL181 | Gloster Meteor F8 [X] | North-East Aircraft Museum, Usworth |
| | WL332 | Gloster Meteor T7 | Stratford Aircraft Collection, Long Marston |
| | WL345 | Gloster Meteor T7 | Privately owned, Hollington, East Sussex |
| | WL349 | Gloster Meteor T7 [Z] | Staverton Airport, on display |
| | WL360 | Gloster Meteor T7 (7920M) [G] | Gloucestershire Aviation Collection, Brockworth |
| | WL375 | Gloster Meteor T7 | Dumfries & Galloway Aviation Museum, Tinwald Downs |
| | WL405 | Gloster Meteor T7 | Martin Baker Aircraft, Chalgrove |
| | WL419 | Gloster Meteor T7 | Martin Baker Aircraft, Chalgrove |
| | WL505 | DH Vampire FB9 (7705M) | Privately owned, Bridgend |
| | WL626 | Vickers Varsity T1 (G-BHDD) [P] | East Midlands Aeropark |
| | WL627 | Vickers Varsity T1 (8488M) [D] | Privately owned, Charlwood, Surrey |
| | WL635 | Vickers Varsity T1 | RAF Machrihanish Police School |
| | WL679 | Vickers Varsity T1 | MoD(PE) RAE Farnborough |
| | WL732 | BP Sea Balliol T21 | RAF Cosford Aerospace Museum |
| | WL738 | Avro Shackleton MR2C (8567M) | *Scrapped at Lossiemouth, March 1990* |
| | WL747 | Avro Shackleton AEW2 | RAF No 8 Sqn, Lossiemouth |
| | WL756 | Avro Shackleton AEW2 | RAF No 8 Sqn, Lossiemouth |
| | WL757 | Avro Shackleton AEW2 | RAF No 8 Sqn, Lossiemouth |
| | WL790 | Avro Shackleton AEW2 | RAF No 8 Sqn, Lossiemouth |
| | WL795 | Avro Shackleton MR2C (8753M) [T] | RAF St Mawgan, on display |
| | WL798 | Avro Shackleton MR2C (8114M) [Z] | RAF Lossiemouth Fire Section |
| | *WL925* | Slingsby Cadet TX3 (really WV925) | Air Cadet Recruiting Team, Cosford |
| | WM145 | AW Meteor NF11 (nose only) | N. Yorks Recovery Group, Chop Gate |
| | WM167 | AW Meteor NF11 (G-LOSM) [M] | Privately owned, Bournemouth |
| | WM223 | AW Meteor TT20 | Second World War Aircraft Preservation Society, Lasham |
| | WM292 | AW Meteor TT20 [841] | Wales Aircraft Museum, Cardiff |

| Reg. | Type | Owner or Operator | Notes |
|---|---|---|---|
| *WM311* | AW Meteor TT20 (8177M) (really WM224) | Privately owned, North Weald | |
| *WM366* | AW Meteor NF13 (4X-FNA) | Second World War Aircraft Preservation Society, Lasham | |
| WM367 | AW Meteor NF13 | Privately owned, Powick, Hereford & Worcs | |
| WM571 | DH Sea Venom FAW 21 [742/VL] | Southampton Hall of Aviation, store | |
| WM729 | DH Vampire NF10 (pod only) [A] | Privately owned, Ruislip | |
| WM913 | Hawker Sea Hawk FB5 [456-J] (A2510/8162M) | Newark Air Museum, Winthorpe | |
| WM961 | Hawker Sea Hawk FB5 [J] (A2517) | Snowdon Mountain Aviation Museum, Caernarfon | |
| WM969 | Hawker Sea Hawk FB5 (A2530) | Imperial War Museum, Duxford | |
| WM993 | Hawker Sea Hawk FB5 (A2522) [034] | Privately owned, Peasedown St John, Avon | |
| WM994 | Hawker Sea Hawk FB5 (A2503/G-SEAH) | Privately owned, Bournemouth | |
| *WN105* | Hawker Sea Hawk FB3 (A2662/A2509/8164M) (really WF299) | Cornwall Aero Park, Helston | |
| WN108 | Hawker Sea Hawk FB5 [033] | Shorts Apprentice School, Belfast | |
| WN149 | BP Balliol T2 (nose only) | Privately owned, Preston | |
| WN493 | WS51 Dragonfly HR5 | FAA Museum, RNAS Yeovilton | |
| WN499 | WS51 Dragonfly HR5 [Y] | Snowdon Mountain Aviation Museum, Caernarfon | |
| WN516 | BP Balliol T2 | North-East Aircraft Museum, Usworth | |
| WN534 | BP Balliol T2 (nose only) | Privately owned, Preston | |
| WN904 | Hawker Hunter F2 (7544M) [3] | RE 39 Regt, Waterbeach, on display | |
| WN907 | Hawker Hunter F2 (7416M) (cockpit only) | Blyth Valley Aviation Collection, Walpole | |
| *WP180* | Hawker Hunter F5 (7582M/ 8473M) [K] (really WP190) | RAF Stanbridge, at main gate | |
| WP185 | Hawker Hunter F5 (7583M) | RAF Abingdon, on display | |
| WP250 | DH Vampire NF10 (nose only) | Friends of Biggin Hill, Sevenoaks | |
| WP255 | DH Vampire NF10 (pod) | Privately owned, Ecclesfield | |
| WP270 | EoN Eton TX1 (8598M) | Greater Manchester Museum of Science and Industry | |
| WP271 | EoN Eton TX1 | Privately owned, stored, Keevil | |
| WP309 | Percival Sea Prince T1 [570/CU] | RNAS Yeovilton Fire Section | |
| WP313 | Percival Sea Prince T1 [568/CU] | FAA Museum, stored Wroughton | |
| WP314 | Percival Sea Prince T1 (8634M) [573/CU] | Privately owned, Charlwood, Surrey | |
| WP321 | Percival Sea Prince T1 (G-BRFC) [750/CU] | Privately owned, Bourn | |
| WP503 | WS51 Dragonfly HR3 [901] | Privately owned, Storwood, East Yorks | |
| WP515 | EE Canberra B2 [CD] | RAF, stored St Athan | |
| WP772 | DH Chipmunk T10 [Q] | AAC, RAF Abingdon | |
| WP776 | DH Chipmunk T10 [817] | RN No 771 Sqn, Culdrose | |
| WP784 | DH Chipmunk T10 PAX | Privately owned, Wellingborough | |
| WP786 | DH Chipmunk T10 [G] | RAF No 6 AEF, Abingdon | |
| WP788 | DH Chipmunk T10 (G-BCHL) | Privately owned, Sleap | |
| WP790 | DH Chipmunk T10 (G-BBNC) [T] | Mosquito Aircraft Museum, London Colney | |
| WP795 | DH Chipmunk T10 [901] | RN Flying Grading Flt, Plymouth | |
| WP800 | DH Chipmunk T10 [2] (G-BCXN) | Privately owned, Duxford | |
| WP801 | DH Chipmunk T10 [911] | RN Flying Grading Flt, Plymouth | |
| WP803 | DH Chipmunk T10 | RAF No 8 Sqn, Lossiemouth | |
| WP805 | DH Chipmunk T10 [D] | RAF No 6 AEF, Abingdon | |
| WP808 | DH Chipmunk T10 (G-BDEU) | Privately owned, Binham | |
| WP809 | DH Chipmunk T10 [778] | RN No 771 Sqn, Culdrose | |
| WP833 | DH Chipmunk T10 [A] | RAF No 4 AEF, Exeter | |
| WP835 | DH Chipmunk T10 (G-BDCB) | Privately owned, Booker | |
| WP837 | DH Chipmunk T10 [L] | RAF No 5 AEF, Cambridge | |
| WP839 | DH Chipmunk T10 [A] | RAF No 8 AEF, Shawbury | |
| WP840 | DH Chipmunk T10 [9] | RAF No 2 AEF, Bournemouth | |
| WP843 | DH Chipmunk T10 (G-BDBP) | Privately owned, Tollerton | |

| Notes | Reg. | Type | Owner or Operator |
|---|---|---|---|
| | WP844 | DH Chipmunk T10 [85] | RAF No 11 AEF, Topcliffe |
| | WP845 | DH Chipmunk T10 PAX | No 1329 Sqn ATC, Stroud |
| | WP855 | DH Chipmunk T10 [5] | RAF No 1 AEF, Manston |
| | WP856 | DH Chipmunk T10 [904] | RN Flying Grading Flt, Plymouth |
| | WP857 | DH Chipmunk T10 (G-BDRJ) [24] | Privately owned, Panshanger |
| | WP859 | DH Chipmunk T10 [E] | RAF No 8 AEF, Shawbury |
| | WP860 | DH Chipmunk T10 | RAF No 12 AEF, Turnhouse |
| | WP863 | DH Chipmunk T10 PAX (8360M/G-ATJI) | No 2293 Sqn ATC, Marlborough |
| | WP864 | DH Chipmunk T10 PAX (8214M) | RAF No 7AEF, Newton |
| | WP869 | DH Chipmunk T10 PAX (8215M) | RAF |
| | WP871 | DH Chipmunk T10 [W] | AAC BFWF, Middle Wallop |
| | WP872 | DH Chipmunk T10 | RAF No 12 AEF, Turnhouse |
| | WP896 | DH Chipmunk T10 [11] | RAF No 10 AEF, Woodvale |
| | WP900 | DH Chipmunk T10 [15] | RAF No 10 AEF, Woodvale |
| | WP901 | DH Chipmunk T10 [B] | RAF No 6 AEF, Abingdon |
| | WP903 | DH Chipmunk T10 (G-BCGC) | RN Gliding Club, Culdrose |
| | WP904 | DH Chipmunk T10 [909] | RN Flying Grading Flt, Plymouth |
| | WP906 | DH Chipmunk T10[816/CU] | RN No 771 Sqn, Culdrose |
| | WP907 | DH Chipmunk T10 PAX (7970M) | Privately owned, Reading |
| | WP912 | DH Chipmunk T10 (8467M) | RAF Cosford Aerospace Museum |
| | WP914 | DH Chipmunk T10 [E] | RAF No 6 AEF, Abingdon |
| | WP920 | DH Chipmunk T10 [10] | RAF No 2 AEF, Bournemouth |
| | WP921 | DH Chipmunk T10 PAX | No 1924 Sqn ATC, Croydon |
| | WP925 | DH Chipmunk T10 [C] | AAC BFWF, Middle Wallop |
| | WP927 | DH Chipmunk T10 PAX (8216M/G-ATJK) | *Burned 5 November 1990* |
| | WP928 | DH Chipmunk T10 [D] | AAC BFWF, Middle Wallop |
| | WP929 | DH Chipmunk T10 [F] | RAF No 8 AEF, Shawbury |
| | WP930 | DH Chipmunk T10 [J] | AAC BFWF, Middle Wallop |
| | WP962 | DH Chipmunk T10 [V] | RAF No 3 AEF, Filton |
| | WP964 | DH Chipmunk T10 [Y] | AAC BFWF, Middle Wallop |
| | WP967 | DH Chipmunk T10 | RAF No 12 AEF, Turnhouse |
| | WP970 | DH Chipmunk T10 [T] | RAF No 5 AEF, Cambridge |
| | WP971 | DH Chipmunk T10 (G-ATHD) | Privately owned, Cranfield |
| | WP972 | DH Chipmunk T10 PAX (8667M) | CSDE, RAF Swanton Morley |
| | WP974 | DH Chipmunk T10 [N] | RAF No 3 AEF, Filton |
| | WP977 | DH Chipmunk T10 (G-BHRD) [N] | Privately owned, Kidlington |
| | WP978 | DH Chipmunk T10 PAX (7467M) | RAF No 2 AEF, Lee-on-Solent |
| | WP979 | DH Chipmunk T10 [J] | CSDE, RAF Swanton Morley |
| | WP980 | DH Chipmunk T10 [E] | RAF EFTS, Swinderby |
| | WP981 | DH Chipmunk T10 [D] | RAF No 5 AEF, Cambridge |
| | WP983 | DH Chipmunk T10 [B] | AAC BFWF, Middle Wallop |
| | WP984 | DH Chipmunk T10 [73] | RAF No 7 AEF, Newton |
| | *WR410* | DH Venom FB54 (really J1790/ G-BLKA) [N] | Vintage Aircraft Team, Cranfield |
| | WR539 | DH Venom FB4 (8399M) [F] | Wales Aircraft Museum, Cardiff |
| | WR960 | Avro Shackleton AEW2 (8772M) | Greater Manchester Museum of Science and Industry |
| | WR963 | Avro Shackleton AEW2 | RAF No 8 Sqn, Lossiemouth |
| | WR965 | Avro Shackleton AEW2 | *Crashed Outer Hebrides 30 April 1990* |
| | WR967 | Avro Shackleton MR2C (8398M) | RAF Lossiemouth, for ground training |
| | WR971 | Avro Shackleton MR3 (8119M) [Q] | Privately owned |
| | WR974 | Avro Shackleton MR3 (8117M) [K] | Privately owned, Charlwood, Surrey |
| | WR977 | Avro Shackleton MR3 (8186M) [B] | Newark Air Museum, Winthorpe |
| | WR982 | Avro Shackleton MR3 (8106M) [J] | Privately owned, Charlwood, Surrey |
| | WR985 | Avro Shackleton MR3 (8103M) [H] | Stratford Aircraft Collection, Long Marston |
| | WS103 | Gloster Meteor T7 [709/VL] | FAA Museum, stored Wroughton |
| | WS692 | Gloster Meteor NF12 (7605M) [C] | Newark Air Museum, Winthorpe |
| | WS726 | Gloster Meteor NF14 (7960M) [G] | No 1855 Sqn ATC, Royton |

| Reg. | Type | Owner or Operator | Notes |
|---|---|---|---|
| WS739 | Gloster Meteor NF14 (7961M) | Newark Air Museum, Winthorpe | |
| WS760 | Gloster Meteor NF14 (7964M) | Classic Jet Aircraft Collection, Loughborough | |
| WS774 | Gloster Meteor NF14 (7959M) | RAF Hospital, Ely, at main gate | |
| WS776 | Gloster Meteor NF14 (7716M) [K] | RAF North Luffenham, at main gate | |
| WS792 | Gloster Meteor NF14 (7965M) [K] | Privately owned, Brighouse Bay, D&G | |
| WS807 | Gloster Meteor NF14 (7973M) [N] | RAF Watton, at main gate | |
| WS832 | Gloster Meteor NF14 [W] | Solway Aviation Society, Carlisle Airport | |
| WS838 | Gloster Meteor NF14 | Midland Air Museum, Coventry | |
| WS840 | Gloster Meteor NF14 (7969M) | RAF Aldergrove for display | |
| WS843 | Gloster Meteor NF14 (7937M) [Y] | RAF Museum, Hendon | |
| *WS844* | Gloster Meteor NF14 (7967M) [JCF] (really WS788) | Yorkshire Air Museum, Elvington | |
| | | | |
| *WT121* | Douglas Skyraider AEW1 [415/CU] (really WT983) | FAA Museum, RNAS Yeovilton | |
| WT212 | EE Canberra B2 | Lovaux Ltd, Macclesfield | |
| WT301 | EE Canberra B6 (Mod) | Defence School, Chattenden | |
| WT308 | EE Canberra B(I)6 | MoD(PE), RAE Farnborough, wfu | |
| WT309 | EE Canberra B(I)6 | MoD(PE) A&AEE, Boscombe Down Apprentice School | |
| WT327 | EE Canberra PR7 | MoD(PE) RAE Bedford | |
| WT333 | EE Canberra B(I)8 | MoD(PE) RAE Bedford | |
| WT339 | EE Canberra B(I)8 (8198M) | RAF Barkston Heath Fire Section | |
| WT346 | EE Canberra B(I)8 (8197M) | RAF Cosford Aerospace Museum | |
| WT478 | EE Canberra T4 [BA] | RAF No 231 OCU, Wyton | |
| WT480 | EE Canberra T4 [BC] | RAF No 231 OCU, Wyton | |
| WT482 | EE Canberra T4 (nose) | Stratford Aircraft Collection, Long Marston | |
| WT483 | EE Canberra T4 [83] | Stratford Aircraft Collection, Long Marston | |
| WT486 | EE Canberra T4 (8102M) [C] | Aldergrove Fire Section | |
| WT488 | EE Canberra T4 | BAe Dunsfold | |
| WT507 | EE Canberra PR7 (8131M/8548M) [44] (nose only) | No 384 Sqn ATC, Mansfield | |
| WT509 | EE Canberra PR7 [CG] | RAF No 100 Sqn, Wyton | |
| WT510 | EE Canberra T22 [854] | RN, stored St Athan | |
| WT518 | EE Canberra PR7 (8133M/8691M) (rear fuselage only) | Wales Aircraft Museum, Cardiff | |
| WT519 | EE Canberra PR7 [CH] | RAF No 100 Sqn, Wyton | |
| WT520 | EE Canberra PR7 (8094M/8184M) [20] | RAF Swinderby | |
| WT525 | EE Canberra T22 [855] | RN, stored St Athan | |
| WT532 | EE Canberra PR7 (8728M/8890M) [Z] | RAF No 2 SoTT, Cosford | |
| WT534 | EE Canberra PR7 (8549M) [43] (nose only) | No 492 Sqn ATC, Shirley, W. Mids | |
| WT535 | EE Canberra T22 [852] | RN, stored St Athan | |
| WT536 | EE Canberra PR7 (8063M) [F] | RAF No 2 SoTT, Cosford | |
| WT537 | EE Canberra PR7 | BAe Samlesbury, on display | |
| WT538 | EE Canberra PR7 [CJ] | RAF No 100 Sqn, Wyton | |
| WT555 | Hawker Hunter F1 (7499M) | Privately owned, London | |
| WT569 | Hawker Hunter F1 (7491M) | No 2117 Sqn ATC, Kenfig Hill, Mid-Glamorgan | |
| WT612 | Hawker Hunter F1 (7496M) | RAF Henlow on display | |
| WT619 | Hawker Hunter F1 (7525M) | Greater Manchester Museum of Science and Industry | |
| WT648 | Hawker Hunter F1 (7530M) (nose section) | RAF St Athan Fire Section | |
| WT651 | Hawker Hunter F1 (7532M) [C] | ROC Lawford Heath, Warwicks, on display | |
| WT660 | Hawker Hunter F1 (7421M) [C] | RAF Carlisle, at main gate | |
| WT680 | Hawker Hunter F1 (7533M) [Z] | No 1429 Sqn ATC at RAE Aberporth | |
| WT684 | Hawker Hunter F1 (7422M) | RAF Brize Norton Fire Section | |
| WT694 | Hawker Hunter F1 (7510M) | RAF Newton, at main gate | |
| WT711 | Hawker Hunter GA11 [833/DD] | RNAS Culdrose, SAH | |
| *WT720* | Hawker Hunter F51 [B] (8565M) (really E-408) | RAF Sealand, on display | |

| Notes | Reg. | Type | Owner or Operator |
|---|---|---|---|
| | WT722 | Hawker Hunter T8C [878/VL] | RN FRADU, Yeovilton |
| | WT723 | Hawker Hunter PR11 [866/VL] | RNAS Yeovilton, Fire Section |
| | WT744 | Hawker Hunter GA11 [868/VL] | RN FRADU, Yeovilton |
| | WT746 | Hawker Hunter F4 (7770M) [A] | Army, Saighton, Chester |
| | WT799 | Hawker Hunter T8C [879] | RN, stored Shawbury |
| | WT804 | Hawker Hunter GA11 [831/DD] | RNAS Culdrose, SAH |
| | WT806 | Hawker Hunter GA11 | RAF Abingdon |
| | WT867 | Slingsby Cadet TX3 | Privately owned, Eaglescott |
| | WT910 | Slingsby Cadet TX1 | Privately owned, Clapham |
| | WT933 | Bristol Sycamore 3 (G-ALSW/7709M) | Newark Air Museum, Winthorpe |
| | WV106 | Douglas Skyraider AEW1 [427/C] | Cornwall Aero Park, Helston |
| | WV198 | S55 Whirlwind HAR21 (G-BJWY/A2576) [K] | The Aeroplane Collection, Warmingham |
| | WV256 | Hawker Hunter GA11 [862/VL] | RN FRADU, Yeovilton |
| | WV267 | Hawker Hunter GA11 [836/DD] | RNAS Culdrose, SAH |
| | WV276 | Hawker Hunter F4 (7847M) [D] | RAF No 1 SoTT, Halton |
| | WV318 | Hawker Hunter T7B | RAF No 208 Sqn, Lossiemouth |
| | WV322 | Hawker Hunter T8C | RAF No 237 OCU, Lossiemouth |
| | WV332 | Hawker Hunter F4 (7673M) (nose only) | No 1254 Sqn ATC, Godalming |
| | WV363 | Hawker Hunter T8C [872/VL] | RN FRADU, Yeovilton |
| | WV372 | Hawker Hunter T7 [877/VL] | RN FRADU, Yeovilton |
| | WV381 | Hawker Hunter GA11 [732/VL] | BNFL, Culham, Oxon |
| | WV382 | Hawker Hunter GA11 [830/VL] | RN Lee-on-Solent, BDRT |
| | WV383 | Hawker Hunter T7 | MoD(PE) RAE Farnborough |
| | WV396 | Hawker Hunter T8C [879/VL] | RN FRADU, Yeovilton |
| | WV483 | Percival Provost T1 (7693M) [N-E] | Privately owned, |
| | WV486 | Percival Provost T1 (7694M) [N-D] | Privately owned, Grazeley, Berks |
| | WV493 | Percival Provost T1 (G-BDYG/7696M) [29] | Royal Scottish Museum of Flight, East Fortune |
| | WV495 | Percival Provost T1 (7697M) [P-C] | Vintage Aircraft Team, Cranfield |
| | WV499 | Percival Provost T1 (7698M) [P-G] | Privately owned, South Woodford, London |
| | WV544 | Percival Provost T1 (7700M) | AAC Netheravon Fire Section |
| | WV562 | Percival Provost T1 (7606M) [P-C] | RAF Cosford Aerospace Museum |
| | WV605 | Percival Provost T1 [T-B] | Norfolk & Suffolk Aviation Museum, Flixton |
| | WV606 | Percival Provost T1 (7622M) [P-B] | Newark Air Museum, Winthorpe |
| | WV679 | Percival Provost T1 (7615M) [O-J] | Privately owned, Dunkeswell |
| | WV686 | Percival Provost T1 (7621M) (G-BLFT) [O-P] | Privately owned, Slough |
| | WV703 | Percival Pembroke C1 (8108M) (*G-IIIM*) | Privately owned, Tattershall Thorpe |
| | WV705 | Percival Pembroke C1 (nose only) | Southampton Hall of Aviation, stored |
| | WV740 | Percival Pembroke C1 (G-BNPH) | Privately owned, Benson |
| | WV746 | Percival Pembroke C1 (8938M) | RAF Cosford Aerospace Museum |
| | WV753 | Percival Pembroke C1 (8113M) | Wales Aircraft Museum, Cardiff |
| | WV781 | Bristol Sycamore HR12 (G-ALTD/7839M) | Snowdon Mountain Aviation Museum, Caernarfon |
| | WV783 | Bristol Sycamore HR12 (G-ALSP/7841M) | RNAY Fleetlands Museum |
| | WV787 | EE Canberra B2/8 (8799M) | Newark Air Museum, Winthorpe |
| | WV795 | Hawker Sea Hawk FGA6 (A2661/8151M) | Jet Heritage, Bournemouth |
| | WV797 | Hawker Sea Hawk FGA6 [491/J] (A2637/8155M) | Midland Air Museum, Coventry |
| | WV798 | Hawker Sea Hawk FGA6 (A2557) [028/CU] | Second World War Aircraft Preservation Society, Lasham |
| | WV826 | Hawker Sea Hawk FGA6 (A2532) [147/Z] | Wales Aircraft Museum, Cardiff |
| | WV843 | Hawker Sea Hawk FGA4 (nose only) | Torbay Aircraft Museum, Paignton |
| | WV856 | Hawker Sea Hawk FGA6 [163] | FAA Museum, RNAS Yeovilton |

| Reg. | Type | Owner or Operator | Notes |
|---|---|---|---|
| WV903 | Hawker Sea Hawk FGA6 (A2632/8153M) [128/C] | RN AES, Lee-on-Solent | |
| WV908 | Hawker Sea Hawk FGA6 (A2660/8154M) [188/A] | RN Historic Flight, RNAS Yeovilton | |
| WV911 | Hawker Sea Hawk FGA4 (A2526) [115/C] | RNAY Fleetlands Museum | |
| WW138 | DH Sea Venom FAW22 [227/O] | FAA Museum, RNAS Yeovilton | |
| WW145 | DH Sea Venom FAW22 [680/LM] | Royal Scottish Museum of Flight, East Fortune | |
| WW217 | DH Sea Venom FAW22 [736] | Newark Air Museum, Winthorpe | |
| WW388 | Percival Provost T1 (7616M) [O-F] | Wales Aircraft Museum, Cardiff | |
| WW397 | Percival Provost T1 (8060M/ G-BKHP) [N-E] | Privately owned, RAF Lyneham | |
| WW421 | Percival Provost T1 (7688M) [O] | Lincolnshire Aviation Museum, East Kirkby | |
| WW442 | Percival Provost T1 (7618M) [N] | Privately owned, Pimlico | |
| WW444 | Percival Provost T1 [D] | Privately owned, Sibson | |
| WW447 | Percival Provost T1 | Privately owned, Grazeley, Berks | |
| WW453 | Percival Provost T1 [W-S] | Privately owned, Strathallan | |
| WW654 | Hawker Hunter GA11 [834/DD] | RNAS Culdrose, SAH | |
| *WX660* | Hover-Air HA-5 Hoverhawk III (really XW660) | Privately owned, Cheltenham | |
| WX788 | DH Venom NF3 | Wales Aircraft Museum, Cardiff | |
| WX853 | DH Venom NF3 (7443M) | De Havilland Heritage Collection, Hatfield | |
| WX905 | DH Venom NF3 (7458M) | Newark Air Museum, Winthorpe | |
| WZ415 | DH Vampire T11 [72] | No 2 Sqn ATC, Pimlico | |
| WZ425 | DH Vampire T11 | Wales Aircraft Museum, Cardiff | |
| WZ450 | DH Vampire T11 (pod only) [23] | No 2371 Sqn ATC, Tile Cross, W. Mids | |
| WZ464 | DH Vampire T11 (N62430) [40] | Vintage Aircraft Team, Cranfield | |
| *WZ476* | DH Vampire T11 (really XE985) | Mosquito Aircraft Museum, stored Hatfield | |
| WZ507 | DH Vampire T11 (G-VTII) | Vintage Aircraft Team, Cranfield | |
| WZ514 | DH Vampire T11 | Privately owned, Meols, Merseyside | |
| WZ515 | DH Vampire T11 [60] | Solway Aviation Society, Carlisle | |
| WZ518 | DH Vampire T11 | North East Aircraft Museum, Usworth | |
| WZ549 | DH Vampire T11 [F] (8118M) | Ulster Heritage Centre, Newtownards | |
| WZ550 | DH Vampire T11 (7902M) [R] | Booker Aircraft Museum | |
| WZ553 | DH Vampire T11 [40] | Newark Air Museum, Winthorpe | |
| WZ557 | DH Vampire T11 | Privately owned, Cranfield | |
| WZ559 | DH Vampire T11 (7736M) [45] (pod only) | RAF Halton Fire Section | |
| WZ581 | DH Vampire T11 [77] | Privately owned, Ruislip | |
| WZ584 | DH Vampire T11 [K] | St Albans College of FE | |
| WZ589 | DH Vampire T11 [19] | Lashenden Air Warfare Museum, Headcorn | |
| WZ590 | DH Vampire T11 [19] | Imperial War Museum, Duxford | |
| WZ608 | DH Vampire T11 [56] (pod only) | Privately owned, East Anglia | |
| WZ616 | DH Vampire T11 [60] | Vintage Aircraft Team, Cranfield | |
| WZ620 | DH Vampire T11 [68] | Privately owned, Keevil | |
| WZ662 | Auster AOP9 (G-BKVK) | Privately owned, Swanton Morley | |
| WZ706 | Auster AOP9 (7851M) | AAC Netheravon | |
| WZ711 | Auster 9/Beagle E3 (G-AVHT) | Privately owned, Middle Wallop | |
| WZ721 | Auster AOP9 | Museum of Army Flying, Middle Wallop | |
| WZ724 | Auster AOP9 (7432M) | AAC Middle Wallop, at main gate | |
| WZ736 | Avro 707A (7868M) | Greater Manchester Museum of Science and Industry | |
| WZ744 | Avro 707C (7932M) | RAF Cosford Aerospace Museum | |
| WZ753 | Slingsby Grasshopper TX1 | Southampton Hall of Aviation | |
| WZ767 | Slingsby Grasshopper TX1 | North East Aircraft Museum, Usworth | |
| WZ779 | Slingsby Grasshopper TX1 | Stratford Aircraft Collection, Long Marston | |
| WZ791 | Slingsby Grasshopper TX1 (8944M) | RAF ACCGS Syerston, preserved | |
| WZ819 | Slingsby Grasshopper TX1 (BGA 3498) | Privately owned, West Malling | |
| WZ822 | Slingsby Grasshopper TX1 | Robertsbridge Aviation Society, E. Sussex | |
| *WZ826* | Vickers Valiant B(K)1 (7872M) (nose only) (really XD826) | Wales Aircraft Museum, Cardiff | |

| Notes | Reg. | Type | Owner or Operator |
|---|---|---|---|
| | WZ845 | DH Chipmunk T10 [6] | RAF No 1 AEF, Manston |
| | WZ846 | DH Chipmunk T10 PAX (G-BCSC/8439M) | No 1404 Sqn ATC, Chatham |
| | WZ847 | DH Chipmunk T10 [F] | RAF No 6 AEF, Abingdon |
| | WZ856 | DH Chipmunk T10 [74] | RAF No 7 AEF, Newton |
| | WZ862 | DH Chipmunk T10 [M] | RAF EFTS, Swinderby |
| | WZ866 | DH Chipmunk T10 PAX (8217M) (G-ATEB) | No 2296 Sqn ATC, Dunoon, Strathclyde |
| | WZ868 | DH Chipmunk T10 (G-BCIW) [H] | Privately owned, Duxford |
| | WZ869 | DH Chipmunk T10 PAX (8019M) [R] | No 391 Sqn ATC, Handforth |
| | WZ872 | DH Chipmunk T10 [E] | RAF No 5 AEF, Cambridge |
| | WZ876 | DH Chipmunk T10 (G-BBWN) | Privately owned, Netherthorpe |
| | WZ877 | DH Chipmunk T10 [75] | RAF No 7AEF, Newton |
| | WZ878 | DH Chipmunk T10 [86] | RAF No 11 AEF, Topcliffe |
| | WZ879 | DH Chipmunk T10 [X] | RAF EFTS, Swinderby |
| | WZ882 | DH Chipmunk T10 [K] | AAC BFWF, Middle Wallop |
| | WZ884 | DH Chipmunk T10 [P] | AAC BFWF, Middle Wallop |
| | XA109 | DH Sea Vampire T22 | Royal Scottish Museum of Flight, East Fortune |
| | XA127 | DH Sea Vampire T22 (nose only) | FAA Museum, RNAS Yeovilton |
| | XA129 | DH Sea Vampire T22 | FAA Museum, stored Wroughton |
| | XA231 | Slingsby Grasshopper TX1 (8888M) | E. Cheshire & S. Manchester Wing ATC HQ, RAF Sealand |
| | XA243 | Slingsby Grasshopper TX1 (8886M) | RAF St Athan, ground instruction |
| | XA244 | Slingsby Grasshopper TX1 | RAF Cosford, stored |
| | XA282 | Slingsby Cadet TX3 | Snowdon Mountain Aviation Museum Caernarfon |
| | XA289 | Slingsby Cadet TX3 | Privately owned, Eaglescott |
| | XA293 | Slingsby Cadet TX3 | Stratford Aircraft Collection, Long Marston |
| | XA454 | Fairey Gannet COD4 | RNAS Yeovilton Fire Section |
| | XA459 | Fairey Gannet ECM6 (A2608) [E/-] | Privately owned, Cirencester |
| | XA460 | Fairey Gannet ECM6 [768/BY] | North-East Wales Institute of HE, Connah's Quay |
| | XA466 | Fairey Gannet COD4 [777/LM] | FAA Museum, stored Wroughton |
| | XA508 | Fairey Gannet T2 (A2472) [627/GN] | Midland Air Museum, Coventry |
| | XA549 | Gloster Javelin FAW1 (7717M) [E] | RAF Museum Store, Swinderby |
| | XA553 | Gloster Javelin FAW1 (7470M) | RAF Stanmore Park, on display |
| | XA564 | Gloster Javelin FAW1 (7464M) | RAF Cosford Aerospace Museum |
| | XA571 | Gloster Javelin FAW1 (nose only) (7663M/7722M) | Booker Aircraft Museum |
| | XA634 | Gloster Javelin FAW4 (7641M) [L] | RAF Leeming, on display |
| | XA699 | Gloster Javelin FAW5 (7809M) | Midland Air Museum, Coventry |
| | XA801 | Gloster Javelin FAW2 (7739M) | RAF Stafford, at main gate |
| | XA847 | EE P1B (8371M) | Privately owned, Southampton Docks |
| | XA862 | WS55 Whirlwind HAR1 (A2542/G-AMJT) [9] | Midland Air Museum, Coventry |
| | XA864 | WS55 Whirlwind HAR1 | FAA Museum, stored Wroughton |
| | XA870 | WS55 Whirlwind HAR1 (A2543) | Cornwall Aero Park, Helston |
| | XA879 | DH Devon C2 | RAE, stored Llanbedr |
| | XA880 | DH Devon C2 | MoD(PE) RAE Llanbedr |
| | XA893 | Avro Vulcan B1 (8591M) (nose only) | RAF Cosford Aerospace Museum |
| | XA903 | Avro Vulcan B1 (nose only) | Wales Aircraft Museum, Cardiff |
| | XA917 | HP Victor B1 (7827M) (nose only) | RAF Marham, ground instruction |
| | XB259 | Blackburn Beverley C1 (G-AOAI) | Museum of Army Transport, Beverley |
| | XB261 | Blackburn Beverley C1 (cockpit) | Imperial War Museum, Duxford |
| | XB285 | Blackburn Beverley C1 | Privately owned, Worminghall, Bucks |
| | XB288 | Blackburn Beverley C1 | Privately owned, Worminghall, Bucks |
| | XB446 | Grumman Avenger ECM6B [992/C] | FAA Museum, RNAS Yeovilton |
| | XB480 | Hiller HT1 (A2577) [537] | FAA Museum, RNAS Yeovilton |
| | XB733 | Canadair Sabre 4 (*G-ATBF*) | Privately owned |
| | XD145 | Saro SR53 | RAF Cosford Aerospace Museum |

| Reg. | Type | Owner or Operator | Notes |
|---|---|---|---|
| XD163 | WS55 Whirlwind HAR10 (8645M) [X] | International Helicopter Museum, Weston-super-Mare | |
| XD165 | WS55 Whirlwind HAR10 (8673M) [B] | RAF No 1 SoTT, Halton | |
| XD186 | WS55 Whirlwind HAR10 (8730M) | RAF Chivenor, on display | |
| XD219 | VS Scimitar F1 (fuselage) | RNAS Yeovilton, fire section | |
| XD234 | VS Scimitar F1 [834] | RAE, derelict Farnborough | |
| XD317 | VS Scimitar F1 [112/R] | FAA Museum, RNAS Yeovilton | |
| XD332 | VS Scimitar F1 (A2574) [194/C] | Cornwall Aero Park, Helston | |
| XD375 | DH Vampire T11 (7887M) | City of Norwich Aviation Museum | |
| XD377 | DH Vampire T11 (8203M) [A] | RAF Cosford | |
| XD382 | DH Vampire T11 (8033M) | Privately owned, Ripley, Derbys | |
| XD425 | DH Vampire T11 [16] | Dumfries & Galloway Aviation Museum, Tinwald Downs | |
| *XD429* | DH Vampire T11 (7604M) [28] (really XD542) | RAF Cranwell, at main gate | |
| XD434 | DH Vampire T11 [25] | Fenland Air Museum, Wisbech | |
| XD435 | DH Vampire T11 | Privately owned, Appleton Thorn, Cheshire | |
| XD445 | DH Vampire T11 [51] | Bomber County Aviation Museum, Hemswell | |
| XD447 | DH Vampire T11 [50] | Stratford Aircraft Collection, Long Marston | |
| XD452 | DH Vampire T11 (7990M) [66] | Privately owned, Whitchurch, Salop | |
| XD453 | DH Vampire T11 (7890M) [64] | No 58 Sqn ATC, Yorkshire Air Museum, Elvington | |
| XD459 | DH Vampire T11 [63] (pod only) | Stratford Aircraft Collection, Long Marston, stored | |
| XD463 | DH Vampire T11 (8023M) | No 1360 Sqn ATC, Stapleford, Notts | |
| XD506 | DH Vampire T11 (7983M) | RAF Swinderby, on display | |
| XD525 | DH Vampire T11 (7882M) (pod only) | Campbell College CCF, Belfast | |
| XD528 | DH Vampire T11 (8159M) | No 2415 Sqn ATC, Penkridge, Staffs | |
| XD534 | DH Vampire T11 [41] | Military Aircraft Preservation Group, Hadfield, Derbys | |
| XD535 | DH Vampire T11 | Aircraft Restoration Flt, North Weald | |
| XD536 | DH Vampire T11 (7734M) [H] | Southall Technical College | |
| XD547 | DH Vampire T11 [Z] (pod only) | Scotland West Aircraft Investigation Group, Aberfoyle | |
| XD593 | DH Vampire T11 [50] | Newark Air Museum, Winthorpe | |
| XD595 | DH Vampire T11 (pod only) | Privately owned, Altrincham | |
| XD596 | DH Vampire T11 (7939M) | Southampton Hall of Aviation | |
| XD599 | DH Vampire T11 [A] | Snowdon Mountain Aviation Museum, Caernarfon | |
| XD602 | DH Vampire T11 (7737M) | Privately owned, Southall | |
| XD616 | DH Vampire T11 [56] | No 1239 Sqn ATC, Hoddesdon, Herts | |
| XD622 | DH Vampire T11 (8160M) | No 2214 Sqn ATC, Usworth | |
| XD624 | DH Vampire T11 [O] | Macclesfield Technical College | |
| XD626 | DH Vampire T11 [Q] | Midland Air Museum, Coventry | |
| XD674 | Hunting Jet Provost T1 (7570M) [T] | RAF Cosford Aerospace Museum | |
| XD816 | Vickers Valiant B(K)1 (nose only) | Brooklands Museum | |
| XD818 | Vickers Valiant B(K)1 (7894M) | RAF Museum, Hendon | |
| XD875 | Vickers Valiant B(K)1 (nose only) | No 163 Sqn ATC, Coventry | |
| XE317 | Bristol Sycamore HR14 (G-AMWO) [S-N] | Newark Air Museum, Winthorpe | |
| XE327 | Hawker Sea Hawk FGA6 (A2556) [644/LH] | Privately owned, Kings Langley, Herts | |
| XE339 | Hawker Sea Hawk FGA6 (8156M/A2635) [149/E] | RNAS, stored Lee-on-Solent | |
| XE340 | Hawker Sea Hawk FGA6 [131/Z] | Privately owned, Strathallan | |
| XE368 | Hawker Sea Hawk FGA6 (A2534) [200/J] | Cornwall Aero Park, Helston | |
| XE369 | Hawker Sea Hawk FGA6 [5] (A2580/8158M/A2633) | RNAS Yeovilton Fire Section | |
| XE521 | Fairey Rotodyne Y (parts) | International Helicopter Museum, Weston-super-Mare | |
| XE531 | Hawker Hunter T12 | *Scrapped at RAE Farnborough* | |
| XE584 | Hawker Hunter FGA9 (front fuselage) | Macclesfield Historical Av Soc, Chelford, Cheshire | |

| Notes | Reg. | Type | Owner or Operator |
|---|---|---|---|
| | XE587 | Hawker Hunter F6 [7] | MoD(PE), RAE Farnborough Apprentice School |
| | XE597 | Hawker Hunter FGA9 (8874M) | RAF Halton Fire Section |
| | XE601 | Hawker Hunter FGA9 | MoD(PE) A&AEE Boscombe Down |
| | XE624 | Hawker Hunter FGA9 (8875M) [G] | RAF Brawdy, on display |
| | XE627 | Hawker Hunter F6A | Imperial War Museum, Duxford |
| | XE643 | Hawker Hunter FGA9 (8586M) (nose only) | RAF Exhibition Flight, Abingdon |
| | XE650 | Hawker Hunter FGA9 (G-9-449) (nose only) | Privately owned, Seighford, Staffs |
| | XE653 | Hawker Hunter F6A (8829M) [D] | RAF TMTS, Scampton |
| | XE656 | Hawker Hunter F6 (8678M) | RAF No 1 SoTT, Halton |
| | XE665 | Hawker Hunter T8C [876/VL] | RN FRADU, Yeovilton |
| | XE668 | Hawker Hunter GA11 [832/DD] | RNAS Culdrose, SAH |
| | XE670 | Hawker Hunter F4 (7762M/ 8585M) (nose only) | RAF Exhibition Flight, Abingdon |
| | XE677 | Hawker Hunter F4 (G-HHUN) | Jet Heritage, Bournemouth |
| | XE682 | Hawker Hunter GA11 | RNAS Culdrose Fire Section |
| | XE685 | Hawker Hunter GA11 [861/VL] | RN FRADU, Yeovilton |
| | XE689 | Hawker Hunter GA11 [864/VL] | RN FRADU, Yeovilton |
| | *XE689* | Hawker Hunter GA11 (8846M) (Really XE673) [680/VL] | *Scrapped January 1990* |
| | XE707 | Hawker Hunter GA11 [865/VL] | RN FRADU, Yeovilton |
| | XE712 | Hawker Hunter GA11 [708] | RN Predannack Fire School |
| | XE793 | Slingsby Cadet TX3 (8666M) | RAF St Athan, instructional use |
| | XE799 | Slingsby Cadet TX3 [R] (8943M) | RAF ACCGS Syerston, preserved |
| | XE849 | DH Vampire T11 (7928M) [V3] | Avon Aviation Museum, Calne, Wilts |
| | XE852 | DH Vampire T11 [H] | No 2247 Sqn ATC, Hawarden |
| | XE855 | DH Vampire T11 | Midland Air Museum, Coventry |
| | XE856 | DH Vampire T11 | Stratford Aircraft Collection, Long Marston |
| | XE864 | DH Vampire T11 | South Yorks Aviation Society, Firbeck |
| | XE872 | DH Vampire T11 [62] | Midland Air Museum, Coventry |
| | XE874 | DH Vampire T11 (8582M) [61] | Privately owned, New Blyth, Grampian |
| | *XE897* | DH Vampire T11 (really XD403) | Privately owned, Strathallan |
| | XE920 | DH Vampire T11 (8196M) [D] | RAF, stored Scampton |
| | XE921 | DH Vampire T11 [64] | Privately owned, Keevil |
| | XE928 | DH Vampire T11 [76] | Privately owned, Keevil |
| | XE935 | DH Vampire T11 [30] | South Yorks Air Museum, Firbeck |
| | XE946 | DH Vampire T11 (7473M) (pod only) | RAF Museum Restoration Centre, Cardington |
| | XE956 | DH Vampire T11 | St Albans College of FE |
| | XE979 | DH Vampire T11 [54] | Privately owned, Pershore |
| | XE982 | DH Vampire T11 (7564M) | Privately owned, Dunkeswell |
| | XE993 | DH Vampire T11 (8161M) | RAF Cosford Fire Section |
| | XE995 | DH Vampire T11 [53] | Privately owned, Torbay |
| | XE998 | DH Vampire T11 [36] | Privately owned, Camberley |
| | XF113 | VS Swift F7 (nose only) [19] | Privately owned, Peasedown St John, Avon |
| | XF114 | VS Swift F7 (G-SWIF) | Jet Heritage Ltd, Bournemouth |
| | XF274 | Gloster Meteor T7 | *Scrapped at RAE Farnborough* |
| | XF289 | Hawker Hunter T8C [875/VL] | RN FRADU, Yeovilton |
| | XF300 | Hawker Hunter GA11 [860/VL] | RN FRADU, Yeovilton |
| | XF301 | Hawker Hunter GA11 [834/VL] | RN FRADU, Yeovilton |
| | XF310 | Hawker Hunter T8C [869/VL] | RN FRADU, Yeovilton |
| | *XF314* | Hawker Hunter F51 [N] (really E-412) | Tangmere Military Aviation Museum |
| | XF319 | Hawker Hunter F4 (7849M) [B] | RAF No 1 SoTT, Halton |
| | XF321 | Hawker Hunter T7 | RNEC Manadon |
| | XF357 | Hawker Hunter T8C [871/VL] | RN FRADU, Yeovilton |
| | XF358 | Hawker Hunter T8C [870/VL] | RN FRADU, Yeovilton |
| | XF368 | Hawker Hunter GA11 [863/VL] | RN FRADU, Yeovilton |
| | XF375 | Hawker Hunter F6 (8736M) [05] | SIF, RAFC Cranwell |
| | XF382 | Hawker Hunter F6A [15] | Midland Air Museum, Coventry |
| | XF383 | Hawker Hunter F6 (8706M) (wears *8506M*) [V] | RAF Wittering, BDRT |
| | *XF383* | Hawker Hunter F51 [71] (really E-409) | Wales Aircraft Museum, Cardiff |
| | XF435 | Hawker Hunter FGA9 (8880M) [52] | RAF |

| Reg. | Type | Owner or Operator | Notes |
|---|---|---|---|
| *XF445* | Hawker Hunter FGA9 (8715M) [T] (really XG264) | RAF Brawdy Fire Section | |
| XF509 | Hawker Hunter F6 (8708M) [73] | RAF Chivenor, at main gate | |
| XF515 | Hawker Hunter F6A (8830M) [C] | RAF TMTS, Scampton | |
| XF516 | Hawker Hunter F6A (8685M) [66] | SIF, RAFC Cranwell | |
| *XF519* | Hawker Hunter FGA9 [J] (8677M/ 8738M) (composite with XJ695) | FSCTE, RAF Manston | |
| XF522 | Hawker Hunter F6 (nose only) | No 1365 Sqn ATC, Aylesbury | |
| XF526 | Hawker Hunter F6 (8679M) [78/E] | RAF St Athan Fire Section | |
| XF527 | Hawker Hunter F6 (8680M) | RAF Halton, on display | |
| XF545 | Percival Provost T1 (7957M) [O-K] | RAF Linton-on-Ouse, on display | |
| XF597 | Percival Provost T1 (G-BKFW) [A-H] | Privately owned, Aldermaston | |
| XF603 | Percival Provost T1 [H] | Rolls-Royce Tech Coll, Filton | |
| XF690 | Percival Provost T1 (G-BGKA/ (8041M) | Privately owned, Newton | |
| XF708 | Avro Shackleton MR3 [203/C] | Imperial War Museum, Duxford | |
| XF785 | Bristol 173 (G-ALBN/7648M) | RAF Museum Store | |
| XF799 | Percival Pembroke C1PR | RAF Northolt, stored | |
| XF836 | Percival Provost T1 (8043M/ G-AWRY) [JG] | Privately owned, Thatcham | |
| XF844 | Percival Provost T1 [70] | RAE Farnborough Apprentice School | |
| XF877 | Percival Provost T1 (G-AWVF) [JX] | Privately owned, Norwich | |
| XF898 | Percival Provost T1 [Z] | Booker Fire Section | |
| XF914 | Percival Provost T1 [P-V] | Vintage Aircraft Team, Cranfield | |
| XF926 | Bristol 188 (8368M) | RAF Cosford Aerospace Museum | |
| XF967 | Hawker Hunter T8C | RAF No 237 OCU, Lossiemouth | |
| XF974 | Hawker Hunter F4 (7949M) [C] | RAF No 1 SoTT, Halton | |
| *XF979* | Hawker Hunter F51 (really E-408) [A] (8565M) | *Repainted as WT720* | |
| XF985 | Hawker Hunter T8C [877/VL] | *Crashed Charminster 10 April 1990* | |
| XF994 | Hawker Hunter T8C [873/VL] | RN FRADU, Yeovilton | |
| XF995 | Hawker Hunter T8B [W] | RAF No 12 Sqn, Lossiemouth | |
| | | | |
| XG154 | Hawker Hunter FGA9 (8863M) [54] | RAF Museum, Hendon | |
| XG160 | Hawker Hunter F6A [B] (8831M) | RAF TMTS, Scampton | |
| XG164 | Hawker Hunter F6 (8681M) | RAF No 1 SoTT, Halton | |
| XG172 | Hawker Hunter F6A [A] (8832M) | RAF TMTS, Scampton | |
| XG194 | Hawker Hunter FGA9 [55] (8839M) | RAF North Luffenham Training Area | |
| *XG195* | Hawker Hunter FGA9 (composite with XG297) | Privately owned, Seighford, Staffs | |
| XG196 | Hawker Hunter F6A [31] (8702M) | RAF Bracknell, on gate | |
| XG209 | Hawker Hunter F6 [69] (8709M) | SIF RAFC, Cranwell | |
| XG210 | Hawker Hunter F6 | RAE Apprentice School, Bedford | |
| XG225 | Hawker Hunter F6A (8713M) [S] | RAF Cosford on display | |
| XG226 | Hawker Hunter F6A (8800M) (fuselage, etc) | Stratford Aircraft Collection, Long Marston | |
| XG226 | Hawker Hunter F6A (8800M) [28] (nose only) | Privately owned, Faygate | |
| XG252 | Hawker Hunter FGA9 (8840M) [U] | RAF Credenhill, on display | |
| XG254 | Hawker Hunter FGA9 (8881M) | Privately owned, Weybourne, Norfolk | |
| XG274 | Hawker Hunter F6 [71] (8710M) | RAF No 1 SoTT, Halton | |
| XG290 | Hawker Hunter F6 [74] (8711M) | RAF CSDE, Swanton Morley | |
| XG297 | Hawker Hunter FGA9 (nose only) | Privately owned, Charnock Richard | |
| XG325 | EE Lightning F1 (nose only) | No 1312 Sqn ATC, Southend, Essex | |
| XG327 | EE Lightning F1 (8188M) | FSCTE, RAF Manston | |
| XG329 | EE Lightning F1 (8050M) | RAF Swinderby | |
| XG331 | EE Lightning F1 (nose only) | Stratford Aircraft Collection, Long Marston | |
| XG337 | EE Lightning F1 (8056M) [M] | RAF Cosford Aerospace Museum | |
| XG452 | Bristol Belvedere HC1 (G-BRMB/7997M) | International Helicopter Museum, Weston-super-Mare | |
| XG454 | Bristol Belvedere HC1 (8366M) | Greater Manchester Museum of Science and Industry | |

| Notes | Reg. | Type | Owner or Operator |
|---|---|---|---|
| | XG474 | Bristol Belvedere HC1 (8367M) [O] | RAF Museum, Hendon |
| | XG502 | Bristol Sycamore HR14 | Museum of Army Flying, Middle Wallop |
| | XG506 | Bristol Sycamore HR14 (7852M) | Bomber County Aviation Museum, Hemswell |
| | XG518 | Bristol Sycamore HR14 (8009M) [S-E] | North East Aircraft Museum, Usworth |
| | XG540 | Bristol Sycamore HR14 (7899M/8345M) [Y-S] | Privately owned, Drighlington, Yorks |
| | XG544 | Bristol Sycamore HR14 | Privately owned, Lower Tremar |
| | XG547 | Bristol Sycamore HR14 (G-HAPR/8010M) [S-T] | International Helicopter Museum, Weston-super-Mare |
| | XG573 | WS55 Whirlwind HAR3 | CDE, Porton Down, Wilts |
| | XG574 | WS55 Whirlwind HAR3 (A2575) [752/PO] | FAA Museum, RNAS Yeovilton |
| | XG577 | WS55 Whirlwind HAR3 (A2571) | RAF Leconfield, derelict |
| | XG592 | WS55 Whirlwind HAS7 [54] | Wales Aircraft Museum, Cardiff |
| | XG594 | WS55 Whirlwind HAS7 [517/PO] | Privately owned, Strathallan |
| | XG596 | WS55 Whirlwind HAS7 (A2651) [66] | International Helicopter Museum, Weston-super-Mare |
| | XG613 | DH Sea Venom FAW21 | Imperial War Museum, Duxford |
| | XG629 | DH Sea Venom FAW22 (pod) | Stratford Aircraft Collection, Long Marston |
| | XG680 | DH Sea Venom FAW22 [735/VL] | North East Aircraft Museum, Usworth |
| | XG691 | DH Sea Venom FAW22 [493/J] | Cornwall Aero Park, Helston |
| | XG692 | DH Sea Venom FAW22 [668/LM] | Midland Warplane Museum, Long Marston |
| | XG730 | DH Sea Venom FAW22 [499/A] | Mosquito Aircraft Museum, London Colney |
| | XG736 | DH Sea Venom FAW22 | Ulster Aviation Society, Newtownards |
| | XG737 | DH Sea Venom FAW22 [220/Z] | Wales Aircraft Museum, Cardiff |
| | XG743 | DH Sea Vampire T22 [597/LM] | Imperial War Museum, Duxford |
| | XG797 | Fairey Gannet ECM6 [766/BY] | Imperial War Museum, Duxford |
| | XG831 | Fairey Gannet ECM6 (A2539) [396] | Cornwall Aero Park, Helston |
| | XG882 | Fairey Gannet T5 (8754M) [771/LM] | *Scrapped at RAF Lossiemouth* |
| | XG883 | Fairey Gannet T5 [773/BY] | Wales Aircraft Museum, Cardiff |
| | XG888 | Fairey Gannet T5 [-/LM] | RNAS Lee-on-Solent, stored |
| | XG900 | Short SC1 | FAA Museum, RNAS Yeovilton |
| | XG905 | Short SC1 | Ulster Folk & Transport Museum, County Down |
| | XH131 | EE Canberra PR9 [AF] | RAF No 1 PRU, Wyton |
| | XH132 | Short SC9 Canberra (8915M) | RAF St Mawgan, BDRT |
| | XH133 | EE Canberra PR9 | RAF, stored St Athan |
| | XH134 | EE Canberra PR9 [AA] | RAF No 1 PRU, Wyton |
| | XH135 | EE Canberra PR9 [AG] | RAF No 1 PRU, Wyton |
| | XH136 | EE Canberra PR9 (8782M) [W] | RAF No 2 SoTT, Cosford |
| | XH165 | EE Canberra PR9 | RAF, stored St Athan |
| | XH168 | EE Canberra PR9 [AB] | RAF No 1 PRU, Wyton |
| | XH169 | EE Canberra PR9 [AC] | RAF No 1 PRU, Wyton |
| | XH170 | EE Canberra PR9 (8739M) | RAF Wyton, on display |
| | XH171 | EE Canberra PR9 (8746M) [U] | RAF No 2 SoTT, Cosford |
| | XH174 | EE Canberra PR9 | RAF, stored St Athan |
| | XH175 | EE Canberra PR9 | RAF, stored St Athan |
| | XH177 | EE Canberra PR9 (nose only) | Wales Aircraft Museum, Cardiff |
| | XH274 | DH Vampire T11 | *Scrapped at RAF Ternhill* |
| | XH278 | DH Vampire T11 (8595M/7866M) | No 2482 Sqn ATC, RAF Henlow |
| | XH312 | DH Vampire T11 [18] | Privately owned, Chester |
| | XH313 | DH Vampire T11 [E] | St Albans College of FE |
| | XH318 | DH Vampire T11 [64] (7761M) | No 424 Sqn ATC, Hants |
| | XH328 | DH Vampire T11 [66] | Privately owned, Cranfield |
| | XH329 | DH Vampire T11 [70] | Privately owned, Keevil |
| | XH330 | DH Vampire T11 [73] | Privately owned, Bridgnorth |
| | XH537 | Avro Vulcan B2MRR (8749M) | RAF Abingdon BDRF |
| | XH558 | Avro Vulcan B2 | RAF Vulcan Display Flight, Scampton |

| Reg. | Type | Owner or Operator | Notes |
|---|---|---|---|
| XH560 | Avro Vulcan K2 | RAF Marham Fire Section | |
| XH567 | EE Canberra B6(mod) | MoD(PE) RAE Bedford | |
| XH568 | EE Canberra B6(mod) | MoD(PE) RAE Bedford | |
| XH583 | EE Canberra T4 (G-27-374) (nose only) | North East Aircraft Museum, Usworth | |
| XH590 | HP Victor K1A | FSCTE, RAF Manston | |
| XH592 | HP Victor K1A (8429M) [L] | RAF Cosford Aerospace Museum | |
| XH593 | HP Victor K1A (8428M) [T] | RAF No 2 SoTT, Cosford | |
| XH616 | HP Victor K1A | FSCTE, RAF Manston | |
| XH648 | HP Victor K1A | Imperial War Museum, Duxford | |
| XH669 | HP Victor K2 | RAF No 55 Sqn, Marham | |
| XH670 | HP Victor SR2 (nose only) | Privately owned, Romford, Essex | |
| XH671 | HP Victor K2 | RAF No 55 Sqn, Marham | |
| XH672 | HP Victor K2 | RAF No 55 Sqn, Marham | |
| XH673 | HP Victor K2 (8911M) | RAF Marham, on display | |
| XH675 | HP Victor K2 | RAF No 55 Sqn, Marham | |
| XH764 | Gloster Javelin FAW9 (7972M) | *Scrapped at RAF Manston* | |
| XH767 | Gloster Javelin FAW9 (7955M) [A] | Avon Aviation Museum, Yatesbury | |
| XH837 | Gloster Javelin FAW7 (8032M) (nose only) | Snowdon Mountain Aviation Museum, Caernarfon | |
| XH892 | Gloster Javelin FAW9 (7982M) [J] | Norfolk & Suffolk Aviation Museum, Flixton | |
| XH897 | Gloster Javelin FAW9 | Imperial War Museum, Duxford | |
| XH903 | Gloster Javelin FAW9 (7938M) | Gloucestershire Aviation Collection, Brockworth | |
| XH980 | Gloster Javelin FAW8 (7867M) [A] | RAF West Raynham, at main gate | |
| XH992 | Gloster Javelin FAW8 (7829M) [P] | Newark Air Museum, Winthorpe | |
| XJ314 | RR Thrust Measuring Rig | FAA Museum, RNAS Yeovilton | |
| XJ319 | DH Sea Devon C20 (G-AMXP) [CU18] | *Privately owned as G-AMXP* | |
| XJ324 | DH Sea Devon C20 (G-AMXZ) | RN Shawbury, stored | |
| XJ348 | DH Sea Devon C20 (G-AMXX/ G-NAVY) | Privately owned, Staverton | |
| XJ380 | Bristol Sycamore HR14 (8628M) | Privately owned, Drighlington, Yorks | |
| XJ389 | Fairey Jet Gyrodyne (XD759/ G-AJJP) | RAF Cosford Aerospace Museum | |
| XJ393 | WS55 Whirlwind HAR3 (A2538) | Privately owned, Pulborough | |
| XJ396 | WS55 Whirlwind HAR10 | RAE Farnborough Fire Section | |
| XJ402 | WS55 Whirlwind HAR3 (A2572) [61] | *Scrapped at RNAS Yeovilton* | |
| XJ409 | WS55 Whirlwind HAR10 | Wales Aircraft Museum, Cardiff | |
| XJ430 | WS55 Whirlwind HAR10 | FSCTE, RAF Manston | |
| XJ435 | WS55 Whirlwind HAR10 (8671M) [V] | RAF No 1 SoTT, Halton | |
| XJ445 | WS55 Whirlwind HAR5 | CDE, Porton Down, Wilts | |
| XJ476 | DH Sea Vixen FAW1 (nose section) | No 424 Sqn ATC, Southampton Hall of Aviation | |
| XJ481 | DH Sea Vixen FAW1 [VL] | RNAY Fleetlands Museum | |
| XJ482 | DH Sea Vixen FAW1 (A2598) [713/VL] | Norfolk & Suffolk Aviation Museum, Flixton | |
| XJ494 | DH Sea Vixen FAW2 | Privately owned, Kings Langley, Herts | |
| XJ560 | DH Sea Vixen FAW2 (8142M) [242] | Newark Air Museum, Winthorpe | |
| XJ565 | DH Sea Vixen FAW2 [127/E] | Mosquito Aircraft Museum, London Colney | |
| XJ571 | DH Sea Vixen FAW2 (8140M) [242/R] | Privately owned, Southampton Airport | |
| XJ575 | DH Sea Vixen FAW2 (A2611) (nose only) | Wellesbourne Aviation Group | |
| XJ580 | DH Sea Vixen FAW2 [131/E] | Christchurch Memorial Group | |
| XJ582 | DH Sea Vixen FAW2 (8139M) [702] | RAF Cottesmore Fire Section | |
| XJ607 | DH Sea Vixen FAW2 (8171M) [701/VL] | Privately owned, Southampton | |

| Notes | Reg. | Type | Owner or Operator |
|---|---|---|---|
| | XJ608 | DH Sea Vixen FAW2 (8802M) | RAF North Luffenham Training Area |
| | XJ609 | DH Sea Vixen FAW2 (8172M) painted 8171M [702/VL] | RAF Abingdon Fire Section |
| | XJ634 | Hawker Hunter F6A (8684M) [29] | SIF, RAFC Cranwell |
| | XJ639 | Hawker Hunter F6A (8687M) [31] | SIF, RAFC Cranwell |
| | XJ676 | Hawker Hunter F6A [32] (8844M) | RAF Lyneham, BDRT |
| | *XJ690* | Hawker Hunter FGA9 (composite with XG195) | Staffordshire Aviation Museum |
| | XJ723 | WS55 Whirlwind HAR10 | OPITB, Montrose |
| | XJ726 | WS55 Whirlwind HAR10 [F] | Snowdon Mountain Aviation Museum, Caernarfon |
| | XJ727 | WS55 Whirlwind HAR10 (8661M) [L] | RAF No 1 SoTT, Halton |
| | XJ729 | WS55 Whirlwind HAR10 (8732M) | RAF Finningley, for display |
| | XJ758 | WS55 Whirlwind HAR10 (8464M) | Privately owned, Oswestry |
| | XJ763 | WS55 Whirlwind HAR10 (G-BKHA) | Privately owned, Tarrant Keyneston, Dorset |
| | XJ772 | DH Vampire T11 [H] | Brooklands Technical College |
| | XJ823 | Avro Vulcan B2A | Privately owned, Carlisle Airport |
| | XJ824 | Avro Vulcan B2A | Imperial War Museum, Duxford |
| | XJ825 | Avro Vulcan K2 (8810M) | RAF Waddington, BDRT |
| | XJ917 | Bristol Sycamore HR14 [H-S] | Cornwall Aero Park, Helston |
| | XJ918 | Bristol Sycamore HR14 (8190M) | RAF Cosford Aerospace Museum |
| | XK149 | Hawker Hunter F6A [34] (8714M) | SIF, RAFC Cranwell |
| | XK378 | Auster AOP9 (TAD200) | Privately owned, Haverfordwest |
| | XK416 | Auster AOP9 (G-AYUA/ 7855M) | Vintage Aircraft Team, Cranfield |
| | XK417 | Auster AOP9 (G-AVXY) | Privately owned, Leicester |
| | XK418 | Auster AOP9 (7976M) | Second World War Aircraft Preservation Society, Lasham |
| | XK421 | Auster AOP9 (8365M) | Stratford Aircraft Collection, Long Marston |
| | XK482 | Saro Skeeter AOP12 (7840M/ G-BJWC) [C] | Helicopter Museum of GB, Squires Gate |
| | XK488 | Blackburn Buccaneer S1 | FAA Museum, RNAS Yeovilton |
| | XK526 | Blackburn Buccaneer S2 (8648M) | RAF Honington, at main gate |
| | XK527 | Blackburn Buccaneer S2D (nose only) (8818M) | Privately owned, New Milton, Hants |
| | XK530 | Blackburn Buccaneer S1 | RAE Bedford Fire Section |
| | XK531 | Blackburn Buccaneer S1 (8403M) [LM] | Defence School, Winterbourne Gunner |
| | XK532 | Blackburn Buccaneer S1 (8867M/A2581) [632/LM] | RAF Lossiemouth, on display |
| | XK533 | Blackburn Buccaneer S1 (nose only) | Royal Scottish Museum of Flight, East Fortune |
| | XK590 | DH Vampire T11 [V] | Wellesbourne Aviation Group |
| | XK623 | DH Vampire T11 [56] (*G-VAMP*) | Snowdon Mountain Aviation Museum, Caernarfon |
| | XK624 | DH Vampire T11 [32] | Norfolk & Suffolk Aviation Museum, Flixton |
| | XK625 | DH Vampire T11 [12] | South Yorkshire Aircraft Preservation Society, Firbeck |
| | XK627 | DH Vampire T11 | Pennine Aviation Museum, Bacup |
| | XK632 | DH Vampire T11 [67] | No 1187 Sqn ATC, Hemel Hempstead |
| | XK637 | DH Vampire T11 [56] | No 1855 Sqn ATC, Royton, Greater Manchester |
| | XK655 | DH Comet 2R (G-AMXA) | *Scrapped July 1990 at Strathallan* |
| | XK659 | DH Comet 2R (G-AMXC) (nose only) | Privately owned, Elland, W. Yorks |
| | XK695 | DH Comet 2R (G-AMXH) | Imperial War Museum, Duxford |
| | XK699 | DH Comet C2 (7971M) | RAF Lyneham on display |
| | XK724 | Folland Gnat F1 (7715M) | RAF Cosford Aerospace Museum |
| | XK740 | Folland Gnat F1 (8396M) | Southampton Hall of Aviation |
| | XK741 | Folland Gnat F1 | Midland Air Museum, Coventry |
| | XK776 | ML Utility 1 | Museum of Army Flying, Middle Wallop |
| | XK824 | Slingsby Grasshopper TX1 | Privately owned, Narborough, Lincs |

| Reg. | Type | Owner or Operator | Notes |
|---|---|---|---|
| XK895 | DH Sea Devon C20 [19/CU] (G-SDEV) | Privately owned, North Weald | |
| XK896 | DH Sea Devon C20 (G-RNAS) | Privately owned, Staverton | |
| XK906 | WS55 Whirlwind HAS7 | AAC Netheravon Fire Section | |
| XK907 | WS55 Whirlwind HAS7 [U] | Midland Air Museum, Coventry | |
| XK911 | WS55 Whirlwind HAS7 (A2603) [519/PO] | RN, stored Wroughton | |
| XK912 | WS55 Whirlwind HAS7 [60/CU] | Privately owned, Crudwell, Wilts | |
| XK936 | WS55 Whirlwind HAS7 [62] | Imperial War Museum, Duxford | |
| XK940 | WS55 Whirlwind HAS7 | *To civil marks G-AYXT* | |
| XK943 | WS55 Whirlwind HAS7 (A2653/8796M) [57] | RAF Abingdon, Fire Section | |
| XK944 | WS55 Whirlwind HAS7 (A2607) | No 617 Sqn ATC, Malpas School, Cheshire | |
| XK968 | WS55 Whirlwind HAR10 (8445M) [E] | FSCTE, RAF Manston | |
| XK969 | WS55 Whirlwind HAR10 (8646M) | FSCTE, RAF Manston | |
| XK970 | WS55 Whirlwind HAR10 (8789M) | RAF Odiham, BDRT | |
| XK986 | WS55 Whirlwind HAR10 (8790M) | RAF Odiham, BDRT | |
| XK987 | WS55 Whirlwind HAR10 (8393M) | MoD Swynnerton, Staffs | |
| XK988 | WS55 Whirlwind HAR10 (A2646) [D] | RNAY Fleetlands Museum | |
| XL149 | Blackburn Beverley C1 (nose only) (7988M) | Newark Air Museum, Winthorpe | |
| XL158 | HP Victor K2 | RAF No 55 Sqn, Marham | |
| XL160 | HP Victor K2 (8910M) | RAF Marham Fire Section | |
| XL161 | HP Victor K2 | RAF No 55 Sqn, Marham | |
| XL162 | HP Victor K2 | RAF No 55 Sqn, Marham | |
| XL163 | HP Victor K2 (8916M) | RAF St Athan Fire Section | |
| XL164 | HP Victor K2 | RAF No 55 Sqn, Marham | |
| XL188 | HP Victor K2 | RAF No 55 Sqn, Marham | |
| XL190 | HP Victor K2 | RAF No 55 Sqn, Marham | |
| XL192 | HP Victor K2 (902M) | RAF Marham Fire Section | |
| XL231 | HP Victor K2 | RAF No 55 Sqn, Marham | |
| XL318 | Avro Vulcan B2 (8733M) | RAF Museum, Hendon | |
| XL319 | Avro Vulcan B2 | North-East Aircraft Museum, Usworth | |
| XL360 | Avro Vulcan B2A | Midland Air Museum, Coventry | |
| XL384 | Avro Vulcan B2 (8505M/ 8670M) | RAF Scampton Fire Section | |
| XL386 | Avro Vulcan B2A (8760M) | FSCTE, RAF Manston | |
| XL388 | Avro Vulcan B2 (nose only) | Privately owned, Walpole, Suffolk | |
| XL391 | Avro Vulcan B2 | Privately owned, Blackpool | |
| XL392 | Avro Vulcan B2 (8745M) | RAF Valley Fire Section | |
| XL426 | Avro Vulcan B2 (G-VJET) | Privately owned, Southend | |
| XL427 | Avro Vulcan B2 (8756M) | RAF Machrihanish Fire Section | |
| XL445 | Avro Vulcan K2 (8811M) | RAF Lyneham Fire Section | |
| XL449 | Fairey Gannet AEW3 | Wales Aircraft Museum, Cardiff | |
| XL472 | Fairey Gannet AEW3 [044/R] | A&AEE Boscombe Down, derelict | |
| XL497 | Fairey Gannet AEW3 [041/R] | RNAS Yeovilton, AMG | |
| XL500 | Fairey Gannet AEW3 (A2701) [LM] | RNAY Fleetlands Museum | |
| XL502 | Fairey Gannet AEW3 (8610M) (G-BMYP) | Privately owned, Carlisle | |
| XL503 | Fairey Gannet AEW3 [070/E] | FAA Museum, RNAS Yeovilton | |
| XL511 | HP Victor K2 | FSCTE, RAF Manston | |
| XL512 | HP Victor K2 | RAF No 55 Sqn, Marham | |
| XL563 | Hawker Hunter T7 | MoD(PE) RAE/IAM Farnborough | |
| XL564 | Hawker Hunter T7 [4] | MoD(PE) ETPS Boscombe Down | |
| XL565 | Hawker Hunter T7 | RAF No 237 OCU, Lossiemouth | |
| XL567 | Hawker Hunter T7 (8723M) [84] (fuselage only) | Jet Heritage, Bournemouth | |
| XL568 | Hawker Hunter T7A [N] | RAF No 12 Sqn, Lossiemouth | |
| XL569 | Hawker Hunter T7 (8833M) [80] | RAF Abingdon, BDRF | |
| XL572 | Hawker Hunter T7 [83] (G-HNTR) | Jet Heritage, Bournemouth | |
| XL573 | Hawker Hunter T7 | RAF No 12 Sqn, Lossiemouth | |
| XL577 | Hawker Hunter T7 (8676M) [01] | SIF, RAFC Cranwell | |
| XL578 | Hawker Hunter T7 [77] | RAF, stored St Athan | |

| Notes | Reg. | Type | Owner or Operator |
|---|---|---|---|
| | XL580 | Hawker Hunter T8M [723] | RN No 899 Sqn, Yeovilton |
| | XL586 | Hawker Hunter T7 | RAF No 237 OCU, Lossiemouth |
| | XL587 | Hawker Hunter T7 (8807M) [Z] | RAF TMTS, Scampton |
| | XL591 | Hawker Hunter T7 | RAF No 208 Sqn, Lossiemouth |
| | XL592 | Hawker Hunter T7 (8836M) [Y] | RAF TMTS, Scampton |
| | XL595 | Hawker Hunter T7 [78] | RAF, stored St Athan |
| | XL598 | Hawker Hunter T8C [880/VL] | RN FRADU, Yeovilton |
| | XL600 | Hawker Hunter T7 [Y/FL] | RNAY Fleetlands Apprentice School |
| | XL601 | Hawker Hunter T7 [874/VL] | RN store, Yeovilton |
| | XL602 | Hawker Hunter T8M | MoD(PE) BAe Dunsfold |
| | XL603 | Hawker Hunter T8M [724/VL] | RN No 899 Sqn, Yeovilton |
| | XL609 | Hawker Hunter T7 (8866M) [YF] | RAF Lossiemouth, BDRT |
| | XL612 | Hawker Hunter T7 [2] | MoD(PE) ETPS Boscombe Down |
| | XL613 | Hawker Hunter T7A | RAF No 237 OCU, Lossiemouth |
| | XL614 | Hawker Hunter T7 [O] | RAF No 237 OCU, Lossiemouth |
| | XL616 | Hawker Hunter T7 | RAF No 237 OCU, Lossiemouth |
| | XL617 | Hawker Hunter T7 [89] (G-HHNT) | *Sold in USA as N617NL Dec 1989* |
| | XL618 | Hawker Hunter T7 (8892M) [05] | RAF Cottesmore, BDRT |
| | XL623 | Hawker Hunter T7 [90] (8770M) | RAF Newton, BDRF |
| | XL629 | EE Lightning T4 | A&AEE Boscombe Down, at main gate |
| | XL703 | SAL Pioneer CC1 (8034M) | RAF Cosford Aerospace Museum |
| | XL728 | WS58 Wessex HAS1 | *To Pendine Ranges* |
| | XL735 | Saro Skeeter AOP12 | Privately owned, Tattershall Thorpe |
| | XL738 | Saro Skeeter AOP12 (7860M) | RNAY Fleetlands Museum |
| | XL762 | Saro Skeeter AOP12 (8017M) | Royal Scottish Museum of Flight, East Fortune |
| | XL763 | Saro Skeeter AOP12 | Southall Technical College |
| | XL764 | Saro Skeeter AOP12 (7940M) | Newark Air Museum, Winthorpe |
| | XL765 | Saro Skeeter AOP12 | Privately owned, Pimlico |
| | XL770 | Saro Skeeter AOP12 (8046M) | Southampton Hall of Aviation, store |
| | XL809 | Saro Skeeter AOP12 (G-BLIX/ PH-HOF) | Privately owned, Clapham, Beds |
| | XL811 | Saro Skeeter AOP12 [157] | The Aircraft Collection, Warmingham |
| | XL812 | Saro Skeeter AOP12 (G-SARO) | Privately owned, Old Buckenham |
| | XL813 | Saro Skeeter AOP12 | Museum of Army Flying, Middle Wallo |
| | XL814 | Saro Skeeter AOP12 | AAC Historic Aircraft Flight, Middle Wallop |
| | XL824 | Bristol Sycamore HR14 (8021M) | Greater Manchester Museum of Scienc and Industry |
| | XL829 | Bristol Sycamore HR14 | Bristol Industrial Museum |
| | XL836 | WS55 Whirlwind HAS7 (A2642) [65] | RNAS Yeovilton Fire Section |
| | XL840 | WS55 Whirlwind HAS7 [56] | Stratford Aircraft Collection, Long Marston |
| | XL846 | WS55 Whirlwind HAS7 (A2625) [85] | RN Predannack Fire School |
| | XL847 | WS55 Whirlwind HAS7 (A2626) [83] | AAC Middle Wallop, Fire Section |
| | XL853 | WS55 Whirlwind HAS7 [LS] (A2630) | RNAY Fleetlands Museum |
| | XL875 | WS55 Whirlwind HAR9 | Air Service Training, Perth |
| | XL880 | WS55 Whirlwind HAR9 (A2714) [33] | RN Lee-on-Solent, Fire Service |
| | XL898 | WS55 Whirlwind HAR9 (8654M) [30/ED] | A&AEE Boscombe Down, derelict |
| | XL899 | WS55 Whirlwind HAR9 [587/CU] | RN Predannack Fire School |
| | XL929 | Percival Pembroke C1 (G-BNPU) | Chelsea College, Shoreham |
| | XL954 | Percival Pembroke C1 | RAF, stored Northolt |
| | XL993 | SAL Twin Pioneer CC1 (8388M) | RAF Cosford Aerospace Museum |
| | XM135 | BAC Lightning F1 [135] | Imperial War Museum, Duxford |
| | XM144 | BAC Lightning F1 (8417M) [J] | RAF Leuchars |
| | XM169 | BAC Lightning F1A (8422M) [W] (nose only) | N. Yorkshire Recovery Group, Chop Gate |
| | XM172 | BAC Lightning F1A (8427M) [B] | Privately owned, Southampton Docks |
| | XM173 | BAC Lightning F1A (8414M) [A] | RAF Bentley Priory, at main gate |
| | XM178 | BAC Lightning F1A (8418M) [Y] | RAF Leuchars decoy |
| | XM191 | BAC Lightning F1A (7854M/ 8590M) (nose only) | RAF Exhibition Flight, Abingdon |
| | XM192 | BAC Lightning F1A (8413M) [K] | RAF Wattisham, at main gate |

| Reg. | Type | Owner or Operator | Notes |
|---|---|---|---|
| XM223 | DH Devon C2 [J] | MoD(PE) RAE West Freugh | |
| XM279 | EE Canberra B(I)8 (nose only) | S Yorks Air Museum, Firbeck | |
| XM296 | DH Heron C4 | FAA Museum, stored Yeovilton | |
| XM300 | WS58 Wessex HAS1 | Wales Aircraft Museum, Cardiff | |
| XM326 | WS58 Wessex HAS1 [515] | RNAS Portland Fire Section | |
| XM327 | WS58 Wessex HAS3 [401/KE] | College of Nautical Studies, Warsash | |
| XM328 | WS58 Wessex HAS3 | RNAS Culdrose, SAH | |
| XM329 | WS58 Wessex HAS1 (A2609) | RN Predannack Fire School | |
| XM330 | WS58 Wessex HAS1 | MoD(PE) RAE Farnborough, stored | |
| XM331 | WS58 Wessex HAS3 | RN Predannack Fire School | |
| XM349 | Hunting Jet Provost T3A [H] | RAF CFS, Scampton | |
| XM350 | Hunting Jet Provost T3A [89] | RAF Church Fenton, Fire Section | |
| XM351 | Hunting Jet Provost T3 [Y] (8078M) | RAF No 2 SoTT, Cosford | |
| XM352 | Hunting Jet Provost T3A [21] | RAF No 1 FTS, Linton-on-Ouse | |
| XM355 | Hunting Jet Provost T3 (8229M) [D] | RAF No 1 SoTT, Halton | |
| XM357 | Hunting Jet Provost T3A [45] | RAF No 1 FTS, Linton-on-Ouse | |
| XM358 | Hunting Jet Provost T3A [53] (8987M) | RAF No 1 SoTT, Halton | |
| XM362 | Hunting Jet Provost T3 (8230M) | RAF No 1 SoTT, Halton | |
| XM365 | Hunting Jet Provost T3A [37] | RAF No 1 FTS, Linton-on-Ouse | |
| XM367 | Hunting Jet Provost T3 [Z] (8083M) | RAF No 2 SoTT, Cosford | |
| XM369 | Hunting Jet Provost T3 (8084M) [C] | RAF No 1 SoTT, Halton | |
| XM370 | Hunting Jet Provost T3A [10] | RAF No 1 FTS, Linton-on-Ouse | |
| XM371 | Hunting Jet Provost T3A [31] (8962M) | RAF No 1 SoTT, Halton | |
| XM372 | Hunting Jet Provost T3A [55] (8917M) | RAF Linton-on-Ouse Fire Section | |
| XM374 | Hunting Jet Provost T3A [18] | RAF No 1 FTS, Linton-on-Ouse | |
| XM375 | Hunting Jet Provost T3 (8231M) [B] | RAF Cottesmore Fire Section | |
| XM376 | Hunting Jet Provost T3A [27] | RAF No 1 FTS, Linton-on-Ouse | |
| XM378 | Hunting Jet Provost T3A [34] | RAF No 1 FTS, Linton-on-Ouse | |
| XM379 | Hunting Jet Provost T3 | Army Apprentice College, Arborfield | |
| XM381 | Hunting Jet Provost T3 (8232M) [A] | RAF No 1 SoTT, Halton | |
| XM383 | Hunting Jet Provost T3A [90] | RAF Scampton, spares use | |
| XM386 | Hunting Jet Provost T3 (8076M) [08] | RAF No 1 SoTT, Halton | |
| XM387 | Hunting Jet Provost T3A [I] | RAF CFS, Scampton | |
| XM401 | Hunting Jet Provost T3A [17] | RAF, Linton-on-Ouse (wfu) | |
| XM402 | Hunting Jet Provost T3 (8055AM) [J] | RAF No 1 SoTT, Halton | |
| XM403 | Hunting Jet Provost T3A [A] | RAF CFS, Scampton | |
| XM404 | Hunting Jet Provost T3 (8055BM) | RAF No 1 SoTT, Halton | |
| XM405 | Hunting Jet Provost T3A [42] | RAF, Linton-on-Ouse (wfu) | |
| XM408 | Hunting Jet Provost T3 (8233M) [D] | RAF No 1 SoTT, Halton | |
| XM409 | Hunting Jet Provost T3 (8082M) [A] | RAF No 1 SoTT, Halton | |
| XM410 | Hunting Jet Provost T3 (8054/AM) [B] | RAF Crash Rescue Training, Halton | |
| XM411 | Hunting Jet Provost T3 (8434M) [L] | RAF No 1 SoTT, Halton | |
| XM412 | Hunting Jet Provost T3A [41] (9011M) | RAF No 1 SoTT, Halton | |
| XM413 | Hunting Jet Provost T3 | Army Apprentice College, Arborfield | |
| XM414 | Hunting Jet Provost T3A [101] (8996M) | RAF No 1 SoTT, Halton | |
| XM417 | Hunting Jet Provost T3 (8054BM) [D] | RAF No 1 SoTT, Halton | |
| XM419 | Hunting Jet Provost T3A [102] (8990M) | RAF CTTS, St Athan | |
| XM424 | Hunting Jet Provost T3A [30] | RAF No 1 FTS, Linton-on-Ouse | |
| XM425 | Hunting Jet Provost T3A [88] (8995M) | RAF No 1 SoTT, Halton | |
| XM426 | Hunting Jet Provost T3 [64] (nose only) | Robertsbridge Aviation Museum | |

| Notes | Reg. | Type | Owner or Operator |
|---|---|---|---|
| | XM455 | Hunting Jet Provost T3A [K] (8960M) | RAF No 2 SoTT, Cosford |
| | XM458 | Hunting Jet Provost T3A [B] | *Scrapped at RAF Scampton* |
| | XM459 | Hunting Jet Provost T3A [F] | RAF CFS, Scampton |
| | XM461 | Hunting Jet Provost T3A [11] | RAF No 1 FTS, Linton-on-Ouse |
| | XM463 | Hunting Jet Provost T3A [38] | RAF No 1 FTS, Linton-on-Ouse |
| | XM464 | Hunting Jet Provost T3A [23] | RAF No 1 FTS, Linton-on-Ouse |
| | XM465 | Hunting Jet Provost T3A [55] | RAF No 1 FTS, Linton-on-Ouse |
| | XM466 | Hunting Jet Provost T3A [31] | RAF No 1 FTS, Linton-on-Ouse |
| | XM467 | Hunting Jet Provost T3 (8085M) [K] | RAF No 1 SoTT, Halton |
| | XM468 | Hunting Jet Provost T3 (8081M) [B] | RAF No 1 SoTT, Halton |
| | XM470 | Hunting Jet Provost T3A [M] | RAF CFS, Scampton |
| | XM471 | Hunting Jet Provost T3A [L] [93] (8968M) | RAF No 2 SoTT, Cosford |
| | XM472 | Hunting Jet Provost T3A [22] | RAF No 1 FTS, Linton-on-Ouse |
| | XM473 | Hunting Jet Provost T3A [53] (8974M) | RAF No 1 SoTT, Halton |
| | XM474 | Hunting Jet Provost T3 (8121M) | No 1330 Sqn ATC, Warrington |
| | XM475 | Hunting Jet Provost T3A [44] | RAF No 1 FTS, Linton-on-Ouse |
| | XM478 | Hunting Jet Provost T3A [33] (8983M) | RAF No 1 FTS, Linton-on-Ouse |
| | XM479 | Hunting Jet Provost T3A [54] | RAF No 1 FTS, Linton-on-Ouse |
| | XM480 | Hunting Jet Provost T3 [02] (8080M) | RAF No 1 SoTT, Halton |
| | *XM515* | DH Vampire T11 (7998M) (really XD515) | Newark Air Museum, Winthorpe |
| | XM529 | Saro Skeeter AOP12 (7979M/ G-BDNS) | Privately owned, Handforth |
| | XM553 | Saro Skeeter AOP12 (G-AWSV) | Privately owned, Middle Wallop |
| | XM555 | Saro Skeeter AOP12 (8027M) | RAF Cosford Aerospace Museum |
| | XM556 | Saro Skeeter AOP12 (G-HELI/7870M) [V] | International Helicopter Museum, Weston-super-Mare |
| | XM561 | Saro Skeeter AOP12 (7980M) | Lincolnshire Aviation Museum, East Kirkby |
| | XM564 | Saro Skeeter AOP12 | Royal Armoured Corps Museum, Bovington |
| | XM569 | Avro Vulcan B2 | Wales Aircraft Museum, Cardiff |
| | XM575 | Avro Vulcan B2A (G-BLMC) | East Midlands Aeropark |
| | XM594 | Avro Vulcan B2 | Newark Air Museum, Winthorpe |
| | XM597 | Avro Vulcan B2 | Royal Scottish Museum of Flight, East Fortune |
| | XM598 | Avro Vulcan B2 (8778M) | RAF Cosford Aerospace Museum |
| | XM602 | Avro Vulcan B2 (8771M) | Privately owned, London |
| | XM603 | Avro Vulcan B2 | Avro Aircraft Restoration Society, BAe Woodford |
| | XM607 | Avro Vulcan B2 (8779M) | RAF Waddington, on display |
| | XM612 | Avro Vulcan B2 | City of Norwich Aviation Museum |
| | XM652 | Avro Vulcan B2 (nose only) | Privately owned, Burntwood, Staffs |
| | XM655 | Avro Vulcan B2 (G-VULC/ N655AV) | Privately owned, Wellesbourne Mountford |
| | XM656 | Avro Vulcan B2 (8757M) (nose only) | RAF Cottesmore Fire Section |
| | XM657 | Avro Vulcan B2A (8734M) | FSCTE, RAF Manston |
| | XM660 | WS55 Whirlwind HAS7 [78] | North East Aircraft Museum, Usworth |
| | XM665 | WS55 Whirlwind HAS7 | Booker Aircraft Museum |
| | XM667 | WS55 Whirlwind HAS7 (A2629) [56/CU] | RN Predannack Fire School |
| | XM685 | WS55 Whirlwind HAS7 (G-AYZJ) [513/PO] | Newark Air Museum, Winthorpe |
| | XM693 | HS Gnat T1 (7891M) | BAe Hamble on display |
| | XM694 | HS Gnat T1 | RAE Bedford Apprentice School |
| | XM697 | HS Gnat T1 (G-NAAT) | Jet Heritage Ltd, Bournemouth |
| | XM706 | HS Gnat T1 (8572M) [12] | RAF Swinderby Fire Section |
| | XM708 | HS Gnat T1 (8573M) | RAF Locking, on display |
| | XM709 | HS Gnat T1 (8617M) [67] | Privately owned |
| | XM715 | HP Victor K2 | RAF No 55 Sqn, Marham |
| | XM717 | HP Victor K2 | RAF No 55 Sqn, Marham |
| | XM833 | WS58 Wessex HAS3 | Second World War Aircraft Preservation Society, Lasham |
| | XM836 | WS58 Wessex HAS3 [651/FL] | RNAY Fleetlands, instructional use |

| Reg. | Type | Owner or Operator | Notes |
|---|---|---|---|
| XM838 | WS58 Wessex HAS3 | RN Predannack Fire School | |
| XM841 | WS58 Wessex HAS1 [510] | RN Predannack Fire School | |
| XM843 | WS58 Wessex HAS1 (A2693) [527/LS] | RNAS Lee-on-Solent on display | |
| XM845 | WS58 Wessex HAS1 (A2682) [530/PO] | RNAS Yeovilton Fire Section | |
| XM868 | WS58 Wessex HAS1 (A2706) [517/PO] | RN AES, Lee-on-Solent | |
| XM870 | WS58 Wessex HAS3 [PO] | RN NACDS, Culdrose | |
| XM874 | WS58 Wessex HAS1 (A2689) [521/CU] | RNAS AES, Lee-on-Solent | |
| XM916 | WS58 Wessex HAS3 [666/PO] | RAF Wroughton Fire Section | |
| XM917 | WS58 Wessex HAS1 (A2692) [528/PO] | RNAS Lee-on-Solent Fire Section | |
| XM919 | WS58 Wessex HAS3 [55] | RNAS Yeovilton Fire Section | |
| XM923 | WS58 Wessex HAS 3 | RNAY Fleetlands, Fire Section | |
| XM927 | WS58 Wessex HAS3 (8814M) [660/PO] | RAF Shawbury, Fire Section | |
| XM987 | BAC Lightning T4 | RAF Coningsby, Fire Section | |
| XN126 | WS55 Whirlwind HAR10 (8655M) [S] | RAF Benson BDRT | |
| XN132 | Sud Alouette AH2 | Privately owned, North Weald | |
| XN137 | Hunting Jet Provost T3 [95] (nose only) | RAF Exhibition Flight, Abingdon | |
| XN185 | Slingsby Sedbergh TX1 (8942M) | RAF ACCGS Syerston, preserved | |
| XN239 | Slingsby Cadet TX3 [G] (8889M) | Imperial War Museum, Duxford | |
| XN246 | Slingsby Cadet TX3 | Southampton Hall of Aviation | |
| XN258 | WS55 Whirlwind HAR9 [589/CU] | Cornwall Aero Park, Helston | |
| XN263 | WS55 Whirlwind HAS7 | Privately owned, Sussex | |
| *XN297* | WS55 Whirlwind HAR9 [12] (really XN311/A2643) | Privately owned, Hull | |
| XN298 | WS55 Whirlwind HAR9 [810/LS] | Privately owned, Stoke-on-Trent | |
| XN299 | WS55 Whirlwind HAS7 [758] | Royal Marines Museum, Portsmouth | |
| XN302 | WS55 Whirlwind HAS7 (A2654) [LS] | RAF Finningley, GI | |
| XN304 | WS55 Whirlwind HAS7 [64] | Norfolk & Suffolk Aviation Museum, Flixton | |
| XN306 | WS55 Whirlwind HAR9 [434/ED] | RNAS Portland Fire Section | |
| XN308 | WS55 Whirlwind HAS7 (A2605) [510/PO] | RNAS Yeovilton Fire Section | |
| XN309 | WS55 Whirlwind HAR9 (A2663) [590/CU] | *IAC Baldonnel, Fire Section* | |
| XN314 | WS55 Whirlwind HAS7 (A2614) | RN Predannack Fire School | |
| XN332 | Saro P531 (G-APNV/A2579) [759] | FAA Museum, stored Wroughton | |
| XN334 | Saro P531 (A2525) | International Helicopter Museum, under restoration, Crawley C.o.T. | |
| XN341 | Saro Skeeter AOP12 (8022M) | RAF St Athan Historic Aircraft Collection | |
| XN344 | Saro Skeeter AOP12 (8018M) | Science Museum, South Kensington | |
| XN351 | Saro Skeeter AOP12 (G-BKSC) | Privately owned, Shempston Farm, Lossiemouth | |
| XN359 | WS55 Whirlwind HAR9 (A2712) [34/ED] | RNAS Lee-on-Solent, Fire Section | |
| XN380 | WS55 Whirlwind HAS7 [67] | Lashenden Air Warfare Museum, Headcorn | |
| XN385 | WS55 Whirlwind HAS7 | RN Historic Flight, stored Wroughton | |
| XN386 | WS55 Whirlwind HAR9 [435/ED] (A2713) | Privately owned, Blackpool | |
| XN387 | WS55 Whirlwind HAR9 (8564M) | RAF Odiham, BDRT | |
| XN412 | Auster AOP9 | Cotswold Aircraft Restoration Group, RAF Innsworth | |
| XN435 | Auster AOP9 (G-BGBU) | Privately owned, Egham | |
| XN437 | Auster AOP9 (G-AXWA) | Privately owned, Welling, Kent | |
| XN441 | Auster AOP9 (G-BGKT) | Privately owned, Reymerston Hall | |
| XN453 | DH Comet 2e | RAE Farnborough Fire Section | |
| XN458 | Hunting Jet Provost T3 [19] (8234M) | RAF CTTS, St Athan | |

| Notes | Reg. | Type | Owner or Operator |
|---|---|---|---|
| | XN459 | Hunting Jet Provost T3A [N] | RAF CFS, Scampton |
| | XN461 | Hunting Jet Provost T3A [28] | RAF No 1 FTS, Linton-on-Ouse |
| | XN462 | Hunting Jet Provost T3A [E] | RAF CFS, Scampton |
| | XN466 | Hunting Jet Provost T3A [29] | RAF No 1 FTS, Linton-on-Ouse |
| | XN467 | Hunting Jet Provost T4 (8559M) [F] | RAF No 1 SoTT, Halton |
| | XN470 | Hunting Jet Provost T3A [41] | RAF No 1 FTS, Linton-on-Ouse |
| | XN471 | Hunting Jet Provost T3A [24] | RAF No 1 FTS, Linton-on-Ouse |
| | XN472 | Hunting Jet Provost T3A [J] (8959M) | RAF No 2 SoTT, Cosford |
| | XN473 | Hunting Jet Provost T3A (8862M) [98] (cockpit only) | RAF Church Fenton Fire Section |
| | XN492 | Hunting Jet Provost T3 [M] (8079M) | RAF No 2 SoTT, Cosford |
| | XN493 | Hunting Jet Provost T3 (nose only) | No 1075 Sqn ATC, Camberley |
| | XN494 | Hunting Jet Provost T3A [43] (9012M) | RAF No 1 SoTT, Halton |
| | XN495 | Hunting Jet Provost T3A [102] (8786M) | RAF Abingdon, BDRF |
| | XN497 | Hunting Jet Provost T3A [52] | RAF No 1 FTS, Linton-on-Ouse |
| | XN498 | Hunting Jet Provost T3A [16] | RAF No 1 FTS, Linton-on-Ouse |
| | XN499 | Hunting Jet Provost T3A [L] | RAF CFS, Scampton |
| | XN500 | Hunting Jet Provost T3A [48] | RAF No 1 FTS, Linton-on-Ouse |
| | XN501 | Hunting Jet Provost T3A [S] (8958M) | RAF No 2 SoTT, Cosford |
| | XN502 | Hunting Jet Provost T3A [D] | RAF CFS, Scampton |
| | XN503 | Hunting Jet Provost T3 (nose only) | RAF Exhibition Flight, Abingdon |
| | XN505 | Hunting Jet Provost T3A [25] | RAF No 1 FTS, Linton-on-Ouse |
| | XN506 | Hunting Jet Provost T3A [19] | RAF No 1 FTS, Linton-on-Ouse |
| | XN508 | Hunting Jet Provost T3A [98] | RAF No 7 FTS, Church Fenton |
| | XN509 | Hunting Jet Provost T3A [50] | RAF No 1 FTS, Linton-on-Ouse |
| | XN510 | Hunting Jet Provost T3A [40] | RAF No 1 FTS, Linton-on-Ouse |
| | XN511 | Hunting Jet Provost T3 [21] (nose only) | Newark Air Museum, Winthorpe |
| | XN512 | Hunting Jet Provost T3 (8435M) | RAF No 1 SoTT, Halton |
| | XN548 | Hunting Jet Provost T3A [32] (8971M) | RAF No 1 SoTT, Halton |
| | XN549 | Hunting Jet Provost T3 [32] (8235M) [P] | RAF No 1 SoTT, Halton |
| | XN551 | Hunting Jet Provost T3A [100] (8984M) | RAF CTTS, St Athan |
| | XN552 | Hunting Jet Provost T3A [32] | RAF No 1 FTS, Linton-on-Ouse |
| | XN553 | Hunting Jet Provost T3A | RAF St Athan Station Flight |
| | XN554 | Hunting Jet Provost T3 (8436M) [K] | RAF No 1 SoTT, Halton |
| | XN574 | Hunting Jet Provost T3A [21] | *Sold to Chassey, France* |
| | XN577 | Hunting Jet Provost T3A [89] [F] (8956M) | RAF No 2 SoTT, Cosford |
| | XN579 | Hunting Jet Provost T3A [14] | RAF No 1 FTS, Linton-on-Ouse |
| | XN581 | Hunting Jet Provost T3A [C] | RAF CFS, Scampton |
| | XN582 | Hunting Jet Provost T3A [H] [95] (8957M) | RAF No 2 SoTT, Cosford |
| | XN584 | Hunting Jet Provost T3A [E] (9014M) | RAF No 1 SoTT, Halton |
| | XN586 | Hunting Jet Provost T3A [91] [S] | RAF No 2 SoTT, Cosford |
| | XN589 | Hunting Jet Provost T3A [46] | RAF No 1 FTS, Linton-on-Ouse |
| | XN592 | Hunting Jet Provost T3 (nose only) | No 1105 Sqn ATC, Winchester |
| | XN593 | Hunting Jet Provost T3A [97] [Q] (8988M) | RAF No 2 SoTT, Cosford |
| | XN594 | Hunting Jet Provost T3 [W] (8077M) | RAF No 2 SoTT, Cosford |
| | XN595 | Hunting Jet Provost T3A [43] | RAF No 1 FTS, Linton-on-Ouse |
| | XN600 | Hunting Jet Provost T3A (nose only) | N. Yorks Recovery Group, Chop Gate |
| | XN602 | Hunting Jet Provost T3 (8088M) | FSCTE, RAF Manston |
| | XN605 | Hunting Jet Provost T3A [J] | RAF Scampton (wfu) |
| | XN606 | Hunting Jet Provost T3A [51] | RAF No 1 FTS, Linton-on-Ouse |

| eg. | Type | Owner or Operator | Notes |
|---|---|---|---|
| N629 | Hunting Jet Provost T3A [49] | RAF No 1 FTS, Linton-on-Ouse | |
| N632 | Hunting Jet Provost T3 (8352M) | RAF Chivenor, crash rescue training | |
| N634 | Hunting Jet Provost T3A [53] | RAF No 1 FTS, Linton-on-Ouse | |
| N635 | Hunting Jet Provost T3 [57] (nose only) | RN Predannack Fire School | |
| N636 | Hunting Jet Provost T3A [15] | RAF No 1 FTS, Linton-on-Ouse | |
| N637 | Hunting Jet Provost T3 (G-BKOU) | Vintage Aircraft Team, Cranfield | |
| N640 | Hunting Jet Provost T3A [99] (9016M) | RAF No 2 SoTT, Cosford | |
| N641 | Hunting Jet Provost T3A (8865M) [47] | RAF Newton Fire Section | |
| N643 | Hunting Jet Provost T3A (8704M) [26] (cockpit only) | RAF Cranwell | |
| N643 | Hunting Jet Provost T3A (8704M) (fuselage only) | BAe Warton Fire Section | |
| N647 | DH Sea Vixen FAW2 (A2610) [707-VL] | Cornwall Aero Park, Helston | |
| N649 | DH Sea Vixen FAW2 [126] | MoD(PE), stored RAE Farnborough | |
| N650 | DH Sea Vixen FAW2 (A2612/ A2620/A2639) [VL] | Wales Aircraft Museum, Cardiff | |
| N651 | DH Sea Vixen FAW2 (A2616) (nose only) | Privately owned, Pucklechurch, Avon | |
| N652 | DH Sea Vixen FAW2 (8817M) | RAF FF&SS, Catterick | |
| N657 | DH Sea Vixen D3 [TR-1] | MoD(PE) RAE Llanbedr Fire Section | |
| N685 | DH Sea Vixen FAW2 (8173M) [P] [03/VL] | BAe Hawarden Apprentice School | |
| N688 | DH Sea Vixen FAW2 (8141M) | RAE Farnborough Fire Section | |
| N691 | DH Sea Vixen FAW2 [N] [247-H] (8143M) | Aces High, North Weald | |
| N692 | DH Sea Vixen FAW2 (A2624) [125/E] | RNAS Yeovilton on display, FONA | |
| N694 | DH Sea Vixen FAW2 | MoD(PE) RAE Llanbedr | |
| N696 | DH Sea Vixen FAW2 [751] (cockpit only) | Privately owned, Suffolk | |
| N699 | DH Sea Vixen FAW2 [752] (8224M) | RAF North Luffenham, for ground instruction | |
| XN714 | Hunting H126 | RAF Cosford Aerospace Museum | |
| XN724 | EE Lightning F2A [F] (8513M) | Privately owned, Newcastle-on-Tyne | |
| XN728 | EE Lightning F2A (8546M) [V] | Privately owned, Balderton, Notts | |
| XN734 | EE Lightning F3A (8346M/ G-27-239/G-BNCA) | Vintage Aircraft Team, Cranfield | |
| XN769 | EE Lightning F2 (8402M) [Z] | London ATCC, West Drayton | |
| XN774 | EE Lightning F2A (8551M) [F] | RAF Coningsby, decoy | |
| XN776 | EE Lightning F2A [C] (8535M) | Royal Scottish Museum of Flight, East Fortune | |
| XN781 | EE Lightning F2A (8538M) [B] | *Scrapped at Withington May 1990* | |
| XN817 | AW Argosy C1 | MoD(PE) RAE West Freugh Fire Section | |
| XN819 | AW Argosy C1 (8205M) (nose only) | Newark Air Museum, Winthorpe | |
| XN855 | AW Argosy E1 (8556M) | FSCTE, RAF Manston | |
| XN923 | HS Buccaneer S1 [13] | Privately owned, Charlwood, Surrey | |
| XN928 | HS Buccaneer S1 (8179M) | Wales Aircraft Museum, Cardiff | |
| XN929 | HS Buccaneer S1 (8051M) (nose only) | RAF Lossiemouth procedures trainer | |
| XN930 | HS Buccaneer S1 (8180M) [632/LM] | RAF Honington, Fire Section | |
| XN934 | HS Buccaneer S1 (A2600) [631] | RN Predannack Fire School | |
| XN953 | HS Buccaneer S1 (A2655/ 8182M) | RN Predannack Fire School | |
| XN957 | HS Buccaneer S1 [630/LM] | FAA Museum, RNAS Yeovilton | |
| XN964 | HS Buccaneer S1 [613/LM] | Newark Air Museum, Winthorpe | |
| XN967 | HS Buccaneer S1 (A2627) [103/E] | Cornwall Aero Park, Helston | |
| *XN972* | HS Buccaneer S1 (8183M) (nose only) (really XN962) | RAF Exhibition Flight, Abingdon | |
| XN973 | HS Buccaneer S1 (nose only) [633] | BAe Warton Fire Section | |
| XN974 | HS Buccaneer S2A | MoD(PE) BAe Warton | |
| XN976 | HS Buccaneer S2B | RAF, Lossiemouth | |

| Notes | Reg. | Type | Owner or Operator |
|---|---|---|---|
| | XN977 | HS Buccaneer S2B [G] | RAF, stored Shawbury |
| | XN979 | HS Buccaneer S2 (nose only) | Cranfield Institute of Technology |
| | XN981 | HS Buccaneer S2B | RAF No 12 Sqn, Lossiemouth |
| | XN982 | HS Buccaneer S2C | MoD(PE) BAe Brough |
| | XN983 | HS Buccaneer S2B | RAF, stored Shawbury |
| | XP107 | WS58 Wessex HAS1 (A2527) | RN Predannack Fire School |
| | XP110 | WS58 Wessex HAS3 [55/FL] | RNAY Fleetlands Apprentice School |
| | XP116 | WS58 Wessex HAS3 (A2618) [520] | RN AES, Lee-on-Solent |
| | XP137 | WS58 Wessex HAS3 [CU] | RN NACDS, Culdrose |
| | XP140 | WS58 Wessex HAS3 (8806M) [653/PO] | RAF Chilmark, BDRT |
| | XP142 | WS58 Wessex HAS3 | FAA Museum, RNAS Yeovilton |
| | XP149 | WS58 Wessex HAS1 (A2669) | RN Predannack Fire School |
| | XP150 | WS58 Wessex HAS3 [406/AN] | RN AES, Lee-on-Solent |
| | XP151 | WS58 Wessex HAS1 (A2684) [047/R] | RN Lee-on-Solent Fire Section |
| | XP155 | WS58 Wessex HAS1 (A2640) | RNAS Culdrose Fire Section |
| | XP157 | WS58 Wessex HAS1 (A2680) | RN AES, Lee-on-Solent |
| | XP158 | WS58 Wessex HAS1 (A2688) [522/CU] | RN AES, Lee-on-Solent |
| | XP159 | WS58 Wessex HAS1 (8877M) [047/R] | RAF Odiham, BDRT |
| | XP160 | WS58 Wessex HAS1 (A2650) [521/CU] | RN AES, Lee-on-Solent |
| | XP165 | WS Scout AH1 | International Helicopter Museum, Weston-super-Mare |
| | XP166 | WS Scout AH1 (G-APVL) | RAe Farnborough, Apprentice School |
| | XP190 | WS Scout AH1 | AAC, stored Wroughton |
| | XP191 | WS Scout AH1 | AAC Middle Wallop, BDRT |
| | XP226 | Fairey Gannet AEW3 (A2667) [073/E] | Newark Air Museum, Winthorpe |
| | XP241 | Auster AOP9 | Tagmore Nurseries, Rabley Heath, Herts |
| | XP242 | Auster AOP9 | AAC Historic Aircraft Flight, stored Middle Wallop |
| | XP244 | Auster AOP9 (7864M) [M7922] | Army Apprentice College, Arborfield |
| | XP248 | Auster AOP9 (7822M) | Vintage Aircraft Team, Cranfield |
| | XP279 | Auster AOP9 (G-BWKK) | Privately owned, Goodwood |
| | XP280 | Auster AOP9 | Leicester Museum of Technology store |
| | XP281 | Auster AOP9 | Imperial War Museum, Duxford |
| | XP282 | Auster AOP9 (G-BGTC) | Privately owned, Tollerton |
| | XP283 | Auster AOP9 (7859M) | Vintage Aircraft Team, Cranfield |
| | XP299 | WS55 Whirlwind HAR10 (8726M) | RAF Cosford Aerospace Museum |
| | XP328 | WS55 Whirlwind HAR10 (G-BKHC) | Privately owned, RAF Lakenheath |
| | XP329 | WS55 Whirlwind HAR10 [V] (8791M) [UN] | Privately owned, Tattershall Thorpe |
| | XP330 | WS55 Whirlwind HAR10 | CAA Fire School, Teesside Airport |
| | XP333 | WS55 Whirlwind HAR10 (8650M) [G] | FSCTE, RAF Manston |
| | XP338 | WS55 Whirlwind HAR10 (8647M) [N] | RAF No 2 SoTT, Cosford |
| | XP344 | WS55 Whirlwind HAR10 (8764M) [X] | RAF North Luffenham |
| | XP345 | WS55 Whirlwind HAR10 [UN] (8792M) | Privately owned, Storwood, East Yorks |
| | XP346 | WS55 Whirlwind HAR10 (8793M) | Stratford Aircraft Collection, Long Marston |
| | XP350 | WS55 Whirlwind HAR10 | Cornwall Aero Park, Helston |
| | XP351 | WS55 Whirlwind HAR10 (8672M) [Z] | RAF Shawbury, gate guardian |
| | XP354 | WS55 Whirlwind HAR10 (8721M) | RAF No 1 SoTT, Halton |
| | XP355 | WS55 Whirlwind HAR10 (8463M/G-BEBC) [A] | City of Norwich Aviation Museum |

| Reg. | Type | Owner or Operator | Notes |
|---|---|---|---|
| XP357 | WS55 Whirlwind HAR10 (8499M) | FSCTE, RAF Manston | |
| XP359 | WS55 Whirlwind HAR10 (8447M) | RAF Stafford, Fire Section | |
| XP360 | WS55 Whirlwind HAR10 [V] | Second World War Aircraft Preservation Society, Lasham | |
| XP361 | WS55 Whirlwind HAR10 (8731M) | RAF Valley, BDRT | |
| XP393 | WS55 Whirlwind HAR10 [U] | RAE Farnborough Fire Section | |
| XP394 | WS55 Whirlwind HAR10 [C] | FSCTE, RAF Manston | |
| XP395 | WS55 Whirlwind HAR10 [A] (8674M) | Privately owned, Tattershall Thorpe | |
| XP398 | WS55 Whirlwind HAR10 (8794M) | Privately owned, Charlwood, Surrey | |
| XP399 | WS55 Whirlwind HAR10 | Privately owned, Raunds, Northants | |
| XP400 | WS55 Whirlwind HAR10 [N] (8444M) | FSCTE, RAF Manston | |
| XP404 | WS55 Whirlwind HAR10 (8682M) | RAF SAREW, Finningley | |
| XP405 | WS55 Whirlwind HAR10 [Y] (8656M) | Junior Infantry Reg't, Shorncliffe, Kent | |
| XP411 | AW Argosy C1 (8442M) [C] | RAF Cosford Aerospace Museum | |
| XP442 | AW Argosy T2 (8454M) [55] | *Scrapped, November 1990* | |
| XP458 | Slingsby Grasshopper TX1 | City of Norwich Aviation Museum | |
| XP502 | HS Gnat T1 (8576M) [02] | RAF St Athan, CTTS | |
| XP503 | HS Gnat T1 (8568M) [73] | RAF No 1 SoTT, Halton | |
| XP504 | HS Gnat T1 (8618M) [68] [04] | RAF No 1 SoTT, Halton | |
| XP505 | HS Gnat T1 [05] | Science Museum, South Kensington | |
| XP511 | HS Gnat T1 (8619M) [65] | RAF No 1 SoTT, Halton | |
| XP516 | HS Gnat T1 (8580M) [16] | MoD(PE) RAE Farnborough | |
| XP530 | HS Gnat T1 (8606M) [60] | RAF No 1 SoTT, Halton | |
| XP532 | HS Gnat T1 (8577M/8615M) [32] | *Scrapped, 1990* | |
| XP533 | HS Gnat T1 (8632M) [Q] | *Sold to USA, May 1990* | |
| XP534 | HS Gnat T1 (8620M) [64] | RAF No 1 SoTT, Halton | |
| XP538 | HS Gnat T1 (8607M) [P] | *Sold to USA as N19GT, April 1990* | |
| XP540 | HS Gnat T1 (8608M) [62] | RAF No 1 SoTT, Halton | |
| XP542 | HS Gnat T1 (8575M) [42] | RAF St Athan, CTTS | |
| XP547 | Hunting Jet Provost T4 [N] [03] (8992M) | RAF No 2 SoTT, Cosford | |
| XP556 | Hunting Jet Provost T4 [B] | RAF, stored Shawbury | |
| XP557 | Hunting Jet Provost T4 (8494M) | RAF No 1 SoTT, Halton | |
| XP558 | Hunting Jet Provost T4 (8627M/A2628) [20] | RAF St Athan, CTTS | |
| XP563 | Hunting Jet Provost T4 [C] | RAF, stored Shawbury | |
| XP567 | Hunting Jet Provost T4 (8510M) [23] | RAF No 1 SoTT, Halton | |
| XP568 | Hunting Jet Provost T4 (fuselage only) | Stratford Aircraft Collection, Long Marston, stored | |
| XP573 | Hunting Jet Provost T4 (8236M) [19] | RAF No 1 SoTT, Halton | |
| XP585 | Hunting Jet Provost T4 (8407M) [24] | RAF No 1 SoTT, Halton | |
| XP627 | Hunting Jet Provost T4 | North East Aircraft Museum, Usworth | |
| XP629 | Hunting Jet Provost T4 [P] | RAF, stored Shawbury | |
| XP638 | Hunting Jet Provost T4 [A] | RAF, stored Shawbury | |
| XP640 | Hunting Jet Provost T4 (8501M) [E] | RAF No 1 SoTT, Halton | |
| XP672 | Hunting Jet Provost T4 (8458M) [27] | RAF No 1 SoTT, Halton | |
| XP677 | Hunting Jet Provost T4 (8587M) (nose only) | No 2530 Sqn ATC, Headley Court, Uckfield, East Sussex | |
| XP680 | Hunting Jet Provost T4 (8460M) | RAF St Athan, BDRT | |
| XP686 | Hunting Jet Provost T4 (8401M/8502M) [G] | RAF No 1 SoTT, Halton | |
| XP688 | Hunting Jet Provost T4 [E] | RAF, stored Shawbury | |
| XP693 | BAC Lightning F6 | MoD(PE) BAe Warton | |
| XP701 | BAC Lightning F3 (8924M) [DD] | Kent Battle of Britain Museum, Hawkinge | |
| XP703 | BAC Lightning F3 (nose only) | Lightning Preservation Group, Bruntingthorpe | |

| Notes | Reg. | Type | Owner or Operator |
|---|---|---|---|
| | XP706 | BAC Lightning F3 (8925M) | Lincolnshire Lightning Preservation Society, Strubby |
| | XP741 | BAC Lightning F3 [AR] (8939M) | FSCTE, RAF Manston |
| | XP745 | BAC Lightning F3 (8453M) [H] | RAF Boulmer, at main gate |
| | XP749 | BAC Lightning F3 (8926M) | Privately owned, Sutton-on-the-Forest |
| | XP750 | BAC Lightning F3 (8927M) | Privately owned, Sutton-on-the-Forest |
| | XP764 | BAC Lightning F3 [DC] (8929M) | Privately owned, Sutton-on-the-Forest |
| | XP769 | DHC Beaver AL1 | *Sold in USA as N21190 May 1990* |
| | XP771 | DHC Beaver AL1 | *Sold in USA as N21200 May 1990* |
| | XP772 | DHC Beaver AL1 | Museum of Army Transport, Beverley |
| | XP775 | DHC Beaver AL1 | Privately owned |
| | XP778 | DHC Beaver AL1 | Privately owned |
| | XP779 | DHC Beaver AL1 | AAC, stored Shawbury |
| | XP806 | DHC Beaver AL1 | Army Apprentice College, Arborfield |
| | XP810 | DHC Beaver AL1 | *Sold in USA as N21208 May 1990* |
| | XP814 | DHC Beaver AL1 | *Sold in USA as N2123X May 1990* |
| | XP820 | DHC Beaver AL1 | AAC Historic Aircraft Flight, Middle Wallop |
| | XP821 | DHC Beaver AL1 [MCO] | Museum of Army Flying, Middle Wallop |
| | XP822 | DHC Beaver AL1 | Museum of Army Flying, Middle Wallop |
| | XP825 | DHC Beaver AL1 | *Sold in USA as N2126S May 1990* |
| | XP827 | DHC Beaver AL1 (fuselage) | AAC Netheravon Fire Section |
| | XP831 | Hawker P1127 (8406M) | RAF Museum, Hendon |
| | XP841 | Handley-Page HP115 | Concorde Museum, RNAS Yeovilton |
| | XP846 | WS Scout AH1 [B, H] (fuselage) | AAC, stored Wroughton |
| | XP847 | WS Scout AH1 | Museum of Army Flying, Middle Wallop |
| | XP848 | WS Scout AH1 | AAC SAE, Middle Wallop |
| | XP849 | WS Scout AH1 | MoD(PE) ETPS Boscombe Down |
| | XP850 | WS Scout AH1 (fuselage) | AAC, stored Wroughton |
| | XP853 | WS Scout AH1 | AAC SAE, Middle Wallop |
| | XP854 | WS Scout AH1 (7898M/ TAD043) | AAC SAE, Middle Wallop |
| | XP855 | WS Scout AH1 | AAC, stored Wroughton |
| | XP856 | WS Scout AH1 | AAC Middle Wallop, BDRT |
| | XP857 | WS Scout AH1 | AAC Middle Wallop Fire Section |
| | XP883 | WS Scout AH1 | AAC No 658 Sqn, Netheravon |
| | XP884 | WS Scout AH1 | AAC SAE, Middle Wallop |
| | XP886 | WS Scout AH1 | Army Apprentice College, Arborfield |
| | XP888 | WS Scout AH1 | AAC SAE, Middle Wallop |
| | XP890 | WS Scout AH1 [G] (fuselage) | AAC, stored Wroughton |
| | XP891 | WS Scout AH1 [S] | AAC No 666 (TA) Sqn, Netheravon |
| | XP893 | WS Scout AH1 | AAC, stored Wroughton |
| | XP899 | WS Scout AH1 [D] | Army Apprentice College, Arborfield |
| | XP902 | WS Scout AH1 | AAC, stored Wroughton |
| | XP903 | WS Scout AH1 (fuselage) | AAC, stored Wroughton |
| | XP905 | WS Scout AH1 | AAC SAE, Middle Wallop |
| | XP907 | WS Scout AH1 | AAC Middle Wallop Fire Section |
| | XP908 | WS Scout AH1 [Y] | AAC No 660 Sqn, Brunei |
| | XP909 | WS Scout AH1 | AAC No 658 Sqn, Netheravon |
| | XP910 | WS Scout AH1 | AAC, stored Wroughton |
| | XP919 | DH Sea Vixen FAW2 (8163M) [706/VL] | City of Norwich Aviation Museum |
| | XP921 | DH Sea Vixen FAW2 (8226M) [753] | RAF North Luffenham Training Area |
| | XP924 | DH Sea Vixen D3 | MoD(PE) RAE Llanbedr |
| | XP925 | DH Sea Vixen FAW2 (nose only) [752] | RAE Farnborough |
| | XP967 | Sud Alouette AH2 | *To G-BSFN* |
| | XP980 | Hawker P.1127 (A2700) | FAA Museum, RNAS Yeovilton |
| | XP984 | Hawker P.1127 (A2658) | RNEC Manadon, for instruction |
| | XR137 | AW Argosy E1 | Snowdon Mountain Aviation Museum, Caernarfon |
| | XR140 | AW Argosy E1 (8579M) (fuselage only) | RAF Halton, Fire Section |
| | XR220 | BAC TSR2 (7933M) | RAF Cosford Aerospace Museum |
| | XR222 | BAC TSR2 | Imperial War Museum, Duxford |
| | XR232 | Sud Alouette AH2 (F-WEIP) | Museum of Army Flying, Middle Wallop |
| | XR240 | Auster AOP9 (G-BDFH) | Privately owned, Booker |
| | XR241 | Auster AOP9 (G-AXRR) | Museum of Army Flying, Middle Wallop |
| | XR243 | Auster AOP9 (8057M) | RAF St Athan Historic Aircraft Collection |

| Reg. | Type | Owner or Operator | Notes |
|---|---|---|---|
| XR244 | Auster AOP9 | AAC Historic Aircraft Flight, Middle Wallop | |
| XR246 | Auster AOP9 (7862M/ G-AZBU) | Privately owned, Reymerston Hall | |
| XR267 | Auster AOP9 (G-BJXR) | Cotswold Aircraft Restoration Group, RAF Innsworth | |
| XR269 | Auster AOP9 (G-BDXY) | Privately owned, Old Buckenham | |
| XR271 | Auster AOP9 | Museum of Artillery, Woolwich | |
| XR363 | SC5 Belfast C1 (G-OHCA) | Privately owned, Southend | |
| XR371 | SC5 Belfast C1 | RAF Cosford Aerospace Museum | |
| XR376 | Sud Alouette AH2 | *Sold to Italy* | |
| XR378 | Sud Alouette AH2 | *To G-BSFS* | |
| XR379 | Sud Alouette AH2 | AAC, Historic Aircraft Flight, Middle Wallop | |
| XR382 | Sud Alouette AH2 | *Sold to France* | |
| XR385 | Sud Alouette AH2 | *To G-BSFU* | |
| XR386 | Sud Alouette AH2 | | |
| XR396 | DH Comet 4C (8882M) (G-BDIU) | RAF Kinloss BDRT | |
| XR436 | Saro Scout AH1 | AAC Middle Wallop, BDRT | |
| XR441 | DH Sea Heron C1 (G-AORG) | Privately owned, Bournemouth | |
| XR442 | DH Sea Heron C1 (G-AORH) | *To* | |
| XR443 | DH Sea Heron C1 (G-ARKU/ G-ODLG) | *To G-ODLG* | |
| XR445 | DH Sea Heron C1 (G-ARKW/ G-ORSJ) | *To G-ORSJ* | |
| XR453 | WS55 Whirlwind HAR10 (8873M) [A] | RAF Odiham, on gate | |
| XR458 | WS55 Whirlwind HAR10 (8662M) [H] | RAF No 1 SoTT, Halton | |
| XR478 | WS55 Whirlwind HAR10 | Defence School, Winterbourne Gunner | |
| XR481 | WS55 Whirlwind HAR10 | RAF, stored Wroughton | |
| XR482 | WS55 Whirlwind HAR10 [G] | Defence School, Winterbourne Gunner | |
| XR483 | WS55 Whirlwind HAR10 | RAF, stored Wroughton | |
| XR485 | WS55 Whirlwind HAR10 [Q] | Norfolk & Suffolk Aviation Museum, Flixton | |
| XR486 | WS55 Whirlwind HCC12 (8727M) (G-RWWW) | Privately owned, Tattershall Thorpe | |
| XR497 | WS58 Wessex HC2 [F] | RAF No 72 Sqn, Aldergrove | |
| XR498 | WS58 Wessex HC2 [X] | RAF No 72 Sqn, Aldergrove | |
| XR499 | WS58 Wessex HC2 [W] | RAF No 72 Sqn, Aldergrove | |
| XR501 | WS58 Wessex HC2 | RAF No 22 Sqn SAR* | |
| XR502 | WS58 Wessex HC2 [Z] | RAF No 72 Sqn, Aldergrove | |
| XR503 | WS58 Wessex HC2 | MoD(PE) RAE Bedford | |
| XR504 | WS58 Wessex HC2 | RAF No 22 Sqn SAR* | |
| XR505 | WS58 Wessex HC2 [WA] | RAF No 2 FTS, Shawbury | |
| XR506 | WS58 Wessex HC2 [V] | RAF No 72 Sqn, Aldergrove | |
| XR507 | WS58 Wessex HC2 | RAF No 22 Sqn SAR* | |
| XR508 | WS58 Wessex HC2 [D] | RAF No 28 Sqn, Sek Kong | |
| XR509 | WS58 Wessex HC2 (8752M) | RAF Benson, BDRT | |
| XR511 | WS58 Wessex HC2 [L] | RAF No 72 Sqn, Aldergrove | |
| XR515 | WS58 Wessex HC2 [B] | RAF No 28 Sqn, Sek Kong | |
| XR516 | WS58 Wessex HC2 [WB] | RAF No 2 FTS, Shawbury | |
| XR517 | WS58 Wessex HC2 [N] | RAF No 72 Sqn, Aldergrove | |
| XR518 | WS58 Wessex HC2 | RAF No 22 Sqn SAR* | |
| XR519 | WS58 Wessex HC2 [WC] | RAF No 2 FTS, Shawbury | |
| XR520 | WS58 Wessex HC2 | RAF No 22 Sqn SAR* | |
| XR521 | WS58 Wessex HC2 [WD] | RAF No 2 FTS, Shawbury | |
| XR522 | WS58 Wessex HC2 [A] | RAF No 28 Sqn, Sek Kong | |
| XR523 | WS58 Wessex HC2 [M] | RAF No 72 Sqn, Aldergrove | |
| XR524 | WS58 Wessex HC2 | RAF No 22 Sqn SAR* | |
| XR525 | WS58 Wessex HC2 [G] | RAF No 72 Sqn, Aldergrove | |
| XR526 | WS58 Wessex HC2 (8147M) | Westlands, Sherborne | |
| XR527 | WS58 Wessex HC2 [K] | RAF No 72 Sqn, Aldergrove | |
| XR528 | WS58 Wessex HC2 [T] | RAF No 72 Sqn, Aldergrove | |
| XR529 | WS58 Wessex HC2 [E] | RAF No 72 Sqn, Aldergrove | |
| XR534 | HS Gnat T1 (8578M) [65] | RAF Valley on display | |
| XR535 | HS Gnat T1 (8569M) [05] | RAF No 1 SoTT, Halton | |
| XR537 | HS Gnat T1 (8642M) [T] (G-NATY) | Jet Heritage Ltd, Bournemouth | |

**Note:** *The SAR Wing and SAREW are based at RAF Finningley. No 22 Sqn SAR has detached flights: A Flt—RAF Chivenor; B Flt—RAF Leuchars; C Flt and SARTU—RAF Valley; E Flt—RAF Coltishall.

| Notes | Reg. | Type | Owner or Operator |
|---|---|---|---|
| | XR538 | HS Gnat T1 (8621M) [69] | RAF No 1 SoTT, Halton |
| | XR544 | HS Gnat T1 | *Scrapped at RAE Farnborough* |
| | XR569 | HS Gnat T1 (8560M) [08] | RAF Linton-on-Ouse Fire Section |
| | XR571 | HS Gnat T1 (8493M) | RAF *Red Arrows* Scampton on display |
| | XR574 | HS Gnat T1 (8631M) [72] | RAF No 1 SoTT, Halton |
| | XR588 | WS58 Wessex HC2 | RAF No 22 Sqn SAR* |
| | XR595 | WS Scout AH1 [M] | AAC, stored Wroughton |
| | XR597 | WS Scout AH1 | AAC SAE, Middle Wallop |
| | XR600 | WS Scout AH1 (fuselage) | AAC Aldergrove, BDRT |
| | XR601 | WS Scout AH1 | Army Apprentice College, Arborfield |
| | XR602 | WS Scout AH1 | AAC, stored Wroughton |
| | XR627 | WS Scout AH1 | AAC, stored Wroughton |
| | XR628 | WS Scout AH1 | AAC, stored Wroughton |
| | XR629 | WS Scout AH1 (fuselage) | AAC, stored Wroughton |
| | XR630 | WS Scout AH1 [U] | AAC Middle Wallop BDRT |
| | XR632 | WS Scout AH1 [Q] | AAC, stored Wroughton |
| | XR635 | WS Scout AH1 | AAC SAE, Middle Wallop |
| | XR637 | WS Scout AH1 (fuselage) | AAC, stored Wroughton |
| | XR639 | WS Scout AH1 [X] (fuselage) | AAC, stored Wroughton |
| | XR643 | Hunting Jet Provost T4 (8516M) [26] | RAF No 1 SoTT, Halton |
| | XR650 | Hunting Jet Provost T4 (8459M) [28] | RAF No 1 SoTT, Halton |
| | XR651 | Hunting Jet Provost T4 (8431M) [A] | RAF Marham, fire section |
| | XR653 | Hunting Jet Provost T4 [H] | RAF, stored Shawbury |
| | XR654 | Hunting Jet Provost T4 (fuselage) | Macclesfield Historical Av Soc, Chelford, Cheshire |
| | XR658 | Hunting Jet Provost T4 (8192M) | North Wales Institute of Higher Education, Connah's Quay |
| | XR662 | Hunting Jet Provost T4 (8410M) [25] | RAF No 1 SoTT, Halton |
| | XR669 | Hunting Jet Provost T4 (8062M) [02] (nose only) | RAF No 1 SoTT, Halton |
| | XR670 | Hunting Jet Provost T4 (8498M) | RAF No 1 SoTT, Halton |
| | XR672 | Hunting Jet Provost T4 [73] (8495M) [C] | RAF No 1 SoTT, Halton |
| | XR673 | Hunting Jet Provost T4 [L] | RAF, stored Shawbury |
| | XR674 | Hunting Jet Provost T4 [D] | RAF, stored Shawbury |
| | XR679 | Hunting Jet Provost T4 [M] (8991M) | RAF No 2 SoTT, Cosford |
| | XR681 | Hunting Jet Provost T4 (8588M) (nose only) | No 1349 Sqn ATC, Odiham |
| | XR700 | Hunting Jet Provost T4 (8589M) (nose only) | RAF Exhibition Flight, Aldergrove |
| | XR701 | Hunting Jet Provost T4 [K] | RAF, stored Shawbury |
| | XR704 | Hunting Jet Provost T4 (8506M) [30] | RAF No 1 SoTT, Halton |
| | XR713 | BAC Lightning F3 (8935M) [C] | RAF No 111 Sqn on display, Leuchars |
| | XR716 | BAC Lightning F3 [AQ] (8940M) | RAF Cottesmore, BDRT |
| | XR718 | BAC Lightning F3 [DA] (8932M) | RAF Wattisham, BDRT |
| | XR720 | BAC Lightning F3 (8930M) | Privately owned, Sutton-on-the-Forest |
| | XR724 | BAC Lightning F6 | RAF, stored Shawbury |
| | XR725 | BAC Lightning F6 | Privately owned, Rossington |
| | XR726 | BAC Lightning F6 | Privately owned, Rossington |
| | XR728 | BAC Lightning F6 [JS] | Lightning Preservation Group, Bruntingthorpe |
| | XR747 | BAC Lightning F6 | Privately owned, Rossington |
| | XR749 | BAC Lightning F3 [Q] (8934M) | RAF Leuchars, BDRT |
| | XR751 | BAC Lightning F3 | Privately owned, Lower Tremar, Cornwall |
| | XR753 | BAC Lightning F6 [BP] (8969M) | RAF Leeming on display |
| | XR754 | BAC Lightning F6 [BC] (8972M) | RAF Honington, BDRT |
| | XR755 | BAC Lightning F6 | Privately owned, Callington, Cornwall |
| | XR757 | BAC Lightning F6 | Privately owned, Rossington |
| | XR759 | BAC Lightning F6 | Privately owned, Rossington |
| | XR770 | BAC Lightning F6 [JS] | Museum of Weapon Technology, Grimsby |
| | XR771 | BAC Lightning F6 | Midland Air Museum, Coventry |
| | XR773 | BAC Lightning F6 [BR] | MoD(PE) BAe Warton |
| | *XR777* | WS Scout AH1 (really XT625) | St George's Barracks, Sutton Coldfield |
| | XR806 | BAC VC10 C1 | RAF No 10 Sqn, Brize Norton |

| Reg. | Type | Owner or Operator | Notes |
|---|---|---|---|
| XR807 | BAC VC10 C1 | RAF No 10 Sqn, Brize Norton | |
| XR808 | BAC VC10 C1 | RAF No 10 Sqn, Brize Norton | |
| XR810 | BAC VC10 C1 | RAF No 10 Sqn, Brize Norton | |
| *XR944* | Wallis WA116 (G-ATTB) | Privately owned, Reymerston Hall | |
| XR953 | HS Gnat T1 (8609M) [63] | RAF No 1 SoTT, Halton | |
| XR954 | HS Gnat T1 (8570M) [30] | RAF No 1 SoTT, Halton | |
| XR955 | HS Gnat T1 (A2678) [SAH-2] | Privately owned, Leavesden | |
| XR977 | HS Gnat T1 (8640M) | RAF Cosford Aerospace Museum | |
| XR980 | HS Gnat T1 (8622M) [70] | RAF No 1 SoTT, Halton | |
| XR984 | HS Gnat T1 (8571M) | RAF | |
| XR998 | HS Gnat T1 (8623M) [71] | RAF No 1 SoTT, Halton | |
| XS100 | HS Gnat T1 (8561M) [57] | RAF No 1 SoTT, Halton | |
| XS101 | HS Gnat T1 (8638M) (G-GNAT) | Privately owned, Cranfield | |
| XS102 | HS Gnat T1 (8624M) [H] (G-MOUR) | Privately owned, Leavesden | |
| XS104 | HS Gnat T1 (8604M) [44] | *To G-FRCE* | |
| XS105 | HS Gnat T1 (8625M) [V] | *Sold to USA as N18GT, April 1990* | |
| XS107 | HS Gnat T1 (8639M) [U] | *Sold to USA, May 1990* | |
| XS109 | HS Gnat T1 (8626M) [75] | RAF No 1 SoTT, Halton | |
| XS110 | HS Gnat T1 (8562M) [20] | *Sold to USA as N7152Z, May 1990* | |
| XS119 | WS58 Wessex HAS3 [55] | RN Predannack Fire School | |
| XS120 | WS58 Wessex HAS1 (8653M) [520/CU] | RAF Wroughton Fire Section | |
| XS122 | WS58 Wessex HAS3 (A2707) [655/PO] | RNEC Manadon, for instruction | |
| XS125 | WS58 Wessex HAS1 (A2648) | RN Predannack Fire School | |
| XS128 | WS58 Wessex HAS1 (A2670) [37] | RNAS Yeovilton, BDRT | |
| XS149 | WS58 Wessex HAS3 [661/GL] | International Helicopter Museum, Weston-super-Mare, Avon | |
| XS153 | WS58 Wessex HAS3 [662/PO] | RNEC Manadon, for instruction | |
| XS176 | Hunting Jet Provost T4 (8514M) [N] | RAF No 1 SoTT, Halton | |
| XS177 | Hunting Jet Provost T4 [N] | RAF St Athan, hack | |
| XS178 | Hunting Jet Provost T4 [P] [05] (8994M) | RAF No 2 SoTT, Cosford | |
| XS179 | Hunting Jet Provost T4 (8237M) [20] | RAF No 1 SoTT, Halton | |
| XS180 | Hunting Jet Provost T4 (8238M) [21] | RAF No 1 SoTT, Halton | |
| XS181 | Hunting Jet Provost T4 [F] | RAF, stored Shawbury | |
| XS186 | Hunting Jet Provost T4 (8408M) [M] | RAF No 1 SoTT, Halton | |
| XS209 | Hunting Jet Provost T4 (8409M) [29] | RAF No 1 SoTT, Halton | |
| XS210 | Hunting Jet Provost T4 (8239M) [22] | RAF No 1 SoTT, Halton | |
| XS215 | Hunting Jet Provost T4 (8507M) [17] | RAF No 1 SoTT, Halton | |
| XS216 | Hunting Jet Provost T4 (nose only) | RAF SAREW Finningley, for rescue training | |
| XS217 | Hunting Jet Provost T4 [O] | RAF, stored Shawbury | |
| XS218 | Hunting Jet Provost T4 (8508M) [18] | RAF | |
| XS219 | Hunting Jet Provost T4 [O] (8993M) | RAF No 2 SoTT, Cosford | |
| XS230 | BAC Jet Provost T5P | MoD(PE) ETPS Boscombe Down | |
| XS231 | BAC Jet Provost T5 (G-ATAJ) | Privately owned, Bruntingthorpe | |
| XS235 | HS Comet 4C | MoD(PE) A&AEE Boscombe Down | |
| XS241 | WS58 Wessex HU5 | MoD(PE) stored, Wroughton | |
| XS416 | BAC Lightning T5 | Privately owned, Rossington | |
| XS417 | BAC Lightning T5 | Newark Air Museum, Winthorpe | |
| XS419 | BAC Lightning T5 | Privately owned, Rossington | |
| XS420 | BAC Lightning T5 | Privately owned, Narborough, Norfolk | |
| XS422 | BAC Lightning T5 | Privately owned, Southampton Docks | |
| XS451 | BAC Lightning T5 (8503M) (G-LTNG) | Privately owned, Plymouth | |
| XS452 | BAC Lightning T5 [BT] (G-BPFE) | Privately owned, Cranfield | |
| XS456 | BAC Lightning T5 | Privately owned, Wainfleet | |
| XS457 | BAC Lightning T5 (nose only) | Museum of Weapon Technology, Grimsby | |
| XS458 | BAC Lightning T5 [DY] | Privately owned, Cranfield | |

| Notes | Reg. | Type | Owner or Operator |
|---|---|---|---|
| | XS459 | BAC Lightning T5 | Privately owned, Narborough, Norfolk |
| | XS463 | WS Wasp HAS1 (A2647) | RN Predannack Fire School |
| | *XS463* | WS Wasp HAS1 (really XT431) | International Helicopter Museum, Weston-super-Mare |
| | XS479 | WS58 Wessex HU5 [XF] (8819M) | JATE, RAF Brize Norton |
| | XS481 | WS58 Wessex HU5 | RN, stored Wroughton |
| | XS482 | WS58 Wessex HU5 [A-D] | RAE Farnborough Apprentice School |
| | XS483 | WS58 Wessex HU5 [T] | RN AES, Lee-on-Solent |
| | XS484 | WS58 Wessex HU5 [821/CU] | RN, stored Wroughton |
| | XS485 | WS58 Wessex HC5C (*Hearts*) | RAF No 84 Sqn, Akrotiri |
| | XS486 | WS58 Wessex HU5 [524] | RN Recruiting Team, Lee-on-Solent |
| | XS488 | WS58 Wessex HU5 [XK] | RN, stored Wroughton |
| | XS489 | WS58 Wessex HU5 [R] | RN, stored Wroughton |
| | XS491 | WS58 Wessex HU5 [XM] | RN, stored Wroughton |
| | XS492 | WS58 Wessex HU5 [623] | RN, stored Wroughton |
| | XS493 | WS58 Wessex HU5 | Department of Naval Recruitment, (846 Sqn), Fleetlands |
| | XS496 | WS58 Wessex HU5 [625/PO] | RN AES, Lee-on-Solent |
| | XS498 | WS58 Wessex HC5C (*Joker*) | RAF No 84 Sqn, Akrotiri |
| | XS506 | WS58 Wessex HU5 [XE] | RN, stored Wroughton |
| | XS507 | WS58 Wessex HU5 [627/PO] | RN AES, Lee-on-Solent |
| | XS508 | WS58 Wessex HU5 | RNAY Fleetlands Museum |
| | XS509 | WS58 Wessex HU5 (A2597) | MoD(PE) ETPS Boscombe Down |
| | XS510 | WS58 Wessex HU5 [626/PO] | RN AES, Lee-on-Solent |
| | XS511 | WS58 Wessex HU5 [M] | RN AES, Lee-on-Solent |
| | XS513 | WS58 Wessex HU5 [419] | RN, Lee-on-Solent, BDRT |
| | XS514 | WS58 Wessex HU5 [L] | RN AES, Lee-on-Solent |
| | XS515 | WS58 Wessex HU5 [N] | RN AES, Lee-on-Solent |
| | XS516 | WS58 Wessex HU5 [Q] | RN AES, Lee-on-Solent |
| | XS517 | WS58 Wessex HC5C (*Diamonds*) | RAF No 84 Sqn, Akrotiri |
| | XS520 | WS58 Wessex HU5 [F] | RN AES, Lee-on-Solent |
| | XS521 | WS58 Wessex HU5 [YB] | Army, Saighton, Cheshire |
| | XS522 | WS58 Wessex HU5 [ZL/VL] | RN AES, Lee-on-Solent |
| | XS523 | WS58 Wessex HU5 [824/CU] | RN, stored Wroughton |
| | XS527 | WS Wasp HAS1 | FAA Museum, RNAS Yeovilton |
| | XS529 | WS Wasp HAS1 [461] | RN AES, Lee-on-Solent |
| | XS535 | WS Wasp HAS1 [432] | RAOC, West Moors, Dorset |
| | XS537 | WS Wasp HAS1 (A2672) [582] | RNAS Portland BDRT |
| | XS538 | WS Wasp HAS1 [451] (A2725) | RN Lee-on-Solent, BDRT |
| | XS539 | WS Wasp HAS1 [435/E] | RN AES, Lee-on-Solent |
| | XS541 | WS Wasp HAS1 [602] | RN, stored Wroughton |
| | XS545 | WS Wasp HAS1 (A2702) [635] | RN, Lee-on-Solent, BDRT |
| | XS562 | WS Wasp HAS1 [605] | RN, stored Wroughton |
| | XS567 | WS Wasp HAS1 [434/E] | RN NBC School, Lee-on-Solent |
| | XS568 | WS Wasp HAS1 [441] | RNAY Fleetlands Apprentice School |
| | XS569 | WS Wasp HAS1 | RNAY Fleetlands Apprentice School |
| | XS570 | WS Wasp HAS1 (A2699) [P] | Warship Preservation Trust, Millbay Docks, Plymouth |
| | XS572 | WS Wasp HAS1 (8845M) [414] | RAF Stafford Fire Section (No 16 MU) |
| | XS576 | DH Sea Vixen FAW2 [125/E] | Imperial War Museum, Duxford |
| | XS577 | DH Sea Vixen D3 | MoD(PE) RAE Llanbedr |
| | XS587 | DH Sea Vixen FAW(TT)2 (8828M) (G-VIXN) | Privately owned, Charlwood, Surrey |
| | XS590 | DH Sea Vixen FAW2 [131/E] | FAA Museum, RNAS Yeovilton |
| | XS596 | HS Andover C1 (PR) | RAF No 60 Sqn, Wildenrath |
| | XS597 | HS Andover C1 | RAF No 60 Sqn, Wildenrath |
| | XS598 | HS Andover C1 (fuselage only) | RAF AMS, Brize Norton |
| | XS603 | HS Andover E3 | RAF No 115 Sqn, Benson |
| | XS605 | HS Andover E3 | RAF No 115 Sqn, Benson |
| | XS606 | HS Andover C1 | MoD(PE) ETPS Boscombe Down |
| | XS607 | HS Andover C1 | MoD(PE) RAE Farnborough |
| | XS610 | HS Andover E3 | RAF No 115 Sqn, Benson |
| | XS637 | HS Andover C1 | RAF No 60 Sqn, Wildenrath |
| | XS639 | HS Andover E3A | RAF No 115 Sqn, Benson |
| | XS640 | HS Andover E3 | RAF No 115 Sqn, Benson |
| | XS641 | HS Andover C1(PR) | RAF No 60 Sqn, Wildenrath |
| | XS642 | HS Andover C1 [C] (8785M) | RAF Benson Fire Section |
| | XS643 | HS Andover E3A | RAF No 115 Sqn, Benson |

| Reg. | Type | Owner or Operator | Notes |
|---|---|---|---|
| XS644 | HS Andover E3A | RAF No 115 Sqn, Benson | |
| XS646 | HS Andover C1 (mod) | MoD(PE) RAE Farnborough | |
| XS650 | Slingsby Swallow TX1 (8801M) | RAF St Athan Historic Aircraft Collection | |
| XS674 | WS58 Wessex HC2 [R] | RAF No 72 Sqn, Aldergrove | |
| XS675 | WS58 Wessex HC2 | RAF No 22 Sqn SAR* | |
| XS676 | WS58 Wessex HC2 [WJ] | RAF No 2 FTS, Shawbury | |
| XS677 | WS58 Wessex HC2 [WK] | RAF No 2 FTS, Shawbury | |
| XS679 | WS58 Wessex HC2 [WG] | RAF No 2 FTS, Shawbury | |
| XS695 | HS Kestrel FGA1 (A2619) [SAH-6] | RNAS Culdrose, SAH | |
| XS709 | HS Dominie T1 [M] | RAF No 6 FTS, Finningley | |
| XS710 | HS Dominie T1 [O] | RAF No 6 FTS, Finningley | |
| XS711 | HS Dominie T1 [L] | RAF No 6 FTS, Finningley | |
| XS712 | HS Dominie T1 [A] | RAF No 6 FTS, Finningley | |
| XS713 | HS Dominie T1 [C] | RAF No 6 FTS, Finningley | |
| XS714 | HS Dominie T1 [P] | RAF No 6 FTS, Finningley | |
| XS726 | HS Dominie T1 [T] | RAF No 6 FTS, Finningley | |
| XS727 | HS Dominie T1 [D] | RAF No 6 FTS, Finningley | |
| XS728 | HS Dominie T1 [E] | RAF No 6 FTS, Finningley | |
| XS729 | HS Dominie T1 [G] | RAF No 6 FTS, Finningley | |
| XS730 | HS Dominie T1 [H] | RAF No 6 FTS, Finningley | |
| XS731 | HS Dominie T1 [J] | RAF No 6 FTS, Finningley | |
| XS732 | HS Dominie T1 [B] | RAF No 6 FTS, Finningley | |
| XS733 | HS Dominie T1 [Q] | RAF No 6 FTS, Finningley | |
| XS734 | HS Dominie T1 [N] | RAF No 6 FTS, Finningley | |
| XS735 | HS Dominie T1 [R] | RAF No 6 FTS, Finningley | |
| XS736 | HS Dominie T1 [S] | RAF No 6 FTS, Finningley | |
| XS737 | HS Dominie T1 [K] | RAF No 6 FTS, Finningley | |
| XS738 | HS Dominie T1 [U] | RAF No 6 FTS, Finningley | |
| XS739 | HS Dominie T1 [F] | RAF No 6 FTS, Finningley | |
| XS743 | Beagle Basset CC1 | MoD(PE) ETPS Boscombe Down | |
| XS770 | Beagle Basset CC1 (G-HRHI) | Privately owned, Cranfield | |
| XS789 | HS Andover CC2 | RAF No 32 Sqn, Northolt | |
| XS790 | HS Andover CC2 | MoD(PE) RAE Farnborough | |
| XS791 | HS Andover CC2 | RAF No 32 Sqn, Northolt | |
| XS792 | HS Andover CC2 | RAF No 32 Sqn, Northolt | |
| XS793 | HS Andover CC2 | RAF No 60 Sqn, Wildenrath | |
| XS794 | HS Andover CC2 | RAF No 32 Sqn, Northolt | |
| XS862 | WS58 Wessex HAS3 [650] | RN AES, Lee-on-Solent | |
| XS863 | WS58 Wessex HAS1 | Imperial War Museum, Duxford | |
| XS865 | WS58 Wessex HAS1 (A2694) [529/CU] | RNAS Lee-on-Solent Fire Section | |
| XS866 | WS58 Wessex HAS1 (A2705) [520/CU] | RN SAH, Culdrose | |
| XS867 | WS58 Wessex HAS1 (A2671) | RNAS Lee-on-Solent Fire Section | |
| XS868 | WS58 Wessex HAS1 (A2691) | RNAY Fleetlands, on gate | |
| XS869 | WS58 Wessex HAS1 (A2649) [508/PO] | FAA Air Medical School, Seafield Park, rescue training | |
| XS870 | WS58 Wessex HAS1 (A2697) [-/PO] | RN BDRT, Lee-on-Solent | |
| XS871 | WS58 Wessex HAS1 (8457M) [AI] | RAF Odiham Fire Section | |
| XS872 | WS58 Wessex HAS1 (A2666) [572/CU] | RNAY Fleetlands Apprentice School | |
| XS873 | WS58 Wessex HAS1 (A2686) [525/CU] | RN Predannack Fire School | |
| XS876 | WS58 Wessex HAS1 (A2695) [523] | RN SAH, Culdrose | |
| XS877 | WS58 Wessex HAS1 (A2687) [16/PO] | RN Culdrose, Engineering Training School | |
| XS878 | WS58 Wessex HAS1 (A2683) | RN, Lee-on-Solent, Fire Section | |
| XS881 | WS58 Wessex HAS1 (A2675) [046/CU] | FAA Museum, stored Wroughton | |
| XS882 | WS58 Wessex HAS1 (A2696) [524] | RN HMS *Naiad*, Portsmouth | |
| XS885 | WS58 Wessex HAS1 (A2668) [12/CU] | RN Exhibition Flight, Lee-on-Solent | |
| XS886 | WS58 Wessex HAS1 (A2685) [527/CU] | No 492 Sqn ATC, Shirley, W. Mids | |
| XS887 | WS58 Wessex HAS1 (A2690) [514/PO] | Cornwall Aero Park, Helston | |
| XS888 | WS58 Wessex HAS1 [521] | RN Exhibition Unit, Fleetlands | |

| Notes | Reg. | Type | Owner or Operator |
|---|---|---|---|
| | XS897 | BAC Lightning F6 | Privately owned, Rossington |
| | XS898 | BAC Lightning F6 [BD] | Privately owned, Cranfield |
| | XS899 | BAC Lightning F6 [BL] | Privately owned, Cranfield |
| | XS903 | BAC Lightning F6 [BA] | Yorkshire Air Museum, Elvington |
| | XS904 | BAC Lightning F6 | MoD(PE) BAe Warton |
| | XS919 | BAC Lightning F6 | Privately owned, Liskeard, Cornwall |
| | XS922 | BAC Lightning F6 [BJ] (8973M) | RAF Wattisham, BDRT |
| | XS923 | BAC Lightning F6 [BE] | Privately owned, Cranfield |
| | XS925 | BAC Lightning F6 [BA] (8961M) | RAF Museum, Hendon |
| | XS928 | BAC Lightning F6 | MoD(PE) BAe Warton |
| | XS932 | BAC Lightning F6 | Privately owned, Rossington |
| | XS933 | BAC Lightning F6 (cockpit only) | Privately owned, Narborough, Norfolk |
| | XS935 | BAC Lightning F6 | Privately owned, Rossington |
| | XS936 | BAC Lightning F6 | Privately owned, Liskeard, Cornwall |
| | XT108 | Agusta-Bell Sioux AH1 [U] | Museum of Army Flying, Middle Wallop |
| | XT131 | Agusta-Bell Sioux AH1 [B] | AAC Historic Aircraft Flight, Middle Wallop |
| | XT133 | Agusta-Bell Sioux AH1 (7923M) | Royal Engineers' Museum, Chatham |
| | XT140 | Agusta-Bell Sioux AH1 | Air Service Training, Perth |
| | XT141 | Agusta-Bell Sioux AH1 (8509M) | RAF AMS, Brize Norton |
| | XT148 | Agusta-Bell Sioux AH1 | Privately owned, Panshanger |
| | XT150 | Agusta-Bell Sioux AH1 (7883M) [R] | AAC Netheravon, on display |
| | XT151 | WS Sioux AH1 [W] | Museum of Army Flying store, Middle Wallop |
| | XT175 | WS Sioux AH1 (TAD175) | CSE Oxford for ground instruction |
| | XT176 | WS Sioux AH1 [U] | FAA Museum, RNAS Yeovilton |
| | XT190 | WS Sioux AH1 | Museum of Army Flying, Middle Wallop |
| | XT200 | WS Sioux AH1 [F] | Newark Air Museum, Winthorpe |
| | XT236 | WS Sioux AH1 (frame only) | Museum of Army Flying, Middle Wallop |
| | XT242 | WS Sioux AH1 (composite with XW179) | Stratford Aircraft Collection, Long Marston |
| | XT255 | WS58 Wessex HAS3 (8751M) | RAF No 14 MU, Carlisle, BDRT |
| | XT257 | WS58 Wessex HAS3 (8719M) | RAF No 1 SoTT, Halton |
| | XT270 | HS Buccaneer S2B | RAF, stored Shawbury |
| | XT271 | HS Buccaneer S2A | RAF No 237 OCU, Lossiemouth |
| | XT272 | HS Buccaneer S2 | MoD(PE) RAE Farnborough |
| | XT273 | HS Buccaneer S2A | RAF No 237 OCU, Lossiemouth |
| | XT274 | HS Buccaneer S2A (8856M) [E] | RAF Abingdon, BDRF |
| | XT275 | HS Buccaneer S2B [A] | RAF, stored Shawbury |
| | XT277 | HS Buccaneer S2A (8853M) [M] | RAF No 2 SoTT, Cosford |
| | XT279 | HS Buccaneer S2B | RAF No 208 Sqn, Lossiemouth |
| | XT280 | HS Buccaneer S2B | RAF No 12 Sqn, Lossiemouth |
| | XT281 | HS Buccaneer S2B (8705M) [ET] | RAF Lossiemouth, ground instruction |
| | XT283 | HS Buccaneer S2A | MoD(PE) A& AEE, Boscombe Down |
| | XT284 | HS Buccaneer S2A (8855M) [T] | RAF Abingdon, BDRF |
| | XT286 | HS Buccaneer S2B | RAF No 208 Sqn, Lossiemouth |
| | XT287 | HS Buccaneer S2B | RAF No 237 OCU, Lossiemouth |
| | XT288 | HS Buccaneer S2B | RAF No 12 Sqn, Lossiemouth |
| | XT415 | WS Wasp HAS1 [FIR3] | Airwork Ltd, Bournemouth |
| | XT420 | WS Wasp HAS1 [606] | RN, stored Wroughton |
| | XT421 | WS Wasp HAS1 [FIR4] | RN, stored Wroughton |
| | XT422 | WS Wasp HAS1 [324] | Privately owned, Burgess Hill |
| | XT426 | WS Wasp HAS1 [FIR2] | RN, stored Wroughton |
| | XT427 | WS Wasp HAS1 [606] | Cornwall Aero Park, Helston |
| | XT429 | WS Wasp HAS1 [445/PLY] | RN, stored Wroughton |
| | XT430 | WS Wasp HAS1 [444] | Defence School, Winterbourne Gunner |
| | XT434 | WS Wasp HAS1 [455] | RNAY Fleetlands Apprentice School |
| | XT437 | WS Wasp HAS1 [423] | RN AES, Lee-on-Solent |
| | XT439 | WS Wasp HAS1 [605] | Cranfield Institute of Technology, gi |
| | XT441 | WS Wasp HAS1 (A2703) | RN Predannack Fire School |
| | XT443 | WS Wasp HAS1 [422/AU] | Westland Training School, Sherborne |
| | XT449 | WS58 Wessex HU5 [C] | RN AES, Lee-on-Solent |
| | XT450 | WS58 Wessex HU5 [V] | RN Predannack Fire School |
| | XT451 | WS58 Wessex HU5 [XN] | RN, stored Wroughton |
| | XT453 | WS58 Wessex HU5 [A] | RN AES, Lee-on-Solent |
| | XT455 | WS58 Wessex HU5 [U] | RN AES, Lee-on-Solent |
| | XT456 | WS58 Wessex HU5 [XZ] (8941M) | RAF No 72 Sqn Aldergrove, BDRT |
| | XT458 | WS58 Wessex HU5 [622] | RN AES, Lee-on-Solent |

| Reg. | Type | Owner or Operator | Notes |
|---|---|---|---|
| XT459 | WS58 Wessex HU5 [D] | RNAS Lee-on-Solent Fire Section | |
| XT460 | WS58 Wessex HU5 [K] | RN, stored Wroughton | |
| XT463 | WS58 Wessex HC5C | RAF No 84 Sqn, Akrotiri | |
| XT466 | WS58 Wessex HU5 [XV] (8921M) | RAF No 2 SoTT, Cosford | |
| XT468 | WS58 Wessex HU5 [628/PO] | RN, stored Wroughton | |
| XT469 | WS58 Wessex HU5 (8920M) | RAF Stafford ground instruction | |
| XT470 | WS58 Wessex HU5 [A] | AAC Netheravon Fire Section | |
| XT471 | WS58 Wessex HU5 | RN, stored Wroughton | |
| XT472 | WS58 Wessex HU5 [XC] | International Helicopter Museum, Weston-super-Mare | |
| XT474 | WS58 Wessex HU5 [820/CU] | RN, stored Wroughton | |
| XT475 | WS58 Wessex HU5 [624/PO] | RN AES, Lee-on-Solent | |
| XT479 | WS58 Wessex HC5C (*Spades*) | RAF No 84 Sqn, Akrotiri | |
| XT480 | WS58 Wessex HU5 [XQ] | RN, stored Wroughton | |
| XT481 | WS58 Wessex HU5 [XF] | RN, stored Wroughton | |
| XT482 | WS58 Wessex HU5 [ZM/VL] | RN AES, Lee-on-Solent | |
| XT484 | WS58 Wessex HU5 [H] | RNAY Fleetlands | |
| XT485 | WS58 Wessex HU5 [621/PO] | RN AES, Lee-on-Solent | |
| XT486 | WS58 Wessex HU5 [XR] (8919M) | RAF JATE, Brize Norton, preserved | |
| XT487 | WS58 Wessex HU5 (A2723) [815/LS] | RNAS Lee-on-Solent Fire Section | |
| XT548 | WS Sioux AH1 [D] | *Hildesheim on display* | |
| XT575 | Vickers Viscount (OE-LAG) | MoD(PE) RAE Bedford | |
| XT595 | McD Phantom FG1 (nose only) (8851M) | RAF Exhibition Flight, Abingdon | |
| XT595 | McD Phantom FG1 (fuselage) (8550M) | RAF Wattisham, BDRT | |
| XT596 | McD Phantom FG1 | FAA Museum, RNAS Yeovilton | |
| XT597 | McD Phantom FG1 | MoD(PE) A&AEE Boscombe Down | |
| XT601 | WS58 Wessex HC2 | RAF No 22 Sqn SAR* | |
| XT602 | WS58 Wessex HC2 | RAF No 22 Sqn SAR* | |
| XT603 | WS58 Wessex HC2 [WF] | RAF No 2 FTS, Shawbury | |
| XT604 | WS58 Wessex HC2 | RAF No 22 Sqn SAR* | |
| XT605 | WS58 Wessex HC2 [E] | RAF No 28 Sqn, Sek Kong | |
| XT606 | WS58 Wessex HC2 | RAF No 2 FTS, Shawbury | |
| XT607 | WS58 Wessex HC2 [P] | RAF No 72 Sqn, Aldergrove | |
| XT614 | WS Scout AH1 [C] | AAC No 660 Sqn, Sek Kong | |
| XT616 | WS Scout AH1 (fuselage) | AAC, stored Wroughton | |
| XT617 | WS Scout AH1 | AAC, stored Wroughton | |
| XT620 | WS Scout AH1 | AAC Aldergrove, BDRT | |
| XT621 | WS Scout AH1 | Royal Military College of Science, Shrivenham | |
| XT623 | WS Scout AH1 | AAC, stored Wroughton | |
| XT624 | WS Scout AH1 [D] | AAC No 660 Sqn, Sek Kong | |
| XT626 | WS Scout AH1 | AAC, stored Wroughton | |
| XT628 | WS Scout AH1 [E] | AAC No 660 Sqn, Sek Kong | |
| XT630 | WS Scout AH1 [G] | AAC No 660 Sqn, Sek Kong | |
| XT631 | WS Scout AH1 [D] | MoD(PE) A&AEE Boscombe Down | |
| XT632 | WS Scout AH1 [U] | AAC No 666 (TA) Sqn, Netheravon | |
| XT633 | WS Scout AH1 | AAC, stored Wroughton | |
| XT634 | WS Scout AH1 [T] | AAC No 666 (TA) Sqn, Netheravon | |
| XT636 | WS Scout AH1 [Z] | AAC No 666 (TA) Sqn, Netheravon | |
| XT637 | WS Scout AH1 (fuselage) | AAC, stored Wroughton | |
| XT638 | WS Scout AH1 [N] | AAC No 666 (TA) Sqn, Netheravon | |
| XT639 | WS Scout AH1 [Y] (fuselage) | AAC, stored Wroughton | |
| XT640 | WS Scout AH1 | AAC SAE, Middle Wallop | |
| XT642 | WS Scout AH1 (fuselage) | AAC, stored Wroughton | |
| XT643 | WS Scout AH1 [Z] | AAC, stored Wroughton | |
| XT644 | WS Scout AH1 [Y] | AAC No 666 (TA) Sqn, Netheravon | |
| XT645 | WS Scout AH1 (fuselage) | AAC, stored Wroughton | |
| XT646 | WS Scout AH1 [Z] | AAC No 666 (TA) Sqn, Netheravon | |
| XT648 | WS Scout AH1 | AAC, stored Wroughton | |
| XT649 | WS Scout AH1 | AAC, stored Wroughton | |
| XT657 | BHC SR.N6 Winchester 5 | British Hovercraft Corpn | |
| XT661 | Vickers Viscount (9G-AAV) | MoD(PE), stored Bedford | |
| XT667 | WS58 Wessex HC2 [F] | RAF No 28 Sqn, Sek Kong | |
| XT668 | WS58 Wessex HC2 [S] | RAF No 72 Sqn, Aldergrove | |
| XT669 | WS58 Wessex HC2 (8894M) [T] | RAF Aldergrove instructional use | |
| XT670 | WS58 Wessex HC2 | RAF No 22 Sqn SAR* | |
| XT671 | WS58 Wessex HC2 [D] | RAF No 72 Sqn, Aldergrove | |
| XT672 | WS58 Wessex HC2 [WE] | RAF No 2 FTS, Shawbury | |
| XT673 | WS58 Wessex HC2 [G] | RAF No 28 Sqn, Sek Kong | |

| Notes | Reg. | Type | Owner or Operator |
|---|---|---|---|
| | XT675 | WS58 Wessex HC2 [C] | RAF No 28 Sqn, Sek Kong |
| | XT676 | WS58 Wessex HC2 [I] | RAF No 72 Sqn, Aldergrove |
| | XT677 | WS58 Wessex HC2 (8016M) | RAF Brize Norton Fire Section |
| | XT678 | WS58 Wessex HC2 [H] | RAF No 28 Sqn, Sek Kong |
| | XT680 | WS58 Wessex HC2 | RAF No 22 Sqn SAR* |
| | XT681 | WS58 Wessex HC2 [U] | RAF No 72 Sqn, Aldergrove |
| | XT752 | Fairey Gannet T5 [-/LM] (G-APYO/WN365) | RNAS, stored Lee-on-Solent |
| | XT755 | WS58 Wessex HU5 [V] | RN, stored Wroughton |
| | XT756 | WS58 Wessex HU5 [ZJ] | RN, stored Wroughton |
| | XT757 | WS58 Wessex HU5 (A2722) | RN Predannack Fire School |
| | XT759 | WS58 Wessex HU5 [XY] | RN, stored Wroughton |
| | XT760 | WS58 Wessex HU5 [618/PO] | RN, stored Wroughton |
| | XT761 | WS58 Wessex HU5 (A27--) | RN AES, Lee-on-Solent |
| | XT762 | WS58 Wessex HU5 | RNAS Culdrose, SAH |
| | XT764 | WS58 Wessex HU5 [G] | RN, stored Wroughton |
| | XT765 | WS58 Wessex HU5 [J] | RN AES, Lee-on-Solent |
| | XT766 | WS58 Wessex HU5 [822/CU] | RN, stored Wroughton |
| | XT768 | WS58 Wessex HU5 | RN, stored Wroughton |
| | XT769 | WS58 Wessex HU5 [823/CU] | RN, stored Wroughton |
| | XT771 | WS58 Wessex HU5 (A27--) [620/PO] | RN AES, Lee-on-Solent |
| | XT772 | WS58 Wessex HU5 (8805M) | RAF Valley, ground instruction |
| | XT773 | WS58 Wessex HU5 | RN, stored Wroughton |
| | XT778 | WS Wasp HAS1 [430] (A27--) | *Scrapped Jan 1990* |
| | XT779 | WS Wasp HAS1 [582] | RN Portland Fire Section |
| | XT780 | WS Wasp HAS1 [636] | RNAY Fleetlands Apprentice School |
| | XT783 | WS Wasp HAS1 [470] | RN, stored Wroughton |
| | XT785 | WS Wasp HAS1 [FIR1] | RN, stored Wroughton |
| | XT786 | WS Wasp HAS1 [441] (A2726) | RN Portland Fire Section |
| | XT788 | WS Wasp HAS1 [442] (G-BMIR) (*XT793*) | Privately owned, Tattershall Thorpe |
| | XT790 | WS Wasp HAS1 [608] | RN, stored Wroughton |
| | XT791 | WS Wasp HAS1 [433] | RN, stored Wroughton |
| | XT793 | WS Wasp HAS1 [456] | RN, stored Wroughton |
| | XT795 | WS Wasp HAS1 [476/LE] | RN, stored Wroughton |
| | XT803 | WS Sioux AH1 [Y] | Privately owned, Panshanger |
| | XT827 | WS Sioux AH1 [D] | AAC HF (spares), Middle Wallop |
| | XT852 | McD Phantom FGR2 | MoD(PE) BAe Scampton |
| | XT853 | McD Phantom FGR2 | MoD(PE) BAe Scampton (wfu) |
| | XT857 | McD Phantom FG1 [MP] (8913M) | RAF Leuchars ground instruction |
| | XT858 | McD Phantom FG1 | MoD(PE) BAe Brough (structures test) |
| | XT859 | McD Phantom FG1 [BK] (8999M) | RAF Leuchars BDRT |
| | XT863 | McD Phantom FG1 [AS] | RAF, stored Abingdon |
| | XT864 | McD Phantom FG1 [BJ] (8998M) | RAF Leuchars on display |
| | XT865 | McD Phantom FG1 [BU] | RAF, stored Wattisham |
| | XT867 | McD Phantom FG1 [BH] | RAF, stored Leuchars |
| | XT870 | McD Phantom FG1 [BS] | RAF, stored Leuchars |
| | XT872 | McD Phantom FG1 [BT] | RAF, stored Wattisham |
| | XT873 | McD Phantom FG1 [BA] | RAF, stored Leuchars |
| | XT874 | McD Phantom FG1 [BE] | RAF, stored Wattisham |
| | XT875 | McD Phantom FG1 [BP] | RAF, stored Wattisham |
| | XT891 | McD Phantom FGR2 [CZ] | RAF No 228 OCU/64 Sqn, Leuchars |
| | XT892 | McD Phantom FGR2 [CQ] | RAF No 228 OCU/64 Sqn, Leuchars |
| | XT894 | McD Phantom FGR2 [X] | RAF No 56 Sqn, Wattisham |
| | XT895 | McD Phantom FGR2 [CJ] | RAF No 228 OCU/64 Sqn, Leuchars |
| | XT896 | McD Phantom FGR2 [CY] | RAF No 228 OCU/64 Sqn, Leuchars |
| | XT897 | McD Phantom FGR2 [CC] | RAF No 228 OCU/64 Sqn, Leuchars |
| | XT898 | McD Phantom FGR2 [CE] | RAF No 228 OCU/64 Sqn, Leuchars |
| | XT899 | McD Phantom FGR2 [N] | RAF No 92 Sqn, Wildenrath |
| | XT900 | McD Phantom FGR2 [CO] | RAF No 228 OCU/64 Sqn, Leuchars |
| | XT901 | McD Phantom FGR2 [CR] | RAF No 228 OCU/64 Sqn, Leuchars |
| | XT902 | McD Phantom FGR2 [K] | RAF No 19 Sqn, Wildenrath |
| | XT903 | McD Phantom FGR2 [CM] | RAF No 228 OCU/64 Sqn, Leuchars |
| | XT905 | McD Phantom FGR2 [CU] | RAF No 228 OCU/64 Sqn, Leuchars |
| | XT906 | McD Phantom FGR2 [CH] | RAF No 228 OCU/64 Sqn, Leuchars |
| | XT907 | McD Phantom FGR2 [CP] | RAF No 228 OCU/64 Sqn, Leuchars |
| | XT909 | McD Phantom FGR2 [CS] | RAF No 228 OCU/64 Sqn, Leuchars |
| | XT910 | McD Phantom FGR2 [Z] | RAF No 56 Sqn, Wattisham |
| | XT911 | McD Phantom FGR2 [T] | RAF, stored St Athan |
| | XT914 | McD Phantom FGR2 [CV] | RAF No 228 OCU/64 Sqn, Leuchars |

| Reg. | Type | Owner or Operator | Notes |
|---|---|---|---|
| XV101 | BAC VC10 C1 | RAF No 10 Sqn, Brize Norton | |
| XV102 | BAC VC10 C1 | RAF No 10 Sqn, Brize Norton | |
| XV103 | BAC VC10 C1 | RAF No 10 Sqn, Brize Norton | |
| XV104 | BAC VC10 C1 | RAF No 10 Sqn, Brize Norton | |
| XV105 | BAC VC10 C1 | RAF No 10 Sqn, Brize Norton | |
| XV106 | BAC VC10 C1 | RAF No 10 Sqn, Brize Norton | |
| XV107 | BAC VC10 C1 | RAF No 10 Sqn, Brize Norton | |
| XV108 | BAC VC10 C1 | RAF No 10 Sqn, Brize Norton | |
| XV109 | BAC VC10 C1 | RAF No 10 Sqn, Brize Norton | |
| XV118 | WS Scout AH1 | AAC, stored Wroughton | |
| XV119 | WS Scout AH1 [T] | AAC, stored Wroughton | |
| XV121 | WS Scout AH1 [V] | AAC No 658 Sqn, Netheravon | |
| XV122 | WS Scout AH1 [A] | AAC, stored Wroughton | |
| XV123 | WS Scout AH1 | AAC, stored Wroughton | |
| XV124 | WS Scout AH1 | AAC, stored Wroughton | |
| XV126 | WS Scout AH1 [X] | AAC No 666 (TA) Sqn, Netheravon | |
| XV127 | WS Scout AH1 | AAC Recruiting Team, Middle Wallop | |
| XV128 | WS Scout AH1 | AAC No 667 Sqn, Middle Wallop | |
| XV129 | WS Scout AH1 [V] | AAC No 666 (TA) Sqn, Netheravon | |
| XV130 | WS Scout AH1 [R] | AAC No 666 (TA) Sqn, Netheravon | |
| XV131 | WS Scout AH1 [Y] | AAC, stored Wroughton | |
| XV134 | WS Scout AH1 [P] | AAC No 666 (TA) Sqn, Netheravon | |
| XV135 | WS Scout AH1 | AAC, stored Wroughton | |
| XV136 | WS Scout AH1 [X] | AAC, stored Wroughton | |
| XV137 | WS Scout AH1 | RM, Falkland Islands | |
| XV138 | WS Scout AH1 | AAC, stored Wroughton | |
| XV139 | WS Scout AH1 | Army Apprentice College, Arborfield | |
| XV140 | WS Scout AH1 [K] | AAC No 666 (TA) Sqn, Netheravon | |
| XV141 | WS Scout AH1 | Army Apprentice College, Arborfield | |
| XV147 | HS Nimrod MR1 (Mod) | MoD(PE) stored RAE Farnborough | |
| XV148 | HS Nimrod MR1 (Mod) | MoD(PE) BAe Woodford, Fire Section | |
| XV154 | HS Buccaneer S2A (8854M) | RAF Lossiemouth, ground instruction | |
| XV155 | HS Buccaneer S2B (8716M) | Lovaux Ltd, Macclesfield | |
| XV156 | HS Buccaneer S2A (8773M) | RAF St Athan Fire Section | |
| XV157 | HS Buccaneer S2B | RAF, stored Shawbury | |
| XV161 | HS Buccaneer S2A | RAF No 237 OCU, Lossiemouth | |
| XV163 | HS Buccaneer S2A | RAF No 237 OCU, Lossiemouth | |
| XV165 | HS Buccaneer S2B | RAF No 12 Sqn, Lossiemouth | |
| XV168 | HS Buccaneer S2B | RAF, stored Shawbury | |
| XV176 | Lockheed Hercules C3P | RAF Lyneham Transport Wing | |
| XV177 | Lockheed Hercules C3P | RAF Lyneham Transport Wing | |
| XV178 | Lockheed Hercules C1P | RAF Lyneham Transport Wing | |
| XV179 | Lockheed Hercules C1P | RAF Lyneham Transport Wing | |
| XV181 | Lockheed Hercules C1P | RAF Lyneham Transport Wing | |
| XV182 | Lockheed Hercules C1P | RAF Lyneham Transport Wing | |
| XV183 | Lockheed Hercules C3P | RAF Lyneham Transport Wing | |
| XV184 | Lockheed Hercules C3P | RAF Lyneham Transport Wing | |
| XV185 | Lockheed Hercules C1P | RAF Lyneham Transport Wing | |
| XV186 | Lockheed Hercules C1P | RAF Lyneham Transport Wing | |
| XV187 | Lockheed Hercules C1P | RAF Lyneham Transport Wing | |
| XV188 | Lockheed Hercules C3P | RAF Lyneham Transport Wing | |
| XV189 | Lockheed Hercules C3P | RAF Lyneham Transport Wing | |
| XV190 | Lockheed Hercules C3P | RAF Lyneham Transport Wing | |
| XV191 | Lockheed Hercules C1P | RAF Lyneham Transport Wing | |
| XV192 | Lockheed Hercules C1K | RAF Lyneham Transport Wing | |
| XV193 | Lockheed Hercules C3P | RAF Lyneham Transport Wing | |
| XV195 | Lockheed Hercules C1P | RAF Lyneham Transport Wing | |
| XV196 | Lockheed Hercules C1P | RAF Lyneham Transport Wing | |
| XV197 | Lockheed Hercules C3P | RAF Lyneham Transport Wing | |
| XV199 | Lockheed Hercules C3P | RAF Lyneham Transport Wing | |
| XV200 | Lockheed Hercules C1P | RAF Lyneham Transport Wing | |
| XV201 | Lockheed Hercules C1K | RAF No 1312 Flt, Mount Pleasant, FI | |
| XV202 | Lockheed Hercules C3P | RAF Lyneham Transport Wing | |
| XV203 | Lockheed Hercules C1K | RAF No 1312 Flt, Mount Pleasant, FI | |
| XV204 | Lockheed Hercules C1K | RAF No 1312 Flt, Mount Pleasant, FI | |
| XV205 | Lockheed Hercules C1P | RAF Lyneham Transport Wing | |
| XV206 | Lockheed Hercules C1P | RAF Lyneham Transport Wing | |
| XV207 | Lockheed Hercules C3P | RAF Lyneham Transport Wing | |
| XV208 | Lockheed Hercules W2 | MoD(PE) MRF Farnborough | |
| XV209 | Lockheed Hercules C3P | RAF Lyneham Transport Wing | |
| XV210 | Lockheed Hercules C1P | RAF Lyneham Transport Wing | |
| XV211 | Lockheed Hercules C1P | RAF Lyneham Transport Wing | |

| Notes | Reg. | Type | Owner or Operator |
|---|---|---|---|
| | XV212 | Lockheed Hercules C3P | RAF Lyneham Transport Wing |
| | XV213 | Lockheed Hercules C1K | RAF No 1312 Flt, Mount Pleasant, FI |
| | XV214 | Lockheed Hercules C3P | RAF Lyneham Transport Wing |
| | XV215 | Lockheed Hercules C1P | RAF Lyneham Transport Wing |
| | XV217 | Lockheed Hercules C3P | RAF Lyneham Transport Wing |
| | XV218 | Lockheed Hercules C1P | RAF Lyneham Transport Wing |
| | XV219 | Lockheed Hercules C3P | RAF Lyneham Transport Wing |
| | XV220 | Lockheed Hercules C3P | RAF Lyneham Transport Wing |
| | XV221 | Lockheed Hercules C3P | RAF Lyneham Transport Wing |
| | XV222 | Lockheed Hercules C3P | RAF Lyneham Transport Wing |
| | XV223 | Lockheed Hercules C3P | RAF Lyneham Transport Wing |
| | XV226 | HS Nimrod MR2 | RAF Kinloss MR Wing |
| | XV227 | HS Nimrod MR2P | RAF Kinloss MR Wing |
| | XV228 | HS Nimrod MR2P | RAF Kinloss MR Wing |
| | XV229 | HS Nimrod MR2P | RAF Kinloss MR Wing |
| | XV230 | HS Nimrod MR2P | RAF Kinloss MR Wing |
| | XV231 | HS Nimrod MR2 | RAF No 236 OCU, St Mawgan |
| | XV232 | HS Nimrod MR2P | RAF Kinloss MR Wing |
| | XV233 | HS Nimrod MR2P | RAF No 42 Sqn, St Mawgan |
| | XV234 | HS Nimrod MR2P | RAF Kinloss MR Wing |
| | XV235 | HS Nimrod MR2 | RAF Kinloss MR Wing |
| | XV236 | HS Nimrod MR2P | RAF Kinloss MR Wing |
| | XV237 | HS Nimrod MR2P | RAF No 42 Sqn, St Mawgan |
| | XV238 | HS Nimrod MR2P | RAF Kinloss MR Wing |
| | XV239 | HS Nimrod MR2P | RAF Kinloss MR Wing |
| | XV240 | HS Nimrod MR2P | RAF No 42 Sqn, St Mawgan |
| | XV241 | HS Nimrod MR2 | RAF Kinloss MR Wing |
| | XV242 | HS Nimrod MR2P | RAF Kinloss MR Wing |
| | XV243 | HS Nimrod MR2P | RAF Kinloss MR Wing |
| | XV244 | HS Nimrod MR2P | RAF Kinloss MR Wing |
| | XV245 | HS Nimrod MR2P | RAF No 42 Sqn, St Mawgan |
| | XV246 | HS Nimrod MR2 | RAF Kinloss MR Wing |
| | XV247 | HS Nimrod MR2P | RAF Kinloss MR Wing |
| | XV248 | HS Nimrod MR2P | RAF Kinloss MR Wing |
| | XV249 | HS Nimrod MR2P | RAF No 42 Sqn, St Mawgan |
| | XV250 | HS Nimrod MR2P | RAF Kinloss MR Wing |
| | XV251 | HS Nimrod MR2P | RAF Kinloss MR Wing |
| | XV252 | HS Nimrod MR2P | RAF Kinloss MR Wing |
| | XV253 | HS Nimrod MR2P | RAF No 42 Sqn, St Mawgan |
| | XV254 | HS Nimrod MR2P | RAF Kinloss MR Wing |
| | XV255 | HS Nimrod MR2P | RAF Kinloss MR Wing |
| | XV257 | HS Nimrod MR2 | MoD(PE), stored BAe Woodford |
| | XV258 | HS Nimrod MR2P | RAF Kinloss MR Wing |
| | XV259 | BAe Nimrod AEW3 | RAF, stored Abingdon |
| | XV260 | HS Nimrod MR2P | RAF Kinloss MR Wing |
| | XV261 | BAe Nimrod AEW3 (8986M) | RAF Abingdon, BDRF |
| | XV262 | BAe Nimrod AEW3 | RAF Abingdon, BDRF |
| | XV263 | BAe Nimrod AEW3P (8967M) | RAF Air Engineer Sqn, Finningley |
| | XV268 | DHC Beaver AL1 | AAC, stored Shawbury |
| | XV269 | DHC Beaver AL1 (8011M) | AAC SAE, Middle Wallop |
| | XV270 | DHC Beaver AL1 | *Sold in USA as N2126T May 1990* |
| | XV271 | DHC Beaver AL1 | Privately owned |
| | XV272 | DHC Beaver AL1 (fuselage only) | AAC Middle Wallop, BDRT |
| | XV277 | HS Harrier GR3 | RN AMG, Yeovilton, for GI |
| | XV279 | HS Harrier GR1 [44] (8566M) | RAF Wittering WLT |
| | XV281 | HS Harrier GR3 (89...M) | RAF Wittering BDRT |
| | XV290 | Lockheed Hercules C3P | RAF Lyneham Transport Wing |
| | XV291 | Lockheed Hercules C1P | RAF Lyneham Transport Wing |
| | XV292 | Lockheed Hercules C1P | RAF Lyneham Transport Wing |
| | XV293 | Lockheed Hercules C1P | RAF Lyneham Transport Wing |
| | XV294 | Lockheed Hercules C3P | RAF Lyneham Transport Wing |
| | XV295 | Lockheed Hercules C1P | RAF Lyneham Transport Wing |
| | XV296 | Lockheed Hercules C1K | RAF Lyneham Transport Wing |
| | XV297 | Lockheed Hercules C1P | RAF Lyneham Transport Wing |
| | XV298 | Lockheed Hercules C1P | RAF Lyneham Transport Wing |
| | XV299 | Lockheed Hercules C3P | RAF Lyneham Transport Wing |
| | XV300 | Lockheed Hercules C1P | RAF Lyneham Transport Wing |
| | XV301 | Lockheed Hercules C3P | RAF Lyneham Transport Wing |
| | XV302 | Lockheed Hercules C3P | RAF Lyneham Transport Wing |
| | XV303 | Lockheed Hercules C3P | RAF Lyneham Transport Wing |
| | XV304 | Lockheed Hercules C3P | RAF Lyneham Transport Wing |
| | XV305 | Lockheed Hercules C3P | RAF Lyneham Transport Wing |

| Reg. | Type | Owner or Operator | Notes |
|---|---|---|---|
| XV306 | Lockheed Hercules C1P | RAF Lyneham Transport Wing | |
| XV307 | Lockheed Hercules C3P | RAF Lyneham Transport Wing | |
| XV328 | BAC Lightning T5 [BZ] | Privately owned, Cranfield | |
| XV332 | HS Buccaneer S2B | RAF No 237 OCU, Lossiemouth | |
| XV333 | HS Buccaneer S2B | RAF No 208 Sqn, Lossiemouth | |
| XV334 | HS Buccaneer S2C | MoD(PE) RAE Farnborough | |
| XV336 | HS Buccaneer S2A | RAF, stored Shawbury | |
| XV337 | HS Buccaneer S2C (8852M) | RAF Abingdon, BDRF | |
| XV338 | HS Buccaneer S2A (nose only) (8774M) | RAF Exhibition Flight, Abingdon | |
| XV341 | HS Buccaneer S2A | RAF Lossiemouth Fire Section | |
| XV342 | HS Buccaneer S2B | RAF No 237 OCU, Lossiemouth | |
| XV344 | HS Buccaneer S2C | MoD(PE) RAE Farnborough | |
| XV349 | HS Buccaneer S2B | RAF, stored Shawbury | |
| XV350 | HS Buccaneer S2B | MoD(PE) BAe Scampton | |
| XV352 | HS Buccaneer S2B | RAF No 208 Sqn, Lossiemouth | |
| XV353 | HS Buccaneer S2B | RAF No 208 Sqn, Lossiemouth | |
| XV355 | HS Buccaneer S2A | RAF No 237 OCU, Lossiemouth | |
| XV356 | HS Buccaneer S2A [B] | RAF, stored Shawbury | |
| XV359 | HS Buccaneer S2B | RAF No 208 Sqn, Lossiemouth | |
| XV361 | HS Buccaneer S2B | RAF No 208 Sqn, Lossiemouth | |
| XV370 | Sikorsky SH-3D (G-ATYU) | RN AES, Lee-on-Solent | |
| XV371 | WS61 Sea King HAS1 | MoD(PE) RAE Farnborough | |
| XV372 | WS61 Sea King HAS1 | Privately owned, Trowbridge, Wilts | |
| XV393 | McD Phantom FGR2 [CA] | RAF No 228 OCU/64 Sqn, Leuchars | |
| XV394 | McD Phantom FGR2 [T] | RAF No 92 Sqn, Wildenrath | |
| XV396 | McD Phantom FGR2 [Y] | RAF No 56 Sqn, Wattisham | |
| XV398 | McD Phantom FGR2 [CI] | RAF No 228 OCU/64 Sqn, Leuchars | |
| XV399 | McD Phantom FGR2 [L] | RAF No 56 Sqn, Wattisham | |
| XV400 | McD Phantom FGR2 [D] | RAF No 56 Sqn, Wattisham | |
| XV401 | McD Phantom FGR2 [CN] | RAF No 228 OCU/64 Sqn, Leuchars | |
| XV402 | McD Phantom FGR2 [C] | RAF No 56 Sqn, Wattisham | |
| XV404 | McD Phantom FGR2 [I] | RAF No 19 Sqn, Wildenrath | |
| XV406 | McD Phantom FGR2 [CK] | RAF No 228 OCU/64 Sqn, Leuchars | |
| XV407 | McD Phantom FGR2 [E] | RAF No 19 Sqn, Wildenrath | |
| XV408 | McD Phantom FGR2 [C] | RAF No 19 Sqn, Wildenrath | |
| XV409 | McD Phantom FGR2 [A] | RAF Coningsby | |
| XV410 | McD Phantom FGR2 [E] | RAF No 56 Sqn, Wattisham | |
| XV411 | McD Phantom FGR2 [L] | RAF No 19 Sqn, Wildenrath | |
| XV412 | McD Phantom FGR2 [P] | RAF No 92 Sqn, Wildenrath | |
| XV414 | McD Phantom FGR2 [R] | RAF Wattisham, BDRT | |
| XV415 | McD Phantom FGR2 [CB] | RAF No 228 OCU/64 Sqn, Leuchars | |
| XV419 | McD Phantom FGR2 [C] | RAF No 228 OCU/64 Sqn, Leuchars | |
| XV420 | McD Phantom FGR2 [BT] | RAF No 56 Sqn, Wattisham | |
| XV421 | McD Phantom FGR2 [F] | RAF No 1435 Flt, Mount Pleasant, FI | |
| XV422 | McD Phantom FGR2 [Y] | RAF No 92 Sqn, Wildenrath | |
| XV423 | McD Phantom FGR2 [F] | RAF No 56 Sqn, Wattisham | |
| XV424 | McD Phantom FGR2 [Q] | RAF No 56 Sqn, Wattisham | |
| XV425 | McD Phantom FGR2 [CD] | RAF No 228 OCU/64 Sqn, Leuchars | |
| XV426 | McD Phantom FGR2 [P] | RAF No 56 Sqn, Wattisham | |
| XV429 | McD Phantom FGR2 [O] | RAF No 56 Sqn, Wattisham | |
| XV430 | McD Phantom FGR2 [S] | RAF No 92 Sqn, Wildenrath | |
| XV432 | McD Phantom FGR2 [N] | RAF No 56 Sqn, Wattisham | |
| XV433 | McD Phantom FGR2 [B] | RAF, stored St Athan | |
| XV435 | McD Phantom FGR2 [R] | RAF No 92 Sqn, Wildenrath | |
| XV438 | McD Phantom FGR2 [J] | RAF No 56 Sqn, Wattisham | |
| XV439 | McD Phantom FGR2 [X] | RAF No 92 Sqn, Wildenrath | |
| XV442 | McD Phantom FGR2 [H] | RAF No 1435 Flt, Mount Pleasant, FI | |
| XV460 | McD Phantom FGR2 [J] | RAF No 19 Sqn, Wildenrath | |
| XV461 | McD Phantom FGR2 [C] | RAF No 1435 Flt, Mount Pleasant, FI | |
| XV462 | McD Phantom FGR2 [G] | RAF No 19 Sqn, Wildenrath | |
| XV464 | McD Phantom FGR2 [AN] | RAF No 92 Sqn, Wildenrath | |
| XV465 | McD Phantom FGR2 [F] | RAF No 19 Sqn, Wildenrath | |
| XV466 | McD Phantom FGR2 [D] | RAF No 1435 Flt, Mount Pleasant, FI | |
| XV467 | McD Phantom FGR2 [Q] | RAF No 92 Sqn, Wildenrath | |
| XV468 | McD Phantom FGR2 [J] | RAF Scampton | |
| XV469 | McD Phantom FGR2 [AO] | RAF No 92 Sqn, Wildenrath | |
| XV470 | McD Phantom FGR2 [CX] | RAF No 228 OCU/64 Sqn, Leuchars | |
| XV472 | McD Phantom FGR2 | RAF No 56 Sqn, Wattisham | |
| XV473 | McD Phantom FGR2 [K] | RAF No 56 Sqn, Wattisham | |
| XV474 | McD Phantom FGR2 [M] | RAF No 56 Sqn, Wattisham | |
| XV475 | McD Phantom FGR2 [H] | RAF No 19 Sqn, Wildenrath | |
| XV476 | McD Phantom FGR2 [S] | RAF No 56 Sqn, Wattisham | |

| Notes | Reg. | Type | Owner or Operator |
|---|---|---|---|
| | XV478 | McD Phantom FGR2 [B] | RAF No 19 Sqn, Wildenrath (wfu) |
| | XV480 | McD Phantom FGR2 [I] | RAF No 56 Sqn, Wattisham |
| | XV481 | McD Phantom FGR2 [H] | RAF No 56 Sqn, Wattisham |
| | XV482 | McD Phantom FGR2 | RAF No 19 Sqn, Wildenrath |
| | XV485 | McD Phantom FGR2 [M] | RAF No 19 Sqn, Wildenrath |
| | XV486 | McD Phantom FGR2 [N] | RAF, stored St Athan |
| | XV487 | McD Phantom FGR2 [B] | RAF No 56 Sqn, Wattisham |
| | XV488 | McD Phantom FGR2 [O] | RAF No 92 Sqn, Wildenrath |
| | XV489 | McD Phantom FGR2 [S] | RAF, stored St Athan |
| | XV490 | McD Phantom FGR2 [CG] | RAF No 228 OCU/64 Sqn, Leuchars |
| | XV492 | McD Phantom FGR2 [W] | RAF No 92 Sqn, Wildenrath |
| | XV494 | McD Phantom FGR2 [AN] | RAF No 92 Sqn, Wildenrath |
| | XV495 | McD Phantom FGR2 | RAF, stored St Athan |
| | XV496 | McD Phantom FGR2 [V] | RAF No 92 Sqn, Wildenrath |
| | XV497 | McD Phantom FGR2 [D] | RAF, stored St Athan |
| | XV498 | McD Phantom FGR2 [U] | RAF No 92 Sqn, Wildenrath |
| | XV499 | McD Phantom FGR2 [CF] | RAF No 228 OCU/64 Sqn, Leuchars |
| | XV500 | McD Phantom FGR2 [J] | RAF, stored St Athan |
| | XV567 | McD Phantom FG1 [AI] | RAF, stored Leuchars |
| | XV568 | McD Phantom FG1 [AT] | RAF, stored Leuchars |
| | XV569 | McD Phantom FG1 [BQ] | RAF, stored Wildenrath |
| | XV570 | McD Phantom FG1 [BN] | RAF, stored Wattisham |
| | XV571 | McD Phantom FG1 [A] | RAF, stored Leuchars |
| | XV572 | McD Phantom FG1 [BG] | RAF, stored Leuchars |
| | XV573 | McD Phantom FG1 [BD] | RAF, stored Leuchars |
| | XV574 | McD Phantom FG1 [Z] | RAF, stored Wattisham |
| | XV575 | McD Phantom FG1 [BO] | RAF, stored Wattisham |
| | XV576 | McD Phantom FG1 [BK] | RAF, stored Wattisham |
| | XV577 | McD Phantom FG1 [AM] | RAF, stored Leuchars |
| | XV579 | McD Phantom FG1 [AR] | RAF, stored Leuchars |
| | XV581 | McD Phantom FG1 [AE] | RAF, stored Wattisham |
| | XV582 | McD Phantom FG1 [M] | RAF, stored Leuchars (wfu) |
| | XV583 | McD Phantom FG1 [BB] | RAF, stored Wattisham |
| | XV584 | McD Phantom FG1 [BF] | RAF, stored Wattisham |
| | XV585 | McD Phantom FG1 [AP] | RAF, stored Leuchars |
| | XV586 | McD Phantom FG1 [AJ] | RAF, stored Leuchars |
| | XV587 | McD Phantom FG1 [BR] | RAF, stored Wattisham |
| | XV588 | McD Phantom FG1 [007] (nose only) | RNAS Culdrose Fire Section |
| | XV588 | McD Phantom FG1 (forward fuselage only) | RAF Leuchars, BDRT |
| | XV590 | McD Phantom FG1 [AX] | RAF, stored Leuchars |
| | XV591 | McD Phantom FG1 [BM] (fuselage) | RAF Leuchars, ground instruction |
| | XV592 | McD Phantom FG1 [BL] | RAF, stored Wattisham |
| | XV615 | BHC SR.N6 Winchester 2 | RN Hong Kong |
| | XV623 | WS Wasp HAS1 [601] (A2724) | RN Portland, BDRT |
| | XV624 | WS Wasp HAS1 [YM] | RN Portland Fire Section |
| | XV625 | WS Wasp HAS1 [471] | RNEC Manadon, for instruction |
| | XV629 | WS Wasp HAS1 | AAC Middle Wallop, BDRT |
| | XV631 | WS Wasp HAS1 | RAE Farnborough, ground instruction |
| | XV638 | WS Wasp HAS1 [430] (8826M)/*A430*) | RAF AMS, Brize Norton |
| | XV639 | WS Wasp HAS1 [612] | RN, stored Wroughton |
| | XV642 | WS61 Sea King HAS2A | MoD(PE) Westlands, Yeovil |
| | XV643 | WS61 Sea King HAS5 [265/N] | RN No 814 Sqn, Culdrose |
| | XV644 | WS61 Sea King HAS1 (A2664) [664] | RN AES, Lee-on-Solent |
| | XV647 | WS61 Sea King HAR5 [820/CU] | RN No 771 Sqn, Culdrose |
| | XV648 | WS61 Sea King HAS5 [582] | RN No 706 Sqn, Culdrose |
| | XV649 | WS61 Sea King AEW2A [183/R] | RN No 849 Sqn, Culdrose |
| | XV650 | WS61 Sea King AEW2A [180/CU] | RN No 849 Sqn, Culdrose |
| | XV651 | WS61 Sea King HAS5 [591] | RN No 706 Sqn, Culdrose |
| | XV653 | WS61 Sea King HAS6 [500] | RN No 810 Sqn, Culdrose |
| | XV654 | WS61 Sea King HAS5 [018/R] | RN No 820 Sqn, Culdrose |
| | XV655 | WS61 Sea King HAS5 [272/N] | RN No 814 Sqn, Culdrose |
| | XV656 | WS61 Sea King AEW2A [186/N] | RN No 849 Sqn, Culdrose |
| | XV657 | WS61 Sea King HAS6 [132] | RN No 826 Sqn, Culdrose |
| | XV659 | WS61 Sea King HAS5 [266/N] | RN No 814 Sqn, Culdrose |
| | XV660 | WS61 Sea King HAS6 [503] | RN No 810 Sqn, Culdrose |
| | XV661 | WS61 Sea King HAS5 [135] | RN No 826 Sqn, Culdrose |
| | XV663 | WS61 Sea King HAS6 [015] | RN No 820 Sqn, Culdrose |
| | XV664 | WS61 Sea King AEW2A [185/N] | RN No 849 Sqn, Culdrose |

| Reg. | Type | Owner or Operator | Notes |
|---|---|---|---|
| XV665 | WS61 Sea King HAS6 [017] | RN No 820 Sqn, Culdrose | |
| XV666 | WS61 Sea King HAR5 [823/CU] | RN No 771 Sqn, Culdrose | |
| XV669 | WS61 Sea King HAS1 [10] (A2659) | RNAS Culdrose, Engineering Training School | |
| XV670 | WS61 Sea King HAS6 [592] | RN No 706 Sqn, Culdrose | |
| XV671 | WS61 Sea King AEW2A [181/CU] | RN No 849 Sqn, Culdrose | |
| XV672 | WS61 Sea King AEW2A [182/R] | RN No 849 Sqn, Culdrose | |
| XV673 | WS61 Sea King HAS5 [588] | RN No 706 Sqn, Culdrose | |
| XV674 | WS61 Sea King HAS5 [274/N] | RN No 814 Sqn, Culdrose | |
| XV675 | WS61 Sea King HAS5 [594] | RN No 706 Sqn, Culdrose | |
| XV676 | WS61 Sea King HAS6 [707] | RN AMG, Culdrose | |
| XV677 | WS61 Sea King HAS6 [501] | RN No 810 Sqn, Culdrose | |
| XV696 | WS61 Sea King HAS5 | RN No 810 Sqn, Culdrose | |
| XV697 | WS61 Sea King AEW2A [187N] | RN No 849 Sqn, Culdrose | |
| XV699 | WS61 Sea King HAS5 [134] | RN stored, Wroughton | |
| XV700 | WS61 Sea King HAS5 [011/R] | RN No 820 Sqn, Culdrose | |
| XV701 | WS61 Sea King HAS6 [010] | RN No 820 Sqn, Culdrose | |
| XV703 | WS61 Sea King HAS6 [011] | MoD(PE), Westlands, Yeovil | |
| XV704 | WS61 Sea King AEW2A [184/R] | RN No 849 Sqn, Culdrose | |
| XV705 | WS61 Sea King HAR5 [821/CU] | RN No 771 Sqn, Culdrose | |
| XV706 | WS61 Sea King HAS6 [510] | RN No 810 Sqn, Culdrose | |
| XV707 | WS61 Sea King AEW2A [185/R] | RN No 849 Sqn, Culdrose | |
| XV708 | WS61 Sea King HAS6 [708] | RN No 819 Sqn, Culdrose | |
| XV709 | WS61 Sea King HAS5 [585] | RN No 706 Sqn, Culdrose | |
| XV710 | WS61 Sea King HAS6 [267/N] | RN No 814 Sqn, Culdrose | |
| XV711 | WS61 Sea King HAS5 [273/N] | RN No 814 Sqn, Culdrose | |
| XV712 | WS61 Sea King HAS6 [014] | RN No 820 Sqn, Culdrose | |
| XV713 | WS61 Sea King HAS5 [508] | RN No 810 Sqn, Culdrose | |
| XV714 | WS61 Sea King AEW2A [180] | RN No 849 Sqn, Culdrose | |
| XV719 | WS58 Wessex HC2 [B] | RAF No 72 Sqn, Aldergrove | |
| XV720 | WS58 Wessex HC2 | RAF No 22 Sqn SAR* | |
| XV721 | WS58 Wessex HC2 [H] | RAF No 72 Sqn, Aldergrove | |
| XV722 | WS58 Wessex HC2 [WH] | RAF No 2 FTS, Shawbury | |
| XV723 | WS58 Wessex HC2 [Q] | RAF No 72 Sqn, Aldergrove | |
| XV724 | WS58 Wessex HC2 | RAF No 22 Sqn SAR* | |
| XV725 | WS58 Wessex HC2 [C] | RAF No 72 Sqn, Aldergrove | |
| XV726 | WS58 Wessex HC2 [J] | RAF No 72 Sqn, Aldergrove | |
| XV728 | WS58 Wessex HC2 [A] | RAF No 72 Sqn, Aldergrove | |
| XV729 | WS58 Wessex HC2 | RAF No 22 Sqn SAR* | |
| XV730 | WS58 Wessex HC2 | RAF No 22 Sqn SAR* | |
| XV731 | WS58 Wessex HC2 [Y] | RAF No 72 Sqn, Aldergrove | |
| XV732 | WS58 Wessex HCC4 | RAF Queen's Flight, Benson | |
| XV733 | WS58 Wessex HCC4 | RAF Queen's Flight, Benson | |
| XV738 | HS Harrier GR3 [B] | RAF No 1 SoTT, Halton | |
| XV740 | HS Harrier GR3 (8989M) | RAF Abingdon, BDRF | |
| XV741 | HS Harrier GR3 [3G] | RAF Cosford Aerospace Museum | |
| XV744 | HS Harrier GR3 [3K] | RAF No 233 OCU, Wittering | |
| XV747 | HS Harrier GR3 (8979M) | RAF Coltishall, BDRT | |
| XV748 | HS Harrier GR3 | MoD (PE) RAE Bedford | |
| XV751 | HS Harrier GR3 [U] | RAF St Athan | |
| XV752 | HS Harrier GR3 [S] | RAF No 4 Sqn, Gütersloh | |
| XV753 | HS Harrier GR3 [3F] (90..M) | RAF No No 1 SoTT, Halton | |
| XV755 | HS Harrier GR3 [M] | RAF No 233 OCU, Wittering | |
| XV758 | HS Harrier GR3 [R] | RAF No 4 Sqn, Gütersloh | |
| XV759 | HS Harrier GR3 [O] | RAF St Athan Fire Section | |
| XV760 | HS Harrier GR3 [K] | RAF No 3 Sqn, Gütersloh | |
| XV762 | HS Harrier GR3 [09] | RAF ASF, Wittering | |
| XV778 | HS Harrier GR3 (9001M) | RAF Valley Fire Section | |
| XV779 | HS Harrier GR3 (8931M) [01/A] | RAF Wittering on display | |
| XV783 | HS Harrier GR3 [N] (90..M) | RAF No 2 SoTT, Cosford | |
| XV784 | HS Harrier GR3 (8909M) | RAF Abingdon, BDRF | |
| XV786 | HS Harrier GR3 [S] | RAF St Athan | |
| XV804 | HS Harrier GR3 [O] | RAF No 4 Sqn, Gütersloh | |
| XV806 | HS Harrier GR3 [E] (90..M) | RAF No 2 SoTT, Cosford | |
| XV808 | HS Harrier GR3 [3J] | RAF No 1 SoTT, Halton | |
| XV810 | HS Harrier GR3 [K] | RAF Abingdon, BDRF | |
| XV814 | DH Comet 4 (G-APDF) | MoD(PE) RAE Farnborough | |
| XV859 | BHC SR.N6 Winchester 6 | RN NHTU, Lee-on-Solent | |
| XV863 | HS Buccaneer S2B | RAF No 208 Sqn, Lossiemouth | |
| XV864 | HS Buccaneer S2B | RAF No 12 Sqn, Lossiemouth | |
| XV865 | HS Buccaneer S2B | RAF No 237 OCU, Lossiemouth | |
| XV866 | HS Buccaneer S2B [Y] | RAF, stored Shawbury | |
| XV867 | HS Buccaneer S2B | RAF No 208 Sqn, Lossiemouth | |

| Notes | Reg. | Type | Owner or Operator |
|---|---|---|---|
| | XV868 | HS Buccaneer S2B | RAF No 12 Sqn, Lossiemouth |
| | XV869 | HS Buccaneer S2B | RAF, stored Shawbury |
| | *XV880* | HS Harrier GR1 (really XV280) (fuselage) | RNAS Yeovilton, fire section |
| | XW175 | HS Harrier T4A | MoD(PE) RAE Bedford |
| | XW198 | WS Puma HC1 [DL] | RAF No 230 Sqn, Gütersloh |
| | XW199 | WS Puma HC1 [DU] | RAF No 230 Sqn, Gütersloh |
| | XW200 | WS Puma HC1 [A] | RAF BFME, Saudi Arabia |
| | XW201 | WS Puma HC1 [B] | RAF BFME, Saudi Arabia |
| | XW202 | WS Puma HC1 [CE] | RAF No 1563 Flt, Belize |
| | XW204 | WS Puma HC1 [C] | RAF BFME, Saudi Arabia |
| | XW206 | WS Puma HC1 [D] | RAF BFME, Saudi Arabia |
| | XW207 | WS Puma HC1 [E] | RAF BFME, Saudi Arabia |
| | XW208 | WS Puma HC1 [DC] | RAF No 33 Sqn, Odiham |
| | XW209 | WS Puma HC1 [CF] | RAF No 33 Sqn, Odiham |
| | XW210 | WS Puma HC1 [CG] | RAF No 1563 Flt, Belize |
| | XW211 | WS Puma HC1 [CH] | RAF No 33 Sqn, Odiham |
| | XW212 | WS Puma HC1 [CI] | RAF No 33 Sqn, Odiham |
| | XW213 | WS Puma HC1 [CJ] | RAF No 1563 Flt, Belize |
| | XW214 | WS Puma HC1 | RAF BFME, Saudi Arabia |
| | XW215 | WS Puma HC1 [DM] | RAF No 230 Sqn, Gütersloh |
| | XW216 | WS Puma HC1 [F] | RAF BFME, Saudi Arabia |
| | XW217 | WS Puma HC1 [G] | RAF BFME, Saudi Arabia |
| | XW218 | WS Puma HC1 [DT] | RAF No 230 Sqn, Gütersloh |
| | XW219 | WS Puma HC1 [DC] | RAF No 230 Sqn, Gütersloh |
| | XW220 | WS Puma HC1 [H] | RAF BFME, Saudi Arabia |
| | XW221 | WS Puma HC1 [CM] | RAF No 33 Sqn, Odiham |
| | XW222 | WS Puma HC1 [J] | RAF BFME, Saudi Arabia |
| | XW223 | WS Puma HC1 [CB] | RAF No 33 Sqn, Odiham |
| | XW224 | WS Puma HC1 | RAF BFME, Saudi Arabia |
| | XW225 | WS Puma HC1 [K] | RAF BFME, Saudi Arabia |
| | XW226 | WS Puma HC1 [T] | RAF BFME, Saudi Arabia |
| | XW227 | WS Puma HC1 [DN] | RAF No 230 Sqn, Gütersloh |
| | XW229 | WS Puma HC1 [DB] | RAF No 230 Sqn, Gütersloh |
| | XW231 | WS Puma HC1 [U] | RAF BFME, Saudi Arabia |
| | XW232 | WS Puma HC1 [DJ] | RAF No 230 Sqn, Gütersloh |
| | XW233 | WS Puma HC1 | RAF No 33 Sqn, Odiham |
| | XW234 | WS Puma HC1 [CO] | RAF No 33 Sqn, Odiham |
| | XW235 | WS Puma HC1 [CP] | RAF No 33 Sqn, Odiham |
| | XW236 | WS Puma HC1 [CQ] | RAF No 1563 Flt, Belize |
| | XW237 | WS Puma HC1 [CR] | RAF No 33 Sqn, Odiham |
| | XW241 | Sud SA330E Puma (F-ZJUX) | MoD(PE) RAE Farnborough (wfu) |
| | XW249 | Cushioncraft CC7 | Cornwall Aero Park, Helston |
| | XW255 | BHC BH-7 Wellington | RN NHTU, Lee-on-Solent |
| | XW264 | HS Harrier T2 (forward fuselage) | CARG store, RAF Innsworth |
| | XW265 | HS Harrier T4A [W] | RAF No 45 Sqn, Gütersloh |
| | XW266 | HS Harrier T4N [719] | RN No 899 Sqn, Yeovilton |
| | XW267 | HS Harrier T4 [U] | RAF SAOEU, Boscombe Down |
| | XW268 | HS Harrier T4N [720] | RN No 899 Sqn, Yeovilton |
| | XW269 | HS Harrier T4 [BD] | MoD (PE) SAOEU, Boscombe Down |
| | XW270 | HS Harrier T4 [04] | RAF Station Flight, Gütersloh |
| | XW271 | HS Harrier T4 [X] | RAF No 233 OCU, Wittering |
| | XW272 | HS Harrier T4 (8783M) (nose only) | BAe, Kingston-upon-Thames |
| | XW276 | Aerospatiale SA341 (F-ZWRI) | North-East Aircraft Museum, Usworth |
| | XW280 | WS Scout AH1 | AAC No 660 Sqn, Brunei |
| | XW281 | WS Scout AH1 [U] | AAC, stored Wroughton |
| | XW282 | WS Scout AH1 [W] | AAC No 666 (TA) Sqn, Netheravon |
| | XW283 | WS Scout AH1 [X] | AAC No 658 Sqn, Netheravon |
| | XW284 | WS Scout AH1 [A] (fuselage only) | AAC, stored Wroughton |
| | XW287 | BAC Jet Provost T5 [P] | RAF No 6 FTS, Finningley |
| | XW289 | BAC Jet Provost T5A [16] | RAF No 3 FTS, Cranwell |
| | XW290 | BAC Jet Provost T5A [41] | RAF, stored Shawbury |
| | XW291 | BAC Jet Provost T5 [N] | RAF No 6 FTS, Finningley |
| | XW292 | BAC Jet Provost T5A [32] | RAF No 3 FTS, Cranwell |
| | XW293 | BAC Jet Provost T5 [Z] | RAF No 6 FTS, Finningley |
| | XW294 | BAC Jet Provost T5A [45] | RAF No 3 FTS, Cranwell |
| | XW295 | BAC Jet Provost T5A [29] | RAF No 3 FTS, Cranwell |
| | XW296 | BAC Jet Provost T5 [Q] | RAF No 6 FTS, Finningley |
| | XW298 | BAC Jet Provost T5 (9013M) | RAF BDRF, Abingdon |
| | XW299 | BAC Jet Provost T5A [60] | RAF No 1 FTS, Linton-on-Ouse |

| Reg. | Type | Owner or Operator | Notes |
|---|---|---|---|
| XW301 | BAC Jet Provost T5A [63] | RAF No 1 FTS, Linton-on-Ouse | |
| XW302 | BAC Jet Provost T5 [T] | RAF No 6 FTS, Finningley | |
| XW303 | BAC Jet Provost T5A [127] | RAF No 7 FTS, Church Fenton | |
| XW304 | BAC Jet Provost T5 [X] | RAF No 6 FTS, Finningley | |
| XW305 | BAC Jet Provost T5A [42] | RAF No 3 FTS, Cranwell | |
| XW306 | BAC Jet Provost T5 [O] | RAF, stored Shawbury | |
| XW307 | BAC Jet Provost T5 [S] | RAF No 6 FTS, Finningley | |
| XW309 | BAC Jet Provost T5 [V] | RAF No 6 FTS, Finningley | |
| XW310 | BAC Jet Provost T5A [37] | RAF, stored Shawbury | |
| XW311 | BAC Jet Provost T5 [W] | RAF No 6 FTS, Finningley | |
| XW312 | BAC Jet Provost T5A [64] | RAF No 1 FTS, Linton-on-Ouse | |
| XW313 | BAC Jet Provost T5A [30] | RAF No 3 FTS, Cranwell | |
| XW315 | BAC Jet Provost T5A [63] (fuselage only) | RAF Abingdon, BDRF, stored | |
| XW315 | BAC Jet Provost T5A (cockpit section only) | Stratford Aircraft Collection, Long Marston, stored | |
| XW316 | BAC Jet Provost T5A [28] | RAF No 3 FTS, Cranwell | |
| XW317 | BAC Jet Provost T5A [25] | RAF No 3 FTS, Cranwell | |
| XW318 | BAC Jet Provost T5A [12] | RAF No 3 FTS, Cranwell | |
| XW319 | BAC Jet Provost T5A [57] | RAF CFS, Scampton | |
| XW320 | BAC Jet Provost T5A [71] (9015M) | RAF No 1 SoTT, Halton | |
| XW321 | BAC Jet Provost T5A [62] | RAF No 1 FTS, Linton-on-Ouse | |
| XW322 | BAC Jet Provost T5B [D] | RAF No 6 FTS, Finningley | |
| XW323 | BAC Jet Provost T5A [44] | RAF No 3 FTS, Cranwell | |
| XW324 | BAC Jet Provost T5 [U] | RAF No 6 FTS, Finningley | |
| XW325 | BAC Jet Provost T5B [E] | RAF No 6 FTS, Finningley | |
| XW326 | BAC Jet Provost T5A [62] | RAF, stored Shawbury | |
| XW327 | BAC Jet Provost T5A [134] | RAF No 7 FTS, Church Fenton (wfu) | |
| XW328 | BAC Jet Provost T5A [22] | RAF No 3 FTS, Cranwell | |
| XW330 | BAC Jet Provost T5A [10] | RAF No 3 FTS, Cranwell | |
| XW332 | BAC Jet Provost T5A [34] | RAF No 3 FTS, Cranwell | |
| XW333 | BAC Jet Provost T5A [61] | RAF CFS, Scampton | |
| XW334 | BAC Jet Provost T5A [131] | RAF, stored Shawbury | |
| XW335 | BAC Jet Provost T5A [27] | RAF No 3 FTS, Cranwell | |
| XW336 | BAC Jet Provost T5A [64] | RAF CFS, Scampton | |
| XW351 | BAC Jet Provost T5A [31] | RAF No 3 FTS, Cranwell | |
| XW352 | BAC Jet Provost T5 [R] | RAF No 6 FTS, Finningley | |
| XW353 | BAC Jet Provost T5A [51] | RAF CFS, Scampton | |
| XW354 | BAC Jet Provost T5A [7] | RAF No 3 FTS, Cranwell | |
| XW355 | BAC Jet Provost T5A [20] | RAF, stored Shawbury | |
| XW357 | BAC Jet Provost T5A [5] | RAF No 3 FTS, Cranwell | |
| XW358 | BAC Jet Provost T5A [130] | RAF No 7 FTS, Church Fenton | |
| XW359 | BAC Jet Provost T5B [65] | RAF No 1 FTS, Linton-on-Ouse | |
| XW360 | BAC Jet Provost T5A [61] | RAF No 1 FTS, Linton-on-Ouse | |
| XW361 | BAC Jet Provost T5A [21] | RAF No 3 FTS, Cranwell | |
| XW362 | BAC Jet Provost T5A [17] | RAF No 3 FTS, Cranwell | |
| XW363 | BAC Jet Provost T5A [36] | RAF No 3 FTS, Cranwell | |
| XW364 | BAC Jet Provost T5A [35] | RAF, stored Shawbury | |
| XW365 | BAC Jet Provost T5A [73] (9018M) | RAF No 1 SoTT, Halton | |
| XW366 | BAC Jet Provost T5A [75] | RAF No 1 FTS, Linton-on-Ouse | |
| XW367 | BAC Jet Provost T5A [26] | RAF No 3 FTS, Cranwell | |
| XW368 | BAC Jet Provost T5A [66] | RAF No 1 FTS, Linton-on-Ouse | |
| XW369 | BAC Jet Provost T5A [65] | RAF CFS, Scampton | |
| XW370 | BAC Jet Provost T5A [72] | RAF No 1 FTS, Linton-on-Ouse | |
| XW372 | BAC Jet Provost T5A [M] | RAF, stored Shawbury | |
| XW373 | BAC Jet Provost T5A [11] | RAF No 3 FTS, Cranwell | |
| XW374 | BAC Jet Provost T5A [38] | RAF No 3 FTS, Cranwell | |
| XW375 | BAC Jet Provost T5A [52] | RAF CFS, Scampton | |
| XW404 | BAC Jet Provost T5A [77] | RAF No 1 FTS, Linton-on-Ouse | |
| XW405 | BAC Jet Provost T5A [J] | RAF, stored Shawbury | |
| XW406 | BAC Jet Provost T5A [23] | RAF No 3 FTS, Cranwell | |
| XW408 | BAC Jet Provost T5A [24] | RAF No 3 FTS, Cranwell | |
| XW409 | BAC Jet Provost T5A [123] | RAF CTTS, St Athan | |
| XW410 | BAC Jet Provost T5A [80] | RAF No 1 FTS, Linton-on-Ouse | |
| XW412 | BAC Jet Provost T5A [15] | RAF No 3 FTS, Cranwell | |
| XW413 | BAC Jet Provost T5A [69] | RAF No 1 FTS, Linton-on-Ouse | |
| XW415 | BAC Jet Provost T5A [53] | RAF CFS, Scampton | |
| XW416 | BAC Jet Provost T5A [19] | RAF No 3 FTS, Cranwell | |
| XW418 | BAC Jet Provost T5A [126] | RAF No 7 FTS, Church Fenton | |
| XW419 | BAC Jet Provost T5A [125] | RAF No 7 FTS, Church Fenton | |
| XW420 | BAC Jet Provost T5A [8] | RAF No 3 FTS, Cranwell | |
| XW421 | BAC Jet Provost T5A [60] | RAF CFS, Scampton | |

| Notes | Reg. | Type | Owner or Operator |
|---|---|---|---|
| | XW422 | BAC Jet Provost T5A [3] | RAF No 3 FTS, Cranwell |
| | XW423 | BAC Jet Provost T5A [14] | RAF, stored Shawbury |
| | XW424 | BAC Jet Provost T5A [62] | Privately owned, Misson, Notts |
| | XW425 | BAC Jet Provost T5A [H] | RAF, stored Shawbury |
| | XW427 | BAC Jet Provost T5A [56] | RAF CFS, Scampton |
| | XW428 | BAC Jet Provost T5A [39] | RAF No 3 FTS, Cranwell |
| | XW429 | BAC Jet Provost T5B [C] | RAF No 6 FTS, Finningley |
| | XW430 | BAC Jet Provost T5A [58] | RAF CFS, Scampton |
| | XW431 | BAC Jet Provost T5B [A] | RAF No 6 FTS, Finningley |
| | XW432 | BAC Jet Provost T5A [76] | RAF No 1 FTS, Linton-on-Ouse |
| | XW433 | BAC Jet Provost T5A [124] | RAF No 7 FTS, Church Fenton |
| | XW434 | BAC Jet Provost T5A [78] | RAF No 1 FTS, Linton-on-Ouse |
| | XW435 | BAC Jet Provost T5A [4] | RAF No 3 FTS, Cranwell |
| | XW436 | BAC Jet Provost T5A [62] | RAF CFS, Scampton |
| | XW437 | BAC Jet Provost T5A [1] | RAF No 3 FTS, Cranwell |
| | XW438 | BAC Jet Provost T5B [B] | RAF No 6 FTS, Finningley |
| | XW527 | HS Buccaneer S2B | RAF No 12 Sqn Lossiemouth |
| | XW528 | HS Buccaneer S2B (8861M) [C] | RAF Coningsby, BDRT |
| | XW529 | HS Buccaneer S2B | RAF ASF Lossiemouth |
| | XW530 | HS Buccaneer S2B | RAF No 12 Sqn, Lossiemouth |
| | XW533 | HS Buccaneer S2B | RAF No 237 OCU, Lossiemouth |
| | XW534 | HS Buccaneer S2B | RAF No 237 OCU, Lossiemouth |
| | XW542 | HS Buccaneer S2B | RAF No 208 Sqn, Lossiemouth |
| | XW543 | HS Buccaneer S2B | RAF No 12 Sqn, Lossiemouth |
| | XW544 | HS Buccaneer S2B (8857M) [Y] | RAF No 2 SoTT, Cosford |
| | XW545 | HS Buccaneer S2B (8859M) | RAF St Athan, BDRT |
| | XW546 | HS Buccaneer S2B | RAF No 237 OCU, Lossiemouth |
| | XW547 | HS Buccaneer S2B | RAF No 12 Sqn, Lossiemouth |
| | XW549 | HS Buccaneer S2B (8860M) | RAF Kinloss, BDRT |
| | XW550 | HS Buccaneer S2B [X] | RAF, stored St Athan |
| | XW566 | SEPECAT Jaguar T2 | MoD(PE) RAE Farnborough store |
| | XW612 | WS Scout AH1 [A] | AAC No 660 Sqn, Sek Kong |
| | XW613 | WS Scout AH1 [B] | AAC No 660 Sqn, Sek Kong |
| | XW614 | WS Scout AH1 | AAC Historic Flight, stored Wroughton |
| | XW616 | WS Scout AH1 | AAC, stored Wroughton |
| | XW626 | DH Comet 4AEW (G-APDS) | MoD(PE), RAE Bedford apprentice school |
| | XW630 | HS Harrier GR3 [T] | RAF St Athan, CTTS |
| | XW635 | Beagle D5/180 (G-AWSW) | Privately owned, Cranwell North |
| | XW664 | HS Nimrod R1P | RAF No 51 Sqn, Wyton |
| | XW665 | HS Nimrod R1P | RAF No 51 Sqn, Wyton |
| | XW666 | HS Nimrod R1P | RAF No 51 Sqn, Wyton |
| | XW750 | HS748 Series 107 (G-ASJT) | MoD(PE) RAE Bedford |
| | XW763 | HS Harrier GR3 (9002M) [3F] | RAF St Athan, fire section |
| | XW764 | HS Harrier GR3 (8981M) | RAF Leeming, BDRT |
| | XW768 | HS Harrier GR3 [N] (90..M) | RAF No 1 SoTT, Halton |
| | XW784 | Mitchell-Procter Kittiwake I (G-BBRN) | Privately owned, Haverfordwest |
| | XW788 | HS125 CC1 | RAF No 32 Sqn, Northolt |
| | XW789 | HS125 CC1 | RAF No 32 Sqn, Northolt |
| | XW790 | HS125 CC1 | RAF No 32 Sqn, Northolt |
| | XW791 | HS125 CC1 | RAF No 32 Sqn, Northolt |
| | XW795 | WS Scout AH1 | AAC, stored Wroughton |
| | XW796 | WS Scout AH1 [X] | AAC, stored Wroughton |
| | XW797 | WS Scout AH1 [G] | AAC No 660 Sqn, Sek Kong |
| | XW798 | WS Scout AH1 | AAC No 660 Sqn, Sek Kong |
| | XW799 | WS Scout AH1 | AAC No 658 Sqn, Netheravon |
| | XW836 | WS Lynx | RNAS Lee-on-Solent, derelict |
| | XW837 | WS Lynx | RNAS Lee-on-Solent, derelict |
| | XW838 | WS Lynx [TAD 009] | AAC SAE, Middle Wallop |
| | XW839 | WS Lynx | RNEC Manadon |
| | XW843 | WS Gazelle AH1 | AAC stored, Wroughton |
| | XW844 | WS Gazelle AH1 | AAC No 661 Sqn, Detmold |
| | XW845 | WS Gazelle HT2 [47/CU] | RN No 705 Sqn, Culdrose |
| | XW846 | WS Gazelle AH1 | AAC, stored Wroughton |
| | XW847 | WS Gazelle AH1 | AAC No 667 Sqn, Middle Wallop |
| | XW848 | WS Gazelle AH1 | AAC No 670 Sqn, Middle Wallop |
| | XW849 | WS Gazelle AH1 [G] | RM 3 CBAS, Yeovilton |
| | XW851 | WS Gazelle AH1 [H] | RM 3 CBAS, Yeovilton |
| | XW852 | WS Gazelle HT3 | RAF No 32 Sqn, Northolt |
| | XW853 | WS Gazelle HT2 [53/CU] | RN No 705 Sqn, Culdrose |
| | XW854 | WS Gazelle HT2 [46/CU] | RN No 705 Sqn, Culdrose |

| Reg. | Type | Owner or Operator | Notes |
|---|---|---|---|
| XW855 | WS Gazelle HT3 | RAF No 32 Sqn, Northolt | |
| XW856 | WS Gazelle HT2 [49/CU] | RN No 705 Sqn, Culdrose | |
| XW857 | WS Gazelle HT2 [55/CU] | RN No 705 Sqn, Culdrose | |
| XW858 | WS Gazelle HT3 [C] (fuselage) | RAF, stored Wroughton | |
| XW860 | WS Gazelle HT2 [44/CU] | RN, stored Wroughton | |
| XW861 | WS Gazelle HT2 [59/CU] | RN, stored Wroughton | |
| XW862 | WS Gazelle HT3 [D] | RAF No 2 FTS, Shawbury | |
| XW863 | WS Gazelle HT2 [42/CU] | RN, stored Wroughton | |
| XW864 | WS Gazelle HT2 [54/CU] | RN No 705 Sqn, Culdrose | |
| XW865 | WS Gazelle AH1 [C] | AAC No 670 Sqn, Middle Wallop | |
| XW866 | WS Gazelle HT3 [E] | RAF No 2 FTS, Shawbury | |
| XW868 | WS Gazelle HT2 [50/CU] | RN No 705 Sqn, Culdrose | |
| XW870 | WS Gazelle HT3 [F] | RAF No 2 FTS, Shawbury | |
| XW871 | WS Gazelle HT2 [44/CU] | RN No 705 Sqn, Culdrose | |
| XW884 | WS Gazelle HT2 [41/CU] | RN No 705 Sqn, Culdrose | |
| XW885 | WS Gazelle AH1 [B] | AAC No 670 Sqn, Middle Wallop | |
| XW886 | WS Gazelle HT2 [48/CU] | RN No 705 Sqn, Culdrose | |
| XW887 | WS Gazelle HT2 [FL] | RN, stored Wroughton | |
| XW888 | WS Gazelle AH1 | AAC SAE, Middle Wallop | |
| XW889 | WS Gazelle AH1 | AAC SAE, Middle Wallop | |
| XW890 | WS Gazelle HT2 [53/CU] | RN, stored Wroughton | |
| XW891 | WS Gazelle HT2 [49] (fuselage) | RN Culdrose, fire section | |
| XW892 | WS Gazelle AH1 [L] | AAC No 662 Sqn, Soest | |
| XW893 | WS Gazelle AH1 | AAC No 665 Sqn, Aldergrove | |
| XW894 | WS Gazelle HT2 [52/CU] | RN No 705 Sqn, Culdrose | |
| XW895 | WS Gazelle HT2 [51/CU] | RN No 705 Sqn, Culdrose | |
| XW897 | WS Gazelle AH1 | AAC No 669 Sqn, Detmold | |
| XW898 | WS Gazelle HT3 [G] | RAF No 2 FTS, Shawbury | |
| XW899 | WS Gazelle AH1 [K] | AAC, No 662 Sqn Soest | |
| XW900 | WS Gazelle AH1 (TAD-900) | AAC SAE, Middle Wallop | |
| XW902 | WS Gazelle HT3 [H] | RAF No 2 FTS, Shawbury | |
| XW903 | WS Gazelle AH1 [E] | AAC No 670 Sqn, Middle Wallop | |
| XW904 | WS Gazelle AH1 | AAC No 7 Flight, Gatow | |
| XW906 | WS Gazelle HT3 [J] | RAF No 2 FTS, Shawbury | |
| XW907 | WS Gazelle HT2 [40/CU] | RN No 705 Sqn, Culdrose | |
| XW908 | WS Gazelle AH1 | AAC SAE, Middle Wallop | |
| XW909 | WS Gazelle AH1 | AAC No 664 Sqn, Minden | |
| XW910 | WS Gazelle HT3 [K] | RAF No 2 FTS, Shawbury | |
| XW911 | WS Gazelle AH1 [I] | AAC No 670 Sqn, Middle Wallop | |
| XW912 | WS Gazelle AH1 | AAC SAE, Middle Wallop | |
| XW913 | WS Gazelle AH1 | AAC No 664 Sqn, Minden | |
| XW916 | HS Harrier GR3 [W] | RAF Wittering Fire Section | |
| XW919 | HS Harrier GR3 [W] (90..M) | RAF No 2 SoTT, Cosford | |
| XW923 | HS Harrier GR3 (cockpit) (8724M) | RAF Wittering for rescue training | |
| XW924 | HS Harrier GR3 [G] | RAF No 4 Sqn, Gütersloh | |
| XW927 | HS Harrier T4 [02] | RAF Station Flight, Gütersloh | |
| XW930 | HS125-1B (G-ATPC) | MoD(PE) RAE Bedford | |
| XW934 | HS Harrier T4 [04] | RAF Station Flight, Gütersloh | |
| XW986 | HS Buccaneer S2B | MoD(PE) RAE Farnborough | |
| XW987 | HS Buccaneer S2B | MoD(PE) A&AEE, Boscombe Down | |
| XW988 | HS Buccaneer S2B | MoD(PE) A&AEE, Boscombe Down | |
| XX101 | Cushioncraft CC7 | International Helicopter Museum, Weston-super-Mare | |
| XX102 | Cushioncraft CC7 | Museum of Army Transport, Beverley | |
| XX105 | BAC 1-11/201 (G-ASJD) | MoD(PE) RAE Bedford | |
| XX108 | SEPECAT Jaguar GR1 (G27-313) | MoD(PE) BAe Warton/A&AEE Boscombe Down | |
| XX109 | SEPECAT Jaguar GR1 (8918M) | RAF Coltishall, ground instruction | |
| XX110 | SEPECAT Jaguar GR1 [EP] (8955M) | RAF No 2 SoTT, Cosford | |
| *XX110* | SEPECAT Jaguar GR1 Replica (BAPC 169) | RAF No 1 SoTT, Halton | |
| XX112 | SEPECAT Jaguar GR1A | RAF No 6 Sqn, Coltishall | |
| XX115 | SEPECAT Jaguar GR1 (JI005) (8821M) (fuselage only) | RAF Abingdon BDRF | |
| XX116 | SEPECAT Jaguar GR1A [02] (JI008) | RAF JMU, Abingdon | |
| XX117 | SEPECAT Jaguar GR1A [06] (JI004) | RAF No 226 OCU, Lossiemouth | |
| XX118 | SEPECAT Jaguar GR1 (JI018) (8815M) (fuselage only) | RAF No 1 SoTT, Halton | |

| Notes | Reg. | Type | Owner or Operator |
|---|---|---|---|
| | XX119 | SEPECAT Jaguar GR1 [01] (8898M) | RAF No 226 OCU, Lossiemouth |
| | XX121 | SEPECAT Jaguar GR1 [EQ] | RAF, stored Shawbury |
| | XX139 | SEPECAT Jaguar T2A | RAF No 226 OCU, Lossiemouth |
| | XX140 | SEPECAT Jaguar T2 [D] (9008M) | RAF No 2 SoTT, Cosford |
| | XX141 | SEPECAT Jaguar T2A [I] | RAF No 226 OCU, Lossiemouth |
| | XX143 | SEPECAT Jaguar T2A [GS/40] (JI002) | RAF No 54 Sqn, Coltishall |
| | XX144 | SEPECAT Jaguar T2A [I] | RAF No 226 OCU, Lossiemouth |
| | XX145 | SEPECAT Jaguar T2 | MoD(PE) ETPS, Boscombe Down |
| | XX146 | SEPECAT Jaguar T2A | RAF JMU, Abingdon |
| | XX150 | SEPECAT Jaguar T2A [W] | RAF No 226 OCU, Lossiemouth |
| | XX154 | HS Hawk T1 [1] | MoD(PE) RAE Llanbedr |
| | XX156 | HS Hawk T1 | MoD(PE) A&AEE, Boscombe Down |
| | XX157 | HS Hawk T1A | RAF No 2 TWU/63 Sqn, Chivenor |
| | XX158 | HS Hawk T1A | RAF No 2 TWU/63 Sqn, Chivenor |
| | XX159 | HS Hawk T1A | RAF No 1 TWU, Brawdy |
| | XX160 | HS Hawk T1 | MoD(PE) RAE Llanbedr |
| | XX161 | HS Hawk T1 | RAF CFS, Valley |
| | XX162 | HS Hawk T1 | RAF No 4 FTS, Valley |
| | XX163 | HS Hawk T1 | RAF CFS, Valley |
| | XX164 | HS Hawk T1 | RAF No 4 FTS, Valley |
| | XX165 | HS Hawk T1 | RAF CFS, Valley |
| | XX167 | HS Hawk T1 | RAF No 4 FTS, Valley |
| | XX168 | HS Hawk T1 | RAF No 4 FTS, Valley |
| | XX169 | HS Hawk T1 | RAF No 4 FTS, Valley |
| | XX170 | HS Hawk T1 | RAF CFS, Valley |
| | XX171 | HS Hawk T1 | RAF No 4 FTS, Valley |
| | XX172 | HS Hawk T1 | RAF No 4 FTS, Valley |
| | XX173 | HS Hawk T1 | RAF No 4 FTS, Valley |
| | XX174 | HS Hawk T1 | RAF No 4 FTS, Valley |
| | XX175 | HS Hawk T1 | RAF CFS, Valley |
| | XX176 | HS Hawk T1 | RAF CFS, Valley |
| | XX177 | HS Hawk T1 | RAF No 4 FTS, Valley |
| | XX178 | HS Hawk T1 | RAF No 4 FTS, Valley |
| | XX179 | HS Hawk T1 | RAF No 4 FTS, Valley |
| | XX181 | HS Hawk T1 | RAF No 1 TWU/79 Sqn, Brawdy |
| | XX183 | HS Hawk T1 | RAF No 4 FTS, Valley |
| | XX184 | HS Hawk T1 | RAF No 4 FTS, Valley |
| | XX185 | HS Hawk T1 | RAF No 4 FTS, Valley |
| | XX186 | HS Hawk T1A | RAF No 2 TWU/63 Sqn, Chivenor |
| | XX187 | HS Hawk T1A | RAF No 1 TWU/79 Sqn, Brawdy |
| | XX188 | HS Hawk T1A | RAF No 1 TWU/234 Sqn, Brawdy |
| | XX189 | HS Hawk T1A [J] | RAF No 2 TWU/151 Sqn, Chivenor |
| | XX190 | HS Hawk T1A | RAF No 1 TWU/234 Sqn, Brawdy |
| | XX191 | HS Hawk T1A | RAF No 1 TWU/79 Sqn, Brawdy |
| | XX193 | HS Hawk T1A | RAF No 1 TWU/234 Sqn, Brawdy |
| | XX194 | HS Hawk T1A | RAF No 1 TWU/234 Sqn, Brawdy |
| | XX195 | HS Hawk T1A | RAF No 2 TWU/63 Sqn, Chivenor |
| | XX196 | HS Hawk T1A | RAF No 2 TWU/63 Sqn, Chivenor |
| | XX198 | HS Hawk T1A | RAF No 1 TWU/79 Sqn, Brawdy |
| | XX199 | HS Hawk T1A | RAF No 1 TWU/79 Sqn, Brawdy |
| | XX200 | HS Hawk T1A | RAF No 1 TWU/79 Sqn, Brawdy |
| | XX201 | HS Hawk T1A [N] | RAF No 2 TWU/151 Sqn, Chivenor |
| | XX202 | HS Hawk T1A [P] | RAF No 2 TWU/151 Sqn, Chivenor |
| | XX203 | HS Hawk T1A | RAF No 2 TWU/63 Sqn, Chivenor |
| | XX204 | HS Hawk T1A [H] | RAF No 2 TWU/151 Sqn, Chivenor |
| | XX205 | HS Hawk T1A [V] | RAF No 2 TWU/151 Sqn, Chivenor |
| | XX217 | HS Hawk T1A | RAF No 2 TWU/63 Sqn, Chivenor |
| | XX218 | HS Hawk T1A | RAF No 1 TWU/234 Sqn, Brawdy |
| | XX219 | HS Hawk T1A [T] | RAF No 2 TWU/151 Sqn, Chivenor |
| | XX220 | HS Hawk T1A | RAF No 1 TWU/234 Sqn, Brawdy |
| | XX221 | HS Hawk T1A | RAF No 1 TWU/79 Sqn, Brawdy |
| | XX222 | HS Hawk T1A | RAF No 1 TWU/79 Sqn, Brawdy |
| | XX224 | HS Hawk T1 | RAF CFS, Valley |
| | XX225 | HS Hawk T1 | RAF No 4 FTS, Valley |
| | XX226 | HS Hawk T1 | RAF No 4 FTS, Valley |
| | XX227 | HS Hawk T1A | RAF *Red Arrows*, Scampton |
| | XX228 | HS Hawk T1A [Q] | RAF No 2 TWU/151 Sqn, Chivenor |
| | XX230 | HS Hawk T1A | RAF No 2 TWU/151 Sqn, Chivenor |
| | XX231 | HS Hawk T1 | RAF No 4 FTS, Valley |
| | XX232 | HS Hawk T1 | RAF No 4 FTS, Valley |

| Reg. | Type | Owner or Operator | Notes |
|---|---|---|---|
| XX233 | HS Hawk T1 | RAF CFS/*Red Arrows*, Scampton | |
| XX234 | HS Hawk T1 | RAF No 4 FTS, Valley | |
| XX235 | HS Hawk T1 | RAF No 4 FTS, Valley | |
| XX236 | HS Hawk T1 | RAF No 4 FTS, Valley | |
| XX237 | HS Hawk T1 | RAF *Red Arrows*, Scampton | |
| XX238 | HS Hawk T1 | RAF CFS, Valley | |
| XX239 | HS Hawk T1 | RAF No 4 FTS, Valley | |
| XX240 | HS Hawk T1 | RAF No 4 FTS, Valley | |
| XX242 | HS Hawk T1 | RAF No 4 FTS, Valley | |
| XX244 | HS Hawk T1 | RAF No 4 FTS, Valley | |
| XX245 | HS Hawk T1 | RAF No 4 FTS, Valley | |
| XX246 | HS Hawk T1A | RAF No 2 TWU/63 Sqn, Chivenor | |
| XX247 | HS Hawk T1A | RAF No 1 TWU/234 Sqn, Brawdy | |
| XX248 | HS Hawk T1A | RAF No 1 TWU/79 Sqn, Brawdy | |
| XX249 | HS Hawk T1 | RAF No 4 FTS, Valley | |
| XX250 | HS Hawk T1 | RAF No 4 FTS, Valley | |
| XX252 | HS Hawk T1A | RAF *Red Arrows*, Scampton | |
| XX253 | HS Hawk T1A | RAF *Red Arrows*, Scampton | |
| XX254 | HS Hawk T1A | RAF No 2 TWU/63 Sqn, Chivenor | |
| XX255 | HS Hawk T1A | RAF No 2 TWU/63 Sqn, Chivenor | |
| XX256 | HS Hawk T1A | RAF No 2 TWU/63 Sqn, Chivenor | |
| XX257 | HS Hawk T1 | RAF Chivenor, BDRT | |
| XX258 | HS Hawk T1A | RAF No 1 TWU/79 Sqn, Brawdy | |
| XX260 | HS Hawk T1A | RAF *Red Arrows*, Scampton | |
| XX261 | HS Hawk T1A | RAF No 1 TWU/79 Sqn, Brawdy | |
| XX263 | HS Hawk T1A | RAF No 2 TWU/63 Sqn, Chivenor | |
| *XX263* | HS Hawk T1 Replica (BAPC 152) | RAF Exhibition Flight, Abingdon | |
| XX264 | HS Hawk T1A | RAF *Red Arrows*, Scampton | |
| XX265 | HS Hawk T1A [U] | RAF No 2 TWU/151 Sqn, Chivenor | |
| XX266 | HS Hawk T1A | RAF *Red Arrows*, Scampton | |
| XX278 | HS Hawk T1A | RAF No 2 TWU/63 Sqn, Chivenor | |
| XX280 | HS Hawk T1A | RAF No 1 TWU/79 Sqn, Brawdy | |
| XX281 | HS Hawk T1A [O] | RAF No 2 TWU/151 Sqn, Chivenor | |
| XX282 | HS Hawk T1A | RAF No 2 TWU/63 Sqn, Chivenor | |
| XX283 | HS Hawk T1A [Z] | RAF No 2 TWU/151 Sqn, Chivenor | |
| XX284 | HS Hawk T1A [E] | RAF No 2 TWU/151 Sqn, Chivenor | |
| XX285 | HS Hawk T1A [R] | RAF No 2 TWU/151 Sqn, Chivenor | |
| XX286 | HS Hawk T1A | RAF No 1 TWU/79 Sqn, Brawdy | |
| XX287 | HS Hawk T1A | RAF No 2 TWU/63 Sqn, Chivenor | |
| XX288 | HS Hawk T1A | RAF No 1 TWU/79 Sqn, Brawdy | |
| XX289 | HS Hawk T1A | RAF No 2 TWU/63 Sqn, Chivenor | |
| XX290 | HS Hawk T1 | RAF No 4 FTS, Valley | |
| XX292 | HS Hawk T1 | RAF No 4 FTS, Valley | |
| XX294 | HS Hawk T1 | RAF *Red Arrows*, Scampton | |
| XX295 | HS Hawk T1 | RAF No 4 FTS, Valley | |
| XX296 | HS Hawk T1 | RAF No 4 FTS, Valley | |
| XX297 | HS Hawk T1A (8933M) | RAF Finningley Fire Section | |
| *XX297* | HS Hawk T1 Replica (BAPC171) | RAF Exhibition Flight, Abingdon | |
| XX299 | HS Hawk T1 | RAF No 4 FTS, Valley | |
| XX301 | HS Hawk T1A [L] | RAF No 2 TWU/151 Sqn, Chivenor | |
| XX302 | HS Hawk T1A | RAF No 1 TWU/234 Sqn, Brawdy | |
| XX303 | HS Hawk T1A | RAF No 1 TWU/234 Sqn, Brawdy | |
| XX304 | HS Hawk T1A | BAe, Brough on rebuild | |
| XX306 | HS Hawk T1A | RAF *Red Arrows*, Scampton | |
| XX307 | HS Hawk T1 | RAF *Red Arrows*, Scampton | |
| XX308 | HS Hawk T1 | RAF *Red Arrows*, Scampton | |
| XX309 | HS Hawk T1 | RAF No 4 FTS, Valley | |
| XX310 | HS Hawk T1 | RAF No 4 FTS, Valley | |
| XX311 | HS Hawk T1 | RAF No 4 FTS, Valley | |
| XX312 | HS Hawk T1 | RAF No 1 TWU/79 Sqn, Brawdy | |
| XX313 | HS Hawk T1 | RAF No 4 FTS, Valley | |
| XX314 | HS Hawk T1 | RAF No 4 FTS, Valley | |
| XX315 | HS Hawk T1A | RAF No 1 TWU/234 Sqn, Brawdy | |
| XX316 | HS Hawk T1A | RAF No 1 TWU/79 Sqn, Brawdy | |
| XX317 | HS Hawk T1A | RAF No 1 TWU/234 Sqn, Brawdy | |
| XX318 | HS Hawk T1A | RAF No 1 TWU/79 Sqn, Brawdy | |
| XX319 | HS Hawk T1A | RAF No 1 TWU/79 Sqn, Brawdy | |
| XX320 | HS Hawk T1A | RAF No 2 TWU/63 Sqn, Chivenor | |
| XX321 | HS Hawk T1A | RAF No 2 TWU/63 Sqn, Chivenor | |
| XX322 | HS Hawk T1A [W] | RAF No 2 TWU/151 Sqn, Chivenor | |

| Notes | Reg. | Type | Owner or Operator |
|---|---|---|---|
| | XX323 | HS Hawk T1A | RAF No 1 TWU/234 Sqn, Brawdy |
| | XX324 | HS Hawk T1A | RAF No 1 TWU/234 Sqn, Brawdy |
| | XX325 | HS Hawk T1A | RAF No 2 TWU/63 Sqn, Chivenor |
| | XX326 | HS Hawk T1A [A] | RAF No 2 TWU/151 Sqn, Chivenor |
| | XX327 | HS Hawk T1A | MoD(PE) RAE Farnborough |
| | XX329 | HS Hawk T1A [C] | RAF No 2 TWU/151 Sqn, Chivenor |
| | XX330 | HS Hawk T1A [D] | RAF No 2 TWU/151 Sqn, Chivenor |
| | XX331 | HS Hawk T1A | RAF No 2 TWU/63 Sqn, Chivenor |
| | XX332 | HS Hawk T1A [F] | RAF No 2 TWU/151 Sqn, Chivenor |
| | XX334 | HS Hawk T1A | RAF No 2 TWU/63 Sqn, Chivenor |
| | XX335 | HS Hawk T1A [I] | RAF No 2 TWU/151 Sqn, Chivenor |
| | XX337 | HS Hawk T1A [K] | RAF No 2 TWU/151 Sqn, Chivenor |
| | XX338 | HS Hawk T1 | RAF No 4 FTS, Valley |
| | XX339 | HS Hawk T1A | RAF No 1 TWU/234 Sqn, Brawdy |
| | XX341 | HS Hawk T1 ASTRA [1] | MoD(PE) ETPS, Boscombe Down |
| | XX342 | HS Hawk T1 [2] | MoD(PE) ETPS, Boscombe Down |
| | XX343 | HS Hawk T1 [3] | MoD(PE) ETPS, Boscombe Down |
| | XX344 | HS Hawk T1 (8847M) | RAF BDRF, Abingdon |
| | XX345 | HS Hawk T1A [Y] | RAF No 2 TWU/151 Sqn, Chivenor |
| | XX346 | HS Hawk T1A | RAF No 2 TWU/63 Sqn, Chivenor |
| | XX347 | HS Hawk T1 | *Crashed at Valley, 9 May 1990* |
| | XX348 | HS Hawk T1A | RAF No 1 TWU, Brawdy |
| | XX349 | HS Hawk T1 | RAF No 2 TWU/63 Sqn, Chivenor |
| | XX350 | HS Hawk T1A | RAF No 1 TWU/234 Sqn, Brawdy |
| | XX351 | HS Hawk T1A | RAF No 1 TWU/234 Sqn, Brawdy |
| | XX352 | HS Hawk T1A | RAF No 2 TWU/63 Sqn, Chivenor |
| | XX370 | WS Gazelle AH1 [A] | AAC No 658 Sqn, Netheravon |
| | XX371 | WS Gazelle AH1 | AAC No 12 Flt, Wildenrath |
| | XX372 | WS Gazelle AH1 [B] | AAC No 658 Sqn, Netheravon |
| | XX375 | WS Gazelle AH1 [C] | AAC No 658 Sqn, Netheravon |
| | XX378 | WS Gazelle AH1 | AAC stored, Wroughton |
| | XX379 | WS Gazelle AH1 [D] | AAC No 658 Sqn, Netheravon |
| | XX380 | WS Gazelle AH1 | RM 3 CBAS, Yeovilton |
| | XX381 | WS Gazelle AH1 | AAC No 2 Flt, Netheravon |
| | XX382 | WS Gazelle HT3 [M] | RAF No 2 FTS, Shawbury |
| | XX383 | WS Gazelle AH1 [E] | AAC No 658 Sqn, Netheravon |
| | XX384 | WS Gazelle AH1 | AAC No 2 Flight, Netheravon |
| | XX385 | WS Gazelle AH1 [A] | AAC No 653 Sqn, Soest |
| | XX386 | WS Gazelle AH1 | AAC No 12 Flt, Wildenrath |
| | XX387 | WS Gazelle AH1 | AAC No 664 Sqn, Miden |
| | XX388 | WS Gazelle AH1 | AAC No 652 Sqn, Hildesheim |
| | XX389 | WS Gazelle AH1 | AAC No 651 Sqn, Hildesheim |
| | XX391 | WS Gazelle HT2 [56/CU] | RN No 705 Sqn, Culdrose |
| | XX392 | WS Gazelle AH1 [W] | AAC, stored Wroughton |
| | XX393 | WS Gazelle AH1 | AAC Middle Wallop |
| | XX394 | WS Gazelle AH1 | AAC No 2 Flt, Netheravon |
| | XX395 | WS Gazelle AH1 [J] | AAC No 662 Sqn, Soest |
| | XX396 | WS Gazelle HT3 (8718M) [N] | RAF Exhibition Flight, Henlow |
| | XX398 | WS Gazelle AH1 | AAC stored, Wroughton |
| | XX399 | WS Gazelle AH1 | AAC No 2 Flt, Netheravon |
| | XX403 | WS Gazelle AH1 [Y] | AAC No 670 Sqn, Middle Wallop |
| | XX405 | WS Gazelle AH1 | AAC stored, Wroughton |
| | XX406 | WS Gazelle HT3 [P] | RAF No 2 FTS, Shawbury |
| | XX407 | WS Gazelle AH1 | AAC No 661 Sqn, Hildesheim |
| | XX408 | WS Gazelle AH1 [33D] | RM, stored Wroughton |
| | XX409 | WS Gazelle AH1 | AAC No 656 Sqn, Netheravon |
| | XX410 | WS Gazelle HT2 [58/CU] | RN AES, Lee-on-Solent |
| | XX411 | WS Gazelle AH1 [X] | AAC Middle Wallop, BDRT |
| | XX411 | WS Gazelle AH1 (tail only) | FAA Museum, RNAS Yeovilton |
| | XX412 | WS Gazelle AH1 [B] | RM 3 CBAS, Yeovilton |
| | XX413 | WS Gazelle AH1 [C] | RM 3 CBAS, Yeovilton |
| | XX414 | WS Gazelle AH1 [N] | AAC No 662 Sqn, Soest |
| | XX416 | WS Gazelle AH1 | AAC No 664 Sqn, Minden |
| | XX417 | WS Gazelle AH1 | AAC No 665 Sqn, Aldergrove |
| | XX418 | WS Gazelle AH1 | AAC No 669 Sqn, Detmold |
| | XX419 | WS Gazelle AH1 | AAC No 669 Sqn, Detmold |
| | XX431 | WS Gazelle HT2 [43/CU] | RN No 705 Sqn, Culdrose |
| | XX432 | WS Gazelle AH1 | AAC No 664 Sqn, Minden |
| | XX433 | WS Gazelle AH1 | AAC No 665 Sqn, Aldergrove |
| | XX434 | WS Gazelle AH1 | RAF Abingdon, BDRF |
| | XX435 | WS Gazelle AH1 [B] | AAC No 653 Sqn, Soest |
| | XX436 | WS Gazelle HT2 [39/CU] | RN No 705 Sqn, Culdrose |

| Reg. | Type | Owner or Operator | Notes |
|---|---|---|---|
| XX437 | WS Gazelle AH1 [C] | AAC No 653 Sqn, Soest | |
| XX438 | WS Gazelle AH1 | AAC No 664 Sqn, Minden | |
| XX439 | WS Gazelle AH1 | AAC No 651 Sqn, Hildesheim | |
| XX440 | WS Gazelle AH1 (G-BCHN) | AAC No 665 Sqn, Aldergrove | |
| XX441 | WS Gazelle HT2 [38/CU] | RN No 705 Sqn, Culdrose | |
| XX442 | WS Gazelle AH1 | AAC No 669 Sqn, Detmold | |
| XX443 | WS Gazelle AH1 [T] | AAC No 663 Sqn, Soest | |
| XX444 | WS Gazelle AH1 | AAC No 656 Sqn, Netheravon | |
| XX445 | WS Gazelle AH1 | AAC No 669 Sqn, Detmold | |
| XX446 | WS Gazelle HT2 [57/CU] | RN No 705 Sqn, Culdrose | |
| XX447 | WS Gazelle AH1 [U] | AAC No 663 Sqn, Soest | |
| XX448 | WS Gazelle AH1 | AAC No 669 Sqn, Detmold | |
| XX449 | WS Gazelle AH1 | AAC No 669 Sqn, Detmold | |
| XX450 | WS Gazelle AH1 [D] | RM 3 CBAS, Yeovilton | |
| XX451 | WS Gazelle HT2 [58/CU] | RN No 705 Sqn, Culdrose | |
| XX452 | WS Gazelle AH1 | AAC Middle Wallop Fire Section | |
| XX453 | WS Gazelle AH1 | AAC No 12 Flt, Wildenrath | |
| XX454 | WS Gazelle AH1 | AAC No 669 Sqn, Detmold | |
| XX455 | WS Gazelle AH1 | AAC No 651 Sqn, Hildesheim | |
| XX456 | WS Gazelle AH1 | AAC No 659 Sqn, Detmold | |
| XX457 | WS Gazelle AH1 | AAC No 2 Flt, Netheravon | |
| XX460 | WS Gazelle AH1 | AAC No 661 Sqn, Hildesheim | |
| XX462 | WS Gazelle AH1 | AAC No 652 Sqn, Hildesheim | |
| XX466 | HS Hunter T66B/T7 [830/DD] | RNAS Culdrose, SAH | |
| XX467 | HS Hunter T66B/T7 | Air Service Training, Perth | |
| XX469 | WS Lynx HAS2 (G-BNCL) (A2657) | Helicopter Museum of GB, Blackpool | |
| XX475 | SA Jetstream T2 [572/CU] (G-AWVJ/N1036S) | RN 750 Sqn, Culdrose | |
| XX476 | SA Jetstream T2 [561/CU] (G-AXGL/N1037S) | RN No 750 Sqn, Culdrose | |
| XX477 | SA Jetstream T1 (8462M) (G-AXXS) | RAF Finningley — ground instruction | |
| XX478 | SA Jetstream T2 [564/CU] (G-AXXT) | RN No 750 Sqn, Culdrose | |
| XX479 | SA Jetstream T2 [563/CU] (G-AXUR) | RN No 750 Sqn, Culdrose | |
| XX480 | SA Jetstream T2 [565/CU] (G-AXXU) | RN No 750 Sqn, Culdrose | |
| XX481 | SA Jetstream T2 [560/CU] (G-AXUP) | RN No 750 Sqn, Culdrose | |
| XX482 | SA Jetstream T1 [J] | RAF No 6 FTS, Finningley | |
| XX483 | SA Jetstream T2 [562/CU] | RN No 750 Sqn, Culdrose | |
| XX484 | SA Jetstream T2 [566/CU] | RN No 750 Sqn, Culdrose | |
| XX485 | SA Jetstream T2 [567/CU] | RN No 750 Sqn, Culdrose | |
| XX486 | SA Jetstream T2 [569/CU] | RN No 750 Sqn, Culdrose | |
| XX487 | SA Jetstream T2 [568/CU] | RN No 750 Sqn, Culdrose | |
| XX488 | SA Jetstream T2 [571/CU] | RN No 750 Sqn, Culdrose | |
| XX490 | SA Jetstream T2 [570/CU] | RN No 750 Sqn, Culdrose | |
| XX491 | SA Jetstream T1 [K] | RAF No 6 FTS, Finningley | |
| XX492 | SA Jetstream T1 [A] | RAF No 6 FTS, Finningley | |
| XX493 | SA Jetstream T1 [L] | RAF No 6 FTS, Finningley | |
| XX494 | SA Jetstream T1 [B] | RAF No 6 FTS, Finningley | |
| XX495 | SA Jetstream T1 [C] | RAF No 6 FTS, Finningley | |
| XX496 | SA Jetstream T1 [D] | RAF No 6 FTS, Finningley | |
| XX497 | SA Jetstream T1 [E] | RAF No 6 FTS, Finningley | |
| XX498 | SA Jetstream T1 [F] | RAF No 6 FTS, Finningley | |
| XX499 | SA Jetstream T1 [G] | RAF No 6 FTS, Finningley | |
| XX500 | SA Jetstream T1 [H] | RAF No 6 FTS, Finningley | |
| XX507 | HS125 CC2 | RAF No 32 Sqn, Northolt | |
| XX508 | HS125 CC2 | RAF No 32 Sqn, Northolt | |
| XX513 | SA Bulldog T1 [A] | RAF No 1 FTS/RNEFTS, Topcliffe | |
| XX515 | SA Bulldog T1 [7] | RAF CFS, Scampton | |
| XX516 | SA Bulldog T1 [C] | RAF No 1 FTS/RNEFTS, Topcliffe | |
| XX518 | SA Bulldog T1 [Z] | RAF Cambridge UAS, Cambridge | |
| XX519 | SA Bulldog T1 [I] | RAF No 1 FTS/RNEFTS, Topcliffe | |
| XX520 | SA Bulldog T1 [2] | RAF CFS, Scampton | |
| XX521 | SA Bulldog T1 [01] | RAF, East Lowlands UAS, Turnhouse | |
| XX522 | SA Bulldog T1 [E] | RAF No 1 FTS/RNEFTS, Topcliffe | |
| XX523 | SA Bulldog T1 [F] | RAF No 1 FTS/RNEFTS, Topcliffe | |
| XX524 | SA Bulldog T1 [04] | RAF, London UAS, Abingdon | |
| XX525 | SA Bulldog T1 [03] | RAF, East Lowlands UAS, Turnhouse | |
| XX526 | SA Bulldog T1 [C] | RAF, Oxford UAS, Abingdon | |
| XX527 | SA Bulldog T1 [G] | RAF No 1 FTS/RNEFTS, Topcliffe | |

| Notes | Reg. | Type | Owner or Operator |
|---|---|---|---|
| | XX528 | SA Bulldog T1 [D] | RAF, Oxford UAS, Abingdon |
| | XX529 | SA Bulldog T1 [H] | RAF No 1 FTS/RNEFTS, Topcliffe |
| | XX530 | SA Bulldog T1 [12] | FSCTE, RAF Manston |
| | XX531 | SA Bulldog T1 [B] | RAF No 1 FTS/RNEFTS, Topcliffe |
| | XX532 | SA Bulldog T1 [J] | RAF, Yorkshire UAS, Finningley |
| | XX533 | SA Bulldog T1 [J] | RAF No 1 FTS/RNEFTS, Topcliffe |
| | XX534 | SA Bulldog T1 [B] | RAF, Birmingham UAS, Cosford |
| | XX535 | SA Bulldog T1 [10] | RAF, London UAS, Abingdon |
| | XX536 | SA Bulldog T1 [D] | RAF No 1 FTS/RNEFTS, Topcliffe |
| | XX537 | SA Bulldog T1 [02] | RAF, East Lowlands UAS, Turnhouse |
| | XX538 | SA Bulldog T1 [P] | RAF No 1 FTS/RNEFTS, Topcliffe |
| | XX539 | SA Bulldog T1 [1] | RAF CFS, Scampton |
| | XX540 | SA Bulldog T1 [K] | RAF No 1 FTS/RNEFTS, Topcliffe |
| | XX541 | SA Bulldog T1 [L] | RAF No 1 FTS/RNEFTS, Topcliffe |
| | XX543 | SA Bulldog T1 [F] | RAF, Yorkshire UAS, Finningley |
| | XX544 | SA Bulldog T1 [01] | RAF, London UAS, Abingdon |
| | XX545 | SA Bulldog T1 PAX [02] | RAF, East Lowlands UAS, Turnhouse |
| | XX546 | SA Bulldog T1 [03] | RAF, London UAS, Abingdon |
| | XX547 | SA Bulldog T1 [05] | RAF, London UAS, Abingdon |
| | XX548 | SA Bulldog T1 [06] | RAF, London UAS, Abingdon |
| | XX549 | SA Bulldog T1 [T] | RAF No 1 FTS/RNEFTS, Topcliffe |
| | XX550 | SA Bulldog T1 [Z] | RAF, Northumbria UAS, Leeming |
| | XX551 | SA Bulldog T1 [M] | RAF No 1 FTS/RNEFTS, Topcliffe |
| | XX552 | SA Bulldog T1 [08] | RAF, London UAS, Abingdon |
| | XX553 | SA Bulldog T1 [07] | RAF, London UAS, Abingdon |
| | XX554 | SA Bulldog T1 [09] | RAF, London UAS, Abingdon |
| | XX555 | SA Bulldog T1 [10] | RAF CFS, Scampton |
| | XX556 | SA Bulldog T1 [S] | RAF, East Midlands UAS, Newton |
| | XX557 | SA Bulldog T1 PAX | RAF Topcliffe, ground instruction |
| | XX558 | SA Bulldog T1 [A] | RAF Birmingham UAS, Cosford |
| | XX559 | SA Bulldog T1 | RAF, Glasgow & Strathclyde UAS, Glasgow |
| | XX560 | SA Bulldog T1 | RAF, Glasgow & Strathclyde UAS, Glasgow |
| | XX561 | SA Bulldog T1 [A] | RAF, Aberdeen, Dundee & St Andrews UAS, Leuchars |
| | XX562 | SA Bulldog T1 [E] | RAF No 13 AEF, Sydenham |
| | XX611 | SA Bulldog T1 | RAF, Glasgow & Strathclyde UAS, Glasgow |
| | XX612 | SA Bulldog T1 [05] | RAF, Wales UAS, St Athan |
| | XX613 | SA Bulldog T1 [A] | RAF, Queen's UAS, Sydenham |
| | XX614 | SA Bulldog T1 [11] | RAF CFS, Scampton |
| | XX615 | SA Bulldog T1 [2] | RAF, Manchester UAS, Woodvale |
| | XX616 | SA Bulldog T1 [3] | RAF, Manchester UAS, Woodvale |
| | XX617 | SA Bulldog T1 [4] | RAF, Manchester UAS, Woodvale |
| | XX619 | SA Bulldog T1 [B] | RAF, Yorkshire UAS, Finningley |
| | XX620 | SA Bulldog T1 [C] | RAF, Yorkshire UAS, Finningley |
| | XX621 | SA Bulldog T1 [D] | RAF, Yorkshire UAS, Finningley |
| | XX622 | SA Bulldog T1 [E] | RAF, Yorkshire UAS, Finningley |
| | XX623 | SA Bulldog T1 [M] | RAF, East Midlands UAS, Newton |
| | XX624 | SA Bulldog T1 [G] | RAF, Yorkshire UAS, Finningley |
| | XX625 | SA Bulldog T1 [01] | RAF, Wales UAS, St Athan |
| | XX626 | SA Bulldog T1 [02] | RAF, Wales UAS, St Athan |
| | XX627 | SA Bulldog T1 [03] | RAF, Wales UAS, St Athan |
| | XX628 | SA Bulldog T1 [04] | RAF, Wales UAS, St Athan |
| | XX629 | SA Bulldog T1 [V] | RAF, Northumbria UAS, Leeming |
| | XX630 | SA Bulldog T1 [A] | RAF, Liverpool UAS, Woodvale |
| | XX631 | SA Bulldog T1 [W, 14] | RAF, Northumbria UAS, Leeming |
| | XX632 | SA Bulldog T1 [D] | RAF, Bristol UAS, Filton |
| | XX633 | SA Bulldog T1 [X] | RAF, Northumbria UAS, Leeming |
| | XX634 | SA Bulldog T1 [C] | RAF, Cambridge UAS, Teversham |
| | XX635 | SA Bulldog T1 (8767M) [S] | RAF St Athan, CTTS |
| | XX636 | SA Bulldog T1 [Y] | RAF, Northumbria UAS, Leeming |
| | XX637 | SA Bulldog T1 [U] | RAF, Northumbria UAS, Leeming |
| | XX638 | SA Bulldog T1 [N] | RAF No 1 FTS/RNEFTS, Topcliffe |
| | XX639 | SA Bulldog T1 [02] | RAF, London UAS, Abingdon |
| | XX640 | SA Bulldog T1 [U] | RAF, Queen's UAS, Sydenham |
| | XX653 | SA Bulldog T1 [E] | RAF, Bristol UAS, Filton |
| | XX654 | SA Bulldog T1 [A] | RAF, Bristol UAS, Filton |
| | XX655 | SA Bulldog T1 [B] | RAF, Bristol UAS, Filton |
| | XX656 | SA Bulldog T1 [C] | RAF, Bristol UAS, Filton |
| | XX657 | SA Bulldog T1 [U] | RAF, Cambridge UAS, Cambridge |

| Reg. | Type | Owner or Operator | Notes |
|---|---|---|---|
| XX658 | SA Bulldog T1 [A] | RAF, Cambridge UAS, Cambridge | |
| XX659 | SA Bulldog T1 [S] | RAF, Cambridge UAS, Cambridge | |
| XX660 | SA Bulldog T1 [A] | BAe Prestwick, spares recovery | |
| XX661 | SA Bulldog T1 [B] | RAF, Oxford UAS, Abingdon | |
| XX663 | SA Bulldog T1 [B] | RAF, Aberdeen, Dundee & St Andrews UAS, Leuchars | |
| XX664 | SA Bulldog T1 [04] | RAF, East Lowlands UAS, Turnhouse | |
| XX665 | SA Bulldog T1 [E] | RAF, Aberdeen, Dundee & St Andrews UAS, Leuchars | |
| XX666 | SA Bulldog T1 [V] | RAF No 1 FTS/RNEFTS, Topcliffe | |
| XX667 | SA Bulldog T1 [D] | RAF, Aberdeen, Dundee & St Andrews UAS, Leuchars | |
| XX668 | SA Bulldog T1 [1] | RAF, Manchester UAS, Woodvale | |
| XX669 | SA Bulldog T1 [B] (8997M) | RAF, Birmingham UAS, instructional use, Cosford | |
| XX670 | SA Bulldog T1 [C] | RAF, Birmingham UAS, Cosford | |
| XX671 | SA Bulldog T1 [D] | RAF, Birmingham UAS, Cosford | |
| XX672 | SA Bulldog T1 [E] | RAF, Birmingham UAS, Cosford | |
| XX685 | SA Bulldog T1 [L] | RAF, Liverpool UAS, Woodvale | |
| XX686 | SA Bulldog T1 [U] | RAF, Liverpool UAS, Woodvale | |
| XX687 | SA Bulldog T1 [A] | RAF, East Midlands UAS, Newton | |
| XX688 | SA Bulldog T1 [S] | RAF, Liverpool UAS, Woodvale | |
| XX689 | SA Bulldog T1 [3] | RAF CFS, Scampton | |
| XX690 | SA Bulldog T1 [A] | RAF, Yorkshire UAS, Finningley | |
| XX691 | SA Bulldog T1 [H] | RAF, Yorkshire UAS, Finningley | |
| XX692 | SA Bulldog T1 [5] | RAF CFS, Scampton | |
| XX693 | SA Bulldog T1 [4] | RAF CFS, Scampton | |
| XX694 | SA Bulldog T1 [E] | RAF, East Midlands UAS, Newton | |
| XX695 | SA Bulldog T1 [A] | RAF, Oxford UAS, Abingdon | |
| XX696 | SA Bulldog T1 [8] | RAF CFS, Scampton | |
| XX697 | SA Bulldog T1 [Q] | RAF, Queen's UAS, Sydenham | |
| XX698 | SA Bulldog T1 [9] | RAF CFS, Scampton | |
| XX699 | SA Bulldog T1 [Q] | RAF No 1 FTS/RNEFTS, Topcliffe | |
| XX700 | SA Bulldog T1 [R] | RAF No 1 FTS/RNEFTS, Topcliffe | |
| XX701 | SA Bulldog T1 [02] | RAF, Southampton UAS, Lee-on-Solent | |
| XX702 | SA Bulldog T1 [bl] | RAF, Glasgow & Strathclyde UAS, Glasgow | |
| XX704 | SA Bulldog T1 [U] | RAF, East Midlands UAS, Newton | |
| XX705 | SA Bulldog T1 [05] | RAF, Southampton UAS, Lee-on-Solent | |
| XX706 | SA Bulldog T1 [01] | RAF, Southampton UAS, Lee-on-Solent | |
| XX707 | SA Bulldog T1 [04] | RAF, Southampton UAS, Lee-on-Solent | |
| XX708 | SA Bulldog T1 [03] | RAF, Southampton UAS, Lee-on-Solent | |
| XX709 | SA Bulldog T1 [C] | RAF, Aberdeen, Dundee St Andrews UAS, Leuchars | |
| XX710 | SA Bulldog T1 [5] | RAF, Manchester UAS, Woodvale | |
| XX711 | SA Bulldog T1 [S] | RAF, Queen's UAS, Sydenham | |
| XX713 | SA Bulldog T1 [6] | RAF CFS, Scampton | |
| XX714 | SA Bulldog T1 [12] | RAF CFS, Scampton | |
| *XX718* | SEPECAT Jaguar GR1 Replica (BAPC150) [GA] | RAF Exhibition Flight, Abingdon | |
| XX719 | SEPECAT Jaguar GR1A | RAF No 6 Sqn, Coltishall | |
| XX720 | SEPECAT Jaguar GR1A (JI003) | RAF No 6 Sqn, Coltishall | |
| XX722 | SEPECAT Jaguar GR1 [EF] | RAF, stored Shawbury | |
| XX723 | SEPECAT Jaguar GR1A [05/35] | RAF No 41 Sqn, Coltishall | |
| XX724 | SEPECAT Jaguar GR1A [GA] | RAF, stored Shawbury | |
| XX725 | SEPECAT Jaguar GR1A (JI010) | RAF BFME, Muharraq | |
| XX726 | SEPECAT Jaguar GR1 [EB] (8947M) | RAF No 1 SoTT, Halton | |
| XX727 | SEPECAT Jaguar GR1 [ER] (8951M) | RAF No 2 SoTT, Cosford | |
| XX729 | SEPECAT Jaguar GR1A (JI012) [GC] | RAF No 54 Sqn, Coltishall | |
| XX730 | SEPECAT Jaguar GR1 [EC] (8952M) | RAF No 2 SoTT, Cosford | |
| XX733 | SEPECAT Jaguar GR1A | RAF BFME, Muharraq | |
| XX734 | SEPECAT Jaguar GR1 (JI014) (8816M) | RAF Coltishall, BDRT | |
| XX736 | SEPECAT Jaguar GR1 (JI013) | RAF, stored Shawbury | |
| XX737 | SEPECAT Jaguar GR1A [EG] (J!015) | RAF, stored Shawbury | |
| XX738 | SEPECAT Jaguar GR1A [GJ] (JI016) | RAF, stored Shawbury | |

| Notes | Reg. | Type | Owner or Operator |
|---|---|---|---|
| | XX739 | SEPECAT Jaguar GR1 (8902M) [I] | RAF No 1 SoTT, Halton |
| | XX741 | SEPECAT Jaguar GR1A [EJ] | RAF No 6 Sqn, Coltishall |
| | XX743 | SEPECAT Jaguar GR1 [EG] (8949M) | RAF No 1 SoTT, Halton |
| | XX744 | SEPECAT Jaguar GR1 [DJ] | RAF, stored Shawbury |
| | XX745 | SEPECAT Jaguar GR1A [04] | RAF No 226 OCU, Lossiemouth |
| | XX746 | SEPECAT Jaguar GR1A [09] (8895M) | RAF No 1 SoTT, Halton |
| | XX747 | SEPECAT Jaguar GR1 [08] (8903M) | RAF No 1 SoTT, Halton |
| | XX748 | SEPECAT Jaguar GR1A | RAF BFME, Muharraq |
| | XX751 | SEPECAT Jaguar GR1 [10] (8937M) | RAF No 2 SoTT, Cosford |
| | XX752 | SEPECAT Jaguar GR1A [GF] | RAF, stored Shawbury |
| | XX753 | SEPECAT Jaguar GR1 [05] | RAF, stored Shawbury |
| | XX754 | SEPECAT Jaguar GR1A | *Crashed Qatar 13 Nov 90* |
| | XX756 | SEPECAT Jaguar GR1 [AM] (8899M) | RAF No 2 SoTT, Cosford |
| | XX757 | SEPECAT Jaguar GR1 [CU] (8948M) | RAF No 1 SoTT, Halton |
| | XX763 | SEPECAT Jaguar GR1 [24] (9009M) | RAF CTTS, St Athan |
| | XX764 | SEPECAT Jaguar GR1 [13] (9010M) | RAF CTTS, St Athan |
| | XX765 | SEPECAT Jaguar ACT | MoD(PE) BAe, stored Warton |
| | XX766 | SEPECAT Jaguar GR1A [EA] | RAF No 6 Sqn, Coltishall |
| | XX767 | SEPECAT Jaguar GR1A [GE/05] | RAF No 54 Sqn, Coltishall |
| | XX818 | SEPECAT Jaguar GR1 [DE] (8945M) | RAF No 1 SoTT, Halton |
| | XX819 | SEPECAT Jaguar GR1 [CE] (8923M) | RAF No 2 SoTT, Cosford |
| | XX821 | SEPECAT Jaguar GR1 [P] (8896M) | SIF, RAFC Cranwell |
| | XX824 | SEPECAT Jaguar GR1 [AD] (9019M) | RAF No 1 SoTT, Halton |
| | XX825 | SEPECAT Jaguar GR1 [BN] (9020M) | RAF No 1 SoTT, Halton |
| | XX826 | SEPECAT Jaguar GR1 [34] (9021M) | RAF No 2 SoTT, Cosford |
| | XX829 | SEPECAT Jaguar T2A [ET] | RAF No 6 Sqn, Coltishall |
| | XX830 | SEPECAT Jaguar T2 | MoD(PE) ETPS, Boscombe Down |
| | XX832 | SEPECAT Jaguar T2A [S] | RAF No 226 OCU, Lossiemouth |
| | XX833 | SEPECAT Jaguar T2A [N²] | MoD(PE) SAOEU, Boscombe Down |
| | XX835 | SEPECAT Jaguar T2 | MoD(PE) RAE Farnborough |
| | XX836 | SEPECAT Jaguar T2A [ER] | RAF, JMU, Abingdon |
| | XX837 | SEPECAT Jaguar T2 [Z] (8978M) | RAF No 1 SoTT, Halton |
| | XX838 | SEPECAT Jaguar T2A [X] | RAF No 226 OCU, Lossiemouth |
| | XX839 | SEPECAT Jaguar T2A [Y] | RAF No 226 OCU, Lossiemouth |
| | XX840 | SEPECAT Jaguar T2A [X] | RAF No 41 Sqn, Coltishall |
| | XX841 | SEPECAT Jaguar T2 | MoD(PE) ETPS, Boscombe Down |
| | XX842 | SEPECAT Jaguar T2A [38] | RAF No 54 Sqn, Coltishall |
| | XX843 | SEPECAT Jaguar T2A [GT] | RAF No 54 Sqn, Coltishall |
| | XX844 | SEPECAT Jaguar T2 [F] (9023M) | RAF No 2 SoTT, Cosford |
| | XX845 | SEPECAT Jaguar T2A [V] | RAF No 41 Sqn, Coltishall |
| | XX846 | SEPECAT Jaguar T2A [Y] | RAF, JMU, Abingdon |
| | XX847 | SEPECAT Jaguar T2 [G] | RAF, JMU, Abingdon |
| | XX885 | HS Buccaneer S2B | RAF No 208 Sqn, Lossiemouth |
| | XX886 | HS Buccaneer S2B | RAF Honington, WLT instructional use |
| | XX887 | HS Buccaneer S2B [N] | RAF, stored Shawbury |
| | XX888 | HS Buccaneer S2B [Z] | RAF, stored Shawbury |
| | XX889 | HS Buccaneer S2B | RAF No 12 Sqn, Lossiemouth |
| | XX892 | HS Buccaneer S2B | RAF No 208 Sqn, Lossiemouth |
| | XX893 | HS Buccaneer S2B | RAF No 237 OCU, Lossiemouth |
| | XX894 | HS Buccaneer S2B | RAF No 12 Sqn, Lossiemouth |
| | XX895 | HS Buccaneer S2B | RAF No 208 Sqn, Lossiemouth |
| | XX896 | HS Buccaneer S2B | RAF, stored Shawbury |
| | XX897 | HS Buccaneer S2B | MoD(PE) RAE Bedford |
| | XX899 | HS Buccaneer S2B | RAF No 12 Sqn, Lossiemouth |
| | XX900 | HS Buccaneer S2B | RAF No 237 OCU, Lossiemouth |
| | XX901 | HS Buccaneer S2B | RAF No 208 Sqn, Lossiemouth |
| | XX910 | WS Lynx HAS2 | RAE, stored Farnborough |

| Reg. | Type | Owner or Operator | Notes |
|---|---|---|---|
| XX914 | BAC VC10 srs 1103 (G-ATDJ/ 8777M) (rear fuselage) | RAF AMS, Brize Norton | |
| XX919 | BAC 1-11/402 (PI-C 1121) | MoD(PE) RAE Farnborough | |
| XX946 | Panavia Tornado (P02) (8883M) | *To RAF Germany, 3/90* | |
| XX947 | Panavia Tornado (P03) (8797M) | RAF Marham for ground instruction | |
| XX948 | Panavia Tornado (P06) (8879M) | RAF No 2 SoTT, Cosford | |
| XX955 | SEPECAT Jaguar GR1A [GK] | RAF No 54 Sqn, Coltishall | |
| XX956 | SEPECAT Jaguar GR1 [BE] (8950M) | RAF No 1 SoTT, Halton | |
| XX958 | SEPECAT Jaguar GR1 [BK] (9022M) | RAF No 2 SoTT, Cosford | |
| XX959 | SEPECAT Jaguar GR1 [CJ] (8953M) | RAF No 2 SoTT, Cosford | |
| XX962 | SEPECAT Jaguar GR1A | RAF BFME, Muharraq | |
| XX965 | SEPECAT Jaguar GR1A | RAF No 226 OCU, Lossiemouth | |
| XX966 | SEPECAT Jaguar GR1A (8904M) [EL] | RAF No 1 SoTT, Halton | |
| XX967 | SEPECAT Jaguar GR1 [AC] (9006M) | RAF No 2 SoTT, Cosford | |
| XX968 | SEPECAT Jaguar GR1 [AJ] (9007M) | RAF No 2 SoTT, Cosford | |
| XX969 | SEPECAT Jaguar GR1A (8897M) [01] | RAF No 2 SoTT, Cosford | |
| XX970 | SEPECAT Jaguar GR1A [18] | RAF No 6 Sqn, Coltishall | |
| XX974 | SEPECAT Jaguar GR1A | RAF No 6 Sqn, Coltishall | |
| XX975 | SEPECAT Jaguar GR1 [07] (8905M) | RAF No 1 SoTT, Halton | |
| XX976 | SEPECAT Jaguar GR1 (8906M) [BD] | RAF No 1 SoTT, Halton | |
| XX977 | SEPECAT Jaguar GR1 | RAF, stored Shawbury | |
| XX979 | SEPECAT Jaguar GR1A [JS] | MoD(PE) A&AEE Boscombe Down | |
| XZ101 | SEPECAT Jaguar GR1A [Q] | RAF No 41 Sqn, Coltishall | |
| XZ103 | SEPECAT Jaguar GR1A [23] | RAF, stored Shawbury | |
| XZ104 | SEPECAT Jaguar GR1A | RAF No 41 Sqn, Coltishall | |
| XZ106 | SEPECAT Jaguar GR1A | RAF, JMU, Abingdon | |
| XZ107 | SEPECAT Jaguar GR1A [H] | RAF No 41 Sqn, Coltishall | |
| XZ108 | SEPECAT Jaguar GR1A [GD/04] | RAF No 54 Sqn, Coltishall | |
| XZ109 | SEPECAT Jaguar GR1A [GL] | RAF No 54 Sqn, Coltishall | |
| XZ111 | SEPECAT Jaguar GR1A [21] | RAF No 6 Sqn, Coltishall | |
| XZ112 | SEPECAT Jaguar GR1A | RAF, JMU, Abingdon | |
| XZ113 | SEPECAT Jaguar GR1A [D] | RAF No 41 Sqn, Coltishall | |
| XZ114 | SEPECAT Jaguar GR1A [B/25] | RAF No 41 Sqn, Coltishall | |
| XZ115 | SEPECAT Jaguar GR1A | RAF No 41 Sqn, Coltishall | |
| XZ117 | SEPECAT Jaguar GR1A | RAF, JMU, Abingdon | |
| XZ118 | SEPECAT Jaguar GR1A | RAF BFME, Muharraq | |
| XZ119 | SEPECAT Jaguar GR1A | RAF BFME, Muharraq | |
| XZ129 | HS Harrier GR3 [3C] | MoD(PE) Cranfield Institute of Technology | |
| XZ130 | HS Harrier GR3 [A] | RAF No 2 SoTT, Cosford | |
| XZ131 | HS Harrier GR3 [3B] | RAF No 233 OCU, Wittering | |
| XZ132 | HS Harrier GR3 [C] | RAF No 4 Sqn, Gütersloh | |
| XZ133 | HS Harrier GR3 [ ] | RAF No 4 Sqn, Gütersloh | |
| XZ135 | HS Harrier GR3 (8848M) (nose only) | RAF Exhibition Flight, Abingdon | |
| XZ138 | HS Harrier GR3 [14] | RAF St Athan Fire Section | |
| XZ145 | HS Harrier T4 [Q] | RAF No 4 Sqn, Gütersloh | |
| XZ146 | HS Harrier T4 [W] | RAF No 233 OCU, Wittering | |
| XZ147 | HS Harrier T4A | RAF No 233 OCU, Wittering | |
| XZ170 | WS Lynx AH9 | MoD(PE) Westlands, Yeovil | |
| XZ171 | WS Lynx AH7 [K] | AAC No 671 Sqn, Middle Wallop | |
| XZ172 | WS Lynx AH7 | AAC, Wroughton | |
| XZ173 | WS Lynx AH1 | AAC No 651 Sqn, Hildesheim | |
| XZ174 | WS Lynx AH1 | AAC No 652 Sqn, Hildesheim | |
| XZ175 | WS Lynx AH1 [A] | AAC No 671 Sqn, Middle Wallop | |
| XZ176 | WS Lynx AH7 | AAC No 654 Sqn, Detmold | |
| XZ177 | WS Lynx AH1 | AAC No 661 Sqn, Hildesheim | |
| XZ178 | WS Lynx AH1 [J] | AAC No 653 Sqn, Soest | |
| XZ179 | WS Lynx AH7 | AAC No 667 Sqn, Middle Wallop | |
| XZ180 | WS Lynx AH7 [T] | RM 3 CBAS, Yeovilton | |
| XZ181 | WS Lynx AH1 [W] | AAC No 663 Sqn, Soest | |
| XZ182 | WS Lynx AH7 [X] | RM 3 CBAS, Yeovilton | |

| Notes | Reg. | Type | Owner or Operator |
|---|---|---|---|
| | XZ183 | WS Lynx AH1 | AAC No 659 Sqn, Detmold |
| | XZ184 | WS Lynx AH1 [K] | AAC No 662 Sqn, Soest |
| | XZ185 | WS Lynx AH1 [L] | AAC No 662 Sqn, Soest |
| | XZ186 | WS Lynx AH7 | AAC No 665 Sqn, Aldergrove |
| | XZ187 | WS Lynx AH7 | AAC No 665 Sqn, Ballykelly |
| | XZ188 | WS Lynx AH7 | AAC No 655 Sqn, Aldergrove |
| | XZ190 | WS Lynx AH1 | AAC No 661 Sqn, Hildesheim |
| | XZ191 | WS Lynx AH1 | AAC No 657 Sqn, Topcliffe |
| | XZ192 | WS Lynx AH7 | AAC No 661 Sqn, Hildesheim |
| | XZ193 | WS Lynx AH1 | AAC No 656 Sqn, Netheravon |
| | XZ194 | WS Lynx AH1 [T] | AAC No 663 Sqn, Soest |
| | XZ195 | WS Lynx AH1 | AAC No 655 Sqn, Ballykelly |
| | XZ196 | WS Lynx AH1 [A] | AAC No 653 Sqn, Soest |
| | XZ197 | WS Lynx AH7 | AAC No 665 Sqn, Aldergrove |
| | XZ198 | WS Lynx AH7 | AAC Fleetlands |
| | XZ199 | WS Lynx AH7 | AAC No 669 Sqn, Detmold |
| | XZ203 | WS Lynx AH1 [C] | AAC No 653 Sqn, Soest |
| | XZ205 | WS Lynx AH7 | RM 3 CBAS, Yeovilton |
| | XZ206 | WS Lynx AH1 [B] | AAC No 671 Sqn, Middle Wallop |
| | XZ207 | WS Lynx AH7 | AAC No 665 Sqn, Ballykelly |
| | XZ208 | WS Lynx AH7 | AAC No 654 Sqn, Detmold |
| | XZ209 | WS Lynx AH1 [M] | AAC No 662 Sqn, Soest |
| | XZ210 | WS Lynx AH1 [U] | AAC No 663 Sqn, Soest |
| | XZ211 | WS Lynx AH1 | AAC No 661 Sqn, Hildesheim |
| | XZ212 | WS Lynx AH1 | AAC No 657 Sqn, Topcliffe |
| | XZ213 | WS Lynx AH1 [TAD213] | AAC SAE, Middle Wallop |
| | XZ214 | WS Lynx AH7 | AAC No 669 Sqn, Soest |
| | XZ215 | WS Lynx AH7 | AAC No 4 Regiment, Detmold |
| | XZ216 | WS Lynx AH1 | AAC No 663 Sqn, Soest |
| | XZ217 | WS Lynx AH7 | AAC No 654 Sqn, Detmold |
| | XZ218 | WS Lynx AH7 | AAC No 655 Sqn, Ballykelly |
| | XZ219 | WS Lynx AH7 | AAC No 654 Sqn, Detmold |
| | XZ220 | WS Lynx AH1 | AAC No 657 Sqn, Oakington |
| | XZ221 | WS Lynx AH7 [N] | AAC No 671 Sqn, Middle Wallop |
| | XZ222 | WS Lynx AH7 | AAC No 667 Sqn, Middle Wallop |
| | XZ227 | WS Lynx HAS3 [405/LO] | RN No 829 Sqn, Portland |
| | XZ228 | WS Lynx HAS3 [443/JP] | RN No 815 Sqn, Portland |
| | XZ229 | WS Lynx HAS3 [403/BX] | RN No 829 Sqn, Portland |
| | XZ230 | WS Lynx HAS3 [335/PO] | RN No 815 Sqn, Portland |
| | XZ231 | WS Lynx HAS3 [604/PO] | RN No 829 Sqn, Portland |
| | XZ232 | WS Lynx HAS3 [353/SD] | RN No 829 Sqn, Portland |
| | XZ233 | WS Lynx HAS3 [435/ED] | RN No 829 Sqn, Portland |
| | XZ234 | WS Lynx HAS3 [326/AW] | RN No 815 Sqn, Portland |
| | XZ235 | WS Lynx HAS3 [605/PO] | RN No 829 Sqn, Portland |
| | XZ236 | WS Lynx HAS3S | MoD(PE) Westlands, Yeovil |
| | XZ237 | WS Lynx HAS3 [412/CW] | RN No 829 Sqn, Portland |
| | XZ238 | WS Lynx HAS3 [645/PO] | RN No 702 Sqn, Portland |
| | XZ239 | WS Lynx HAS3 [321] | RN No 208 Flt, Gibraltar |
| | XZ240 | WS Lynx HAS3 [344/GW] | RN No 815 Sqn, Portland |
| | XZ241 | WS Lynx HAS3S [352/SD] | RN No 829 Sqn, Portland |
| | XZ243 | WS Lynx HAS3 [635] (wreck) | RNAS Portland, BDRT |
| | XZ245 | WS Lynx HAS3 [431/CY] | RN No 815 Sqn, Portland |
| | XZ246 | WS Lynx HAS3 [434/ED] | RN No 829 Sqn, Portland |
| | XZ248 | WS Lynx HAS3 [345] | RN No 815 Sqn, Portland |
| | XZ249 | WS Lynx HAS2 | RN Predannack Fire School |
| | XZ250 | WS Lynx HAS3 [603] | RN No 829 Sqn, Portland |
| | XZ252 | WS Lynx HAS3 [644/PO] | RN No 702 Sqn, Portland |
| | XZ254 | WS Lynx HAS3 [322] | RN No 815 Sqn, Portland |
| | XZ255 | WS Lynx HAS3 [466/AT] | RN No 829 Sqn, Portland |
| | XZ256 | WS Lynx HAS3 [350/CL] | RN No 829 Sqn, Portland |
| | XZ257 | WS Lynx HAS3 [634/PO] | RN No 702 Sqn, Portland |
| | XZ280 | BAe Nimrod AEW3 | RAF, stored Abingdon |
| | XZ281 | BAe Nimrod AEW3 | RAF, stored Abingdon |
| | XZ282 | BAe Nimrod AEW3 (9000M) | RAF NMSU, Kinloss |
| | XZ283 | BAe Nimrod AEW3 | RAF, stored Abingdon |
| | XZ284 | HS Nimrod MR2 | RAF Kinloss MR Wing |
| | XZ285 | BAe Nimrod AEW3 | RAF, stored Abingdon |
| | XZ286 | BAe Nimrod AEW3 | *Scrapped at Abingdon March 1990* |
| | XZ287 | BAe Nimrod AEW3 | RAF, stored Abingdon |
| | XZ290 | WS Gazelle AH1 | AAC, stored Wroughton |
| | XZ291 | WS Gazelle AH1 | AAC No 12 Flt, Wildenrath |
| | XZ292 | WS Gazelle AH1 | AAC No 654 Sqn, Detmold |

| Reg. | Type | Owner or Operator | Notes |
|---|---|---|---|
| XZ294 | WS Gazelle AH1 | AAC No 664 Sqn, Minden | |
| XZ295 | WS Gazelle AH1 | AAC No 12 Flt, Wildenrath | |
| XZ296 | WS Gazelle AH1 | AAC No 664 Sqn, Minden | |
| XZ298 | WS Gazelle AH1 | AAC No 669 Sqn, Detmold | |
| XZ299 | WS Gazelle AH1 | AAC No 657 Sqn, Topcliffe | |
| XZ300 | WS Gazelle AH1 | AAC No 664 Sqn, Minden | |
| XZ301 | WS Gazelle AH1 | AAC No 664 Sqn, Minden | |
| XZ302 | WS Gazelle AH1 | AAC No 655 Sqn, Ballykelly | |
| XZ303 | WS Gazelle AH1 [8] | AAC No 663 Sqn, Soest | |
| XZ304 | WS Gazelle AH1 | AAC No 664 Sqn, Minden | |
| XZ305 | WS Gazelle AH1 | AAC No 665 Sqn, Aldergrove | |
| XZ307 | WS Gazelle AH1 | AAC No 665 Sqn, Aldergrove | |
| XZ308 | WS Gazelle AH1 [L] | AAC No 670 Sqn, Middle Wallop | |
| XZ309 | WS Gazelle AH1 | AAC No 664 Sqn, Minden | |
| XZ310 | WS Gazelle AH1 | AAC No 661 Sqn, Hildesheim | |
| XZ311 | WS Gazelle AH1 | AAC No 664 Sqn, Minden | |
| XZ312 | WS Gazelle AH1 | AAC No 2 Flight, Netheravon | |
| XZ313 | WS Gazelle AH1 [S] | AAC No 670 Sqn, Middle Wallop | |
| XZ314 | WS Gazelle AH1 | AAC No 656 Sqn, Netheravon | |
| XZ315 | WS Gazelle AH1 | AAC No 665 Sqn, Aldergrove | |
| XZ316 | WS Gazelle AH1 [R] | AAC No 670 Sqn, Middle Wallop | |
| XZ317 | WS Gazelle AH1 [Q] | AAC No 670 Sqn, Middle Wallop | |
| XZ318 | WS Gazelle AH1 | AAC No 670 Sqn, Middle Wallop | |
| XZ320 | WS Gazelle AH1 | AAC, stored Wroughton | |
| XZ321 | WS Gazelle AH1 | AAC No 665 Sqn, Aldergrove | |
| XZ322 | WS Gazelle AH1 [N] | AAC No 670 Sqn, Middle Wallop | |
| XZ323 | WS Gazelle AH1 | AAC SAE, Middle Wallop | |
| XZ324 | WS Gazelle AH1 | AAC, stored Wroughton | |
| XZ325 | WS Gazelle AH1 [T] | AAC No 670 Sqn, Middle Wallop | |
| XZ326 | WS Gazelle AH1 [C] | RM, stored Wroughton | |
| XZ327 | WS Gazelle AH1 [B1] | AAC No 670 Sqn, Middle Wallop | |
| XZ328 | WS Gazelle AH1 | AAC No 657 Sqn, Topcliffe | |
| XZ329 | WS Gazelle AH1 [J] | AAC No 670 Sqn, Middle Wallop | |
| XZ330 | WS Gazelle AH1 [D] | AAC No 658 Sqn, Netheravon | |
| XZ331 | WS Gazelle AH1 | AAC, stored Wroughton | |
| XZ332 | WS Gazelle AH1 [O] | AAC No 670 Sqn, Middle Wallop | |
| XZ333 | WS Gazelle AH1 [A] | AAC No 670 Sqn, Middle Wallop | |
| XZ334 | WS Gazelle AH1 [M] | AAC No 662 Sqn, Soest | |
| XZ335 | WS Gazelle AH1 | AAC No 3 Flt, Topcliffe | |
| XZ337 | WS Gazelle AH1 | AAC No 664 Sqn, Minden | |
| XZ338 | WS Gazelle AH1 [X] | AAC No 670 Sqn, Middle Wallop | |
| XZ339 | WS Gazelle AH1 | MoD(PE) Westlands, Yeovil | |
| XZ340 | WS Gazelle AH1 | AAC, stored Wroughton | |
| XZ341 | WS Gazelle AH1 | AAC No 667 Sqn, Middle Wallop | |
| XZ342 | WS Gazelle AH1 [E] | AAC No 653 Sqn, Soest | |
| XZ343 | WS Gazelle AH1 | AAC stored, Wroughton | |
| XZ344 | WS Gazelle AH1 | AAC No 3 Flt, Topcliffe | |
| XZ345 | WS Gazelle AH1 | AAC No 3 Flt, Topcliffe | |
| XZ346 | WS Gazelle AH1 | AAC No 665 Sqn, Aldergrove | |
| XZ347 | WS Gazelle AH1 | AAC No 3 Flt, Topcliffe | |
| XZ348 | WS Gazelle AH1 (wreckage) | AAC stored, Wroughton | |
| XZ349 | WS Gazelle AH1 [M] | AAC No 670 Sqn, Middle Wallop | |
| XZ355 | SEPECAT Jaguar GR1A | RAF No 41 Sqn, Middle Wallop | |
| XZ356 | SEPECAT Jaguar GR1A | RAF BFME, Muharraq | |
| XZ357 | SEPECAT Jaguar GR1A | RAF No 41 Sqn, Coltishall | |
| XZ358 | SEPECAT Jaguar GR1A | RAF BFME, Muharraq | |
| XZ360 | SEPECAT Jaguar GR1A [N] | Stored, Shawbury | |
| XZ361 | SEPECAT Jaguar GR1A [25] | RAF No 54 Sqn, Coltishall | |
| XZ362 | SEPECAT Jaguar GR1A [ED] | RAF No 6 Sqn, Coltishall | |
| XZ363 | SEPECAT Jaguar GR1A | RAF No 41 Sqn, Coltishall | |
| *XZ363* | SEPECAT Jaguar GR1A Replica [A] (BAPC 151) | RAF Exhibition Flight, Abingdon | |
| XZ364 | SEPECAT Jaguar GR1A | RAF BFME, Muharraq | |
| XZ366 | SEPECAT Jaguar GR1A [22] | RAF, stored Shawbury | |
| XZ367 | SEPECAT Jaguar GR1A | RAF BFME, Muharraq | |
| XZ368 | SEPECAT Jaguar GR1 [8900M] [AG] | RAF No 2 SoTT, Cosford | |
| XZ369 | SEPECAT Jaguar GR1A | RAF No 6 Sqn, Coltishall | |
| XZ370 | SEPECAT Jaguar GR1 [BN] (9004M) | RAF No 2 SoTT, Cosford | |
| XZ371 | SEPECAT Jaguar GR1 (8907M) [AP] | RAF No 2 SoTT, Cosford | |
| XZ372 | SEPECAT Jaguar GR1A | RAF No 6 Sqn, Coltishall | |

| Notes | Reg. | Type | Owner or Operator |
|---|---|---|---|
| | XZ373 | SEPECAT Jaguar GR1A | RAF No 54 Sqn, Coltishall |
| | XZ374 | SEPECAT Jaguar GR1 (9005M) | RAF No 2 SoTT, Cosford |
| | XZ375 | SEPECAT Jaguar GR1A | RAF BFME, Muharraq |
| | XZ377 | SEPECAT Jaguar GR1A | RAF No 6 Sqn, Coltishall |
| | XZ378 | SEPECAT Jaguar GR1A [EP] | RAF No 6 Sqn, Coltishall |
| | XZ381 | SEPECAT Jaguar GR1A [GB] | RAF No 54 Sqn, Coltishall |
| | XZ382 | SEPECAT Jaguar GR1 (8908M) [AE] | RAF No 1 SoTT, Halton |
| | XZ383 | SEPECAT Jaguar GR1 (8901M) [AF] | RAF No 2 SoTT, Cosford |
| | XZ384 | SEPECAT Jaguar GR1 [BC] (8954M) | RAF No 2 SoTT, Cosford |
| | XZ385 | SEPECAT Jaguar GR1A [GM] | RAF No 54 Sqn, Coltishall |
| | XZ387 | SEPECAT Jaguar GR1A [GG] | *Crashed Solway Firth 12/9/90* |
| | XZ389 | SEPECAT Jaguar GR1 [BL] (8946M) | RAF No 1 SoTT, Halton |
| | XZ390 | SEPECAT Jaguar GR1A (9003M) | RAF No 2 SoTT, Cosford |
| | XZ391 | SEPECAT Jaguar GR1A [GN] | RAF, stored Shawbury |
| | XZ392 | SEPECAT Jaguar GR1A [GQ] | RAF No 54 Sqn, Coltishall |
| | XZ394 | SEPECAT Jaguar GR1A [GN] | RAF No 54 Sqn, Coltishall |
| | XZ396 | SEPECAT Jaguar GR1A [22] | RAF No 6 Sqn, Coltishall |
| | XZ398 | SEPECAT Jaguar GR1A [GA/01] (JI007) | RAF No 54 Sqn, Coltishall |
| | XZ399 | SEPECAT Jaguar GR1A [03] | RAF No 226 OCU, Lossiemouth |
| | XZ400 | SEPECAT Jaguar GR1A [GH/07] | RAF No 54 Sqn, Coltishall |
| | XZ431 | HS Buccaneer S2B | RAF No 12 Sqn, Lossiemouth |
| | XZ432 | HS Buccaneer S2B | RAF No 12 Sqn, Lossiemouth |
| | XZ439 | BAe Sea Harrier FRS2 [2] | MoD(PE) BAe Dunsfold |
| | XZ440 | BAe Sea Harrier FRS1 [126/N] | RN No AIU, Lee-on-Solent |
| | XZ445 | BAe Harrier T4A [722] | RNAS Yeovilton for spares |
| | XZ451 | BAe Sea Harrier FRS1 [005/R] | *Crashed off Sardinia, 1 December 1989* |
| | XZ455 | BAe Sea Harrier FRS1 [715] | RN No 899 Sqn, Yeovilton |
| | XZ457 | BAe Sea Harrier FRS1 [003/R] | RN No 801 Sqn, Yeovilton |
| | XZ459 | BAe Sea Harrier FRS1 [006/R] | RN No 801 Sqn, Yeovilton |
| | XZ460 | BAe Sea Harrier FRS1 [128/N] | *Crashed off Sardinia 8 May 1990* |
| | XZ492 | BAe Sea Harrier FRS1 [712] | RN No 899 Sqn, Yeovilton |
| | XZ493 | BAe Sea Harrier FRS1 [716] | RN St Athen, store |
| | XZ494 | BAe Sea Harrier FRS1 [716] | RN No 899 Sqn, Yeovilton |
| | XZ495 | BAe Sea Harrier FRS1 | RN AMG, Yeovilton |
| | XZ497 | BAe Sea Harrier FRS1 | MoD(PE) BAe Dunsfold |
| | XZ498 | BAe Sea Harrier FRS1 [001/R] | RN AMG, Yeovilton |
| | XZ499 | BAe Sea Harrier FRS1 [001/R] | RN No 801 Sqn, Yeovilton |
| | XZ550 | Slingsby Venture T2 (wreck) | RAF, CGMF, Syerston |
| | XZ551 | Slingsby Venture T2 | RAF No 633 VGS, Cosford |
| | XZ552 | Slingsby Venture T2 [A] | RAF Linton-on-Ouse, stored |
| | XZ553 | Slingsby Venture T2 | RAF No 663 VGS, Kinloss |
| | XZ554 | Slingsby Venture T2 [4] | RAF No 633 VGS, Cosford |
| | XZ555 | Slingsby Venture T2 | RAF Linton-on-Ouse, stored |
| | XZ556 | Slingsby Venture T2 [56] | RAF Ternhill, stored |
| | XZ557 | Slingsby Venture T2 [7] | RAF Little Rissington, stored |
| | XZ558 | Slingsby Venture T2 [8] | RAF No 624 VGS, Chivenor |
| | XZ559 | Slingsby Venture T2 [9] | RAF Syerston, stored |
| | XZ560 | Slingsby Venture T2 [0] | RAF No 633 VGS, Cosford |
| | XZ561 | Slingsby Venture T2 (wreck) | RAF CGMF, Syerston |
| | XZ562 | Slingsby Venture T2 | RAF Syerston, stored |
| | XZ563 | Slingsby Venture T2 [3] | RAF No 624 VGS, Chivenor |
| | XZ564 | Slingsby Venture T2 | RAF No 663 VGS, Kinloss |
| | XZ570 | WS61 Sea King HAS5 (mod) | MoD(PE) Westlands, Yeovil |
| | XZ571 | WS61 Sea King HAS5 [136] | RN No 826 Sqn, Culdrose |
| | XZ574 | WS61 Sea King HAS5 [506] | RN No 810 Sqn, Culdrose |
| | XZ575 | WS61 Sea King HAS5 [599] | RN No 706 Sqn, Culdrose |
| | XZ576 | WS61 Sea King HAS6 | MoD(PE) Westlands, Yeovil |
| | XZ577 | WS61 Sea King HAS5 [138] | RN No 826 Sqn, Culdrose |
| | XZ578 | WS61 Sea King HAS5 [581] | RN No 706 Sqn, Culdrose |
| | XZ579 | WS61 Sea King HAS6 [017/R] | RNAY Fleetlands |
| | XZ580 | WS61 Sea King HAS6 | RN No 810 Sqn, Culdrose |
| | XZ581 | WS61 Sea King HAS6 [704/PW] | RN No 819 Sqn, Prestwick |
| | XZ582 | WS61 Sea King HAS5 [264/N] | *Ditched off Bermuda, 27 October 1989* |
| | XZ585 | WS61 Sea King HAR3 | RNAY Fleetlands on rebuild |
| | XZ586 | WS61 Sea King HAR3 [S] | RAF No 78 Sqn, Mount Pleasant, FI |
| | XZ587 | WS61 Sea King HAR3 | RAF No 202 Sqn SAR* |
| | XZ588 | WS61 Sea King HAR3 | RAF No 202 Sqn SAR* |
| | XZ589 | WS61 Sea King HAR3 | RAF No 202 Sqn SAR* |

| Reg. | Type | Owner or Operator | Notes |
|---|---|---|---|
| XZ590 | WS61 Sea King HAR3 | RAF No 202 Sqn SAR* | |
| XZ591 | WS61 Sea King HAR3 [S] | RAF No 202 Sqn, SAR* | |
| XZ592 | WS61 Sea King HAR3 | RAF SKTU, RNAS Culdrose | |
| XZ593 | WS61 Sea King HAR3 | RAF No 202 Sqn SAR* | |
| XZ594 | WS61 Sea King HAR3 | RAF No 202 Sqn SAR* | |
| XZ595 | WS61 Sea King HAR3 | RAF No 202 Sqn SAR* | |
| XZ596 | WS61 Sea King HAR3 | RAF No 202 Sqn SAR* | |
| XZ597 | WS61 Sea King HAR3 | RAF No 78 Sqn, Mount Pleasant, FI | |
| XZ598 | WS61 Sea King HAR3 | RAF No 202 Sqn SAR* | |
| XZ599 | WS61 Sea King HAR3 [S] | RAF No 202 Sqn SAR* | |
| XZ605 | WS Lynx AH1 [72X] | RM Fleetlands | |
| XZ606 | WS Lynx AH7 | AAC No 654 Sqn, Detmold | |
| XZ607 | WS Lynx AH1 [E] | AAC No 671 Sqn, Middle Wallop | |
| XZ608 | WS Lynx AH7 | AAC No 651 Sqn, Hildesheim | |
| XZ609 | WS Lynx AH1 | AAC No 657 Sqn, Topcliffe | |
| XZ610 | WS Lynx AH7 | AAC No 669 Sqn, Detmold | |
| XZ611 | WS Lynx AH1 [H] | AAC No 671 Sqn, Middle Wallop | |
| XZ612 | WS Lynx AH7 [Y] | RM Fleetlands | |
| XZ613 | WS Lynx AH7 | AAC No 667 Sqn, Middle Wallop | |
| XZ614 | WS Lynx AH1 [Z] | RM 3 CBAS, Yeovilton | |
| XZ615 | WS Lynx AH1 | AAC No 651 Sqn, Hildesheim | |
| XZ616 | WS Lynx AH7 | AAC No 654 Sqn, Detmold | |
| XZ617 | WS Lynx AH7 [F] | AAC No 671 Sqn, Middle Wallop | |
| XZ631 | Panavia Tornado GR1T | MoD(PE) BAe Warton | |
| XZ641 | WS Lynx AH7 | AAC SAE, Middle Wallop | |
| XZ642 | WS Lynx AH7 | AAC No 654 Sqn, Detmold | |
| XZ643 | WS Lynx AH1 | AAC No 663 Sqn, Soest | |
| XZ644 | WS Lynx AH1 | AAC No 657 Sqn, Topcliffe | |
| XZ645 | WS Lynx AH1 | AAC No 659 Sqn, Detmold | |
| XZ646 | WS Lynx AH7 | AAC No 669 Sqn, Detmold | |
| XZ647 | WS Lynx AH7 [N] | AAC Fleetlands | |
| XZ648 | WS Lynx AH7 [D] | AAC No 671 Sqn, Middle Wallop | |
| XZ649 | WS Lynx AH7 | AAC No 665 Sqn, Aldergrove | |
| XZ650 | WS Lynx AH7 | AAC No 664 Sqn, Minden | |
| XZ651 | WS Lynx AH7 | AAC No 651 Sqn, Hildesheim | |
| XZ652 | WS Lynx AH1 | AAC No 656 Sqn, Netheravon | |
| XZ653 | WS Lynx AH7 | AAC No 659 Sqn, Detmold | |
| XZ654 | WS Lynx AH1 | AAC SAE, Middle Wallop | |
| XZ655 | WS Lynx AH1 | AAC No 652 Sqn, Hildesheim | |
| XZ661 | WS Lynx AH1 | AAC No 652 Sqn, Hildesheim | |
| XZ662 | WS Lynx AH1 | AAC No 652 Sqn, Hildesheim | |
| XZ663 | WS Lynx AH1 [X] | AAC No 653 Sqn, Soest | |
| XZ664 | WS Lynx AH7 | AAC Fleetlands | |
| XZ665 | WS Lynx AH7 | AAC Fleetlands | |
| XZ666 | WS Lynx AH7 | AAC Fleetlands | |
| XZ667 | WS Lynx AH1 [B] | AAC No 653 Sqn, Soest | |
| XZ668 | WS Lynx AH1 [E] | AAC No 653 Sqn, Soest | |
| XZ669 | WS Lynx AH1 [D] | AAC No 653 Sqn, Soest | |
| XZ670 | WS Lynx AH7 | AAC Fleetlands | |
| XZ671 | WS Lynx AH9 | MoD(PE) Westlands, Yeovil | |
| XZ672 | WS Lynx AH1 [N] | AAC No 662 Sqn, Soest | |
| XZ673 | WS Lynx AH7 | AAC Fleetlands | |
| XZ674 | WS Lynx AH1 | AAC No 664 Sqn, Minden | |
| XZ675 | WS Lynx AH1 [M] | AAC No 671 Sqn, Middle Wallop | |
| XZ676 | WS Lynx AH1 | AAC No 656 Sqn, Netheravon | |
| XZ677 | WS Lynx AH1 | AAC No 651 Sqn, Hildesheim | |
| XZ678 | WS Lynx AH1 | AAC No 651 Sqn, Hildesheim | |
| XZ679 | WS Lynx AH7 | AAC, No 659 Sqn, Detmold | |
| XZ680 | WS Lynx AH7 | MoD(PE), Westlands, Yeovil | |
| XZ681 | WS Lynx AH1 | AAC Middle Wallop, BDRT | |
| XZ689 | WS Lynx HAS3 [420/EX] | RN No 815 Sqn, Portland | |
| XZ690 | WS Lynx HAS3 [635/PO] | RN No 702 Sqn, Portland | |
| XZ691 | WS Lynx HAS3 [320/AZ] | RN No 815 Sqn, Portland | |
| XZ692 | WS Lynx HAS3 [643/PO] | RN No 702 Sqn, Portland | |
| XZ693 | WS Lynx HAS3 [640/PO] | RN No 702 Sqn, Portland | |
| XZ694 | WS Lynx HAS3 [360] | RN No 815 Sqn, Portland | |
| XZ695 | WS Lynx HAS3S [431/CY] | RN No 815 Sqn, Portland | |
| XZ696 | WS Lynx HAS3 [411/EB] | RN No 815 Sqn, Portland | |
| XZ697 | WS Lynx HAS3 | RN Fleetlands | |

**Note:** *The SAR Wing and SAREW are based at RAF Finningley, with the SKTU at RNAS Culdrose and with No 202 Sqn SAR detached flights: A Flt—RAF Boulmer; B Flt—RAF Brawdy; C Flt—RAF Manston; D Flt—RAF Lossiemouth; E Flt—RAF Leconfield.

| Notes | Reg. | Type | Owner or Operator |
|---|---|---|---|
| | XZ698 | WS Lynx HAS3 [479] | RN Lynx Support Flight, Portland |
| | XZ699 | WS Lynx HAS3 [302/PO] | RN AMG, Portland |
| | XZ719 | WS Lynx HAS3 [BT] | RN No 829 Sqn, Portland |
| | XZ720 | WS Lynx HAS3 [336] | RN No 829 Sqn, Portland |
| | XZ721 | WS Lynx HAS3 | RN AMG, Portland |
| | XZ722 | WS Lynx HAS3 [327] | RN No 815 Sqn, Portland |
| | XZ723 | WS Lynx HAS3 [454/PN] | RN No 829 Sqn, Portland |
| | XZ724 | WS Lynx HAS3 | RN AMG, Portland |
| | XZ725 | WS Lynx HAS3 [432] | RN No 815 Sqn, Portland |
| | XZ726 | WS Lynx HAS3 [464/DN] | RN No 829 Sqn, Portland |
| | XZ727 | WS Lynx HAS3 [360/MC] | RN No 815 Sqn, Portland |
| | XZ728 | WS Lynx HAS3 [300/PO] | RN No 815 Sqn, Portland |
| | XZ729 | WS Lynx HAS3 [471/PB] | RN No 829 Sqn, Portland |
| | XZ730 | WS Lynx HAS3 [341/AG] | RN No 815 Sqn, Portland |
| | XZ731 | WS Lynx HAS3 [641/PO] | RN No 702 Sqn, Portland |
| | XZ732 | WS Lynx HAS3 [303] | RN No 815 Sqn, Portland |
| | XZ733 | WS Lynx HAS3 [328/BA] | RN Fleetlands |
| | XZ734 | WS Lynx HAS3 [475/HM] | *Written off Gibraltar Jul 90* |
| | XZ735 | WS Lynx HAS3 [602/PO] | RN No 829 Sqn, Portland |
| | XZ736 | WS Lynx HAS3 [424/MV] | RN No 829 Sqn, Portland |
| | XZ918 | WS61 Sea King HAS5 [589] | RN No 706 Sqn, Culdrose |
| | XZ920 | WS61 Sea King HAR5 [822/CU] | RN No 771 Sqn, Culdrose |
| | XZ921 | WS61 Sea King HAS5 [593] | RN No 706 Sqn, Culdrose |
| | XZ922 | WS61 Sea King HAS6 | RN AMG, Culdrose |
| | XZ930 | WS Gazelle HT3 [Q] | RAF No 2 FTS, Shawbury |
| | XZ931 | WS Gazelle HT3 [R] | RAF No 2 FTS, Shawbury |
| | XZ932 | WS Gazelle HT3 [S] | RAF No 2 FTS, Shawbury |
| | XZ933 | WS Gazelle HT3 [T] | RAF No 2 FTS, Shawbury |
| | XZ934 | WS Gazelle HT3 [U] | RAF No 2 FTS, Shawbury |
| | XZ935 | WS Gazelle HT3 | RAF No 32 Sqn, Northolt |
| | XZ936 | WS Gazelle HT3 | MoD(PE) ETPS, Boscombe Down |
| | XZ937 | WS Gazelle HT3 [Y] | RAF No 2 FTS, Shawbury |
| | XZ938 | WS Gazelle HT2 [45/CU] | RN No 705 Sqn, Culdrose |
| | XZ939 | WS Gazelle HT3 [Z] | MoD(PE) ETPS, Boscombe Down |
| | XZ940 | WS Gazelle HT3 | RAF No 7 Sqn, hack |
| | XZ941 | WS Gazelle HT3 [B] | RAF No 2 FTS, Shawbury |
| | XZ942 | WS Gazelle HT2 [42/CU] | RN No 705 Sqn, Culdrose |
| | XZ964 | BAe Harrier GR3 | RAF No 233 OCU, Wittering |
| | XZ965 | BAe Harrier GR3 [L] | RAF No 4 Sqn, Gütersloh |
| | XZ966 | BAe Harrier GR3 [K] | RAF No 4 Sqn, Gütersloh |
| | XZ967 | BAe Harrier GR3 [F] | RAF No 4 Sqn, Gütersloh |
| | XZ968 | BAe Harrier GR3 [3G] | RAF No 233 OCU, Wittering |
| | XZ969 | BAe Harrier GR3 [D] | RAF St Athan |
| | XZ970 | BAe Harrier GR3 [H] | RAF No 4 Sqn, Gütersloh |
| | XZ971 | BAe Harrier GR3 [D] | RAF No 1417 Flt, Belize |
| | XZ987 | BAe Harrier GR3 [C] | RAF No 1417 Flt, Belize |
| | XZ990 | BAe Harrier GR3 [F] | RAF No 1417 Flt, Belize |
| | XZ991 | BAe Harrier GR3 [X] | RAF No 4 Sqn, Gütersloh |
| | XZ993 | BAe Harrier GR3 [M] | RAF No 4 Sqn, Gütersloh |
| | XZ994 | BAe Harrier GR3 | RAF Wittering |
| | XZ995 | BAe Harrier GR3 [C] | RAF Wittering |
| | XZ996 | BAe Harrier GR3 [G] | RAF No 1417 Flt, Belize |
| | XZ997 | BAe Harrier GR3 [V] | RAF No 4 Sqn, Gütersloh |
| | XZ998 | BAe Harrier GR3 [D] | RAF Wittering |
| | ZA101 | BAe Hawk 100 (G-HAWK/XX155) | BAe Warton |
| | ZA105 | WS61 Sea King HAR3 [S] | RAF SKTU, Culdrose |
| | ZA110 | BAe Jetstream T2 [573/CU] (G-AXUO) | RN No 750 Sqn, Culdrose |
| | ZA111 | BAe Jetstream T2 [574/CU] (G-AXFV) | RN No 750 Sqn, Culdrose |
| | ZA126 | WS61 Sea King HAS6 [509] | RN No 810 Sqn, Culdrose |
| | ZA127 | WS61 Sea King HAS5 [504] | RN No 810 Sqn, Culdrose |
| | ZA128 | WS61 Sea King HAS5 [598] | RN No 706 Sqn, Culdrose |
| | ZA129 | WS61 Sea King HAS6 [012] | RN No 820 Sqn, Culdrose |
| | ZA130 | WS61 Sea King HAS6 [701] | RN No 819 Sqn, Prestwick |
| | ZA131 | WS61 Sea King HAS5 [133] | RN No 826 Sqn, Culdrose |
| | ZA133 | WS61 Sea King HAS5 [505] | RN No 810 Sqn, Culdrose |
| | ZA134 | WS61 Sea King HAS6 [702] | RN No 819 Sqn, Prestwick |
| | ZA135 | WS61 Sea King HAS6 [705/PW] | RN No 819 Sqn, Prestwick |
| | ZA136 | WS61 Sea King HAS6 [706/PW] | RN No 819 Sqn, Prestwick |
| | ZA137 | WS61 Sea King HAS5 [137] | RN No 826 Sqn, Culdrose |
| | ZA140 | BAe VC10 K2 (G-ARVL) [A] | RAF No 101 Sqn, Brize Norton |

| Reg. | Type | Owner or Operator | Notes |
|---|---|---|---|
| ZA141 | BAe VC10 K2 (G-ARVG) [B] | RAF No 101 Sqn, Brize Norton | |
| ZA142 | BAe VC10 K2 (G-ARVI) [C] | RAF No 101 Sqn, Brize Norton | |
| ZA143 | BAe VC10 K2 (G-ARVK) [D] | RAF No 101 Sqn, Brize Norton | |
| ZA144 | BAe VC10 K2 (G-ARVC) [E] | RAF No 101 Sqn, Brize Norton | |
| ZA147 | BAe VC10 K3 (5H-MMT) [F] | RAF No 101 Sqn, Brize Norton | |
| ZA148 | BAe VC10 K3 (5Y-ADA) [G] | RAF No 101 Sqn, Brize Norton | |
| ZA149 | BAe VC10 K3 (5X-UVJ) [H] | RAF No 101 Sqn, Brize Norton | |
| ZA150 | BAe VC10 K3 (5H-MOG) [J] | RAF No 101 Sqn, Brize Norton | |
| ZA166 | WS61 Sea King HAS5 [590] | RN AMG, Culdrose | |
| ZA167 | WS61 Sea King HAS5 [264/N] | RN No 814 Sqn, Culdrose | |
| ZA168 | WS61 Sea King HAS6 [703/PW] | RN No 819 Sqn, Prestwick | |
| ZA169 | WS61 Sea King HAS6 [011] | RN No 820 Sqn, Culdrose | |
| ZA170 | WS61 Sea King HAS5 [584] | RN No 706 Sqn, Culdrose | |
| ZA175 | BAe Sea Harrier FRS1 [711] | RN No 899 Sqn, Yeovilton | |
| ZA176 | BAe Sea Harrier FRS1 [122/N] | RN No 800 Sqn, Yeovilton | |
| ZA193 | BAe Sea Harrier FRS1 [004/R] | RN No 801 Sqn, Yeovilton | |
| ZA195 | BAe Sea Harrier FRS2 | MoD(PE) A&AEE, Boscombe Down | |
| ZA250 | BAe Harrier T52 (G-VTOL) | Brooklands Aviation Museum, | |
| ZA254 | Panavia Tornado F2 | MoD(PE) BAe Warton | |
| ZA267 | Panavia Tornado F2T | MoD(PE) A&AEE Boscombe Down | |
| ZA283 | Panavia Tornado F2 | MoD(PE) BAe Warton | |
| ZA291 | WS61 Sea King HC4 | RN AMG, Yeovilton | |
| ZA292 | WS61 Sea King HC4 [ZW] | RN No 707 Sqn, Yeovilton | |
| ZA293 | WS61 Sea King HC4 [VP] | RN No 846 Sqn, Saudi Arabia | |
| ZA295 | WS61 Sea King HC4 [ZU] | RN No 707 Sqn, Yeovilton | |
| ZA296 | WS61 Sea King HC4 [VK] | RN No 846 Sqn, Saudi Arabia | |
| ZA297 | WS61 Sea King HC4 [F] | RN AMG, Yeovilton | |
| ZA298 | WS61 Sea King HC4 [WA] (G-BJNM) | RN No 848 Sqn, Saudi Arabia | |
| ZA299 | WS61 Sea King HC4 [ZV] | RN No 707 Sqn, Yeovilton | |
| ZA310 | WS61 Sea King HC4 | RN No 848 Sqn, Yeovilton | |
| ZA312 | WS61 Sea King HC4 [B] | RN No 845 Sqn, Saudi Arabia | |
| ZA313 | WS61 Sea King HC4 [E] | RN No 845 Sqn, Saudi Arabia | |
| ZA314 | WS61 Sea King HC4 [WD] | RN No 848 Sqn, Saudi Arabia | |
| ZA319 | Panavia Tornado GR1T [B-11] | RAF TTTE, Cottesmore | |
| ZA320 | Panavia Tornado GR1T [B-01] | RAF TTTE, Cottesmore | |
| ZA321 | Panavia Tornado GR1 [B-58] | RAF TTTE, Cottesmore | |
| ZA322 | Panavia Tornado GR1 [B-50] | RAF TTTE, Cottesmore | |
| ZA323 | Panavia Tornado GR1T [B-14] | RAF TTTE, Cottesmore | |
| ZA324 | Panavia Tornado GR1T [B-02] | RAF TTTE, Cottesmore | |
| ZA325 | Panavia Tornado GR1T [B-03] | RAF TTTE, Cottesmore | |
| ZA326 | Panavia Tornado GR1T | MoD(PE) RAE Bedford | |
| ZA327 | Panavia Tornado GR1 [O] | RAF No 617 Sqn, Marham | |
| ZA328 | Panavia Tornado GR1 | MoD(PE) BAe Warton | |
| ZA330 | Panavia Tornado GR1T [B-08] | RAF TTTE, Cottesmore | |
| ZA352 | Panavia Tornado GR1T [B-04] | RAF TTTE, Cottesmore | |
| ZA353 | Panavia Tornado GR1 [B-53] | RAF TTTE, Cottesmore | |
| ZA354 | Panavia Tornado GR1 | MoD(PE) BAe Warton | |
| ZA355 | Panavia Tornado GR1 [B-54] | RAF TTTE, Cottesmore | |
| ZA356 | Panavia Tornado GR1T [B-07] | RAF TTTE, Cottesmore | |
| ZA357 | Panavia Tornado GR1T [T] | RAF No 13 Sqn, Honington | |
| ZA358 | Panavia Tornado GR1T | RAF TWCU/45 Sqn, Honington | |
| ZA359 | Panavia Tornado GR1 [B-55] | RAF TTTE, Cottesmore | |
| ZA360 | Panavia Tornado GR1 | RAF TWCU/45 Sqn, Honington | |
| ZA361 | Panavia Tornado GR1 [B-57] | RAF TTTE, Cottesmore | |
| ZA362 | Panavia Tornado GR1T | RAF TWCU/45 Sqn, Honington | |
| ZA365 | Panavia Tornado GR1T [GZ] | RAF No 20 Sqn, Laarbruch | |
| ZA367 | Panavia Tornado GR1T | RAF TWCU/45 Sqn, Honington | |
| ZA368 | Panavia Tornado GR1T | RAF TWCU/45 Sqn, Honington | |
| ZA369 | Panavia Tornado GR1A [II] | RAF No 2 Sqn, Laarbruch | |
| ZA370 | Panavia Tornado GR1A [A] | RAF No 2 Sqn, Laarbruch | |
| ZA371 | Panavia Tornado GR1A [C] | RAF No 2 Sqn, Laarbruch | |
| ZA372 | Panavia Tornado GR1A [E] | RAF No 2 Sqn, Laarbruch | |
| ZA373 | Panavia Tornado GR1A [H] | RAF No 2 Sqn, Laarbruch | |
| ZA374 | Panavia Tornado GR1 [CN] | RAF BFME, Saudi Arabia | |
| ZA375 | Panavia Tornado GR1 [BN] | RAF No 14 Sqn, Bruggen | |
| ZA376 | Panavia Tornado GR1 [JL] | RAF No 27 Sqn, Marham | |
| ZA392 | Panavia Tornado GR1 [EK] | RAF BFME, Saudi Arabia | |
| ZA393 | Panavia Tornado GR1 [CQ] | RAF No 17 Sqn, Bruggen | |
| ZA394 | Panavia Tornado GR1A [I] | RAF No 2 Sqn, Laarbruch | |
| ZA395 | Panavia Tornado GR1A [N] | RAF No 2 Sqn, Laarbruch | |
| ZA396 | Panavia Tornado GR1 [GE] | RAF BFME, Muharraq | |

| Notes | Reg. | Type | Owner or Operator |
|---|---|---|---|
| | ZA397 | Panavia Tornado GR1A [O] | RAF No 2 Sqn, Laarbruch |
| | ZA398 | Panavia Tornado GR1A [S] | RAF No 2 Sqn, Laarbruch |
| | ZA399 | Panavia Tornado GR1 [GA] | RAF BFME, Saudi Arabia |
| | ZA400 | Panavia Tornado GR1A [T] | RAF No 2 Sqn, Laarbruch |
| | ZA401 | Panavia Tornado GR1A [GJ] | MoD(PE), A&AEE, Boscombe Down |
| | ZA402 | Panavia Tornado GR1 | MoD(PE) BAe Warton |
| | ZA403 | Panavia Tornado GR1 [CO] | RAF No 17 Sqn, Bruggen |
| | ZA404 | Panavia Tornado GR1A [W] | RAF No 2 Sqn, Laarbruch |
| | ZA405 | Panavia Tornado GR1A [Y] | RAF No 2 Sqn, Laarbruch |
| | ZA406 | Panavia Tornado GR1A [DN] | RAF No 31 Sqn, Bruggen |
| | ZA407 | Panavia Tornado GR1 | RAF TWCU/45 Sqn, Honington |
| | ZA409 | Panavia Tornado GR1T | RAF TWCU/45 Sqn, Honington |
| | ZA410 | Panavia Tornado GR1T [EX] | RAF No 15 Sqn, Laarbruch |
| | ZA411 | Panavia Tornado GR1T [GY] | RAF No 20 Sqn, Laarbruch |
| | ZA412 | Panavia Tornado GR1T [FX] | RAF No 16 Sqn, Laarbruch |
| | ZA446 | Panavia Tornado GR1 [F] | RAF No 15 Sqn, Laarbruch |
| | *ZA446* | Panavia Tornado GR1 (Replica) (BAPC155) [F] | RAF Exhibition Flight, Abingdon |
| | ZA447 | Panavia Tornado GR1 [EA] | RAF BFME, Saudi Arabia |
| | ZA449 | Panavia Tornado GR1 | MoD(PE), RAE Bedford |
| | ZA450 | Panavia Tornado GR1 [EC] | RAF No 15 Sqn, Laarbruch |
| | ZA452 | Panavia Tornado GR1 [GK] | RAF BFME, Saudi Arabia |
| | ZA453 | Panavia Tornado GR1 [EG] | RAF No 15 Sqn, Laarbruch |
| | ZA454 | Panavia Tornado GR1 [EH] | *Crashed CFB Goose Bay, 30 April 1990* |
| | ZA455 | Panavia Tornado GR1 [EJ] | RAF BFME, Saudi Arabia |
| | ZA456 | Panavia Tornado GR1 [GB] | RAF No 20 Sqn, Laarbruch |
| | ZA457 | Panavia Tornado GR1 [CE] | RAF BFME, Saudi Arabia |
| | ZA458 | Panavia Tornado GR1 [FB] | RAF No 16 Sqn, Laarbruch |
| | ZA459 | Panavia Tornado GR1 [EL] | RAF BFME, Muharraq |
| | ZA460 | Panavia Tornado GR1 [FD] | RAF BFME, Saudi Arabia |
| | ZA461 | Panavia Tornado GR1 [DK] | RAF BFME, Saudi Arabia |
| | ZA462 | Panavia Tornado GR1 [EM] | RAF No 15 Sqn, Laarbruch |
| | ZA463 | Panavia Tornado GR1 [GL] | RAF No 20 Sqn, Laarbruch |
| | ZA464 | Panavia Tornado GR1 [GM] | *Crashed into North Sea, 14 Aug 1990* |
| | ZA465 | Panavia Tornado GR1 [FK] | RAF BFME, Saudi Arabia |
| | ZA466 | Panavia Tornado GR1 [FH] | RAF BFME, *Badley damaged Tabuk 18 Oct 90* |
| | ZA467 | Panavia Tornado GR1 [FF] | RAF No 16 Sqn, Laarbruch |
| | ZA469 | Panavia Tornado GR1 [GD] | RAF BFME, Saudi Arabia |
| | ZA470 | Panavia Tornado GR1 [FL] | RAF No 16 Sqn, Laarbruch |
| | ZA471 | Panavia Tornado GR1 [ER] | RAF BFME, Saudi Arabia |
| | ZA472 | Panavia Tornado GR1 [EE] | RAF No 15 Sqn, Laarbruch |
| | ZA473 | Panavia Tornado GR1 [FM] | RAF BFME, Saudi Arabia |
| | ZA474 | Panavia Tornado GR1 [FG] | RAF No 16 Sqn, Laarbruch |
| | ZA475 | Panavia Tornado GR1 [FC] | RAF No 16 Sqn, Laarbruch |
| | ZA490 | Panavia Tornado GR1 [GG] | RAF No 20 Sqn, Laarbruch |
| | ZA491 | Panavia Tornado GR1 [GC] | RAF No 20 Sqn, Laarbruch |
| | ZA492 | Panavia Tornado GR1 [FE] | RAF BFME, Saudi Arabia |
| | ZA494 | Panavia Tornado GR1 [15] (89--M) | *Scrapped at Honington, 1990* |
| | ZA540 | Panavia Tornado GR1T [JQ] | RAF No 27 Sqn, Marham |
| | ZA541 | Panavia Tornado GR1T | RAF TWCU/45 Sqn, Honington |
| | ZA542 | Panavia Tornado GR1 [JA] | RAF No 27 Sqn, Marham |
| | ZA543 | Panavia Tornado GR1 | RAF TWCU/45 Sqn, Honington |
| | ZA544 | Panavia Tornado GR1T [BX] | RAF No 14 Sqn, Bruggen |
| | ZA545 | Panavia Tornado GR1 | *Crashed 14 August 1990 off Spurn Head* |
| | ZA546 | Panavia Tornado GR1 [JB] | RAF No 27 Sqn, Marham |
| | ZA547 | Panavia Tornado GR1 [JC] | RAF No 27 Sqn, Marham |
| | ZA548 | Panavia Tornado GR1T | RAF TWCU/45 Sqn, Honington |
| | ZA549 | Panavia Tornado GR1T | RAF No 15 Sqn, Laarbruch |
| | ZA550 | Panavia Tornado GR1 [JD] | RAF No 27 Sqn, Marham |
| | ZA551 | Panavia Tornado GR1T | RAF TWCU/45 Sqn, Honington |
| | ZA552 | Panavia Tornado GR1T [X] | RAF No 2 Sqn, Laarbruch |
| | ZA553 | Panavia Tornado GR1 [JE] | RAF No 27 Sqn, Marham |
| | ZA554 | Panavia Tornado GR1 [DM] | RAF No 31 Sqn, Bruggen |
| | ZA555 | Panavia Tornado GR1T | *Scrapped at RAF Honington* |
| | ZA556 | Panavia Tornado GR1 | RAF TWCU/45 Sqn, Honington |
| | ZA557 | Panavia Tornado GR1 | RAF TWCU/45 Sqn, Honington |
| | ZA559 | Panavia Tornado GR1 | RAF TWCU/45 Sqn, Honington |
| | ZA560 | Panavia Tornado GR1 [MC] | RAF No 9 Sqn, Bruggen |
| | ZA561 | Panavia Tornado GR1 [JH] | *Crashed 16 August 1990 off Spurn Head* |
| | ZA562 | Panavia Tornado GR1T [JT] | RAF No 27 Sqn, Marham |
| | ZA563 | Panavia Tornado GR1 [EP] | RAF No 155 Sqn, Laarbruch |

| Reg. | Type | Owner or Operator | Notes |
|---|---|---|---|
| ZA564 | Panavia Tornado GR1 [JK] | RAF No 27 Sqn, Marham | |
| ZA585 | Panavia Tornado GR1 [G] | RAF No 617 Sqn, Marham | |
| ZA587 | Panavia Tornado GR1 [GN] | RAF No 20 Sqn, Laarbruch | |
| ZA588 | Panavia Tornado GR1 [CP] | RAF No 17 Sqn, Bruggen | |
| ZA589 | Panavia Tornado GR1 [DC] | RAF No 31 Sqn, Bruggen | |
| ZA590 | Panavia Tornado GR1 | RAF No 15 Sqn, Laarbruch | |
| ZA591 | Panavia Tornado GR1 | RAF No 16, Sqn, Laarbruch | |
| ZA592 | Panavia Tornado GR1 [MB] | RAF No 617 Sqn, Marham | |
| ZA594 | Panavia Tornado GR1T [EY] | RAF No 15 Sqn, Laarbruch | |
| ZA595 | Panavia Tornado GR1T | RAF TWCU/45 Sqn, Honington | |
| ZA596 | Panavia Tornado GR1 | RAF TWCU/45 Sqn, Honington | |
| ZA597 | Panavia Tornado GR1 [M] | RAF/BAe Samlesbury, on rebuild | |
| ZA598 | Panavia Tornado GR1T [S] | RAF No 617 Sqn, Marham | |
| ZA599 | Panavia Tornado GR1T | RAF No 155 Sqn, Laarbruch | |
| ZA600 | Panavia Tornado GR1 [CM] | RAF No 17 Sqn, Bruggen | |
| ZA601 | Panavia Tornado GR1 | RAF No 15 Sqn, Laarbruch | |
| ZA602 | Panavia Tornado GR1T [AZ] | RAF No 9 Sqn, Bruggen | |
| ZA604 | Panavia Tornado GR1T | RAF TWCU/45 Sqn, Honington | |
| ZA606 | Panavia Tornado GR1 | RAF TWCU/45 Sqn, Honington | |
| ZA607 | Panavia Tornado GR1 [AN] | RAF No 9 Sqn, Bruggen | |
| ZA608 | Panavia Tornado GR1 [A] | RAF No 617 Sqn, Marham | |
| ZA609 | Panavia Tornado GR1 [J] | RAF No 617 Sqn, Marham | |
| ZA611 | Panavia Tornado GR1 [A] | MoD(PE) BAe Warton | |
| ZA612 | Panavia Tornado GR1T [CX] | RAF No 17 Sqn, Bruggen | |
| ZA613 | Panavia Tornado GR1 [N] | RAF No 617 Sqn, Marham | |
| ZA614 | Panavia Tornado GR1 [E] | RAF No 617 Sqn, Marham | |
| ZA625 | Slingsby Venture T2 [1] | RAF Benson, stored | |
| ZA626 | Slingsby Venture T2 [C] | RAF No 624 VGS, Chivenor | |
| ZA627 | Slingsby Venture T2 [7] | RAF No 613 VGS, Halton | |
| ZA628 | Slingsby Venture T2 | RAF No 613 VGS, Halton | |
| ZA629 | Slingsby Venture T2 [9] | *To G-BSWM, October 1990* | |
| ZA630 | Slingsby Venture T2 | RAF Henlow, stored | |
| ZA631 | Slingsby Venture T2 | RAF Syerston, stored | |
| ZA632 | Slingsby Venture T2 [2] | RAF Ternhill, stored | |
| ZA633 | Slingsby Venture T2 [3] | RAF No 635 VGS, Samlesbury | |
| ZA634 | Slingsby Venture T2 | RAF No 635 VGS, Samlesbury | |
| ZA652 | Slingsby Venture T2 | RAF Syerston, stored | |
| ZA653 | Slingsby Venture T2 | RAF No 633 VGS, Cosford | |
| ZA654 | Slingsby Venture T2 [4] | RAF Little Rissington, stored | |
| ZA655 | Slingsby Venture T2 [V] | *To G-BSWL, October 1990* | |
| ZA656 | Slingsby Venture T2 | RAF Benson, stored | |
| ZA657 | Slingsby Venture T2 [7] | RAF Linton-on-Ouse, stored | |
| ZA658 | Slingsby Venture T2 | RAF Syerston, stored | |
| ZA659 | Slingsby Venture T2 | RAF No 663 VGS, Kinloss | |
| ZA660 | Slingsby Venture T2 | RAF ACCGS, Syerston | |
| ZA661 | Slingsby Venture T2 [3] | RAF Henlow, stored | |
| ZA662 | Slingsby Venture T2 | RAF No 635 VGS, Samlesbury | |
| ZA663 | Slingsby Venture T2 | RAF Syerston, stored | |
| ZA664 | Slingsby Venture T2 [X] | RAF Benson, stored | |
| ZA665 | Slingsby Venture T2 | RAF Little Rissington, stored | |
| ZA666 | Slingsby Venture T2 | RAF Henlow, stored | |
| ZA670 | B-V Chinook HC1 [BG] | RAF No 18 Sqn, Gütersloh | |
| ZA671 | B-V Chinook HC1 [O] | RAF BFME, Saudia Arabia | |
| ZA673 | B-V Chinook HC1 [FF] | RAF No 240 OCU, Odiham | |
| ZA674 | B-V Chinook HC1 [BA] | RAF No 18 Sqn, Gütersloh | |
| ZA675 | B-V Chinook HC1 [BB] | RAF BFME, Saudi Arabia | |
| ZA676 | B-V Chinook HC1 [FG] | RAF Fleetlands | |
| ZA677 | B-V Chinook HC1 [U] | RAF BFME, Saudi Arabia | |
| ZA678 | B-V Chinook HC1 [EZ] (wreck) | RAF Odiham | |
| ZA679 | B-V Chinook HC1 [Z] | RAF BFME, Saudi Arabia | |
| ZA680 | B-V Chinook HC1 [EM] | RAF No 7 Sqn, Odiham | |
| ZA681 | B-V Chinook HC1 [ES] | RAF No 7 Sqn, Odiham | |
| ZA682 | B-V Chinook HC1 [N] | RAF BFME, Saudi Arabia | |
| ZA683 | B-V Chinook HC1 [W] | RAF BFME, Saudi Arabia | |
| ZA684 | B-V Chinook HC1 [L] | RAF BFME, Saudi Arabia | |
| ZA704 | B-V Chinook HC1 [FJ] | RAF No 240 OCU, Odiham | |
| ZA705 | B-V Chinook HC1 [FO] | RAF No 240 OCU, Odiham | |
| ZA707 | B-V Chinook HC1 [V] | RAF BFME, Saudi Arabia | |
| ZA708 | B-V Chinook HC1 [BK] | RAF No 18 Sqn, Gütersloh | |
| ZA709 | B-V Chinook HC1 [B] | RAF No 78 Sqn, Mount Pleasant, FI | |
| ZA710 | B-V Chinook HC1 [EY] | RAF No 7 Sqn, Odiham | |
| ZA711 | B-V Chinook HC1 [A] | RAF No 78 Sqn, Mount Pleasant, FI | |

| Notes | Reg. | Type | Owner or Operator |
|---|---|---|---|
| | ZA712 | B-V Chinook HC1 [R] | RAF BFME, Saudi Arabia |
| | ZA713 | B-V Chinook HC1 [EN] | RAF Fleetlands |
| | ZA714 | B-V Chinook HC1 [EX] | RAF No 7 Sqn, Odiham |
| | ZA717 | B-V Chinook HC1 [C] | RAF, stored Wroughton |
| | ZA718 | B-V Chinook HC2 [EQ] | MoD(PE) A&AEE, Boscombe Down |
| | ZA720 | B-V Chinook HC1 [P] | RAF BFME, Saudi Arabia |
| | ZA726 | WS Gazelle AH1 | AAC No 663 Sqn, Soest |
| | ZA728 | WS Gazelle AH1 [E] | RM 3 CBAS, Yeovilton |
| | ZA729 | WS Gazelle AH1 | AAC No 654 Sqn, Detmold |
| | ZA730 | WS Gazelle AH1 | AAC No 665 Sqn, Aldergrove |
| | ZA731 | WS Gazelle AH1 [A] | AAC No 29 Flt, Suffield, Canada |
| | ZA733 | WS Gazelle AH1 | AAC No 665 Sqn, Aldergrove |
| | ZA734 | WS Gazelle AH1 | AAC No 25 Flt, Belize |
| | ZA735 | WS Gazelle AH1 | AAC, stored Wroughton |
| | ZA736 | WS Gazelle AH1 [S] | AAC No 29 Flt, Suffield, Canada |
| | ZA737 | WS Gazelle AH1 [V] | AAC No 670 Sqn, Middle Wallop |
| | ZA765 | WS Gazelle AH1 | AAC No 25 Flt, Belize |
| | ZA766 | WS Gazelle AH1 | AAC Wroughton, stored |
| | ZA767 | WS Gazelle AH1 | AAC No 25 Flt, Belize |
| | ZA768 | WS Gazelle AH1 [F] | AAC No 670 Sqn, Middle Wallop |
| | ZA769 | WS Gazelle AH1 [K] | AAC No 670 Sqn, Middle Wallop |
| | ZA771 | WS Gazelle AH1 [Z] | AAC No 670 Sqn, Middle Wallop |
| | ZA772 | WS Gazelle AH1 | AAC No 656 Sqn, Netheravon |
| | ZA773 | WS Gazelle AH1 | AAC No 665 Sqn, Aldergrove |
| | ZA774 | WS Gazelle AH1 | AAC No 665 Sqn, Aldergrove |
| | ZA775 | WS Gazelle AH1 | AAC No 656 Sqn, Netheravon |
| | ZA776 | WS Gazelle AH1 [F] | RM 3 CBAS, Yeovilton |
| | ZA777 | WS Gazelle AH1 | AAC No 661 Sqn, Hildesheim |
| | ZA802 | WS Gazelle HT3 [W] | RAF No 2 FTS, Shawbury |
| | ZA803 | WS Gazelle HT3 [X] | RAF No 2 FTS, Shawbury |
| | ZA804 | WS Gazelle HT3 [I] | RAF No 2 FTS, Shawbury |
| | ZA934 | WS Puma HC1 [L] | RAF BFME, Saudi Arabia |
| | ZA935 | WS Puma HC1 [M] | RAF BFME, Saudi Arabia |
| | ZA936 | WS Puma HC1 [N] | RAF BFME, Saudi Arabia |
| | ZA937 | WS Puma HC1 [O] | RAF BFME, Saudi Arabia |
| | ZA938 | WS Puma HC1 | RAF BFME, Saudi Arabia |
| | ZA939 | WS Puma HC1 [P] | RAF BFME, Saudi Arabia |
| | ZA940 | WS Puma HC1 [CY] | RAF No 33 Sqn, Odiham |
| | ZA941 | WS Puma HC1 | MoD(PE) RAE Farnborough |
| | ZA947 | Douglas Dakota C3 | MoD(PE) RAE Farnborough |
| | | | |
| | ZB506 | WS61 Sea King Mk 4X | MoD(PE) RAE Bedford |
| | ZB507 | WS61 Sea King Mk 4X | MoD(PE) RAE Farnborough |
| | ZB600 | BAe Harrier T4 [Z] | RAF No 233 OCU, Wittering |
| | ZB601 | BAe Harrier T4 [Y] | RN No 899 Sqn, Yeovilton |
| | ZB602 | BAe Harrier T4 [R] | RAF No 233 OCU, Wittering |
| | ZB603 | BAe Harrier T4 [Q] | RAF No 233 OCU, Wittering |
| | ZB604 | BAe Harrier T4N [722] | RN No 899 Sqn, Yeovilton |
| | ZB605 | BAe Harrier T4N [721] | RN St Athan |
| | ZB615 | SEPECAT Jaguar T2A | MoD(PE) IAM Farnborough |
| | ZB625 | WS Gazelle HT3 [N] | RAF No 2 FTS, Shawbury |
| | ZB626 | WS Gazelle HT3 [L] | RAF No 2 FTS, Shawbury |
| | ZB627 | WS Gazelle HT3 [A] | RAF No 2 FTS, Shawbury |
| | ZB628 | WS Gazelle HT3 [V] | RAF No 2 FTS, Shawbury |
| | ZB629 | WS Gazelle HT3 | RAF No 32 Sqn, Northolt |
| | ZB646 | WS Gazelle HT2 | MoD(PE) RAE Farnborough |
| | ZB647 | WS Gazelle HT2 [59/CU] | RN No 705 Sqn, Culdrose |
| | ZB648 | WS Gazelle HT2 [37/CU] | RN No 705 Sqn, Culdrose |
| | ZB649 | WS Gazelle HT2 [VL] | RN FONA, Yeovilton |
| | ZB665 | WS Gazelle AH1 [AH] | AAC, UNFICYP, Nicosia |
| | ZB666 | WS Gazelle AH1 [G] | AAC No 670 Sqn, Middle Wallop |
| | ZB667 | WS Gazelle AH1 | AAC, UNFICYP, Nicosia |
| | ZB668 | WS Gazelle AH1 | AAC, UNFICYP, Nicosia |
| | ZB669 | WS Gazelle AH1 [A1] | AAC No 670 Sqn, Middle Wallop |
| | ZB670 | WS Gazelle AH1 | AAC No 665 Sqn, Aldergrove |
| | ZB671 | WS Gazelle AH1 | AAC No 29 Flt, Suffield, Canada |
| | ZB672 | WS Gazelle AH1 | AAC No 3 Flt, Topcliffe |
| | ZB673 | WS Gazelle AH1 [P] | AAC No 670 Sqn, Middle Wallop |
| | ZB674 | WS Gazelle AH1 | AAC, stored Wroughton |
| | ZB675 | WS Gazelle AH1 [C1] | AAC No 670 Sqn, Middle Wallop |
| | ZB676 | WS Gazelle AH1 | AAC, stored Wroughton |
| | ZB677 | WS Gazelle AH1 | AAC No 29 Flt, Suffield, Canada |

| Reg. | Type | Owner or Operator | Notes |
|---|---|---|---|
| ZB678 | WS Gazelle AH1 | AAC No 16 Flt, Dhekelia, Cyprus | |
| ZB679 | WS Gazelle AH1 | AAC No 16 Flt, Dhekelia, Cyprus | |
| ZB680 | WS Gazelle AH1 [B] | AAC No 29 Flt, Suffield, Canada | |
| ZB681 | WS Gazelle AH1 | AAC No 665 Sqn, Aldergrove | |
| ZB682 | WS Gazelle AH1 | AAC No 665 Sqn, Aldergrove | |
| ZB683 | WS Gazelle AH1 (wreck) | AAC, stored Wroughton | |
| ZB684 | WS Gazelle AH1 | AAC No 655 Sqn, Ballykelly | |
| ZB685 | WS Gazelle AH1 | AAC No 665 Sqn, Aldergrove | |
| ZB686 | WS Gazelle AH1 | AAC No 655 Sqn, Ballykelly | |
| ZB687 | WS Gazelle AH1 (wreck) | Army, Thatcham, Berks | |
| ZB688 | WS Gazelle AH1 [H] | AAC No 670 Sqn, Middle Wallop | |
| ZB689 | WS Gazelle AH1 | AAC No 661 Sqn, Hildesheim | |
| ZB690 | WS Gazelle AH1 | AAC No 16 Flt, Dhekelia, Cyprus | |
| ZB691 | WS Gazelle AH1 [D1] | AAC No 670 Sqn, Middle Wallop | |
| ZB692 | WS Gazelle AH1 [W] | AAC No 670 Sqn, Middle Wallop | |
| ZB693 | WS Gazelle AH1 [Y] | AAC No 670 Sqn, Middle Wallop | |
| ZD230 | BAC Super VC10 (G-ASGA) | MoD(PE), BAe Filton | |
| ZD232 | BAC Super VC10 (G-ASGD) (8699M) | RAF Brize Norton Fire Section | |
| ZD233 | BAC Super VC10 (G-ASGE) | FSCTE, RAF Manston | |
| ZD235 | BAC Super VC10 (G-ASGG) [G] | RAF, stored Abingdon | |
| ZD239 | BAC Super VC10 (G-ASGK) | FSCTE, RAF Manston | |
| ZD240 | BAC Super VC10 (G-ASGL) | MoD(PE), BAe Filton | |
| ZD241 | BAC Super VC10 (G-ASGM) | RAF, stored Abingdon | |
| ZD242 | BAC Super VC10 (G-ASGP) | MoD(PE), BAe, Filton | |
| ZD243 | BAC Super VC10 (G-ASGR) | RAF, stored Abingdon | |
| ZD249 | WS Lynx HAS3 | MoD(PE) A&AEE, Boscombe Down | |
| ZD250 | WS Lynx HAS3 [333] | RN No 815 Sqn, Portland | |
| ZD251 | WS Lynx HAS3 [348/CM] | RN No 829 Sqn, Portland | |
| ZD252 | WS Lynx HAS3S [301/PO] | RN No 815 Sqn, Portland | |
| ZD253 | WS Lynx HAS3S | RN, Portland, AMG | |
| ZD254 | WS Lynx HAS3 [631/PO] | RN No 702 Sqn, Portland | |
| ZD255 | WS Lynx HAS3 [450/SS] | RN No 829 Sqn, Portland | |
| ZD256 | WS Lynx HAS3 [330/BZ] | RN No 829 Sqn, Portland | |
| ZD257 | WS Lynx HAS3 [475/HM] | RN No 815 Sqn, Portland | |
| ZD258 | WS Lynx HAS3 | RN, Portland, AMG | |
| ZD259 | WS Lynx HAS3 [323/AB] | RN No 815 Sqn, Portland | |
| ZD260 | WS Lynx HAS3 [346/BW] | RN No 829 Sqn, Portland | |
| ZD261 | WS Lynx HAS3 [472/AM] | RN No 815 Sqn, Portland | |
| ZD262 | WS Lynx HAS3 [632/PO] | RN, Portland, AMG | |
| ZD263 | WS Lynx HAS3 [630/PO] | RN No 702 Sqn, Portland | |
| ZD264 | WS Lynx HAS3 [407/YK] | RN No 815 Sqn, Portland | |
| ZD265 | WS Lynx HAS3 [338/CT] | RN No 829 Sqn, Portland | |
| ZD266 | WS Lynx HAS3S | MoD(PE) Westlands, Yeovil | |
| ZD267 | WS Lynx HAS3S | MoD(PE) A&AEE, Boscombe Down | |
| ZD268 | WS Lynx HAS3S [417/NM] | RN No 815 Sqn, Portland | |
| ZD272 | WS Lynx AH1 [F] | AAC No 653 Sqn, Soest | |
| ZD273 | WS Lynx AH1 | AAC No 656 Sqn, Netheravon | |
| ZD274 | WS Lynx AH1 | AAC No 656 Sqn, Netheravon | |
| ZD275 | WS Lynx AH1 | AAC No 657 Sqn, Topcliffe | |
| ZD276 | WS Lynx AH1 | AAC No 661 Sqn, Hildesheim | |
| ZD277 | WS Lynx AH1 | AAC No 657 Sqn, Topcliffe | |
| ZD278 | WS Lynx AH1 [P] | AAC No 662 Sqn, Soest | |
| ZD279 | WS Lynx AH1 [L] | AAC No 671 Sqn, Middle Wallop | |
| ZD280 | WS Lynx AH1 [Y] | AAC No 663 Sqn, Soest | |
| ZD281 | WS Lynx AH1 | AAC No 656 Sqn, Netheravon | |
| ZD282 | WS Lynx AH1 [V] | RM 3 CBAS, Yeovilton | |
| ZD283 | WS Lynx AH1 | AAC No 652 Sqn, Hildesheim | |
| ZD284 | WS Lynx AH1 [W] | RM 3 CBAS, Yeovilton | |
| ZD285 | WS Lynx AH7 | AAC, Fleetlands | |
| ZD318 | BAe Harrier GR5A | MoD(PE) A&AEE, Boscombe Down | |
| ZD319 | BAe Harrier GR5A | MoD(PE) A&AEE, Boscombe Down | |
| ZD320 | BAe Harrier GR5A | MoD(PE) A&AEE, Boscombe Down | |
| ZD321 | BAe Harrier GR5A | MoD(PE) A&AEE, Boscombe Down/BAe Dunsfold | |
| ZD322 | BAe Harrier GR5 [A] | RAF No 233 OCU, Wittering | |
| ZD323 | BAe Harrier GR5 [AN] | RAF No 3 Sqn, Gütersloh | |
| ZD324 | BAe Harrier GR5 [B] | RAF No 233 OCU, Wittering | |
| ZD326 | BAe Harrier GR5 [I] | RAF No 223 OCU, Wittering | |
| ZD327 | BAe Harrier GR5 [AJ] | RAF No 3 Sqn, Gütersloh | |
| ZD328 | BAe Harrier GR5 [AD] | RAF No 3 Sqn, Gütersloh | |

| Notes | Reg. | Type | Owner or Operator |
|---|---|---|---|
| | ZD329 | BAe Harrier GR5 [AI] | RAF No 3 Sqn, Gütersloh |
| | ZD330 | BAe Harrier GR5 [AM] | RAF No 3 Sqn, Gütersloh |
| | ZD345 | BAe Harrier GR5 [A] | RAF Wittering |
| | ZD346 | BAe Harrier GR5 [E] | RAF No 233 OCU, Wittering |
| | ZD347 | BAe Harrier GR5 [K] | RAF No 233 OCU, Wittering |
| | ZD348 | BAe Harrier GR5 [G] | RAF No 233 OCU, Wittering |
| | ZD349 | BAe Harrier GR5 [AK] | RAF No 3 Sqn, Gütersloh |
| | ZD350 | BAe Harrier GR5 [05] | RAF No 1 Sqn, Wittering |
| | ZD351 | BAe Harrier GR5 [03] | RAF No 1 Sqn, Wittering |
| | ZD352 | BAe Harrier GR5 [U] | MoD(PE) SAOEU, Boscombe Down |
| | ZD353 | BAe Harrier GR5 [H] | RAF No 233 OCU, Wittering |
| | ZD354 | BAe Harrier GR5 [09] | RAF No 1 Sqn, Wittering |
| | ZD355 | BAe Harrier GR5 [01] | *Written off, Denmark, 17/10/90* |
| | ZD375 | BAe Harrier GR5 [-] | RAF No 1 Sqn, Wittering |
| | ZD376 | BAe Harrier GR5 [F] | RAF No 233 OCU, Wittering |
| | ZD377 | BAe Harrier GR5 [AE] | RAF No 3 Sqn, Gütersloh |
| | ZD378 | BAe Harrier GR5 [AL] | RAF No 3 Sqn, Gütersloh |
| | ZD379 | BAe Harrier GR5 [10] | RAF No 1 Sqn, Wittering |
| | ZD380 | BAe Harrier GR5 [04] | MoD(PE), BAe Dunsfold |
| | ZD400 | BAe Harrier GR5 [02] | RAF No 1 Sqn, Wittering |
| | ZD401 | BAe Harrier GR5 [AA] | RAF No 3 Sqn, Gütersloh |
| | ZD402 | BAe Harrier GR5 [04] | RAF No 1 Sqn, Wittering |
| | ZD403 | BAe Harrier GR5 [08] | RAF No 1 Sqn, Wittering |
| | ZD404 | BAe Harrier GR5 [07] | RAF No 1 Sqn, Wittering |
| | ZD405 | BAe Harrier GR5 [12] | RAF No 1 Sqn, Wittering |
| | ZD406 | BAe Harrier GR5 [AB] | RAF No 3 Sqn, Gütersloh |
| | ZD407 | BAe Harrier GR5 [AC] | RAF No 3 Sqn, Gütersloh |
| | ZD408 | BAe Harrier GR5 [11] | RAF No 1 Sqn, Wittering |
| | ZD409 | BAe Harrier GR5 [06] | RAF No 1 Sqn, Wittering |
| | ZD410 | BAe Harrier GR5 [AF] | RAF No 3 Sqn, Gütersloh |
| | ZD411 | BAe Harrier GR5 [AG] | RAF No 3 Sqn, Gütersloh |
| | ZD412 | BAe Harrier GR5 [AH] | RAF No 3 Sqn, Gütersloh |
| | ZD430 | BAe Harrier GR5A | MoD(PE), BAe Dunsfold |
| | ZD431 | BAe Harrier GR5A | RAF, stored Shawbury |
| | ZD432 | BAe Harrier GR5A | RAF, Wittering |
| | ZD433 | BAe Harrier GR5A | RAF Wittering, Maintenance School |
| | ZD434 | BAe Harrier GR5A | RAF, stored Shawbury |
| | ZD435 | BAe Harrier GR5A | RAF, stored Shawbury |
| | ZD436 | BAe Harrier GR5A | RAF, stored Shawbury |
| | ZD437 | BAe Harrier GR5A | RAF, stored Shawbury |
| | ZD438 | BAe Harrier GR5A | RAF, stored Shawbury |
| | ZD461 | BAe Harrier GR5A | MoD(PE) A&AEE, Boscombe Down |
| | ZD462 | BAe Harrier GR5A | RAF, stored Shawbury |
| | ZD463 | BAe Harrier GR5A | RAF, stored Shawbury |
| | ZD464 | BAe Harrier GR5A | RAF, stored Shawbury |
| | ZD465 | BAe Harrier GR5A | RAF, stored Shawbury |
| | ZD466 | BAe Harrier GR5A | MoD(PE), Rolls-Royce, Filton |
| | ZD467 | BAe Harrier GR5A | RAF, Wittering |
| | ZD468 | BAe Harrier GR5A | RAF, stored Shawbury |
| | ZD469 | BAe Harrier GR5A | RAF, stored Shawbury |
| | ZD470 | BAe Harrier GR5A | A&AEE, Boscombe Down |
| | *ZD472* | Harrier GR5 Replica [01] (BAPC191) | RAF Exhibition Flight, Abingdon |
| | ZD476 | WS61 Sea King HC4 [ZS] | RN No 707 Sqn, Yeovilton |
| | ZD477 | WS61 Sea King HC4 [A] | RN No 845 Sqn, Saudi Arabia |
| | ZD478 | WS61 Sea King HC4 [VM] | RN No 846 Sqn, Saudi Arabia |
| | ZD479 | WS61 Sea King HC4 [VJ] | RN No 846 Sqn, Saudi Arabia |
| | ZD480 | WS61 Sea King HC4 | RN No 845 Sqn, Saudi Arabia |
| | ZD559 | WS Lynx AH5 | MoD(PE) RAE Bedford |
| | ZD560 | WS Lynx AH7 | MoD(PE) ETPS Boscombe Down |
| | ZD565 | WS Lynx HAS3 [633/PO] | RN No 702 Sqn, Portland |
| | ZD566 | WS Lynx HAS3 [637/PO] | RN No 702 Sqn, Portland |
| | ZD567 | WS Lynx HAS3S [322/AV] | RN No 815 Sqn, Portland |
| | ZD574 | B-V Chinook HC1 [FH] | RAF No 240 OCU, Odiham |
| | ZD575 | B-V Chinook HC1 [H] | RAF BFME, Saudi Arabia |
| | ZD576 | B-V Chinook HC1 [G] | RAF BFME, Saudi Arabia |
| | ZD578 | BAe Sea Harrier FRS1 [129/N] | RN No 800 Sqn, Yeovilton |
| | ZD579 | BAe Sea Harrier FRS2 | RN, AMG, Yeovilton |
| | ZD580 | BAe Sea Harrier FRS1 [714] | RN No 899 Sqn, Yeovilton |
| | ZD581 | BAe Sea Harrier FRS1 [718] | RN No 899 Sqn, Yeovilton |
| | ZD582 | BAe Sea Harrier FRS1 [002/R] | RN No 801 Sqn, Yeovilton |
| | ZD607 | BAe Sea Harrier FRS1 [127/N] | RN No 800 Sqn, Yeovilton |

| Reg. | Type | Owner or Operator | Notes |
|---|---|---|---|
| ZD608 | BAe Sea Harrier FRS1 [710] | RN No 899 Sqn, Yeovilton | |
| ZD609 | BAe Sea Harrier FRS1 | RN No 801 Sqn, Yeovilton | |
| ZD610 | BAe Sea Harrier FRS1 [713] | RN No 899 Sqn, Yeovilton | |
| ZD611 | BAe Sea Harrier FRS1 [717] | RN, St Athan | |
| ZD612 | BAe Sea Harrier FRS1 [128/N] | RN No 800 Sqn, Yeovilton | |
| ZD613 | BAe Sea Harrier FRS1 [000/R] | RN No 801 Sqn, Yeovilton | |
| ZD614 | BAe Sea Harrier FRS1 [125/N] | RN No 800 Sqn, Yeovilton | |
| ZD615 | BAe Sea Harrier FRS1 [124/N] | RN No 800 Sqn, Yeovilton | |
| ZD620 | BAe 125 CC3 | RAF No 32 Sqn, Northolt | |
| ZD621 | BAe 125 CC3 | RAF No 32 Sqn, Northolt | |
| ZD625 | WS61 Sea King HC4 [ZX] | RN No 707 Sqn, Yeovilton | |
| ZD626 | WS61 Sea King HC4 [ZY] | RN No 707 Sqn, Yeovilton | |
| ZD627 | WS61 Sea King HC4 [ZZ] | RN No 707 Sqn, Yeovilton | |
| ZD630 | WS61 Sea King HAS6 | RN, Fleetlands | |
| ZD631 | WS61 Sea King HAS6 | RN, Fleetlands | |
| ZD633 | WS61 Sea King HAS6 [512] | RN, No 810 Sqn, Culdrose | |
| ZD634 | WS61 Sea King HAS6 | RN, Fleetlands | |
| ZD636 | WS61 Sea King HAS6 [705/PW] | RN No 819 Sqn, Prestwick | |
| ZD637 | WS61 Sea King HAS6 [510] | RN No 810 Sqn, Culdrose | |
| ZD643 | Schleicher Vanguard TX1 (BGA2884) | Privately owned | |
| ZD644 | Schleicher Vanguard TX1 (BGA2883) | *Privately owned as BGA3697* | |
| ZD645 | Schleicher Vanguard TX1 (BGA2885) | *Privately owned as BGA3674* | |
| ZD646 | Schleicher Vanguard TX1 (BGA2886) | *Privately owned as BGA3679* | |
| ZD647 | Schleicher Vanguard TX1 (BGA2887) | *Privately owned as BGA2887* | |
| ZD648 | Schleicher Vanguard TX1 (BGA2888) | *Scrapped at RAF Syerston* | |
| ZD649 | Schleicher Vanguard TX1 (BGA2889) | Privately owned | |
| ZD650 | Schleicher Vanguard TX1 (BGA2890) | Privately owned | |
| ZD651 | Schleicher Vanguard TX1 (BGA2891) | Privately owned | |
| ZD652 | Schleicher Vanguard TX1 (BGA2892) | *Privately owned as BGA3673* | |
| ZD657 | Schleicher Valiant TX1 (BGA2893) | RAF No 622 VGS, Upavon | |
| ZD658 | Schleicher Valiant TX1 (BGA2894) | RAF stored, Syerston | |
| ZD659 | Schleicher Valiant TX1 (BGA2895) | RAF No 645 VGS, Catterick | |
| ZD660 | Schleicher Valiant TX1 (BGA2896) | RAF stored, Syerston | |
| ZD661 | Schleicher Valiant TX1 (BGA2897) (wreck) | Privately owned, Cranfield | |
| ZD667 | BAe Harrier GR3 [U] | RAF No 4 Sqn, Gütersloh | |
| ZD668 | BAe Harrier GR3 [J] | RAF No 4 Sqn, Gütersloh | |
| ZD669 | BAe Harrier GR3 [I] | RAF No 4 Sqn, Gütersloh | |
| ZD670 | BAe Harrier GR3 [3C] | RAF No 233 OCU, Wittering | |
| ZD703 | BAe 125 CC3 | RAF No 32 Sqn, Northolt | |
| ZD704 | BAe 125 CC3 | RAF No 32 Sqn, Northolt | |
| ZD707 | Panavia Tornado GR1 [BK] | RAF BFME, Saudi Arabia | |
| ZD708 | Panavia Tornado GR1 | BAe Warton | |
| ZD709 | Panavia Tornado GR1 [AH] | RAF No 9 Sqn, Bruggen | |
| ZD711 | Panavia Tornado GR1T [DY] | RAF No 31 Sqn, Bruggen | |
| ZD712 | Panavia Tornado GR1T [BY] | RAF No 14 Sqn, Bruggen | |
| ZD713 | Panavia Tornado GR1T | RAF TWCU/45 Sqn, Honington | |
| ZD714 | Panavia Tornado GR1 [BE] | RAF No 14 Sqn, Bruggen | |
| ZD715 | Panavia Tornado GR1 [DB] | RAF BFME, Saudi Arabia | |
| ZD716 | Panavia Tornado GR1 [O] | MoD(PE) SAOEU Boscombe Down | |
| ZD717 | Panavia Tornado GR1 [CD] | RAF BFME, Muharraq | |
| ZD718 | Panavia Tornado GR1 [BH] | RAF BFME, Saudi Arabia | |
| ZD719 | Panavia Tornado GR1 [AD] | RAF No 9 Sqn, Bruggen | |
| ZD720 | Panavia Tornado GR1 [CK] | MoD(PE), BAe Warton | |
| ZD739 | Panavia Tornado GR1 [AC] | RAF No 9 Sqn, Bruggen | |
| ZD740 | Panavia Tornado GR1 [DA] | RAF No 31 Sqn, Bruggen | |
| ZD741 | Panavia Tornado GR1T [DZ] | RAF No 31 Sqn, Bruggen | |
| ZD742 | Panavia Tornado GR1T [CZ] | RAF No 17 Sqn, Bruggen | |

| Notes | Reg. | Type | Owner or Operator |
|---|---|---|---|
| | ZD743 | Panavia Tornado GR1T | RAF TWCU/45 Sqn, Honington |
| | ZD744 | Panavia Tornado GR1 [BD] | RAF BFME, Saudi Arabia |
| | ZD745 | Panavia Tornado GR1 [BM] | RAF BFME, Saudi Arabia |
| | ZD746 | Panavia Tornado GR1 [AB] | RAF No 9 Sqn, Bruggen |
| | ZD747 | Panavia Tornado GR1 [AL] | RAF No 9 Sqn, Bruggen |
| | ZD748 | Panavia Tornado GR1 [AK] | RAF No 9 Sqn, Bruggen |
| | ZD749 | Panavia Tornado GR1 [U] | MoD(PE) SAOEU Boscombe Down |
| | ZD788 | Panavia Tornado GR1 [CB] | RAF No 17 Sqn, Bruggen |
| | ZD789 | Panavia Tornado GR1 [AM] | RAF No 9 Sqn, Bruggen |
| | ZD790 | Panavia Tornado GR1 [DL] | RAF No 31 Sqn, Bruggen |
| | ZD791 | Panavia Tornado GR1 [BG] | RAF BFME, Muharraq |
| | ZD792 | Panavia Tornado GR1 [CF] | RAF BFME, Saudi Arabia |
| | ZD793 | Panavia Tornado GR1 [CA] | RAF No 17 Sqn, Bruggen |
| | ZD809 | Panavia Tornado GR1 [BA] | RAF No 14 Sqn, Bruggen |
| | ZD810 | Panavia Tornado GR1 [AA] | RAF No 9 Sqn, Bruggen |
| | ZD811 | Panavia Tornado GR1 [DF] | RAF No 31 Sqn, Bruggen |
| | ZD812 | Panavia Tornado GR1T [FV] | RAF No 16 Sqn, Laarbruch |
| | ZD842 | Panavia Tornado GR1T | RAF TWCU/45 Sqn, Honington |
| | ZD843 | Panavia Tornado GR1 [DH] | RAF BFME, Saudi Arabia |
| | ZD844 | Panavia Tornado GR1 [DE] | RAF No 31 Sqn, Bruggen |
| | ZD845 | Panavia Tornado GR1 [AF] | RAF BFME, Saudi Arabia |
| | ZD846 | Panavia Tornado GR1 [BL] | RAF No 14 Sqn, Bruggen |
| | ZD847 | Panavia Tornado GR1 [CH] | RAF BFME, Saudi Arabia |
| | ZD848 | Panavia Tornado GR1 [BC] | RAF No 14 Sqn, Bruggen |
| | ZD849 | Panavia Tornado GR1 [CC] | RAF Tabuk, Saudi Arabia |
| | ZD850 | Panavia Tornado GR1 [CL] | RAF No 9 Sqn, Bruggen |
| | ZD851 | Panavia Tornado GR1 [AJ] | RAF No 9 Sqn, Bruggen |
| | ZD890 | Panavia Tornado GR1 [AE] | RAF No 9 Sqn, Bruggen |
| | ZD892 | Panavia Tornado GR1 [BJ] | RAF BFME, Muharraq |
| | ZD893 | Panavia Tornado GR1 [AG] | RAF No 9 Sqn, Bruggen |
| | ZD895 | Panavia Tornado GR1 [BF] | RAF BFME, Saudi Arabia |
| | ZD899 | Panavia Tornado F2T | MoD(PE) BAe Warton |
| | ZD900 | Panavia Tornado F2T | MoD(PE) A&AEE, Boscombe Down |
| | ZD901 | Panavia Tornado F2T [AB] | RAF, stored St Athan |
| | ZD902 | Panavia Tornado F2T | MoD(PE), RAE Farnborough |
| | ZD903 | Panavia Tornado F2T [AB] | RAF, stored St Athan |
| | ZD904 | Panavia Tornado F2T [AE] | RAF, stored St Athan |
| | ZD905 | Panavia Tornado F2 [AV] | RAF, stored St Athan |
| | ZD906 | Panavia Tornado F2 [AN] | RAF, stored St Athan |
| | ZD932 | Panavia Tornado F2 [AM] | RAF, stored St Athan |
| | ZD933 | Panavia Tornado F2 [AO] | RAF, stored St Athan |
| | ZD934 | Panavia Tornado F2T [AD] | RAF, stored St Athan |
| | ZD935 | Panavia Tornado F2T | RAF, stored St Athan |
| | ZD936 | Panavia Tornado F2 [AP] | RAF, stored St Athan |
| | ZD937 | Panavia Tornado F2 [AQ] | RAF, stored St Athan |
| | ZD938 | Panavia Tornado F2 [AR] | RAF, stored St Athan |
| | ZD939 | Panavia Tornado F2 [AS] | RAF, stored St Athan |
| | ZD940 | Panavia Tornado F2 | RAF, stored St Athan |
| | ZD941 | Panavia Tornado F2 [AU] | RAF, stored St Athan |
| | ZD948 | Lockheed TriStar KC1 (G-BFCA) | RAF No 216 Sqn, Brize Norton |
| | ZD949 | Lockheed TriStar K1 (G-BFCB) | RAF No 216 Sqn, Brize Norton |
| | ZD950 | Lockheed TriStar KC1 (G-BFCC) | MoD(PE) A&AEE, Boscombe Down |
| | ZD951 | Lockheed TriStar K1 (G-BFCD) | RAF No 216 Sqn, Brize Norton |
| | ZD952 | Lockheed TriStar KC1 (G-BFCE) | RAF No 216 Sqn, Brize Norton |
| | ZD953 | Lockheed TriStar K1 (G-BFCF) | RAF No 216 Sqn, Brize Norton |
| | ZD974 | Schempp-Hirth Janus C (BGA2875) | RAF CGMF, Syerston |
| | ZD975 | Schempp-Hirth Janus C (BGA2876) | RAF CGMF, Syerston |
| | ZD980 | B-V Chinook HC1 [J] | RAF BFME, Saudi Arabia |
| | ZD981 | B-V Chinook HC1 [I] | RAF BFME, Saudi Arabia |
| | ZD982 | B-V Chinook HC1 [FI] | RAF No 240 OCU, Odiham |
| | ZD983 | B-V Chinook HC1 [BF] | RAF No 18 Sqn, Gütersloh |
| | ZD984 | B-V Chinook HC1 [BT] | RAF No 7 Sqn, Odiham |
| | ZD990 | BAe Harrier T4A [T] | RAF No 233 OCU, Wittering |
| | ZD991 | BAe Harrier T4 [V] | RAF No 233 OCU, Wittering |
| | ZD992 | BAe Harrier T4 [Y] | RAF No 4 Sqn, Gütersloh |
| | ZD993 | BAe Harrier T4 [U] | RAF No 233 OCU, Wittering |
| | ZD996 | Panavia Tornado GR1A [I] | RAF No 31 Sqn, Bruggen |
| | ZE116 | Panavia Tornado GR1A [DG] | RAF No 31 Sqn, Bruggen |
| | ZE154 | Panavia Tornado F3T [AD] | RAF No 229 OCU/65 Sqn, Coningsby |

| Reg. | Type | Owner or Operator | Notes |
|---|---|---|---|
| ZE155 | Panavia Tornado F3 | MoD(PE) BAe Warton | |
| ZE156 | Panavia Tornado F3 [FJ] | RAF No 25 Sqn, Leeming | |
| ZE157 | Panavia Tornado F3T [BF] | RAF No 29 Sqn, Coningsby | |
| ZE158 | Panavia Tornado F3 | RAF No 43 Sqn, Leuchars | |
| ZE159 | Panavia Tornado F3 [DO] | RAF No 11 Sqn, Dhahran, Saudi Arabia | |
| ZE160 | Panavia Tornado F3T [HA] | RAF Coningsby, ASF | |
| ZE161 | Panavia Tornado F3 | RAF No 43 Sqn, Leuchars | |
| ZE162 | Panavia Tornado F3 [DM] | RAF No 11 Sqn, Dhahran, Saudi Arabia | |
| ZE163 | Panavia Tornado F3T[CF] | RAF No 5 Sqn, Coningsby | |
| ZE164 | Panavia Tornado F3 [DQ] | RAF No 11 Sqn, Dhahran, Saudi Arabia | |
| ZE165 | Panavia Tornado F3 [DU] | RAF No 11 Sqn, Dhahran, Saudi Arabia | |
| ZE166 | Panavia Tornado F3T [AF] | RAF No 229 OCU/65 Sqn, Coningsby | |
| ZE167 | Panavia Tornado F3 [AR] | RAF, stored St Athan | |
| ZE168 | Panavia Tornado F3 [AO] | RAF, stored St Athan | |
| ZE199 | Panavia Tornado F3T | RAF No 111 Sqn, Leuchars | |
| ZE200 | Panavia Tornado F3 | RAF No 43 Sqn, Leuchars | |
| ZE201 | Panavia Tornado F3 [AQ] | RAF Coningsby, ASF | |
| ZE202 | Panavia Tornado F3T [AH] | RAF No 229 OCU/65 Sqn, Coningsby | |
| ZE203 | Panavia Tornado F3 [DA] | RAF No 11 Sqn, Dhahran, Saudi Arabia | |
| ZE204 | Panavia Tornado F3 [DB] | RAF No 11 Sqn, Dhahran, Saudi Arabia | |
| ZE205 | Panavia Tornado F3T | RAF No 29 Sqn, Coningsby | |
| ZE206 | Panavia Tornado F3 [DC] | RAF No 11 Sqn, Dhahran, Saudi Arabia | |
| ZE207 | Panavia Tornado F3 [BJ] | RAF No 29 Sqn, Coningsby | |
| ZE208 | Panavia Tornado F3T [DZ] | RAF No 11 Sqn, Leeming | |
| ZE209 | Panavia Tornado F3 [AS] | RAF No 229 OCU/65 Sqn, Coningsby | |
| ZE210 | Panavia Tornado F3 [DD] | RAF No 11 Sqn, Dhahran, Saudi Arabia | |
| ZE250 | Panavia Tornado F3T [EQ] | RAF No 23 Sqn, Leeming | |
| ZE251 | Panavia Tornado F3 [HB] | RAF No 111 Sqn, Leuchars | |
| ZE252 | Panavia Tornado F3 [AY] | RAF No 229 OCU/65 Sqn, Coningsby | |
| ZE253 | Panavia Tornado F3T [AB] | RAF No 229 OCU/65 Sqn, Coningsby | |
| ZE254 | Panavia Tornado F3 [BG] | RAF No 29 Sqn, Coningsby | |
| ZE255 | Panavia Tornado F3 [BH] | RAF No 29 Sqn, Coningsby | |
| ZE256 | Panavia Tornado F3T [AJ] | RAF No 229 OCU/65 Sqn, Coningsby | |
| ZE257 | Panavia Tornado F3 [BD] | RAF No 29 Sqn, Coningsby | |
| ZE258 | Panavia Tornado F3 [BE] | RAF No 29 Sqn, Coningsby | |
| ZE287 | Panavia Tornado F3T [AE] | RAF No 229 OCU/65 Sqn, Coningsby | |
| ZE288 | Panavia Tornado F3 [BI] | RAF No 29 Sqn, Coningsby | |
| ZE289 | Panavia Tornado F3 [BA] | RAF No 29 Sqn, Coningsby | |
| ZE290 | Panavia Tornado F3T [FE] | RAF No 25 Sqn, Leeming | |
| ZE291 | Panavia Tornado F3 [AZ] | RAF No 229 OCU/65 Sqn, Coningsby | |
| ZE292 | Panavia Tornado F3 [AU] | RAF No 229 OCU/65 Sqn, Coningsby | |
| ZE293 | Panavia Tornado F3T [AC] | RAF No 229 OCU/65 Sqn, Coningsby | |
| ZE294 | Panavia Tornado F3 [AQ] | RAF No 229 OCU/65 Sqn, Coningsby | |
| ZE295 | Panavia Tornado F3 [AR] | RAF No 229 OCU/65 Sqn, Coningsby | |
| ZE296 | Panavia Tornado F3T [AM] | RAF No 229 OCU/65 Sqn, Coningsby | |
| ZE338 | Panavia Tornado F3 [BB] | RAF No 29 Sqn, Coningsby | |
| ZE339 | Panavia Tornado F3 [AX] | RAF No 229 OCU/65 Sqn, Coningsby | |
| ZE340 | Panavia Tornado F3T [AG] | RAF No 229 OCU/65 Sqn, Coningsby | |
| ZE341 | Panavia Tornado F3 [BC] | RAF No 29 Sqn, Coningsby | |
| ZE342 | Panavia Tornado F3 [BK] | RAF No 29 Sqn, Coningsby | |
| ZE343 | Panavia Tornado F3T [AI] | RAF No 229 OCU/65 Sqn, Coningsby | |
| ZE350 | McD Phantom F-4J(UK) [T] | RAF No 74 Sqn, Wattisham | |
| ZE351 | McD Phantom F-4J(UK) [I] | RAF No 74 Sqn, Wattisham | |
| ZE352 | McD Phantom F-4J(UK) [G] | RAF No 74 Sqn, Wattisham | |
| ZE353 | McD Phantom F-4J(UK) [E] | RAF No 74 Sqn, Wattisham | |
| ZE354 | McD Phantom F-4J(UK) [R] | RAF No 74 Sqn, Wattisham | |
| ZE355 | McD Phantom F-4J(UK) [S] | RAF No 74 Sqn, Wattisham | |
| ZE356 | McD Phantom F-4J(UK) [Q] | RAF No 74 Sqn, Wattisham | |
| ZE357 | McD Phantom F-4J(UK) [N] | RAF No 74 Sqn, Wattisham | |
| ZE359 | McD Phantom F-4J(UK) [J] | RAF No 74 Sqn, Wattisham | |
| ZE360 | McD Phantom F-4J(UK) [O] | RAF No 74 Sqn, Wattisham | |
| ZE361 | McD Phantom F-4J(UK) [P] | RAF No 74 Sqn, Wattisham | |
| ZE362 | McD Phantom F-4J(UK) [V] | RAF No 74 Sqn, Wattisham | |
| ZE363 | McD Phantom F-4J(UK) [W] | RAF No 74 Sqn, Wattisham | |
| ZE364 | McD Phantom F-4J(UK) [Z] | RAF No 74 Sqn, Wattisham | |
| ZE368 | WS61 Sea King HAR3 | RAF No 202 Sqn SAR* | |
| ZE369 | WS61 Sea King HAR3 | RAF No 202 Sqn SAR* | |
| ZE370 | WS61 Sea King HAR3 | RAF No 202 Sqn SAR* | |
| ZE375 | WS Lynx AH7 [B] | AAC No 671 Sqn, Middle Wallop | |
| ZE376 | WS Lynx AH7 | MoD(PE) Westlands, Yeovil | |
| ZE378 | WS Lynx AH7 | MoD(PE) Westlands, Yeovil | |
| ZE379 | WS Lynx AH7 | AAC No 665 Sqn, Aldergrove | |
| ZE380 | WS Lynx AH7 | AAC No 657 Sqn, Topcliffe | |

| Notes | Reg. | Type | Owner or Operator |
|---|---|---|---|
| | ZE381 | WS Lynx AH7 | AAC No 665 Sqn, Aldergrove |
| | ZE382 | WS Lynx AH7 | AAC No 657 Sqn, Topcliffe |
| | ZE395 | BAe 125 CC3 | RAF No 32 Sqn, Northolt |
| | ZE396 | BAe 125 CC3 | RAF No 32 Sqn, Northolt |
| | ZE410 | Agusta A109A (AE-334) | AAC No 8 Flight, Netheravon |
| | ZE411 | Agusta A109A (AE-331) | AAC No 8 Flight, Netheravon |
| | ZE412 | Agusta A109A | AAC No 8 Flight, Netheravon |
| | ZE413 | Agusta A109A | AAC No 8 Flight, Netheravon |
| | ZE418 | WS61 Sea King HAS5 [502] | RN No 810 Sqn, Culdrose |
| | ZE419 | WS61 Sea King HAS6 | RN Fleetlands |
| | ZE420 | WS61 Sea King HAS5 [134] | RN No 826 Sqn, Culdrose |
| | ZE422 | WS61 Sea King HAS5 [130] | RN No 826 Sqn, Culdrose |
| | ZE425 | WS61 Sea King HC4 [D] | RN No 845 Sqn, Yeovilton |
| | ZE426 | WS61 Sea King HC4 [A] | RN Yeovilton, AMG |
| | ZE427 | WS61 Sea King HC4 [WB] | RN No 848 Sqn, Saudi Arabia |
| | ZE428 | WS61 Sea King HC4 [WC] | RN No 848 Sqn, Saudi Arabia |
| | ZE432 | BAC 1-11/479 (DQ-FBV) | MoD(PE) ETPS Boscombe Down |
| | ZE433 | BAC 1-11/479 (DQ-FBQ) | MoD(PE) RAE Bedford |
| | ZE438 | BAe Jetstream T3 [576] | RN FONA/Heron Flight, Yeovilton |
| | ZE439 | BAe Jetstream T3 [577/CU] | RN FONA/Heron Flight, Yeovilton |
| | ZE440 | BAe Jetstream T3 [578] | RN No 750 Sqn, Culdrose |
| | ZE441 | BAe Jetstream T3 [579] | RN No 750 Sqn, Culdrose |
| | ZE477 | WS Lynx 3 | International Helicopter Museum, Weston-super-Mare |
| | ZE495 | Grob Viking T1 (BGA3000) | RAF CGMF, Syerston |
| | ZE496 | Grob Viking T1 (BGA3001) | RAF No 615 VGS, Kenley |
| | ZE497 | Grob Viking T1 (BGA3002) | RAF No 662 VGS, Arbroath |
| | ZE498 | Grob Viking T1 (BGA3003) | RAF No 618 VGS, West Malling |
| | ZE499 | Grob Viking T1 (BGA3004) | RAF CGMF, Syerston |
| | ZE500 | Grob Viking T1 (BGA3005) | *Written off* |
| | ZE501 | Grob Viking T1 (BGA3006) | RAF ACCGS, Syerston |
| | ZE502 | Grob Viking T1 (BGA3007) | RAF No 626 VGS, Predannack |
| | ZE503 | Grob Viking T1 (BGA3008) | RAF No 625 VGS, South Cerney |
| | ZE504 | Grob Viking T1 (BGA3009) | RAF No 645 VGS, Catterick |
| | ZE520 | Grob Viking T1 (BGA3010) | RAF No 618 VGS, West Malling |
| | ZE521 | Grob Viking T1 (BGA3011) | RAF No 611 VGS, Swanton Morley |
| | ZE522 | Grob Viking T1 (BGA3012) | RAF No 625 VGS, South Cerney |
| | ZE523 | Grob Viking T1 (BGA3013) | Privately owned |
| | ZE524 | Grob Viking T1 (BGA3014) | RAF No 611 VGS, Swanton Morley |
| | ZE525 | Grob Viking T1 (BGA3015) (wreck) | RAF CGMF, Syerston |
| | ZE526 | Grob Viking T1 (BGA3016) | RAF CGMF, Syerston |
| | ZE527 | Grob Viking T1 (BGA3017) | RAF No 643 VGS, Scampton |
| | ZE528 | Grob Viking T1 (BGA3018) | RAF No 614 VGS, Wethersfield |
| | ZE529 | Grob Viking T1 (BGA3019) | RAF CGMF, Syerston |
| | ZE530 | Grob Viking T1 (BGA3020) | RAF No 645 VGS, Catterick |
| | ZE531 | Grob Viking T1 (BGA3021) | RAF No 631, VGS, Sealand |
| | ZE532 | Grob Viking T1 (BGA3022) | RAF, ACCGS Syerston |
| | ZE533 | Grob Viking T1 (BGA3023) | RAF No 622 VGS, Upavon |
| | ZE534 | Grob Viking T1 (BGA3024) | RAF No 662 VGS, Arbroath |
| | ZE550 | Grob Viking T1 (BGA3025) | RAF No 622 VGS, Upavon |
| | ZE551 | Grob Viking T1 (BGA3026) | RAF No 611 VGS, Swanton Morley |
| | ZE552 | Grob Viking T1 (BGA3027) | RAF No 625 VGS, South Cerney |
| | ZE553 | Grob Viking T1 (BGA3028) | RAF No 611 VGS, Swanton Morley |
| | ZE554 | Grob Viking T1 (BGA3029) | RAF No 631 VGS, Sealand |
| | ZE555 | Grob Viking T1 (BGA3030) | RAF No 631 VGS, Sealand |
| | ZE556 | Grob Viking T1 (BGA3031) | RAF No 661 VGS, Kirknewton |
| | ZE557 | Grob Viking T1 (BGA3032) | RAF No 661 VGS, Kirknewton |
| | ZE558 | Grob Viking T1 (BGA3033) | RAF No 634 VGS, St Athan |
| | ZE559 | Grob Viking T1 (BGA3034) | RAF No 645 VGS, Catterick |
| | ZE560 | Grob Viking T1 (BGA3035) | RAF No 611 VGS, Swanton Morley |
| | ZE561 | Grob Viking T1 (BGA3036) | RAF CGMF, Syerston |
| | ZE562 | Grob Viking T1 (BGA3037) | RAF No 631 VGS, Sealand |
| | ZE563 | Grob Viking T1 (BGA3038) | RAF No 636 VGS, Swansea |
| | ZE564 | Grob Viking T1 (BGA3039) | RAF No 661 VGS, Kirknewton |
| | ZE584 | Grob Viking T1 (BGA3040) | RAF CGMF, Syerston |
| | ZE585 | Grob Viking T1 (BGA3041) | RAF CGMF, Syerston |
| | ZE586 | Grob Viking T1 (BGA3042) | RAF No 625 VGS, South Cerney |
| | ZE587 | Grob Viking T1 (BGA3043) | RAF No 622 VGS, Upavon |
| | ZE588 | Grob Viking T1 (BGA3044) | Privately owned |
| | ZE589 | Grob Viking T1 (BGA3045) | RAF No 634 VGS, St Athan |
| | ZE590 | Grob Viking T1 (BGA3046) | RAF No 634 VGS, St Athan |
| | ZE591 | Grob Viking T1 (BGA3047) | RAF No 662 VGS, Arbroath |

| Reg. | Type | Owner or Operator | Notes |
|---|---|---|---|
| ZE592 | Grob Viking T1 (BGA3048) | RAF No 615 VGS, Kenley | |
| ZE593 | Grob Viking T1 (BGA3049) | RAF No 631 VGS, Sealand | |
| ZE594 | Grob Viking T1 (BGA3050) | RAF No 621 VGS, Weston-super-Mare | |
| ZE595 | Grob Viking T1 (BGA3051) | RAF No 662 VGS, Arbroath | |
| ZE600 | Grob Viking T1 (BGA3052) | RAF ACCGS, Syerston | |
| ZE601 | Grob Viking T1 (BGA3053) | RAF No 625 VGS, South Cerney | |
| ZE602 | Grob Viking T1 (BGA3054) | RAF No 617 VGS, Manston | |
| ZE603 | Grob Viking T1 (BGA3055) | RAF No 617 VGS, Manston | |
| ZE604 | Grob Viking T1 (BGA3056) | RAF ACCGS, Syerston | |
| ZE605 | Grob Viking T1 (BGA3057) | RAF No 618 VGS, West Malling | |
| ZE606 | Grob Viking T1 (BGA3058) | RAF No 643 VGS, Scampton | |
| ZE607 | Grob Viking T1 (BGA3059) | RAF ACCGS, Syerston | |
| ZE608 | Grob Viking T1 (BGA3060) | RAF No 625 VGS, South Cerney | |
| ZE609 | Grob Viking T1 (BGA3061) | RAF No 622 VGS, Upavon | |
| ZE610 | Grob Viking T1 (BGA3062) | RAF No 621 VGS, Weston-super-Mare | |
| ZE611 | Grob Viking T1 (BGA3063) | RAF No 621 VGS, Weston-super-Mare | |
| ZE612 | Grob Viking T1 (BGA3064) (wreck) | RAF CGMF, Syerston | |
| ZE613 | Grob Viking T1 (BGA3065) | RAF No 621 VGS, Weston-super-Mare | |
| ZE614 | Grob Viking T1 (BGA3066) | RAF CGMF, Syerston | |
| ZE625 | Grob Viking T1 (BGA3067) | RAF No 643 VGS, Scampton | |
| ZE626 | Grob Viking T1 (BGA3068) | RAF ACCGS, Syerston | |
| ZE627 | Grob Viking T1 (BGA3069) | RAF CGMF, Syerston | |
| ZE628 | Grob Viking T1 (BGA3070) | RAF ACCGS, Syerston | |
| ZE629 | Grob Viking T1 (BGA3071) | RAF ACCGS, Syerston | |
| ZE630 | Grob Viking T1 (BGA3072) | RAF No 636 VGS, Swansea | |
| ZE631 | Grob Viking T1 (BGA3073) | RAF No 643 VGS, Scampton | |
| ZE632 | Grob Viking T1 (BGA3074) | RAF No 614 VGS, Wethersfield | |
| ZE633 | Grob Viking T1 (BGA3075) | RAF No 615 VGS, Kenley | |
| ZE634 | Grob Viking T1 (BGA3076) (wreck) | RAF CGMF, Syerston | |
| ZE635 | Grob Viking T1 (BGA3077) | RAF No 631 VGS, Sealand | |
| ZE636 | Grob Viking T1 (BGA3078) | RAF No 643 VGS, Scampton | |
| ZE637 | Grob Viking T1 (BGA3079) | RAF CGMF, Syerston | |
| ZE650 | Grob Viking T1 (BGA3080) | RAF CGMF, Syerston | |
| ZE651 | Grob Viking T1 (BGA3081) | RAF CGMF, Syerston | |
| ZE652 | Grob Viking T1 (BGA3082) | RAF No 615 VGS, Kenley | |
| ZE653 | Grob Viking T1 (BGA3083) | RAF No 614 VGS, Wethersfield | |
| ZE654 | Grob Viking T1 (BGA3084) | RAF No 618 VGS, West Malling | |
| ZE655 | Grob Viking T1 (BGA3085) | RAF No 618 VGS, West Malling | |
| ZE656 | Grob Viking T1 (BGA3086) | RAF No 617 VGS, Manston | |
| ZE657 | Grob Viking T1 (BGA3087) | RAF No 618 VGS, West Malling | |
| ZE658 | Grob Viking T1 (BGA3088) | RAF No 621 VGS, Weston-super-Mare | |
| ZE659 | Grob Viking T1 (BGA3089) | RAF No 645 VGS, Catterick | |
| ZE677 | Grob Viking T1 (BGA3090) | RAF No 615 VGS, Kenley | |
| ZE678 | Grob Viking T1 (BGA3091) | RAF No 645 VGS, Catterick | |
| ZE679 | Grob Viking T1 (BGA3092) | RAF No 631 VGS, Sealand | |
| ZE680 | Grob Viking T1 (BGA3093) | RAF No 617 VGS, Manston | |
| ZE681 | Grob Viking T1 (BGA3094) | RAF No 617 VGS, Manston | |
| ZE682 | Grob Viking T1 (BGA3095) | RAF No 636 VGS, Swansea | |
| ZE683 | Grob Viking T1 (BGA3096) | RAF No 662 VGS, Arbroath | |
| ZE684 | Grob Viking T1 (BGA3097) | RAF No 661 VGS, Kirknewton | |
| ZE685 | Grob Viking T1 (BGA3098) | RAF No 661 VGS, Kirknewton | |
| ZE686 | Grob Viking T1 (BGA3099) | MoD(PE), Slingsby, Kirkbymoorside | |
| ZE690 | BAe Sea Harrier FRS1 | RN, stored St Athan | |
| ZE691 | BAe Sea Harrier FRS1 | RN, stored St Athan | |
| ZE692 | BAe Sea Harrier FRS1 | RN, stored St Athan | |
| ZE693 | BAe Sea Harrier FRS1 [005/R] | RN No 801 Sqn, Yeovilton | |
| ZE694 | BAe Sea Harrier FRS1 [126/N] | RN No 800 Sqn, Yeovilton | |
| ZE695 | BAe Sea Harrier FRS1 | RN stored, St Athan | |
| ZE696 | BAe Sea Harrier FRS1 [717] | RN No 899 Sqn, Yeovilton | |
| ZE697 | BAe Sea Harrier FRS1 [123/N] | RN No 800 Sqn, Yeovilton | |
| ZE698 | BAe Sea Harrier FRS1 [007/R] | RN No 801 Sqn, Yeovilton | |
| ZE700 | BAe 146 CC2 | RAF Queen's Flight, Benson | |
| ZE701 | BAe 146 CC2 | RAF Queen's Flight, Benson | |
| ZE702 | BAe 146 CC2 | RAF Queen's Flight, Benson | |
| ZE704 | Lockheed TriStar C2 (N508PA) | RAF No 216 Sqn, Brize Norton | |
| ZE705 | Lockheed TriStar C2 (N509PA) | RAF No 216 Sqn, Brize Norton | |
| ZE706 | Lockheed TriStar K2 (N503PA) | MoD(PE)/Marshall, Cambridge | |
| ZE728 | Panavia Tornado F3T [AA] | RAF No 229 OCU/65 Sqn, Coningsby | |
| ZE729 | Panavia Tornado F3 [CD] | RAF No 5 Sqn, Coningsby | |
| ZE730 | Panavia Tornado F3 [DF] | RAF No 111 Sqn, Leuchars | |
| ZE731 | Panavia Tornado F3 | RAF No 111 Sqn, Leuchars | |

| Notes | Reg. | Type | Owner or Operator |
|---|---|---|---|
| | ZE732 | Panavia Tornado F3 [CH] | RAF No 5 Sqn, Coningsby |
| | ZE733 | Panavia Tornado F3 [FH] | RAF No 111 Sqn, Leuchars |
| | ZE734 | Panavia Tornado F3 [CJ] | RAF No 5 Sqn, Coningsby |
| | ZE735 | Panavia Tornado F3T [AL] | RAF No 229 OCU/65 Sqn, Coningsby |
| | ZE736 | Panavia Tornado F3 [CK] | RAF No 5 Sqn, Coningsby |
| | ZE737 | Panavia Tornado F3 | RAF No 43 Sqn, Leuchars |
| | ZE755 | Panavia Tornado F3 [CG] | RAF No 5 Sqn, Coningsby |
| | ZE756 | Panavia Tornado F3 | MoD(PE), BAe Warton |
| | ZE757 | Panavia Tornado F3 | MoD(PE), BAe Warton |
| | ZE758 | Panavia Tornado F3 [CB] | RAF No 5 Sqn, Coningsby |
| | ZE759 | Panavia Tornado F3T [CI] | RAF No 58 Sqn, Coningsby |
| | ZE760 | Panavia Tornado F3 [AP] | RAF No 229 OCU/65 Sqn, Coningsby |
| | ZE761 | Panavia Tornado F3 [CC] | RAF No 5 Sqn, Coningsby |
| | ZE762 | Panavia Tornado F3 [CA] | RAF No 5 Sqn, Coningsby |
| | ZE763 | Panavia Tornado F3 | RAF No 43 Sqn, Leuchars |
| | ZE764 | Panavia Tornado F3 [HC] | RAF No 111 Sqn, Leuchars |
| | ZE785 | Panavia Tornado F3 [AO] | RAF No 229 OCU/65 Sqn, Coningsby |
| | ZE786 | Panavia Tornado F3T [DT] | RAF No 11 Sqn, Leeming |
| | ZE787 | Panavia Tornado F3 [DB] | RAF No 11 Sqn, Leeming |
| | ZE788 | Panavia Tornado F3 [DC] | RAF No 11 Sqn, Leeming |
| | ZE789 | Panavia Tornado F3 [FI] | RAF No 43 Sqn, Leuchars |
| | ZE790 | Panavia Tornado F3 [DE] | RAF No 11 Sqn, Leeming |
| | ZE791 | Panavia Tornado F3 [FF] | RAF No 25 Sqn, Leeming |
| | ZE792 | Panavia Tornado F3 | RAF No 111 Sqn, Leuchars |
| | ZE793 | Panavia Tornado F3T [AK] | RAF No 229 OCU/65 Sqn, Coningsby |
| | ZE794 | Panavia Tornado F3 | RAF No 111 Sqn, Leuchars |
| | ZE808 | Panavia Tornado F3 [GF] | RAF No 43 Sqn, Leuchars |
| | ZE809 | Panavia Tornado F3 [EZ] | RAF No 23 Sqn, Leeming |
| | ZE810 | Panavia Tornado F3 [EN] | RAF No 23 Sqn, Leeming |
| | ZE811 | Panavia Tornado F3 | RAF No 111 Sqn, Leuchars |
| | ZE812 | Panavia Tornado F3 [EA] | RAF No 23 Sqn, Leeming |
| | ZE830 | Panavia Tornado F3T [ET] | RAF No 111 Sqn, Leuchars |
| | ZE831 | Panavia Tornado F3 [EW] | RAF No 23 Sqn, Leeming |
| | ZE832 | Panavia Tornado F3 [EB] | RAF No 111 Sqn, Leuchars |
| | ZE834 | Panavia Tornado F3 [ED] | RAF No 23 Sqn, Leeming |
| | ZE835 | Panavia Tornado F3 [CE] | RAF No 5 Sqn, Coningsby |
| | ZE836 | Panavia Tornado F3 [EF] | RAF No 23 Sqn, Leeming |
| | ZE837 | Panavia Tornado F3T | RAF No 111 Sqn, Leuchars |
| | ZE838 | Panavia Tornado F3 | RAF No 25 Sqn, Leeming |
| | ZE839 | Panavia Tornado F3 [FJ] | RAF No 25 Sqn, Leeming |
| | ZE858 | Panavia Tornado F3 [FB] | RAF No 43 Sqn, Leuchars |
| | ZE862 | Panavia Tornado F3T | RAF F3 OEU, Coningsby |
| | ZE887 | Panavia Tornado F3 [DE] | RAF No 43 Sqn, Leuchars |
| | ZE888 | Panavia Tornado F3T | RAF No 43 Sqn, Leuchars |
| | ZE889 | Panavia Tornado F3 | RAF F3 OEU, Coningsby |
| | ZE907 | Panavia Tornado F3 [DK] | RAF No 11 Sqn, Dhahran, Saudi Arabia |
| | ZE908 | Panavia Tornado F3T | RAF No 111 Sqn, Leuchars |
| | ZE911 | Panavia Tornado F3 | RAF F3 OEU, Coningsby |
| | ZE934 | Panavia Tornado F3T [DV] | RAF No 11 Sqn, Dhahran, Saudi Arabia |
| | ZE936 | Panavia Tornado F3 [DF] | RAF No 11 Sqn, Dhahran, Saudi Arabia |
| | ZE941 | Panavia Tornado F3T [DW] | RAF No 115 Sqn, Dhahran |
| | ZE942 | Panavia Tornado F3 [DG] | RAF No 115 Sqn, Dhahran |
| | ZE961 | Panavia Tornado F3 [DH] | RAF No 11 Sqn, Dhahran |
| | ZE962 | Panavia Tornado F3 [DI] | RAF No 11 Sqn, Dhahran |
| | ZE963 | Panavia Tornado F3 [DX] | RAF No 11 Sqn, Dhahran |
| | ZE964 | Panavia Tornado F3T [DS] | RAF No 11 Sqn, Dhahran |
| | ZE965 | Panavia Tornado F3 | RAF No 43 Sqn, Leuchars |
| | ZE966 | Panavia Tornado F3 [ ] | RAF No 43 Sqn, Leuchars |
| | ZE967 | Panavia Tornado F3 | RAF No 43 Sqn, Leuchars |
| | ZE968 | Panavia Tornado F3 [DJ] | RAF No 11 Sqn, Leeming |
| | ZE969 | Panavia Tornado F3 [DL] | RAF No 11 Sqn, Dhahran |
| | ZE982 | Panavia Tornado F3 [DD] | RAF No 11 Sqn, Leeming |
| | ZE983 | Panavia Tornado F3 | MoD(PE), BAe Warton |
| | | | |
| | ZF115 | WS61 Sea King HC4 | MoD(PE) ETPS, Boscombe Down |
| | ZF116 | WS61 Sea King HC4 | MoD(PE) A&AEE, Boscombe Down |
| | ZF117 | WS61 Sea King HC4 [D] | RN No 845 Sqn, Saudi Arabia |
| | ZF118 | WS61 Sea King HC4 [VL] | RN No 846 Sqn, Saudi Arabia |
| | ZF119 | WS61 Sea King HC4 [VO] | RN No 846 Sqn, Saudi Arabia |
| | ZF120 | WS61 Sea King HC4 [20/PO] | RN AMG, Portland |
| | ZF121 | WS61 Sea King HC4 [21/PO] | RN No 772 Sqn, Portland |
| | ZF122 | WS61 Sea King HC4 [22/PO] | RN No 772 Sqn, Portland |
| | ZF123 | WS61 Sea King HC4 [23] | RN No 772 Sqn, Portland |

| Reg. | Type | Owner or Operator | Notes |
|---|---|---|---|
| ZF124 | WS61 Sea King HC4 [24/PO] | RN No 772 Sqn, Portland | |
| ZF130 | BAe 125-600B (G-BLUW) | MoD(PE) BAe Dunsfold | |
| ZF135 | Shorts Tucano T1 | MoD(PE) Shorts, Belfast | |
| ZF136 | Shorts Tucano T1 | MoD(PE) Shorts, Belfast | |
| ZF137 | Shorts Tucano T1 | MoD(PE) Shorts, Belfast | |
| ZF138 | Shorts Tucano T1 | RAF No 7 FTS, Church Fenton | |
| ZF139 | Shorts Tucano T1 | RAF No 7 FTS, Church Fenton | |
| ZF140 | Shorts Tucano T1 | MoD(PE) Shorts, Belfast | |
| ZF141 | Shorts Tucano T1 | RAF No 7 FTS, Church Fenton | |
| ZF142 | Shorts Tucano T1 | RAF No 7 FTS, Church Fenton | |
| ZF143 | Shorts Tucano T1 | RAF No 7 FTS, Church Fenton | |
| ZF144 | Shorts Tucano T1 | RAF No 3 FTS, Cranwell | |
| ZF145 | Shorts Tucano T1 | RAF No 7 FTS, Church Fenton | |
| ZF160 | Shorts Tucano T1 | RAF No 7 FTS, Church Fenton | |
| ZF161 | Shorts Tucano T1 | RAF No 7 FTS, Church Fenton | |
| ZF162 | Shorts Tucano T1 | RAF No 7 FTS, Church Fenton | |
| ZF163 | Shorts Tucano T1 | RAF No 7 FTS, Church Fenton | |
| ZF164 | Shorts Tucano T1 | RAF No 7 FTS, Church Fenton | |
| ZF165 | Shorts Tucano T1 | RAF No 7 FTS, Church Fenton | |
| ZF166 | Shorts Tucano T1 | RAF No 7 FTS, Church Fenton | |
| ZF167 | Shorts Tucano T1 | RAF No 7 FTS, Church Fenton | |
| ZF168 | Shorts Tucano T1 | RAF No 7 FTS, Church Fenton | |
| ZF169 | Shorts Tucano T1 | RAF No 7 FTS, Church Fenton | |
| ZF170 | Shorts Tucano T1 | RAF No 7 FTS, Church Fenton | |
| ZF171 | Shorts Tucano T1 | RAF No 7 FTS, Church Fenton | |
| ZF172 | Shorts Tucano T1 | RAF No 7 FTS, Church Fenton | |
| ZF200 | Shorts Tucano T1 | RAF No 7 FTS, Church Fenton | |
| ZF201 | Shorts Tucano T1 | RAF CFS, Scampton | |
| ZF202 | Shorts Tucano T1 | RAF CFS, Scampton | |
| ZF203 | Shorts Tucano T1 | RAF CFS, Scampton | |
| ZF204 | Shorts Tucano T1 | RAF CFS, Scampton | |
| ZF205 | Shorts Tucano T1 | RAF CFS, Scampton | |
| ZF206 | Shorts Tucano T1 | RAF CFS, Scampton | |
| ZF207 | Shorts Tucano T1 | RAF No 7 FTS, Church Fenton | |
| ZF208 | Shorts Tucano T1 | RAF No 7 FTS, Church Fenton | |
| ZF209 | Shorts Tucano T1 | RAF No 7 FTS, Church Fenton | |
| ZF210 | Shorts Tucano T1 | RAF No 7 FTS, Church Fenton | |
| ZF211 | Shorts Tucano T1 | RAF No 7 FTS, Church Fenton | |
| ZF212 | Shorts Tucano T1 | RAF CFS, Scampton | |
| ZF238 | Shorts Tucano T1 | RAF No 7 FTS, Church Fenton | |
| ZF239 | Shorts Tucano T1 | RAF No 7 FTS, Church Fenton | |
| ZF240 | Shorts Tucano T1 | RAF No 7 FTS, Church Fenton | |
| ZF241 | Shorts Tucano T1 | RAF No 7 FTS, Church Fenton | |
| ZF242 | Shorts Tucano T1 | RAF No 7 FTS, Church Fenton | |
| ZF243 | Shorts Tucano T1 | RAF No 7 FTS, Church Fenton | |
| ZF244 | Shorts Tucano T1 | RAF No 7 FTS, Church Fenton | |
| ZF245 | Shorts Tucano T1 | RAF No 7 FTS, Church Fenton | |
| ZF263 | Shorts Tucano T1 | RAF No 7 FTS, Church Fenton | |
| ZF264 | Shorts Tucano T1 | RAF No 7 FTS, Church Fenton | |
| ZF265 | Shorts Tucano T1 | RAF | |
| ZF266 | Shorts Tucano T1 | RAF No 7 FTS, Church Fenton | |
| ZF267 | Shorts Tucano T1 | RAF | |
| ZF268 | Shorts Tucano T1 | RAF | |
| ZF269 | Shorts Tucano T1 | RAF | |
| ZF270 | Shorts Tucano T1 | RAF | |
| ZF284 | Shorts Tucano T1 | RAF | |
| ZF285 | Shorts Tucano T1 | RAF | |
| ZF286 | Shorts Tucano T1 | RAF | |
| ZF287 | Shorts Tucano T1 | RAF | |
| ZF288 | Shorts Tucano T1 | RAF | |
| ZF289 | Shorts Tucano T1 | RAF | |
| ZF290 | Shorts Tucano T1 | RAF | |
| ZF291 | Shorts Tucano T1 | RAF | |
| ZF292 | Shorts Tucano T1 | RAF | |
| ZF293 | Shorts Tucano T1 | RAF | |
| ZF294 | Shorts Tucano T1 | RAF | |
| ZF295 | Shorts Tucano T1 | RAF | |
| ZF315 | Shorts Tucano T1 | RAF | |
| ZF316 | Shorts Tucano T1 | RAF | |
| ZF317 | Shorts Tucano T1 | RAF | |
| ZF318 | Shorts Tucano T1 | RAF | |
| ZF319 | Shorts Tucano T1 | RAF | |

| Notes | Reg. | Type | Owner or Operator |
|---|---|---|---|
| | ZF320 | Shorts Tucano T1 | RAF |
| | ZF338 | Shorts Tucano T1 | RAF |
| | ZF339 | Shorts Tucano T1 | RAF |
| | ZF340 | Shorts Tucano T1 | RAF |
| | ZF341 | Shorts Tucano T1 | RAF |
| | ZF342 | Shorts Tucano T1 | RAF |
| | ZF343 | Shorts Tucano T1 | RAF |
| | ZF344 | Shorts Tucano T1 | RAF |
| | ZF345 | Shorts Tucano T1 | RAF |
| | ZF346 | Shorts Tucano T1 | RAF |
| | ZF347 | Shorts Tucano T1 | RAF |
| | ZF348 | Shorts Tucano T1 | RAF |
| | ZF349 | Shorts Tucano T1 | RAF |
| | ZF350 | Shorts Tucano T1 | RAF |
| | ZF372 | Shorts Tucano T1 | RAF |
| | ZF373 | Shorts Tucano T1 | RAF |
| | ZF374 | Shorts Tucano T1 | RAF |
| | ZF375 | Shorts Tucano T1 | RAF |
| | ZF376 | Shorts Tucano T1 | RAF |
| | ZF377 | Shorts Tucano T1 | RAF |
| | ZF378 | Shorts Tucano T1 | RAF |
| | ZF379 | Shorts Tucano T1 | RAF |
| | ZF380 | Shorts Tucano T1 | RAF |
| | ZF405 | Shorts Tucano T1 | RAF |
| | ZF406 | Shorts Tucano T1 | RAF |
| | ZF407 | Shorts Tucano T1 | RAF |
| | ZF408 | Shorts Tucano T1 | RAF |
| | ZF409 | Shorts Tucano T1 | RAF |
| | ZF410 | Shorts Tucano T1 | RAF |
| | ZF411 | Shorts Tucano T1 | RAF |
| | ZF412 | Shorts Tucano T1 | RAF |
| | ZF413 | Shorts Tucano T1 | RAF |
| | ZF414 | Shorts Tucano T1 | RAF |
| | ZF415 | Shorts Tucano T1 | RAF |
| | ZF416 | Shorts Tucano T1 | RAF |
| | ZF417 | Shorts Tucano T1 | RAF |
| | ZF418 | Shorts Tucano T1 | RAF |
| | ZF444 | BN2A Islander (G-WOTG) | RAF Parachute Association, Weston-on-the-Green |
| | ZF445 | Shorts Tucano T1 | RAF |
| | ZF446 | Shorts Tucano T1 | RAF |
| | ZF447 | Shorts Tucano T1 | RAF |
| | ZF448 | Shorts Tucano T1 | RAF |
| | ZF449 | Shorts Tucano T1 | RAF |
| | ZF450 | Shorts Tucano T1 | RAF |
| | ZF483 | Shorts Tucano T1 | RAF |
| | ZF484 | Shorts Tucano T1 | RAF |
| | ZF485 | Shorts Tucano T1 | RAF |
| | ZF486 | Shorts Tucano T1 | RAF |
| | ZF487 | Shorts Tucano T1 | RAF |
| | ZF488 | Shorts Tucano T1 | RAF |
| | ZF489 | Shorts Tucano T1 | RAF |
| | ZF490 | Shorts Tucano T1 | RAF |
| | ZF491 | Shorts Tucano T1 | RAF |
| | ZF492 | Shorts Tucano T1 | RAF |
| | ZF510 | Shorts Tucano T1 | RAF |
| | ZF511 | Shorts Tucano T1 | RAF |
| | ZF512 | Shorts Tucano T1 | RAF |
| | ZF513 | Shorts Tucano T1 | RAF |
| | ZF514 | Shorts Tucano T1 | RAF |
| | ZF515 | Shorts Tucano T1 | RAF |
| | ZF516 | Shorts Tucano T1 | RAF |
| | ZF520 | Piper PA-31 Navajo Chieftain 350 (N35823/G-BLZK) | MoD(PE) RAE Farnborough |
| | ZF521 | Piper PA-31 Navajo Chieftain 350 (N27509) | MoD(PE) RAE Farnborough |
| | ZF522 | Piper PA-31 Navajo Chieftain 350 (N4261A/G-RNAV/N27728) | MoD(PE) RAE Farnborough |
| | ZF534 | BAe EAP | MoD(PE) BAe Warton |
| | ZF537 | WS Lynx AH7 [C] | AAC No 671 Sqn, Middle Wallop |
| | ZF538 | WS Lynx AH7 | AAC No 657 Sqn, Topcliffe |
| | ZF539 | WS Lynx AH7 | AAC No 657 Sqn, Topcliffe |

| Reg. | Type | Owner or Operator | Notes |
|---|---|---|---|
| ZF540 | WS Lynx AH7 | AAC No 667 Sqn, Middle Wallop | |
| ZF557 | WS Lynx HAS3CTS [670] | RN No 700L Sqn, Portland | |
| ZF558 | WS Lynx HAS3CTS [672] | RN No 700L Sqn, Portland | |
| ZF559 | WS Lynx HAS3 | RN, stored Wroughton | |
| ZF560 | WS Lynx HAS3S | RN, Fleetlands | |
| ZF561 | WS Lynx HAS3 | RN, stored Wroughton | |
| ZF562 | WS Lynx HAS3CTS | RN No 700L Sqn, Portland | |
| ZF563 | WS Lynx HAS3CTS [671] | RN No 700L Sqn, Portland | |
| ZF573 | BN2T Islander (G-SRAY) | MoD(PE), Bembridge | |
| ZF577 | BAC Lightning F53 (668) | Haydon Baillie Aircraft & Naval Museum | |
| ZF578 | BAC Lightning F53 (670) | Wales Aircraft Museum, Cardiff Airport | |
| ZF579 | BAC Lightning F53 (671) | Haydon Baillie Aircraft & Naval Museum | |
| ZF580 | BAC Lightning F53 (672) | BAe Samlesbury gate | |
| ZF581 | BAC Lightning F53 (675) | Haydon Baillie Aircraft & Naval Museum | |
| ZF582 | BAC Lightning F53 (676) | Haydon Baillie Aircraft & Naval Museum | |
| ZF583 | BAC Lightning F53 (681) | Solway Aviation Society, Carlisle | |
| ZF584 | BAC Lightning F53 (682) | Ferranti Ltd, South Gyle, Edinburgh | |
| ZF585 | BAC Lightning F53 (683) | Haydon Baillie Aircraft & Naval Museum | |
| ZF586 | BAC Lightning F53 (688) | Haydon Baillie Aircraft & Naval Museum | |
| ZF587 | BAC Lightning F53 (691) | Haydon Baillie Aircraft & Naval Museum | |
| ZF588 | BAC Lightning F53 (693) | East Midlands Aero Park | |
| ZF589 | BAC Lightning F53 (700) | Haydon Baillie Aircraft & Naval Museum | |
| ZF590 | BAC Lightning F53 (679) | Haydon Baillie Aircraft & Naval Museum | |
| ZF591 | BAC Lightning F53 (685) | Haydon Baillie Aircraft & Naval Museum | |
| ZF592 | BAC Lightning F53 (686) | Haydon Baillie Aircraft & Naval Museum | |
| ZF593 | BAC Lightning F53 (692) | *USAF Museum, Wright-Patterson AFB, Ohio 12 April 1990* | |
| ZF594 | BAC Lightning F53 (696) | North-East Aircraft Museum, Usworth | |
| ZF595 | BAC Lightning T55 (714) | Haydon Baillie Aircraft & Naval Museum | |
| ZF596 | BAC Lightning T55 (715) | Haydon Baillie Aircraft & Naval Museum | |
| ZF597 | BAC Lightning T55 (711) | Haydon Baillie Aircraft & Naval Museum | |
| ZF598 | BAC Lightning T55 (713) | Midland Air Museum, Coventry | |
| ZF622 | Piper PA-31 Navajo Chieftain 350 | MoD(PE) A&AEE Boscombe Down | |
| ZF641 | WS/Agusta EH-101 [PP1] | MoD(PE) EHI, Milan | |
| ZF644 | WS EH-101 Merlin [PP4] | MoD(PE) Westlands, Yeovil | |
| ZF649 | WS EH-101 Merlin HAS1 [PP5] | MoD(PE) Westlands, Yeovil | |
| | | | |
| *ZG101* | WS EH-101 (mock-up) [GB] | Westlands/Agusta, Yeovil | |
| ZG468 | WS70 Black Hawk | Westland Helicopters, Yeovil | |
| ZG471 | BAe Harrier GR7 [CE] | RAF No 4 Sqn, Gütersloh | |
| ZG472 | BAe Harrier GR7 | MoD(PE) A&AEE Boscombe Down | |
| ZG473 | BAe Harrier GR7 [CA] | RAF No 4 Sqn, Gütersloh | |
| ZG474 | BAe Harrier GR7 [CB] | RAF No 4 Sqn, Gütersloh | |
| ZG475 | BAe Harrier GR7 | MoD(PE) SAOEU Boscombe Down | |
| ZG476 | BAe Harrier GR7 | MoD(PE) BAe Dunsfold | |
| ZG477 | BAe Harrier GR7 [CC] | RAF No 4 Sqn, Gütersloh | |
| ZG478 | BAe Harrier GR7 [CD] | RAF No 4 Sqn, Gütersloh | |
| ZG479 | BAe Harrier GR7 | RAF | |
| ZG480 | BAe Harrier GR7 | RAF | |
| ZG500 | BAe Harrier GR7 | RAF | |
| ZG501 | BAe Harrier GR7 | RAF | |
| ZG502 | BAe Harrier GR7 | RAF | |
| ZG503 | BAe Harrier GR7 | RAF | |
| ZG504 | BAe Harrier GR7 | RAF | |
| ZG505 | BAe Harrier GR7 | RAF | |
| ZG506 | BAe Harrier GR7 | RAF | |
| ZG507 | BAe Harrier GR7 | RAF | |
| ZG508 | BAe Harrier GR7 | RAF | |
| ZG509 | BAe Harrier GR7 | RAF | |
| ZG510 | BAe Harrier GR7 | RAF | |
| ZG511 | BAe Harrier GR7 | RAF | |
| ZG512 | BAe Harrier GR7 | RAF | |
| ZG530 | BAe Harrier GR7 | RAF | |
| ZG531 | BAe Harrier GR7 | RAF | |
| ZG532 | BAe Harrier GR7 | RAF | |
| ZG533 | BAe Harrier GR7 | RAF | |
| ZG705 | Panavia Tornado GR1A [A] | RAF No 13 Sqn, Honington | |
| ZG706 | Panavia Tornado GR1A [E] | RAF SAOEU, Boscombe Down | |
| ZG707 | Panavia Tornado GR1A [B] | RAF No 13 Sqn, Honington | |
| ZG708 | Panavia Tornado GR1A [C] | RAF No 13 Sqn, Honington | |
| ZG709 | Panavia Tornado GR1A [I] | RAF No 13 Sqn, Honington | |
| ZG710 | Panavia Tornado GR1A [D] | RAF No 13 Sqn, Honington | |

| Notes | Reg. | Type | Owner or Operator |
|---|---|---|---|
| | ZG711 | Panavia Tornado GR1A [E] | RAF No 13 Sqn, Honington |
| | ZG712 | Panavia Tornado GR1A [F] | RAF No 13 Sqn, Honington |
| | ZG713 | Panavia Tornado GR1A [G] | RAF No 13 Sqn, Honington |
| | ZG714 | Panavia Tornado GR1A [H] | RAF No 13 Sqn, Honington |
| | ZG725 | Panavia Tornado GR1A [J] | RAF No 13 Sqn, Honington |
| | ZG726 | Panavia Tornado GR1 | RAF |
| | ZG727 | Panavia Tornado GR1 | RAF |
| | ZG728 | Panavia Tornado F3 | RAF |
| | ZG729 | Panavia Tornado GR1 | RAF |
| | ZG730 | Panavia Tornado F3 | RAF |
| | ZG731 | Panavia Tornado F3 | RAF |
| | ZG732 | Panavia Tornado F3 | RAF |
| | ZG733 | Panavia Tornado F3 | RAF |
| | ZG734 | Panavia Tornado F3 | RAF |
| | ZG735 | Panavia Tornado F3 | RAF |
| | ZG750 | Panavia Tornado GR1T | RAF |
| | ZG751 | Panavia Tornado F3 | RAF |
| | ZG752 | Panavia Tornado GR1T | RAF |
| | ZG753 | Panavia Tornado F3 | RAF |
| | ZG754 | Panavia Tornado GR1T | RAF |
| | ZG755 | Panavia Tornado F3 | RAF |
| | ZG756 | Panavia Tornado GR1T | RAF |
| | ZG757 | Panavia Tornado F3 | RAF |
| | ZG768 | Panavia Tornado F3 | RAF |
| | ZG769 | Panavia Tornado GR1T | RAF |
| | ZG770 | Panavia Tornado F3 | RAF |
| | ZG771 | Panavia Tornado GR1T | RAF |
| | ZG772 | Panavia Tornado F3 | RAF |
| | ZG773 | Panavia Tornado GR1 | RAF |
| | ZG774 | Panavia Tornado F3 | RAF |
| | ZG775 | Panavia Tornado GR1 | RAF |
| | ZG776 | Panavia Tornado F3 | RAF |
| | ZG777 | Panavia Tornado GR1 | RAF |
| | ZG778 | Panavia Tornado F3 | RAF |
| | ZG779 | Panavia Tornado GR1 | RAF |
| | ZG780 | Panavia Tornado F3 | RAF |
| | ZG791 | Panavia Tornado GR1 | RAF |
| | ZG792 | Panavia Tornado GR1 | RAF |
| | ZG793 | Panavia Tornado F3 | RAF |
| | ZG794 | Panavia Tornado GR1 | RAF |
| | ZG795 | Panavia Tornado F3 | RAF |
| | ZG796 | Panavia Tornado F3 | RAF |
| | ZG797 | Panavia Tornado F3 | RAF |
| | ZG798 | Panavia Tornado F3 | RAF |
| | ZG799 | Panavia Tornado F3 | RAF |
| | ZG816 | WS61 Sea King HAS6 [013/R] | RN No 820 Sqn, Culdrose |
| | ZG817 | WS61 Sea King HAS6 [511/CU] | RN No 810 Sqn, Culdrose |
| | ZG818 | WS61 Sea King HAS6 [273] | RN No 814 Sqn, Culdrose |
| | ZG819 | WS61 Sea King HAS6 [018/R] | RN No 820 Sqn, Culdrose |
| | ZG820 | WS61 Sea King HC4 [F] | RN No 845 Sqn, Saudi Arabia |
| | ZG821 | WS61 Sea King HC4 [WE] | RN No 848 Sqn, Saudi Arabia |
| | ZG822 | WS61 Sea King HC4 [WF] | RN No 848 Sqn, Saudi Arabia |
| | ZG829 | WS61 Sea King HC4 | MoD(PE) ETPS, Boscombe Down |
| | ZG844 | PBN 2T Turbine Defender AL.1 (G-BLNE) | MoD(PE) A&AEE, Boscombe Down |
| | ZG845 | PBN 2T Turbine Defender AL.1 (G-BLNT) | AAC Defender Training Flight, Middle Wallop |
| | ZG846 | PBN 2T Turbine Defender AL.1 (G-BLNU) | AAC No 1 Flt, Aldergrove |
| | ZG847 | PBN 2T Turbine Defender AL.1 (G-BLNV) | AAC No 1 Flt, Aldergrove |
| | ZG848 | PBN 2T Turbine Defender AL.1 (G-BLNY) | AAC Defender Training Flight, Middle Wallop |
| | ZG856 | BAe Harrier GR7 | MoD(PE) for RAF |
| | ZG857 | BAe Harrier GR7 | MoD(PE) for RAF |
| | ZG858 | BAe Harrier GR7 | MoD(PE) for RAF |
| | ZG859 | BAe Harrier GR7 | MoD(PE) for RAF |
| | ZG860 | BAe Harrier GR7 | MoD(PE) for RAF |
| | ZG861 | BAe Harrier GR7 | MoD(PE) for RAF |
| | ZG862 | BAe Harrier GR7 | MoD(PE) for RAF |
| | ZG875 | WS61 Sea King HAS6 [270/N] | RN, No 814 Sqn, Culdrose |
| | ZG876 | WS61 Sea King HAS6 | MoD(PE) for RN |

| Reg. | Type | Owner or Operator | Notes |
|---|---|---|---|
| ZG879 | Powerchute Raider Mk 1 | MoD(PE)/Powerchute | |
| ZG884 | WS Lynx AH9 | MoD(PE) A&AEE, Boscombe Down | |
| ZG885 | WS Lynx AH9 | MoD(PE) for AAC | |
| ZG886 | WS Lynx AH9 | MoD(PE) for AAC | |
| ZG887 | WS Lynx AH9 | MoD(PE) for AAC | |
| ZG888 | WS Lynx AH9 | MoD(PE) for AAC | |
| ZG889 | WS Lynx AH9 | MoD(PE) for AAC | |
| ZG914 | WS Lynx AH9 | MoD(PE) for AAC | |
| ZG915 | WS Lynx AH9 | MoD(PE) for AAC | |
| ZG916 | WS Lynx AH9 | MoD(PE) for AAC | |
| ZG917 | WS Lynx AH9 | MoD(PE) for AAC | |
| ZG918 | WS Lynx AH9 | MoD(PE) for AAC | |
| ZG919 | WS Lynx AH9 | MoD(PE) for AAC | |
| ZG920 | WS Lynx AH9 | MoD(PE) for AAC | |
| ZG921 | WS Lynx AH9 | MoD(PE) for AAC | |
| ZG922 | WS Lynx AH9 | MoD(PE) for AAC | |
| ZG923 | WS Lynx AH9 | MoD(PE) for AAC | |
| ZG945 | BAe Sea Harrier FRS51 | *To Indian Navy as IN611* | |
| ZG946 | BAe Sea Harrier FRS51 | *To Indian Navy as IN612* | |
| ZG947 | BAe Sea Harrier FRS51 | *For Indian Navy as IN613* | |
| ZG948 | BAe Sea Harrier FRS51 | *For Indian Navy as IN614* | |
| ZG949 | BAe Sea Harrier FRS51 | *For Indian Navy as IN615* | |
| ZG950 | BAe Sea Harrier FRS51 | *For Indian Navy as IN616* | |
| ZG951 | BAe Sea Harrier FRS51 | *For Indian Navy as IN617* | |
| ZG952 | BAe Sea Harrier FRS51 | *For Indian Navy as IN618* | |
| ZG953 | BAe Sea Harrier FRS51 | *For Indian Navy as IN619* | |
| ZG954 | BAe Sea Harrier FRS51 | *For Indian Navy as IN620* | |
| ZG955 | BAe Sea Harrier FRS51 | *For Indian Navy as IN621* | |
| ZG956 | BAe Sea Harrier FRS51 | *For Indian Navy as IN622* | |
| ZG957 | BAe Sea Harrier FRS51 | *For Indian Navy as IN623* | |
| ZG969 | Pilatus PC-9 (HB-HQE) | BAe Brough | |
| ZG980 | WS61 Sea King 42B | *To IN535, Indian Navy* | |
| ZG984 | BAe Harrier T60 | *To Indian Navy as IN653* | |
| ZG989 | PBN 2T Turbine Defender Astor (G-DLRA) | MoD(PE) A&AEE, Boscombe Down | |
| ZG993 | PBN 2T Turbine Defender AL.1 (G-BOMD) | AAC No 1 Flight, Aldergrove | |
| ZG994 | PBN 2T Turbine Defender AL.1 (G-BPLN) | AAC No 1 Flight, Aldergrove | |
| ZH101 | Boeing E-3D Sentry AEW1 | RAF No 8 Sqn, Waddington | |
| ZH102 | Boeing E-3D Sentry AEW1 | RAF No 8 Sqn, Waddington | |
| ZH103 | Boeing E-3D Sentry AEW1 | MoD(PE) for RAF No 8 Sqn, Waddington | |
| ZH104 | Boeing E-3D Sentry AEW1 | MoD(PE) for RAF No 8 Sqn, Waddington | |
| ZH105 | Boeing E-3D Sentry AEW1 | MoD(PE) for RAF No 8 Sqn, Waddington | |
| ZH106 | Boeing E-3D Sentry AEW1 | MoD(PE) for RAF No 8 Sqn, Waddington | |
| ZH107 | Boeing E-3D Sentry AEW1 | MoD(PE) for RAF No 8 Sqn, Waddington | |
| ZH115 | Grob Vigilant T1 | RAF ACCGS, Syerston | |
| ZH116 | Grob Vigilant T1 | RAF No 632 VGS, Ternhill | |
| ZH117 | Grob Vigilant T1 | RAF No 632 VGS, Ternhill | |
| ZH118 | Grob Vigilant T1 | RAF No 632 VGS, Ternhill | |
| ZH119 | Grob Vigilant T1 | RAF No 616 VGS, Henlow | |
| ZH120 | Grob Vigilant T1 | RAF No 616 VGS, Henlow | |
| ZH121 | Grob Vigilant T1 | RAF No 616 VGS, Henlow | |
| ZH122 | Grob Vigilant T1 | RAF No 616 VGS, Henlow | |
| ZH123 | Grob Vigilant T1 | RAF No 642 VGS, Linton-on-Ouse | |
| ZH124 | Grob Vigilant T1 | RAF No 642 VGS, Linton-on-Ouse | |
| ZH125 | Grob Vigilant T1 | MoD (PE), A&AEE, Boscombe Down | |
| ZH126 | Grob Vigilant T1 | RAF No 642 VGS, Linton-on-Ouse | |
| ZH127 | Grob Vigilant T1 | RAF No 642 VGS, Linton-on-Ouse | |
| ZH128 | Grob Vigilant T1 | RAF No 612 VGS, Benson | |
| ZH129 | Grob Vigilant T1 | RAF No 612 VGS, Benson | |
| ZH144 | Grob Vigilant T1 | RAF No 612 VGS, Benson | |
| ZH145 | Grob Vigilant T1 | RAF No 632 VGS, Ternhill | |
| ZH146 | Grob Vigilant T1 | RAF No 637 VGS, Little Rissington | |
| ZH147 | Grob Vigilant T1 | RAF No 637 VGS, Little Rissington | |
| ZH148 | Grob Vigilant T1 | RAF No 637 VGS, Little Rissington | |
| ZH184 | Grob Vigilant T1 | RAF | |
| ZH185 | Grob Vigilant T1 | RAF | |
| ZH186 | Grob Vigilant T1 | RAF | |
| ZH187 | Grob Vigilant T1 | RAF | |
| ZH188 | Grob Vigilant T1 | RAF | |

| Notes | Reg. | Type | Owner or Operator |
|---|---|---|---|
| | ZH189 | Grob Vigilant T1 | RAF |
| | ZH190 | Grob Vigilant T1 | RAF |
| | ZH191 | Grob Vigilant T1 | RAF |
| | ZH192 | Grob Vigilant T1 | RAF |
| | ZH193 | Grob Vigilant T1 | RAF |
| | ZH194 | Grob Vigilant T1 | RAF |
| | ZH195 | Grob Vigilant T1 | RAF |
| | ZH196 | Grob Vigilant T1 | RAF |
| | ZH197 | Grob Vigilant T1 | RAF |
| | ZH200 | BAe Hawk 200 | MoD(PE), BAe Warton |
| | ZH204 | Shorts Tucano T51 | *To Kenya AF as 811* |
| | ZH205 | Shorts Tucano T51 | *To Kenya AF as 812* |
| | ZH205 | Grob Vigilant T1 | RAF Syerston |
| | ZH206 | Shorts Tucano T51 | *To Kenya AF as 813* |
| | ZH206 | Grob Vigilant T1 | RAF Syerston |
| | ZH207 | Shorts Tucano T51 | *To Kenya AF as 814* |
| | ZH207 | Grob Vigilant T1 | RAF Syerston |
| | ZH208 | Shorts Tucano T51 | *To Kenya AF as 815* |
| | ZH208 | Grob Vigilant T1 | RAF |
| | ZH209 | Shorts Tucano T51 | *To Kenya AF as 816* |
| | ZH209 | Grob Vigilant T1 | RAF |
| | ZH210 | Shorts Tucano T51 | *To Kenya AF as 817* |
| | ZH210 | Grob Vigilant T1 | RAF |
| | ZH211 | Grob Vigilant T1 | RAF |
| | ZH219 | WS Lynx Mk 99 | *To 90-0701 Korean Navy* |
| | ZH220 | WS Lynx Mk 99 | *To 90-0702 Korean Navy* |
| | ZH221 | WS Lynx Mk 99 | *For Korean Navy* |
| | ZH222 | WS Lynx Mk 99 | *For Korean Navy* |
| | ZH223 | WS Lynx Mk 99 | *For Korean Navy* |
| | ZH224 | WS Lynx Mk 99 | *For Korean Navy* |
| | ZH225 | WS Lynx Mk 99 | *For Korean Navy* |
| | ZH226 | WS Lynx Mk 99 | *For Korean Navy* |
| | ZH247 | Grob Vigilant T1 | MoD(PE) for RAF |
| | ZH248 | Grob Vigilant T1 | MoD(PE) for RAF |
| | ZH249 | Grob Vigilant T1 | RAF |
| | ZH263 | Grob Vigilant T1 | MoD(PE) for RAF |
| | ZH264 | Grob Vigilant T1 | MoD(PE) for RAF |
| | ZH265 | Grob Vigilant T1 | MoD(PE) for RAF |
| | ZH266 | Grob Vigilant T1 | MoD(PE) for RAF |
| | ZH267 | Grob Vigilant T1 | MoD(PE) for RAF |
| | ZH268 | Grob Vigilant T1 | MoD(PE) for RAF |
| | ZH269 | Grob Vigilant T1 | MoD(PE) for RAF |
| | ZH270 | Grob Vigilant T1 | MoD(PE) for RAF |
| | ZH271 | Grob Vigilant T1 | MoD(PE) for RAF |
| | ZH272 | Grob Vigilant T1 | MoD(PE) for RAF |

# RAF Maintenance Command/ Support Command 'M' number cross-reference

1764M/K4972
2365M/K6038
4354M/BL614
5377M/EP120
5405M/LF738
5466M/*BN230* (LF751)
5690M/MK356
5718M/BM597
5758M/DG202
6457M/ML427
6490M/LA255
6850M/TE184
6944M/RW386
6946M/RW388
6948M/DE673
6960M/MT847
7000M/TE392
7008M/EE549
7014M/N6720
7015M/NL985
7035M/*K2567* (DE306)
7060M/VF301
7090M/EE531
7118M/LA198
7119M/LA226
7150M/PK683
7151M/VT229
7154M/WB188
7174M/VX272
7175M/VV106
7200M/VT812
7241M/*X4474*
7243M/TE462
7244M/*X4277*
7245M/RW382
7246M/TD248
7256M/TB752
7257M/TB252
7279M/TB752
7281M/TB252
7285M/VV119
7288M/PK724
7293M/RW393
7323M/VV217
7325M/R5868
7326M/VN485
7362M/475081 (VP546)
7416M/WN907
7421M/WT660
7422M/WT684
7428M/WK198
7432M/WZ724
7443M/WX853
7451M/TE476
7458M/WX905
7464M/XA564
7467M/WP978
7470M/XA553
7473M/XE946
7491M/WT569
7496M/WT612
7499M/WT555
7510M/WT694
7525M/WT619
7530M/WT648
7532M/WT651
7533M/WT680
7544M/WN904
7548M/PS915
7554M/FS890
7564M/XE982
7570M/XD674
7582M/*WP180* (WP190)
7583M/WP185
7602M/WE600
7604M/*XD429* (XD542)
7605M/WS692
7606M/WV562
7607M/TJ138
7615M/WV679
7616M/WW388
7618M/WW442
7621M/WV686
7622M/WV606
7625M/WD356
7630M/VZ304
7631M/VX185
7641M/XA634
7645M/WD293
7646M/VX461
7648M/XF785
7656M/WJ573
7663M/XA571
7673M/WV332
7688M/WW421
7693M/WV483
7696M/WV493
7697M/WV495
7698M/WV499
7700M/WV544
7703M/WG725
7704M/TW536
7705M/WL505
7706M/WB584
7709M/WT933
7711M/PS915
7712M/WK281
7715M/XK724
7716M/WS776
7717M/XA549
7718M/WA577
7719M/WK277
7722M/XA571
7729M/WB758
7734M/XD536
7736M/WZ559
7737M/XD602
7739M/XA801
7741M/VZ477
7750M/*WK864* (WL168)
7751M/WL131
7755M/WG760
7758M/PM651
7759M/PK664
7761M/XH318
7762M/XE670
7770M/WT746
7796M/WJ676
7805M/TW117
7806M/TA639
7809M/XA699
7816M/WG763
7817M/TX214
7822M/XP248
7825M/WK991
7827M/XA917
7829M/XH992
7839M/WV781
7840M/XK482
7841M/WV783
7847M/WV276
7849M/XF319
7851M/WZ706
7852M/XG506
7854M/XM191
7855M/XK416
7859M/XP283
7860M/XL738
7862M/XR246
7864M/XP244
7865M/TX226
7866M/XH278
7867M/XH980
7868M/WZ736
7869M/WK935
7870M/XM556
7872M/*WZ826* (XD826)
7881M/WD413
7882M/XD525
7883M/XT150
7887M/XD375
7890M/XD453
7891M/XM693
7894M/XD818
7895M/WF784
7898M/XP854
7899M/XG540
7900M/WA576
7902M/WZ550
7906M/WH132
7917M/WA591
7920M/WL360
7923M/XT133
7928M/XE849
7930M/WH301
7931M/RD253
7932M/WZ744
7933M/XR220
7937M/WS843
7938M/XH903
7939M/XD596
7940M/XL764
7949M/XF974
7955M/XH767
7957M/XF545
7959M/WS774
7960M/WS726
7961M/WS739
7964M/WS760
7965M/WS792
7967M/*WS844* (WS788)
7969M/WS840
7970M/WP907
7971M/XK699
7972M/XH764
7973M/WS807
7976M/XK418
7979M/XM529
7980M/XM561
7982M/XH892
7983M/XD506
7986M/WG777
7988M/XL149
7990M/XD452
7997M/XG452
7998M/*XM515* (XD515)
8005M/WG768
8009M/XG518
8010M/XG547
8012M/VS562
8016M/XT677
8017M/XL762
8018M/XN344
8019M/WZ869
8021M/XL824
8022M/XN341
8023M/XD463
8027M/XM555
8032M/XH837
8033M/XD382
8034M/XL703
8041M/XF690
8043M/XF836
8046M/XL770
8049M/WE168
8050M/XG329
8051M/XN929
8052M/WH166
8054BM/XM417
8055AM/XM402
8055BM/XM404
8056M/XG337
8057M/XR243
8060M/WW397
8062M/XR669
8063M/WT536
8070M/EP120
8071M/TE476
8072M/PK624
8073M/TB252
8074M/TE392
8075M/RW382
8076M/XM386
8077M/XN594
8078M/XM351
8079M/XN492
8080M/XM480
8081M/XM468
8082M/XM409
8083M/XM367
8085M/XM467
8086M/TB752
8088M/XN602
8092M/WK654
8094M/WT520
8101M/WH984
8102M/WT486
8103M/WR985
8106M/WR982
8108M/WV703
8113M/WV753
8114M/WL798
8117M/WR974
8118M/WZ549
8119M/WR971
8121M/XM474
8128M/WH775
8130M/WH798
8131M/WT507
8133M/WT518
8139M/XJ582
8140M/XJ571
8141M/XN688
8142M/XJ560
8143M/XN691
8147M/XR526
8151M/WV795
8153M/WV903
8154M/WV908
8155M/WV797
8156M/XE339
8158M/XE369
8159M/XD528
8160M/XD622
8161M/XE993
8162M/WM913
8163M/XP919
8164M/*WN105* (WF299)
8165M/WH791
8169M/WH364
8171M/XJ607
8172M/XJ609
8173M/XN685
8176M/WH791
8177M/*WM311* (WM224)
8179M/XN928
8180M/XN930
8182M/XN953
8183M/*XN972* (XN962)
8184M/WT520
8186M/WR977
8187M/WH791
8188M/XG327
8189M/WD646
8190M/XJ918
8192M/XR658
8196M/XE920
8197M/WT346
8198M/WT339
8203M/XD377
8205M/XN819
8206M/WG419
8207M/WD318

8208M/WG303
8209M/WG418
8210M/WG471
8211M/WK570
8212M/WK587
8213M/WK626
8214M/WP864
8215M/WP869
8216M/WP927
8217M/WZ866
8224M/XN699
8226M/XP921
8229M/XM355
8230M/XM362
8231M/XM375
8232M/XM381
8233M/XM408
8234M/XN458
8235M/XN549
8236M/XP573
8237M/XS179
8238M/XS180
8239M/XS210
8344M/WH960
8345M/XG540
8346M/XN734
8350M/WH840
8352M/XN632
8355M/*KG374* (KN645)
8357M/WK576
8359M/WF825
8360M/WP863
8361M/WB670
8362M/WG477
8363M/WG463
8364M/WG464
8365M/XK421
8366M/XG454
8367M/XG474
8368M/XF926
8369M/WE139
8370M/N1671
8371M/XA847
8372M/K8042
8373M/P2617
8375M/NX611
8376M/RF398
8377M/R9125
8378M/*T9707*
8379M/DG590
8380M/Z7197
8382M/VR930
8383M/K9942
8384M/X4590
8385M/N5912
8386M/NV778
8387M/T6296
8388M/XL993
8389M/VX573
8390M/SL542
8392M/SL674
8393M/XK987
8394M/WG422
8395M/WF408
8396M/XK740
8398M/WR967
8399M/WR539
8401M/XP686
8402M/XN769
8403M/XK531
8406M/XP831
8407M/XP585
8408M/XS186
8409M/XS209
8410M/XR662
8413M/XM192
8414M/XM173
8417M/XM144
8418M/XM178
8422M/XM169
8427M/XM172
8428M/XH593
8429M/XH592
8431M/XR651
8434M/XM411
8435M/XN512
8436M/XN554
8437M/WG362
8439M/WZ846
8440M/WD935
8442M/XP411
8444M/XP400
8445M/XK968
8447M/XP359
8453M/XP745
8454M/XP442
8457M/XS871
8458M/XP672
8459M/XR650
8460M/XP680
8462M/XX477
8463M/XP355
8464M/XJ758
8465M/W1048
8466M/L-866
8467M/WP912
8468M/MM5701 (BT474)
8470M/584219
8471M/701152
8472M/120227 (VN679)
8473M/*WP180* (WP190)
8475M/360043 (PJ876)
8477M/4101 (DG200)
8478M/10639 (RN228)
8479M/730301
8482M/112372 (VK893)
8483M/420430
8484M/5439
8485M/997
8487M/J-1172
8488M/WL627
8490M/WH703
8491M/WJ880
8492M/WJ872
8493M/XR571
8494M/XP557
8495M/XR672
8498M/XR670
8499M/XP357
8501M/XP640
8502M/XP686
8503M/XS451
8505M/XL384
8506M/XR704
8507M/XS215
8508M/XS218
8509M/XT141
8510M/XP567
8513M/XN724
8514M/XS176
8515M/WH869
8516M/XR643
8535M/XN776
8538M/XN781
8546M/XN728
8548M/WT507
8549M/WT534
8550M/XT595
8551M/XN774
8554M/TG511
8556M/XN855
8559M/XN467
8560M/XR569
8561M/XS100
8564M/XN387
8565M/*T120* (E-408)
8566M/XV279
8567M/WL738
8568M/XP503
8569M/XR535
8570M/XR954
8571M/XR984
8572M/XM706
8573M/XM708
8575M/XP542
8576M/XP502
8577M/XP532
8578M/XR534
8579M/XR140
8580M/XP516
8581M/WJ775
8582M/XE874
8585M/XE670
8586M/XE643
8587M/XP677
8588M/XR681
8589M/XR700
8590M/XM191
8591M/XA813
8595M/XH278
8596M/LH208
8598M/WP270
8602M/*PF179* (XR541)
8604M/XS104
8606M/XP530
8608M/XP540
8609M/XR953
8610M/XL502
8611M/WF128
8615M/XP532
8617M/XM709
8618M/XP504
8619M/XP511
8620M/XP534
8621M/XR538
8622M/XR980
8623M/XR998
8624M/XS102
8626M/XS109
8627M/XP558
8628M/XJ380
8630M/WG362
8631M/XR574
8634M/WP314
8638M/XS101
8640M/XR977
8642M/XR537
8645M/XD163
8646M/XK969
8647M/XP338
8648M/XK526
8650M/XP333
8653M/XS120
8654M/XL898
8655M/XN126
8656M/XP405
8657M/VZ634
8661M/XJ727
8662M/XR458
8664M/WJ603
8666M/XE793
8667M/WP972
8668M/WJ821
8670M/XL384
8671M/XJ435
8672M/XP351
8673M/XD165
8674M/XP395
8676M/XL577
8677M/*XF519* (XJ695)
8678M/XE656
8679M/XF526
8680M/XF527
8681M/XG164
8682M/XP404
8683M/WJ870
8684M/XJ634
8685M/XF516
8687M/XJ639
8689M/WK144
8691M/WT518
8693M/WH863
8695M/WJ817
8696M/WH773
8699M/ZD232
8702M/XG196
8703M/VW453
8704M/XN643
8705M/XT281
8706M/XF383
8708M/XF509
8709M/XG209
8710M/XG274
8711M/XG290
8713M/XG225
8714M/XK149
8715M/*XF445* (XG264)
8716M/XV155
8718M/XX396
8719M/XT257
8721M/XP354
8722M/WJ640
8723M/XL567
8724M/XW923
8726M/XP299
8727M/XR486
8728M/WT532
8729M/WJ815
8730M/XD186
8731M/XP361
8732M/XJ729
8733M/XL318
8734M/XM657
8736M/XF375
8738M/*XF519* (XJ695)
8739M/XH170
8740/WE173
8741M/XW329
8743M/WD790
8745M/XL392
8746M/XH171
8747M/WJ629
8749M/XH537
8751M/XT255
8752M/XR509
8753M/WL795
8754M/XG882
8755M/*WH699* (WJ637)
8756M/XL427
8757M/XM656
8760M/XL386
8762M/WH740
8763M/WH665
8764M/XP344
8767M/XX635
8768M/A-522
8769M/A-528
8770M/XL623
8771M/XM602
8772M/WR960
8773M/XV156
8774M/XV338
8777M/XX914
8778M/XM598
8779M/XM607
8780M/WK102
8781M/WE982
8782M/XH136
8783M/XW272
8784M/VP976
8785M/XS642
8786M/XN495
8789M/XK970
8790M/XK986
8791M/XP329
8792M/XP345
8793M/XP346
8794M/XP398
8796M/XK943
8797M/XX947
8799M/WV787
8800M/XG226
8801M/XS650
8802M/XJ608
8805M/XT772
8806M/XP140
8807M/XL587
8810M/XJ825
8813M/VT260
8814M/XM927
8815M/XX118
8816M/XX734
8817M/XN652
8818M/XK527
8819M/XS479
8820M/VP952
8821M/XX115
8822M/VP957
8823M/VP965
8826M/XV638
8828M/XS587
8829M/XE653
8830M/XF515
8831M/XG160
8832M/XG172
8833M/XL569
8836M/XL592
8838M/*34037* (429356)
8839M/XG194
8840M/XG252

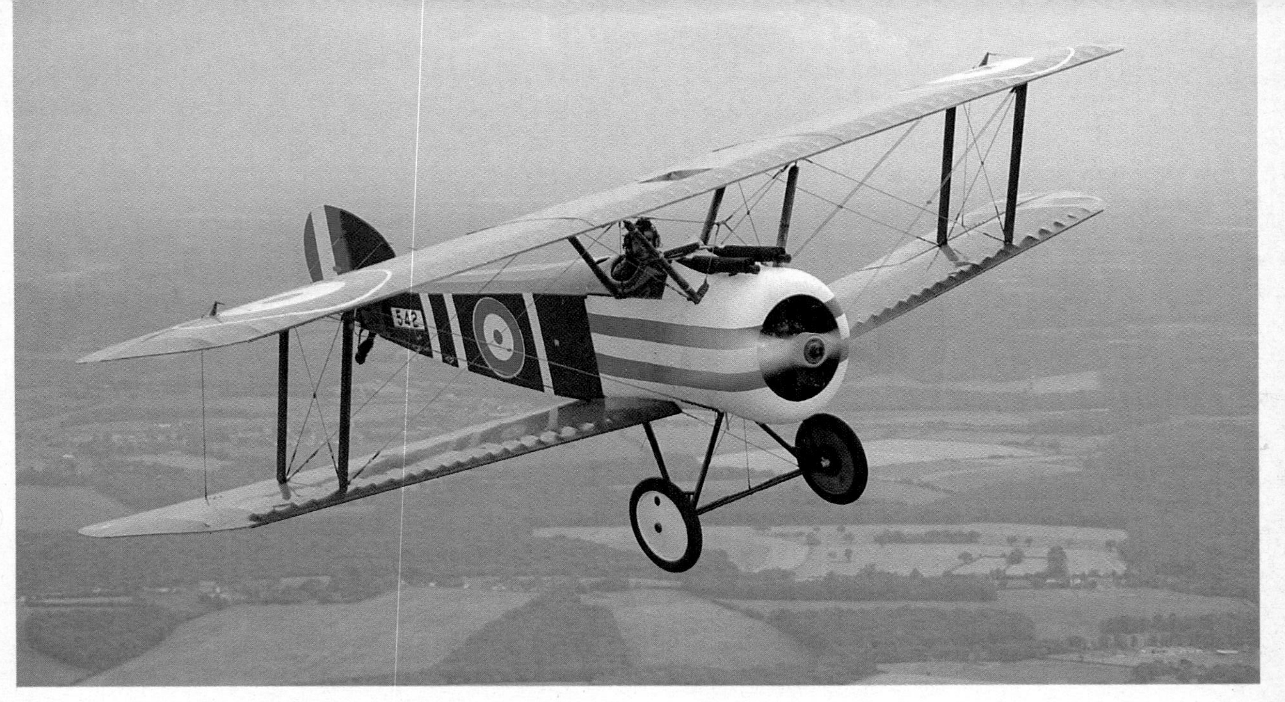


The Sopwith Camel Replica G-BPOB carries the serial 542. *PRM*

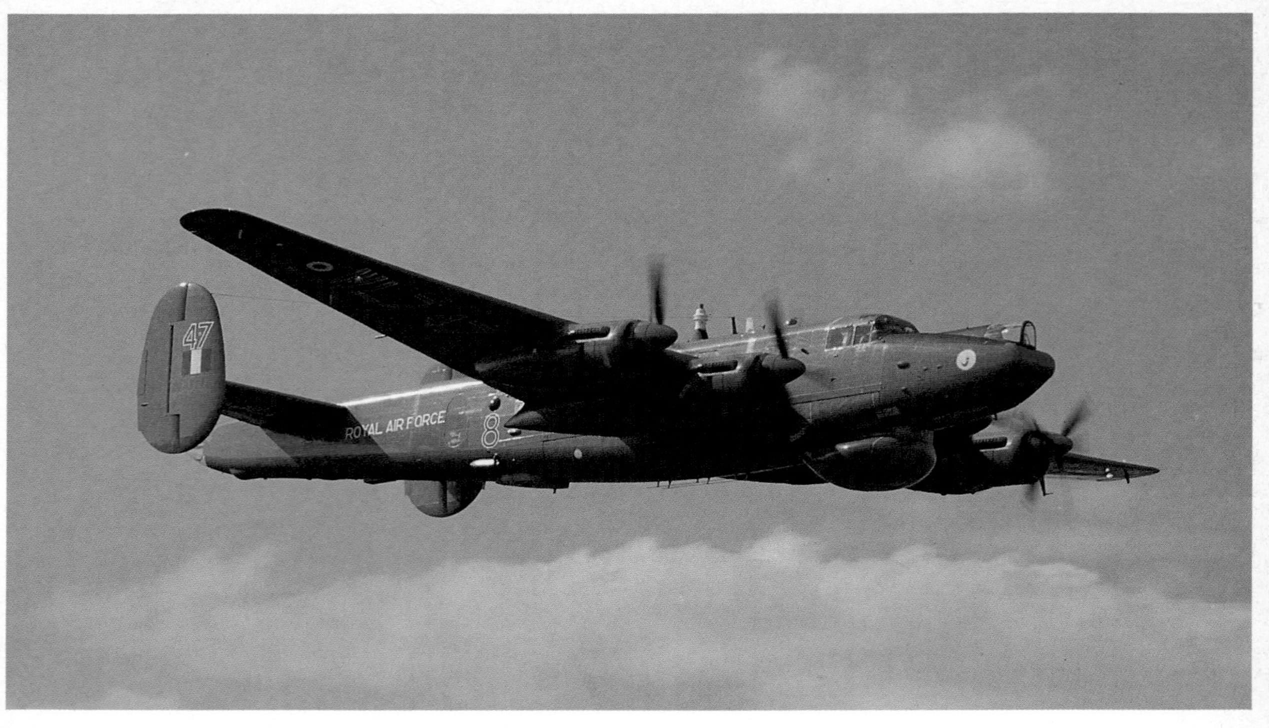


Avro Shackleton AEW2. WL747 of No 8 Squadron is based at RAF Lossiemouth. *PRM*

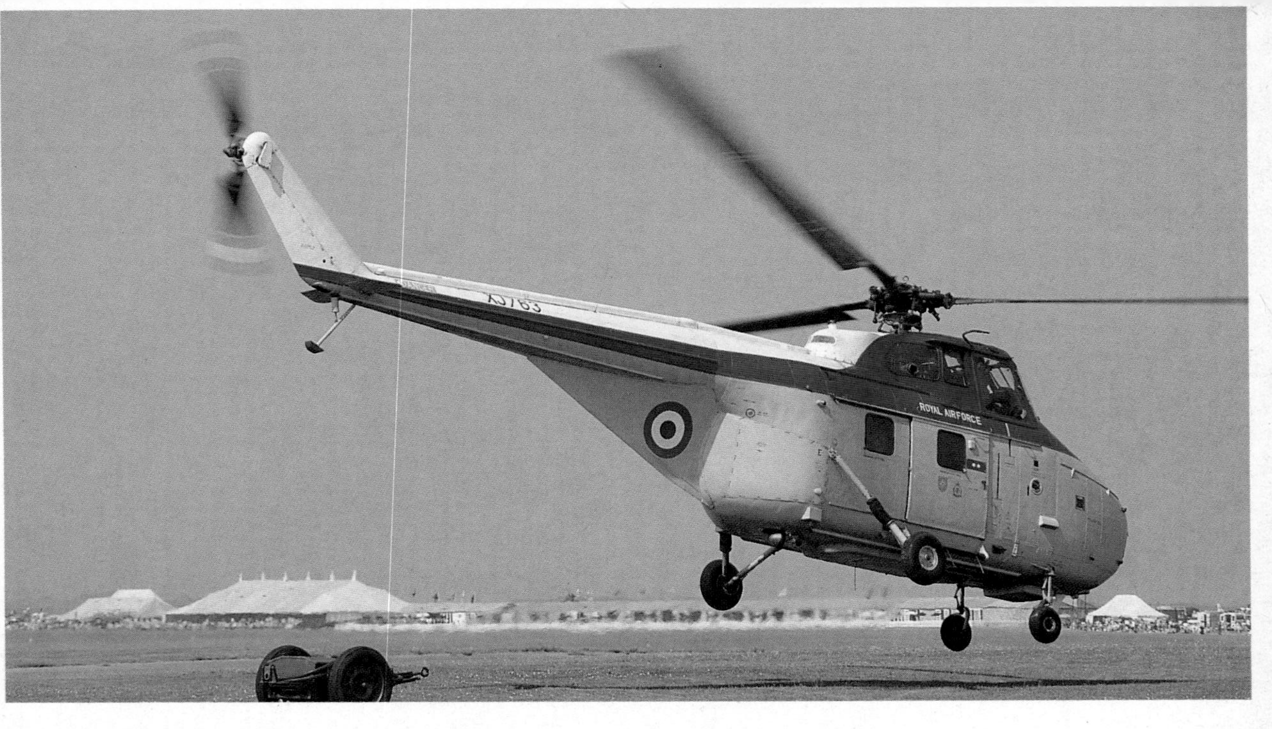


Whirlwind HAR10, XJ763 is now privately owned and is allocated the civil registration G-BKHA. *PRM*

HP Victor K2, XL188 of No 55 Squadron, RAF Marham, demonstrates a sprightly take-off. *PRM*

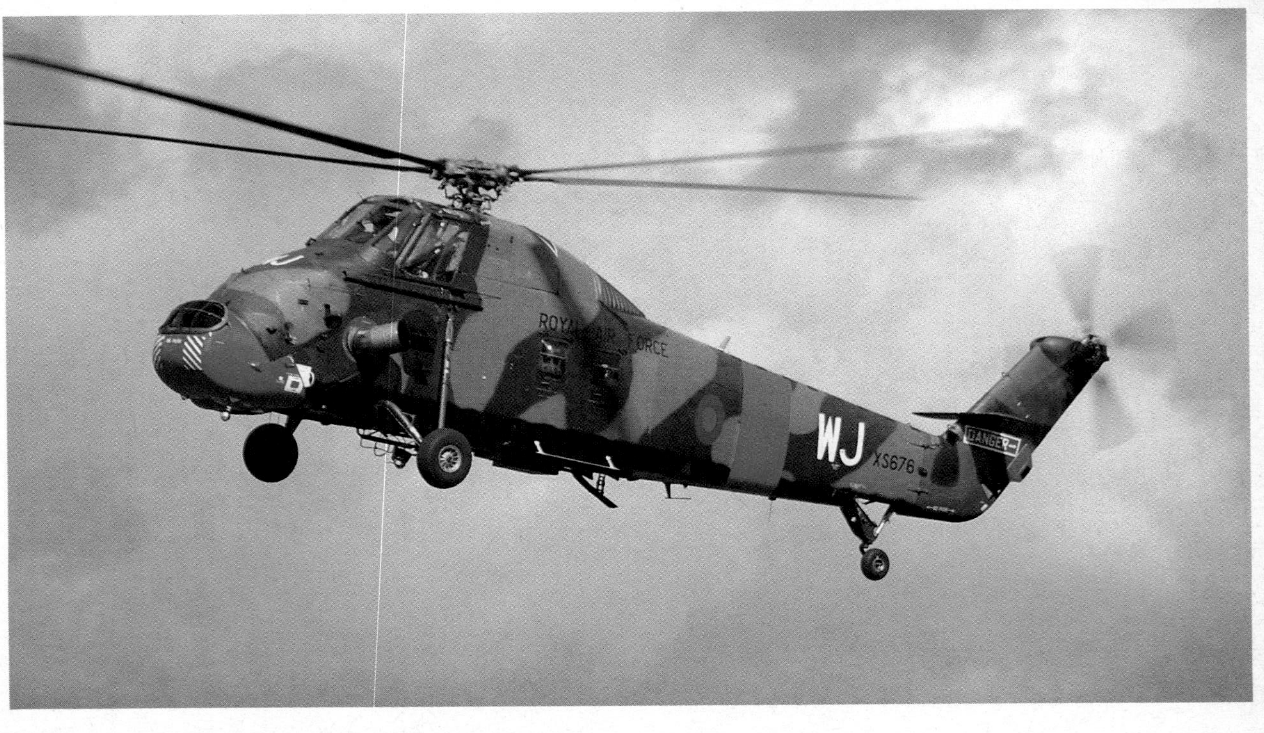


WS58 Wessex HC2, XS676, belongs to No 2FTS at Shawbury. *PRM*

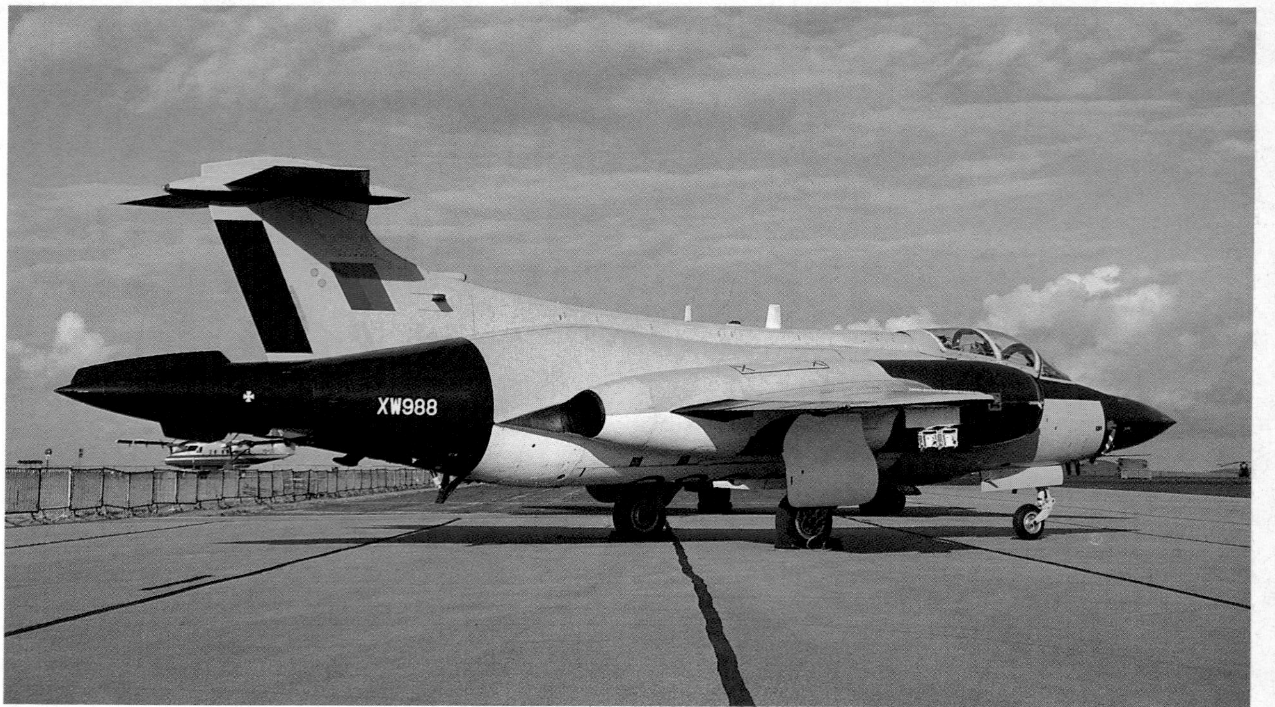

The unusual colour scheme carried by this Buccaneer S2B (XW988), reflects its 'posting' to MoD (PE) A&AEE Boscombe Down. *PRM*

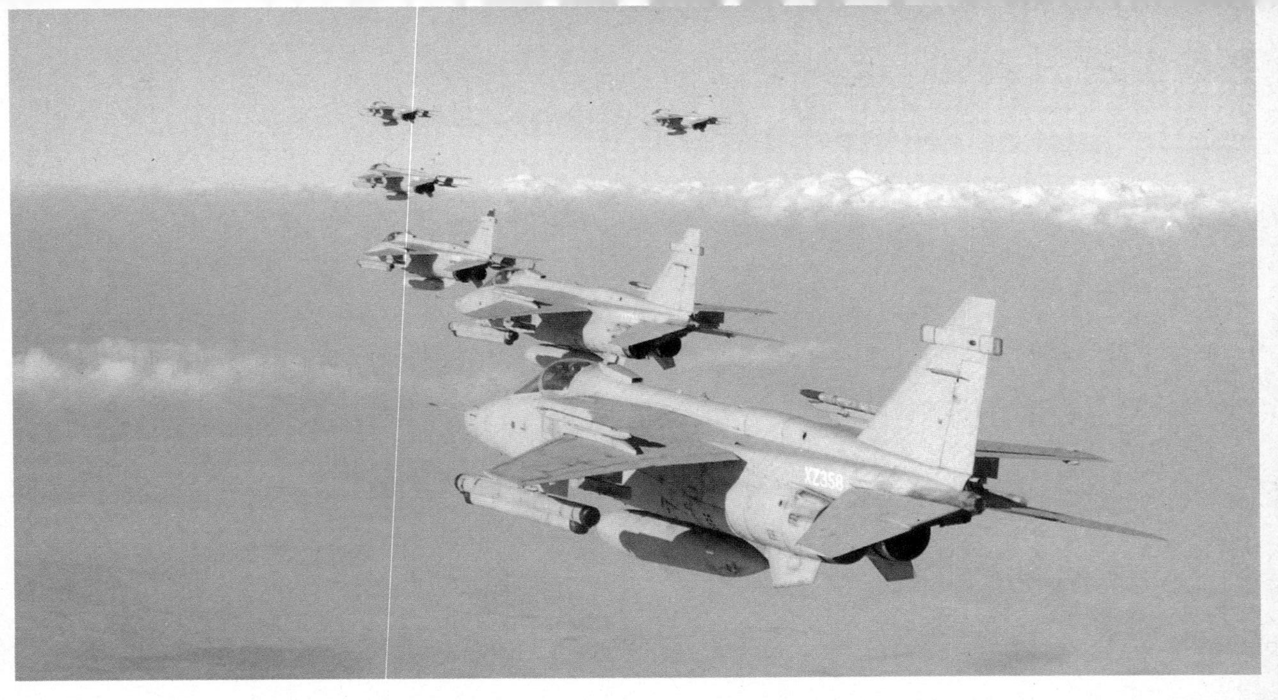


Six Jaguars operating in the Gulf region during the crisis in the Middle East, equipped with overwing Sidewinder rails and 'Desert Pink' colour scheme. The aircraft in the foreground is XZ358. *Sqn Ldr Tony Paxton*

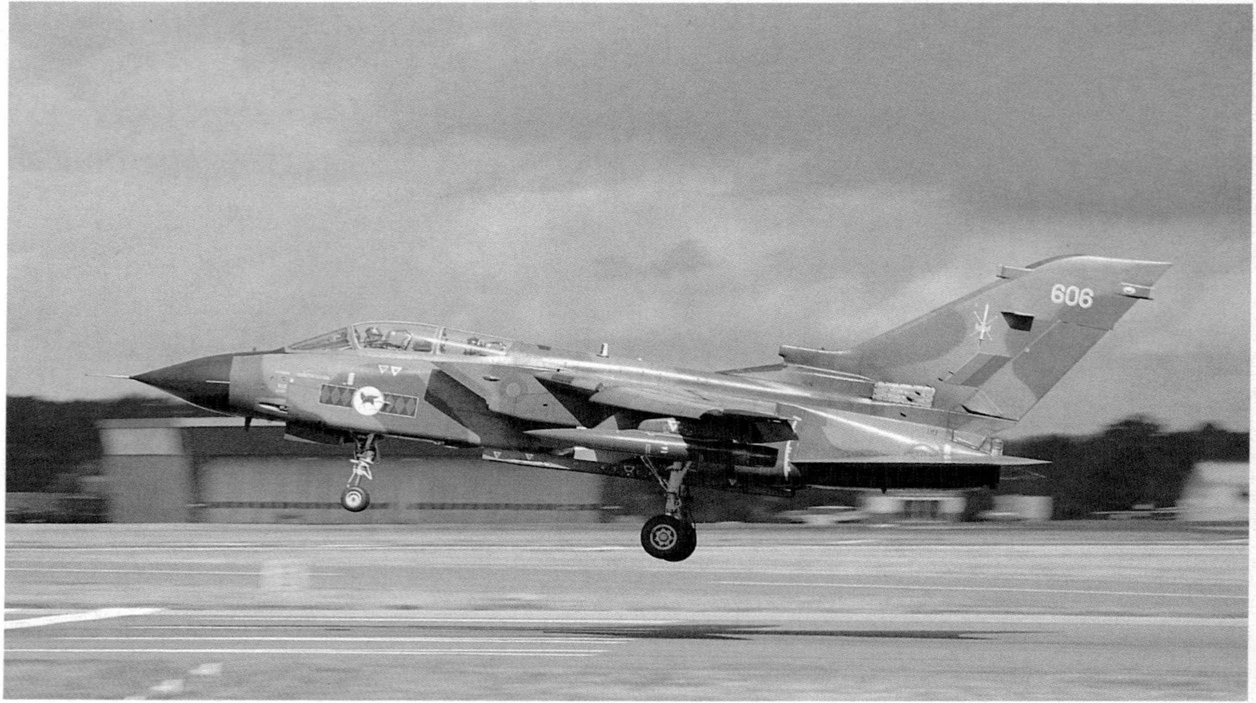

Panavia Tornado GR1 assigned to TWCU/No 45 Squadron at RAF Honington. *PRM*

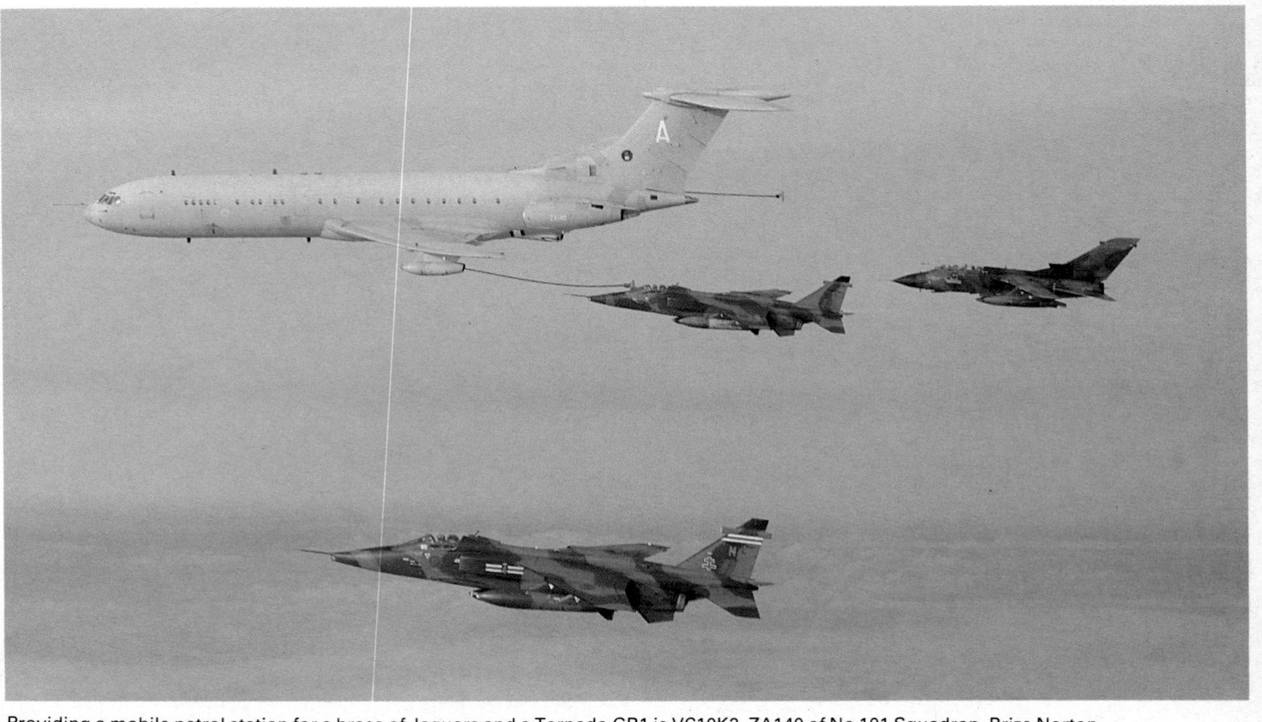

Providing a mobile petrol station for a brace of Jaguars and a Tornado GR1 is VC10K2, ZA140 of No 101 Squadron, Brize Norton.
*Sqn Ldr Michael Rondot*

Heading a line-up of Army Lynx is ZD277. *PRM*

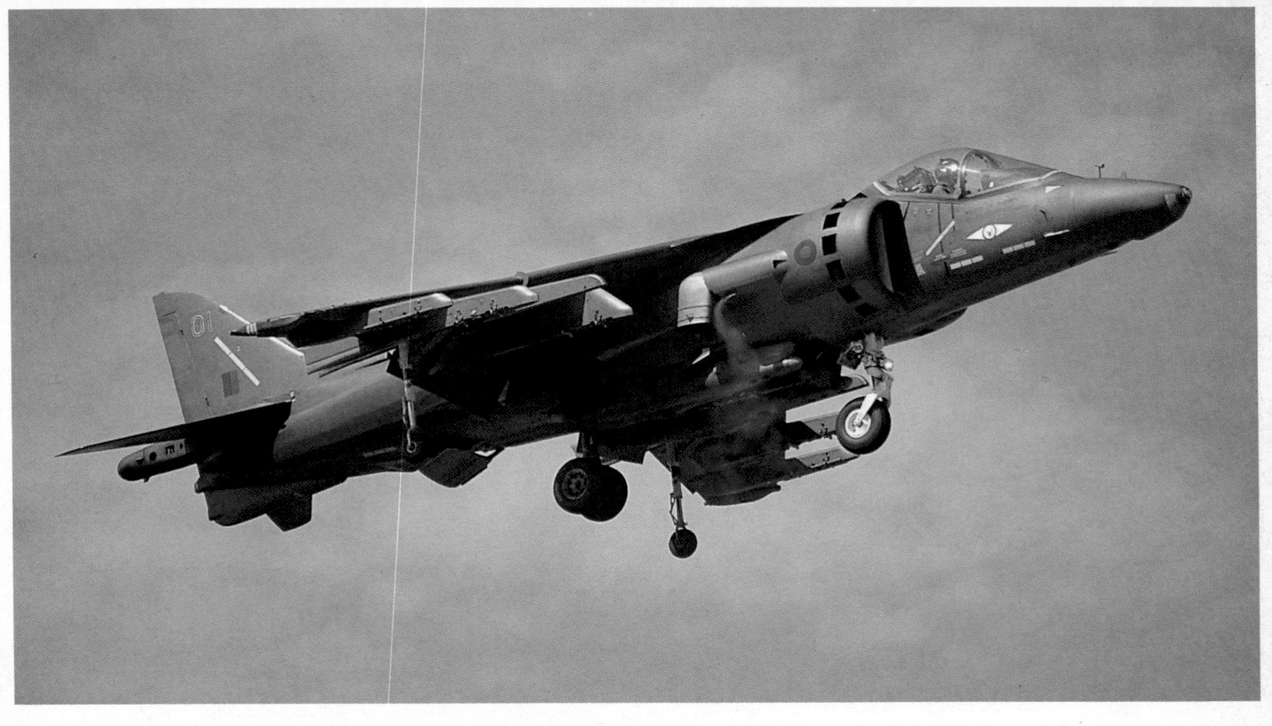


Flying with No 1 Squadron at RAF Wittering is Harrier GR5, ZD355/01. *PRM*

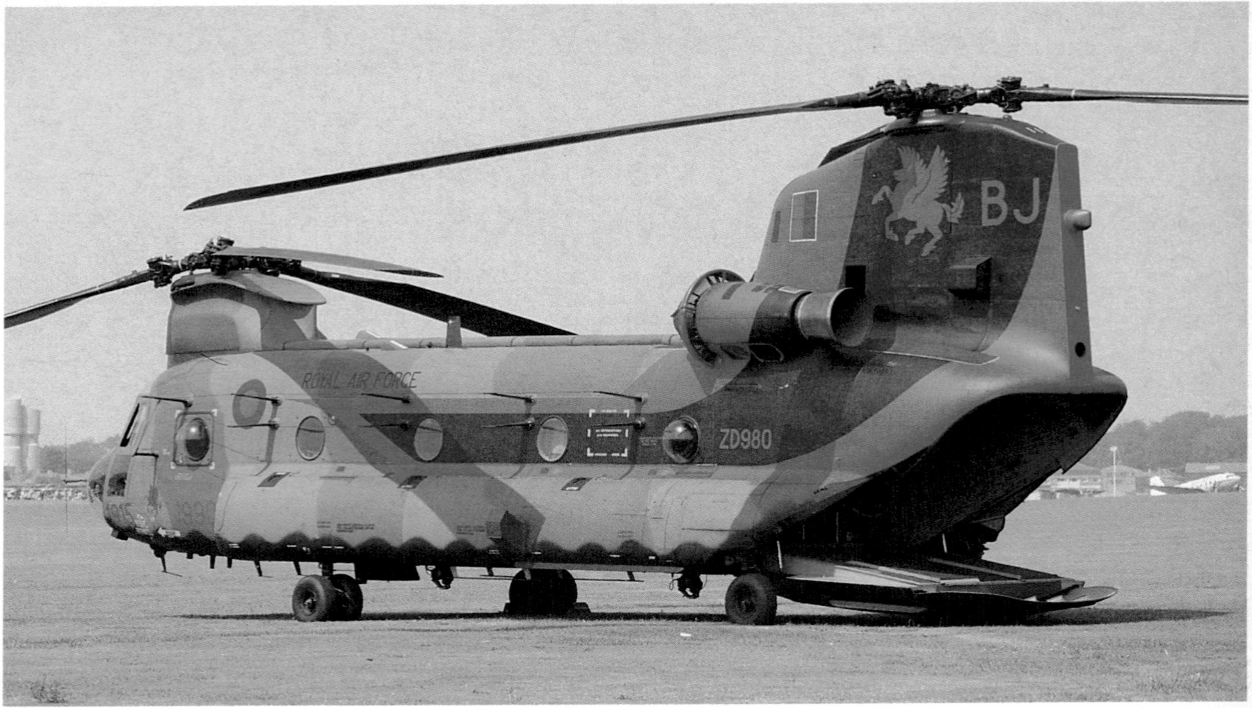

Carrying special anniversary markings is Chinook HC1 ZD980 of No 18 Squadron. *PRM*

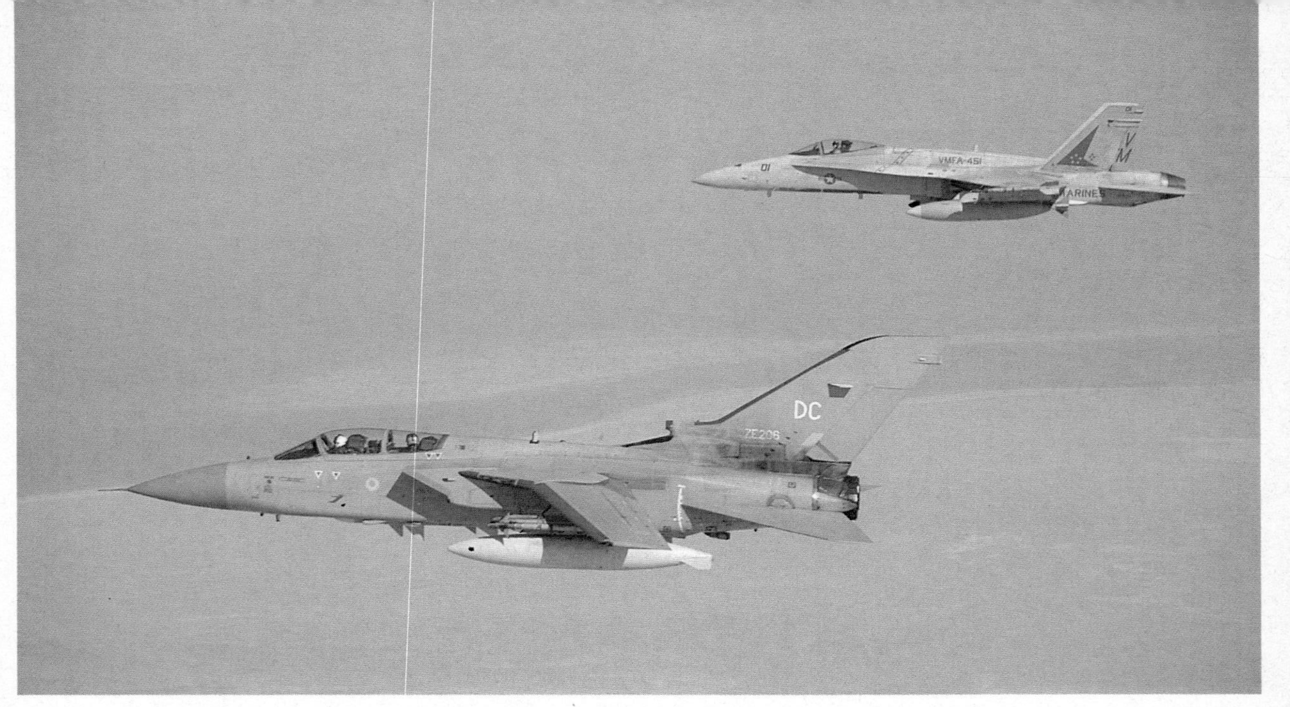


RAF Tornado F3 ZE206 of No 11 Squadron flying in formation with a US Marine Corps F-18 Hornet during the Gulf crisis. *Sqn Ldr Tony Paxton*

Scheduled to enter service with the Royal Navy in 1992 is the EH-101 Merlin helicopter. *PRM*

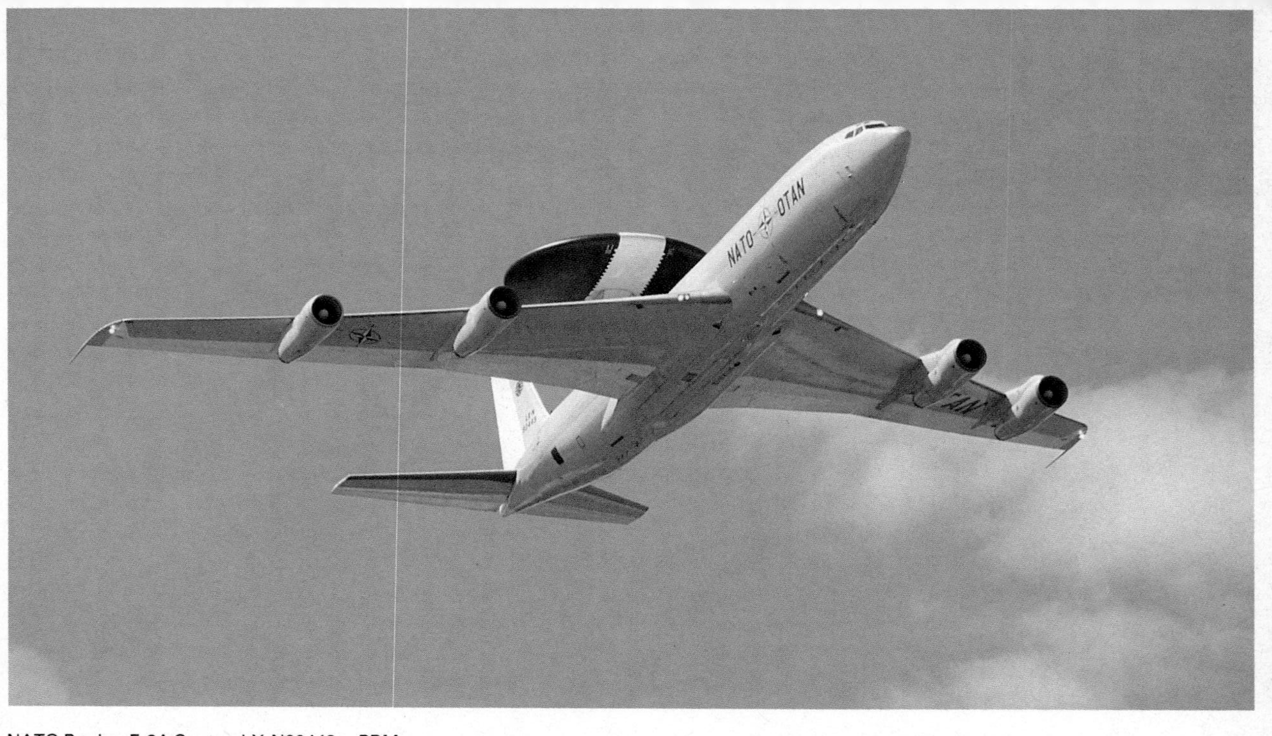


NATO Boeing E-3A Sentry, LX-N90443. *PRM*

RNethAF F-16 Fighting Falcon demonstrates its sleek lines as J-060 climbs-out at the start of a flying display. *PRM*

8845M/XS572
8847M/XX344
8848M/XZ135
8851M/XT595
8852M/XV337
8853M/XT277
8854M/XV154
8855M/XT284
8856M/XT274
8857M/XW544
8859M/XW545
8860M/XW549
8861M/XW528
8862M/XN473
8863M/XG154
8864M/WJ678
8865M/XN641
8866M/XL609
8867M/XK532
8868M/WH775
8869M/WH957
8870M/WH964
8871M/WJ565
8873M/XR453
8874M/XE597
8875M/XE624
8876M/*VM791* (XA312)
8877M/XP159
8879M/XX948
8880M/XF435
8881M/XG254
8882M/XR396
8884M/VX275
8886M/XA243
8887M/WK162
8888M/XA231
8889M/XN239
8890M/WT532
8892M/XL618
8894M/XT669
8895M/XX746
8896M/XX821
8897M/XX969
8898M/XX119
8899M/XX756
8900M/XZ368
8901M/XZ383
8902M/XX739
8903M/XX747
8904M/XX966
8905M/XX975
8906M/XX976
8907M/XZ371
8908M/XZ382
8909M/XV784
8910M/XL160
8911M/XH673
8913M/XT857
8915M/XH132
8916M/XL163
8917M/XM372
8918M/XX109
8919M/XT486
8920M/XT469
8921M/XT466
8923M/XX819
8924M/XP701
8925M/XP706
8926M/XP749
8927M/XP750
8929M/XP764
8930M/XR720
8931M/XV779
8932M/XR718
8933M/XX297
8934M/XR749
8935M/XR713
8937M/XX751
8938M/WV746
8939M/XP741
8940M/XR716
8941M/XT456
8942M/XN185
8943M/XE799
8944M/WZ791
8945M/XX818
8946M/XZ389
8947M/XX726
8948M/XX757
8949M/XX743
8950M/XX956
8951M/XX727
8952M/XX730
8953M/XX959
8954M/XZ384
8955M/XX110
8956M/XN577
8957M/XN582
8958M/XN501
8959M/XN472
8960M/XM455
8961M/XS925
8962M/XM371
8967M/XV263
8968M/XM471
8969M/XR753
8971M/XN548
8972M/XR754
8973M/XS922
8974M/XM473
8978M/XX837
8979M/XV747
8981M/XW764
8983M/XM478
8984M/XN551
8985M/WK127
8986M/XV261
8987M/XM358
8988M/XN593
8989M/XV740
8990M/XM419
8991M/XR679
8992M/XP547
8993M/XS219
8994M/XS178
8995M/XM425
8996M/XM414
8997M/XX669
8998M/XT864
8999M/XT859
9000M/XZ282
9001M/XV778
9002M/XW763
9003M/XZ390
9004M/XZ370
9005M/XZ374
9006M/XX967
9007M/XX968
9008M/XX140
9009M/XX763
9010M/XX764
9011M/XM412
9012M/XN494
9013M/XW298
9014M/XN584
9015M/XW320
9016M/XN640
9017M/
9018M/XW365
9019M/XX824
9020M/XX825
9021M/XX826
9022M/XX958
9023M/XX844
9024M/XL192

# RN Engineering 'A' airframe number cross-reference

*A430*/XV638
A646/SX300
A680/DE373
A696/SX300
A2001/*P4139* (HS618)
A2054/SX300
A2055/SX336
A2127/DE373
A2439/WF219
A2472/XA508
A2483/WF259
A2503/WM994
A2509/*WN105* (WF299)
A2510/WM913
A2511/*WM983* (XE489)
A2517/WM961
A2522/WM993
A2525/XN334
A2526/WV911
A2527/XP107
A2530/WM969
A2531/WG718
A2532/WV826
A2534/XE368
A2538/XJ393
A2539/XG831
A2542/XA862
A2543/XA870
A2556/XE327
A2557/WV798
A2571/XG577
A2572/XJ402
A2574/XD332
A2575/XG574
A2576/WV198
A2577/XB480
A2579/XN332
A2580/XE369
A2581/XK532
A2597/XS509
A2598/XJ482
A2600/XN934
A2603/XK911
A2605/XN308
A2607/XK944
A2608/XA459
A2609/XM329
A2610/XN647
A2612/XN650
A2614/XN314
A2616/XN651
A2618/XP116
A2619/XS695
A2620/XN650
A2624/XN692
A2625/XL846
A2626/XL847
A2627/XN967
A2628/XP558
A2629/XM667
A2630/XL853
A2632/WV903
A2633/XE369
A2635/XE339
A2637/WV797
A2639/XN650
A2640/XP155
A2642/XL836
A2643/*XN297* (XN311)
A2645/WF225
A2646/XK988
A2647/XS463
A2648/XS125
A2649/XS869
A2650/XP160
A2651/XG596
A2653/XK943
A2654/XN302
A2655/XN953
A2657/XX469
A2658/XP984
A2659/XV669
A2660/WV908
A2661/WV795
A2662/*WN105* (WF299)
A2664/XV644
A2666/XS872
A2667/XP226
A2668/XS885
A2669/XP149
A2670/XS128
A2671/XS867
A2672/XS537
A2673/WF122
A2674/WF125
A2675/XS881
A2678/XR955
A2680/XP157
A2682/XM845
A2683/XS878
A2684/XP151
A2685/XS886
A2686/XS873
A2687/XS877
A2688/XP158
A2689/XM874
A2690/XS887
A2691/XS868
A2692/XM917
A2693/XM843
A2694/XS865
A2695/XS876
A2696/XS882
A2697/XS870
A2699/XS570
A2700/XP930
A2701/XL500
A2702/XS545
A2703/XT441
A2705/XS866
A2706/XM868
A2707/XS122
A2710/
A2712/XN359
A2713/XN386
A2714/XL880
A2715/
A2716/
A2717/
A2718/
A2719/
A2720/
A2721/
A2722/XT757
A2723/XT487
A2724/XV623
A2725/XS538
A2726/XT786
A2727/
A2728/
A2729/
A2730/
A2731/
A2732/
A2733/
A2734/
A2735/
A2736/
A2737/
A2738/
A2739/
A2740/
A2741/
A2742/
A2743/
A2744/
A2745/
A2746/
A2747/
A2748/
A2749/
A2750/

# RAF Gliding and Soaring Association Markings

| Notes | Identity | Type, Previous Identity and Competition Number | Club and Location |
|---|---|---|---|
| | R1 | Schempp-Hirth Janus C (BGA 2723) | Cranwell GC, RAF Cranwell |
| | R2 | Schempp-Hirth Janus CE | RAFG&SA Centre, RAF Bicester |
| | R3 | Schleicher ASK-13 | RAFG&SA Centre, RAF Bicester |
| | R4 | Schleicher ASK-13 | Anglia GC, RAF Wattisham |
| | R5 | Schleicher Ka-7 | Cranwell GC, RAF Cranwell |
| | R6 | Schempp-Hirth Discus B | Wrekin GC, RAF Cosford |
| | R7 | Schleicher ASK-13 | Clevelands GC, RAF Dishforth |
| | R8 | Grob G102 Astir CS (OY-XGE) | RAFG&SA Centre, RAF Bicester |
| | R9 | Schempp-Hirth Janus B (BGA 2359) | Four Counties GC, RAF Syerston |
| | R10 | Schempp-Hirth Discus B [R10] | Four Counties GC, RAF Syerston |
| | R11 | Schempp-Hirth Discus B | Chilterns GC, RAF Halton |
| | R12 | Schempp-Hirth Discus B | Bannerdown GC, RAF Hullavington |
| | R15 | Schempp-Hirth Discus B | Anglia GC, RAF Wattisham |
| | R16 | Schempp-Hirth Ventus CT [16] | RAFG&SA Centre, RAF Bicester |
| | R17 | Schempp-Hirth Discus B | Fenlands GC, RAF Marham |
| | R18 | Schleicher ASW-19 B [R18] (BGA 2836) | Fenlands GC, RAF Marham |
| | R19 | Schleicher ASW-24 | RAFG&SA Centre, RAF Bicester |
| | R20 | Schleicher ASK-21 | Bannerdown GC, RAF Hullavington |
| | R21 | Schleicher ASK-21 | RAFG&SA Centre, RAF Bicester |
| | R22 | Schleicher ASK-21 | Wrekin GC, RAF Cosford |
| | R23 | Schempp-Hirth Discus B | Clevelands GC, RAF Dishforth |
| | R24 | Schempp-Hirth Ventus B [24] | Clevelands GC, RAF Dishforth |
| | R25 | Schleicher ASK-21 | Fulmar GC, RAF Kinloss |
| | R26 | Schempp-Hirth Nimbus 3DT [26] | RAFG&SA Centre, RAF Bicester |
| | R27 | Schempp-Hirth Ventus B [27] | Bannerdown GC, RAF Hullavington |
| | R28 | Schempp-Hirth Ventus CT | Cranwell GC, RAF Cranwell |
| | R29 | Schleicher Ka-7 | Humber GC, RAF Scampton |
| | R30 | Glaser-Dirks DG-300 [R30] | Humber GC, RAF Scampton |
| | R31 | Schleicher ASK-13 (BGA 2533) | Fulmar GC, RAF Kinloss |
| | R32 | Schleicher ASK-18 | Fulmar GC, RAF Kinloss |
| | R33 | Schleicher ASK-18 | Bannerdown GC, RAF Hullavington |
| | R34 | Schleicher ASK-13 | Chilterns GC, RAF Halton |
| | R35 | Schleicher ASK-21 | Cranwell GC, RAF Cranwell |
| | R36 | Schleicher ASK-18 | Four Counties GC, RAF Syerston |
| | R37 | Schleicher ASK-13 | Wrekin GC, RAF Cosford |
| | R40 | Schleicher ASK-21 (BGA2922) | RAFG&SA Centre, RAF Bicester |
| | R41 | Schleicher ASK-13 | Chilterns GC, RAF Halton |
| | R42 | Schleicher K-8B | Anglia GC, RAF Wattisham |
| | R43 | Schleicher ASK-18 | Wrekin GC, RAF Cosford |
| | R44 | Schleicher K-8B | Wrekin GC, RAF Cosford |
| | R45 | Schleicher K-8B | Fulmar GC, RAF Kinloss |
| | R46 | Schleicher ASK-13 | Fenlands GC, RAF Marham |
| | R47 | Schleicher K-8B | Chilterns GC, RAF Halton |
| | R48 | Schleicher ASK-18 | RAFG&SA Centre, RAF Bicester |
| | R49 | Schleicher ASK-18 | Fenlands GC, RAF Marham |
| | R50 | Grob G103 A Twin II Acro | RAFG&SA Centre, RAF Bicester |
| | R51 | Schleicher ASK-13 | Anglia GC, RAF Wattisham |
| | R52 | Grob G103A Twin II Acro | Clevelands GC, RAF Dishforth |
| | R57 | Grob G102 Astir CS | Four Counties GC, RAF Syerston |
| | R58 | Grob G103A Twin II Acro (BGA 2873) | Four Counties GC, RAF Syerston |
| | R60 | Grob G102 Astir 77 | Clevelands GC, RAF Dishforth |
| | R63 | Grob G102 Astir 77 | Humber GC, RAF Scampton |
| | R65 | Grob G102 Astir 77 | Cranwell GC, RAF Cranwell |
| | R67 | Grob G102 Astir 77 | Anglia GC, RAF Wattisham |
| | R68 | Grob G102 Astir 77 | Wrekin GC, RAF Cosford |
| | R69 | Grob G102 Astir CS | Cranwell GC, RAF Cranwell |
| | R75 | Schleicher K-8B | Fenlands GC, RAF Marham |
| | R77 | Grob G102 Astir CS | RAFG&SA Centre, RAF Bicester |
| | R78 | Grob G102 Astir 77 | Bannerdown GC, RAF Hullavington |
| | R80 | Schleicher ASK-13 | Bannerdown GC, RAF Hullavington |

| Identity | Type, Previous Identity and Competition Number | Club and Location | Notes |
|---|---|---|---|
| R82 | Grob G102 Astir 77 | Fulmar GC, RAF Kinloss | |
| R83 | Schleicher ASK-13 (BGA 1427) | Four Counties GC, RAF Syerston | |
| R84 | Grob G102 Astir 77 | Chilterns GC, RAF Halton | |
| R86 | Schleicher ASK-13 | Fenlands GC, RAF Marham | |
| R88 | Schleicher ASK-13 | Humber GC, RAF Scampton | |
| R95 | Schleicher K-8B | RAFG & SA Centre, RAF Bicester | |
| R96 | Schleicher K-8B | RAFG & SA Centre, RAF Bicester | |
| R97 | Grob G102 Astir (BGA 3216) | Bannerdown GC, RAF Hullavington | |
| R98 | Schleicher K-8B | Humber GC, RAF Scampton | |

# RN Gliding and Soaring Association Markings

| Identity | Type, Previous Identity and Competition Number | Club and Location | Notes |
|---|---|---|---|
| N12 | Grob G102 Astir II (BGA 2630) | Portsmouth Naval GC, RNAS Lee-on-Solent | |
| N13 | SZD-30 Pirat (BGA 2031) | Portsmouth Naval GC, RNAS Lee-on-Solent | |
| N14 | Slingsby T50 Skylark 4 (BGA 1239) | Portsmouth Naval GC, RNAS Lee-on-Solent | |
| N21 | Slingsby T21B Sedbergh (BGA 673) | Portsmouth Naval GC, RNAS Lee-on-Solent | |
| N22 | Omnipol L-13 Blanik (BGA 2407) | Portsmouth Naval GC, RNAS Lee-on-Solent | |
| N23 | Slingsby T49B Capstan (BGA 1196) | Portsmouth Naval GC, RNAS Lee-on-Solent | |
| N27 | Schleicher Ka-7 (BGA 1157) | Portsmouth Naval GC, RNAS Lee-on-Solent | |
| N29 | Schleicher ASK-13 (BGA 3254) | Portsmouth Naval GC, RNAS Lee-on-Solent | |
| N31 | Slingsby T.49B Capstan (BGA 1134) | Heron GC, RNAS Yeovilton | |
| N32 | LET L-13 Blanik (BGA 2066) | Heron GC, RNAS Yeovilton | |
| N33 | Schempp-Hirth H.S.7 Mini-Nimbus (BGA 2353) | Heron GC, RNAS Yeovilton | |
| N34 | Grob G102 Astir (BGA 2289) [480] | Heron GC, RNAS Yeovilton | |
| N35 | Grob G103 Twin Astir (BGA 3191) | Heron GC, RNAS Yeovilton | |
| N51 | Centrair 101A Pegase (BGA 2987/EVM) | Seahawk GC, RNAS Culdrose | |
| N52 | SZD-30 Pirat II (BGA 1551/CHG) | Seahawk GC, RNAS Culdrose | |
| N53 | LET L-13 Blanik (BGA 2263/DPC) | Seahawk GC, RNAS Culdrose | |
| N54 | Slingsby T49B Capstan (BGA 1360/BZG) | Seahawk GC, RNAS Culdrose | |
| N55 | Slingsby T49B Capstan (BGA 1118/BPD) | Seahawk GC, RNAS Culdrose | |

# Army Gliding and Soaring Association Markings

| Identity | Type, Previous Identity and Competition Number | Club and Location | Notes |
|---|---|---|---|
| AGA 1 | Rolladen-Schneider LS4 [412] | Wyvern GC, RAF Upavon | |
| AGA 2 | Schempp-Hirth HS7 Mini-Nimbus C (BGA2553/EBK) [52] | Kestrel GC, RAF Odiham | |
| AGA 3 | Schempp-Hirth Cirrus 75 [A7] (BGA2114/DGX) | Kestrel GC, RAF Odiham | |
| AGA 4 | Schempp-Hirth Discus [12] | Wyvern GC, RAF Upavon | |
| AGA 6 | Grob G102 Astir CS [212] | Wyvern GC, RAF Upavon | |
| AGA 8 | Schleicher ASK-21 [EKG] (BGA2742) | Wyvern GC, RAF Upavon | |
| AGA 9 | Schleicher ASK-23 [A6] | Wyvern GC, RAF Upavon | |
| AGA 11 | Schleicher ASK-21 [A3] | Kestrel GC, RAF Odiham | |
| AGA 14 | Schleicher ASK-13 [A2] | Wyvern GC, RAF Upavon | |
| AGA 15 | Schleicher ASK-13 [A1] (BGA2385/DUE) | Kestrel GC, RAF Odiham | |
| AGA 16 | Schleicher ASK-18 | Kestrel GC, RAF Odiham | |
| AGA 18 | Schleicher ASK-23 [A5] | Kestrel GC, RAF Odiham | |

# RN Landing Platform and Shore Station Code-letters

**Alpha-Numeric Sequence**

| Notes | Sqn code | Deck letters | Name and Pennant Number | Type/task/squadron |
|---|---|---|---|---|
| | 323 | AB | HMS *Ambuscade* (F172) | Type 21 (815 Sqn) |
| | 430 | AC | HMS *Achilles* (F12) | Leander |
| | 455 | AE | HMS *Ariadne* (F72) | Leander |
| | 341 | AG | HMS *Avenger* (F185) | Type 21 (815 Sqn) |
| | 327 | AL | HMS *Alacrity* (F174) | Type 21 (815 Sqn) |
| | 472 | AM | HMS *Andromeda* (F57) | Leander (815 Sqn) |
| | | AS | RFA *Argus* (A135) | Aviation Training ship |
| | 466 | AT | HMS *Argonaut* (F56) | Leander (829 Sqn) |
| | 322 | AV | HMS *Active* (F171) | Type 21 (815 Sqn) |
| | 326 | AW | HMS *Arrow* (F173) | Type 21 (815 Sqn) |
| | 365/6 | AY | HMS *Argyll* (F232) | Type 23 |
| | 320 | AZ | HMS *Amazon* (F169) | Type 21 (815 Sqn) |
| | 328 | BA | HMS *Brave* (F94) | Type 22 (829 Sqn) |
| | — | BD | RFA *Sir Bedivere* (L3004) | Landing ship |
| | — | BE | RFA *Blue Rover* (A270) | Fleet tanker |
| | 333 | BM | HMS *Birmingham* (D86) | Type 42 (815 Sqn) |
| | 342 | BT | HMS *Brilliant* (F90) | Type 22 (829 Sqn) |
| | — | BV | HMS *Black Rover* (A273) | Fleet tanker |
| | 346/7 | BW | HMS *Broadsword* (F88) | Type 22 (829 Sqn) |
| | 403 | BX | HMS *Battleaxe* (F89) | Type 22 (829 Sqn) |
| | 330 | BZ | HMS *Brazen* (F91) | Type 22 (829 Sqn) |
| | 335 | CF | HMS *Cardiff* (D108) | Type 42 (815 Sqn) |
| | — | CH | HMS *Challenger* (K07) | Seabed ops |
| | 350/1 | CL | HMS *Cumberland* (F85) | Type 22 (829 Sqn) |
| | 348/9 | CM | HMS *Chatham* (F87) | Type 22 (829 Sqn) |
| | 463 | CP | HMS *Cleopatra* (F28) | Leander |
| | 338/9 | CT | HMS *Campbeltown* (F86) | Type 22 (829 Sqn) |
| | — | CU | RNAS Culdrose (HMS *Seahawk*) | |
| | 336 | CV | HMS *Coventry* (F98) | Type 22 (829 Sqn) |
| | 412/3 | CW | HMS *Cornwall* (F99) | Type 22 (829 Sqn) |
| | 431 | CY | HMS *Charybdis* (F75) | Leander (815 Sqn) |
| | — | DC | HMS *Dumbarton Castle* (P268) | Fishery protection |
| | — | DG | RFA *Diligence* (A132) | Maintenance |
| | 464 | DN | HMS *Danae* (F47) | Leander (829 Sqn) |
| | 411 | EB | HMS *Edinburgh* (D97) | Type 42 (815 Sqn) |
| | 434/5 | ED | HMS *Endurance* (A171) | Ice Patrol (829 Sqn) |
| | 420 | EX | HMS *Exeter* (D89) | Type 42 (815 Sqn) |
| | — | FA | RFA *Fort Austin* (A386) | Support ship |
| | 343 | FG | RFA *Fort Grange* (A385) | Support ship |
| | — | FL | RNAY Fleetlands | |
| | — | FS | HMS *Fearless* (L10) | Assault |
| | 410 | GC | HMS *Gloucester* (D96) | Type 42 (815 Sqn) |
| | 321 | GIB | Gibraltar Airport | – (815 Sqn) |
| | — | GD | RFA *Sir Galahad* (L3005) | Landing ship |
| | — | GN | RFA *Green Rover* (A268) | Fleet tanker |
| | — | GR | RFA *Sir Geraint* (L3027) | Landing ship |
| | — | GV | RFA *Gold Rover* (A271) | Fleet tanker |
| | 344 | GW | HMS *Glasgow* (D88) | Type 42 (815 Sqn) |
| | — | GY | RFA *Grey Rover* (A269) | Fleet tanker |
| | 475 | HM | HMS *Hermione* (F58) | Leander (815 Sqn) |
| | 325 | HR | HMS *Herald* | Survey ship |
| | — | ID | HMS *Intrepid* (L11) | Assault |
| | 465 | JO | HMS *Juno* (F52) | Leander |
| | 443 | JP | HMS *Jupiter* (F60) | Leander (815 Sqn) |
| | — | L | HMS *Illustrious* (R06) | Carrier |
| | 365/6 | LA | HMS *Lancaster* (F233) | Type 23 |
| | — | LC | HMS *Leeds Castle* (P258) | Fishery protection |
| | 405 | LO | HMS *London* (F95) | Type 22 (829 Sqn) |
| | 332 | LP | HMS *Liverpool* (D92) | Type 42 (815 Sqn) |
| | — | LS | RNAS Lee-on-Solent (HMS *Daedalus*) | |
| | 363/4 | MA | HMS *Marlborough* (F231) | Type 23 |
| | 360 | MC | HMS *Manchester* (D95) | Type 42 (815 Sqn) |
| | 424 | MV | HMS *Minerva* (F45) | Leander (829 Sqn) |
| | — | N | HMS *Invincible* (R05) | Carrier |
| | 345 | NC | HMS *Newcastle* (D87) | Type 42 (815 Sqn) |

| Sqn code | Deck letters | Name and Pennant Number | Type/task/squadron | Notes |
|---|---|---|---|---|
| 361/2 | NF | HMS *Norfolk* (F230) | Type 23 | |
| 417 | NM | HMS *Nottingham* (D91) | Type 42 (815 Sqn) | |
| 347 | OD | RFA *Olmeda* (A124) | Fleet tanker | |
| 347 | ON | RFA *Olna* (A123) | Fleet tanker | |
| 347 | OW | RFA *Olwen* (A122) | Fleet tanker | |
| 454 | PN | HMS *Penelope* (F127) | Leander (829 Sqn) | |
| — | PO | RNAS Portland (HMS *Osprey*) | | |
| — | PV | RFA *Sir Percival* (L3036) | Landing ship | |
| — | PW | Prestwick Airport (HMS *Gannet*) | | |
| — | R | HMS *Ark Royal* (R09) | Carrier | |
| 436 | RG | RFA *Regent* (A486) | Support ship | |
| 437 | RS | RFA *Resource* (A480) | Support ship | |
| 432 | SC | HMS *Scylla* (F71) | Leander (815 Sqn) | |
| 352 | SD | HMS *Sheffield* (F96) | Type 23 (829 Sqn) | |
| 334 | SN | HMS *Southampton* (D90) | Type 42 | |
| 450 | SS | HMS *Sirius* (F40) | Leander (815 Sqn) | |
| — | TM | RFA *Sir Tristram* (L3505) | Landing ship | |
| 347 | TS | RFA *Tidespring* (A75) | Fleet tanker | |
| 375 | VB | HMS *Beaver* (F93) | Type 22 (829 Sqn) | |
| — | VL | RNAS Yeovilton (HMS *Heron*) | | |
| — | WU | RNAY Wroughton | | |
| 376 | XB | HMS *Boxer* (F92) | Type 22 | |
| 407 | YK | HMS *York* (D98) | Type 42 (815 Sqn) | |
| — | — | HMS *Iron Duke* (F234) | Type 23 | |
| — | — | HMS *Monmouth* (F235) | Type 23 | |
| — | — | HMS *Montrose* (F236) | Type 23 | |
| — | — | RFA *Fort Victoria* | Auxiliary Oiler Replenishment | |
| — | — | RFA *Fort George* | Auxiliary Oiler Replenishment | |

# Ships' Numeric Code — Deck Letters Analysis

| | 0 | 1 | 2 | 3 | 4 | 5 | 6 | 7 | 8 | 9 |
|---|---|---|---|---|---|---|---|---|---|---|
| **32** | AZ | GIB | AV | AB | | | AW | AL | BA | |
| **33** | BZ | | LP | BM | SN | CF | CV | | CT | CT |
| **34** | | AG | BT | FG | GW | NC | BW | BW | CM | CM |
| **35** | CL | CL | | | | | | | | |
| **36** | MC | NF | NF | MA | MA | AY | AY | | | |
| **37** | | | | | | VB | XB | | | |
| **40** | | | | BX | | LO | | YK | | |
| **41** | GC | EB | CW | CW | | | | NM | | |
| **42** | EX | | | | MV | | | | | |
| **43** | AC | CY | SC | | ED | ED | RG | RS | | |
| **44** | | | | JP | | | | | | |
| **45** | SS | | | | PN | AE | | | | |
| **46** | | | | CP | DN | JO | AT | | | |
| **47** | | | AM | | | HM | | | | |

# RN Code-Squadron-Base-Aircraft Cross-check

| *Code Numbers* | *Deck/Base Letters* | *Unit* | *Location* | *Aircraft Type(s)* |
|---|---|---|---|---|
| 000–005 | R | 801 Sqn | Yeovilton | Sea Harrier FRS1 |
| 010–020 | R | 820 Sqn | Culdrose | Sea King HAS5 |
| 122–129 | N | 800 Sqn | Yeovilton | Sea Harrier FRS1 |
| 130–139 | — | 826 Sqn | Culdrose | Sea King HAS5 |
| 180–187 | — | 849 Sqn | Culdrose | Sea King AEW2A |
| 264–274 | N | 814 Sqn | Culdrose | Sea King HAS5 |
| 300–306 | PO | 815 Sqn | Portland | Lynx HAS2/HAS3 |
| 320–479 | * | 815/829 Sqns | Portland | Lynx HAS2/HAS3 |
| 500–510 | — | 810 Sqn | Culdrose | Sea King HAS5 |
| 538–559 | CU | 705 Sqn | Culdrose | Gazelle HT2 |
| 560–575 | CU | 750 Sqn | Culdrose | Jetstream T2 |
| 576–579 | CU | 750 Sqn | Culdrose | Jetstream T3 |
| 580–599 | — | 706 Sqn | Culdrose | Sea King HAS5 |
| 600–605 | PO | 829 Sqn | Portland | Lynx HAS2/HAS3 |
| 606–612 | PO | 829 Sqn | Portland | Lynx HAS2/HAS3 |
| 620–628 | PO | 772 Sqn | Portland | Sea King HC4 |
| 630–638 | PO | 702 Sqn | Portland | Lynx HAS2/HAS3 |
| 640–648 | PO | 702 Sqn | Portland | Lynx HAS2/HAS3 |
| 701–708 | PW | 819 Sqn | Prestwick | Sea King HAS6 |
| 710–716 | VL | 899 Sqn | Yeovilton | Sea Harrier FRS1 |
| 717-718, 723 | VL | 899 Sqn | Yeovilton | Harrier T4N |
| 719–720 | VL | 899 Sqn | Yeovilton | Hunter T8M |
| 721–722 | VL | 899 Sqn | Yeovilton | Sea Harrier FRS1 |
| 738–739 | VL | Station Flt | Yeovilton | Chipmunk T10 |
| 816–817 | — | 771 Sqn | Culdrose | Chipmunk T10 |
| 820–826 | CU | 771 Sqn | Culdrose | Sea King HAR5 |
| 830–838 | VL | FRADU | Yeovilton | Hunter GA11 |
| 840–848 | VL | FRADU | Yeovilton | Canberra TT18 |
| 860–868 | VL | FRADU | Yeovilton | Hunter GA11 |
| 869–880 | VL | FRADU | Yeovilton | Hunter T7/T8 |
| 901–912 | — | FGF | Plymouth | Chipmunk T10 |

*See foregoing separate ships' Deck Letter Analysis

Note that only the 'last two' digits of the Code are worn by some aircraft types, especially helicopters.

# British-based Historic Aircraft in Overseas Markings

Some 'Historic' aircraft carry the markings of overseas air arms and can be seen in the UK, mainly preserved in museums and collections or taking part in air shows.

| *Serial* | *Type (alternative identity)* | *Owner, operator and location* | *Notes* |
|---|---|---|---|
| **Argentina** | | | |
| A-515 | FMA IA58 Pucara (ZD485) | RAF Cosford Aerospace Museum | |
| A-517 | FMA IA58 Pucara (G-BLRP) | Privately owned, Channel Islands | |
| A-522 | FMA IA58 Pucara (8768M) | FAA Museum, RNAS Yeovilton | |
| A-528 | FMA IA58 Pucara (8769M) | Museum of Army Flying, Middle Wallop | |
| A-533 | FMA IA58 Pucara (ZD486) | Museum of Army Flying, Middle Wallop | |
| A-549 | FMA IA58 Pucara (ZD487) | Imperial War Museum, Duxford | |
| AE-406 | Bell UH-1H | Museum of Army Flying, Middle Wallop | |
| AE-409 | Bell UH-1H [656] | Museum of Army Flying, Middle Wallop | |
| AE-422 | Bell UH-1H | FAA Museum, RNAS Yeovilton | |
| AE-520 | Vertol CH-47C Chinook | RAF, stored Wroughton | |
| PA-12 | SA330L Puma HC1 (ZE449) | Westlands, Sherborne | |
| 0729 | Beech T-34C Turbo Mentor [1-A-411] | FAA Museum, RNAS Yeovilton | |
| 0767 | Macchi MB339AA [4-A-116] | Rolls-Royce, Filton | |
| **Australia** | | | |
| A2-4 | Supermarine Seagull V (VH-ALB) | RAF Museum, Hendon | |
| A16-199 | Lockheed Hudson IV (G-BEOX) (FH174) [SF-R] | RAF Museum, Hendon | |
| A17-48 | DH Tiger Moth (N48DH) (G-BPHR) | Privately owned, Norfolk | |
| **Belgium** | | | |
| FT-36 | Lockheed T-33A | Dumfries & Galloway Aviation Museum, Tinwald Downs | |
| HD-75 | Hanriot HD1 (OO-APJ/G-AFDX/N75, | RAF Museum, Hendon | |
| MT-11 | Fouga CM-170R Magister (G-BRFU) | Vintage Aircraft Team, Cranfield | |
| **Canada** | | | |
| *232* | Hawker Sea Fury FB11 (N232J) | Privately owned, North Weald | |
| *671* | DHC Chipmunk 22 (G-BNZC) | British Aerial Museum, Duxford | |
| 920 | VS Stranraer (CF-BXO) [Q-N] | RAF Museum, Hendon | |
| 5481 | Hawker Hurricane (G-ORGI) | Privately owned, Sandown | |
| 9059 | Bristol Bolingbroke IVT | Privately owned, Portsmouth | |
| 9893 | Bristol Bolingbroke IVT | Imperial War Museum store | |
| 9940 | Bristol Bolingbroke IVT | Royal Scottish Museum of Flight, East Fortune | |
| 10201 | Bristol Bolingbroke IVT (G-BPIV) | British Aerial Museum, Duxford | |
| *16693* | Auster J/1N Alpha (G-BLPG) [693] | Privately owned, Headcorn | |
| 18393 | Avro Canada CF-100 (G-BCYK) | Imperial War Museum, Duxford | |
| *20385* | CCF T-6J Harvard IV (G-BGPB) | Harvard Formation Team, North Weald | |
| 23140 | NA Sabre [AX] (fuselage) | Midland Air Museum, Coventry | |
| **Czechoslovakia** | | | |
| 1304 | Mikoyan MiG 21 PF | Privately owned, Bournemouth | |
| **Denmark** | | | |
| E-402 | Hawker Hunter F51 | Lovaux Ltd, Bournemouth | |
| E-407 | Hawker Hunter F51 | Privately owned, Cranfield | |
| E-419 | Hawker Hunter F51 | North-East Aircraft Museum, Usworth | |
| E-421 | Hawker Hunter F51 | Brooklands Museum, Weybridge | |
| E-423 | Hawker Hunter F51 (G-9-444) | Second World War Aircraft Preservation Society, Lasham | |
| E-424 | Hawker Hunter F51 | S Yorks Air Museum, Firbeck | |
| E-425 | Hawker Hunter F51 | Midland Air Museum, Coventry | |
| E-427 | Hawker Hunter F51 (G-9-447) | Privately owned, Bruntingthorpe | |
| E-430 | Hawker Hunter F51 | Privately owned, Charlwood, Surrey | |
| ET-272 | Hawker Hunter T7 (cockpit only) | Jet Heritage, Bournemouth | |
| ET-273 | Hawker Hunter T7 | Historical Aviation Society, Chelford | |
| L-866 | Consolidated Catalina (8466M) | RAF Cosford Aerospace Museum | |
| R-756 | Lockheed F-104G | Midland Air Museum, Coventry | |

| Notes | Serial | Type (alternative identity) | Owner, operator and location |
|---|---|---|---|
| | **Egypt** | | |
| | 705 | Yak 18 (G-OYAK) | Privately owned, Earls Colne |
| | **France** | | |
| | 9 | Dassault Mystère IVA [004] | RAF Bentwaters |
| | 16 | Dassault Mystère IVA | RAF Lakenheath |
| | 19 | Deperdussin Replica (BAPC136) | Leisure Sport, Thorpe Park |
| | 25 | Dassault Mystère IVA | RAF Woodbridge |
| | 36 | Dassault Mystère IVA [EABDR 8] | RAF Upper Heyford BDRT |
| | 37 | Nord 3400 [MAB] (G-ZARA) | Privately owned, Stixwuld |
| | 45 | SNCAN Stampe SV4C (G-BHFG) | Privately owned, Enstone |
| | 46 | Dassault Mystère IVA [EABDR 9] | RAF Upper Heyford |
| | 50 | Dassault Mystère IVA | RAF Woodbridge |
| | 57 | Dassault Mystère IVA [8-MT] | Imperial War Museum, Duxford |
| | 59 | Dassault Mystère IVA [314-TH] | Wales Aircraft Museum, Cardiff |
| | 65 | Nord 3202 (G-BMBF) | Privately owned, Stamford |
| | 68 | Nord 3400 [MHA] | Privately owned, Coventry |
| | 70 | Dassault Mystère IVA [8-NV] | Midland Air Museum, Coventry |
| | 75 | Dassault Mystère IVA [11] | RAF Lakenheath |
| | 79 | Dassault Mystère IVA [8-NB] | Norfolk & Suffolk Aviation Museum, Flixton |
| | 83 | Dassault Mystère IVA [8-MS] | Newark Air Museum, Winthorpe |
| | 84 | Dassault Mystère IVA [8-NF] | Robertsbridge Aviation Society, Headcorn |
| | 85 | Dassault Mystère IVA | Privately owned, Bruntingthorpe |
| | 97 | Dassault Mystère IVA [10] | RAF Molesworth |
| | 99 | Dassault Mystère IVA | RAF Lakenheath |
| | 101 | Dassault Mystère IVA [8-MN] | Bomber County Aviation Museum, Hemswell |
| | 104 | Dassault Mystère IVA | RAF Bentwaters, BDRT |
| | 113 | Dassault Mystère IVA | RAF Lakenheath |
| | 120 | SNCAN Stampe SV4C (G-AZGC) | Privately owned, Booker |
| | 121 | Dassault Mystère IVA [8-MY] | City of Norwich Aviation Museum |
| | 126 | Dassault Mystère IVA | RAF Lakenheath |
| | 127 | Dassault Mystère IVA [EABDR 7] | RAF Upper Heyford |
| | 129 | Dassault Mystère IVA [EABDR 6] | RAF Upper Heyford |
| | 133 | Dassault Mystère IVA | RAF Woodbridge |
| | 145 | Dassault Mystère IVA | RAF Lakenheath |
| | 146 | Dassualt Mystère IVA [8-MC] | North East Aircraft Museum, Usworth |
| | 192 | MH1521M Bronssard (G-BKPT) | Privately owned, Newbury |
| | 241 | Dassault Mystère IVA [2] | RAF Lakenheath |
| | 276 | Dassault Mystère IVA | RAF Woodbridge |
| | 285 | Dassault Mystère IVA | RAF Lakenheath |
| | 300 | Dassault Mystère IVA [5] | RAF Lakenheath |
| | 309 | Dassault Mystère IVA [8] | RAF Lakenheath |
| | 318 | Dassault Mystère IVA [8-NY] | Dumfries & Galloway Aviation Museum, Tinwald Downs |
| | 319 | Dassault Mystère IVA [8-ND] | Rebel Air Museum, Andrewsfield |
| | 1076 | Morane MS230 (G-AVEB) | Privately owned, Booker |
| | 133722 | CV F4U-7 Corsair (NX1337A) [15F-22] | Privately owned, Duxford |
| | 14286 | Lockheed T-33A [WK] | Imperial War Museum, Duxford |
| | 16718 | Lockheed T-33A [314-UJ] | City of Norwich Aviation Museum |
| | 42163 | NA F-100D Super Sabre [11-YG] | Dumfries & Galloway Aviation Museum, Tinwald Downs |
| | 42165 | NA F-100D Super Sabre [11-ML] | Imperial War Museum, Duxford |
| | 42204 | NA F-100D Super Sabre [11-MQ] | RAF Alconbury |
| | 54433 | Lockheed T-33A [WD] | Norfolk & Suffolk Aviation Museum, Flixton |
| | 63938 | NA F-100F Super Sabre [11-MU] | Lashenden Air Warfare Museum, Headcorn |
| | *S3398* | Spad XIII Replica (G-BFYO) [2] | FAA Museum, RNAS Yeovilton |
| | S4523 | Spad S-XIII (N4727V) [1] | Imperial War Museum, Duxford |
| | **Germany** | | |
| | *C19/18* | Albatros Replica (BAPC 118) | South Yorks Air Museum, Firbeck |
| | *D5397/17* | Albatros D.VA Replica (G-BFXL) | FAA Museum, RNAS Yeovilton |
| | LG+01 | Bucker Bu.133C Jungmeister (G-AYSJ) | Privately owned Duxford |
| | *BU+CK* | CASA 1-131E Jungmann (G-BUCK) | Privately owned, White Waltham |
| | *6J+PR* | CASA 2111D (G-AWHB) | Aces High Ltd, North Weald |
| | *N7+AA* | CASA 352L (G-BFHF) | *To Auto und Technik Museum, Sinsheim, Germany* |

| Serial | Type (alternative identity) | Owner, operator and location | Notes |
|---|---|---|---|
| *VK+AZ* | CASA 352L (G-BFHG) | Aces High Ltd, North Weald | |
| *A1+BT* | CZL Super Aero (G-APRR) | Privately owned, Elstree | |
| — | Fieseler Fi103 (V-1) (8583M) | RAF Cosford Aerospace Museum | |
| 442795 | Fieseler Fi103 (V-1) (BAPC 199) | Science Museum, South Kensington | |
| 475081 | Fieseler Fi156C Storch (VP546/ 7362M) [GM+AK] | RAF Cosford Aerospace Museum | |
| 28368 | Flettner Fl282/B-V20 Kolibri (frame only) | Midland Air Museum, Coventry | |
| 100143 | Focke-Achgelis Fa330A | Imperial War Museum, Duxford | |
| 100502 | Focke-Achgelis Fa330A | Lincolnshire Aviation Museum, East Kirkby | |
| 100509 | Focke-Achgelis Fa330A | Science Museum, stored South Kensington | |
| 100545 | Focke-Achgelis Fa330A | Torbay Aircraft Museum, Paignton | |
| 100549 | Focke-Achgelis Fa330A | Greater Manchester Museum of Science and Industry | |
| *8* | Focke Wulf FW190 Replica (G-WULF) | Privately owned, Elstree | |
| *7334* | Focke Wulf FW190 Replica (G-SYFW) [2+1] | Privately owned, Guernsey | |
| 584219/38 | Focke Wulf FW190F-8/U1 (8470M) | RAF Museum, Hendon | |
| 733682 | Focke Wulf FW190A-8/R6 | Imperial War Museum, Lambeth | |
| *4253/18* | Fokker D.VII Replica (G-BFPL) | Privately owned, Duxford | |
| *5125/18* | Fokker D.VII Replica (BAPC 110) | Leisure Sport, Thorpe Park | |
| 8417/18 | Fokker D.VII | RAF Museum store | |
| *102/18* | Fokker Dr.1 Dreidekker Replica (BAPC 88) | FAA Museum, RNAS Yeovilton | |
| *150/17* | Fokker Dr.1 Dreidekker Replica (BAPC 139) | Leisure Sport, Thorpe Park | |
| *152/17* | Fokker Dr.1 Dreidekker Replica (G-ATJM) | Privately owned, North Weald | |
| *425/17* | Fokker Dr.1 Dreidekker Replica (BAPC 133) | FAA Museum, Yeovilton | |
| *425/17* | Fokker Dr.1 Dreidekker Replica (G-BEFR) | Privately owned, Dunkeswell | |
| *422/15* | Fokker EIII replica (G-AVJO) | Privately owned, Booker | |
| 22912 | Hansa Brandenburg W.29 Replica (BAPC 138) | Leisure Sport, Thorpe Park | |
| 701152 | Heinkel He111H-23 (8471M) [NT+SL] | RAF Museum, Hendon | |
| 120227 | Heinkel He162A-2 Salamander (VN679/8472M) [2] | RAF Museum, Hendon | |
| 120235 | Heinkel He162A Salamander | Imperial War Museum, Lambeth | |
| +14 | Hispano HA1112 (C4K-172/G-BJZZ/ G-HUNN) | Privately owned, Micheldever | |
| — | Hispano HA 1112 (G-BOML) | Privately owned, Duxford | |
| 494083 | Junkers Ju87D-5 (8474M) [RI+JK] | RAF Museum, Hendon | |
| 360043 | Junkers Ju88R-1 (PJ876/8475M) [D5+EV] | RAF Museum, Hendon | |
| 22+35 | Lockheed F104G Starfighter | Second World War Aircraft Preservation Society, Lasham | |
| 22+57 | Lockheed F104G Starfighter | Starfighter Preservation Group, Ingoldmells | |
| 7198/18 | LVG C.VI (G-AANJ) | Shuttleworth Collection, Old Warden | |
| *6357* | Messerschmitt Bf109 Replica (BAPC74) | Kent Battle of Britain Museum, Hawkinge | |
| *14* | Messerschmitt Bf109 Replica (BAPC67) | Kent Battle of Britain Museum, Hawkinge | |
| 1190 | Messerschmitt Bf109E-3 | Privately owned, Bournemouth | |
| *1480* | Messerschmitt Bf109 [6] (BAPC 66) | Kent Battle of Britain Museum, Hawkinge | |
| 4101 | Messerschmitt Bf109E-3 (DG200/ 8477M) [12] | RAF Museum, Hendon | |
| 10639 | Messerschmitt Bf109G-2 (Trop) (RN228/8478M) (G-USTV) | Imperial War Museum, Benson | |
| 730301 | Messerschmitt Bf110G-4 (8479M) [D5+RL] | RAF Museum, Hendon | |
| 191316 | Messerschmitt Me163B Komet | Science Museum, South Kensington | |
| 191614 | Messerschmitt Me163B Komet (8481M) | RAF Cosford Aerospace Museum | |
| 191659 | Messerschmitt Me163B Komet [15] | Royal Scottish Museum of Flight, East Fortune | |
| 191660 | Messerschmitt Me163B Komet [3] | Imperial War Museum, Duxford | |

| Notes | Serial | Type (alternative identity) | Owner, operator and location |
|---|---|---|---|
| | 112372 | Messerschmitt Me262A-2a (VK893/ 8482M) [9K-XK] | RAF Cosford Aerospace Museum |
| | 420430 | Messerschmitt Me410A-1/U2 (8483M) [3U+CC] | RAF Cosford Aerospace Museum |
| | *7A+WN* | Morane-Saulnier MS500 (G-AZMH) | Privately owned, Chalmington, Dorset |
| | *FI+S* | Morane-Saulnier MS505 (G-BIRW) Criquet | Royal Scottish Museum of Flight, East Fortune |
| | *TA+RC* | Morane-Saulnier MS 505 Criquet (G-BPHZ) | Privately owned, Duxford |
| | *NJ+C11* | Nord 1002 (G-ATBG) | Privately owned, Sutton Bridge |
| | *14* | Pilatus P-2 (J-108/G-BJAX) | Privately owned, Andrewsfield |
| | *CC+43* | Pilatus P-2 (U-143/G-CJCI) | Privately owned, Micheldever |
| | 97+04 | Putzer Elster B (G-APVF) | Privately owned, Henlow |
| | **Greece** | | |
| | 52-6541 | Republic F-84F Thunderflash | North East Aircraft Museum, Usworth |
| | *51-6151* | Canadair F-86D Sabre (really 51-6171) | North East Aircraft Museum, Usworth |
| | **Hungary** | | |
| | 501 | Mikoyan MiG 21 PF | Privately owned, Bournemouth |
| | 503 | Mikoyan MiG 21 SMT (G-BRAM) | Aces High, North Weald |
| | **India** | | |
| | Q497 | EE Canberra T4 (WH847) | BAe Warton Fire Service |
| | **Iraq** | | |
| | 333 | DH Vampire T55 (pod only) | Military Aircraft Preservation Group, Hadfield, Derbys |
| | **Israel** | | |
| | 28 | NA P-51D Mustang | Privately owned, Fowlmere, Cambs |
| | 41 | NA P-51D Mustang (472028) | Privately owned, N. Yorkshire |
| | **Italy** | | |
| | MM5701 | Fiat CR42 (BT474/8468M) [13-95] | RAF Museum, Hendon |
| | MM53211 | Fiat G.46-4 (BAPC 79) | Privately owned, Lympne |
| | MM53432 | NA T-6D [RM-11] | Privately owned, South Wales |
| | MM53692 | CCF T-6G Texan | RAeS Medway Branch, Rochester |
| | MM53795 | CCF Harvard IV (G-BJST) [SC-66] | Privately owned, RAF Kemble |
| | MM53796 | CCF Harvard IV [SC-52] | Privately owned, RAF Kemble |
| | MM54099 | CCF T-6G Harvard [RR-56] | Privately owned, Audley End |
| | **Japan** | | |
| | 24 | Kawasaki Ki100-1B (8476M) (BAPC83) | RAF Cosford Aerospace Museum |
| | 5439 | Mitsubishi Ki46-III(8484M)(BAPC84) | RAF Cosford Aerospace Museum |
| | *AI-110* | Mitsubishi Zero Replica (N15798) | Privately owned, North Weald |
| | 997 | Yokosuka MXY 7 Ohka 11 (8485M) (BAPC98) | Greater Manchester Museum of Science and Industry |
| | 15-1585 | Yokosuka MXY 7 Ohka 11 (BAPC58) | Fleet Air Arm Museum, Yeovilton |
| | – | Yokosuka MXY 7 Ohka 11(8486M) (BPAC99) | RAF Cosford Aerospace Museum |
| | – | Yokosuka MXY 7 Ohka 11(BPAC159) | Defence School, Chattenden |
| | **Morocco** | | |
| | 92 | MH1521 Broussard (G-BJGW) | Privately owned, Duxford |
| | **Netherlands** | | |
| | 204/V | Lockheed SP-2H Neptune | RAF Cosford Aerospace Museum |
| | E-15 | Fokker S-11 Instructor (G-BIYU) | Privately owned, Chessington |
| | E-31 | Fokker S-11 Instructor (G-BEPV) | Strathallan Aircraft Collection |
| | N-202 | Hawker Hunter F6 (nose only) [10] | Pinewood Studios, Elstree |
| | N-250 | Hawker Hunter F6 (nose only) [G-9-185] | Science Museum, South Kensington |
| | N-315 | Hawker Hunter T7 | Privately owned, Batley |
| | R-163 | Piper L-21B Super Cub (G-BIRH) | Privately owned, Lee-on-Solent |
| | R-167 | Piper L-21B Super Cub (G-LION) | Privately owned, Nayland |
| | **New Zealand** | | |
| | NZ5628 | CV F4U-4B Corsair (N240CA) | Privately owned, Duxford |

| Serial | Type (alternative identity) | Owner, operator and location | Notes |
|---|---|---|---|
| **Norway** | | | |
| 56321 | Saab S91B Safir (G-BKPY) [U-AB] | Newark Air Museum, Winthorpe | |
| **Poland** | | | |
| 1120 | MiG-15 | IWM, South Lambeth | |
| 1420 | MiG-15 (G-BMZF) | FAA Museum, RNAS Yeovilton | |
| **Portugal** | | | |
| 1513 | NA Harvard II | Privately owned, Cranfield | |
| 1681 | NA T-6G Texan (G-BSBD) | Warbirds of GB, Thruxton | |
| 1730 | CCF Harvard IV (G-BSBE) | Warbirds of GB, Thruxton | |
| 1736 | CCF Harvard IV (G-BSBF) | Warbirds of GB, Thruxton | |
| 1753 | CCF Harvard IV (G-BSBG) | Warbirds of GB, Thruxton | |
| 1780 | CCF Harvard IV (G-BSBC) | Warbirds of GB, Thruxton | |
| 1788 | CCF Harvard IV (G-BSBB) | Warbirds of GB, Thruxton | |
| 3460 | Dornier 27 (G-BMFG) | Privately owned | |
| 3497 | Dornier 27 (G-BMFH) | Privately owned | |
| 6316 | Amiot AAC1 [IZ+NK] | Imperial War Museum, Duxford | |
| **Qatar** | | | |
| QA10 | Hawker Hunter FGA 78 | Lovaux Ltd., Bournemouth | |
| QA12 | Hawker Hunter FGA 78 | Lovaux Ltd., Bournemouth | |
| **South Africa** | | | |
| 6130 | Lockheed Ventura II (AJ469) | RAF Museum Store, Henlow | |
| **Spain** | | | |
| E3B-369 | CASA 1.131E (G-BPDM) [781-32] | Privately owned, Staverton | |
| *EM-01* | DH60G Moth (G-AAOR) [30-76] | Privately owned, Shoreham | |
| HD5-1 | Dornier Do24T-3 [58-1] | RAF Museum, Hendon | |
| T2-124 | Messerschmitt Bf-109K [FE-124] | Warbirds of GB, Bitteswell | |
| C4E-88 | Messerschmitt Bf-109E | Tangmere Military Aviation Museum | |
| **Sweden** | | | |
| 29640 | Saab J-29F [20-08] | Midland Air Museum, Coventry | |
| 35075 | Saab J-35J Draken [40] | Imperial War Museum, Duxford | |
| **Switzerland** | | | |
| C-558 | EKW C3605 | Privately owned, Booker | |
| U-110 | Pilatus P-2 (G-PTWO) | Privately owned, North Weald | |
| U-142 | Pilatus P-2 (G-BONE) | Privately owned, Southend | |
| J-1008 | DH Vampire FB6 | Mosquito Aircraft Museum, London Colney | |
| J-1172 | DH Vampire FB6 (8487M) | Greater Manchester Museum of Science and Industry | |
| J-1605 | DH Venom FB50 (G-BLID) | Privately owned, Charlwood, Surrey | |
| J-1614 | DH Venom FB50 (G-BLIE) | Privately owned, Glasgow | |
| J-1632 | DH Venom FB50 (G-VNOM) | Privately owned, Cranfield | |
| J-1704 | DH Venom FB54 | RAF Cosford Aerospace Museum | |
| J-1758 | DH Venom FB54 (G-BLSD/N203DM) | Aces High Ltd, North Weald | |
| **Uganda** | | | |
| PAW-3 | Bell 206 JetRanger | Privately owned, Panshanger (stored) | |
| U-708 | Bell 206 JetRanger | Privately owned, Panshanger (stored) | |
| **USA** | | | |
| *01534* | Northrop F-5E Tiger II (Replica) | RAF Alconbury on display | |
| O-17899 | Convair VT-29B | Imperial War Museum, Duxford | |
| *11042* | Wolf WII Replica (G-BMZX) [7] | Privately owned, Haverfordwest | |
| *11083* | Wolf WII Replica (G-BNAI) [5] | Privately owned, Haverfordwest | |
| *101* | CV F4U-4 Corsair (NX49092) (really 97280) | Warbirds of GB, Biggin Hill | |
| 111989 | Cessna L-19A Bird Dog (N33600) | Museum of Army Flying, Middle Wallop | |
| 115042 | NA T-6G Texan (G-BGHU) [TA-042] | Privately owned, Headcorn | |
| 115302 | Piper L-18C Super Cub (G-BJTP) [TP] | Privately owned, Winterbourne, Bristol | |
| *1164* | Beech C-45 (G-BKGL) (really RCAF 5193) | British Aerial Museum, Duxford | |
| 122179 | CV F4U-5NL Corsair [NP-9] (N179FT) | Warbirds of GB, Biggin Hill | |
| *122351* | Beech C-45G (G-BKRG) | Aces High, North Weald | |
| *124485* | Boeing B-17G (G-BEDF/485784) [DF-A] | B-17 Preservation, Duxford | |

| Notes | Serial | Type (alternative identity) | Owner, operator and location |
|---|---|---|---|
| | *1411* | Grumman Widgeon (N444M) | Privately owned, Biggin Hill |
| | 14419 | Lockheed T-33A | Midland Air Museum, Coventry |
| | 140547 | NA T-28C Trojan (N2800Q) | Privately owned, Duxford |
| | 146289 | NA T-28C Trojan (N99153) | Norfolk & Suffolk Aviation Museum, Flixton |
| | 14700 | NA T-6G Texan | Privately owned, Coventry |
| | *150225* | Westland Wessex (G-AWOX) [123] | International Helicopter Museum, Weston-super-Mare |
| | *151632* | NA TB-25N Mitchell (NL9494Z) (really 430925) | Privately owned, Coventry |
| | 153008 | McD F-4N Phantom | RAF Alconbury, BDRT |
| | 155848 | McD F-4S Phantom (WT-11/ VMFA-232] | FAA Museum, RNAS Yeovilton |
| | 159233 | AV-8A Harrier [CG-33] (VMA-231) | FAA Museum, RNAS Yeovilton |
| | 16769 | Lockheed T-33A | RAF Mildenhall Fire Section |
| | 17473 | Lockheed T-33A | RAF Cosford Aerospace Museum |
| | *17640* | Goodyear FG-1D Corsair (NX55JP) (really 88439) | Warbirds of GB, Bournemouth |
| | 17657 | Douglas A-26K Invader (FY64) (nose only) | Booker Aircraft Museum |
| | *18-2001* | Piper L-18C Super Cub (G-BIZV) (really 52-2401) | Privately owned, White Waltham |
| | 19036 | Lockheed T-33A | Newark Air Museum, Winthorpe |
| | 19252 | Lockheed T-33A | Tangmere Military Aviation Museum |
| | *226671* | Republic P-47M Thunderbolt [MX-X] (NX47DD) | The Fighter Collection, Duxford |
| | *23* | Fairchild PT-23 (N49272) | Privately owned, Cosford |
| | *231983* | Boeing B-17G (F-BDRS) [IY-G] (really 44-83735) | Imperial War Museum, Duxford |
| | *236800* | Piper L-4A Cub (G-BHPK) [44-A] (really 42-38410) | Privately owned, Tibenham |
| | 24198 | Lockheed VC-140B Jetstar | RAF Mildenhall, BDRT |
| | *243809* | Waco CG-4A Hadrian (BAPC 185) | Museum of Army Flying, Middle Wallop |
| | 24535 | Kaman HH-43F Huskie | Midland Air Museum, Coventry |
| | *26* | Boeing-Stearman N2S (G-BAVO) | Privately owned, Liverpool |
| | *2807* | NA T-6G Texan (G-BHTH) [V-103] | Privately owned, Kidlington |
| | *29261* | Culver Cadet (G-CDET) | Privately owned, Booker |
| | 29963 | Lockheed T-33A | Wales Aircraft Museum, Cardiff |
| | 315509 | Douglas C-47A (G-BHUB) | Imperial War Museum, Duxford |
| | 31923 | Aeronca O-58B (G-BRHP) | Privately owned, White Waltham |
| | *329417* | Piper L-4A Cub (G-BDHK) (really 42-38400) | Privately owned, Coleford |
| | 32947 | Piper L-4H Cub (G-BGXA) [44-F] | Privately owned, Martley, Worcs |
| | 329601 | Piper L-4H Cub (G-AXHR) [D-44] | Privately owned, Nayland |
| | 329854 | Piper L-4H Cub (G-BMKC) [R-44] | Privately owned, Booker |
| | 329934 | Piper L-4H Cub (G-BCPH) [72-B] | Privately owned, Booker |
| | 330485 | Piper L-4H Cub (G-AJES) [44-C] | Privately owned, Dunkeswell |
| | 33340 | Beech T-34A Mentor (N34AB) | Warbirds of GB, Bournemouth |
| | *34037* | NA TB-25N Mitchell (N9115Z/ 8838M) (really 429366) | RAF Museum, Hendon |
| | 343251 | Boeing Stearman (G-NZSS) | Privately owned, Cumbernauld |
| | 361 | Boeing Stearman (G-ELAN) | Privately owned, White Waltham |
| | 37699 | McD F-4C Phantom (FY63) | RAF Upper Heyford, BDRT |
| | 40707 | McD F-4C Phantom (FY64) | RAF Lakenheath, BDRT |
| | *413048* | Piper L-4J Cub (G-BCXJ) [39-E] (really 44-80752) | Privately owned, Compton Abbas |
| | 41-33275 | NA AT6D Harvard (G-BICE) [CE] | Privately owned, Ipswich |
| | 413573 | NA P-51D Mustang (N6526D) [B6-V] | RAF Museum, stored Halton |
| | *41386* | Thomas-Morse S4 Scout Replica (G-MJTD) | Privately owned, Hitchin |
| | 414151 | NA-51D Mustang (NL314BG) [HO-M] | Warbirds of GB, Bournemouth |
| | 42157 | NA F-100D Super Sabre | North East Aviation Museum, Usworth |
| | 42174 | NA F-100D Super Sabre [UH] | Midland Air Museum, Coventry |
| | 42196 | NA F-100D Super Sabre [LT] | Norfolk & Suffolk Aviation Museum, Flixton |
| | 42223 | NA F-100D Super Sabre | Newark Air Museum, Winthorpe |
| | 430823 | TB-25J Mitchell (N1042B) [69] | Aces High Ltd, North Weald |
| | 431171 | NA B-25J Mitchell (N7614C) | Imperial War Museum, Duxford |
| | 43-1952 | Aeronca O-58B (G-BRPR) | Privately owned |
| | *44* | Piper PA-18-95 Super Cub (G-BJLH) [K-33] | Privately owned, Felthorpe |
| | 442 | Boeing A75 Stearman (G-BPTB) | Privately owned |

| Serial | Type (alternative identity) | Owner, operator and location | Notes |
|---|---|---|---|
| 44-30861 | NA TB-25J Mitchell (N9089Z) | Aces High Ltd, North Weald | |
| 44-4393 | Bell RP-63C Kingcobra (N62822) | Privately owned, Duxford | |
| 44-79609 | Piper L-4H Cub (G-BHXY) [PR] | Privately owned, Bryngwyn Bach, Clwyd | |
| 44-83184 | Fairchild 24R Argus III [7] (G-RGUS) | Privately owned, Tongham | |
| 454467 | Piper J-3C-65 Cub (G-BILI) [44-J] | Privately owned, Bristol | |
| 454537 | Piper L-4J Cub (G-BFDL) [44-J] | Privately owned, Meppershall | |
| 461748 | Boeing B-29A Superfortress (G-BHDK) [Y] | Imperial War Museum, Duxford | |
| *463221* | NA P-51D Mustang (N51JJ) (really 473149) [G4-S] | The Fighter Collection, Duxford | |
| 472216 | NA P-51D Mustang (G-BIXL) [AJ-L] | Privately owned, North Weald | |
| *472258* | NA P-51D Mustang (really 473979) [WZ-I] | Imperial War Museum, Lambeth | |
| 472773 | NA P-51D Mustang [AJ-C] (G-SUSY) | Privately owned, Micheldever | |
| *472917* | CAC-18 Mustang 23 [AJ-A] (G-HAEC) | Privately owned, Duxford | |
| 473877 | NA P-51D Mustang (N167F) [AJ-N] | Privately owned, Duxford | |
| 479766 | Piper L-4H Cub (G-BKHG) [63-D] | Privately owned, Goldcliff | |
| 480015 | Piper L-4H Cub (G-AKIB) | Privately owned, Bodmin | |
| 480133 | Piper L-4J Cub (G-BDCD) [44-B] | Privately owned, Slinfold | |
| 480321 | Piper L-4J Cub (G-FRAN) [44-H] | Privately owned, Stapleford | |
| 480480 | Piper L-4J Cub (G-BECN) [44-E] | Privately owned, Milden | |
| 480594 | Piper L-4J Cub (G-BEDJ) | Privately owned, Ashford Hill | |
| *483009* | NA AT-6D Texan (really 244450) (G-BPSE) | Aces High, North Weald | |
| 483868 | Boeing B-17G Fortress (N5237V) [A-N] | RAF Museum, Hendon | |
| 511371 | NA P-51D Mustang (NL1051S) [VF-S] | Privately owned, Southend | |
| 51-15227 | NA T-6G Harvard (G-BKRA) [10] | Privately owned, Shoreham | |
| 51-15673 | Piper L-18C Super Cub (G-CUBI) | Privately owned, Felixkirk | |
| 53319 | Grumman TBM 3E Avenger (N3966A) [319-RB] | Privately owned, North Weald | |
| *540* | Piper L-4H Cub (G-BCNX) (really 43-29877) | Privately owned, Monewden | |
| *54137* | CCF Harvard IV (G-CTKL) [69] | Privately owned, Shoreham | |
| 54-21261 | Lockheed T-33A (N33VC) | Privately owned, Duxford | |
| 542447 | Piper L-21B Super Cub (G-SCUB) | Privately owned, Anwick | |
| 542457 | Piper L-21B Super Cub (G-LION/R-167) | Privately owned, Nayland | |
| 54439 | Lockheed T-33A | North East Aviation Museum, Usworth | |
| 60312 | McDonnell F-101F Voodoo [AR] | RAF Alconbury, BDRT | |
| 60689 | Boeing B-52D Stratofortress | Imperial War Museum, Duxford | |
| *607327* | Piper L-21B Super Cub [09-L] (G-ARAO) | Privately owned, Lambley | |
| 612414 | Boeing CH-47A Chinook | RAF Odiham, instructional use | |
| *63000* | NA F-100D Super Sabre (really 42160) | Wales Aircraft Museum, Cardiff | |
| *63000* | NA F-100D Super Sabre [FW-000] (really 42212) | RAF Upper Heyford, at gate | |
| *63319* | NA F-100D Super Sabre (really 42269) [319-FW] | RAF Lakenheath, at gate | |
| 63-414 | McD F-4C Phantom (37414) | RAF Woodbridge, BDRT | |
| 63-419 | McD F-4C Phantom (37419) | RAF Alconbury, BDRT | |
| *63-428* | Republic F-105G Thunderchief (really 24428) | RAF Upper Heyford, BDRT | |
| 63449 | McD F-4C Phantom (37449) [LD] | RAF Upper Heyford, BDRT | |
| 63-471 | McD F-4C Phantom (37471) [LN] | RAF Lakenheath, BDRT | |
| 63-610 | McD F-4C Phantom (37610) | RAF Lakenheath, BDRT | |
| 66692 | Lockheed U2CT | RAF Alconbury, BDRT | |
| *6771* | Republic F-84F Thunderstreak (really 52-7133) (ex-FU-6) | RAF Museum/RAeS Medway Branch, Rochester | |
| 68-060 | GD F-111E (pod) | Dumfries & Galloway Aviation Museum, Tinwald Downs | |
| 70270 | McDonnell F-101B Voodoo | RAF Woodbridge | |
| *70-494* | Republic F-105G Thunderchief [LN] (really 62-4434) | RAF Lakenheath, BDRT | |
| 70524 | Lockheed C-130A Hercules | RAF Mildenhall, BDRT | |
| 7797 | Aeronca L-16A (G-BFAF) | Privately owned, Finmere | |
| 80-219 | Fairchild GA-10A (00219) | RAF Alconbury, GI use | |
| 80260 | McDonnell F-101B Voodoo | RAF Bentwaters BDRT | |
| 80483 | Grumman F7F-3 Tigercat [483-JW] (N6178C) | Privately owned, Duxford | |

| Notes | Serial | Type (alternative identity) | Owner, operator and location |
|---|---|---|---|
| | 82062 | DHC U-6A Beaver | Midland Air Museum, Coventry |
| | *855* | Ryan PT-22 (N56421) | Privately owned, Cosford |
| | 88297 | Goodyear FG-1D Corsair (N8297) [29] | Privately owned, Duxford |
| | *897* | Aeronca 11AC Chief (G-BJEV) | Privately owned, Little Gransden |
| | *91007* | Lockheed T-33A (G-TJET) (really 51-8566) [TR-007] | Privately owned, Cranfield |
| | 93542 | CCF Harvard IV (G-BRLV) | Privately owned, North Weald |
| | *985* | Boeing A75N-1 Stearman (G-ERIX) (really 42-16930) | Privately owned, Sutton Bridge |
| | **Yugoslavia** | | |
| | 13064 | Republic P-47D Thunderbolt | RAF Museum Restoration Centre, Cardington |
| | 30146 | Soko P-2 Kraguj [146] (G-BRXD) | Privately owned, Shoreham |
| | 30149 | Soko P-2 Kraguj [149] (G-BRXK) | Privately owned, Shoreham |

# Irish Army Air Corps Military Aircraft Markings

| Notes | Serial | Type (alternative identity) | Owner, operator and location |
|---|---|---|---|
| | 34 | Miles Magister | Irish Aviation Museum Store, Castlemoate House, Dublin |
| | 141 | Avro Anson | Irish Aviation Museum Store, Castlemoate House, Dublin |
| | 164 | DH Chipmunk T20 | Engineering Wing, Baldonnel (stored) |
| | 168 | DH Chipmunk T20 | Training Wing, Gormanston (stored) |
| | 172 | DH Chipmunk T20 | Training Wing, Gormanston (stored) |
| | 173 | DH Chipmunk T20 | South East Aviation Enthusiasts, Waterford |
| | 176 | DH Dove 4 | South East Aviation Enthusiasts, Waterford |
| | 177 | Percival Provost T51 (G-BLIW) | Privately owned, Shoreham |
| | 178 | Percival Provost T51 (G-BKOS) | Privately owned, Thatcham |
| | 181 | Percival Provost T51 | Privately owned, Thatcham |
| | 183 | Percival Provost T51 | Irish Aviation Museum Store, Castlemoate House, Dublin |
| | 184 | Percival Provost T51 | South East Aviation Enthusiasts, Waterford |
| | 187 | DH Vampire T55 | Aviation Society of Ireland, stored, Waterford |
| | 189 | Percival Provost T51 | Baldonnel, Fire Section |
| | 191 | DH Vampire T55 | Irish Aviation Museum Store, Castlemoate House, Dublin |
| | 192 | DH Vampire T55 | South East Aviation Enthusiasts, Waterford |
| | 193 | DH Vampire T55 | Baldonnel Fire Section |
| | 195 | Sud Alouette III | No 1 Support Wing, Baldonnel |
| | 196 | Sud Alouette III | No 1 Support Wing, Baldonnel |
| | 197 | Sud Alouette III | No 1 Support Wing, Baldonnel |
| | 198 | DH Vampire T11 (XE977) | On display, Baldonnel |
| | 199 | DH Chipmunk T22 | Training Wing store, Gormanston |
| | 202 | Sud Alouette III | No 1 Support Wing, Baldonnel |
| | 203 | Cessna FR172H | No 2 Support Wing, Gormanston |
| | 205 | Cessna FR172H | No 2 Support Wing, Gormanston |
| | 206 | Cessna FR172H | No 2 Support Wing, Gormanston |
| | 207 | Cessna FR172H | No 2 Support Wing, Gormanston |
| | 208 | Cessna FR172H | No 2 Support Wing, Gormanston |
| | 209 | Cessna FR172H | No 2 Support Wing, Gormanston |
| | 210 | Cessna FR172H | No 2 Support Wing, Gormanston |
| | 211 | Sud Alouette III | No 1 Support Wing, Baldonnel |
| | 212 | Sud Alouette III | No 1 Support Wing, Baldonnel |
| | 213 | Sud Alouette III | No 1 Support Wing, Baldonnel |
| | 214 | Sud Alouette III | No 1 Support Wing, Baldonnel |
| | 215 | Fouga Super Magister | No 1 Support Wing, Baldonnel |
| | 216 | Fouga Super Magister | No 1 Support Wing, Baldonnel |
| | 217 | Fouga Super Magister | No 1 Support Wing, Baldonnel |

| Serial | Type (alternative identity) | Owner, operator and location | Notes |
|---|---|---|---|
| 218 | Fouga Super Magister | No 1 Support Wing, Baldonnel | |
| 219 | Fouga Super Magister | No 1 Support Wing, Baldonnel | |
| 220 | Fouga Super Magister | No 1 Support Wing, Baldonnel | |
| 221 | Fouga Super Magister [3-KE] | Engineering Wing, Baldonnel | |
| 222 | SIAI SF-260W Warrior | Training Wing, Baldonnel | |
| 223 | SIAI SF-260W Warrior | Training Wing, Baldonnel | |
| 225 | SIAI SF-260W Warrior | Training Wing, Baldonnel | |
| 226 | SIAI SF-260W Warrior | Training Wing, Baldonnel | |
| 227 | SIAI SF-260W Warrior | Training Wing, Baldonnel | |
| 228 | SIAI SF-260W Warrior | Training Wing, Baldonnel | |
| 229 | SIAI SF-260W Warrior | Training Wing, Baldonnel | |
| 230 | SIAI SF-260W Warrior | Training Wing, Baldonnel | |
| 231 | SIAI SF-260W Warrior | Training Wing, Baldonnel | |
| 232 | Beech King Air 200 (EI-BCY) | Transport & Training Squadron, Baldonnel | |
| 233 | SIAI SF-260MC | Engineering Wing, Baldonnel (stored) | |
| 234 | Beech King Air 200 (EI-BFJ) | Transport & Training Squadron, Baldonnel | |
| 235 | SIAI SF-260W Warrior | Training Wing, Baldonnel | |
| 237 | Aerospatiale Gazelle | Advanced Flying Training School, Baldonnel | |
| 238 | HS125/700B | Transport & Training Squadron, Baldonnel | |
| 240 | Beech King Air 200 | Transport & Training Squadron, Baldonnel | |
| 241 | Aerospatiale Gazelle | Advanced Flying Training School, Baldonnel | |
| 243 | Cessna FR172P | No 2 Support Wing, Gormanston | |
| 244 | SA365F Dauphin II | No 3 Support Wing, Baldonnel | |
| 245 | SA365F Dauphin II | No 3 Support Wing, Baldonnel | |
| 246 | SA365F Dauphin II | No 3 Support Wing, Baldonnel | |
| 247 | SA365F Dauphin II | No 3 Support Wing, Baldonnel | |
| 248 | SA365F Dauphin II | No 3 Support Wing, Baldonnel | |
| 249 | Grumman Gulfstream III (N8226M) | Transport & Training Squadron, Baldonnel | |

# Overseas Military Aircraft Markings

Aircraft included in this section are a selection of those likely to be seen visiting UK civil and military airfields on transport flights, exchange visits, exercises and for air shows. It is not a comprehensive list of *all* aircraft operated by the air arms concerned.

| Notes | Serial |
|---|---|
| | **ALGERIA** |
| | **Force Aerienne Algerienne** |
| | **Lockheed C-130H Hercules** |
| | 4911 (7T-WHT) |
| | 4912 (7T-WHS) |
| | 4913 (7T-WHY) |
| | 4914 (7T-WHZ) |
| | 4924 (7T-WHR) |
| | 4926 (7T-WHQ) |
| | 4928 (7T-WHJ) |
| | 4930 (7T-WHI) |
| | 4934 (7T-WHF) |
| | 4935 (7T-WHE) |
| | **Lockheed C-130H-30 Hercules** |
| | 4987 (7T-WHD) |
| | 4989 (7T-WHL) |
| | 4997 (7T-WHA) |
| | **AUSTRALIA** |
| | **Royal Australian Air Force** |
| | **Boeing 707-338C** |
| | 33 Sqn, Richmond, NSW |
| | A20-623 |
| | A20-624 |
| | A20-627 |
| | A20-629 |
| | **Boeing 707-368C** |
| | 33 Sqn, Richmond, NSW |
| | A20-103 |
| | A20-261 |
| | **Lockheed C-130H Hercules** |
| | 36 Sqn, Richmond, NSW |
| | A97-001 |
| | A97-002 |
| | A97-003 |
| | A97-004 |
| | A97-005 |
| | A97-006 |
| | A97-007 |
| | A97-008 |
| | A97-009 |
| | A97-010 |
| | A97-011 |
| | A97-012 |
| | **Lockheed C130E Hercules** |
| | 37 Sqn, Richmond, NSW |
| | A97-159 |
| | A97-160 |
| | A97-167 |
| | A97-168 |
| | A97-171 |
| | A97-172 |
| | A97-177 |
| | A97-178 |
| | A97-180 |
| | A97-181 |
| | A97-189 |
| | A97-190 |
| | **Lockheed P-3C Orion** |
| | Edinburgh, NSW |
| | 10 Sqn* |
| | 11 Sqn † |
| | A9-656† |
| | A9-657† |
| | A9-658† |
| | A9-659† |
| | A9-660† |
| | A9-661† |
| | A9-662† |
| | A9-663† |
| | A9-664† |
| | A9-665† |
| | A9-751* |
| | A9-752* |
| | A9-753* |
| | A9-754* |
| | A9-755* |
| | A9-756* |
| | A9-757* |
| | A9-758* |
| | A9-759* |
| | A9-760* |
| | **AUSTRIA** |
| | **Oesterreichische Luftstreitkrafte** |
| | **Saab 105ÖE (yellow)** |
| | I Staffel, Linz |
| | 1101/A |
| | 1102/B |
| | 1104/D |
| | 1105/E |
| | 1106/F |
| | 1107/G |
| | 1108/H |
| | 1109/I |
| | 1110/J |
| | **Saab 105ÖE (green)** |
| | III Staffel, Linz |
| | 1111/A |
| | 1112/B |
| | 1114/D |
| | 1116/F |
| | 1117/G |
| | 1119/I |
| | 1120/J |

| Serial | Notes |
|---|---|

**Saab 105ÖE (red)**
II Staffel, Graz
1122/B
1123/C
1124/D
1125/E
1126/F
1127/G
1128/H
1129/I
1130/J

**Saab 105ÖE (blue)**
I Staffel, Zeltweg
1131/A
1132/B
1133/C
1134/D
1135/E
1136/F
1137/G
1139/I
1140/J

**Short SC7 Skyvan 3M**
Flachenstaffel, Tulln
5S-TA
5S-TB

**BELGIUM**
**Force Aerienne Belge/ Belgische Luchtmacht**

**D-BD Alpha Jet**
7/11 Smaldeel, 9 Wing, Brustem
AT01
AT02
AT03
AT05
AT06
AT08
AT09
AT10
AT11
AT12
AT13
AT14
AT15
AT16
AT17
AT18
AT19
AT20
AT21
AT22
AT23
AT24
AT25
AT26
AT27
AT28
AT29
AT30
AT31
AT32
AT33

**Dassault Mirage 5BA**
8 Smaldeel (3Wg) Bierset
BA03
BA08
BA10
BA11
BA15
BA16
BA17
BA18
BA20
BA21
BA22
BA26
BA30
BA31
BA33
BA42
BA43
BA44
BA45
BA53
BA54
BA60

**Dassault Mirage 5BD**
8 Smaldeel, Bierset; 42 Smaldeel, Florennes
BD01 8 Sm
BD03 8 Sm
BD04 8 Sm
BD08 42 Sm
BD09 8 Sm
BD10 8 Sm
BD11 8 Sm
BD12 8 Sm
BD13 8 Sm

**Dassault Mirage 5BR**
42 Smaldeel, Florennes
BR03
BR04
BR07
BR08
BR09
BR10
BR12
BR13
BR14
BR15
BR16
BR17
BR19
BR21
BR22
BR23
BR24
BR25
BR26
BR27

**Swearingen Merlin IIIA**
21 Smaldeel, Melsbroek
CF01
CF02
CF04
CF05
CF06

**Lockheed C-130H Hercules**
20 Smaldeel, Melsbroek
CH01
CH02

| Notes | Serial | |
|---|---|---|
| | CH03 | |
| | CH04 | |
| | CH05 | |
| | CH06 | |
| | CH07 | |
| | CH08 | |
| | CH09 | |
| | CH10 | |
| | CH11 | |
| | CH12 | |

**Dassault Falcon 20E**

21 Smaldeel, Melsbroek

| Notes | Serial | |
|---|---|---|
| | CM01 | |
| | CM02 | |

**Hawker-Siddeley HS748 Srs 2A**

21 Smaldeel, Melsbroek

| Notes | Serial | |
|---|---|---|
| | CS01 | |
| | CS02 | |
| | CS03 | |

**General Dynamics F-16A**

349/350 Smaldeel, Bevekom (1 Wg); 1 Smaldeel, Florennes; OCS, Bevekom; 2/23/31 Smaldeel, Kleine Brogel (10 Wg)

| Notes | Serial | |
|---|---|---|
| | FA01 | 349 Sm |
| | FA02 | 350 Sm |
| | FA03 | 349 Sm |
| | FA04 | 350 Sm |
| | FA05 | 349 Sm |
| | FA09 | 349 Sm |
| | FA10 | 349 Sm |
| | FA16 | 349 Sm |
| | FA17 | 349 Sm |
| | FA18 | 350 Sm |
| | FA19 | 350 Sm |
| | FA20 | 349 Sm |
| | FA21 | 349 Sm |
| | FA22 | 350 Sm |
| | FA23 | 350 Sm |
| | FA25 | 349 Sm |
| | FA26 | 349 Sm |
| | FA27 | 349 Sm |
| | FA28 | 350 Sm |
| | FA30 | 350 Sm |
| | FA31 | 349 Sm |
| | FA32 | 350 Sm |
| | FA34 | 349 Sm |
| | FA36 | 350 Sm |
| | FA37 | 349 Sm |
| | FA38 | 350 Sm |
| | FA39 | 350 Sm |
| | FA40 | 349 Sm |
| | FA43 | 349 Sm |
| | FA44 | 350 Sm |
| | FA45 | 349 Sm |
| | FA46 | 349 Sm |
| | FA47 | 349 Sm |
| | FA48 | 349 Sm |
| | FA49 | 350 Sm |
| | FA50 | 350 Sm |
| | FA51 | 350 Sm |
| | FA53 | 350 Sm |
| | FA55 | 349 Sm |
| | FA56 | 2 Sm |
| | FA57 | 23 Sm |
| | FA58 | 31 Sm |
| | FA60 | 31 Sm |
| | FA61 | 23 Sm |
| | FA64 | 31 Sm |
| | FA65 | 23 Sm |
| | FA66 | 31 Sm |
| | FA67 | 23 Sm |
| | FA68 | 31 Sm |
| | FA69 | 23 Sm |
| | FA70 | 31 Sm |
| | FA71 | 23 Sm |
| | FA72 | 31 Sm |
| | FA73 | 23 Sm |
| | FA74 | 31 Sm |
| | FA75 | 23 Sm |
| | FA76 | 31 Sm |
| | FA77 | 23 Sm |
| | FA78 | 31 Sm |
| | FA80 | 31 Sm |
| | FA81 | 23 Sm |
| | FA82 | 31 Sm |
| | FA83 | 23 Sm |
| | FA84 | 31 Sm |
| | FA86 | 31 Sm |
| | FA87 | 23 Sm |
| | FA88 | 31 Sm |
| | FA89 | 23 Sm |
| | FA90 | 31 Sm |
| | FA91 | 23 Sm |
| | FA92 | 31 Sm |
| | FA93 | 23 Sm |
| | FA94 | 31 Sm |
| | FA95 | 23 Sm |
| | FA96 | 1 Sm |
| | FA97 | 1 Sm |
| | FA98 | 2 Sm |
| | FA99 | 2 Sm |
| | FA100 | 2 Sm |
| | FA101 | 2 Sm |
| | FA102 | 2 Sm |
| | FA103 | 1 Sm |
| | FA104 | 2 Sm |
| | FA106 | 2 Sm |
| | FA107 | 1 Sm |
| | FA108 | 2 Sm |
| | FA109 | 1 Sm |
| | FA110 | 2 Sm |
| | FA111 | 1 Sm |
| | FA112 | 2 Sm |
| | FA113 | 1 Sm |
| | FA114 | 2 Sm |
| | FA115 | 1 Sm |
| | FA116 | 2 Sm |
| | FA117 | 1 Sm |
| | FA118 | 2 Sm |
| | FA119 | 1 Sm |
| | FA120 | 2 Sm |
| | FA121 | 1 Sm |
| | FA122 | 2 Sm |
| | FA123 | 1 Sm |
| | FA124 | 2 Sm |
| | FA125 | |
| | FA126 | |
| | FA127 | |
| | FA128 | |
| | FA129 | |
| | FA130 | |
| | FA131 | |
| | FA132 | |
| | FA133 | |
| | FA134 | |
| | FA135 | |
| | FA136 | |

| Serial | Notes |
|---|---|

**General Dynamics F-16B**
349/350 Smaldeel, Bevekom (1 Wg); 1 Smaldeel, Florennes; OCS, Bevekom; 2/23/31 Smaldeel, Kleine Brogel (10 Wg)

FB01 OCS
FB02 349 Sm
FB03 350 Sm
FB04 OCS
FB05 OCS
FB07 OCS
FB08 OCS
FB09 OCS
FB10 10 Wg
FB11 350 Sm
FB12 OCS
FB13 10 Wg
FB14 10 Wg
FB15 10 Wg
FB17 10 Wg
FB18 31 Sm
FB19 10 Wg
FB20 10 Wg
FB21 1 Sm
FB22 2 Sm
FB23 1 Sm
FB24 2 Sm

**Fouga CM170 Magister**
33 Sm, 9 Wing, Brustem

MT3
MT04
MT13
MT14
MT23
MT28
MT29
MT30
MT31
MT33
MT34
MT35
MT36
MT40
MT44
MT46
MT48
MT49

**Siai Marchetti SF.260MB**
Ecole de Pilotage Elementaire, (5 Sm) Gossoncourt

ST02
ST03
ST04
ST06
ST07
ST08
ST09
ST11
ST12
ST15
ST16
ST17
ST18
ST19
ST20
ST21
ST22
ST23
ST24
ST25
ST26
ST27
ST29
ST30
ST31
ST32
ST33
ST34
ST35
ST36

**Belgische Landmacht**

**Britten-Norman BN-2A Islander**
*15/16 Smaldeel, Brasschaat;
†SvHLV, Brasschaat

B01/LA†
B02/LB*
B03/LC*
B04/LD†
B07/LG†
B08/LH†
B09/LI*
B10/LJ†
B11/LK†
B12/LL†

**Sud Alouette II**
16 Sm, Butzweilerhof;
17 Sm, Werl;
18 Sm, Merzbrück;
†SvHLV, Brasschaat

A04 16 Sm
A05 †
A08 18 Sm
A09 17 Sm
A12 17 Sm
A14 16 Sm
A15 17 Sm
A16 †
A18 16 Sm
A22 16 Sm
A23 18 Sm
A24 †
A25 16 Sm
A26 †
A27 18 Sm
A29 18 Sm
A31 †
A32 18 Sm
A34 17 Sm
A35 †
A37 18 Sm
A38 17 Sm
A40 17Sm
A41 †
A42 18 Sm
A43 †
A44 †
A45 18 Sm
A46 17 Sm
A47 18 Sm
A48 17 Sm
A49 16 Sm
A50 16 Sm
A53 †
A54 †
A55 †
A57 16 Sm
A59 16 Sm

| Notes | Serial |
|---|---|
| | A61 16 Sm |
| | A62 17 Sm |
| | A64 16 Sm |
| | A65 16 Sm |
| | A66 † |
| | A67 16 Sm |
| | A68 17 Sm |
| | A69 † |
| | A70 18 Sm |
| | A72 † |
| | A73 † |
| | A74 16 Sm |
| | A75 18 Sm |
| | A76 16 Sm |
| | A77 † |
| | A78 16 Sm |
| | A79 16 Sm |
| | A80 18 Sm |
| | A81 16 Sm |
| | A90 † |
| | A92 16 Sm |
| | A93 † |
| | A94 † |
| | A95 † |

**Belgische Zeemacht**
**Sud Alouette III**
40 Smaldeel, Koksijde
M1 (OT-ZPA)
M2 (OT-ZPB)
M3 (OT-ZPC)
M4 (OT-ZPD)

**Westland Sea King Mk48**
40 Smaldeel, Koksijde
RS01
RS02
RS03
RS04
RS05

**BRAZIL**
**Forca Aerea Brazileira**
**Boeing KC-137**
2 GT 2 Esq Afonsos
2401
2402
2403
2404

**Lockheed C-130E Hercules**
1 GT Afonsos
C-130 2451
C-130 2453
C-130 2454
C-130 2455
C-130 2456
C-130 2458
C-130 2460

**Lockheed KC-130H Hercules**
1 GT 1 Esq Afonsos
C-130 2461
C-130 2462

**Lockheed C-130H Hercules**
1 GT 1 Esq Afonsos
C-130 2463
C-130 2464
C-130 2465
C-130 2466
C-130 2467

**Lockheed RC-130E Hercules**
6 GAV 1 Esq Recife
C-130 2459

**CANADA**
**Canadian Forces**
**McDonnell Douglas CF-18A Hornet**
409/421/439 Squadrons, 1st CAD, Sollingen Germany
188709 439 Sqn
188723
188728 421 Sqn
188729 409 Sqn
188731 439 Sqn
188733 439 Sqn
188738 439 Sqn
188739 409 Sqn
188740 409 Sqn
188741 421 Sqn
188742 409 Sqn
188743 439 Sqn
188744 439 Sqn
188745
188746 421 Sqn
188747 421 Sqn
188748 409 Sqn
188751 421 Sqn
188752
188753 409 Sqn
188754 421 Sqn
188755
188756 439 Sqn
188757 421 Sqn
188758 439 Sqn
188759 439 Sqn
188760 421 Sqn
188761
188764
188766 439 Sqn
188767 409 Sqn
188768 439 Sqn
188769 409 Sqn
188770
188795 421 Sqn
188796

**McDonnell Douglas CF-18B Hornet**
1st CAD, Sollingen, Germany
188918 409 Sqn
188922
188923
188926 421 Sqn
188927 409 Sqn
188928

**Canadair CC-109 Cosmopolitan**
412 Sqn, Lahr, Germany
109157
199160

**Lockheed CC-130E Hercules**
*429 Sqn, Winnipeg
†435 Sqn, Edmonton

| Serial | Notes |
|---|---|
| ‡436 Sqn, Trenton | |
| 130305* | |
| 130306* | |
| 130307* | |
| 130308‡ | |
| 130310* | |
| 130311† | |
| 130313† | |
| 130314‡ | |
| 130315‡ | |
| 130316† | |
| 130317‡ | |
| 130319‡ | |
| 130320‡ | |
| 130321‡ | |
| 130322‡ | |
| 130323‡ | |
| 130324‡ | |
| 130325‡ | |
| 130326‡ | |
| 130327‡ | |
| 130328‡ | |
| **Lockheed CC-130H Hercules** | |
| 130332† | |
| 130333† | |
| 130334† | |
| 130335† | |
| 130336† | |
| 130337† | |
| **Canadair CT-133 Silver Star** | |
| GTTF, Sollingen Germany | |
| 133052 | |
| 133094 | |
| 133345 | |
| 133450 | |
| 133542 | |
| **Bell CH-136 Kiowa** | |
| 444 Sqn, Lahr, Germany | |
| 136224 | |
| 136225 | |
| 136227 | |
| 136228 | |
| 136229 | |
| 136230 | |
| 136231 | |
| 136232 | |
| 136233 | |
| 136234 | |
| 136236 | |
| 136237 | |
| **Boeing CC-137 (B.707-374C)** | |
| 437 Sqn, Trenton | |
| 13701 | |
| 13702 | |
| 13703 | |
| 13704 | |
| 13705 | |
| **Lockheed CP-140 Aurora** | |
| 404/405/415 Sqns, Greenwood; *407 Sqn, Comox | |
| 140101 | |
| 140102* | |

| Serial | Notes |
|---|---|
| 140103 | |
| 140104 | |
| 140105* | |
| 140106 | |
| 140107 | |
| 140108 | |
| 140109* | |
| 140110 | |
| 140111 | |
| 140112* | |
| 140113 | |
| 140114 | |
| 140115 | |
| 140116 | |
| 140117* | |
| 140118* | |
| **Lockheed CP-140A Arctura** | |
| 140119 | |
| 140120 | |
| 140121 | |
| **Canadair CC-144 Challenger** | |
| 412 Sqn, Lahr Germany; Ottawa-Uplands | |
| 144601 | |
| 144602 | |
| 144604 | |
| 144605 | |
| 144608 | |
| 144609 | |
| 144613 | |
| 144614 | |
| 144615 | |
| 144616 | |
| **CHILE** | |
| **Fuerza Aérea de Chile** | |
| **Lockheed C-130H Hercules** | |
| Grupo 10, Santiago | |
| 995 | |
| 996 | |
| **DENMARK** | |
| **Kongelige Danske Flyvevaabnetv** | |
| **Saab A-35XD Draken** | |
| Eskadrille 725, Karup | |
| A001 | |
| A002 | |
| A004 | |
| A005 | |
| A006 | |
| A007 | |
| A008 | |
| A009 | |
| A010 | |
| A011 | |
| A012 | |
| A014 | |
| A017 | |
| A018 | |
| A019 | |
| A020 | |
| **Saab S-35XD Draken** | |
| Eskadrille 729, Karup | |
| AR102 | |

| Notes | Serial |
|---|---|
| | AR104 |
| | AR105 |
| | AR106 |
| | AR107 |
| | AR108 |
| | AR109 |
| | AR110 |
| | AR111 |
| | AR112 |
| | AR113 |
| | AR114 |
| | AR115 |
| | AR116 |
| | AR117 |
| | AR118 |
| | AR119 |
| | AR120 |

**Saab Sk-35XD Draken**
*Eskadrille 725, Karup
†Eskadrille 729, Karup

| Notes | Serial |
|---|---|
| | AT151† |
| | AT152† |
| | AT153* |
| | AT154* |
| | AT155† |
| | AT156† |
| | AT157* |
| | AT158* |
| | AT160* |

**Lockheed C-130H Hercules**
Eskadrille 721, Vaerlose

| Notes | Serial |
|---|---|
| | B678 |
| | B679 |
| | B680 |

**General Dynamics F-16**
Eskadrille 723, Aalborg;
Eskadrille 726, Aalborg;
Eskadrille 727, Skrydstrup;
Eskadrille 730, Skrydstrup

**F-16A**

| Notes | Serial | |
|---|---|---|
| | E004 | Esk 726 |
| | E005 | Esk 726 |
| | E006 | Esk 726 |
| | E007 | Esk 726 |
| | E008 | Esk 726 |
| | E016 | Esk 726 |
| | E017 | Esk 726 |
| | E018 | Esk 726 |
| | E174 | Esk 730 |
| | E176 | Esk 723 |
| | E177 | Esk 723 |
| | E178 | Esk 726 |
| | E180 | Esk 723 |
| | E181 | Esk 730 |
| | E182 | Esk 730 |
| | E183 | Esk 723 |
| | E184 | Esk 723 |
| | E187 | Esk 730 |
| | E188 | Esk 730 |
| | E189 | Esk 726 |
| | E190 | Esk 723 |
| | E191 | Esk 730 |
| | E192 | Esk 730 |
| | E193 | Esk 730 |
| | E194 | Esk 730 |
| | E195 | Esk 723 |
| | E196 | Esk 723 |
| | E197 | Esk 727 |
| | E198 | Esk 730 |
| | E199 | Esk 727 |
| | E200 | Esk 723 |
| | E202 | Esk 730 |
| | E203 | Esk 723 |
| | E596 | Esk 726 |
| | E597 | Esk 730 |
| | E598 | Esk 730 |
| | E599 | Esk 730 |
| | E600 | Esk 730 |
| | E601 | Esk 727 |
| | E602 | Esk 727 |
| | E603 | Esk 730 |
| | E604 | Esk 726 |
| | E605 | Esk 730 |
| | E606 | Esk 730 |
| | E607 | Esk 726 |
| | E608 | Esk 723 |
| | E609 | Esk 727 |
| | E610 | Esk 727 |
| | E611 | Esk 727 |

**F-16B**

| Notes | Serial | |
|---|---|---|
| | ET022 | Esk 726 |
| | ET197 | Esk 726 |
| | ET198 | Esk 726 |
| | ET199 | Esk 726 |
| | ET204 | Esk 727 |
| | ET205 | Esk 730 |
| | ET206 | Esk 727 |
| | ET207 | Esk 730 |
| | ET208 | Esk 727 |
| | ET210 | Esk 726 |
| | ET612 | Esk 730 |
| | ET613 | Esk 727 |
| | ET614 | Esk 727 |
| | ET615 | Esk 727 |

**Grumman Gulfstream III**
Eskadrille 721, Vaerlose

| Notes | Serial |
|---|---|
| | F249 |
| | F313 |
| | F330 |

**Saab T-17 Supporter**
*Flyveskolen, Avno (FLSK);
†Haerens Flyvetjaeneste (Danish Army), Vandel;
‡Eskadrille 721, Vaerlose

| Notes | Serial | |
|---|---|---|
| | T401 | Aalborg Stn Flt |
| | T402 | ‡ |
| | T403 | Skrydstrup Stn Flt |
| | T404 | Karup Stn Flt |
| | T405 | Karup Stn Flt |
| | T407 | Karup Stn Flt |
| | T408 | ‡ |
| | T409 | ‡ |
| | T410 | Karup Stn Flt |
| | T411 | Karup Stn Flt |
| | T412 | † |
| | T413 | † |
| | T414 | † |
| | T415 | † |
| | T417 | † |
| | T418 | † |
| | T419 | ‡ |
| | T420 | * |
| | T421 | * |
| | T422 | * |

| Serial | Notes |
|---|---|
| T423 * | |
| T425 * | |
| T426 * | |
| T427 * | |
| T428 * | |
| T429 Aalborg Stn Flt | |
| T430 * | |
| T431 * | |
| T432 * | |

**Sikorsky S-61A Sea King**
Eskadrille 722, Vaerlose
Detachments at:
Aalborg, Ronne, Skvydstrup

U240
U275
U276
U277
U278
U279
U280
U481

**Sovaernets Flyvetjaeneste (Navy)**

**Westland Lynx Mk 80/90***
Eskadrille 722, Vaerlose

S035
S134
S142
S170
S175
S181
S191
S249*
S256*

**Haerens Flyvetjaeneste (Army)**

**Hughes 500M**
Vandel

H201
H202
H203
H205
H206
H207
H209
H210
H211
H212
H213
H244
H245
H246

**ECUADOR**

**Lockheed C-130H Hercules**

FAE-812
FAE-893

**EGYPT**

**Al Quwwat al-Jawwiya Ilmisriya**

**Lockheed C-130H Hercules**
16 Sqn, Cairo West

1271/SU-BAB
1272/SU-BAC
1273/SU-BAD
1274/SU-BAE
1275/SU-BAF
1277/SU-BAI
1278/SU-BAJ
1279/SU-BAK
1280/SU-BAL
1281/SU-BAM
1282/SU-BAN
1283/SU-BAP
1284/SU-BAQ
1285/SU-BAR
1286/SU-BAS
1287/SU-BAT
1288/SU-BAU
1289/SU-BAV
1290/SU-BEW
1291/SU-BEX
1292/SU-BEY
1293/SU-BKS
1294/SU-BKT

**FRANCE**

**Armee de l'Air**

**Aerospatiale TB-30 Epsilon**
GE315, Cognac

1 315-UA
2 315-UB
3 FZ
4 315-UC
5 315-UD
6 315-UE
7 315-UF
8 315-UG
9 315-UH
10 315-UI
11 315-UJ
12 315-UK
13 315-UL
14 315-UM
15 315-UN
16 315-UO
17 315-UP
18 315-UQ
19 315-UR
20 315-US
21 315-UT
23 315-UV
24 315-UW
25 315-UX
26 315-UY
27 315-UZ
28 315-VA
29 315-VB
30 315-VC
31 315-VD
32 315-VE
33 315-VF
34 315-VG
35 315-VH
36 315-VI
37 315-VJ
38 315-VK
39 315-VL
40 315-VM
41 315-VN
42 315-VO
43 315-VP
44 315-VQ
45 315-VR
46 315-VS

| Notes | Serial | |
|---|---|---|
| | 47 | 315-VT |
| | 48 | 315-VU |
| | 49 | 315-VV |
| | 50 | 315-VW |
| | 51 | 2-BD |
| | 52 | 315-VX |
| | 53 | 315-VY |
| | 54 | 315-VZ |
| | 56 | 315-WA |
| | 57 | F-ZVLB |
| | 58 | 315-WB |
| | 59 | 2-BE |
| | 60 | 315-WC |
| | 61 | 315-WD |
| | 62 | 315-WE |
| | 63 | 315-WF |
| | 64 | 315-WG |
| | 65 | 315-WH |
| | 66 | 315-WI |
| | 67 | 315-WJ |
| | 68 | 315-WK |
| | 69 | 315-WL |
| | 70 | 315-WM |
| | 71 | 315-WN |
| | 72 | 315-WO |
| | 73 | 315-WP |
| | 74 | 315-WQ |
| | 75 | 315-WR |
| | 76 | 315-WS |
| | 77 | 315-WT |
| | 78 | 315-WU |
| | 79 | 315-WV |
| | 80 | 315-WW |
| | 81 | 315-WX |
| | 82 | 315-WY |
| | 83 | 315-WZ |
| | 84 | 315-XA |
| | 85 | 315-XB |
| | 86 | 315-XC |
| | 87 | 315-XD |
| | 88 | 315-XE |
| | 89 | 315-XF |
| | 90 | 315-XG |
| | 91 | 315-XH |
| | 92 | 315-XI |
| | 93 | 315-XJ |
| | 94 | 315-XK |
| | 95 | 315-XL |
| | 96 | 315-XM |
| | 97 | 315-XN |
| | 98 | 315-XO |
| | 99 | 315-XP |
| | 100 | 315-XQ |
| | 101 | 315-XR |
| | 102 | 315-XS |
| | 103 | 315-XT |
| | 104 | 315-XU |
| | 105 | 315-XV |
| | 106 | 315-XW |
| | 107 | 315-XX |
| | 108 | 315-XY |
| | 109 | 315-XZ |
| | 110 | 315-YA |
| | 111 | 315-YB |
| | 112 | 315-YC |
| | 113 | 315-YD |
| | 114 | 315-YE |
| | 115 | 315-YF |
| | 116 | 315-YG |
| | 117 | 315-YH |
| | 118 | 315-YI |
| | 119 | 315-YJ |

| Notes | Serial | |
|---|---|---|
| | 120 | 315-YK |
| | 121 | 315-YL |
| | 122 | 315-YM |
| | 123 | 315-YN |
| | 124 | 315-YO |
| | 125 | 315-YP |
| | 126 | 315-YQ |
| | 127 | 315-YR |
| | 128 | 315-YS |
| | 129 | 315-YT |
| | 130 | 315-YU |
| | 131 | 315-YV |
| | 132 | 315-YW |
| | 133 | 315-YX |
| | 134 | 315-YY |
| | 135 | 315-YZ |
| | 136 | 315-ZA |
| | 137 | 315-ZB |
| | 138 | 315-ZC |
| | 139 | 315-ZD |
| | 140 | 315-ZE |
| | 141 | 315-ZF |
| | 142 | 315-ZG |
| | 143 | 315-ZH |
| | 144 | 315-ZI |
| | 145 | 315-ZJ |
| | 146 | 315-ZK |
| | 148 | 315-ZL |
| | 149 | 315-ZM |
| | 150 | 315-ZN |
| | 152 | 315-ZO |
| | 153 | 315-ZP |
| | 154 | 315-ZQ |
| | 155 | 315-ZR |
| | 158 | 315-ZS |
| | 159 | 315-ZT |

**Boeing C-135FR**
ERV 93, Avord, Istres and Mont de Marsan

| Notes | Serial | |
|---|---|---|
| | 38470 | 93-CA |
| | 38471 | 93-CB |
| | 38472 | 93-CC |
| | 38474 | 93-CE |
| | 38475 | 93-CF |
| | 312735 | 93-CG |
| | 12736 | 93-CH |
| | 12737 | 93-CI |
| | 12738 | 93-CJ |
| | 12739 | 93-CK |
| | 312740 | 93-CL |

**Boeing E-3F Sentry**
EDA-36, Avord

| Notes | Serial | |
|---|---|---|
| | 201 | 36-CA |
| | 202 | 36-CB |

**CASA 212**
CEV

| Notes | Serial | |
|---|---|---|
| | | MO |
| | | MP |
| | 388 | MS |

**Cessna 310**
CEV

| Notes | Serial | |
|---|---|---|
| | 045 | AU |
| | 46 | AV |
| | 185 | AU |
| | 186 | BI |
| | 187 | BJ |
| | 188 | BK |
| | 190 | BL |

| Serial | | Notes |
|---|---|---|
| 192 | BM | |
| 193 | BG | |
| 0194 | BH | |
| 242 | AW | |
| 244 | AX | |
| 820 | CL | |
| 981 | BF | |

**Cessna 404**

| Serial | | Notes |
|---|---|---|
| 692 | DX | |
| 815 | DY | |

**Cessna 411**
CEV

| Serial | | Notes |
|---|---|---|
| 6 | AD | |
| 8 | AE | |
| 185 | AC | |
| 248 | AB | |

**D-BD Alpha Jet**
*Patrouille de France;
EC 1/8, EC 2/8 Cazaux;
GE 314, Tours; CEAM (330), Mont de Marsan

| Serial | | | Notes |
|---|---|---|---|
| 01 | | | |
| 02 | F-ZWRU | | |
| E1 | (CEV) | | |
| E3 | 8-NC | 2/8 | |
| E4 | | | |
| E5 | | | |
| E7 | | | |
| E8 | | | |
| E9 | | | |
| E10 | 8-NL | 2/8 | |
| E11 | 8-NR | 2/8 | |
| E12 | 8-NO | 2/8 | |
| E13 | 314-LH | | |
| E14 | | | |
| E15 | 314-TT | | |
| E17 | 8-NK | | |
| E18 | 8-MH | 1/8 | |
| E19 | F-TERH* (6) | | |
| E20 | | | |
| E21 | 314-UD | | |
| E22 | 314-LD | | |
| E23 | 314-UB | | |
| E24 | 8-MP | 1/8 | |
| E25 | F-TERJ* (1) | | |
| E26 | 314-TI | | |
| E27 | 8-MU | 1/8 | |
| E28 | 314-LM | | |
| E29 | 8-MF | 1/8 | |
| E30 | 8-NI | 2/8 | |
| E31 | 314-UE | | |
| E32 | | | |
| E33 | 8-NN | 2/8 | |
| E34 | | | |
| E35 | 314-LI | | |
| E36 | F-TERC*(4) | | |
| E37 | 314-TE | | |
| E38 | 314-TP | | |
| E39 | 314-TS | | |
| E40 | 8-MD | 1/8 | |
| E41 | 314-LB | | |
| E42 | 314-TL | | |
| E43 | 314-TI | | |
| E44 | (CEV) | | |
| E45 | 314-LG | | |
| E46 | | | |
| E47 | 314-LO | | |
| E48 | | | |
| E49 | 314-TQ | | |
| E50 | 314-UH | | |
| E51 | | | |
| E52 | F-TERB* (8) | | |
| E53 | | | |
| E55 | F-TERE* (9) | | |
| E58 | 314-TD | | |
| E59 | F-TERI* (7) | | |
| E60 | (CEV) | | |
| E61 | | | |
| E63 | | | |
| E64 | 8-NH | 2/8 | |
| E65 | 314-TG | | |
| E66 | 8-NP | 2/8 | |
| E67 | 8-MR | 1/8 | |
| E68 | 8-MK | 1/8 | |
| E69 | 314-LY | | |
| E70 | | | |
| E72 | | | |
| E73 | 314-UA | | |
| E74 | | | |
| E75 | | | |
| E76 | | | |
| E77 | 314-LI | | |
| E79 | 314-LX | | |
| E80 | (CEV) | | |
| E81 | 314-LP | | |
| E82 | | | |
| E83 | 8-NS | 2/8 | |
| E84 | | | |
| E85 | 8-NM | 2/8 | |
| E86 | 314-TJ | | |
| E87 | 314-LL | | |
| E88 | 314-TV | | |
| E89 | 314-TG | | |
| E90 | 314-TU | | |
| E91 | 330-BR | | |
| E92 | 314-TB | | |
| E93 | 8-MS | 1/8 | |
| E94 | | | |
| E95 | 8-MO | 1/8 | |
| E96 | | | |
| E97 | 314-LE | | |
| E98 | | | |
| E99 | 8-MW | 1/8 | |
| E100 | (CEV) | | |
| E101 | 8-MD | 1/8 | |
| E102 | 8-ME | 1/8 | |
| E103 | 314-TO | | |
| E104 | 314-LC | | |
| E105 | 314-TF | | |
| E106 | 314-LV | | |
| E107 | F-TERK* (5) | | |
| E108 | 8-NQ | 2/8 | |
| E109 | 314-LK | | |
| E110 | | | |
| E112 | | | |
| E113 | 314-TW | | |
| E114 | | | |
| E115 | 314-LQ | | |
| E116 | | | |
| E117 | 8-MI | 1/8 | |
| E118 | 8-NT | 2/8 | |
| E119 | 314-TR | | |
| E120 | | | |
| E121 | 8-NK | 2/8 | |
| E122 | 314-UG | | |
| E123 | 314-LJ | | |
| E124 | 8-MC | 1/8 | |
| E125 | 314-TN | | |
| E126 | | | |
| E127 | 314-LW | | |

| Notes | Serial | | |
|---|---|---|---|
| | E128 | 314-TX | |
| | E129 | 8-NB | 2/8 |
| | E130 | 8-MT | 1/8 |
| | E131 | 314-TY | |
| | E132 | | |
| | E133 | 8-NU | 2/8 |
| | E134 | | |
| | E135 | 314-TK | |
| | E136 | | |
| | E137 | 8-MI | 1/8 |
| | E138 | | |
| | E139 | 314-UF | |
| | E140 | | |
| | E141 | 8-MQ | 1/8 |
| | E142 | 8-MB | 1/8 |
| | E143 | 314-LT | |
| | E144 | 314-LA | |
| | E145 | | |
| | E146 | 8-MG | 1/8 |
| | E147 | 8-NE | 2/8 |
| | E148 | 8-NJ | 2/8 |
| | E149 | | |
| | E150 | 8-NF | 2/8 |
| | E151 | | |
| | E152 | 314-TA | |
| | E153 | 314-TM | |
| | E154 | | |
| | E155 | | |
| | E156 | F-TERG* (2) | |
| | E157 | 314-UC | |
| | E158 | 314-UC | |
| | E159 | | |
| | E160 | 314-LZ | |
| | E161 | 8-NG | 2/8 |
| | E162 | 314-LF | |
| | E163 | | |
| | E164 | 8-MJ | 1/8 |
| | E165 | | |
| | E166 | 8-MN | 1/8 |
| | E167 | 8-MV | 1/8 |
| | E168 | | |
| | E169 | | |
| | E170 | F-TERM* (0) | |
| | E171 | F-TERN | |
| | E172 | F-TERO* (3) | |
| | E173 | | |
| | E174 | | |
| | E175 | 314-LU | |
| | E176 | 330-BT | |

**Dassault Mystère 20**
CEV
SIET 98/120, Cazaux
*ET.60, Villacoublay
†ET.3/65, Villacoublay
‡CIFAS 328, Bordeaux
CITAC-339, Luxeuil

| Serial | |
|---|---|
| 1 | CV (CEV) |
| 22 | CS (CEV) |
| 49 | (SIET 98/120) |
| 79 | CT (CEV) |
| 86 | CG (CEV) |
| 093 | * |
| 104 | CW (CEV) |
| 115 | 339-WL |
| 124 | CC (CEV) |
| 131 | CD (CEV) |
| 138 | CR (CEV) |
| 145 | CU (CEV) |
| 167 | * |
| 182 | JA‡ |
| 186 | 339-WM |
| 188 | CX (CEV) |
| 238 | * |
| 260 | * |
| 263 | CY (CEV) |
| 268 | * |
| 288 | CZ (CEV) |
| 291 | P† |
| 309 | 339-WP |
| 324 | O* |
| 342 | * |
| 375 | (CEV) |
| 422 | † |
| 451 | 339-WN |
| 483 | 339-WO |

**Dassault Falcon 50**
ET.60 Villacoublay
005
78 F-RAFJ

**Dassault Falcon 900**
ET.60, Villacoublay
002
004 F-RAFQ

**Dassault Mirage IVA/IVP***
EB 1/91, Mont-de-Marsan;
EB 2/91, Cazaux;
EB 1/94 Istres;
CIFAS 328 Bordeaux-Merignac

| Serial | | |
|---|---|---|
| 1 | AP | |
| 2 | AA | |
| 4 | AC | |
| 5 | AD | |
| 6 | AE | |
| 7 | AF | |
| 8/01* | AG | |
| 11* | AJ | 1/91 |
| 12 | AK | |
| 13* | AL | |
| 14 | AM | |
| 15 | AN | |
| 19 | AR | |
| 20 | AS | |
| 21 | AT | |
| 23* | AV | 1/91 |
| 24 | AW | |
| 25* | AX | 1/91 |
| 26* | AY | 1/91 |
| 27 | AZ | |
| 31* | BD | 1/91 |
| 32 | BE | |
| 34 | BG | |
| 36* | BI | 1/91 |
| 37 | BJ | |
| 39 | BL | |
| 42 | BO | |
| 44 | BQ | |
| 45* | BR | CIFAS 328 |
| 46 | BS | |
| 47 | BT | |
| 48* | BU | |
| 49* | BV | 1/91 |
| 51* | BX | |
| 52* | BY | CIFAS 328 |
| 53* | BZ | 1/91 |
| 54* | CA | 1/91 |
| 55* | CB | |
| 56* | CC | |
| 57* | CD | 1/91 |

| Serial | | | Notes |
|---|---|---|---|
| 59* | CF | 1/91 | |
| 61* | CH | 2/91 | |
| 62* | CI | 1/91 | |

**Dassault Mirage F.1C**
EC 5, Orange;
EC 12, Cambrai;
EC 30, Rheims; CEAM (330)
Mont de Marsan

| Serial | | | Notes |
|---|---|---|---|
| 2 | 30-MG | 2/30 | |
| 3 | 12-YJ | 1/2 | |
| 4 | 330-AM | | |
| 5 | 12-KR | 3/12 | |
| 6 | 30-MA | 2/30 | |
| 8 | | | |
| 9 | 30-SK | 1/30 | |
| 10 | | | |
| 14 | 12-YG | 1/12 | |
| 15 | 12-KP | 3/12 | |
| 16 | 5-OH | 2/5 | |
| 17 | 5-OF | 2/5 | |
| 18 | | | |
| 19 | 12-YK | 1/12 | |
| 20 | 30-MN | 2/30 | |
| 21 | | | |
| 22 | | | |
| 23 | | | |
| 24 | 30-SR | 1/30 | |
| 25 | | | |
| 26 | | | |
| 27 | 30-FB | 3/30 | |
| 29 | | | |
| 30 | 12-ZJ | 2/12 | |
| 31 | 12-ZA | 2/12 | |
| 32 | 5-AU | 3/5 | |
| 33 | | | |
| 35 | | | |
| 36 | | | |
| 37 | 2-KJ | 3/12 | |
| 38 | | | |
| 39 | | | |
| 40 | | | |
| 41 | 30-FG | 3/30 | |
| 42 | 5-AK | 3/5 | |
| 43 | 12-ZD | 2/12 | |
| 44 | | | |
| 47 | 5-OQ | 2/5 | |
| 48 | 30-SO | 1/30 | |
| 49 | 5-OI | 2/5 | |
| 50 | 12-KH | 3/12 | |
| 52 | 30-MH | 2/30 | |
| 54 | 12-YA | 1/12 | |
| 55 | | | |
| 60 | 30-MM | 2/30 | |
| 62 | | | |
| 63 | | | |
| 64 | 30-SA | 1/30 | |
| 67 | | | |
| 68 | 30-FN | 3/30 | |
| 69 | | | |
| 70 | 5-AI | 3/5 | |
| 71 | | | |
| 72 | 12-KC | 3/12 | |
| 73 | | | |
| 74 | 30-SE | 1/30 | |
| 75 | | | |
| 76 | | | |
| 77 | | | |
| 78 | 12-ZF | 2/12 | |
| 79 | 30-L | 4/30 | |
| 80 | 5-AD | 3/5 | |
| 81 | 30-LA | 4/30 | |
| 82 | 30-FA | 3/30 | |
| 83 | 12-ZB | 2/12 | |
| 84 | | | |
| 85 | 12-ZQ | 2/12 | |
| 87 | 330-AP | | |
| 90 | 12-YN | 1/12 | |
| 100 | | | |
| 101 | 12-YL | 1/12 | |
| 102 | 5-AC | 3/5 | |
| 103 | 30-LC | 4/30 | |
| 201 | 30-FM | 3/30 | |
| 202 | 30-FF | 3/30 | |
| 203 | 12-YE | 1/12 | |
| 205 | | | |
| 206 | | | |
| 207 | 12-YC | 1/12 | |
| 210 | 30-SN | 1/30 | |
| 211 | 12-YF | 1/12 | |
| 213 | 12-ZR | 2/12 | |
| 214 | 12-KG | 3/12 | |
| 216 | 30-SG | 1/30 | |
| 217 | 12-KE | 3/12 | |
| 218 | 5-OM | 2/5 | |
| 219 | 30-FH | 3/30 | |
| 220 | 30-MC | 2/30 | |
| 221 | 30-MP | 2/30 | |
| 223 | 330-AD | | |
| 224 | 30-MD | 2/30 | |
| 225 | 30-ME | 2/30 | |
| 226 | 12-YO | 1/12 | |
| 227 | | | |
| 228 | 30-SB | 1/30 | |
| 229 | 12-YD | 1/12 | |
| 230 | 30-SD | 1/30 | |
| 231 | 12-ZE | 2/12 | |
| 232 | 30-MJ | 2/30 | |
| 233 | 30-LG | 4/30 | |
| 234 | | | |
| 235 | 12-YB | 1/12 | |
| 236 | 12-KB | 3/12 | |
| 237 | 30-LE | 4/30 | |
| 238 | 30-LD | 4/30 | |
| 239 | 30-LJ | 4/30 | |
| 240 | 12-YP | 1/12 | |
| 241 | | | |
| 242 | 30-MF | 2/30 | |
| 243 | 30-LL | 4/30 | |
| 244 | 12-YH | 1/12 | |
| 245 | 12-KO | 1/12 | |
| 246 | 30-SL | 1/30 | |
| 247 | | | |
| 248 | | | |
| 249 | 12-KQ | 3/12 | |
| 251 | 12-ZP | 2/12 | |
| 252 | 30-MB | 2/30 | |
| 253 | 30-LM | 4/30 | |
| 254 | 12-ZM | 2/12 | |
| 255 | 12-KD | 3/12 | |
| 256 | 12-KA | 3/12 | |
| 257 | 12-YI | 1/12 | |
| 258 | | | |
| 259 | 30-SH | 1/30 | |
| 260 | 30-MI | 2/30 | |
| 261 | 12-ZI | 2/12 | |
| 262 | | | |
| 264 | 12-KN | 3/12 | |
| 265 | 30-LO | 4/30 | |
| 267 | | | |
| 268 | 30-MQ | 2/30 | |
| 271 | 30-SF | 1/30 | |
| 272 | 12-YH | 1/12 | |

| Serial | Code | Unit |
|---|---|---|
| 273 | 12-ZN | 2/12 |
| 274 | 12-ZH | 2/12 |
| 275 | | |
| 277 | | |
| 278 | 5-OE | 2/5 |
| 279 | 5-AO | 3/5 |
| 280 | 12-KM | 3/12 |
| 281 | 30-MR | 2/30 |
| 282 | | |
| 283 | 12-ZC | 2/12 |

**Dassault Mirage F.1CR**

ER 33 Strasbourg; CEAM Mont de Marsan; EAA601 Chateaudun (330), Mont de Marsan; CEV, Istres

| Serial | Code | Unit |
|---|---|---|
| 601 | (CEV) | |
| 602 | (CEV) | |
| 603 | 33-CB | 1/33 |
| 604 | 33-CE | 1/33 |
| 605 | 33-NF | 2/33 |
| 606 | 33-TS | 3/33 |
| 607 | 33-NM | 2/33 |
| 608 | 33-TN | 3/33 |
| 609 | 33-CA | 1/33 |
| 610 | 33-CH | 1/33 |
| 611 | | |
| 612 | 33-NJ | 2/33 |
| 613 | 33-CL | 1/33 |
| 614 | 330-AA | |
| 615 | 33-CU | 1/33 |
| 616 | 33-CS | 1/33 |
| 617 | 33-CC | 1/33 |
| 619 | 330-AC | |
| 620 | | |
| 622 | 33-CR | 1/33 |
| 623 | 33-CM | 1/33 |
| 624 | 33-NE | 2/33 |
| 625 | | |
| 627 | 33-NI | 2/33 |
| 628 | 330-AB | |
| 629 | 33-CG | 1/33 |
| 630 | 33-NL | 2/33 |
| 631 | | |
| 632 | 33-TM | 3/33 |
| 634 | 33-CK | 1/33 |
| 635 | | |
| 636 | 33-TL | 3/33 |
| 637 | 33-TC | 3/33 |
| 638 | | |
| 640 | 33-TE | 3/33 |
| 641 | 33-NT | 2/33 |
| 642 | 33-NC | 2/33 |
| 643 | 33-CO | 1/33 |
| 644 | 33-NS | 2/33 |
| 645 | | |
| 646 | 33-NH | 2/33 |
| 647 | 33-TR | 3/33 |
| 648 | 33-CF | 1/33 |
| 649 | 330-AE | |
| 650 | 33-CJ | 1/33 |
| 651 | 33-NB | 2/33 |
| 653 | 33-TB | 3/33 |
| 654 | 33-TF | 3/33 |
| 655 | 33-TH | 3/33 |
| 656 | 33-CN | 1/33 |
| 657 | | |
| 658 | 33-TI | 3/33 |
| 659 | 33-TG | 3/33 |
| 660 | 33-ND | 2/33 |
| 661 | 33-TA | 3/33 |
| 662 | 33-NA | 2/33 |
| 664 | 33-TJ | 3/33 |
| 665 | | |
| 666 | | |
| 667 | | |
| 668 | | |
| 669 | | |
| 670 | | |

**Dassault Mirage 2000B**

CEAM, Mont de Marsan (330);
ECT 2/2, Dijon;
EC 3/2, Dijon

| Serial | Code | Unit |
|---|---|---|
| 501 | 2-EQ | (CEV) |
| 502 | 2-FA | 2/2 |
| 503 | 330-AX | |
| 504 | | |
| 505 | 2-FB | 2/2 |
| 506 | 2-FC | 2/2 |
| 507 | 2-FD | 2/2 |
| 508 | 2-FE | 2/2 |
| 509 | 2-FF | 2/2 |
| 510 | 2-FG | 2/2 |
| 511 | 2-FH | 2/2 |
| 512 | 2-FI | 2/2 |
| 513 | 2-FJ | 2/2 |
| 514 | 2-FK | 2/2 |
| 515 | 330-AN | |
| 516 | 2-LD | 3/2 |
| 517 | 5-OP | 2/5 |
| 518 | 5-OJ | 2/5 |
| 519 | 5-NR | 1/5 |
| 520 | 5-NP | 1/5 |
| 521 | 5-OL | 2/5 |
| 522 | 330-AZ | |
| 523 | | |
| 524 | | |
| 525 | | |

**Dassault Mirage 2000C**

EC 1/2, ECT 2/2, EC 3/2, Dijon;
EC 5, Orange;
CEAM (330), Mont de Marsan

| Serial | Code | Unit |
|---|---|---|
| 01 | | |
| 03 | | (CEV) |
| 04 | | |
| 1 | 2-EP | (CEV) |
| 2 | | (CEV) |
| 3 | 2-EG | 1/2 |
| 4 | 2-EJ | 1/2 |
| 5 | | |
| 6 | 2-LH | 3/2 |
| 8 | 2-EC | 1/2 |
| 9 | 2-LO | 3/2 |
| 11 | 2-EF | 1/2 |
| 12 | 2-EH | 1/2 |
| 13 | 2-EI | 1/2 |
| 14 | 2-FN | 2/2 |
| 15 | 2-EK | 1/2 |
| 16 | 2-EL | 1/2 |
| 17 | 2-EM | 1/2 |
| 18 | 2-FL | 2/2 |
| 19 | 2-LA | 3/2 |
| 20 | 2-LE | 3/2 |
| 21 | 2-LF | 3/2 |
| 22 | 2-LG | 3/2 |
| 25 | 2-LK | 3/2 |
| 27 | 2-LM | 3/2 |
| 28 | 2-LN | 3/2 |
| 29 | 2-ED | 1/2 |
| 30 | 2-EO | 1/2 |
| 32 | 2-EP | 1/2 |
| 33 | 2-LQ | 3/2 |

| Serial | | | Notes |
|---|---|---|---|
| 34 | 2-LI | 3/2 | |
| 35 | 2-EE | 1/2 | |
| 36 | 2-EN | 1/2 | |
| 37 | 2-LS | 3/2 | |
| 38 | 330-AT | | |
| 39 | | | |
| 40 | 330-AI | | |
| 41 | 5-NB | 1/5 | |
| 42 | 5-NC | 1/5 | |
| 43 | | | |
| 44 | 5-NE | 1/5 | |
| 45 | 5-OM | 2/5 | |
| 46 | 5-NG | 1/5 | |
| 47 | 5-NH | 1/5 | |
| 48 | | | |
| 49 | 5-NJ | 1/5 | |
| 51 | 5-OG | 2/5 | |
| 52 | 5-OC | 2/5 | |
| 53 | 5-NN | 1/5 | |
| 54 | 5-NO | 1/5 | |
| 55 | 5-OH | 2/5 | |
| 56 | 5-OA | 2/5 | |
| 57 | 5-AJ | 3/5 | |
| 58 | 5-ND | 1/5 | |
| 59 | 5-OB | 2/5 | |
| 61 | 5-OD | 2/5 | |
| 62 | 5-AL | 3/5 | |
| 63 | 5-OK | 2/5 | |
| 64 | 330-AQ | | |
| 65 | 330-AH | | |
| 66 | 330-AS | | |
| 67 | | | |
| 68 | 330-AW | | |
| 69 | | | |
| 70 | | | |
| 71 | 5-NF | 1/5 | |
| 72 | 5-NK | 1/5 | |
| 73 | 5-NM | 1/5 | |
| 74 | | | |
| 75 | | | |
| 76 | | | |
| 77 | | | |
| 78 | | | |
| 79 | | | |
| 80 | | | |
| 81 | | | |
| 82 | | | |
| 83 | | | |
| 84 | | | |
| 85 | | | |
| 86 | | | |
| 87 | | | |
| 88 | | | |
| 89 | | | |
| 90 | | | |

**Dassault Mirage 2000N**
CEAM (330), Mont de Marsan;
EC.1/4, EC.2/4 Luxeuil;
EC.3/4 Istres

| Serial | | | Notes |
|---|---|---|---|
| 301 | | | |
| 302 | 4-CA | 3/4 | |
| 303 | | | |
| 304 | 3-CB | 3/4 | |
| 305 | 4-BB | 2/4 | |
| 306 | 4-CC | 3/4 | |
| 307 | 4-BC | 2/4 | |
| 308 | 4-CD | 3/4 | |
| 309 | 4-BD | 2/4 | |
| 310 | 4-CE | 3/4 | |
| 311 | 4-BE | 2/4 | |
| 312 | 4-CF | 3/4 | |
| 313 | 4-BF | 2/4 | |
| 314 | 4-CG | 3/4 | |
| 315 | 4-BG | 2/4 | |
| 316 | 4-CH | 3/4 | |
| 317 | 4-BH | 2/4 | |
| 318 | 4-CI | 3/4 | |
| 319 | 4-BI | 2/4 | |
| 320 | 4-CJ | 3/4 | |
| 322 | 4-CK | 3/4 | |
| 323 | 4-BK | 2/4 | |
| 324 | 4-CL | 3/4 | |
| 325 | 4-BL | 2/4 | |
| 326 | 4-CM | 3/4 | |
| 327 | 4-BM | 2/4 | |
| 328 | 4-CN | 3/4 | |
| 329 | 4-BN | 2/4 | |
| 330 | 4-CO | 3/4 | |
| 331 | 4-BO | 2/4 | |
| 332 | 330-AR | | |
| 333 | 330-AG | | |
| 334 | 330-AV | | |
| 335 | 330-AP | | |
| 336 | 4-AB | 1/4 | |
| 337 | 4-AC | 1/4 | |
| 338 | | | |
| 339 | 4-AE | 1/4 | |
| 340 | 4-AA | 1/4 | |
| 341 | | | |
| 342 | 4-AH | 1/4 | |
| 343 | 4-AI | 1/4 | |
| 344 | 4-AJ | 1/4 | |
| 345 | 4-AK | 1/4 | |
| 346 | 4-AL | 1/4 | |
| 347 | 4-AM | 1/4 | |
| 348 | 4-AN | 1/4 | |
| 349 | 4-AO | 1/4 | |
| 350 | 4-AP | 1/4 | |
| 351 | 4-AQ | 1/4 | |
| 352 | | | |
| 353 | | | |
| 354 | | | |
| 355 | | | |
| 356 | | | |
| 357 | | | |
| 358 | | | |
| 359 | | | |
| 360 | | | |

**Dassault Rafale-A**

| Serial | | Notes |
|---|---|---|
| 01 | AMD-BA | |

**Dassault Rafale-C**

| Serial | | Notes |
|---|---|---|
| 01 | AMD-BA | |
| 02 | | |
| 03 | | |

**DHC6 Twin Otter**
*ET 65 Villacoublay;
†GAM 56 Evreux

| Serial | | Notes |
|---|---|---|
| 292 | OW† | |
| 298 | OY† | |
| 300 | OZ† | |
| 603 | CY* | |
| 683 | 65-CT* | |
| 730 | CA* | |
| 742 | 65-CB* | |
| 743 | 65-CZ* | |
| 745 | CV* | |
| 786 | | |
| 790 | | |

**Douglas DC8F**
*EE.51 Evreux
†ET3/60 Charles de Gaulle

*Notes* *Serial*

45570 F-RAFE*
45819 F-RAFC†
46013 F-RAFG†
46043 F-RAFD†
46130 F-RAFF†

**Embraer Xingu**
* GE 319 Avord;
† ETE 43 Bordeaux;
‡ETE 44 Aix-en-Provence
CITAC339, Luxeuil, CEAM,
Mont de Marsan
054 YX*
064 YY*
072 YA*
073 YB*
075 YC*
076 YD*
078 YE*
080 YF*
082 YG*
084 YH*
086 YI‡
089 YJ*
091 YK*
092 YL*
095 YM*
096 YN‡
098 YO*
099 YP*
101 IB (CEAM)
102 YS*
103 YT*
105 YU*
107 YV*
108 IA (CEAM)
111 YQ*

**Lockheed**
**C-130H Hercules**
***C-130H-30 Hercules**
ET-2/61, Orleans
5114 61-PA
5116 61-PB
5119 61-PC
5140 61-PD
5142* 61-PE
5144* 61-PF
5150* 61-PG
5151* 61-PH
5152* 61-PI
5153* 61-PJ

**Morane Saulnier 760**
**Paris**
ETE 41 Metz;
ETE 43 Bordeaux;
ETE 44 Aix-en-Provence;
ET 65 Villacoublay; CEAM
(330) Mont de Marsan
1 330-DB
14 312-DF
19 41-AR
23
24 65-LA
25 41-AP
26 65-LN
27 DE
29 65-LC
30 65-LW
34 43-BB
35
36 43-BD
38 41-AK
44 65-LM
45 43-BC
51
53 DD
54
56 41-AD
57 65-LK
58 65-LB
59 41-AC
60 41-AT
62 65-LV
68 NB (CEV)
70 65-LF
71 65-LE
73
75 65-LZ
77 330-DD
78 65-LI
79 NL (CEV)
80 65-LT
81 65-LL
83 NC (CEV)
91 65-LU
92 330-DA
93 65-LD
94 330-DC
95
97 65-LH
100 NG (CEV)
113 NI (CEV)
114 NJ (CEV)
115 OV (CEV)
116 ON (CEV)
117 AZ (CEV)
118 NQ (CEV)
119 NL (CEV)

**Nord 262 Fregate**
†EdC 70 Chateaudun;
*ET 65 Villacoublay;
ETE 41 Metz;
ETE 44, Aix-en-Provence;
GE 316 Toulouse;
CEAM (330) Mont de
Marsan;
CEV, Istres
01 (CEV)
3 OH (CEV)
55 MH (CEV)
58 MJ (CEV)
64 AA*
66 AB (ETE 44)
67 MI (CEV)
68 AC*
76 316-DA
77 AK*
78 AF*
80 AW*
81 AH*
83 316-DB
86 316-DD
87 316-DC
88 AL (ETE 44)
89 AZ*
91 AT*
93 MB (CEV)
94 AU (ETE 41)
95 AR*
105 AE*
106 MA†
107 AX*
108 AG*

| Serial | | | Notes |
|---|---|---|---|
| 109 | AM* | | |
| 110 | AS* | | |

**Transall C-160**
**Transall C-160H†**
ETOM 55, Dakar
EE 59, Evreux (C160H);
ET 61 Orleans (C160A/F);
ET 64 Evreux (C160NG)

| Serial | | | Notes |
|---|---|---|---|
| A02 | 61-ZB | | |
| A04 | 61-BI | (CEV) | |
| A06 | 61-MI | | |
| F1 | 61-MA | | |
| F2 | 61-MB | | |
| F3 | 61-MC | | |
| F4 | 61-MD | | |
| F5 | 61-ME | | |
| F11 | 61-MF | | |
| F12 | 61-MG | | |
| F13 | 61-MH | | |
| F15 | 61-MJ | | |
| F16 | 61-MK | | |
| F17 | 61-ML | | |
| F18 | 61-MM | | |
| F42 | 61-MN | | |
| F43 | 61-MO | | |
| F44 | 61-MP | | |
| F45 | 61-MQ | | |
| F46 | 61-MR | | |
| F48 | 61-MT | | |
| F49 | 61-MU | | |
| F51 | 61-MW | | |
| F52 | 61-MX | | |
| F53 | 61-MY | | |
| F54 | 61-MZ | | |
| F55 | 61-ZC | | |
| F86 | 61-ZD | | |
| F87 | 61-ZE | | |
| F88 | 61-ZF | | |
| F89 | 61-ZG | | |
| F90 | 61-ZH | | |
| F91 | 61-ZI | | |
| F92 | 61-ZJ | | |
| F93 | 61-ZK | | |
| F94 | 61-ZL | | |
| F95 | 61-ZM | | |
| F96 | 61-ZN | | |
| F97 | 61-ZO | | |
| F98 | 61-ZP | | |
| F99 | 61-ZQ | | |
| F100 | 61-ZR | | |
| F153 | 61-ZS | | |
| F154 | 61-ZT | | |
| F155 | 61-ZU | | |
| F157 | 61-ZW | | |
| F158 | 61-ZX | | |
| F159 | 61-ZY | | |
| F160 | 61-ZZ | | |
| F201 | 64-GA | | |
| F202 | 64-GB | | |
| F203 | 64-GC | | |
| F204 | 64-GD | | |
| F205 | 64-GE | | |
| F206 | 64-GF | | |
| F207 | 64-GG | | |
| F208 | 64-GH | | |
| F210 | 64-GJ | | |
| F211 | 64-GK | | |
| F212 | 64-GL | | |
| F213 | 64-GM | | |
| F214 | 64-GN | | |
| F215 | 64-GO | | |
| F216 | F-ZJUP | | |
| F217 | 64-GQ | | |
| F218 | 64-GR | | |
| F221 | F-ZJUU | | |
| F222 | 64-GV | | |
| F223 | 64-GW | | |
| F224 | 64-GX | | |
| F225 | 64-GY | | |
| F226 | 64-GZ | | |
| F227 | 64-GP | | |
| F230† | F-ZJUA | | |
| F231† | F-ZJUB | | |
| F232† | | | |
| H01† | 59-BA | | |
| H02† | 59-BB | | |
| H03† | 59-BC | | |
| H04† | 59-BD | | |

**SEPECAT**
**Jaguar A**
EC 1/7, 2/7, 3/7 St Dizier;
EC 1/11, 2/11, 3/11 Toul;
EC 4/11 Bordeaux;
CEAM (330) Mont de Marsan
CIIAC-339, Luxeuil

| Serial | | | Notes |
|---|---|---|---|
| A1 | 11-RW | 3/11 | |
| A2 | 11-MD | 2/11 | |
| A3 | | (CEV) | |
| A5 | | | |
| A7 | 11-EA | 1/11 | |
| A8 | 11-EB | 1/11 | |
| A9 | 11-MS | 2/11 | |
| A10 | 11-YD | 4/11 | |
| A11 | 7-PL | 2/7 | |
| A12 | | | |
| A13 | 11-EM | 1/11 | |
| A14 | 7-PG | 2/7 | |
| A15 | | | |
| A16 | 11-YL | 4/11 | |
| A17 | | | |
| A19 | 7-IB | 3/7 | |
| A21 | 7-IA | 3/7 | |
| A22 | 7-IN | 3/7 | |
| A23 | 7-HK | 1/7 | |
| A24 | 7-HH | 1/7 | |
| A25 | | | |
| A26 | 11-MC | 2/11 | |
| A27 | 7-IO | 3/7 | |
| A28 | | | |
| A29 | 11-YF | 4/11 | |
| A31 | | | |
| A32 | | | |
| A33 | 7-IH | 3/7 | |
| A34 | | | |
| A35 | 7-HG | 1/7 | |
| A36 | 7-IE | 3/7 | |
| A37 | 7-HA | 1/7 | |
| A38 | | | |
| A39 | 7-IP | 3/7 | |
| A40 | 7-HQ | 1/7 | |
| A41 | | | |
| A43 | | | |
| A44 | 7-ID | 3/7 | |
| A46 | 7-II | 3/7 | |
| A47 | 7-HP | 1/7 | |
| A48 | 7-HI | 1/7 | |
| A49 | 7-HM | 1/7 | |
| A50 | 11-YM | 4/11 | |
| A53 | | | |
| A54 | | | |
| A55 | 7-IL | 3/7 | |
| A58 | 11-RH | 3/11 | |
| A59 | 7-IQ | 3/7 | |

| Notes | Serial | | |
|---|---|---|---|
| | A60 | | |
| | A61 | | |
| | A64 | | |
| | A65 | 7-IS | 3/7 |
| | A66 | 7-IM | 3/7 |
| | A67 | 7-IT | 3/7 |
| | A70 | 7-HC | 1/7 |
| | A72 | 7-HJ | 1/7 |
| | A73 | 7-HR | 1/7 |
| | A74 | 7-IF | 3/7 |
| | A75 | | |
| | A76 | 7-HL | 1/7 |
| | A79 | 7-HQ | 1/7 |
| | A80 | | |
| | A82 | 11-YB | 4/11 |
| | A83 | 11-YL | 4/11 |
| | A84 | 11-YJ | 4/11 |
| | A87 | 11-RX | 3/11 |
| | A88 | 11-EC | 1/11 |
| | A89 | 11-MM | 2/11 |
| | A90 | 11-MB | 2/11 |
| | A91 | 11-YG | 4/11 |
| | A92 | 11-RS | 3/11 |
| | A93 | 11-MV | 2/11 |
| | A94 | 11-ES | 1/11 |
| | A95 | 11-MQ | 2/11 |
| | A96 | 11-RA | 3/11 |
| | A97 | 11-RG | 3/11 |
| | A98 | 11-MT | 2/11 |
| | A99 | 11-EI | 1/11 |
| | A100 | 11-ER | 1/11 |
| | A101 | 11-MP | 2/11 |
| | A103 | 11-MA | 2/11 |
| | A104 | 11-EK | 1/11 |
| | A107 | | |
| | A108 | | |
| | A112 | 11-MO | 2/11 |
| | A113 | 11-MW | 2/11 |
| | A115 | 11-YA | 4/11 |
| | A117 | 11-MH | 2/11 |
| | A118 | 11-YI | 4/11 |
| | A119 | 11-RO | 3/11 |
| | A120 | 11-MR | 1/11 |
| | A121 | 11-YN | 4/11 |
| | A122 | | |
| | A123 | 11-MG | 2/11 |
| | A124 | 11-ME | 2/11 |
| | A126 | 11-YC | 4/11 |
| | A127 | 11-EW | 1/11 |
| | A128 | 11-MF | 2/11 |
| | A129 | 11-EE | 1/11 |
| | A130 | | |
| | A131 | | (CEV) |
| | A133 | 11-EF | 1/11 |
| | A135 | 11-RJ | 3/11 |
| | A136 | | |
| | A137 | 11-EJ | 1/11 |
| | A138 | | |
| | A139 | | |
| | A140 | 11-EL | 1/11 |
| | A141 | 11-YO | 4/11 |
| | A142 | 11-RQ | 3/11 |
| | A144 | | |
| | A145 | | |
| | A146 | | |
| | A148 | 11-YD | 4/11 |
| | A149 | 11-RK | 3/11 |
| | A150 | 11-YK | 4/11 |
| | A151 | 11-EU | 1/11 |
| | A152 | | |
| | A153 | 11-RB | 3/11 |
| | A154 | 11-YN | 4/11 |
| | A156 | | |

| Notes | Serial | | |
|---|---|---|---|
| | A157 | 11-EN | 1/11 |
| | A158 | 11-RM | 3/11 |
| | A159 | 11-RV | 3/11 |
| | A160 | (CEAM) | |

**SEPECAT Jaguar E**

| Serial | | |
|---|---|---|
| E1 | | (CEV) |
| E2 | | |
| E3 | | |
| E4 | 7-PF | 2/7 |
| E5 | | |
| E6 | 11-RF | 3/11 |
| E7 | | |
| E8 | 7-IG | 3/7 |
| E9 | 7-PQ | 2/7 |
| E10 | 339-WF | |
| E11 | 7-PE | 2/7 |
| E12 | | |
| E13 | 11-RD | 3/11 |
| E15 | 339-WG | |
| E16 | 7-HO | 1/7 |
| E17 | 7-PN | 2/7 |
| E18 | | |
| E19 | | |
| E20 | 11-EV | 1/11 |
| E21 | 339-WI | |
| E22 | 7-PC | 2/7 |
| E23 | | |
| E24 | 11-EG | 1/11 |
| E25 | | |
| E27 | 7-IK | 3/7 |
| E28 | 7-IJ | 3/7 |
| E29 | | |
| E30 | 7-PO | 2/7 |
| E32 | 11-YY | 16/11 |
| E33 | | |
| E35 | 7-PK | 2/7 |
| E36 | 7-PP | 2/7 |
| E37 | 7-IG | 3/7 |
| E38 | | |
| E39 | 11-YZ | 4/11 |
| E40 | 7-PH | 2/7 |

**Aeronavale/Marine**

**Aerospatiale SA.321G Super Frelon**

32 F, Lanveoc;
33 F, San Mandrier

| Serial | |
|---|---|
| 101 | (32F) |
| 102 | (32F) |
| 105 | (33F) |
| 106 | (32F) |
| 118 | (32F) |
| 120 | (32F) |
| 122 | (32F) |
| 134 | (32F) |
| 137 | (32F) |
| 141 | (32F) |
| 144 | (32F) |
| 148 | (33F) |
| 149 | (32F) |
| 150 | (33F) |
| 60 | (32F) |
| 162 | (32F) |
| 163 | (33F) |
| 164 | (32F) |
| 165 | (32F) |

**Breguet 1050 Alizé**

4F, Lann Bihoue;
6F, Nimes-Garons;

| Serial | Notes |
|---|---|
| ES 20, Frejus; | |
| ES 59, Hyeres | |
| 11 (4F) | |
| 12 (4F) | |
| 17 (4F) | |
| 22 (4F) | |
| 24 (59S) | |
| 25 (4F) | |
| 26 (6F) | |
| 28 | |
| 31 (59S) | |
| 33 (4F) | |
| 36 (4F) | |
| 41 (59S) | |
| 43 (4F) | |
| 47 (6F) | |
| 48 (4F) | |
| 50 (59S) | |
| 51 (6F) | |
| 52 (4F) | |
| 53 (6F) | |
| 55 (59S) | |
| 56 (59S) | |
| 59 (6F) | |
| 60 (4F) | |
| 64 (6F) | |
| 65 (6F) | |
| 67 (59S) | |
| 68 (6F) | |
| 73 (6F) | |
| 76 (59S) | |
| 87 (59S) | |
| **Breguet 1150 Atlantic/Atlantic 2‡** | |
| 21F/22F, Nimes-Garons; | |
| 23F/24F, Lann Bihoue | |
| 03 (21F/22F) | |
| 04 (21F/22F) | |
| 1 (21F/22F) | |
| 2 (21F/22F) | |
| 3 (21F/22F) | |
| 5 (21F/22F) | |
| 7 (23F/24F) | |
| 9 (21F/22F) | |
| 11 (21F/22F) | |
| 13 (21F/22F) | |
| 15 (21F/22F) | |
| 17 (23F/24F) | |
| 21 (23F/24F) | |
| 23 (23F/24F) | |
| 24 (23F/24F) | |
| 25 (23F/24F) | |
| 27 (21F/22F) | |
| 31 (21F/22F) | |
| 35 (21F/22F) | |
| 37 (21F/22F) | |
| 38 (21F/22F) | |
| 41 (21F/22F) | |
| 44 (23F/24F) | |
| 45 (23F/24F) | |
| 47 (21F/22F) | |
| 48 (23F/24F) | |
| 49 (21F/22F) | |
| 50 (23F/24F) | |
| 51 (21F/22F) | |
| 52 (21F/22F) | |
| 53 (21F/22F) | |
| 54 (23F/24F) | |
| 55 (23F/24F) | |
| 56 (21F/22F) | |
| 57 (23F/24F) | |
| 61 (21F/22F) | |

| Serial | Notes |
|---|---|
| 65 (23F/24F) | |
| 66 (23F/24F) | |
| 67 (21F/22F) | |
| 68 (23F/24F) | |
| ‡01 CEV | |
| ‡02 CEV | |
| ‡03 CEV | |
| ‡04 CEV | |
| ‡1 (23F/24F) | |
| ‡2 | |
| ‡3 | |
| **Dassault Etendard IVM** | |
| 16F, Landivisiau; | |
| ES 59, Hyeres | |
| 1 (59S) | |
| 3 (59S) | |
| 5 (59S) | |
| 7 (16F) | |
| 9 (16F) | |
| 11 (59S) | |
| 13 (59S) | |
| 14 (59S) | |
| 15 (59S) | |
| 16 (59S) | |
| 21 (16F) | |
| 22 (16F) | |
| 26 (59S) | |
| 29 (59S) | |
| 30 (59S) | |
| 32 (16F) | |
| 34 (59S) | |
| 36 (59S) | |
| 37 (59S) | |
| 40 (59S) | |
| 41 (59S) | |
| 42 (59S) | |
| 51 (59S) | |
| 52 (59S) | |
| 53 (59S) | |
| 56 (59S) | |
| 57 (59S) | |
| 59 (59S) | |
| 60 (16F) | |
| **Dassault Etendard IVP/IVMP*** | |
| 16F, 57S Landivisiau | |
| 101 (57S) | |
| 107 | |
| 108 | |
| 109 (16F) | |
| 114 | |
| 115 | |
| 117 (16F) | |
| 118 | |
| 120 (16F) | |
| 153* (16F) | |
| 162* (16F) | |
| 163* (16F) | |
| 166* (16F) | |
| **Dassault Super Etendard** | |
| 11F, Landivisiau; | |
| 14F, Landivisiau; | |
| 17F, Hyeres | |
| 1 (14F) | |
| 2 (14F) | |
| 3 (14F) | |

## Overseas Serials

| Notes | Serial |
|---|---|
| | 4 (17F) |
| | 5 (11F) |
| | 6 (14F) |
| | 7 (11F) |
| | 8 (11F) |
| | 9 (11F) |
| | 10 (14F) |
| | 11 (11F) |
| | 12 (11F) |
| | 13 (11F) |
| | 14 (11F) |
| | 15 (17F) |
| | 16 (14F) |
| | 17 (14F) |
| | 18 (11F) |
| | 19 (14F) |
| | 20 (11F) |
| | 21 |
| | 23 (11F) |
| | 24 (17F) |
| | 25 (11F) |
| | 26 (11F) |
| | 27 |
| | 28 (14F) |
| | 29 (14F) |
| | 30 (11F) |
| | 31 (14F) |
| | 32 (14F) |
| | 33 (17F) |
| | 34 (11F) |
| | 35 (17F) |
| | 37 (11F) |
| | 38 (17F) |
| | 39 |
| | 41 (11F) |
| | 42 |
| | 43 (14F) |
| | 44 (14F) |
| | 45 (14F) |
| | 46 (17F) |
| | 47 (17F) |
| | 48 (11F) |
| | 49 (17F) |
| | 50 (14F) |
| | 51 (14F) |
| | 52 (14F) |
| | 53 (14F) |
| | 54 (14F) |
| | 55 (11F) |
| | 57 (17F) |
| | 59 (17F) |
| | 60 (14F) |
| | 61 (17F) |
| | 62 (14F) |
| | 63 (11F) |
| | 64 (11F) |
| | 65 (14F) |
| | 66 (14F) |
| | 68 (17F) |
| | 69 (11F) |
| | 71 (14F) |
| | **Dassault Falcon 10(MER)** |
| | ES 3, Hyeres; |
| | ES 57, Landivisiau |
| | 32 (57S) |
| | 101 (57S) |
| | 129 (57S) |
| | 133 (57S) |
| | 143 (57S) |
| | 185 (3S) |

| Notes | Serial |
|---|---|
| | **Dassault Falcon Guardian** |
| | ES 9 Noumea; |
| | ES 12 Papeete |
| | CEPA, Istres |
| | 48 (12S) |
| | 65 (9S) |
| | 72 (12S) |
| | 77 (9S) |
| | 80 (CEPA) |
| | **Embraer Xingu** |
| | ES 2, Lann Bihoué; |
| | ES 11, Le Bourget; |
| | ES 20, Frejus; |
| | ES 52, Lann Bihoué; |
| | ES 56, Nimes-Garons |
| | 55 |
| | 65 (52S) |
| | 66 (52S) |
| | 67 (52S) |
| | 68 (52S) |
| | 69 (52S) |
| | 70 (56S) |
| | 71 (2S) |
| | 74 (11S) |
| | 77 (56S) |
| | 79 (56S) |
| | 81 (3S) |
| | 83 (52S) |
| | 85 (52S) |
| | 87 (52S) |
| | 90 (52S) |
| | **LTV F-8E (FN) Crusader** |
| | 12F, Landivisiau |
| | 3 |
| | 4 |
| | 5 |
| | 6 |
| | 7 |
| | 8 |
| | 10 |
| | 11 |
| | 17 |
| | 19 |
| | 23 |
| | 27 |
| | 29 |
| | 31 |
| | 32 (CEV) |
| | 34 |
| | 35 |
| | 37 |
| | 39 |
| | **Morane Saulnier 760 Paris** |
| | ES 57, Landivisiau |
| | 32 |
| | 33 |
| | 40 |
| | 41 |
| | 42 |
| | 46 |
| | 47 |
| | 85 |
| | 87 |
| | 88 |

| Serial | Notes |
|---|---|
| **Nord 262 Fregate** | |
| ES 2, Lann Bihoué; | |
| ES 3, Hyeres; | |
| ES 11, Le Bourget; | |
| ES 56, Nimes-Garons | |
| 16 (2S) | |
| 28 (2S) | |
| 43 (56S) | |
| 45 (56S) | |
| 46 (56S) | |
| 51 (56S) | |
| 52 (56S) | |
| 53 (56S) | |
| 59 (2S) | |
| 60 (2S) | |
| 61 (11S) | |
| 62 (3S) | |
| 63 (2S) | |
| 65 (2S) | |
| 69 (56S) | |
| 70 (56S) | |
| 71 (2S) | |
| 72 (56S) | |
| 73 (56S) | |
| 75 (3S) | |
| 79 (2S) | |
| 100 (56S) | |
| 102 (11S) | |
| 104 (3S) | |
| **Piper Navajo** | |
| ES 3, Hyeres; | |
| ES 20 Fréjus | |
| 227 (3S) | |
| 232 (3S) | |
| 903 (3S) | |
| 904 (3S) | |
| 906 (3S) | |
| 912 (3S) | |
| 914 (3S) | |
| 916 (3S) | |
| 925 (3S) | |
| 927 (20S) | |
| 929 (3S) | |
| 931 (3S) | |
| **Westland Lynx HAS2 (FN)*; HAS4 (FN)†** | |
| 31F, San Mandrier; | |
| 34F, Lanvéoc; | |
| 35F, Lanvéoc; | |
| ES 20, St Raphael | |
| 260* (20S) | |
| 262* (35F) | |
| 263* (34F) | |
| 264* (34F) | |
| 265* | |
| 266* (34F) | |
| 267* | |
| 268* | |
| 269* (34F) | |
| 270* (34F) | |
| 271* (35F) | |
| 272* (20S) | |
| 273* (34F) | |
| 274* (34F) | |
| 275* (34F) | |
| 276* (34F) | |
| 278* (34F) | |
| 621* (34F) | |
| 622* (34F) | |

| Serial | Notes |
|---|---|
| 623* (34F) | |
| 624* (34F) | |
| 625* (34F) | |
| 626* (34F) | |
| 627* (35F) | |
| 801† (20S) | |
| 802† (34F) | |
| 803† (31F) | |
| 804† (35F) | |
| 805† (31F) | |
| 806† (34F) | |
| 807† (34F) | |
| 808† (34F) | |
| 809† (31F) | |
| 810† (31F) | |
| 811† (31F) | |
| 812† (34F) | |
| 813† (31F) | |
| 814† (34F) | |
| **GERMANY** | |
| **Luftwaffe, Marineflieger** | |
| **Boeing 707-307C** | |
| FBS-BMVg, Köln-Bonn | |
| 10+01 | |
| 10+02 | |
| 10+03 | |
| 10+04 | |
| **Tupolev Tu.154M** | |
| TG-44, Wreizen | |
| 11+01 | |
| 11+02 | |
| 11+03 | |
| **Tupolev Tu.134A** | |
| TG-44, Wreizen | |
| 11+10 | |
| 11+11 | |
| 11+12 (DDR-SDR) | |
| 11+13 | |
| 11+14 | |
| 11+15 | |
| **Ilyushin Il.62MT/Il.62MK*** | |
| TG-44, Wreizen | |
| †11+20 (DDR-SEN) | |
| *11+21 (DDR-SEV) | |
| †11+22 (DDR-SEP) | |
| **Canadair CL601 Challenger** | |
| FBS-BMVg, Köln-Bonn | |
| 12+01 | |
| 12+02 | |
| 12+03 | |
| 12+04 | |
| 12+05 | |
| 12+06 | |
| 12+07 | |
| **HFB 320 Hansa Jet ECM** | |
| JbG32 Lechfeld; | |
| 16+21 | |
| 16+23 | |
| 16+24 | |
| 16+25 | |
| 16+26 | |
| 16+27 | |
| 16+28 | |

| Notes | Serial |
|---|---|
| | **VFW 614** |
| | FBS-BMVg, Köln-Bonn |
| | 17+01 |
| | 17+02 |
| | 17+03 |
| | **McD RF-4E Phantom** |
| | AkG 51, Bremgarten; |
| | AkG 52, Leck; |
| | Tslw 1, Kaufbeuren; |
| | WTD 61, Ingolstadt |
| | 35+01 WTD 61 |
| | 35+02 AkG 52 |
| | 35+03 AkG 51 |
| | 35+04 AkG 51 |
| | 35+05 AkG 52 |
| | 35+06 AkG 51 |
| | 35+07 AkG 51 |
| | 35+08 AkG 52 |
| | 35+09 AkG 52 |
| | 35+10 AkG 52 |
| | 35+11 AkG 51 |
| | 35+12 AkG 51 |
| | 35+13 AkG 52 |
| | 35+17 AkG 52 |
| | 35+18 AkG 52 |
| | 35+19 AkG 51 |
| | 35+20 AkG 52 |
| | 35+21 AkG 52 |
| | 35+22 AkG 51 |
| | 35+24 AkG 52 |
| | 35+25 AkG 51 |
| | 35+26 AkG 52 |
| | 35+28 AkG 51 |
| | 35+29 AkG 51 |
| | 35+31 AkG 52 |
| | 35+32 AkG 52 |
| | 35+33 AkG 51 |
| | 35+34 AkG 51 |
| | 35+35 AkG 51 |
| | 35+36 AkG 52 |
| | 35+37 AkG 52 |
| | 35+38 AkG 51 |
| | 35+39 AkG 52 |
| | 35+40 AkG 51 |
| | 35+41 AkG 52 |
| | 35+42 AkG 52 |
| | 35+43 AkG 52 |
| | 35+44 AkG 51 |
| | 35+46 AkG 51 |
| | 35+48 AkG 51 |
| | 35+49 AkG 51 |
| | 35+50 AkG 51 |
| | 35+51 AkG 51 |
| | 35+52 AkG 52 |
| | 35+53 AkG 52 |
| | 35+54 AkG 52 |
| | 35+56 AkG 51 |
| | 35+57 AkG 51 |
| | 35+58 AkG 51 |
| | 35+59 AkG 51 |
| | 35+60 AkG 52 |
| | 35+61 AkG 51 |
| | 35+62 AkG 52 |
| | 35+63 AkG 51 |
| | 35+64 AkG 51 |
| | 35+65 AkG 52 |
| | 35+66 AkG 52 |
| | 35+67 AkG 52 |
| | 35+68 AkG 52 |
| | 35+71 AkG 51 |

| Notes | Serial |
|---|---|
| | 35+72 AkG 52 |
| | 35+73 AkG 51 |
| | 35+74 AkG 52 |
| | 35+75 AkG 51 |
| | 35+76 AkG 52 |
| | 35+77 AkG 52 |
| | 35+78 AkG 51 |
| | 35+79 AkG 52 |
| | 35+82 AkG 51 |
| | 35+83 WTD 61 |
| | 35+84 AkG 52 |
| | 35+86 AkG 51 |
| | 35+87 AkG 52 |
| | 35+88 AkG 51 |
| | **McD F-4F Phantom** |
| | JG 71, Wittmundhaven; |
| | JG 72, Hopsten; |
| | JG 73, Pferdsfeld; |
| | JG 74, Neuburg/Donau; |
| | TSLw 1, Kaufbeuren; |
| | WTD 61, Ingolstadt |
| | 37+01 JG 72 |
| | 37+03 JG 73 |
| | 37+04 TSLw 1 |
| | 37+05 JG 74 |
| | 37+06 JG 71 |
| | 37+07 JG 72 |
| | 37+08 JG 71 |
| | 37+09 JG 73 |
| | 37+10 JG 71 |
| | 37+11 JG 72 |
| | 37+12 JG 72 |
| | 37+13 JG 73 |
| | 37+14 TSLw 1 |
| | 37+15 WTD-61 |
| | 37+16 WTD-61 |
| | 37+17 JG 72 |
| | 37+18 JG 73 |
| | 37+19 JG 71 |
| | 37+20 JG 74 |
| | 37+21 JG 74 |
| | 37+22 JG 71 |
| | 37+23 JG 71 |
| | 37+24 JG 74 |
| | 37+25 JG 72 |
| | 37+26 JG 73 |
| | 37+28 JG 74 |
| | 37+29 JG 72 |
| | 37+30 JG 73 |
| | 37+31 JG 71 |
| | 37+32 JG 74 |
| | 37+33 JG 72 |
| | 37+34 JG 73 |
| | 37+35 JG 71 |
| | 37+36 JG 74 |
| | 37+37 JG 72 |
| | 37+38 JG 71 |
| | 37+39 JG 71 |
| | 37+40 JG 74 |
| | 37+41 JG 72 |
| | 37+42 JG 73 |
| | 37+43 JG 71 |
| | 37+44 JG 74 |
| | 37+45 JG 72 |
| | 37+46 JG 71 |
| | 37+47 JG 71 |
| | 37+48 JG 74 |
| | 37+49 JG 72 |
| | 37+50 JG 73 |
| | 37+51 JG 71 |
| | 37+52 JG 74 |

| Serial | | Notes |
|---|---|---|
| 37+53 | JG 72 | |
| 37+54 | JG 73 | |
| 37+55 | JG 71 | |
| 37+56 | JG 74 | |
| 37+58 | JG 73 | |
| 37+60 | JG 74 | |
| 37+61 | JG 73 | |
| 37+63 | JG 73 | |
| 37+64 | JG 74 | |
| 37+65 | JG 72 | |
| 37+66 | JG 73 | |
| 37+67 | JG 71 | |
| 37+69 | JG 72 | |
| 37+70 | JG 73 | |
| 37+71 | JG 71 | |
| 37+73 | JG 72 | |
| 37+75 | JG 71 | |
| 37+76 | JG 72 | |
| 37+77 | JG 72 | |
| 37+78 | JG 73 | |
| 37+79 | JG 71 | |
| 37+81 | JG 72 | |
| 37+82 | JG 73 | |
| 37+83 | JG 71 | |
| 37+84 | JG 74 | |
| 37+85 | JG 72 | |
| 37+86 | JG 71 | |
| 37+88 | JG 71 | |
| 37+89 | JG 72 | |
| 37+90 | JG 72 | |
| 37+91 | WTD 61 | |
| 37+92 | JG 74 | |
| 37+93 | JG 72 | |
| 37+94 | JG 73 | |
| 37+96 | JG 74 | |
| 37+97 | JG 72 | |
| 37+98 | JG 73 | |
| 38+00 | JG 74 | |
| 38+01 | JG 72 | |
| 38+02 | JG 73 | |
| 38+03 | JG 71 | |
| 38+04 | JG 74 | |
| 38+05 | JG 72 | |
| 38+06 | JG 73 | |
| 38+07 | JG 71 | |
| 38+08 | JG 74 | |
| 38+09 | JG 72 | |
| 38+10 | JG 73 | |
| 38+11 | JG 73 | |
| 38+12 | JG 74 | |
| 38+13 | JG 73 | |
| 38+14 | JG 73 | |
| 38+16 | JG 74 | |
| 38+17 | JG 72 | |
| 38+18 | JG 73 | |
| 38+20 | JG 74 | |
| 38+21 | JG 72 | |
| 38+24 | JG 74 | |
| 38+25 | JG 72 | |
| 38+26 | JG 73 | |
| 38+27 | JG 71 | |
| 38+28 | JG 74 | |
| 38+29 | JG 72 | |
| 38+30 | JG 73 | |
| 38+31 | JG 71 | |
| 38+32 | JG 74 | |
| 38+33 | JG 72 | |
| 38+34 | JG 73 | |
| 38+36 | JG 74 | |
| 38+37 | JG 72 | |
| 38+38 | JG 71 | |
| 38+39 | JG 71 | |
| 38+40 | JG 74 | |
| 38+42 | JG 73 | |
| 38+43 | JG 71 | |
| 38+44 | JG 74 | |
| 38+45 | JG 72 | |
| 38+46 | JG 73 | |
| 38+47 | JG 71 | |
| 38+48 | JG 74 | |
| 38+49 | JG 72 | |
| 38+50 | JG 73 | |
| 38+51 | JG 71 | |
| 38+53 | JG 72 | |
| 38+54 | JG 73 | |
| 38+55 | JG 71 | |
| 38+56 | JG 74 | |
| 38+57 | JG 72 | |
| 38+58 | JG 73 | |
| 38+59 | JG 71 | |
| 38+60 | JG 74 | |
| 38+61 | JG 71 | |
| 38+62 | JG 73 | |
| 38+63 | JG 71 | |
| 38+64 | JG 74 | |
| 38+66 | JG 71 | |
| 38+67 | JG 72 | |
| 38+68 | JG 74 | |
| 38+69 | JG 71 | |
| 38+70 | JG 71 | |
| 38+72 | JG 74 | |
| 38+73 | JG 74 | |
| 38+74 | JG 73 | |
| 38+75 | JG 73 | |

**D-BD Alpha Jet**

JbG 41, Husum;
JbG 43, Oldenburg;
JbG 44, Beja (Portugal);
JbG 49, Fürstenfeldbruck;
WTD 61, Ingolstadt

| Serial | | Notes |
|---|---|---|
| 40+01 | WTD 61 | |
| 40+02 | WTD 61 | |
| 40+03 | JbG 49 | |
| 40+04 | JbG 43 | |
| 40+05 | JbG 49 | |
| 40+06 | JbG 49 | |
| 40+07 | JbG 49 | |
| 40+08 | JbG 44 | |
| 40+09 | JbG 41 | |
| 40+11 | JbG 43 | |
| 40+12 | JbG 49 | |
| 40+13 | JbG 43 | |
| 40+14 | JbG 43 | |
| 40+15 | JbG 41 | |
| 40+16 | JbG 41 | |
| 40+17 | JbG 49 | |
| 40+18 | JbG 49 | |
| 40+20 | JbG 43 | |
| 40+21 | JbG 41 | |
| 40+22 | JbG 41 | |
| 40+23 | JbG 49 | |
| 40+24 | JbG 43 | |
| 40+25 | JbG 49 | |
| 40+26 | JbG 41 | |
| 40+27 | JbG 43 | |
| 40+28 | JbG 41 | |
| 40+29 | JbG 49 | |
| 40+30 | JbG 49 | |
| 40+31 | JbG 43 | |
| 40+32 | JbG 43 | |
| 40+33 | JbG 41 | |
| 40+34 | JbG 41 | |
| 40+35 | JbG 49 | |

| Notes | Serial | |
|---|---|---|
| | 40+36 | JbG 43 |
| | 40+37 | JbG 49 |
| | 40+38 | JbG 43 |
| | 40+39 | JbG 41 |
| | 40+40 | JbG 49 |
| | 40+41 | JbG 41 |
| | 40+42 | JbG 44 |
| | 40+43 | JbG 43 |
| | 40+44 | JbG 43 |
| | 40+45 | JbG 41 |
| | 40+46 | JbG 43 |
| | 40+47 | JbG 49 |
| | 40+48 | JbG 43 |
| | 40+49 | JbG 49 |
| | 40+50 | JbG 43 |
| | 40+51 | JbG 41 |
| | 40+52 | JbG 44 |
| | 40+53 | JbG 44 |
| | 40+54 | JbG 43 |
| | 40+56 | WTD-61 |
| | 40+57 | JbG 43 |
| | 40+58 | JbG 43 |
| | 40+59 | TSLw 3 |
| | 40+60 | JbG 41 |
| | 40+61 | JbG 43 |
| | 40+62 | JbG 41 |
| | 40+63 | JbG 41 |
| | 40+64 | JbG 49 |
| | 40+65 | JbG 49 |
| | 40+66 | JbG 44 |
| | 40+67 | JbG 49 |
| | 40+68 | JbG 41 |
| | 40+69 | JbG 43 |
| | 40+70 | JbG 41 |
| | 40+71 | JbG 44 |
| | 40+72 | JbG 44 |
| | 40+73 | JbG 49 |
| | 40+74 | JbG 41 |
| | 40+75 | JbG 43 |
| | 40+76 | JbG 49 |
| | 40+77 | JbG 49 |
| | 40+78 | TSLw 3 |
| | 40+79 | JbG 43 |
| | 40+80 | JbG 43 |
| | 40+81 | JbG 41 |
| | 40+82 | JbG 49 |
| | 40+84 | JbG 49 |
| | 40+85 | JbG 49 |
| | 40+86 | JbG 44 |
| | 40+88 | JbG 41 |
| | 40+89 | JbG 41 |
| | 40+90 | JbG 49 |
| | 40+91 | JbG 49 |
| | 40+92 | JbG 43 |
| | 40+93 | JbG 49 |
| | 40+94 | JbG 44 |
| | 40+95 | JbG 43 |
| | 40+96 | JbG 49 |
| | 40+97 | JbG 44 |
| | 40+98 | JbG 44 |
| | 40+99 | JbG 41 |
| | 41+00 | JbG 43 |
| | 41+01 | JbG 43 |
| | 41+02 | JbG 41 |
| | 41+03 | JbG 41 |
| | 41+04 | JbG 49 |
| | 41+05 | JbG 43 |
| | 41+06 | JbG 41 |
| | 41+07 | JbG 44 |
| | 41+08 | JbG 44 |
| | 41+09 | JbG 49 |
| | 41+10 | JbG 49 |

| Notes | Serial | |
|---|---|---|
| | 41+11 | JbG 49 |
| | 41+12 | JbG 43 |
| | 41+13 | JbG 43 |
| | 41+14 | JbG 41 |
| | 41+15 | JbG 41 |
| | 41+16 | JbG 43 |
| | 41+17 | JbG 43 |
| | 41+18 | JbG 43 |
| | 41+19 | JbG 44 |
| | 41+20 | JbG 41 |
| | 41+21 | JbG 41 |
| | 41+22 | JbG 44 |
| | 41+23 | JbG 44 |
| | 41+24 | JbG 41 |
| | 41+25 | JbG 49 |
| | 41+26 | JbG 49 |
| | 41+27 | JbG 43 |
| | 41+28 | JbG 43 |
| | 41+29 | JbG 43 |
| | 41+30 | JbG 44 |
| | 41+31 | JbG 41 |
| | 41+32 | JbG 41 |
| | 41+33 | JbG 41 |
| | 41+34 | JbG 43 |
| | 41+35 | JbG 49 |
| | 41+36 | JbG 49 |
| | 41+37 | JbG 49 |
| | 41+38 | JbG 49 |
| | 41+39 | JbG 43 |
| | 41+40 | JbG 43 |
| | 41+41 | JbG 41 |
| | 41+42 | JbG 43 |
| | 41+43 | JbG 43 |
| | 41+44 | JbG 49 |
| | 41+45 | JbG 49 |
| | 41+46 | JbG 43 |
| | 41+47 | JbG 41 |
| | 41+48 | JbG 41 |
| | 41+49 | JbG 49 |
| | 41+50 | JbG 49 |
| | 41+51 | JbG 43 |
| | 41+52 | JbG 44 |
| | 41+53 | JbG 41 |
| | 41+54 | JbG 41 |
| | 41+55 | JbG 49 |
| | 41+56 | JbG 49 |
| | 41+57 | JbG 43 |
| | 41+58 | JbG 43 |
| | 41+59 | JbG 41 |
| | 41+60 | JbG 41 |
| | 41+61 | JbG 49 |
| | 41+62 | JbG 41 |
| | 41+63 | JbG 43 |
| | 41+64 | JbG 43 |
| | 41+65 | JbG 41 |
| | 41+66 | JbG 41 |
| | 41+67 | JbG 49 |
| | 41+68 | JbG 49 |
| | 41+70 | JbG 43 |
| | 41+71 | JbG 41 |
| | 41+72 | JbG 41 |
| | 41+73 | JbG 41 |
| | 41+74 | JbG 41 |
| | 41+75 | JbG 41 |

**Panavia Tornado Strike/Trainer*/ECR†**
TTTE RAF Cottesmore;
JbG 31, Nörvenich;
JbG 32, Lechfeld;
JbG 33, Büchel;

| Serial | | Notes |
|---|---|---|
| JbG 34, Memmingen; | | |
| JbG 38, Jever; | | |
| MBB, Manching; | | |
| MFG1, Schleswig; | | |
| MFG2, Eggebek; | | |
| TSLw 1, Kaufbeuren; | | |
| WTD61, Ingolstadt | | |
| 98+01 | WTD 61 | |
| 98+02 | WTD 61 | |
| 98+03 | WTD 61 | |
| 98+79 | WTD 61 | |
| 43+00 | | |
| *43+01 | G-20 TTTE | |
| *43+02 | G-21 TTTE | |
| *43+03 | G-22 TTTE | |
| *43+04 | G-23 TTTE | |
| *43+05 | G-24 TTTE | |
| *43+06 | G-25 TTTE | |
| *43+07 | G-26 TTTE | |
| *43+08 | G-27 TTTE | |
| *43+09 | G-28 TTTE | |
| *43+10 | G-29 TTTE | |
| *43+11 | G-30 TTTE | |
| 43+12 | G-70 TTTE | |
| 43+13 | G-71 TTTE | |
| 43+14 | G-72 TTTE | |
| *43+15 | G-31 TTTE | |
| *43+16 | G-32 TTTE | |
| *43+17 | G-33 TTTE | |
| 43+18 | JbG 34 | |
| 43+19 | JbG 31 | |
| 43+20 | G-73 TTTE | |
| *43+22 | JbG 38 | |
| *43+23 | G-34 TTTE | |
| 43+25 | G-75 TTTE | |
| 43+26 | JbG 38 | |
| 43+27 | MFG 1 | |
| 43+28 | JbG 38 | |
| *43+29 | JbG 31 | |
| 43+30 | JbG 38 | |
| *43+31 | JbG-31 | |
| 43+32 | JbG 38 | |
| *43+33 | JbG 38 | |
| 43+34 | JbG 38 | |
| *43+35 | JbG 38 | |
| 43+36 | JbG 38 | |
| *43+37 | JbG 38 | |
| 43+38 | JbG 38 | |
| 43+40 | JbG 38 | |
| 43+41 | JbG 31 | |
| *43+42 | MFG 1 | |
| *43+43 | MFG 1 | |
| *43+44 | MFG 1 | |
| *43+45 | MFG 1 | |
| 43+46 | MFG 1 | |
| 43+47 | MFG 1 | |
| 43+48 | MFG 1 | |
| 43+50 | MFG 1 | |
| 43+52 | MFG 1 | |
| 43+53 | MFG 1 | |
| 43+54 | MFG 1 | |
| 43+55 | MFG 1 | |
| 43+57 | MFG 1 | |
| 43+58 | MFG 1 | |
| 43+59 | MFG 1 | |
| 43+60 | MFG 1 | |
| 43+61 | MFG 1 | |
| 43+62 | MFG 1 | |
| 43+63 | MFG 1 | |
| 43+64 | MFG 1 | |
| 43+65 | MFG 1 | |
| 43+67 | MFG 1 | |

| Serial | | Notes |
|---|---|---|
| 43+68 | MFG 1 | |
| 43+69 | MFG 1 | |
| 43+70 | JbG 38 | |
| 43+71 | MFG 1 | |
| 43+72 | MFG 1 | |
| 43+73 | MFG 1 | |
| 43+74 | MFG 1 | |
| 43+75 | MFG 1 | |
| 43+76 | MFG 1 | |
| 43+77 | MFG 1 | |
| 43+78 | MFG 1 | |
| 43+79 | MFG 1 | |
| 43+80 | MFG 1 | |
| 43+81 | MFG 1 | |
| 43+82 | MFG 1 | |
| 43+83 | MFG 1 | |
| 43+84 | MFG 1 | |
| 43+85 | MFG 1 | |
| 43+86 | MFG 1 | |
| 43+87 | MFG 1 | |
| 43+88 | MFG 1 | |
| 43+89 | MFG 1 | |
| *43+90 | JbG 38 | |
| *43+91 | JbG 38 | |
| *43+92 | JbG 31 | |
| *43+94 | JbG 31 | |
| 43+95 | JbG 32 | |
| 43+96 | JbG 31 | |
| *43+97 | JbG 31 | |
| 43+98 | JbG 31 | |
| 43+99 | JbG 31 | |
| 44+00 | JbG 31 | |
| *44+01 | JbG 38 | |
| 44+02 | JbG 31 | |
| 44+03 | JbG 31 | |
| 44+04 | JbG 31 | |
| *44+05 | JbG 38 | |
| 44+06 | JbG 31 | |
| 44+07 | JbG 31 | |
| 44+08 | JbG 38 | |
| 44+09 | JbG 31 | |
| *44+10 | JbG 38 | |
| 44+11 | JbG 38 | |
| 44+12 | JbG 31 | |
| 44+13 | JbG 38 | |
| 44+14 | JbG 34 | |
| *44+15 | JbG 38 | |
| 44+16 | JbG 31 | |
| 44+17 | JbG 38 | |
| 44+19 | JbG 31 | |
| *44+20 | JbG 38 | |
| 44+21 | JbG 31 | |
| 44+22 | JbG 31 | |
| 44+23 | JbG 31 | |
| 44+24 | JbG 38 | |
| *44+25 | JbG 38 | |
| 44+26 | JbG 31 | |
| 44+27 | JbG 31 | |
| 44+28 | JbG 31 | |
| 44+29 | JbG 31 | |
| 44+30 | JbG 31 | |
| 44+31 | JbG 31 | |
| 44+32 | JbG 38 | |
| 44+33 | JbG 31 | |
| 44+34 | JbG 31 | |
| 44+35 | JbG 31 | |
| *44+36 | JbG 32 | |
| *44+37 | JbG 32 | |
| *44+38 | JbG 32 | |
| *44+39 | JbG 32 | |
| 44+40 | JbG 33 | |
| 44+41 | JbG 31 | |

# Overseas Serials

| Notes | Serial | | Notes | Serial | |
|---|---|---|---|---|---|
| | 44+42 | JbG 32 | | 45+17 | JbG 33 |
| | 44+43 | JbG 32 | | 45+18 | JbG 34 |
| | 44+44 | JbG 31 | | 45+19 | JbG 33 |
| | 44+46 | JbG 32 | | 45+20 | JbG 33 |
| | 44+48 | JbG 31 | | 45+21 | JbG 33 |
| | 44+49 | JbG 31 | | 45+22 | JbG 33 |
| | 44+50 | JbG 32 | | 45+23 | JbG 33 |
| | 44+51 | JbG 32 | | 45+24 | JbG 33 |
| | 44+52 | JbG 31 | | 45+25 | JbG 33 |
| | 44+53 | JbG 32 | | 45+26 | TSLw 1 |
| | 44+54 | JbG 32 | | 45+27 | MFG 2 |
| | 44+55 | JbG 32 | | 45+28 | MFG 2 |
| | 44+56 | JbG 32 | | 45+29 | MFG 2 |
| | 44+57 | JbG 32 | | 45+30 | MFG 2 |
| | 44+58 | JbG 32 | | 45+31 | MFG 2 |
| | 44+59 | JbG 32 | | 45+32 | MFG 2 |
| | 44+60 | JbG 32 | | 45+33 | MFG 2 |
| | 44+61 | JbG 32 | | 45+34 | MFG 2 |
| | 44+62 | JbG 32 | | 45+35 | MFG 2 |
| | 44+63 | JbG 32 | | 45+36 | MFG 2 |
| | 44+64 | JbG 32 | | 45+37 | MFG 2 |
| | 44+65 | JbG 38 | | 45+38 | MFG 2 |
| | 44+66 | JbG 32 | | 45+39 | MFG 2 |
| | 44+67 | JbG 32 | | 45+40 | MFG 2 |
| | 44+68 | JbG 32 | | 45+41 | MFG 2 |
| | 44+69 | JbG 32 | | 45+42 | MFG 2 |
| | 44+70 | JbG 32 | | 45+43 | MFG 2 |
| | 44+71 | JbG 32 | | 45+44 | MFG 2 |
| | *44+72 | JbG 33 | | 45+45 | MFG 2 |
| | *44+73 | JbG 33 | | 45+46 | MFG 2 |
| | *44+74 | JbG 33 | | 45+47 | MFG 2 |
| | *44+75 | JbG 33 | | 45+48 | MFG 2 |
| | 44+76 | JbG 32 | | 45+49 | MFG 2 |
| | 44+77 | JbG 32 | | 45+50 | MFG 2 |
| | 44+78 | JbG 32 | | 45+51 | MFG 2 |
| | 44+79 | JbG 32 | | 45+52 | MFG 2 |
| | 44+80 | JbG 32 | | 45+53 | MFG 2 |
| | 44+81 | JbG 32 | | 45+54 | MFG 2 |
| | 44+82 | JbG 32 | | 45+55 | MFG 2 |
| | 44+83 | JbG 32 | | 45+56 | MFG 2 |
| | 44+84 | JbG 32 | | 45+57 | MFG 2 |
| | 44+85 | JbG 32 | | 45+58 | MFG 2 |
| | 44+86 | JbG 33 | | 45+59 | MFG 2 |
| | 44+87 | JbG 33 | | *45+60 | JbG 38 |
| | 44+88 | JbG 33 | | *45+61 | JbG 34 |
| | 44+89 | JbG 33 | | *45+62 | JbG 38 |
| | 44+90 | JbG 33 | | *45+63 | JbG 38 |
| | 44+91 | JbG 33 | | 45+64 | TSLw 1 |
| | 44+92 | JbG 33 | | 45+65 | MFG 2 |
| | 44+94 | JbG 33 | | 45+66 | MFG 2 |
| | 44+95 | JbG 33 | | 45+67 | MFG 2 |
| | 44+96 | JbG 33 | | 45+68 | MFG 2 |
| | 44+97 | JbG 33 | | 45+69 | MFG 2 |
| | 44+98 | JbG 33 | | *45+70 | JbG 33 |
| | 44+99 | JbG 34 | | 45+71 | MFG 2 |
| | 45+00 | JbG 33 | | 45+72 | MFG 2 |
| | 45+01 | JbG 33 | | *45+73 | JbG 31 |
| | 45+02 | JbG 33 | | 45+74 | MFG 2 |
| | 45+03 | JbG 33 | | 45+76 | JbG 34 |
| | 45+04 | JbG 33 | | *45+77 | JbG 33 |
| | 45+05 | JbG 33 | | 45+78 | JbG 32 |
| | 45+06 | JbG 33 | | 45+79 | JbG 34 |
| | 45+07 | JbG 33 | | 45+80 | JbG 38 |
| | 45+08 | JbG 33 | | 45+81 | JbG 34 |
| | 45+09 | JbG 33 | | 45+82 | JbG 34 |
| | 45+10 | JbG 33 | | 45+83 | JbG 34 |
| | 45+11 | JbG 33 | | 45+84 | JbG 34 |
| | *45+12 | MFG 2 | | 45+85 | JbG 34 |
| | *45+13 | MFG 2 | | 45+86 | JbG 34 |
| | *45+14 | MFG 2 | | 45+87 | JbG 34 |
| | *45+15 | MFG 2 | | 45+88 | JbG 34 |
| | *45+16 | MFG 2 | | 45+89 | JbG 33 |

| Serial | | Notes |
|---|---|---|
| 45+90 | JbG 34 | |
| 45+91 | JbG 34 | |
| 45+92 | JbG 34 | |
| 45+93 | JbG 34 | |
| 45+94 | JbG 34 | |
| 45+95 | JbG 34 | |
| 45+96 | JbG 34 | |
| 45+97 | JbG 34 | |
| 45+98 | JbG 34 | |
| *45+99 | JbG 34 | |
| 46+00 | JbG 34 | |
| 46+01 | JbG 34 | |
| 46+02 | JbG 34 | |
| 46+03 | JbG 34 | |
| *46+04 | MFG 1 | |
| *46+05 | MFG 2 | |
| *46+06 | JbG 32 | |
| 46+07 | JbG 34 | |
| 46+08 | JbG 34 | |
| 46+09 | JbG 34 | |
| 46+10 | MFG 1 | |
| 46+11 | MFG 1 | |
| 46+12 | MFG 2 | |
| 46+13 | MFG 1 | |
| 46+14 | MFG 1 | |
| 46+15 | MFG 1 | |
| 46+16 | MFG 1 | |
| 46+17 | MFG 1 | |
| 46+18 | JbG 38 | |
| 46+19 | MFG 2 | |
| 46+20 | MFG 2 | |
| 46+21 | JbG 38 | |
| 46+22 | MFG 2 | |
| †46+23 | JbG 38 | |
| †46+24 | JbG 38 | |
| †46+25 | TSLw 1 | |
| †46+26 | JbG 38 | |
| †46+27 | JbG 38 | |
| †46+28 | JbG 38 | |
| †46+29 | JbG 38 | |
| †46+30 | JbG 38 | |
| †46+31 | JbG 38 | |
| †46+32 | JbG 38 | |
| †46+33 | JbG 38 | |
| †46+34 | | |
| †46+35 | | |
| †46+36 | | |
| †46+37 | | |
| †46+38 | | |
| †46+39 | | |
| †46+40 | | |
| †46+41 | | |
| †46+42 | | |
| †46+43 | | |
| †46+44 | | |
| †46+45 | | |
| †46+46 | | |
| †46+47 | | |
| †46+48 | | |
| †46+49 | | |
| †46+50 | | |
| †46+51 | | |
| †46+52 | | |
| †46+53 | | |
| †46+54 | | |
| †46+55 | | |
| †46+56 | | |
| †46+57 | | |

**Transall C-160**
LTG 61, Landsberg;
LTG 62, Wunstorf;
LTG 63, Hohn;
WTD61 Ingolstadt

| Serial | | Notes |
|---|---|---|
| 50+06 | LTG 63 | |
| 50+07 | LTG 61 | |
| 50+08 | LTG 61 | |
| 50+09 | LTG 62 | |
| 50+10 | LTG 62 | |
| 50+17 | LTG 62 | |
| 50+29 | LTG 62 | |
| 50+33 | LTG 63 | |
| 50+34 | LTG 62 | |
| 50+35 | LTG 62 | |
| 50+36 | LTG 62 | |
| 50+37 | LTG 62 | |
| 50+38 | LTG 62 | |
| 50+40 | LTG 61 | |
| 50+41 | LTG 63 | |
| 50+42 | LTG 63 | |
| 50+43 | LTG 61 | |
| 50+44 | LTG 61 | |
| 50+45 | LTG 63 | |
| 50+46 | LTG 62 | |
| 50+47 | LTG 61 | |
| 50+48 | LTG 61 | |
| 50+49 | LTG 61 | |
| 50+50 | LTG 63 | |
| 50+51 | LTG 61 | |
| 50+52 | LTG 62 | |
| 50+53 | LTG 62 | |
| 50+54 | LTG 63 | |
| 50+55 | LTG 62 | |
| 50+56 | LTG 63 | |
| 50+57 | LTG 61 | |
| 50+58 | LTG 63 | |
| 50+59 | LTG 63 | |
| 50+61 | LTG 63 | |
| 50+62 | LTG 61 | |
| 50+64 | LTG 61 | |
| 50+65 | LTG 62 | |
| 50+66 | LTG 61 | |
| 50+67 | LTG 63 | |
| 50+68 | LTG 61 | |
| 50+69 | LTG 63 | |
| 50+70 | WTD 61 | |
| 50+71 | LTG 63 | |
| 50+72 | LTG 61 | |
| 50+73 | LTG 62 | |
| 50+74 | LTG 61 | |
| 50+75 | WTD 61 | |
| 50+76 | LTG 63 | |
| 50+77 | LTG 63 | |
| 50+78 | LTG 62 | |
| 50+79 | LTG 63 | |
| 50+81 | LTG 62 | |
| 50+82 | LTG 63 | |
| 50+83 | LTG 62 | |
| 50+84 | LTG 63 | |
| 50+85 | LTG 61 | |
| 50+86 | LTG 61 | |
| 50+87 | LTG 63 | |
| 50+88 | LTG 61 | |
| 50+89 | LTG 62 | |
| 50+90 | LTG 63 | |
| 50+91 | LTG 62 | |
| 50+92 | LTG 61 | |
| 50+93 | LTG 61 | |
| 50+94 | LTG 63 | |
| 50+95 | LTG 63 | |
| 50+96 | LTG 61 | |
| 50+97 | LTG 62 | |
| 50+98 | LTG 61 | |
| 50+99 | LTG 61 | |

| Notes | Serial | |
|---|---|---|
| | 51+00 | LTG 62 |
| | 51+01 | LTG 62 |
| | 51+02 | LTG 63 |
| | 51+03 | LTG 62 |
| | 51+04 | LTG 61 |
| | 51+05 | LTG 62 |
| | 51+06 | LTG 63 |
| | 51+07 | LTG 62 |
| | 51+08 | LTG 63 |
| | 51+09 | LTG 63 |
| | 51+10 | LTG 61 |
| | 51+11 | LTG 62 |
| | 51+12 | LTG 63 |
| | 51+13 | LTG 61 |
| | 51+14 | LTG 63 |
| | 51+15 | LTG 61 |

**Dornier Do.28D-2 Skyservant**

LTG61, Landsberg;
LTG 62, Wunsdorf;
LTG 63, Hohn;
WTD 61, Ingolstadt;
FBS-BMVg, Köln-Bonn
MFG 5, Kiel-Holtenau

| Notes | Serial | |
|---|---|---|
| | 58+05 | WTD 61 |
| | 58+08 | LTG 62 |
| | 58+09 | LTG 62 |
| | 58+14 | LTG 62 |
| | 58+15 | JbG 31 |
| | 58+18 | FBS BMVg |
| | 58+20 | JbG 31 |
| | 58+23 | FBS-BMVg |
| | 58+26 | LTG 63 |
| | 58+28 | JG 73 |
| | 58+29 | LTG 62 |
| | 58+30 | LTG 62 |
| | 58+32 | JG 74 |
| | 58+34 | LTG 62 |
| | 58+36 | LTG 62 |
| | 58+37 | LTG 62 |
| | 58+38 | LTG 62 |
| | 58+39 | LTG 62 |
| | 58+46 | LTG 62 |
| | 58+47 | JG 74 |
| | 58+49 | JbG 49 |
| | 58+50 | JbG 38 |
| | 58+52 | LTG 62 |
| | 58+53 | JbG 32 |
| | 58+54 | AkG 51 |
| | 58+55 | JbG 32 |
| | 58+58 | JbG 33 |
| | 58+59 | JbG 34 |
| | 58+60 | AkG 52 |
| | 58+61 | JbG 34 |
| | 58+62 | JG 72 |
| | 58+65 | JG 71 |
| | 58+66 | JbG 38 |
| | 58+67 | JbG 38 |
| | 58+68 | LTG 62 |
| | 58+69 | LTG 62 |
| | 58+70 | LTG 62 |
| | 58+71 | LTG 62 |
| | 58+72 | AkG 51 |
| | 58+73 | JbG 31 |
| | 58+74 | JbG 41 |
| | 58+76 | JbG 41 |
| | 58+77 | JbG 49 |
| | 58+78 | JbG 31 |
| | 58+79 | LTG 62 |
| | 58+80 | JbG 33 |
| | 58+81 | LTG 62 |
| | 58+82 | JbG 43 |
| | 58+83 | LTG 62 |
| | 58+84 | JbG 43 |
| | 58+85 | JG 74 |
| | 58+86 | JbG 49 |
| | 58+87 | JbG 49 |
| | 58+89 | JbG 49 |
| | 58+90 | JbG 49 |
| | 58+92 | JG 72 |
| | 58+94 | JG 73 |
| | 58+98 | AkG 52 |
| | 58+99 | JG 71 |
| | 59+00 | FBS-BMVg |
| | 59+01 | FBS-BMVg |
| | 59+02 | FBS-BMVg |
| | 59+03 | FBS-BMVg |
| | 59+04 | FBS-BMVg |
| | 59+05 | FBS-BMVg |
| | 59+06 | MFG5 |
| | 59+07 | MFG5 |
| | 59+08 | MFG5 |
| | 59+09 | MFG5 |
| | 59+10 | MFG5 |
| | 59+11 | MFG5 |
| | 59+12 | MFG5 |
| | 59+13 | MFG5 |
| | 59+14 | MFG5 |
| | 59+15 | MFG5 |
| | 59+16 | MFG5 |
| | 59+17 | MFG5 |
| | 59+18 | MFG5 |
| | 59+19 | MFG5 |
| | 59+20 | MFG5 |
| | 59+21 | MFG5 |
| | 59+22 | MFG5 |
| | 59+23 | MFG5 |
| | 59+24 | MFG5 |
| | 59+25 | MFG5 |

**Breguet 1151 Atlantic**

MFG3, Nordholz

| Notes | Serial |
|---|---|
| | 61+01 |
| | 61+02 |
| | 61+03 |
| | 61+04 |
| | 61+05 |
| | 61+06 |
| | 61+08 |
| | 61+09 |
| | 61+10 |
| | 61+11 |
| | 61+12 |
| | 61+13 |
| | 61+14 |
| | 61+15 |
| | 61+16 |
| | 61+17 |
| | 61+18 |
| | 61+19 |
| | 61+20 |

**Westland Lynx Mk88**

MFG 3, Nordholz

| Notes | Serial |
|---|---|
| | 83+01 |
| | 83+02 |
| | 83+03 |
| | 83+04 |
| | 83+05 |
| | 83+06 |

| Serial | | Notes |
|---|---|---|
| 83+07 | | |
| 83+08 | | |
| 83+09 | | |
| 83+10 | | |
| 83+11 | | |
| 83+12 | | |
| 83+13 | | |
| 83+14 | | |
| 83+15 | | |
| 83+16 | | |
| 83+17 | | |
| 83+18 | | |
| 83+19 | | |

**Heeresfliegertruppe**
**Sikorsky/VFW CH-53G**
HFlgRgt-15, Rheine-Bentlage
HFlgRgt-25, Laupheim
HFlgRgt-35, Mendig
HFWS, Bückeburg
WTD 61, Ingolstadt

| Serial | | Notes |
|---|---|---|
| 84+01 | WTD 61 | |
| 84+02 | WTD 61 | |
| 84+03 | 15 | |
| 84+04 | 35 | |
| 84+05 | 35 | |
| 84+06 | 35 | |
| 84+07 | HFWS | |
| 84+08 | 35 | |
| 84+09 | 25 | |
| 84+10 | 25 | |
| 84+11 | HFWS | |
| 84+12 | 15 | |
| 84+13 | HFWS | |
| 84+14 | HFWS | |
| 84+15 | 25 | |
| 84+16 | HFWS | |
| 84+17 | 25 | |
| 84+18 | HFWS | |
| 84+19 | HFWS | |
| 84+20 | 35 | |
| 84+21 | HFWS | |
| 84+22 | 35 | |
| 84+23 | 35 | |
| 84+24 | 35 | |
| 84+25 | 35 | |
| 84+26 | 35 | |
| 84+27 | 35 | |
| 84+28 | 35 | |
| 84+29 | 35 | |
| 84+30 | 35 | |
| 84+31 | 35 | |
| 84+32 | 35 | |
| 84+33 | 35 | |
| 84+34 | 35 | |
| 84+35 | 35 | |
| 84+36 | 35 | |
| 84+37 | 35 | |
| 84+38 | 35 | |
| 84+39 | 35 | |
| 84+40 | 25 | |
| 84+41 | HFWS | |
| 84+42 | 25 | |
| 84+43 | 25 | |
| 84+44 | 25 | |
| 84+45 | 25 | |
| 84+46 | 25 | |
| 84+47 | 25 | |
| 84+48 | 25 | |
| 84+49 | HFWS | |
| 84+50 | 25 | |
| 84+51 | 25 | |
| 84+52 | 25 | |
| 84+53 | 25 | |
| 84+54 | 25 | |
| 84+55 | 25 | |
| 84+56 | 25 | |
| 84+57 | 25 | |
| 84+58 | 25 | |
| 84+59 | 25 | |
| 84+60 | 25 | |
| 84+62 | 25 | |
| 84+63 | 25 | |
| 84+64 | 25 | |
| 84+65 | 35 | |
| 84+66 | 35 | |
| 84+67 | 35 | |
| 84+68 | 15 | |
| 84+69 | 15 | |
| 84+70 | 15 | |
| 84+71 | 15 | |
| 84+72 | 15 | |
| 84+73 | 15 | |
| 84+74 | 15 | |
| 84+75 | 15 | |
| 84+76 | 15 | |
| 84+77 | 15 | |
| 84+78 | 15 | |
| 84+79 | 15 | |
| 84+80 | 15 | |
| 84+82 | 15 | |
| 84+83 | 15 | |
| 84+84 | 15 | |
| 84+85 | 15 | |
| 84+86 | 15 | |
| 84+87 | 15 | |
| 84+88 | 15 | |
| 84+89 | 15 | |
| 84+90 | 15 | |
| 84+91 | 15 | |
| 84+92 | 35 | |
| 84+93 | 35 | |
| 84+94 | 35 | |
| 84+95 | 25 | |
| 84+96 | 25 | |
| 84+97 | 25 | |
| 84+98 | 15 | |
| 84+99 | 15 | |
| 85+00 | 15 | |
| 85+01 | 35 | |
| 85+02 | 35 | |
| 85+03 | 35 | |
| 85+04 | 25 | |
| 85+05 | 25 | |
| 85+06 | 25 | |
| 85+07 | 15 | |
| 85+08 | 15 | |
| 85+09 | 15 | |
| 85+10 | 35 | |
| 85+11 | 25 | |
| 85+12 | 15 | |

**Westland Sea**
**King HAS41**
MFG 5, Kiel-Holtenau

| Serial | Notes |
|---|---|
| 89+50 | |
| 89+51 | |
| 89+52 | |
| 89+53 | |
| 89+54 | |
| 89+55 | |
| 89+56 | |
| 89+57 | |
| 89+58 | |

| Notes | Serial |
|---|---|
| | 89+59 |
| | 89+60 |
| | 89+61 |
| | 89+62 |
| | 89+63 |
| | 89+64 |
| | 89+65 |
| | 89+66 |
| | 89+67 |
| | 89+68 |
| | 89+69 |
| | 89+70 |
| | 89+71 |

**Dornier Do228**
WTD-61, Ingolstadt
98+78

**English Electric Canberra B2**
MGA, Manching
99+34
99+35

## GHANA
**Airforce**

**Short SC7 Skyvan**
No 1 Transport Sqn, Takoradi
G450
G451
G452
G453
G454
G455

## GREECE
**Elliniki Aeroporia**

**Lockheed C-130H Hercules**
356 Moira, Elefsis
741
742
743
744
745
746
747
748
749
750
751
752

## ISRAEL
**Heyl Ha'Avir**

**Lockheed C-130H Hercules**
4X-FBA/102
4X-FBB/106
4X-FBC/309

**Lockheed C-130E Hercules**
4X-FBD/311
4X-FBE/304
4X-FBF/301
4X-FBG/310
4X-FBH/312
4X-FBI/314
4X-FBJ/305
4X-FBK/318
4X-FBL/313
4X-FBM/316
4X-FBN/307
4X-FBP/208

**Lockeed C-130H Hercules**
4X-FBQ/420
4X-FBS/427
4X-FBT/435
4X-FBU/448
4X-FBW/436
4X-FBX/428

**Lockheed KC-130H Hercules**
4X-FBY/522
4X-FBZ/545

## ITALY
**Aeronautica Militare Italiano**

**Aeritalia G222**
46 Brigata Aerea, Pisa
14°Stormo, Pratica di Mare;
RSV, Pratica di Mare

| Serial | Code |
|---|---|
| MM62101 | RS-45 |
| MM62102 | 46-20 |
| MM62104 | 46-91 |
| MM62105 | 46-82 |
| MM62108 | 46-30 |
| MM62109 | 46-96 |
| MM62110 | 46-81 |
| MM62111 | 46-83 |
| MM62112 | 46-85 |
| MM62113 | 46-34 |
| MM62114 | 46-80 |
| MM62115 | 46-22 |
| MM62116 | 46-35 |
| MM62117 | 46-25 |
| MM62118 | 46-24 |
| MM62119 | 46-21 |
| MM62120 | 46-90 |
| MM62121 | 46-86 |
| MM62122 | 46-23 |
| MM62123 | 46-28 |
| MM62124 | 46-88 |
| MM62125 | 46-87 |
| MM62126 | 46-26 |
| MM62127 | 46-27 |
| MM62128 | RS-46 |
| MM62129 | RS-44 |
| MM62130 | 46-31 |
| MM62132 | 46-32 |
| MM62133 | 46-93 |
| MM62134 | 46-33 |
| MM62143 | 46-36 |
| MM62144 | 46-98 |
| MM62145 | 46-50 |
| MM62146 | 46-51 |
| MM62147 | 46-52 |

**Aeritalia G222TCM**

| Serial | Code |
|---|---|
| MM62103 | 46-37 |
| MM62135 | 46-94 |
| MM62136 | 46-97 |
| MM62137 | 46-95 |

| Serial | | Notes |
|---|---|---|
| **Aeritalia G222RM** | | |
| 14° Stormo, Pratica di Mare | | |
| MM62107 | | |
| MM62138 | | |
| MM62139 | 14-20 | |
| MM62140 | 14-21 | |
| MM62141 | 14-22 | |
| MM62142 | | |
| **Aermacchi MB339** | | |
| *Frecce Tricolori, 313° Gruppo, Rivotto; 61ª Brigata Aerea, Lecce; 14° Stormo, Pratica di Mare; RSV, Pratica di Mare | | |
| MM54438 | 61-93 | |
| MM54439 | 13* | |
| MM54440 | | |
| MM54442 | 61-95 | |
| MM54443 | 61-50 | |
| MM54445 | 8* | |
| MM54446 | 61-01 | |
| MM54447 | 61-02 | |
| MM54448 | 61-03 | |
| MM54449 | 61-00 | |
| MM54450 | 14-30 | |
| MM54451 | 61-86 | |
| MM54452 | | |
| MM54453 | 61-05 | |
| MM54454 | 61-06 | |
| MM54455 | 61-07 | |
| MM54456 | RS-10 | |
| MM54457 | 61-11 | |
| MM54458 | 61-12 | |
| MM54459 | 61-13 | |
| MM54460 | 61-14 | |
| MM54461 | 61-15 | |
| MM54462 | 61-16 | |
| MM54463 | 61-17 | |
| MM54464 | 61-20 | |
| MM54465 | 61-21 | |
| MM54467 | 61-23 | |
| MM54468 | RS-26 | |
| MM54469 | 61-25 | |
| MM54470 | 61-26 | |
| MM54471 | 61-27 | |
| MM54472 | 61-30 | |
| MM54473 | 4* | |
| MM54475 | 3* | |
| MM54476 | | |
| MM54477 | 11* | |
| MM54478 | 10* | |
| MM54479 | 1* | |
| MM54480 | 0* | |
| MM54482 | 5* | |
| MM54483 | | |
| MM54484 | 12* | |
| MM54485 | 7* | |
| MM54486 | 2* | |
| MM54487 | 61-31 | |
| MM54488 | 61-32 | |
| MM54489 | 61-33 | |
| MM54490 | 61-34 | |
| MM54491 | 61-35 | |
| MM54492 | 61-36 | |
| MM54493 | 61-37 | |
| MM54494 | 61-40 | |
| MM54496 | 61-42 | |
| MM54497 | 61-43 | |
| MM54498 | 61-44 | |
| MM54499 | 61-45 | |
| MM54500 | 61-46 | |

| Serial | | Notes |
|---|---|---|
| MM54501 | 61-47 | |
| MM54503 | 61-51 | |
| MM54504 | 61-52 | |
| MM54505 | 61-53 | |
| MM54506 | 61-54 | |
| MM54507 | 61-55 | |
| MM54508 | 61-56 | |
| MM54509 | 61-57 | |
| MM54510 | 61-60 | |
| MM54511 | 61-61 | |
| MM54512 | 61-62 | |
| MM54513 | 61-63 | |
| MM54514 | 61-64 | |
| MM54515 | 61-65 | |
| MM54516 | 61-66 | |
| MM54517 | 61-67 | |
| MM54518 | 61-70 | |
| MM54532 | 61-71 | |
| MM54533 | 61-72 | |
| MM54534 | 61-73 | |
| MM54535 | 61-74 | |
| MM54536 | 9* | |
| MM54537 | | |
| MM54538 | 61-75 | |
| MM54539 | 61-76 | |
| MM54540 | 61-77 | |
| MM54541 | RS-27 | |
| MM54542 | 61-81 | |
| MM54543 | 61-82 | |
| MM54544 | 61-83 | |
| MM54545 | 61-84 | |
| MM54546 | 61-85 | |
| MM54547 | 61-87 | |
| MM54548 | 61-90 | |
| MM54549 | 61-91 | |
| MM54550 | 61-92 | |
| MM54551 | 6* | |
| MM54553 | 61-94 | |
| MM54554 | 61-95 | |
| **Breguet 1150 Atlantic** | | |
| 30° Stormo, Cagliari | | |
| 41° Stormo, Catania | | |
| MM40108 | 41-70 | |
| MM40109 | 30-71 | |
| MM40110 | 41-72 | |
| MM40111 | 41-73 | |
| MM40112 | 30-74 | |
| MM40113 | 30-75 | |
| MM40114 | 41-76 | |
| MM40115 | 41-77 | |
| MM40116 | 30-78 | |
| MM40117 | 41-02 | |
| MM40118 | 30-03 | |
| MM40119 | 30-04 | |
| MM40120 | 41-05 | |
| MM40121 | 41-06 | |
| MM40122 | 30-07 | |
| MM40123 | 30-10 | |
| MM40124 | 41-11 | |
| MM40125 | 30-12 | |
| **Dassault Falcon 50** | | |
| 31° Stormo, Roma Ciampino | | |
| MM62020 | | |
| MM62021 | | |
| MM62026 | | |
| **Grumman Gulfstream III** | | |
| 31° Stormo, Roma Ciampino | | |
| MM62022 | | |
| MM62025 | | |

| Notes | Serial | |
|---|---|---|
| | **Lockheed C-130H Hercules** | |
| | 46 Brigata Aerea, Pisa | |
| | MM61988 | 46-02 |
| | MM61989 | 46-03 |
| | MM61990 | 46-04 |
| | MM61991 | 46-05 |
| | MM61992 | 46-06 |
| | MM61993 | 46-07 |
| | MM61994 | 46-08 |
| | MM61995 | 46-09 |
| | MM61997 | 46-11 |
| | MM61998 | 46-12 |
| | MM61999 | 46-13 |
| | MM62001 | 46-15 |
| | **McDonnell Douglas DC9-32** | |
| | 31° Stormo, Roma Ciampino | |
| | MM62012 | |
| | MM62013 | |
| | **Panavia Tornado** | |
| | *TTTE RAF Cottesmore | |
| | 50° Stormo, Piacenza | |
| | 36° Stormo, Giola del Colle | |
| | 50° Stormo, Piacenza | |
| | RSV, Pratica di Mare | |
| | MM586 | |
| | MM7002 | |
| | MM7003 | I-93* |
| | MM7004 | 6-04 |
| | MM7005 | |
| | MM7006 | 50-03 |
| | MM7007 | 50-12 |
| | MM7008 | 50-02 |
| | MM7009 | 50-44 |
| | MM7010 | 50-06 |
| | MM7011 | 50-10 |
| | MM7012 | 50-11 |
| | MM7013 | 50-05 |
| | MM7014 | 6-14 |
| | MM7015 | |
| | MM7016 | 6-16 |
| | MM7017 | 50-14 |
| | MM7018 | 50-24 |
| | MM7019 | 19 |
| | MM7020 | 6-20 |
| | MM7021 | 6-21 |
| | MM7022 | 6-22 |
| | MM7023 | |
| | MM7024 | |
| | MM7025 | 6-25 |
| | MM7026 | 6-26 |
| | MM7027 | |
| | MM7028 | 6-38 |
| | MM7029 | 6-25 |
| | MM7030 | 50-36 |
| | MM7031 | 6-31 |
| | MM7033 | |
| | MM7034 | |
| | MM7035 | 35 |
| | MM7036 | 50-36 |
| | MM7037 | 36-37 |
| | MM7038 | 36-33 |
| | MM7039 | 50-52 |
| | MM7040 | 36-35 |
| | MM7041 | 6-01 |
| | MM7042 | 6-42 |
| | MM7043 | 6-43 |
| | MM7044 | 6-66 |
| | MM7046 | 36-34 |

| Notes | Serial | |
|---|---|---|
| | MM7047 | 6-04 |
| | MM7048 | 36-54 |
| | MM7049 | |
| | MM7050 | 50 |
| | MM7051 | 36-32 |
| | MM7052 | 36-41 |
| | MM7053 | 6-33 |
| | MM7054 | 6-46 |
| | MM7055 | 36-47 |
| | MM7056 | 36-52 |
| | MM7057 | 36-54 |
| | MM7058 | 36-57 |
| | MM7059 | 6-35 |
| | MM7060 | |
| | MM7061 | 61 |
| | MM7062 | 36-53 |
| | MM7063 | 36-43 |
| | MM7064 | 6-24 |
| | MM7065 | 6-55 |
| | MM7066 | 66 |
| | MM7067 | 67 |
| | MM7068 | 36-46 |
| | MM7069 | 6-61 |
| | MM7070 | 70 |
| | MM7071 | 71 |
| | MM7072 | 6-72 |
| | MM7073 | 73 |
| | MM7074 | 74 |
| | MM7075 | 75 |
| | MM7076 | 76 |
| | MM7078 | |
| | MM7079 | |
| | MM7080 | 80 |
| | MM7081 | RS-01 |
| | MM7082 | RS-02 |
| | MM7083 | 6-70 |
| | MM7084 | 84 |
| | MM7085 | 36-50 |
| | MM7086 | 86 |
| | MM7087 | 6-65 |
| | MM7088 | 88 |
| | MM55000 | I-42* |
| | MM55001 | I-40* |
| | MM55002 | I-41* |
| | MM55003 | I-43* |
| | MM55004 | I-44* |
| | MM55005 | 50-13 |
| | MM55006 | 50-50 |
| | MM55007 | 6-51 |
| | MM55008 | |
| | MM55009 | 6-15 |
| | MM55010 | 36-56 |
| | MM55011 | 36-55 |
| | **Piaggio-Douglas PD-808; †PD-808-GE; *PD-808-RM; ‡PD-808-TA** | |
| | 14° Stormo, Pratica di Mare; | |
| | 31° Stormo, Roma-Ciampino | |
| | RSV, Pratica di Mare | |
| | MM577‡ | RS-37 |
| | MM578‡ | RS-49 |
| | MM61948 | (14) |
| | MM61949 | (14) |
| | MM61950 | 14-50 |
| | MM61951 | (31) |
| | MM61952† | (14) |
| | MM61953‡ | (14) |
| | MM61954‡ | 14-52 |
| | MM61955† | (14) |
| | MM61956* | 14-51 |
| | MM61957‡ | RS-50 |

| Serial | Notes |
|---|---|
| MM61958† (14) | |
| MM61959† (14) | |
| MM61960† (14) | |
| MM61961† (14) | |
| MM61962† (14) | |
| MM61963† (14) | |
| MM62014* (14) | |
| MM62015* (14) | |
| MM62016* 14-55 | |
| MM62017* (14) | |

**JORDAN**
**Al Quwwat al-Jawwiya al Malakiya al-Urduniya**

**Lockheed C-130B Hercules**
3 Sqn, Amman
340
341

**Lockheed C-130H Hercules**
3 Sqn, Amman
344
345
346
347

**KUWAIT**
**Kuwait Air Force**

**McDonnell Douglas DC9-32**
KAF 320
KAF 321

**Lockheed L100-30 Hercules**
KAF 322
KAF 323
KAF 324
KAF 325

**LUXEMBOURG**
**NATO**
**Boeing E-3A**
NAEWF, Geilenkirchen
LX-N90442
LX-N90443
LX-N90444
LX-N90445
LX-N90446
LX-N90447
LX-N90448
LX-N90449
LX-N90450
LX-N90451
LX-N90452
LX-N90453
LX-N90454
LX-N90455
LX-N90456
LX-N90457
LX-N90458
LX-N90459

**Boeing 707-329C**
NAEWF, Geilenkirchen
LX-N19996
LX-N20198
LX-N20199

**MOROCCO**
**Force Aerienne Royaume Marocaine**

**CAP-230**
Green March
06 CN-ABI
07 CN-ABJ
08 CN-ABK
09 CN-ABL

**Lockheed C-130H Hercules**
4535 CN-AOA
4551 CN-AOC
4575 CN-AOD
4581 CN-AOE
4583 CN-AOF
4713 CN-AOG
4717 CN-AOH
4733 CN-AOI
4738 CN-AOJ
4739 CN-AOK
4742 CN-AOL
4875 CN-AOM
4876 CN-AON
4877 CN-AOO
4888 CN-AOP
4892 CN-AOQ
4907 CN-AOR
4909 CN-AOS
4940 CN-AOT

**NETHERLANDS**
**Koninklijke Luchtmacht**

**Fokker F-27-100 Friendship**
334 Sqn, Soesterberg
C-1
C-2
C-3

**Fokker F-27-300M Troopship**
334 Sqn, Soesterberg
C-4
C-5
C-6
C-7
C-8
C-9
C-10
C-11
C-12

**General Dynamics F-16A/F16B***
306 Sqn, 311 Sqn, and 312 Sqn, Volkel; 313 Sqn and 315 Sqn, Twente; 314 Sqn, Gilze-Rijen; 316 Sqn Eindhoven
322 Sqn, and 323 Sqn, Leeuwarden
J001 313 Sqn
J002 313 Sqn
J003
J004
J005
J006
J054 315 Sqn
J055 315 Sqn

| *Notes* | *Serial* | |
|---|---|---|
| | J057 | 315 Sqn |
| | J058 | 315 Sqn |
| | J059 | 315 Sqn |
| | J060 | 315 Sqn |
| | J061 | 315 Sqn |
| | J062 | 315 Sqn |
| | J063 | 315 Sqn |
| | J064* | 315 Sqn |
| | J065* | 315 Sqn |
| | J066* | 315 Sqn |
| | J067* | 315 Sqn |
| | J068* | 313 Sqn |
| | J135 | 314 Sqn |
| | J136 | 314 Sqn |
| | J137 | 314 Sqn |
| | J138 | 314 Sqn |
| | J139 | 314 Sqn |
| | J140 | 314 Sqn |
| | J141 | 314 Sqn |
| | J142 | 314 Sqn |
| | J143 | 314 Sqn |
| | J144 | 314 Sqn |
| | J145 | 313 Sqn |
| | J146 | 314 Sqn |
| | J192 | 311 Sqn |
| | J193 | 311 Sqn |
| | J194 | 311 Sqn |
| | J195 | 311 Sqn |
| | J196 | 311 Sqn |
| | J197 | 311 Sqn |
| | J198 | 311 Sqn |
| | J199 | 323 Sqn |
| | J200 | 313 Sqn |
| | J201 | 322 Sqn |
| | J202 | 322 Sqn |
| | J203 | 322 Sqn |
| | J204 | 322 Sqn |
| | J205 | 322 Sqn |
| | J206 | 322 Sqn |
| | J207 | 315 Sqn |
| | J208* | 314 Sqn |
| | J209* | 314 Sqn |
| | J210* | 314 Sqn |
| | J211* | 314 Sqn |
| | J212 | 323 Sqn |
| | J213 | 323 Sqn |
| | J214 | 323 Sqn |
| | J215 | 322 Sqn |
| | J218 | 322 Sqn |
| | J220 | 322 Sqn |
| | J223 | 322 Sqn |
| | J226 | 322 Sqn |
| | J228 | 322 Sqn |
| | J230 | 322 Sqn |
| | J231 | 323 Sqn |
| | J232 | 323 Sqn |
| | J234 | 323 Sqn |
| | J235 | 323 Sqn |
| | J236 | 323 Sqn |
| | J238 | 322 Sqn |
| | J239 | 322 Sqn |
| | J240 | 322 Sqn |
| | J241 | 322 Sqn |
| | J243 | 322 Sqn |
| | J246 | 323 Sqn |
| | J248 | 323 Sqn |
| | J249 | 323 Sqn |
| | J250 | 323 Sqn |
| | J251 | 322 Sqn |
| | J253 | 323 Sqn |
| | J254 | 323 Sqn |
| | J255 | 323 Sqn |

| *Notes* | *Serial* | |
|---|---|---|
| | J256 | 323 Sqn |
| | J259* | 323 Sqn |
| | J260* | 322 Sqn |
| | J261* | 322 Sqn |
| | J262* | 323 Sqn |
| | J264* | 323 Sqn |
| | J265* | 323 Sqn |
| | J266* | 323 Sqn |
| | J267* | 323 Sqn |
| | J270* | 323 Sqn |
| | J359 | 313 Sqn |
| | J360 | 323 Sqn |
| | J361 | 313 Sqn |
| | J362 | 314 Sqn |
| | J363 | 314 Sqn |
| | J364 | 314 Sqn |
| | J365 | 313 Sqn |
| | J366 | 313 Sqn |
| | J367 | 315 Sqn |
| | J368* | 314 Sqn |
| | J369* | 314 Sqn |
| | J508 | 315 Sqn |
| | J509 | 315 Sqn |
| | J510 | 315 Sqn |
| | J511 | 313 Sqn |
| | J512 | 315 Sqn |
| | J513 | 315 Sqn |
| | J514 | 315 Sqn |
| | J515 | 315 Sqn |
| | J516 | 315 Sqn |
| | J616 | 311 Sqn |
| | J617 | 311 Sqn |
| | J618 | 311 Sqn |
| | J619 | 311 Sqn |
| | J620 | 311 Sqn |
| | J622 | 311 Sqn |
| | J623 | 311 Sqn |
| | J624 | 311 Sqn |
| | J627 | 306 Sqn |
| | J628 | 306 Sqn |
| | J630 | 306 Sqn |
| | J631 | 306 Sqn |
| | J632 | 306 Sqn |
| | J633 | 306 Sqn |
| | J635 | 306 Sqn |
| | J636 | 306 Sqn |
| | J637 | 306 Sqn |
| | J638 | 306 Sqn |
| | J640 | 306 Sqn |
| | J641 | 306 Sqn |
| | J642 | 306 Sqn |
| | J643 | 306 Sqn |
| | J644 | 306 Sqn |
| | J645 | 306 Sqn |
| | J646 | 306 Sqn |
| | J647 | 306 Sqn |
| | J648 | 306 Sqn |
| | J649* | 306 Sqn |
| | J650* | 323 Sqn |
| | J651* | 312 Sqn |
| | J652* | 311 Sqn |
| | J653* | 306 Sqn |
| | J654* | 311 Sqn |
| | J655* | 306 Sqn |
| | J656* | 312 Sqn |
| | J657* | 323 Sqn |
| | J864 | 312 Sqn |
| | J866 | 312 Sqn |
| | J867 | 312 Sqn |
| | J868 | 312 Sqn |
| | J869 | 312 Sqn |
| | J870 | 312 Sqn |

| Serial | | Notes |
|---|---|---|
| J871 | 312 Sqn | |
| J872 | 312 Sqn | |
| J873 | 312 Sqn | |
| J874 | 312 Sqn | |
| J875 | 312 Sqn | |
| J876 | 312 Sqn | |
| J877 | 312 Sqn | |
| J878 | 312 Sqn | |
| J879 | 312 Sqn | |
| J880 | 312 Sqn | |
| J881 | 312 Sqn | |
| J882* | 323 Sqn | |
| J884* | 312 Sqn | |
| J885* | 311 Sqn | |

**MBB Bo.105**
**Bo.105CB;**
***Bo.105CD**
299 Sqn, Deelen

| Serial | Notes |
|---|---|
| B37 | |
| B38 | |
| B39 | |
| B40 | |
| B41 | |
| B42 | |
| B43 | |
| B44 | |
| B45 | |
| B46 | |
| B47 | |
| B48 | |
| B63 | |
| B64 | |
| B66 | |
| B67 | |
| B68 | |
| B69 | |
| B70 | |
| B71 | |
| B72 | |
| B73 | |
| B74 | |
| B75 | |
| B76 | |
| B77 | |
| B78 | |
| B79 | |
| B80 | |
| B83* | |

**Northrop NF-5A**
316 Sqn, Eindhoven

| Serial | | Notes |
|---|---|---|
| K3005 | 316 Sqn | |
| K3012 | 316 Sqn | |
| K3014 | 316 Sqn | |
| K3017 | 316 Sqn | |
| K3031 | 316 Sqn | |
| K3033 | 316 Sqn | |
| K3042 | 316 Sqn | |
| K3047 | 316 Sqn | |
| K3061 | 316 Sqn | |
| K3062 | 314 Sqn | |
| K3069 | 316 Sqn | |

**Northrop NF-5B**
316 Sqn, Eindhoven

| Serial | | Notes |
|---|---|---|
| K4001 | 316 Sqn | |
| K4006 | 316 Sqn | |
| K4009 | 316 Sqn | |
| K4013 | 316 Sqn | |
| K4014 | 316 Sqn | |
| K4015 | 316 Sqn | |
| K4016 | 316 Sqn | |
| K4017 | 316 Sqn | |
| K4019 | 316 Sqn | |
| K4024 | 316 Sqn | |
| K4027 | 316 Sqn | |
| K4029 | 316 Sqn | |

**Sud Alouette III**
*Grasshoppers
298 Sqn, Soesterberg;
300 Sqn, Deelen

| Serial | Notes |
|---|---|
| A177 | |
| A208 | |
| A209 | |
| A217 | |
| A218 | |
| A226 | |
| A227 | |
| A235 | |
| A246 | |
| A247 | |
| A253 | |
| A260 | |
| A261 | |
| A266 | |
| A267 | |
| A275 | |
| A281 | |
| A292 | |
| A293 | |
| A301 | |
| A302 | |
| A307 | |
| A319 | |
| A324 | |
| A336 | |
| A342 | |
| A343 | |
| A350* | |
| A366 | |
| A374 | |
| A383 | |
| A390* | |
| A391 | |
| A398* | |
| A399 | |
| A407 | |
| A414 | |
| A451 | |
| A452 | |
| A453 | |
| A464 | |
| A465* | |
| A470 | |
| A471 | |
| A482 | |
| A483 | |
| A488 | |
| A489 | |
| A494 | |
| A495 | |
| A499* | |
| A500 | |
| A514 | |
| A515 | |
| A521 | |
| A522 | |
| A528 | |
| A529 | |
| A535 | |
| A536 | |
| A542 | |
| A549 | |
| A550 | |

| Notes | Serial |
|---|---|
| | **Marine Luchtvaart Dienst** |
| | **Fokker** |
| | **F-27-200MPA** |
| | 336 Sqn, Hato, Antilles |
| | M-1 |
| | M-2 |
| | |
| | **Lockheed** |
| | **P-3C Orion** |
| | 320 Sqn, Valkenburg and Keflavik |
| | 300 |
| | 301 |
| | 302 |
| | 303 |
| | 304 |
| | 305 |
| | 306 |
| | 307 |
| | 308 |
| | 309 |
| | 310 |
| | 311 |
| | 312 |
| | |
| | **Westland Lynx** |
| | *UH14A (7 Sqn) |
| | †SH14B (860 Sqn) |
| | ‡SH14C (860 Sqn) |
| | De Kooij |
| | 260* K |
| | 261* K |
| | 262* K |
| | 264† |
| | 265† |
| | 266† |
| | 267† K |
| | 268† |
| | 269† K |
| | 270† K |
| | 271† KN |
| | 272† |
| | 273† K |
| | 274† K |
| | 276‡ K |
| | 277‡ K |
| | 278‡ K |
| | 279‡ |
| | 280‡ K |
| | 281‡ |
| | 282‡ K |
| | 283‡ K |
| | |
| | **NEW ZEALAND** |
| | **Royal New Zealand Air Force** |
| | **Boeing 727-22C** |
| | 40 Sqn, Whenuapai |
| | NZ7271 |
| | NZ7272 |
| | |
| | **Lockheed** |
| | **C-130H Hercules** |
| | 40 Sqn, Whenuapai |
| | NZ7001 |
| | NZ7002 |
| | NZ7003 |
| | NZ7004 |
| | NZ7005 |
| | |
| | **Lockheed** |
| | **P-3K Orion** |
| | 5 Sqn, Whenuapai |
| | NZ4201 |

| Notes | Serial | |
|---|---|---|
| | NZ4202 | |
| | NZ4203 | |
| | NZ4204 | |
| | NZ4205 | |
| | NZ4206 | |
| | | |
| | **NIGERIA** | |
| | **Federal Nigerian Air Force** | |
| | **Lockheed** | |
| | **C-130H Hercules** | |
| | Lagos | |
| | NAF-910 | |
| | NAF-911 | |
| | NAF-912 | |
| | NAF-913 | |
| | NAF-914 | |
| | NAF-915 | |
| | NAF-917 | |
| | NAF-918 | |
| | *NAF-918* (NAF 916) | |
| | | |
| | **NORWAY** | |
| | **Kongelige Norske Luftforsvaret** | |
| | **Dassault** | |
| | **Falcon 20 ECM** | |
| | 335 Skv, Gardermoen | |
| | 041 | |
| | 053 | |
| | | |
| | **General Dynamics** | |
| | **F-16A/*F-16B** | |
| | 331 Skv and 334 Skv, Bodø; 332 Skv, Rygge; 338 Skv, Orland | |
| | 272 | 332 Skv |
| | 273 | 332 Skv |
| | 274 | 332 Skv |
| | 275 | 332 Skv |
| | 276 | 332 Skv |
| | 277 | 332 Skv |
| | 278 | 332 Skv |
| | 279 | 332 Skv |
| | 281 | 332 Skv |
| | 282 | 332 Skv |
| | 284 | 332 Skv |
| | 285 | 332 Skv |
| | 288 | 338 Skv |
| | 289 | 338 Skv |
| | 291 | 338 Skv |
| | 292 | 338 Skv |
| | 293 | 338 Skv |
| | 295 | 338 Skv |
| | 297 | 338 Skv |
| | 298 | 338 Skv |
| | 299 | 338 Skv |
| | 302* | 332 Skv |
| | 304* | 332 Skv |
| | 305* | 332 Skv |
| | 306* | 332 Skv |
| | 307* | 332 Skv |
| | 658 | 334 Skv |
| | 659 | 334 Skv |
| | 660 | 334 Skv |
| | 661 | 334 Skv |
| | 662 | 334 Skv |
| | 663 | 334 Skv |
| | 664 | 334 Skv |
| | 665 | 334 Skv |
| | 666 | 334 Skv |
| | 667 | 334 Skv |
| | 668 | 334 Skv |
| | 669 | 334 Skv |

| Serial | | Notes |
|---|---|---|
| 670 | 334 Skv | |
| 671 | 334 Skv | |
| 672 | 331 Skv | |
| 673 | 331 Skv | |
| 674 | 331 Skv | |
| 675 | 331 Skv | |
| 677 | 331 Skv | |
| 678 | 331 Skv | |
| 680 | 331 Skv | |
| 681 | 331 Skv | |
| 682 | 331 Skv | |
| 683 | 331 Skv | |
| 685 | 331 Skv | |
| 686 | 331 Skv | |
| 687 | 331 Skv | |
| 688 | 331 Skv | |
| 689* | 338 Skv | |
| 690* | 332 Skv | |
| 691* | 332 Skv | |
| 692* | 334 Skv | |
| 693* | 338 Skv | |
| 711* | 331 Skv | |
| 712* | 331 Skv | |

**Lockheed**
**C-130H Hercules**
335 Skv, Gardermoen
952
953
954
955
956
957

**Lockheed**
**P-3C Orion**
333 Skv, Andøya
3296
3297
3298
3299

**Northrop F-5A**
336 Skv, Rygge
128
130
132
134
208
210
215
220
222
225
895
896
898
902

**Northrop F-5B**
336 Skv, Rygge
135
136
241
242
243
244
387
594
595
906
907
908
909

**Westland**
**Sea King Mk43/† Mk 43A**
330 Skv, Bodø
060
062
066
069†
070
071
072
073
074
189†

**Westland Lynx**
**Mk86**
Bardufoss
337 Skv
207
216
228
232
237

**Lockheed P-3N Orion**
333Skv Andøya
602
603

**OMAN**
**Al Quwwat al Jawwiya al Sultanat Oman**

**BAC 1-11**
**srs 485GD**
4 Sqn, Seeb
551
552
553

**Lockheed**
**C-130H Hercules**
4 Sqn, Seeb
501
502
503

**Short Skyvan 3M**
2 Sqn, Seeb
901
902
903
904
905
906
907
908
910
911
912
913
914
915
916

**PAKISTAN**
**Air Force**

**Boeing 707-340C**
68-19866 12 Sqn

**PORTUGAL**
**Forca Aerea Portuguesa**

**Cessna T-37C**
102 Esq, Sintra
2401
2402

| Notes | Serial |
|---|---|
| | 2403 |
| | 2404 |
| | 2406 |
| | 2407 |
| | 2410 |
| | 2411 |
| | 2412 |
| | 2414 |
| | 2415 |
| | 2417 |
| | 2418 |
| | 2419 |
| | 2420 |
| | 2421 |
| | 2422 |
| | 2423 |
| | 2424 |
| | 2425 |
| | 2426 |
| | 2427 |
| | 2428 |
| | 2429 |
| | 2430 |

**Dassault Falcon 20C**
504 Esq, Lisbon/Montijo
8101
8102
8103

**Dassault Falcon 50**
504 Esq, Lisbon/Montijo
7401
7402

**Lockheed C-130H Hercules**
501 Esq, Lisbon/Montijo
6801
6802
6803
6804
6805

**SAUDI ARABIA**
**Al Quwwat al-Jawwiya as Sa' udiya**

**Lockheed C-130 Hercules**
†1 Sqn, Riyadh
‡4 Sqn, Jeddah
*16 Sqn, Jeddah

| | |
|---|---|
| 112 | VC-130H† |
| 451 | C-130E‡ |
| 452 | C-130E‡ |
| 455 | C-130E‡ |
| 456 | KC-130H‡ |
| 457 | KC-130H‡ |
| 458 | KC-130H‡ |
| 459 | KC-130H‡ |
| 460 | C-130H‡ |
| 461 | C-130H‡ |
| 462 | C-130H‡ |
| 463 | C-130H‡ |
| 464 | C-130H‡ |
| 465 | C-130H‡ |
| 466 | C-130H‡ |
| 467 | C-130H‡ |
| 468 | C-130H‡ |
| 469 | C-130H‡ |
| 470 | C-130H‡ |
| 1601 | C-130H* |
| 1602 | C-130H* |
| 1603 | C-130H* |
| 1604 | C-130H* |
| 1605 | C-130H* |
| 1606 | C-130E* |
| 1607 | C-130E* |
| 1608 | C-130E* |
| 1609 | C-130E* |
| 1610 | C-130E* |
| 1611 | C-130E* |
| 1612 | C-130H* |
| 1613 | C-130H* |
| 1614 | C-130H* |
| 1615 | C-130H* |
| 1616 | KC-130H* |
| 1617 | KC-130H* |
| 1618 | C-130H* |
| 1619 | C-130H* |
| 1621 | KC-130H* |

**Lockheed Jetstar**
1 Sqn, Riyadh
101
102

**SINGAPORE**
**Republic of Singapore Air Force**

**Lockheed C-130B Hercules**
122 Sqn, Changi
720
721
724
725

**Lockheed C-130H Hercules**
122 Sqn, Changi
730
731
732
733

**Lockheed KC-130H Hercules**
122 Sqn, Changi
734
745

**SPAIN**
**Ejercito del Aire**

**Airtech CN235**
Ala 35, Getafe

| | |
|---|---|
| T-19C-01 | 35-60. |
| T-19C-02 | 35-61 |
| T.19B-03 | 25-21 |

**Boeing 707-381B†/368C‡**
Ala 45, Madrid

| | |
|---|---|
| †T.17-1 | 45-10 |
| †T.17-2 | 45-11 |
| ‡T.17-3 | 45-12 |

**CASA 101 Aviojet**
Grupo de Escuelas de Matacan (74);
AGA, San Javier (79)

| | |
|---|---|
| E.25-01 | 79-01 |
| E.25-02 | 793-02 |
| E.25-03 | 79-03 |
| E.25-05 | 79-05 |

| Serial | | Notes |
|---|---|---|
| E.25-06 | 79-06 | |
| E.25-07 | 79-07 | |
| E.25-08 | 79-08 | |
| E.25-09 | 79-09 | |
| E.25-10 | 79-10 | |
| E.25-11 | 79-11 | |
| E.25-12 | 79-12 | |
| E.25-13 | 79-13 | |
| E.25-14 | 79-14 | |
| E.25-15 | 79-15 | |
| E.25-16 | 79-16 | |
| E.25-17 | 79-17 | |
| E.25-18 | 79-18 | |
| E.25-19 | | |
| E.25-20 | 79-20 | |
| E.25-21 | 79-21 | |
| E.25-22 | 79-22 | |
| E.25-23 | 79-23 | |
| E.25-24 | 79-24 | |
| E.25-25 | 79-25 | |
| E.25-26 | 79-26 | |
| E.25-27 | 79-27 | |
| E.25-28 | 79-28 | |
| E.25-29 | 79-29 | |
| E.25-30 | 79-30 | |
| E.25-31 | 79-31 | |
| E.25-32 | 74-01 | |
| E.25-33 | 74-02 | |
| E.25-34 | 79-34 | |
| E.25-35 | 74-03 | |
| E.25-36 | 79-36 | |
| E.25-37 | 74-04 | |
| E.25-38 | 79-38 | |
| E.25-39 | 74-05 | |
| E.25-40 | 74-06 | |
| E.25-41 | 79-41 | |
| E.25-42 | 793-32 | |
| E.25-43 | 79-43 | |
| E.25-44 | 79-44 | |
| E.25-45 | 79-45 | |
| E.25-46 | 79-46 | |
| E.25-47 | 79-47 | |
| E.25-48 | 79-48 | |
| E.25-49 | 79-49 | |
| E.25-50 | 79-40 | |
| E.25-51 | 74-07 | |
| E.25-52 | 74-08 | |
| E.25-53 | 74-09 | |
| E.25-54 | 74-10 | |
| E.25-55 | | |
| E.25-56 | 74-11 | |
| E.25-57 | 74-12 | |
| E.25-58 | | |
| E.25-59 | 74-13 | |
| E.25-60 | 74-14 | |
| E.25-61 | 74-15 | |
| E.25-62 | 74-16 | |
| E.25-63 | 74-17 | |
| E.25-64 | 74-18 | |
| E.25-65 | 74-19 | |
| E.25-66 | 74-20 | |
| E.25-67 | 74-21 | |
| E.25-68 | 74-22 | |
| E.25-69 | 74-23 | |
| E.25-70 | 74-24 | |
| E.25-71 | 74-25 | |
| E.25-72 | 74-26 | |
| E.25-73 | 74-27 | |
| E.25-74 | 74-28 | |
| E.25-75 | 74-29 | |
| E.25-76 | 74-30 | |
| E.25-77 | 74-31 | |
| E.25-78 | 79-02 | |
| E.25-79 | 74-32 | |
| E.25-80 | 74-33 | |
| E.25-81 | 74-34 | |
| E.25-83 | 74-35 | |
| E.25-84 | 79-04 | |
| E.25-86 | 74-37 | |
| E.25-87 | 74-38 | |
| E.25-88 | 74-39 | |

**CASA 212 Aviocar**
**212 (XT.12),**
**212A (T.12B),**
**212B (TR.12A),**
**212D (TE.12B),**
**212E (T.12C).**
Ala35, Getafe; 403 Esc Cuatro Vientos;

408 Esc, Getafe;
461 Esc Gando, Las Palmas;
Grupo 72, Alcantarilla;
Grupo Esc Matacan (74);
AGA (Ala79), San Javier.

| Serial | | Notes |
|---|---|---|
| XT.12A-1 | 54-10 | |
| XT.12 -2 | 54-12 | |
| TR.12A-3 | 403-01 | |
| TR.12A-4 | 403-02 | |
| TR.12A-5 | 403-03 | |
| TR.12A-6 | 403-04 | |
| TR.12A-7 | 403-05 | |
| TR.12A-8 | 79-90 | |
| TE.12B-9 | 79-91 | |
| TE.12B-10 | 79-92 | |
| T.12B-12 | 35-01 | |
| T.12B-13 | 74-70 | |
| T.12B-14 | 46-30 | |
| T.12B-15 | | |
| T.12B-16 | 744-16 | |
| T.12B-17 | | |
| T.12B-18 | 46-31 | |
| T.12B-19 | 46-32 | |
| T.12B-20 | 35-04 | |
| T.12B-21 | 35-05 | |
| T.12B-22 | 35-06 | |
| T.12B-23 | 72-01 | |
| T.12B-24 | 35-07 | |
| T.12B-25 | 744-25 | |
| T.12B-26 | 72-02 | |
| T.12B-27 | 46-33 | |
| T.12B-28 | 72-03 | |
| T.12B-29 | 35-08 | |
| T.12B-30 | 744-30 | |
| T.12B-31 | 46-34 | |
| T.12B-33 | 72-04 | |
| T.12B-34 | 744-34 | |
| T.12B-35 | 46-35 | |
| T.12B-36 | 35-09 | |
| T.12B-37 | 72-05 | |
| T.12B-38 | 35-10 | |
| T.12B-39 | 745-39 | |
| TE.12B-40 | 79-93 | |
| TE.12B-41 | 79-94 | |
| TE.12B-42 | 744-42 | |
| T.12C-43 | 46-50 | |
| T.12C-44 | 35-50 | |
| T.12B-46 | 745-46 | |
| T.12B-47 | 72-06 | |
| T.12B-48 | 35-11 | |
| T.12B-49 | 46-36 | |
| T.12B-50 | 745-50 | |
| T.12B-51 | 744-51 | |
| T.12B-52 | 72-07 | |
| T.12B-53 | 35-12 | |

| Notes | Serial |
|---|---|
| | T.12B-54 35-13 |
| | T.12B-55 46-37 |
| | T.12B-56 74-79 |
| | T.12B-57 72-08 |
| | T.12B-58 46-38 |
| | T.12C-59 35-51 |
| | T.12C-60 35-52 |
| | T.12C-61 35-53 |
| | T.12B-63 35-14 |
| | T.12B-64 46-39 |
| | T.12B-65 74-80 |
| | T.12B-66 72-09 |
| | T.12B-67 74-81 |
| | T.12B-68 35-15 |
| | T.12B-69 35-16 |
| | T.12B-70 |
| | T.12B-71 35-18 |
| | TR.12D-72 408-01 |
| | TR.12D-73 408-02 |
| | TR.12D-74 408-03 |

**Dassault Falcon 20**
Grupo 45, Madrid
T.11-1 45-02
T.11-2 45-03
TM.11-3 45-04
TM.11-4 45-01
T.11-5 45-05

**Dassault Falcon 50**
Grupo 45, Madrid
T.16-1 45-20

**Dassault Falcon 900**
Grupo 45, Madrid
T.18-1 45-40

**Fokker F.27M Friendship 400MPA**
802 Esc, Gando
D.2-01
D.2-02
D.2-03

**Lockheed C-130H Hercules/ C-130H-30†**
311 Esc/312 Esc (Ala31), Zaragoza
TL.10-1† 31-01
T.10-2 31-02
T.10-3 31-03
T.10-4 31-04
T.10-8 31-05
T.10-9 31-06
T.10-10 31-07

**Lockheed KC-130H Hercules**
312 Esc (Ala31), Zaragosa
TK.10-5 31-50
TK.10-6 31-51
TK.10-7 31-52
TK.10-11 31-53
TK.10-12 31-54

**Arma Aerea de l'Armada Espanola**
**Cessna 550 Citation 2**
Esc 004, Rota
U.20-1 01-405
U.20-2 01-406
U.20-3 01-407

**SUDAN**
**Silakh Al Jawwiya as Sudaniya**
**Lockheed C-130H Hercules**
1100
1101
1102
1103
1104
1105

**SWEDEN**
**Kungliga Svenska Flygvapnet**
**Beechcraft Super King Air (Tp.101)**
†F17, Ronneby
‡F21, Lulea
101002 012‡
101003 013†

**Lockheed C-130E Hercules (Tp.84)**
F7, Satenäs
84001 841
84002 842

**Lockheed C-130H Hercules (Tp.84)**
F7, Satenäs
84003 843
84004 844
84005 845
84006 846
84007 847
84008 848

**SAAB SF.340B (TP.100)**
10000P1 001

**Swearingen Metro III (Tp.88)**
88002 882
88003 883

**Vertol 107-II-4 (Hkp.4B)**
*F15, Soderhamm
†F21, Lulea
‡F17 Ronneby
04451 91‡
04452 92‡
04453 93‡
04454 94†
04455 95*
04456 96
04457 97‡
04458 98‡
04459 99‡
04460 90‡

**Marine Flygtjanst**
**Vertol 107-II-5 (Hkp.4C)**
1HKP Div, Berga
04061 61
04063 63
04064 64

**Kawasaki-Vertol KV.107-II (Hkp.4C)**
*1 HKPDiv, Berga
†2 HKPDiv, Säve
*04065 65

| Serial | Notes |
|---|---|
| †04067 67 | |
| *04068 68 | |
| *04069 69 | |
| †04070 70 | |
| *04071 71 | |
| †04072 72 | |
| 04073 73 | |
| 04074 74 | |
| 04075 75 | |

**SWITZERLAND**
**Schweizerische Flugwaffe**
**Beech E-50**
**Twin Bonanza**
Transport Corps, Dubendorf

| Serial | Notes |
|---|---|
| A-711 | |
| A-712 | |
| A-713 | |

**TURKEY**
**Turk Hava Kuvvetleri**
**Transall C.160D**
221 Filo, Erkilet

| Serial | Notes |
|---|---|
| 019 12-019 | |
| 020 12-020 | |
| 021 12-021 | |
| 022 12-022 | |
| 023 12-023 | |
| 024 12-024 | |
| 025 12-025 | |
| 026 12-026 | |
| 027 12-027 | |
| 028 12-028 | |
| 029 12-029 | |
| 030 12-030 | |
| 031 12-031 | |
| 032 12-032 | |
| 033 12-033 | |
| 034 12-034 | |
| 035 12-035 | |
| 036 12-036 | |
| 037 12-037 | |
| 038 12-038 | |
| 039 12-039 | |
| 040 12-040 | |

**Lockheed**
**C-130E Hercules**
222 Filo, Erkilet

| Serial | Notes |
|---|---|
| 00991 12-991 | |
| 01468 12-468 | |
| 01947 12-947 | |
| 13186 12-186 | |
| 13187 12-187 | |
| 13188 12-188 | |
| 13189 12-189 | |
| 17949 12-949 | |

**UNITED ARAB EMIRATES**
**United Arab Emirates Air Force**
*Abu Dhabi*
**Lockheed**
**C-130H Hercules**

| Serial | Notes |
|---|---|
| 1211 | |
| 1212 | |
| 1213 | |
| 1214 | |

**Lockheed**
**L.100-30 Hercules**
*Dubai*

| Serial | Notes |
|---|---|
| 311 | |
| 312 | |

# US Military Aircraft Markings

All USAF aircraft have been allocated a fiscal year (FY) number since 1921. Individual aircraft are given a serial according to the fiscal year in which they are ordered. The numbers commence at 0001 and are prefixed with the year of allocation. For example F-111E 68-0001 was the first aircraft ordered in 1968. The fiscal year (FY) serial is carried on the technical bloc which is usually stencilled on the left-hand side of the aircraft just below the cockpit. The number displayed on the fin is a corruption of the FY serial. Most tactical aircraft carry the fiscal year in small figures followed by the last three digits of the serial in large figures. For example F-111F 70-2362 carries 70362 on its tail. Large transport and tanker aircraft such as C-130s and KC-135s usually display a five-figure number commencing with the last digit of the appropriate fiscal year and four figures of the production number. An example of this is EC-135H 61-0282 which displays 10282 on its fin. Aircraft of more than 10 years vintage which might duplicate a five-figure number of a more modern type in service, are prefixed 0-.

USN serials follow a straightforward numerical sequence which commenced, for the present series, with the allocation of 00001 to an SB2C Helldiver by the Bureau of Aeronautics in 1940. Numbers in the 163000 series are presently being issued. They are usually carried in full on the rear fuselage of the aircraft and displayed either as a four- or five-figure sequence or in full on the fin.

# UK based USAF Aircraft

The following aircraft are normally based in the UK. They are listed in numerical order of type with individual aircraft in serial number order, as depicted on the aircraft. The number in brackets is either the alternative presentation of the five-figure number commencing with the last digit of the fiscal year, or the fiscal year where a five-figure serial is presented on the aircraft. Where it is possible to identify the allocation of aircraft to individual squadrons by means of colours carried on fin or cockpit edge, this is also provided.

| Serial | | | | Notes |
|---|---|---|---|---|
| **Lockheed TR-1A/TR-1B*** | | | | |
| 95RS/17RW, RAF Alconbury | | | | |
| *FY80* | | | | |
| 01065* | | | | |
| 01079 | | | | |
| 01081 | | | | |
| 01083 | | | | |
| 01085 | | | | |
| 01086 | | | | |
| 01088 | | | | |
| 01092 | | | | |
| 01093 | | | | |
| 01094 | | | | |
| 01099 | | | | |
| **Fairchild A-10A Thunderbolt II** | | | | |
| **AR:** 10TFW: | | | | |
| 509TFS grey (gy) Alconbury | | | | |
| 511TFS black (bk) Alconbury | | | | |
| **WR:** 81TFW: | | | | |
| 78TFS red (r) Woodbridge | | | | |
| 91TFS blue (bl) Woodbridge | | | | |
| 92TFS yellow (y) Bentwaters | | | | |
| 510TFS purple (pr) Bentwaters | | | | |
| 76-514 | (60514) | pr | WR | |
| 76-522 | (60522) | r | WR | |
| 76-527 | (60527) | bk | AR | |
| 76-548 | (60548) | bk | AR | |
| 76-550 | (60550) | bl | WR | |
| 76-553 | (60553) | y | WR | |
| 77-233 | (70233) | bk | AR | |
| 77-235 | (70235) | bk | AR | |
| 77-236 | (70236) | bk | AR | |
| 77-237 | (70237) | bk | AR | |
| 77-238 | (70238) | bk | AR | |
| 77-241 | (70241) | bk | AR | |
| 77-242 | (70242) | bk | AR | |
| 77-246 | (70246) | bk | AR | |
| 77-247 | (70247) | bk | AR | |
| 77-250 | (70250) | bk | AR | |
| 77-254 | (70254) | bk | AR | |
| 77-259 | (70259) | bk | AR | |
| 77-262 | (70262) | bk | AR | |
| 77-263 | (70263) | bk | AR | |
| 77-264 | (70264) | bk | AR | |
| 77-276 | (70276) | bk | AR | |
| 79-217 | (90217) | r | WR | |
| 79-218 | (90218) | y | WR | |
| 79-220 | (90220) | gy | AR | |
| 79-221 | (90221) | pr | WR | |

| Serial | | | Notes |
|---|---|---|---|
| 79-224 | (90224) gy | AR | |
| 79-225 | (90225) bl | WR | |
| 80-143 | (00143) r | WR | |
| 80-144 | (00144) gy | AR | |
| 80-145 | (00145) y | WR | |
| 80-147 | (00147) pr | WR | |
| 80-155 | (00155) pr [510 TFS] | WR | |
| 80-157 | (00157) bk | AR | |
| 80-158 | (00158) bl | WR | |
| 80-159 | (00159) y | WF | |
| 80-160 | (00160) pr | WR | |
| 80-167 | (00167) r | WR | |
| 80-168 | (00168) y | WR | |
| 30-169 | (00169) pr | WR | |
| 80-170 | (00170) gy | AR | |
| 80-171 | (00171) bl | WR | |
| 80-172 | (00172) gy | AR | |
| 80-179 | (00179) r | WR | |
| 80-180 | (00180) bl | WR | |
| 80-181 | (00181) m | 81 TFW | |
| 80-192 | (00192) y | 92 TFS | |
| 80-194 | (00194) gy | AR | |
| 80-195 | (00195) pr | WR | |
| 80-203 | (00203) r | WR | |
| 80-204 | (00204) bl | WR | |
| 80-205 | (00205) bl | WR | |
| 80-206 | (00206) y | WR | |
| 80-207 | (00207) y | WR | |
| 80-208 | (00208) gy | AR | |
| 80-215 | (00215) | WR | |
| 80-216 | (00216) pr | WR | |
| 80-217 | (00217) y | WR | |
| 80-220 | (00220) bl | WR | |
| 80-228 | (00228) pr | WR | |
| 80-229 | (00229) gy | AR | |
| 80-233 | (00233) r | WR | |
| 80-234 | (00234) bl | WR | |
| 80-235 | (00235) r | WR | |
| 80-236 | (00236) r | WR | |
| 80-237 | (00237) gy | AR | |
| 80-270 | (00270) r | WR | |
| 80-271 | (00271) | WR | |
| 80-272 | (00272) y | WR | |
| 80-274 | (00274) pr | WR | |
| 80-276 | (00276) y | WR | |
| 80-277 | (00277) gy | AR | |
| 80-278 | (00278) r | 78 TFS | |
| 80-279 | (00279) pr | WR | |
| 80-280 | (00280) bl | WR | |
| 80-281 | (00281) y | WR | |
| 81-939 | (10939) gy | AR | |
| 81-941 | (10941) r | WR | |
| 81-942 | (10942) bl | WR | |
| 81-943 | (10943) y | WR | |
| 81-944 | (10944) pr | WR | |
| 81-947 | (10947) gy | AR | |
| 81-948 | (10948) gy | AR | |
| 81-950 | (10950) r | WR | |
| 81-951 | (10951) bl | WR | |
| 81-952 | (10952) pr | WR | |
| 81-953 | (10953) gy | AR | |
| 81-954 | (10954) | WR | |
| 81-956 | (10956) bl | WR | |
| 81-960 | (10960) r | WR | |
| 81-961 | (10961) r | WR | |
| 81-962 | (10962) bl | WR | |
| 81-963 | (10963) y | WR | |
| 81-964 | (10964) | AR | |
| 81-965 | (10965) pr | WR | |
| 81-966 | (10966) pr | WR | |
| 81-967 | (10967) bk | AR | |
| 81-976 | (10976) bl | WR | |
| 81-977 | (10977) y | WR | |
| 81-978 | (10978) r | 78 TFS | |

| Serial | | | Notes |
|---|---|---|---|
| 81-979 | (10979) bk/gy | 10 TFW | |
| 81-980 | (10980) | WR | |
| 81-982 | (10982) r | WR | |
| 81-983 | (10983) bl | WR | |
| 81-984 | (10984) r | WR | |
| 81-985 | (10985) y | WR | |
| 81-987 | (10987) gy | AR | |
| 81-988 | (10988) pr | WR | |
| 81-990 | (10990) gy | AR | |
| 819-91 | (10991) bl | 91 TFS | |
| 81-992 | (10992) y | WR | |
| 82-646 | (20646) pr | WR | |
| 82-649 | (20649) bl | WR | |
| 82-650 | (20650) pr | WR | |
| 82-654 | (20654) r | WR | |
| 82-655 | (20655) bl | WR | |
| 82-656 | (20656) y | WR | |
| 82-657 | (20657) gy | AR | |
| 82-658 | (20658) r | WR | |

**Sikorsky MH-53J**
39SOW 121 SOS
RAF Woodbridge

| Serial | Notes |
|---|---|
| 01626 (FY70) | |
| 14431 (FY66) | |
| 88284 (FY68) | |
| 95784 (FY69) | |
| 95796 (FY69) | |

**General Dynamics EF-111A Raven**
**UH:** RAF Upper Heyford
66ECW/42ECS grey

| Serial | | Notes |
|---|---|---|
| 66-015 | (60015) | |
| 66-016 | (60016) | |
| 66-019 | (60019) | |
| 66-023 | (60023) | |
| 66-037 | (60037) | |
| 66-039 | (60039) | |
| 66-047 | (60047) | |
| 66-050 | (60050) | |
| 66-055 | (60055) | |
| 66-056 | (60056) | |
| 67-034 | (70034) | |
| 67-035 | (70035) | |

**General Dynamics F-111E**
**UH:** 20TFW, RAF Upper Heyford
55TFS blue/white (bl)
77TFS red (r)
79TFS yellow/black (y)

| Serial | | Notes |
|---|---|---|
| 67-119 | (70119) y | |
| 67-120 | (70120) r | |
| 67-121 | (70121) bl | |
| 67-122 | (70122) y | |
| 67-123 | (70123) y | |
| 68-002 | (80002) y | |
| 68-004 | (80004) bl | |
| 68-005 | (80005) bl | |
| 68-006 | (80006) bl | |
| 68-007 | (80007) r | |
| 68-009 | (80009) r | |
| 68-010 | (80010) y | |
| 68-011 | (80011) r | |
| 68-013 | (80013) r | |
| 68-014 | (80014) bl | |
| 68-015 | (80015) r | |
| 68-016 | (80016) y | |
| 68-017 | (80017) r | |
| 68-020 | (80020) m (20 TFW) | |
| 68-021 | (80021) r | |
| 68-022 | (80022) y | |
| 68-023 | (80023) bl | |

| Notes | Serial |
|---|---|
| | 68-025 (80025) r |
| | 68-026 (80026) bl |
| | 68-027 (80027) bl |
| | 68-028 (80028) bl |
| | 68-029 (80029) bl |
| | 68-030 (80030) y |
| | 68-031 (80031) y |
| | 68-032 (80032) bl |
| | 68-033 (80033) r |
| | 68-034 (80034) bl |
| | 68-035 (80035) r |
| | 68-036 (80036) bl |
| | 68-037 (80037) bl |
| | 68-038 (80038) r |
| | 68-039 (80039) r |
| | 68-041 (80041) r |
| | 68-043 (80043) bl |
| | 68-044 (80044) bl |
| | 68-046 (80046) bl |
| | 68-047 (80047) r |
| | 68-048 (80048) r |
| | 68-049 (80049) y |
| | 68-050 (80050) r |
| | 68-051 (80051) r |
| | 68-052 (80052) y |
| | 68-053 (80053) y |
| | 68-054 (80054) bl |
| | 680-55 (80055) bl (55 TFS) |
| | 68-056 (80056) bl |
| | 68-059 (80059) r |
| | 68-061 (80061) bl |
| | 68-062 (80062) y |
| | 68-063 (80063) y |
| | 68-064 (80064) y |
| | 68-065 (80065) bl |
| | 68-067 (80067) r |
| | 68-068 (80068) y |
| | 68-069 (80069) bl |
| | 68-071 (80071) r |
| | 68-072 (80072) y |
| | 68-073 (80073) y |
| | 68-074 (80074) bl |
| | 68-075 (80075) bl |
| | 68-076 (80076) bl |
| | 68-077 (80077) r (77 TFS) |
| | 68-078 (80078) r |
| | 68-079 (80079) y (79 TFS) |
| | 68-080 (80080) y |
| | 68-082 (80082) y |
| | 68-083 (80083) y |
| | 68-084 (80084) y |

**General Dynamics F-111F**
**LN:** 48TFW, RAF Lakenheath
492 TFS blue (bl)
493 TFS yellow (y)
494 TFS red (r)
495 TFS green (gn)

| Notes | Serial |
|---|---|
| | 70-362 (02362) y |
| | 70-363 (02363) gn |
| | 70-364 (02364) r |
| | 70-365 (02365) bl |
| | 70-369 (02369) gn |
| | 70-370 (02370) r |
| | 70-371 (02371) y |
| | 70-372 (02372) gn |
| | 70-373 (02373) bl |
| | 70-374 (02374) y |
| | 70-376 (02376) r |
| | 70-378 (02378) gn |
| | 70-379 (02379) bl |
| | 70-381 (02381) r |
| | 70-382 (02382) bl |
| | 70-383 (02383) bl |
| | 70-384 (02384) y |
| | 70-385 (02385) y |
| | 70-386 (02386) r |
| | 70-387 (02387) gn |
| | 70-390 (02390) m (48 TFW) |
| | 70-391 (02391) (495 TFS) |
| | 70-392 (02392) gn |
| | 70-394 (02394) (492 TFS) |
| | 70-396 (02396) y |
| | 70-398 (02398) y |
| | 70-399 (02399) y |
| | 70-401 (02401) r |
| | 70-402 (02402) gn |
| | 70-403 (02403) (493 TFS) |
| | 70-404 (02404) y |
| | 70-405 (02405) r |
| | 70-406 (02406) bl |
| | 70-408 (02408) r |
| | 70-409 (02409) r |
| | 70-411 (02411) gn |
| | 70-412 (02412) |
| | 70-413 (02413) bl |
| | 70-414 (02414) gn |
| | 70-415 (02415) gn |
| | 70-416 (02416) r |
| | 70-417 (02417) y |
| | 70-419 (02419) gn |
| | 71-883 (10883) gn |
| | 71-884 (10884) bl |
| | 71-885 (10885) bl |
| | 71-886 (10886) y |
| | 71-887 (10887) y |
| | 71-888 (10888) y |
| | 71-889 (10889) y |
| | 71-890 (10890) bl |
| | 71-891 (10891) y |
| | 71-892 (10892) r |
| | 71-893 (10893) gn |
| | 71-894 (10894) m |
| | 72-442 (21442) bl |
| | 72-443 (21443) r |
| | 72-444 (21444) r |
| | 72-445 (21445) bl |
| | 72-446 (21446) bl |
| | 72-448 (21448) m (48 TFW) |
| | 72-449 (21449) y |
| | 72-450 (21450) y |
| | 72-451 (21451) y |
| | 72-452 (21452) y |
| | 73-707 (30707) r |
| | 73-708 (30708) gn |
| | 73-710 (30710) r |
| | 73-711 (30711) r |
| | 73-712 (30712) (494 TFS) |
| | 73-713 (30713) gn |
| | 73-715 (30715) r |
| | 74-177 (40177) bl |
| | 74-178 (40178) r |
| | 74-180 (40180) gn |
| | 74-181 (40181) bl |
| | 74-182 (40182) bl |
| | 74-184 (40184) r |
| | 74-185 (40185) bl |

**Lockheed C-130E/H Hercules**
313 TAG, RAF Mildenhall
Continuous presence of two-month deployments of 18 aircraft from 314TAW, 317TAW or 463TAW — see USAF (US) Section serials

| Serial | Notes |
|---|---|
| **Lockheed C-130 Hercules** | |
| 67SOS/39 SOW, RAF Woodbridge | |
| 50973 (FY65) HC-130H | |
| 60220 (FY66) HC-130P | |
| 60223 (FY66) HC-130P | |
| 95820 (FY69) HC-130N | |
| 95823 (FY69) HC-130N | |
| 95826 (FY69) HC-130N | |
| 95827 (FY69) HC-130N | |
| 95831 (FY69) HC-130N | |
| **Boeing C-135** | |
| 513ACCW/10 ACCS, RAF Mildenhall | |
| *FY61* | |
| 10282 EC-135H | |
| 10285 EC-135H | |
| 10286 EC-135H | |
| 10291 EC-135H | |
| 12667 WC-135B | |

# UK based US Navy Aircraft

| Serial |
|---|
| **Beech UC-12M Super King Air** |
| **8G:** Naval Air Facility, Mildenhall |
| 3837 (163837) 8G |
| 3840 (163840) 8G |
| 3843 (163843) 8G |

# European based USAF Aircraft

These aircraft are normally based in Western Europe with the USAFE. They are shown in numerical order of type designation, with individual aircraft in serial number order as carried on the aircraft. An alternative five-figure presentation of the serial is shown in brackets where appropriate. Fiscal year (FY) details are also provided if necessary. The unit allocation and operating bases are given for most aircraft.

| Serial | | |
|---|---|---|
| **Bell UH-1N** | | |
| 58 MAS Ramstein | | |
| *FY69* | | |
| 96606 | | |
| 96608 | | |
| 96609 | | |
| 96619 | | |
| **McDonnell Douglas RF-4C Phantom** | | |
| **ZR:** 26TRW/38TRS | | |
| Zweibrucken green/white | | |
| 68-554 | (80554) | |
| 68-555 | (80555) | |
| 68-557 | (80557) | |
| 68-561 | (80561) | |
| 68-565 | (80565) | |
| 68-567 | (80567) | |
| 68-570 | (80570) | |
| 68-580 | (80580) | |
| 68-583 | (80583) | |
| 68-589 | (80589) | |
| 69-359 | (90359) | |
| 69-369 | (90369) | |
| 69-370 | (90370) [26TRW] | |
| 69-383 | (90383) [38TRS] | |
| 71-249 | (10249) | |
| 71-251 | (10251) | |
| 71-254 | (10254) | |
| 71-259 | (10259) | |
| 72-152 | (20152) | |
| 72-153 | (20153) | |
| **McDonnell Douglas F-4G Phantom** | | |
| **SP:** 52TFW | | |
| Spangdahlem | | |
| 23 TFS blue/white (bl) | | |
| 81 TFS yellow/black (y) | | |
| 480 TFS red/white (r) | | |
| 69-202 | (97202) | bl |
| 69-209 | (97209) | r |
| 69-210 | (97210) | r |
| 69-212 | (97212) | bl |
| 69-228 | (97228) | bl |
| 69-232 | (97232) | r |
| 69-234 | (97234) | r |
| 69-237 | (90237) | y |
| 69-241 | (90241) | bl |
| 69-242 | (90242) | bl |
| 69-245 | (90245) | bl |
| 69-247 | (90247) | |
| 69-248 | (90248) [480TFS] | r |
| 69-250 | (90250) | r |
| 69-253 | (90253) | r |
| 69-255 | (90255) [23TFS] | bl |
| 69-258 | (90258) | y |
| 69-259 | (90259) | bl |
| 69-262 | (97262) | r |
| 69-263 | (90263) | y |
| 69-267 | (97267) | |
| 69-268 | (97268) [81TFS] | y |
| 69-269 | (90269) | r |
| 69-270 | (90270) | bl |
| 69-270 | (97270) | r |
| 69-274 | (90274) | r |
| 69-278 | (90278) | bl |
| 69-285 | (90285) | y |
| 69-286 | (90286) | y |
| 69-286 | (97286) | r |
| 69-291 | (97291) | bl |
| 69-293 | (97293) | y |
| 69-295 | (97295) | y |
| 69-546 | (97546) | bl |
| 69-556 | (97556) | y |
| 69-558 | (97558) | r |
| 69-566 | (97566) | bl |
| 69-571 | (97571) | bl |
| 69-579 | (97579) | r |
| 69-582 | (97582) [52TFW] | m |
| 69-587 | (97587) SP | y |
| **McDonnell Douglas C-9A Nightingale *VIP** | | |
| 435TAW/55AAS Rhein Main | | |
| *FY71* | | |
| 10876 | | |
| 10878* | | |

| Serial |
|---|
| 10879 |
| 10881 |
| 10882* |
| 10960 |

**Fairchild A-10A Thunderbolt II**

**AR:** 10TFW: RAF Alconbury
**WR:** 81 TFW: RAF Woodbridge/ Bentwaters
Forward Operating Locations (FOL)
Det 1 Sembach AR WR
Det 2 WGAF Leipheim WR
Det 3 WGAF Ahlhorn AR
Det 4 WGAF Norvenich WR
Det 5 WGAF Jever AR
At each, eight aircraft on rotation from the six UK-based Squadrons at RAF Alconbury and RAF Woodbridge/Bentwaters — see USAF/UK-based section.

**Beech C-12**

*58 MAS Ramstein
‡JUSMG Torrejon
**MAAG Athens
§MAAG, Ankara
‡‡JUSMG Turkey

| | | |
|---|---|---|
| 31212 | (FY73)‡ | C-12A |
| 31216 | (FY73)§ | C-12A |
| 31218 | (FY73)** | C-12A |
| 40161 | (FY84)* | C-12F |
| 40162 | (FY84)* | C-12F |
| 40163 | (FY84)* | C-12F |
| 40164 | (FY84)* | C-12F |
| 40165 | (FY84)* | C-12F |
| 40166 | (FY84)* | C-12F |
| 60173 | (FY76)§ | C-12A |

**McDonnell Douglas F-15C/‡F-15D Eagle**

**CR:** 32TFG/32TFS Soesterberg
orange/green (or)
**BT:** 36TFW Bitburg
22TFS red (r)
53TFS yellow/black (y)
525TFS blue (bl)
**IS:** 57FIS Keflavik
black/white (bk)

| | | | |
|---|---|---|---|
| 79-007 | (90007)‡ | BT | bl |
| 79-010 | (90010)‡ | BT | r |
| 79-011 | (90011)‡ | BT | r |
| 79-012 | (90012)‡ | BT | bl |
| 79-016 | (90016) | CR | or |
| 79-020 | (90020) | CR | or |
| 79-021 | (90021) | CR | or |
| 79-022 | (90022) | BT | r |
| 79-024 | (90024) | CR | or |
| 79-025 | (90025) | [525TFS] | |
| 79-026 | (90026) | CR | or |
| 79-027 | (90027) | CR | or |
| 79-028 | (90028) | CR | or |
| 79-029 | (90029) | CR | or |
| 79-030 | (90030) | CR | or |
| 79-034 | (90034) | CR | or |
| 79-035 | (90035) | BT | bl |
| 79-036 | (90036) | BT | bl |
| 79-037 | (90037) | BT | bl |
| 79-043 | (90043) | BT | bl |
| 79-045 | (90045) | BT | bl |
| 79-046 | (90046) | BT | bl |
| 79-047 | (90047) | BT | bl |
| 79-048 | (90048) | BT | bl |
| 79-052 | (90052) | BT | r |
| 79-057 | (90057) | BT | r |
| 79-058 | (90058) | BT | bl |
| 79-062 | (90062) | BT | bl |
| 79-063 | (90063) | BT | r |
| 79-064 | (90064) | BT | r |
| 79-068 | (90068) | BT | r |
| 79-069 | (90069) | BT | bl |
| 79-072 | (90072) | BT | r |
| 79-073 | (90073) | BT | bl |
| 79-074 | (90074) | BT | r |
| 79-076 | (90076) | BT | bl |
| 79-077 | (90077) | BT | r |
| 79-078 | (90078) | BT | r |
| 79-079 | (90079) | BT | r |
| 80-003 | (00003) | BT | r |
| 80-004 | (00004) | BT | r |
| 80-005 | (00005) | BT | r |
| 80-010 | (00010) | BT | r |
| 80-011 | (00011) | BT | bl |
| 80-012 | (00012) | BT | bl |
| 80-013 | (00013) | BT | bl |
| 80-014 | (00014) | BT | bl |
| 80-015 | (00015) | BT | bl |
| 80-019 | (00019) | BT | bl |
| 80-021 | (00021) | BT | r |
| 80-022 | (00022) [22TFS] | | r |
| 80-023 | (00023) | BT | r |
| 80-026 | (00026) | BT | r |
| 80-027 | (00027) | IS | bk |
| 80-028 | (00028) | BT | bl |
| 80-029 | (00029) | BT | bl |
| 80-030 | (00030) | IS | bk |
| 80-031 | (00031) | BT | r |
| 80-033 | (00033) | [A.F. Iceland] | |
| 80-034 | (00034) | IS | bk |
| 80-035 | (00035) | IS | bk |
| 80-038 | (00038) | IS | bk |
| 80-039 | (00039) | IS | bk |
| 80-040 | (00040) | IS | bk |
| 80-041 | (00041) | IS | bk |
| 80-042 | (00042) | IS | bk |
| 80-043 | (00043) | IS | bk |
| 80-044 | (00044) | IS | bk |
| 80-045 | (00045) | IS | bk |
| 80-046 | (00046) | IS | bk |
| 80-047 | (00047) | IS | bk |
| 80-048 | (00048) | IS | bk |
| 80-049 | (00049) | IS | bk |
| 80-050 | (00050) | IS | bk |
| 80-052 | (00052) | IS | bk |
| 80-055 | (00055)‡ | BT | bl |
| 80-056 | (00056)‡ | IS | bk |
| 80-057 | (00057)‡ | IS | bk |
| 80-060 | (00060)‡ | BT | bl |
| 81-027 | (10027) | CR | or |
| 81-028 | (10028) | BT | bl |
| 81-045 | (10045) | CR | or |
| 81-046 | (10046) | CR | or |
| 81-047 | (10047) | CR | or |
| 81-048 | (10048) | CR | or |
| 81-065 | (10065)‡ | CR | or |
| 84-001 | (40001) | BT | m |
| 84-002 | (40002) | BT | y |
| 84-003 | (40003) | BT | m |
| 84-004 | (40004) | BT | r |
| 84-005 | (40005) | BT | m |
| 84-006 | (40006) | BT | m |
| 84-007 | (40007) | BT | r |
| 84-008 | (40008) | BT | y |
| 84-009 | (40009) | BT | r |
| 84-010 | (40010) | BT | r |
| 84-013 | (40013) | BT | m |
| 84-014 | (40014) | BT | y |
| 84-015 | (40015) | BT | y |
| 84-016 | (40016) | BT | y |
| 84-017 | (40017) | BT | r |
| 84-019 | (40019) | BT | y |
| 84-020 | (40020) | BT | y |
| 84-021 | (40021) | BT | r |
| 84-022 | (40022) [22 TFS] | | r |
| 84-023 | (40023) | BT | y |
| 84-024 | (40024) | BT | r |
| 84-025 | (40025) | BT | m |
| 84-026 | (40026) | BT | y |
| 84-027 | (40027) | BT | y |
| 84-043 | (40043)‡ | BT | y |
| 84-044 | (40044)‡ | BT | y |

**General Dynamics F-16C/‡F-16D**

**HR:** 50TFW Hahn
10TFS blue/yellow (bl)
313TFS orange (or)
496TFS yellow (y)
**RS:** 86TFW Ramstein
512TFS green/black (gn)
526TFS red/black (r)
**SP:** 52TFW Spangdahlem
23TFS blue/white (bl)
81TFS yellow/black (y)
480TFS red/white (r)
**TJ:** 401TFW Crotone
612TFS blue/white (bl)
613TFS yellow/black (y)
614TFS red/black (r)

| | | | |
|---|---|---|---|
| 83-130 | (31130) | HR | or |
| 84-238 | (41238) | HR | bl |
| 842-50 | (41250) [50TFW] | | |
| 84-264 | (41264) | HR | or |
| 84-266 | (41266) | HR | y |
| 84-267 | (41267) | HR | y |
| 84-271 | (41271) | HR | y |
| 84-274 | (41274) | HR | or |
| 84-275 | (41275) | HR | bl |
| 84-276 | (41276) | HR | y |
| 84-278 | (41278) | HR | bl |
| 84-279 | (41279) | HR | or |
| 84-282 | (41282) | HR | bl |
| 84-283 | (41283) | HR | or |
| 84-284 | (41284) | HR | y |
| 84-287 | (41287) | HR | or |
| 84-288 | (41288) | HR | or |
| 84-290 | (41290) | HR | bl |
| 84-291 | (41291) | HR | y |
| 84-292 | (41292) | HR | or |
| 84-294 | (41294) | HR | or |
| 84-295 | (41295) | HR | bl |
| 84-296 | (41296) [496TFS] | | |
| 84-297 | (41297) | HR | y |
| 84-298 | (41298) | HR | y |
| 84-299 | (41299) | HR | y |
| 84-300 | (41300) | HR | bl |
| 84-301 | (41301) | HR | or |
| 84-302 | (41302) | HR | or |
| 84-303 | (41303) | HR | or |
| 84-304 | (41304) | HR | y |
| 84-305 | (41305) | HR | y |
| 84-306 | (41306) | HR | y |
| 84-307 | (41307) | HR | y |

| Serial | | | |
|---|---|---|---|
| 84-308 | (41308) | HR | or |
| 84-309 | (41309) | HR | or |
| 84-310 | (41310) [10 TFS] | | |
| 84-311 | (41311) | HR | or |
| 84-313 | (41313) [313 TFS] | | |
| 84-315 | (41315) | HR | y |
| 84-316 | (41316) | HR | or |
| 84-317 | (41317) | HR | y |
| 84-318 | (41318) | HR | y |
| 84-324 | (41324)‡ | HR | or |
| 84-325 | (41325)‡ | HR | y |
| 84-326 | (41326)‡ | HR | y |
| 84-327 | (41327)‡ | HR | or |
| 84-328 | (41328)‡ | HR | bl |
| 84-331 | (41331)‡ | HR | bl |
| 84-374 | (41374) | HR | bl |
| 84-375 | (41375) | HR | or |
| 84-376 | (41376) | HR | bl |
| 84-377 | (41377) | HR | bl |
| 84-382 | (41382) | HR | bl |
| 84-383 | (41383) | HR | or |
| 84-384 | (41384) | HR | y |
| 84-385 | (41385) | HR | y |
| 84-386 | (41386) | HR | y |
| 84-387 | (41387) | HR | bl |
| 84-388 | (41388) | HR | bl |
| 84-390 | (41390) | HR | bl |
| 84-391 | (41391) | HR | y |
| 84-392 | (41392) | HR | bl |
| 84-393 | (41393) | HR | or |
| 84-394 | (41394) | HR | or |
| 85-398 | (51398) | RS | r |
| 85-400 | (51400) | RS | gn |
| 85-402 | (51402) | RS | r |
| 85-403 | (51403) | HR | bl |
| 85-404 | (51404) | HR | y |
| 85-405 | (51405) | HR | y |
| 85-406 | (51406) | HR | y |
| 85-407 | (51407) | HR | bl |
| 85-408 | (51408) | RS | r |
| 85-409 | (51409) | HR | bl |
| 85-410 | (51410) | RS | r |
| 85-411 | (51411) | HR | bl |
| 85-413 | (51413) | HR | or |
| 85-415 | (51415) | HR | bl |
| 85-416 | (51416) | HR | bl |
| 85-417 | (51417) | HR | or |
| 85-418 | (51418) | HR | bl |
| 85-422 | (51422) | RS | r |
| 85-426 | (51426) [526 TFS] | | |
| 85-428 | (51428) | RS | gn |
| 85-434 | (51434) | RS | r |
| 85-436 | (51436) | RS | gn |
| 85-438 | (51438) | RS | gn |
| 85-440 | (51440) | RS | gn |
| 85-442 | (51442) | RS | r |
| 85-444 | (51444) | RS | r |
| 85-446 | (51446) | RS | r |
| 85-448 | (51448) | RS | r |
| 85-449 | (51449) | RS | r |
| 85-450 | (51450) | RS | r |
| 85-451 | (51451) | RS | r |
| 85-453 | (51453) | RS | r |
| 85-454 | (51454) | RS | gn |
| 85-455 | (51455) | RS | gn |
| 85-456 | (51456) | RS | gn |
| 85-457 | (51457) | RS | gn |
| 85-458 | (51458) | RS | gn |
| 85-459 | (51459) | RS | gn |
| 85-460 | (51460) | RS | r |
| 85-461 | (51461) | RS | r |
| 85-464 | (51464) | RS | r |

| Serial | | | |
|---|---|---|---|
| 85-465 | (51465) | RS | r |
| 85-466 | (51466) | RS | gn |
| 85-467 | (51467) | RS | gn |
| 85-468 | (51468) | RS | gn |
| 85-469 | (51469) | RS | gn |
| 85-470 | (51470) [512TFS] | | |
| 85-471 | (51471) | RS | gn |
| 85-472 | (51472) | RS | gn |
| 85-473 | (51473) | RS | gn |
| 85-474 | (51474) | RS | gn |
| 85-475 | (51475) | RS | r |
| 85-476 | (51476) | RS | r |
| 85-477 | (51477) | RS | r |
| 85-478 | (51478) | RS | r |
| 85-479 | (51479) | RS | gn |
| 85-480 | (51480) | RS | gn |
| 85-481 | (51481) | RS | gn |
| 85-484 | (51484) | RS | r |
| 85-485 | (51485) | RS | gn |
| 85-486 | (51486) [86TFW] | | |
| 85-509 | (51509)‡ | RS | gn |
| 85-511 | (51511)‡ | RS | r |
| 85-546 | (51546) | RS | r |
| 85-552 | (51552) [52TFW] | | |
| 85-572 | (51572)‡ | SP | r |
| 86-042 | (60042)‡ | SP | y |
| 86-043 | (60043)‡ | SP | bl |
| 86-044 | (60044)‡ | TJ | bl |
| 86-047 | (60047)‡ | TJ | r |
| 86-049 | (60049)‡ | TJ | y |
| 86-050 | (60050)‡ | TJ | r |
| 86-209 | (60209) | RS | r |
| 86-216 | (60216) | SP | y |
| 86-219 | (60219) | SP | r |
| 86-222 | (60222) | SP | r |
| 86-223 | (60223) [23 TFS] | | |
| 86-224 | (60224) | SP | bl |
| 86-225 | (60225) | SP | r |
| 86-226 | (60226) | SP | r |
| 86-227 | (60227) | SP | y |
| 86-228 | (60228) | SP | r |
| 86-229 | (60229) | SP | y |
| 86-230 | (60230) | SP | y |
| 86-231 | (60231) | SP | bl |
| 86-232 | (60232) | SP | bl |
| 86-237 | (60237) | SP | bl |
| 86-242 | (60242) | SP | bl |
| 86-243 | (60243) | SP | bl |
| 86-244 | (60244) | SP | bl |
| 86-245 | (60245) | SP | y |
| 86-246 | (60246) | SP | bl |
| 86-248 | (60248) | SP | y |
| 86-249 | (60249) | SP | y |
| 86-254 | (60254) | SP | r |
| 86-255 | (60255) | RS | gn |
| 86-258 | (60258) | SP | y |
| 86-259 | (60259) | SP | r |
| 86-260 | (60260) | SP | y |
| 86-261 | (60261) | SP | y |
| 86-262 | (60262) | TJ | bl |
| 86-263 | (60263) | TJ | bl |
| 86-270 | (60270) | TJ | bl |
| 86-287 | (60287) | SP | y |
| 86-288 | (60288) | TJ | r |
| 86-289 | (60289) [612TFS] | | |
| 86-302 | (60302) | TJ | bl |
| 86-303 | (60303) | TJ | bl |
| 86-313 | (60313) | TJ | bl |
| 86-315 | (60315) | TJ | bl |
| 86-324 | (60324) | TJ | bl |
| 86-325 | (60325) | TJ | bl |
| 86-326 | (60326) | TJ | bl |

| Serial | | | |
|---|---|---|---|
| 86-327 | (60327) | TJ | bl |
| 86-328 | (60328) | TJ | bl |
| 86-329 | (60329) | TJ | bl |
| 86-330 | (60330) | TJ | bl |
| 86-338 | (60338) | TJ | bl |
| 86-339 | (60339) | TJ | bl |
| 86-340 | (60340) | TJ | bl |
| 86-341 | (60341) | TJ | y |
| 86-342 | (60342) | TJ | y |
| 86-343 | (60343) [613TFS] | | |
| 87-345 | (60345) [613TFS] | | |
| 86-346 | (60346) | TJ | y |
| 86-347 | (60347) | TJ | y |
| 86-348 | (60348) | TJ | y |
| 86-349 | (60349) | TJ | y |
| 86-350 | (60350) | TJ | bl |
| 86-358 | (60358) | TJ | r |
| 86-360 | (60360) | TJ | bl |
| 86-361 | (60361) | TJ | y |
| 86-362 | (60362) | TJ | y |
| 86-363 | (60363) | TJ | y |
| 86-364 | (60364) | TJ | y |
| 86-365 | (60365) | TJ | bl |
| 86-366 | (60366) | TJ | y |
| 86-367 | (60367) | TJ | bl |
| 86-368 | (60368) | TJ | y |
| 86-369 | (60369) | TJ | y |
| 86-370 | (60370) | TJ | y |
| 86-371 | (60371) | TJ | y |
| 87-217 | (70217) | TJ | y |
| 87-218 | (70218) | TJ | y |
| 87-219 | (70219) | TJ | y |
| 87-220 | (70220) | TJ | y |
| 87-221 | (70221) [614TFS] | | |
| 87-222 | (70222) | TJ | y |
| 87-223 | (70223) | TJ | r |
| 87-224 | (70224) | TJ | r |
| 87-225 | (70225) | TJ | r |
| 87-226 | (70226) | TJ | r |
| 87-227 | (70227) | TJ | r |
| 87-228 | (70228) | TJ | r |
| 87-229 | (70229) | TJ | r |
| 87-230 | (70230) | TJ | r |
| 87-237 | (70237) | TJ | bl |
| 87-238 | (70238) | TJ | r |
| 87-239 | (70239) | TJ | r |
| 87-240 | (70240) | TJ | r |
| 87-241 | (70241) | TJ | r |
| 87-242 | (70242) | TJ | r |
| 87-243 | (70243) | TJ | r |
| 87-244 | (70244) | TJ | r |
| 87-245 | (70245) | TJ | r |
| 87-246 | (70246) | TJ | r |
| 87-247 | (70247) | TJ | r |
| 87-248 | (70248) | TJ | r |
| 87-249 | (70249) | TJ | bl |
| 87-257 | (70257) | TJ | r |
| 87-258 | (70258) | TJ | r |
| 87-259 | (70259) | TJ | r |
| 87-260 | (70260) | SP | r |
| 87-268 | (70268) | SP | bl |
| 87-270 | (70270) | SP | r |
| 87-271 | (70271) | TJ | y |
| 87-281 | (70281) [81 TFS] | | |
| 87-282 | (70282) | SP | bl |
| 87-283 | (70283) | SP | bl |
| 87-284 | (70284) | TJ | y |
| 87-287 | (70287) | TJ | y |
| 87-336 | (70336) | SP | r |
| 87-337 | (70337) [16th AF) | | |
| 88-174 | (80174)‡ | HR | y |
| 88-398 | (80398) | TJ | y |

## USAF (EUR based)

| Serial | | | |
|---|---|---|---|
| 88-399 | (80399) | SP | y |
| 88-400 | (80400) [480TFS] | | |
| 88-401 | (80401) [401TFW] | | |
| 89- | (9 ) | | |
| 89- | (9 ) | | |
| 89- | (9 ) | | |
| 89- | (9 ) | | |
| 89- | (9 ) | | |
| 89- | (9 ) | | |
| 89- | (9 ) | | |
| 89- | (9 ) | | |
| 89- | (9 ) | | |
| 89- | (9 ) | | |

**Grumman C-20A Gulfstream III**
58 MAS, Ramstein

*FY83*
30500
30501
30502

**Gates C-21A Learjet**
*58MAS Ramstein
†7005ABS Stuttgart

*FY84*
40081†
40082†
40083†
40084*
40085*
40086*

**Boeing T-43A**
58 MAS, Ramstein

20283 (FY72)

**Lockheed C-130E Hercules**
435TAW 37TAS; Rhein Main:
*7405 OS

| Serial | |
|---|---|
| 01260 | (FY70) |
| 01264 | (FY70) |
| 01271 | (FY70) |
| 01274 | (FY70) |
| 10935 | (FY68) |
| 10938 | (FY68) |
| 10943 | (FY68) |
| 10947 | (FY68) |
| 17681 | (FY64) |
| 18240 | (FY64) |
| 21819 | (FY62)* |
| 21822 | (FY62)* |
| 21828 | (FY62)* |
| 37814 | (FY63)* |
| 37885 | (FY63) |
| 40502 | (FY64) |
| 40527 | (FY64) |
| 40550 | (FY64) |
| 96566 | (FY69) |
| 96582 | (FY69) |
| 96583 | (FY69) |

**Lockheed EC-130H Hercules**
**SB:** 66ECW/43 ECS, Sembach

*FY73*
31583
31584
31585
31588
31594
31595

**Lockheed MC-130E Hercules**
39 SOW/7SOS Rhein Main

*FY64*
40523
40555
40566

**Boeing C.135B**
58 MAS, Ramstein
24125

# European based US Army Aircraft

**Bell AH-1S (FM) Cobra**
2-1 Avn, Ansbach
2-4 Avn, 3-4 Avn, Mainz
2-227 Avn, Hanau
3-1 Avn, Illesheim
3-3 Avn, 2-3 Avn, Giebelstadt
3-227 Avn, Hanau
4-7 Air Cavalry, Budingen
4-2nd Armoured Cavalry Regiment: Feucht
4-11th Armoured Cavalry Regiment: Fulda

*FY68*

| Serial | | |
|---|---|---|
| 15007 | 2-4 | Avn |
| 15015 | 3-3 | Avn |
| 15036 | 4-11 | ACR |
| 15038 | 2-1 | Avn |
| 15046 | 2-1 | Avn |
| 15057 | 3-1 | Avn |
| 15069 | 2-1 | Avn |
| 15084 | 2-227 | Avn |
| 15085 | 2 | ACR |
| 15092 | 2-227 | Avn |
| 15093 | 2-4 | Avn |
| 15104 | 2-4 | Avn |
| 15105 | 2 | ACR |
| 15106 | 2-3 | Avn |
| 15110 | 4-11 | ACR |
| 15112 | 3-1 | Avn |
| 15116 | 4-2 | ACR |
| 15131 | 3-4 | Avn |
| 15134 | 2-1 | Avn |
| 15152 | 2-1 | Avn |
| 15173 | 2-1 | Avn |
| 15180 | 4-11 | ACR |
| 15208 | 4-11 | ACR |

*FY66*

| Serial | | |
|---|---|---|
| 15249 | 2-227 | Avn |
| 15250 | 4-2 | ACR |
| 15252 | 11 | ACR |
| 15254 | 4-2 | ACR |
| 15261 | 4-2 | ACR |
| 15263 | 2-4 | Avn |
| 15264 | 2-3 | Avn |
| 15266 | 4-2 | ACR |
| 15275 | 3-227 | Avn |
| 15289 | 2-4 | Avn |
| 15290 | 4-2 | ACR |
| 15292 | 3-4 | Avn |
| 15293 | 1-1 | Avn |
| 15295 | 4-2 | ACR |
| 15315 | 2-227 | Avn |
| 15316 | 3-3 | Avn |
| 15321 | 3-4 | Avn |
| 15322 | 2-1 | Avn |
| 15325 | 4-11 | ACR |
| 15328 | 2-227 | Avn |
| 15335 | 4-11 | ACR |
| 15348 | 3-3 | Avn |
| 15350 | 3-3 | Avn |
| 15356 | 11 | ACR |

*FY67*

| Serial | | |
|---|---|---|
| 15450 | 4-2 | ACR |
| 15452 | 3-4 | Avn |
| 15455 | 2 | ACR |
| 15457 | 3-227 | Avn |
| 15460 | 2-4 | Avn |
| 15470 | 4-11 | ACR |
| 15475 | 4-11 | ACR |
| 15477 | 3-3 | Avn |
| 15479 | 2-3 | Avn |
| 15480 | 2-227 | Avn |
| 15489 | 3-4 | Avn |
| 15491 | 3-4 | Avn |
| 15497 | 4-2 | ACR |
| 15506 | 2-1 | Avn |
| 15507 | 4-11 | ACR |
| 15512 | 2-3 | Avn |
| 15520 | 1-1 | Avn |
| 15522 | 2-3 | Avn |
| 15528 | 2-3 | Avn |
| 15530 | 2-3 | Avn |
| 15535 | 3-3 | Avn |
| 15540 | 3-4 | Avn |
| 15548 | 2-3 | Avn |
| 15551 | 3-1 | Avn |
| 15565 | 3-3 | Avn |
| 15571 | 2-4 | Avn |
| 15572 | 4-11 | ACR |
| 15587 | 3-1 | Avn |
| 15593 | 4-11 | ACR |
| 15610 | 4-2 | ACR |
| 15613 | 3-4 | Avn |
| 15614 | 2-4 | Avn |
| 15617 | 2-227 | Avn |
| 15621 | 4-2 | ACR |
| 15633 | 3-1 | Avn |
| 15642 | 3-4 | Avn |
| 15643 | 4-2 | ACR |
| 15650 | 2-227 | Avn |

| Serial | |
|---|---|
| 5652 | 2-227 Avn |
| 5658 | 11 ACR |
| 5659 | 4-2 ACR |
| 5662 | 4-11 ACR |
| 15664 | 3-3 Avn |
| 5665 | 3-4 Avn |
| 5666 | 11 ACR |
| 5675 | 11 ACR |
| 5679 | 3-4 Avn |
| 5682 | 2-4 Avn |
| 5683 | 4-2 ACR |
| 15689 | 4-2 ACR |
| 15701 | 4-2 ACR |
| 15710 | 2-227 Avn |
| 15716 | 4-7 Cav |
| 15717 | 2-3 Avn |
| 15721 | 3-3 Avn |
| 15736 | 3-3 Avn |
| 15741 | 4-11 ACR |
| 15745 | 2-4 Avn |
| 15757 | 3-227 Avn |
| 15764 | 2-3 Avn |
| 15769 | 3-4 Avn |
| 15771 | 2-227 Avn |
| 15772 | 2-4 Avn |
| 15776 | 4-7 Cav |
| 15784 | 2-4 Avn |
| 15789 | 3-1 Avn |
| 15790 | 3-3 Avn |
| 15805 | 2-1 Avn |
| 15815 | 2-1 Avn |
| 15822 | 4-2 ACR |
| 15829 | 3-1 Avn |
| 15833 | 3-3 Avn |
| 15842 | 4-2 ACR |
| 15852 | 4-11 ACR |
| 15860 | 3-4 Avn |
| 15863 | 3-3 Avn |
| *FY70* | |
| 15947 | 3-4 Avn |
| 15950 | 4-2 ACR |
| 15951 | 4-7 Cav |
| 15952 | 4-11 ACR |
| 15958 | 11 ACR |
| 15959 | 3-4 Avn |
| 15961 | 3-4 Avn |
| 15970 | 2-3 Avn |
| 15971 | 3-3 Avn |
| 15995 | 4-2 ACR |
| 16012 | 3-3 Avn |
| 16016 | 3-3 Avn |
| 16048 | 3-3 Avn |
| 16091 | 2-1 Avn |
| *FY69* | |
| 16422 | 4-11 ACR |
| 16426 | 2 ACR |
| 16429 | 2-3 Avn |
| 16432 | 2-227 Avn |
| 16433 | 2-4 Avn |
| 16434 | 2-227 Avn |
| 16436 | 3-227 Avn |
| 16439 | 11 ACR |
| 16445 | 2-4 Avn |
| *FY68* | |
| 17023 | 4-7 Cav |
| 17028 | 2-227 Avn |
| 17047 | 4-11 ACR |
| 17049 | 2-4 Avn |
| 17062 | 4-7 Cav |
| 17063 | 2-227 Avn |

| Serial | |
|---|---|
| 17074 | 4-11 ACR |
| 17076 | 2-1 Avn |
| 17078 | 4-2 ACR |
| 17079 | 2-227 Avn |
| 17085 | 3-227 Avn |
| 17087 | 1-1 Avn |
| 17088 | 4-11 ACR |
| 17092 | 2-227 Avn |
| 17095 | 3-4 Avn |
| 17101 | 3-227 Avn |
| 17105 | 4-2 ACR |
| 17108 | 3-1 Avn |
| 17111 | 3-4 Avn |
| 17112 | 4-11 ACR |
| *FY71* | |
| 20998 | 4-11 ACR |
| 21003 | 4-2 ACR |
| 21014 | 3-227 Avn |
| 21033 | 4-2 ACR |
| 21035 | 4-2 ACR |
| *FY78* | |
| 23089 | 3-3 Avn |
| 23095 | 4-11 ACR |
| 23118 | 2-3 Avn |
| 23119 | 1-2 Cav |
| *FY79* | |
| 23189 | 2-3 Avn |
| 23190 | 2-3 Avn |
| 23194 | 2-3 Avn |
| 23199 | 3-3 Avn |
| 23200 | 3-3 Avn |
| 23235 | 3-3 Avn |
| *FY81* | |
| 23526 | 4-11 ACR |
| 23527 | 4-11 ACR |
| 23528 | 3-4 Avn |
| 23529 | 3-4 Avn |
| 23530 | 3-4 Avn |
| 23531 | 2-4 Avn |
| 23533 | 3-4 Avn |
| 23534 | 3-4 Avn |
| 23535 | 2-4 Avn |
| 23536 | 2-4 Avn |
| 23537 | 2-3 Avn |
| 23538 | 2-3 Avn |
| 23539 | 3-3 Avn |
| 23540 | 2-3 Avn |

**Grumman V-1 Mohawk**

†1MIB, Wiesbaden
‡2MIB, Stuttgart

| | | |
|---|---|---|
| 14244 | (FY64) | RV-1D‡ |
| 14246 | (FY64) | RV-1D‡ |
| 14247 | (FY64) | RV-1D‡ |
| 14258 | (FY64) | RV-1D† |
| 14262 | (FY64) | RV-1D† |
| 14267 | (FY64) | RV-1D† |
| 14273 | (FY64) | RV-1D† |
| 15943 | (FY68) | OV-1D† |
| 15950 | (FY68) | OV-1D‡ |
| 15953 | (FY68) | OV-1D‡ |
| 15956 | (FY68) | OV-1D‡ |
| 15957 | (FY68) | OV-1D† |
| 15962 | (FY68) | OV-1D‡ |
| 16993 | (FY68) | OV-1D† |
| 16996 | (FY68) | OV-1D‡ |
| 17004 | (FY69) | OV-1D‡ |
| 17008 | (FY69) | OV-1D‡ |
| 17021 | (FY69) | OV-1D† |
| 18900 | (FY67) | OV-1D† |
| 18905 | (FY67) | OV-1D† |
| 18908 | (FY67) | OV-1D‡ |
| 18909 | (FY67) | OV-1D† |
| 18910 | (FY67) | OV-1D† |
| 18919 | (FY67) | OV-1D† |
| 18925 | (FY67) | OV-1D† |
| 18927 | (FY67) | OV-1D† |
| 25876 | (FY62) | OV-1D‡ |
| 25891 | (FY62) | RV-1D‡ |
| 25897 | (FY62) | RV-1D† |
| 25902 | (FY62) | OV-1D‡ |
| 25919 | (FY62) | RV-1D† |

**Beech C-12 Super King Air ($=C-12C, *=C-12D, †=RC-12D, ‡=C-12F)**

25AvCo, Stuttgart;
HQ/USEUCOM;
3rd Btn, 58 AvRgt, Coleman Barracks
207AvCo Heidelberg
Corps of Engineers, Wiesbaden
V Corps, Wiesbaden
1MIB, Wiesbaden
2MIB/330 ASACo, Stuttgart

| | | |
|---|---|---|
| 22253$ | (FY73) | 25AvCo |
| 22254$ | (FY73) | VII Corps |
| 22255$ | (FY73) | 6 Avn Det |
| 22260$ | (FY73) | Corps of Eng's |
| 22261$ | (FY73) | VCorps |
| 22262$ | (FY73) | Berlin Bgde |
| 22549$ | (FY76) | HQ/USEUCOM |
| 22550$ | (FY76) | HQ/USEUCOM |
| 22556$ | (FY76) | 6 Avn Det |
| 22557$ | (FY76) | 207AvCo |
| 22564$ | (FY76) | 3-58 Avn |
| 22931$ | (FY77) | 6 Avn Det |
| 22932$ | (FY77) | 6 Avn Det |
| 22944$ | (FY77) | 3-58 Avn |
| 22950$ | (FY77) | 207AvCo |
| 23126$ | (FY78) | 207AvCo |
| 23127$ | (FY78) | 207AvCo |
| 23128$ | (FY78) | 207AvCo |
| 23141† | (FY78) | 1MIB |
| 23142† | (FY78) | 1MIB |
| 23143† | (FY78) | 1MIB |
| 23144† | (FY78) | 2MIB/330ASA Co |
| 23371† | (FY80) | 2MIB/330ASA Co |
| 23373† | (FY80) | 2MIB/330ASA Co |
| 23374† | (FY80) | 2MIB/330ASA Co |
| 23375† | (FY80) | 1MIB |
| 23376† | (FY80) | 2MIB/330ASA Co |
| 23377† | (FY80) | 1MIB |
| 23378† | (FY80) | 2MIB/330ASA Co |
| 23542† | (FY81) | 1MIB |
| 24380† | (FY84) | 207AvCo |

**Beech U-21A King Air**

| | | |
|---|---|---|
| 18000 | (FY66) | 3-58 Avn |
| 18010 | (FY66) | 3-58 Avn |
| 18013 | (FY66) | 3-58 Avn |
| 18014 | (FY66) | 3-58 Avn |
| 18021 | (FY66) | 3-58 Avn |
| 18027 | (FY66) | 3-58 Avn |

| Serial | | |
|---|---|---|
| 18030 | (FY66) | 3-58 Avn |
| 18049 | (FY67) | 3-58 Avn |
| 18058 | (FY67) | V Corps |
| 18078 | (FY67) | VII Corps |
| 18080 | (FY67) | 3-58 Avn |
| 18116 | (FY67) | 3-58 Avn |

**Boeing-Vertol CH-47D Chinook**

A Co, 5 Batt, 159 Av Reg't Schwabisch Hall
7-158 Avn Mainz-Finthen
'D' Co, 502 Avn Reg't, Coleman Barracks
'E' Co, 502 Avn Reg't Aviano

*FY86*

61671 7-158 Avn
61672 7-158 Avn
61673 7-158 Avn
61674 7-158 Avn
61675 7-158 Avn
61676 7-158 Avn
61677 7-158 Avn
61678 7-158 Avn

*FY87*

70071 7-158 Avn
70072 7-158 Avn
70073 7-158 Avn
70074 7-158 Avn
70075 7-158 Avn
70076 7-158 Avn
70077 7-158 Avn
70078 7-158 Avn
70079 5/159 ACo
70080 5/159 ACo
70081 5/159 ACo
70082 5/159 ACo
70083 5/159 ACo
70084 5/159 ACo
70085 5/159 ACo
70086 5/159 ACo
70087 5/159 ACo
70088 5/159 ACo
70089 5/159 ACo
70090 5/159 ACo
70091 5/159 ACo
70092 5/159 ACo
70093 5/159 ACo
70094 5/159 ACo
70096 502 DCo
70097 502 DCo
70098 502 DCo
70099 502 DCo
70100 502 DCo
70101 502 DCo
70102 502 DCo
70103 502 DCo
70104 502 DCo
70105 502 DCo
70106 502 DCo
70107 502 DCo
70109 502 DCo
70110 502 DCo
70111 502 DCo
70112 502 DCo

*FY88*

80098 502 ECo
80099 502 ECo
80100 502 ECo
80101 502 ECo
80102 502 ECo
80103 502 ECo
80104 502 ECo
80106 502 ECo

*FY89*

90138 502 ECo
90139 502 ECo
90140 502 ECo
90141 502 ECo
90142 502 ECo
90143 502 ECo
90144 502 ECo
90145 502 ECo

**Sikorsky UH-60A Black Hawk**

2nd Armored Cavalry Regiment, 4th Sqn, Feucht
4-11th Armored Cavalry Regiment, Fulda
'H' Co, 1st Avn Reg't, Hanau
'H' Co, 'I' Co, 3rd Avn Reg't, Giebelstadt, Ansbach
'H' Co, 'I' Co, 4th Avn Reg't, Mainz-Finthen/Wiesbaden, 3rd Btn, 58 Avn Reg't, Coleman Barracks
'B' Co, 6th Btn, 158 Avn Reg't, Wiesbaden, 8th Btn, 158 Avn Reg't, Hanau
'C' Co, 6th Btn, 159 Avn Reg't, Schwabisch Hall, 7th Btn, 159 Avn Reg't, Nellingen
'H' Co, 'I' Co, 227 Avn Reg't, Hanau, 2/6 Cavalry, Illesheim, 5/6 Cavalry, Wiesbaden
357th Avn Det/SHAPE, Chievres
207th Aviation Co: Heidelberg
15th Med Det (HA), Grafenwohr
45 Med Co, Nellingen
63rd Med Det (HA), Landstuhl
159th Med Det (HA), Lemwerder
236th Med Co (HA), Landstuhl
421st Medical Btn: Nellingen

*FY77*

22723 159 Med Det
22727 236 Med Co

*FY78*

22969 236 Med Co
22986 236 Med Co
22990 159 Med Det
22991 421 Med Btn
22995 236 Med Co
22996 45 Med Co
22997 45 Med Co
23000 159 Med Det
23001 63 Med Det
23003 159 Med Det
23271 236 Med Co

*FY80*

23425 3 HCo
23427 3 HCo
23428 3 HCo
23431 3 HCo
23432 3 HCo
23433 3 HCo
23434 236 Med Co
23436 3 HCo
23438 3 HCo
23439 3 HCo
23440 3 HCo
23442 3 HCo
23443 3 HCo
23444 3 HCo
23489 6/159 CCo
23490 3 HCo

*FY81*

23548 4-2 ACR
23551 45 Med Co
23568 8-158 Avn
23571 3 HCo
23572 6/158 BCo
23573 4-11 ACR
23575 6/158 BCo
23578 6/158 BCo
23579 421 Med Btn
23580 6/158 BCo
23581 227 HCo
23582 6/158 BCo
23583 227 HCo
23584 227 HCo
23586 227 HCo
23587 6/158 BCo
23589 6/158 BCo
23590 6/158 BCo
23591 6/158 BCo
23592 236 Med Co
23593 6/158 BCo
23594 1 HCo
23595 4-2 ACR
23596 236 Med Co
23597 6/158 BCo
23598 4-11 ACR
23599 6/158 BCo
23602 4-11 ACR
23603 227 HCo
23604 227 HCo
23605 227 HCo
23606 4-11 ACR
23607 4 HCo
23608 4-11 ACR
23609 227 HCo
23610 227 HCo
23613 1 HCo
23614 227 HCo
23615 227 HCo
23617 227 HCo
23618 227 HCo
23622 3 HCo
23623 8 ICo
23624 4 HCo
23625 4-11 ACR
23626 4 HCo

*FY82*

23660 4-2 ACR
23661 1 HCo
23662 1 HCo
23663 1 HCo
23664 1 HCo
23665 4-11 ACR
23666 4 HCo
23667 4 HCo
23668 4-11 ACR
23669 4 HCo
23672 6/159 CCo
23673 4-2 ACR
23675 421 Med Btn
23676 236 Med Co
23682 4 HCo
23683 4 HCo
23684 4 HCo

| Serial | |
|---|---|
| 23685 | 4 HCo |
| 23686 | 4 HCo |
| 23690 | 4-2 ACR |
| 23691 | 1 HCo |
| 23692 | 3 HCo |
| 23693 | 4-2 ACR |
| 23694 | 1 HCo |
| 23695 | 6/159 CCo |
| 23697 | 4-11 ACR |
| 23698 | 6/159 CCo |
| 23699 | 4-2 ACR |
| 23700 | 207 AvCo |
| 23701 | 207 AvCo |
| 23702 | 1 ICo |
| 23703 | 4-2 ACR |
| 23704 | 4-2 ACR |
| 23720 | 63 Med Det |
| 23721 | 6/159 CCo |
| 23722 | 6/159 CCo |
| 23723 | 421 Med Btn |
| 23726 | 236 Med Co |
| 23727 | 45 Med Co |
| 23729 | 236 Med Co |
| 23730 | 45 Med Co |
| 23731 | 45 Med Co |
| 23733 | 421 Med Btn |
| 23735 | 421 Med Btn |
| 23736 | 421 Med Btn |
| 23737 | 45 Med Co |
| 23738 | 45 Med Co |
| 23739 | 159 Med Co |
| 23740 | 421 Med Btn |
| 23741 | 63 Med Det |
| 23743 | 421 Med Btn |
| 23744 | 1 HCo |
| 23745 | 421 Med Btn |
| 23746 | 421 Med Btn |
| 23749 | 45 Med Co |
| 23750 | 45 Med Co |
| 23751 | 421 Med Btn |
| 23753 | 421 Med Btn |
| 23754 | 45 Med Co |
| 23755 | 421 Med Btn |
| 23756 | 421 Med Btn |
| 23761 | 3-58 Avn |
| 23855 | 6/159 CCo |
| *FY84* | |
| 24291 | 2/6 Cav |
| *FY85* | |
| 24418 | 3 HCo |
| *FY86* | |
| 24498 | 357 Avn Det |
| 24530 | 2/6 Cav |
| 24531 | 2/6 Cav |
| 24532 | 2/6 Cav |
| 24533 | |
| 24538 | 207 AvCo |
| 24550 | 421 Med Btn |
| 24551 | 236 Med Co |
| 24552 | 6/158 BCo |
| 24553 | 6/158 BCo |
| 24554 | 6/158 BCo |
| 24555 | 6/158 BCo |
| 24570 | 3 HCo |
| 24579 | 6/158 BCo |
| 24581 | 236 Med Co |
| 24583 | 357 Av Det |
| 24584 | 357 Av Det |
| 24621 | 3-1 Avn |

| Serial | |
|---|---|
| *FY87* | |
| 24642 | 4-2 ACR |
| 24643 | 4-2 ACR |
| 24644 | 4-2 ACR |
| 24645 | 4-2 ACR |
| 24646 | 4-2 ACR |
| 24647 | 4-2 ACR |
| 24656 | 4-2 ACR |
| 26000 | 4-2 ACR |
| 26001 | 4-2 ACR |
| 26002 | 4-2 ACR |
| 26003 | 4-2 ACR |
| 26004 | 4-2 ACR |
| *FY88* | |
| 26019 | 5/6 Cav |
| 26020 | 4-229 Avn |
| 26021 | 5/6 Cav |
| 26023 | 6/159 CCo |
| 26024 | 3-58 Avn |
| 26025 | 6/159 CCo |
| 26026 | 6/159 CCo |
| 26027 | 6/159 CCo |
| 26028 | 6/159 CCo |
| 26031 | 4-11 ACR |
| 26034 | 4-229 Avn |
| 26037 | 4-229 Avn |
| 26038 | 4-11 ACR |
| 26039 | 4-11 ACR |
| 26040 | 4-11 ACR |
| 26041 | 4-11 ACR |
| 26042 | 4-11 ACR |
| 26055 | |
| 26056 | 6/158 BCo |
| 26058 | |
| 26059 | 5/6 Cav |
| 26062 | 6/159 Avn |
| 26080 | 3-1 Avn |
| 26083 | 6/159 CCo |
| 26086 | 3-227 Avn |
| *FY89* | |
| 26145 | 3-227 Avn |
| 26146 | 3-227 Avn |
| 26151 | 2-1 Avn |
| 26153 | 3-1 Avn |
| 26164 | 2-1 Avn |
| 26165 | 2-1 Avn |

**McD AH-64A Apache**

2-1 Avn, Ansbach
3rd Btn, 1st Avn Reg't, Ansbach
2/6 Cav, Illesheim
5/6 Cav, Wiesbaden
2-227 Avn, 3-227 Avn, Hanau
4th Btn, 229 Avn Reg't, Illesheim

| Serial | |
|---|---|
| *FY84* | |
| 24218 | 2/6 Cav |
| 24257 | 2/6 Cav |
| 24258 | 2/6 Cav |
| 24260 | 2/6 Cav |
| 24262 | 2/6 Cav |
| 24263 | 2/6 Cav |
| 24266 | 2/6 Cav |
| 24290 | 2/6 Cav |
| 24291 | 2/6 Cav |
| 24292 | 2/6 Cav |
| 24293 | 2/6 Cav |
| 24294 | 5/6 Cav |
| 24295 | 2/6 Cav |
| 24296 | 2/6 Cav |
| 24297 | 2/6 Cav |
| 24298 | 2/6 Cav |
| 24299 | 2/6 Cav |
| 24302 | 2/6 Cav |
| 24303 | 2/6 Cav |
| 24304 | 2/6 Cav |
| *FY85* | |
| 25397 | 5/6 Cav |
| 25398 | 2/6 Cav |
| 25460 | 3-1 Avn |
| 25469 | 5/6 Cav |
| 25470 | 5/6 Cav |
| 25471 | 5/6 Cav |
| 25472 | 5/6 Cav |
| 25473 | 3-1 Avn |
| 25474 | 5/6 Cav |
| 25475 | 5/6 Cav |
| 25476 | 5/6 Cav |
| 25478 | 3-1 Cav |
| 25479 | 3-1 Cav |
| 25480 | 5/6 Cav |
| 25482 | 5/6 Cav |
| 25483 | 5/6 Cav |
| 25484 | 5/6 Cav |
| 25485 | 5/6 Cav |
| 25487 | 5/6 Cav |
| 25488 | 5/6 Cav |
| *FY86* | |
| 8940 | 4-229 Avn |
| 8941 | 4-229 Avn |
| 8942 | 4-229 Avn |
| 8943 | 4-229 Avn |
| 8946 | 4-229 Avn |
| 8947 | 4-229 Avn |
| 8948 | 4-229 Avn |
| 8949 | 4-229 Avn |
| 8950 | 4-229 Avn |
| 8951 | 4-229 Avn |
| 8952 | 4-229 Avn |
| 8953 | 4-229 Avn |
| 8954 | 4-229 Avn |
| 8955 | 4-229 Avn |
| 8956 | 3-1 Avn |
| 8957 | 4-229 Avn |
| 8958 | 3-1 Avn |
| 8959 | 4-229 Avn |
| 8960 | 4-229 Avn |
| 8961 | 4-229 Avn |
| 8970 | 3-227 Avn |
| 8981 | 5/6 Cav |
| 8983 | 5/6 Cav |
| 9010 | 2-1 Avn |
| 9011 | 2-1 Avn |
| 9026 | 2-227 Avn |
| 9029 | 2-227 Avn |
| 9030 | 3-1 Avn |
| 9032 | 2-1 Avn |
| 9039 | 3-1 Avn |
| 9044 | 3-1 Avn |
| 9045 | 2-227 Avn |
| 9048 | 2-1 Avn |
| 9058 | 2-1 Avn |
| *FY87* | |
| 408 | 3-1 Avn |
| 409 | 3-1 Avn |
| 412 | 2-1 Avn |
| 413 | 3-1 Avn |
| 417 | 2-1 Avn |
| 419 | 2-1 Avn |
| 420 | 3-1 Avn |
| 423 | 3-1 Avn |
| 428 | 3-1 Avn |

## US Army (EUR based)

| Serial | |
|---|---|
| 432 | 2-1 Avn |
| 433 | 3-227 Avn |
| 434 | 3-227 Avn |
| 436 | 3-1 Avn |
| 437 | 2-1 Avn |
| 438 | 3-227 Avn |
| 439 | 3-1 Avn |
| 440 | 3-227 Avn |
| 441 | 3-227 Avn |
| 442 | 3-1 Avn |
| 443 | 3-227 Avn |
| 444 | 3-227 Avn |
| 445 | 3-227 Avn |
| 446 | 3-227 Avn |
| 447 | 3-227 Avn |
| 449 | 3-227 Avn |
| 450 | 3-227 Avn |
| 451 | 3-227 Avn |
| 452 | 2-1 Avn |
| 454 | 3-227 Avn |
| 455 | 3-227 Avn |
| 457 | 3-227 Avn |
| 458 | 2-1 Avn |
| 459 | 2-1 Avn |
| 464 | 2-1 Avn |
| 470 | 2-1 Avn |
| 473 | 2-1 Avn |
| 474 | 2-1 Avn |
| 476 | 2-1 Avn |
| 477 | 2-1 Avn |
| 478 | 2-1 Avn |
| 479 | 2-1 Avn |
| 481 | 2-1 Avn |
| 482 | 2-1 Avn |
| 496 | 2-227 Avn |
| 503 | 2-227 Avn |
| 505 | 2-227 Avn |
| 506 | 2-227 Avn |
| 507 | 2-227 Avn |
| 510 | 2-227 Avn |
| *FY88* | |
| 197 | 2-227 Avn |
| 198 | 2-227 Avn |
| 213 | |
| 215 | |

# European based US Navy Aircraft

*Serial*

**Grumman C-2A Greyhound**
(VR-24 Sigonella)
162143 [JM23]
162144 [JM24]
162145 [JM25]
162153 [JM21]
162158 [JM27]
162159 [JM22]
163172 [JM26]
162176 [JM20]

**Lockheed †P-3A/EP-3E/ VP-3A‡*/UP-3A Orion**
(VQ-2: Rota)
148888 [JQ-23]
149668 [JQ-21]
149677 [JQ-20]*
150494 [JQ-25]
150495 NAF Keflavik*
150496 CinCLANT‡
150505 [JQ-24]
150511 HQ USMC‡
150515 CinCAFSE‡
151368 [JQ-27]†

**Beech UC-12M Super King Air**
**8C:** NAF Sigonella†
**8D:** NAF Rota*
3838 (163838)†
3839 (163839)*
3841 (163841)†
3842 (163842)*
3844 (163844)†

**NA CT-39G Sabreliner**
(VR-24 Sigonella)
159361 [31]
159362 [32]
159363 [33]

**Lockheed C-130F/KC-130F*/ TC-130Q‡ Hercules**
(VR-22: Rota)
148892 [JL 05]*
148895 [JL 06]*
149790 [JL00]
149794 [JL01]
149797 [JL02]
149801 [JL03]
150687 [JL04]*
159348 [JL04]‡

# US based USAF Aircraft

The following aircraft are normally based in the USA but are likely to be seen visiting the UK from time to time. The types are in numerical order, commencing with the B-**1B** and concluding with the C-**141**. The aircraft are listed in numerical progression by the serial actually carried externally. Fiscal year information is provided, together with details of mark variations and in some cases operating units.

*Serial Wing*

**Rockwell B-1B Lancer**
28 BW Ellsworth AFB, South Dakota
96 BW Dyess AFB, Texas
319 BW Grand Forks AFB, North Dakota
384 BW McConnell AFB, Kansas
AFFTC Air Force Flight Test Center, Edwards AFB, California

| Serial | Wing |
|---|---|
| *FY83* | |
| 30065 | 96 BW |
| 30066 | 96 BW |
| 30067 | 96 BW |
| 30068 | 96 BW |
| 30069 | 96 BW |
| 30070 | 96 BW |
| 30071 | 96 BW |
| *FY84* | |
| 40049 | 6512TS [ED] |
| 40050 | 96 BW |
| 40051 | 96 BW |
| 40053 | 96 BW |
| 40054 | 96 BW |
| 40055 | 96 BW |
| 40056 | 96 BW |
| 40057 | 96 BW |
| 40058 | 96 BW |
| *FY85* | |
| 50059 | 96 BW |
| 50060 | 96 BW |
| 50061 | 96 BW |
| 50062 | 96 BW |
| 50064 | 28 BW |
| 50065 | 96 BW |
| 50066 | 96 BW |
| 50067 | 96 BW |
| 50068 | 6512TS [ED] |
| 50069 | 96 BW |
| 50070 | 96 BW |
| 50071 | 96 BW |
| 50072 | 96 BW |
| 50073 | 96 BW |
| 50074 | 96 BW |
| 50075 | 96 BW |
| 50077 | 96 BW |
| 50078 | 28 BW |

| erial | Wing |
|---|---|
| 079 | 28 BW |
| 080 | 28 BW |
| 081 | 28 BW |
| 082 | 28 BW |
| 083 | 28 BW |
| 084 | 28 BW |
| 085 | 28 BW |
| 086 | 28 BW |
| 087 | 28 BW |
| 088 | 28 BW |
| 089 | 28 BW |
| 0090 | 28 BW |
| 0091 | 28 BW |
| 0092 | 28 BW |
| *Y86* | |
| 0093 | 28 BW |
| 0094 | 28 BW |
| 0095 | 28 BW |
| 0096 | 28 BW |
| 0097 | 28 BW |
| 0098 | 28 BW |
| 0099 | 28 BW |
| 0100 | 28 BW |
| 0101 | 28 BW |
| 0102 | 28 BW |
| 0103 | 28 BW |
| 0104 | 28 BW |
| 0105 | 28 BW |
| 0106 | 28 BW |
| 0107 | 28 BW |
| 0108 | 319 BW |
| 0109 | 28 BW |
| 0110 | 319 BW |
| 0111 | 319 BW |
| 0112 | 319 BW |
| 0113 | 319 BW |
| 0114 | 319 BW |
| 0115 | 319 BW |
| 0116 | 319 BW |
| 0117 | 319 BW |
| 0118 | 319 BW |
| 0119 | 319 BW |
| 0120 | 319 BW |
| 0121 | 319 BW |
| 0122 | 319 BW |
| 0123 | 319 BW |
| 0124 | 384 BW |
| 0125 | 384 BW |
| 0126 | 384 BW |
| 0127 | 384 BW |
| 0128 | 384 BW |
| 0129 | 384 BW |
| 0130 | 384 BW |
| 0131 | 384 BW |
| 0132 | 96 BW |
| 0133 | 384 BW |
| 0134 | 384 BW |
| 0135 | 384 BW |
| 0136 | 384 BW |
| 0137 | 384 BW |
| 0138 | 384 BW |
| 0139 | 384 BW |
| 0140 | 384 BW |

### oeing E-3 Sentry

52 AW&CW
963 AW&CS (bk)
964 AW&CS(r)
965 AW&CS(y)
966 AW&CS(TS) (bl)
inker AFB, Oklahoma

| Serial | Wing | |
|---|---|---|
| *FY80* | | |
| 00137 | E-3C | y |
| 00138 | E-3C | y |
| 00139 | E-3C | y |
| *FY81* | | |
| 10004 | E-3C | y |
| 10005 | E-3C | y |
| *FY71* | | |
| 11407 | E-3B | bl |
| 11408 | E-3B | r |
| *FY82* | | |
| 20006 | E-3C | r |
| 20007 | E-3C | y |
| *FY83* | | |
| 30008 | E-3C | bk |
| 30009 | E-3C | r |
| *FY73* | | |
| 31674 | JE-3C | Boeing |
| 31675 | E-3B | r |
| *FY75* | | |
| 50556 | E-3B | r |
| 50557 | E-3B | bk |
| 50558 | E-3B | r |
| 50559 | E-3B | r |
| 50560 | E-3B | r |
| *FY76* | | |
| 61604 | E-3B | y |
| 61605 | E-3B | r |
| 61606 | E-3B | r |
| 61607 | E-3C | y |
| *FY77* | | |
| 70351 | E-3B | bk |
| 70352 | E-3B | m |
| 70353 | E-3B | bl |
| 70354 | E-3B | bk |
| 70355 | E-3B | bk |
| 70356 | E-3B | y |
| *FY78* | | |
| 80576 | E-3B | bk |
| 80577 | E-3C | r |
| 80578 | E-3B | bk |
| *FY79* | | |
| 90001 | E-3B | bl |
| 90002 | E-3C | r |
| 90003 | E-3B | r |

### Boeing E-4B

1ACCS/55SRW
Offutt AFB, Nebraska

| | |
|---|---|
| 31676 | (FY73) |
| 31677 | (FY73) |
| 40787 | (FY74) |
| 50125 | (FY75) |

### Lockheed C-5 Galaxy

(*ANG, Air National Guard
†AFRES, Air Force Reserve)
60 MAW: Travis AFB, California
137 MAS/105 MAG*: Stewart AFB, New York
433 MAW/68 MAS†: Kelly AFB, Texas
436 MAW: Dover AFB, Delaware
439 MAW/337 MAS†: Westover AFB, Massachusetts
443 MAW: Altus AFB, Oklahoma
459 MAW: Andrews AFB, Maryland

| Serial | Wing |
|---|---|
| **C-5A Galaxy** | |
| *FY70* | |
| 00445 | 433 MAW† |
| 00446 | 433 MAW† |
| 00447 | 439 MAW† |
| 00448 | 439 MAW† |
| 00449 | 60 MAW |
| 00450 | 60 MAW |
| 00451 | 60 MAW |
| 00452 | 436 MAW |
| 00453 | 436 MAW |
| 00454 | 436 MAW |
| 00455 | 436 MAW |
| 00456 | 436 MAW |
| 00457 | 60 MAW |
| 00458 | 436 MAW |
| 00459 | 60 MAW |
| 00460 | 436 MAW |
| 00461 | 60 MAW |
| 00462 | 60 MAW |
| 00463 | 436 MAW |
| 00464 | 436 MAW |
| 00465 | 436 MAW |
| 00466 | 436 MAW |
| 00467 | 436 MAW |
| *FY66* | |
| 68304 | 439 MAW† |
| 68305 | 433 MAW† |
| 68306 | 433 MAW† |
| 68307 | 433 MAW† |
| *FY67* | |
| 70167 | 60 MAW |
| 70168 | 433 MAW† |
| 70169 | 137 MAS* |
| 70170 | 137 MAS* |
| 70171 | 433 MAW† |
| 70173 | 436 MAW |
| 70174 | 137 MAS* |
| *FY68* | |
| 80211 | 439 MAW† |
| 80212 | 137 MAS* |
| 80213 | 60 MAW |
| 80214 | 436 MAW |
| 80215 | 439 MAW† |
| 80216 | 433 MAW† |
| 80217 | 436 MAW |
| 80219 | 439 MAW† |
| 80220 | 433 MAW† |
| 80221 | 433 MAW† |
| 80222 | 439 MAW† |
| 80223 | 433 MAW† |
| 80224 | 137 MAS* |
| 80225 | 439 MAW† |
| 80226 | 137 MAS* |
| *FY69* | |
| 90001 | 60 MAW |
| 90002 | 433 MAW† |
| 90003 | 439 MAW† |
| 90004 | 433 MAW† |
| 90005 | 439 MAW† |
| 90006 | 433 MAW† |
| 90007 | 60 MAW |
| 90008 | 137 MAS* |
| 90009 | 137 MAS* |
| 90010 | 60 MAW |
| 90011 | 439 MAW† |
| 90012 | 137 MAS* |
| 90013 | 439 MAW† |
| 90014 | 443 MAW |

## USAF (US based)

| Serial | Wing |
|---|---|
| 90015 | 137 MAS* |
| 90016 | 433 MAW† |
| 90017 | 439 MAW† |
| 90018 | 60 MAW |
| 90019 | 439 MAW† |
| 90020 | 439 MAW† |
| 90021 | 137 MAS* |
| 90022 | 439 MAW† |
| 90023 | 60 MAW |
| 90024 | 60 MAW |
| 90025 | 60 MAW |
| 90026 | 436 MAW |
| 90027 | 436 MAW |

**C-5B Galaxy**

| Serial | Wing |
|---|---|
| *FY83* | |
| 31285 | 436 MAW |
| *FY84* | |
| 40059 | 436 MAW |
| 40060 | 60 MAW |
| 40061 | 436 MAW |
| 40062 | 60 MAW |
| *FY85* | |
| 50001 | 436 MAW |
| 50002 | 60 MAW |
| 50003 | 436 MAW |
| 50004 | 60 MAW |
| 50005 | 436 MAW |
| 50006 | 60 MAW |
| 50007 | 436 MAW |
| 50008 | 60 MAW |
| 50009 | 436 MAW |
| 50010 | 60 MAW |
| *FY86* | |
| 60011 | 436 MAW |
| 60012 | 60 MAW |
| 60013 | 436 MAW |
| 60014 | 60 MAW |
| 60015 | 436 MAW |
| 60016 | 60 MAW |
| 60017 | 436 MAW |
| 60018 | 60 MAW |
| 60019 | 436 MAW |
| 60020 | 60 MAW |
| 60021 | 443 MAW |
| 60022 | 443 MAW |
| 60023 | 443 MAW |
| 60024 | 443 MAW |
| 60025 | 443 MAW |
| 60026 | 443 MAW |
| *FY87* | |
| 70027 | 443 MAW |
| 70028 | 60 MAW |
| 70029 | 436 MAW |
| 70030 | 60 MAW |
| 70031 | 436 MAW |
| 70032 | 60 MAW |
| 70033 | 436 MAW |
| 70034 | 60 MAW |
| 70035 | 436 MAW |
| 70036 | 60 MAW |
| 70037 | 436 MAW |
| 70038 | 60 MAW |
| 70039 | 436 MAW |
| 70040 | 60 MAW |
| 70041 | 436 MAW |
| 70042 | 60 MAW |
| 70043 | 436 MAW |
| 70044 | 60 MAW |
| 70045 | 436 MAW |

**Boeing E-8A†/YE-8B‡**

*FY86*
60416 (N770JS)
60417 (N8411)

*FY88*
80322

**McDonnell-Douglas KC-10A Extender**
*2 BW, Barksdale AFB, California
†22 ARW, March AFB, California
‡68 ARW, Seymour-Johnson AFB, North Carolina

*FY82*
20191 †
20192 ‡
20193 †

*FY83*
30075 *
30076 †
30077 ‡
30078 †
30079 *
30080 †
30081 *
30082 *

*FY84*
40185 †
40186 *
40187 †
40188 *
40189 †
40190 *
40191 †
40192 *

*FY85*
50027 †
50028 *
50029 ‡
50030 ‡
50031 ‡
50032 *
50033 *
50034 *

*FY86*
60027 *
60028 ‡
60029 ‡
60030 ‡
60031 ‡
60032 ‡
60033 ‡
60034 ‡
60035 ‡
60036 ‡
60037 ‡
60038 ‡

*FY87*
70117 †
70118 †
70119 †
70120 †
70121 ‡
70122 ‡
70123 ‡
70124 ‡

*FY79*
90433 *
90434 *
91710 *
91711 *
91712 *
91713 *
91946 †
91947 †
91948 †
91949 †
91950 †
91951 †

**Boeing C-18A/EC-18B*/C-18B†/EC-18D‡**
(Air Force Systems Command)
Wright-Patterson AFB, Ohio

| Serial | Wing |
|---|---|
| *FY81* | |
| 10891* | 4950 TW |
| 10892* | 4950 TW |
| 10893‡ | 4950 TW |
| 10894* | 4950 TW |
| 10895‡ | 4950 TW |
| 10896* | 4950 TW |
| 10898 | 4950 TW |

**Grumman C-20B/*C20C Gulfstream III**
89 MAW Andrews AFB

*FY85*
50049*
50050*

*FY86*
60200
60201
60202
60203
60204
60205
60206
60403*

**Boeing C-22A/C-22B*/C-22C†**
HQ ANG East, Andrews AFB
310 MAS, Howard AFB

| Serial | Wing |
|---|---|
| *FY83* | |
| 34610* | HQ ANG |
| 34612* | HQ ANG |
| 34615* | HQ ANG |
| 34616* | HQ ANG |
| 34618† | HQ ANG |
| *FY84* | |
| 40193 | 310 MAS |

**Boeing VC-25A**
89 MAW, Andrews AFB

*FY86*
28000

**British Aerospace C-29A**
375MAW
*FY88*
80269
80270
80271
80272
80273
80274

| erial | Wing |
|---|---|

**eing T-43A**
3 FTW, Mather AFB
ANG West, Buckley ANGB

*Y71*

| | |
|---|---|
| 402 | NT, 323 FTW |
| 404 | NT, 323 FTW |
| 405 | NT, 323 FTW |
| 406 | NT, 323 FTW |

*Y72*

| | |
|---|---|
| 282 | NT, 323 FTW |
| 284 | HQ ANG |
| 285 | NT, 323 FTW |
| 287 | HQ ANG |
| 288 | HQ ANG |

*Y73*

| | |
|---|---|
| 1149 | NT, 323 FTW |
| 1150 | NT, 323 FTW |
| 1151 | NT, 323 FTW |
| 1152 | NT, 323 FTW |
| 1153 | NT, 323 FTW |
| 1154 | HQ ANG |
| 1155 | NT, 323 FTW |
| 1156 | NT, 323 FTW |

**oeing B-52G**
**tratofortress**
BW Barksdale AFB, Louisiana
2 BW Loring AFB, Maine
3 BW Castle AFB, California
7 BW Eaker AFB, Arkansas
20 BW Mather AFB, California
79 BW Wurtsmith AFB, Michigan
16 BW Griffiss AFB, New York
512 TS (AFSC) Wright-Patterson AFB, Ohio

*FY57*

| Serial | Wing |
|---|---|
| 76469 | 320 BW |
| 76470 | 93 BW |
| 76471 | 2 BW |
| 76472 | 379 BW |
| 76473 | 2 BW |
| 76474 | 379 BW |
| 76475 | 2 BW |
| 76476 | 2 BW |
| 76477 | 93 BW |
| 76480 | 2 BW |
| 76483 | 93 BW |
| 76485 | 2 BW |
| 76486 | 93 BW |
| 76487 | 93 BW |
| 76488 | 320 BW |
| 76490 | 416 BW |
| 76491 | 2 BW |
| 76492 | 379 BW |
| 76495 | 320 BW |
| 76497 | 2 BW |
| 76498 | 416 BW |
| 76499 | 93 BW |
| 76501 | 416 BW |
| 76502 | 320 BW |
| 76503 | 2 BW |
| 76504 | 2 BW |
| 76505 | 93 BW |
| 76508 | 2 BW |
| 76509 | 2 BW |
| 76510 | 42 BW |
| 76511 | 93 BW |
| 76512 | 2 BW |
| 76514 | 93 BW |
| 76515 | 416 BW |
| 76516 | 416 BW |
| 76517 | 2 BW |
| 76518 | 2 BW |
| 76519 | 6512TS [ED] |
| 76520 | 2 BW |

*FY58*

| Serial | Wing |
|---|---|
| 80158 | 2 BW |
| 80159 | 379 BW |
| 80160 | 416 BW |
| 80162 | 97 BW |
| 80163 | 93 BW |
| 80164 | 416 BW |
| 80165 | 416 BW |
| 80166 | 93 BW |
| 80167 | 93 BW |
| 80168 | 379 BW |
| 80170 | 416 BW |
| 80171 | 2 BW |
| 80173 | 379 BW |
| 80175 | 379 BW |
| 80176 | 416 BW |
| 80177 | 2 BW |
| 80178 | 320 BW |
| 80179 | 93 BW |
| 80181 | 2 BW |
| 80182 | 379 BW |
| 80183 | 93 BW |
| 80184 | 2 BW |
| 80185 | 2 BW |
| 80191 | 93 BW |
| 80192 | 93 BW |
| 80193 | 416 BW |
| 80194 | 379 BW |
| 80195 | 42 BW |
| 80197 | 320 BW |
| 80199 | 93 BW |
| 80200 | 379 BW |
| 80202 | 2 BW |
| 80203 | 2 BW |
| 80204 | 379 BW |
| 80205 | 2 BW |
| 80206 | 93 BW |
| 80207 | 93 BW |
| 80210 | 2 BW |
| 80211 | 93 BW |
| 80212 | 2 BW |
| 80213 | 2 BW |
| 80214 | 2 BW |
| 80216 | 2 BW |
| 80217 | 379 BW |
| 80218 | 2 BW |
| 80220 | 93 BW |
| 80221 | 93 BW |
| 80222 | 2 BW |
| 80223 | 93 BW |
| 80225 | 2 BW |
| 80226 | 320 BW |
| 80227 | 379 BW |
| 80230 | 320 BW |
| 80231 | 416 BW |
| 80233 | 2 BW |
| 80234 | 320 BW |
| 80235 | 320 BW |
| 80236 | 97 BW |
| 80237 | 379 BW |
| 80238 | 2 BW |
| 80239 | 416 BW |
| 80240 | 42 BW |
| 80241 | 42 BW |
| 80242 | 2 BW |
| 80243 | 97 BW |
| 80244 | 93 BW |
| 80245 | 2 BW |
| 80247 | 379 BW |
| 80248 | 93 BW |
| 80249 | 379 BW |
| 80250 | 2 BW |
| 80252 | 2 BW |
| 80253 | 320 BW |
| 80254 | 93 BW |
| 80255 | 42 BW |
| 80257 | 2 BW |
| 80258 | 2 BW |

*FY59*

| Serial | Wing |
|---|---|
| 92564 | 2 BW |
| 92565 | 2 BW |
| 92566 | 416 BW |
| 92567 | 416 BW |
| 92568 | 416 BW |
| 92569 | 2 BW |
| 92570 | 2 BW |
| 92571 | BW |
| 92572 | 93 BW |
| 92573 | 42 BW |
| 92575 | 93 BW |
| 92577 | 93 BW |
| 92578 | 42 BW |
| 92579 | 379 BW |
| 92580 | 2 BW |
| 92581 | 416 BW |
| 92582 | 2 BW |
| 92583 | 416 BW |
| 92584 | 93 BW |
| 92585 | 42 BW |
| 92586 | NASA |
| 92588 | 2 BW |
| 92589 | 379 BW |
| 92590 | 2 BW |
| 92591 | 379 BW |
| 92593 | 320 BW |
| 92594 | 93 BW |
| 92595 | 42 BW |
| 92598 | 2 BW |
| 92599 | 2 BW |
| 92601 | 416 BW |
| 92602 | 416 BW |

**Lockheed C-130 Hercules**
**‡ — AC-130, $ — EC-130, £ — HC-130**
**• — LC-130, § — MC-130**
**‡ — WC-130**
* — ANG: Air National Guard
102 ARS New York ANG
105 TAS Tennessee ANG
109 TAS Minnesota ANG
115 TAS California ANG
129 ARS California ANG
130 TAS West Virginia ANG
135 TAS Maryland ANG
139 TAS New York ANG
142 TAS Delaware ANG
143 TAS Rhode Island ANG
144 TAS Alaska ANG
154 TAS Arkansas ANG
155 TAS Tennessee ANG
156 TAS North Carolina ANG
158 TAS Georgia ANG
164 TAS Ohio ANG
165 TAS Kentucky ANG
167 TAS West Virginia ANG

| Serial | Wing |
|---|---|

180 TAS Missouri ANG
181 TAS Texas ANG
183 TAS Mississippi ANG
185 TAS Oklahoma ANG
187 TAS Wyoming ANG
193 SOS Pennsylvania ANG
† — AFRES: Air Force Reserve
63 TAS, Selfridge, Michigan
64 TAS, Chicago O'Hare, Illinois
95 TAS, Milwaukee, Wisconsin
96 TAS, St Paui, Minnesota
301 ARS, Homestead, Florida
303 TAS, March, California
304 ARS, Portland, Oregon
305 ARS, Selfridge, Michigan
327 TAS, Willow Grove, Pennsylvania
328 TAS, Niagara Falls, New York
356 TAS, Rickenbacker, Ohio
357 TAS, Maxwell, Alabama
700 TAS, Dobbins, Georgia
711 SOS, Eglin, Florida
731 TAS, Peterson, Colorado
757 TAS, Youngston, Ohio
758 TAS, Pittsburgh, Pennsylvania
815 TAS, Keesler, Missouri

*FY60:* **C-130B**
00294 731 TAS†
00295 731 TAS†
00296 731 TAS†
00299 731 TAS†
00300 731 TAS†
00303 731 TAS†
00310 731 TAS†

*FY80:* **C-130H**
00320 158 TAS*
00321 158 TAS*
00322 158 TAS*
00323 158 TAS*
00324 158 TAS*
00325 158 TAS*
00326 158 TAS*
00332 158 TAS*

*FY70:* **C-130E**
01259 317 TAW
01260 435 TAW
01261 317 TAW
01262 317 TAW
01263 317 TAW
01264 435 TAW
01265 317 TAW
01266 317 TAW
01267 317 TAW
01268 317 TAW
01269 317 TAW
01270 317 TAW
01271 435 TAW
01272 317 TAW
01273 317 TAW
01274 435 TAW
01275 317 TAW
01276 317 TAW

*FY81:* **C-130H**
10626 700 TAS†
10627 700 TAS†
10628 700 TAS†
10629 700 TAS†
10630 700 TAS†
10631 700 TAS†

*FY68:* **C-130E**
10934 317 TAW
10935 435 TAW
10937 317 TAW
10938 435 TAW
10939 317 TAW
10940 317 TAW
10941 317 TAW
10942 317 TAW
10943 435 TAW
10947 435 TAW
10948 314 TAW
10949 314 TAW
80950 314 TAW

*FY61:* **C-130B**
10948 731 TAS†
10949 156 TAS*
10950 156 TAS*
10951 757 TAS†
10952 164 TAS*
10954 303 TAS† [S]
10956 303 TAS†
10957 303 TAS†
10958 303 TAS†
10959 731 TAS†
10960 303 TAS†
10961 164 TAS*
10962 156 TAS*
10963 164 TAS*
10964 165 TAS*
10966 187 TAS*
10967 303 TAS†
10968 303 TAS† [2]
10969 303 TAS†
10971 757 TAS†

*FY61:* **C-130E**
12358 115 TAS*
12359 115 TAS*
12360‡ 53 WRS
12361 314 TAW
12362 314 TAW
12363 314 TAW
12364 314 TAW
12365‡ 815 TAS†
12366‡ 815 TAS†
12367 115 TAS* [4]
12368 314 TAW
12369 314 TAW
12370 115 TAS*
12371 314 TAW
12372 115 TAS*

*FY61:* **C-130B**
12634 165 TAS*
12635 187 TAS*
12636 156 TAS*
12638 156 TAS*
12639 TAS*
12640 156 TAS*
12643 187 TAS*
12645 107 TFS*
12647 303 TAS† [3]

*FY64:* **C-130H**
14852£ 301 ARS†
14854 463 TAW
14855£ 304 ARS†
14857£ 6514 TS
14858£
14859$ 41 ECS
14861‡ 815 TAS†
14862$ 41 ECS
14866 815 TAS†

*FY64:* **C-130P**
14853£ 305 ARS†
14856£ 304 ARS†
14860£ 304 ARS†
14863£ 301 ARS†
14864£ 304 ARS†
14865£ 304 ARS†

*FY64:* **C-130E**
17681 435 TAW
18240 435 TAW
47680 314 TAW

*FY82:* **C-130H**
20054 144 TAS*
20055 144 TAS*
20056 144 TAS*
20057 144 TAS*
20058 144 TAS*
20059 144 TAS*
20060 144 TAS*
20061 144 TAS*

*FY72:* **C-130E**
21288 21 TAS
21289 345 TAS
21290 21 TAS
21291 314 TAW
21292 314 TAW
21293 314 TAW
21294 314 TAW
21295 314 TAW
21296 314 TAW
21298 314 TAW
21299 345 TAS

*FY72:* **C-130H**
21302£

*FY62:* **C-130E**
21784 154 TAS*
21786 109 TAS*
21787 154 TAS*
21788 154 TAS*
21789 63 TAS†
21790 154 TAS*
21791$ 7 ACCS
21792 115 TAS*
21793 115 TAS*
21794 356 TAS†
21795 154 TAS*
21798 154 TAS*
21799 115 TAS*
21801 115 TAS*
21803 63 TAS†
21804 154 TAS*
21806 96 TAS†
21807 356 TAS†
21808 356 TAS†
21810 63 TAS†
21811 115 TAS*
21812 109 TAS*
21816 63 TAS†
21817 109 TAS*
21818$ 7 ACCS
21819 7405 OS
21820 356 TAS†
21821 314 TAW
21822 7405 OS
21823 63 TAS†
21824 154 TAS*
21825$ 7 ACCS [KS]

| Serial | Wing |
|---|---|
| 21826 | 115 TAS* |
| 21827 | 314 TAW |
| 21828 | 7405 OS |
| 21829 | 109 TAS* |
| 21830 | 63 TAS† |
| 21832$ | 7 ACCS [KS] |
| 21833 | 115 TAS* |
| 21834 | 96 TAS† |
| 21835 | 96 TAS† |
| 21836$ | 7 ACCS |
| 21837 | 109 TAS* |
| 21838 | 356 TAS† |
| 21839 | 96 TAS† |
| 21842 | 115 TAS* |
| 21843§ | 1 SOS |
| 21844 | 96 TAS† |
| 21846 | 109 TAS* |
| 21847 | 96 TAS† |
| 21848 | 96 TAS† |
| 21849 | 356 TAS† |
| 21850 | 356 TAS† |
| 21851 | 115 TAS* |
| 21852 | 96 TAS† |
| 21855§ | 8 SOS |
| 21856 | 109 TAS* |
| 21857$ | 7 ACCS |
| 21858 | 63 TAS† |
| 21859 | 167 TAS* |
| 21860 | 63 TAS† |
| 21862 | 115 TAS* |
| 21863$ | 7 ACCS [KS] |
| 21864 | 109 TAS* |
| 21866 | 356 TAS† |

*FY62:* **C-130B**

| Serial | Wing |
|---|---|
| 23487 | 757 TAS† |
| 23493 | 757 TAS† |
| 23495 | 188 TFS* |
| 23496 | 303 TAS† |

*FY83:* **C-130H**

| Serial | Wing |
|---|---|
| 30486 | 139 TAS* |
| 30487 | 139 TAS* |
| 30488 | 139 TAS* |
| 30489 | 139 TAS* |
| 30490• | 139 TAS* |
| 30491• | 139 TAS* |
| 30492• | 139 TAS* |
| 30493• | 139 TAS* |
| 31212§ | 6152 TS [ED] |

*FY73:* **C-130H**

| Serial | Wing |
|---|---|
| 31580$ | 41 ECS |
| 31581$ | |
| 31582 | 21 TAS |
| 31583$ | 43 ECS [SB] |
| 31584$ | 43 ECS [SB] |
| 31585$ | 43 ECS [SB] |
| 31586$ | 41 ECS |
| 31587$ | 41 ECS |
| 31588$ | 43 ECS [SB] |
| 31590$ | 41 ECS |
| 31592$ | 41 ECS |
| 31594$ | 43 ECS [SB] |
| 31595$ | 43 ECS [SB] |
| 31597 | 21 TAS |
| 31598 | 21 TAS |

*FY53:* **C-130A**

| Serial | Wing |
|---|---|
| 33129‡ | 711 SOS† |

*FY63:* **C-130E**

| Serial | Wing |
|---|---|
| 37764 | 328 TAS† |
| 37765 | 314 TAW |
| 37767 | 314 TAW |
| 37768 | 314 TAW |
| 37769 | 314 TAW |
| 37770 | 328 TAS† |
| 37771 | 314 TAW |
| 37773$ | 193 SOS* |
| 37776 | 314 TAW |
| 37777 | 167 TAS* |
| 37778 | 314 TAW |
| 37779 | 317 TAW |
| 37781 | 314 TAW |
| 37782 | 143 TAS* |
| 37783$ | 193 SOS* |
| 37784 | 314 TAW |
| 37785§ | 1 SOS |
| 37786 | 314 TAW |
| 37788 | 143 TAS* |
| 37790 | 314 TAW |
| 37791 | 314 TAW |
| 37792 | 167 TAS* |
| 37793 | 314 TAW |
| 37794 | 314 TAW |
| 37795 | 314 TAW |
| 37796 | 314 TAW |
| 37799 | 314 TAW |
| 37800 | 167 TAS* |
| 37803 | 345 TAS |
| 37804 | 345 TAS |
| 37805 | 328 TAS† |
| 37806 | 314 TAW |
| 37807 | 317 TAW |
| 37808 | 314 TAW |
| 37809 | 317 TAW |
| 37811 | 143 TAS* |
| 37812 | 167 TAS* |
| 37813 | 317 TAW |
| 37814 | 7405 OS |
| 37815 | 193 SOS* |
| 37816 | 193 SOS* |
| 37817 | 328 TAS† |
| 37818 | 167 TAS* |
| 37819 | 345 TAS |
| 37820 | 314 TAW |
| 37821 | 317 TAW |
| 37822 | 328 TAS† |
| 37823 | 317 TAW |
| 37824 | 143 TAS* |
| 37825 | 135 TAS* |
| 37826 | 327 TAS† |
| 37828 | 193 SOS* |
| 37829 | 317 TAW |
| 37830 | 314 TAW |
| 37831 | 314 TAW |
| 37832 | 327 TAS† |
| 37833 | 327 TAS† |
| 37834 | 327 TAS† |
| 37835 | 314 TAW |
| 37836 | 314 TAW |
| 37837 | 345 TAS |
| 37838 | 314 TAW |
| 37839 | 314 TAW |
| 37840 | 143 TAS* |
| 37841 | 314 TAW |
| 37842 | 62 MAW |
| 37845 | 317 TAW |
| 37846 | 317 TAW |
| 37847 | 154 TAS* |
| 37848 | 327 TAS† |
| 37849 | 317 TAW |
| 37850 | 314 TAW |
| 37851 | 167 TAS* |
| 37852 | 328 TAS† |
| 37853 | 356 TAS† |
| 37854 | 314 TAW |
| 37856 | 328 TAS† |
| 37857 | 314 TAW |
| 37858 | 167 TAS* |
| 37859 | 143 TAS* |
| 37860 | 314 TAW |
| 37861 | 314 TAW |
| 37863 | 328 TAS† |
| 37864 | 328 TAS† |
| 37865 | 345 TAS |
| 37866 | 314 TAW |
| 37867 | 327 TAS† |
| 37868 | 143 TAS* |
| 37869$ | 193 SOS* |
| 37871 | 317 TAW |
| 37872 | 167 TAS* |
| 37874 | 314 TAW |
| 37876 | 314 TAW |
| 37877 | 167 TAS* |
| 37879 | 21 TAS |
| 37880 | 314 TAW |
| 37881 | 167 TAS* |
| 37882 | 314 TAW |
| 37883 | 327 TAS† |
| 37884 | 317 TAW |
| 37885 | 435 TAW |
| 37887 | 314 TAW |
| 37888 | 314 TAW |
| 37889 | 143 TAS* |
| 37890 | 317 TAW |
| 37891 | 314 TAW |
| 37892 | 327 TAS† |
| 37893 | 314 TAW |
| 37894 | 314 TAW |
| 37895 | 135 TAS* |
| 37896 | 314 TAW |
| 37897 | 167 TAS* |
| 37898 | 314 TAW |
| 37899 | 317 TAW |
| 39810 | 317 TAW |
| 39811 | 314 TAW |
| 39812 | 314 TAW |
| 39813 | 314 TAW |
| 39814 | 314 TAW |
| 39815 | 314 TAW |
| 39816$ | 193 SOS* |
| 39817$ | 193 SOS* |

*FY84:* **C-130H**

| Serial | Wing |
|---|---|
| 40204 | 700 TAS† |
| 40205 | 700 TAS† |
| 40206 | 142 TAS* |
| 40207 | 142 TAS* |
| 40208 | 142 TAS* |
| 40209 | 142 TAS* |
| 40210 | 142 TAS* |
| 40211 | 142 TAS* |
| 40212 | 142 TAS* |
| 40213 | 142 TAS* |
| 40475§ | 6512 TS [ED] |
| 40476§ | 6512 TS [ED] |

*FY64:* **C-130E**

| Serial | Wing |
|---|---|
| 40495 | 317 TAW |
| 40496 | 317 TAW |
| 40497 | 21 TAS |
| 40498 | 317 TAW |
| 40499 | 317 TAW |
| 40500 [D4] | AFLC |
| 40501 | 317 TAW |
| 40502 | 435 TAW |
| 40503 | 345 TAS |

## USAF (US based)

| Serial | Wing |
|---|---|
| 40504 | 317 TAW |
| 40510 | 135 TAS* |
| 40512 | 154 TAS* |
| 40513 | 314 TAW |
| 40514 | 135 TAS* |
| 40515 | 135 TAS* |
| 40517 | 317 TAW |
| 40518 | 314 TAW |
| 40519 | 314 TAW |
| 40520 | 135 TAS* |
| 40521 | 135 TAS* |
| 40523§ | 7 SOS |
| 40524 | 62 MAW |
| 40525 | 317 TAW |
| 40526 | 115 TAS* |
| 40527 | 435 TAW |
| 40529 | 317 TAW |
| 40530 | 314 TAW |
| 40531 | 317 TAW |
| 40533 | 314 TAW |
| 40534 | 345 TAS |
| 40535 | 314 TAW |
| 40537 | 317 TAW |
| 40538 | 314 TAW |
| 40539 | 317 TAW |
| 40540 | 317 TAW |
| 40541 | 317 TAW |
| 40542 | 317 TAW |
| 40544 | 135 TAS* |
| 40550 | 435 TAW |
| 40551§ | 8 SOS |
| 40552‡ | 53 WRS |
| 40553‡ | 53 WRS |
| 40554‡ | 53 WRS |
| 40555§ | 7 SOS |
| 40556 | 345 TAS |
| 40557 | 314 TAW |
| 40559§ | 8 SOS |
| 40560 | 314 TAW |
| 40561§ | 8 SOS |
| 40562§ | 8 SOS |
| 40565§ | 1 SOS |
| 40566§ | 7 SOS |
| 40567§ | 8 SOS |
| 40568§ | 8 SOS |
| 40569 | 314 TAW |
| 40570 | 317 TAW |
| 40571§ | 1 SOS |
| 40572§ | 8 SOS |

*FY54:* **C-130A**

| Serial | Wing |
|---|---|
| 41623‡ | 711 SOS† |
| 41628‡ | 711 SOS† |
| 41630‡ | 711 SOS† |
| 41634 | 155 TAS* |
| 41635 | TAS* |
| 41637 | 155 TAS* |
| 41639 | |

*FY74:* **C-130H**

| Serial | Wing |
|---|---|
| 41658 | 17 TAS |
| 41659 | 17 TAS |
| 41660 | 463 TAW |
| 41661 | 463 TAW |
| 41662 | 463 TAW |
| 41663 | 463 TAW |
| 41664 | 463 TAW |
| 41665 | 463 TAW |
| 41666 | 463 TAW |
| 41667 | 463 TAW |
| 41668 | 17 TAS |
| 41669 | 463 TAW |
| 41670 | 463 TAW |
| 41671 | 463 TAW |
| 41673 | 463 TAW |
| 41674 | 463 TAW |
| 41675 | 463 TAW |
| 41676 | 463 TAW |
| 41677 | 463 TAW |
| 41679 | 463 TAW |
| 41680 | 463 TAW |
| 41681 | 463 TAW |
| 41682 | 463 TAW |
| 41684 | 463 TAW |
| 41685 | 463 TAW |
| 41687 | 463 TAW |
| 41688 | 463 TAW |
| 41689 | 463 TAW |
| 41690 | 463 TAW |
| 41691 | 463 TAW |
| 41692 | 17 TAS |
| 42061 | 463 TAW |
| 42062 | 17 TAS |
| 42063 | 463 TAW |
| 42065 | 463 TAW |
| 42066 | 17 TAS |
| 42067 | 463 TAW |
| 42069 | 463 TAW |
| 42070 | 17 TAS |
| 42071 | 17 TAS |
| 42072 | 463 TAW |
| 42130 | 463 TAW |
| 42131 | 17 TAS |
| 42132 | 463 TAW |
| 42133 | 345 TAS |
| 42134 | 463 TAW |

*FY55:* **C-130A**

| Serial | Wing |
|---|---|
| 50011‡ | 711 SOS‡ |
| 50014‡ | 711 SOS† |
| 50022 | 3246 TW |
| 50023 | |
| 50029‡ | 711 SOS† |
| 50035 | TAS† |
| 50046‡ | 711 SOS† |

*FY85:* **C-130H**

| Serial | Wing |
|---|---|
| 50011§ | 6512 TS [ED] |
| 50012§ | AFSC |
| 50035 | 357 TAS† |
| 50036 | 357 TAS† |
| 50037 | 357 TAS† |
| 50038 | 357 TAS† |
| 50039 | 357 TAS† |
| 50040 | 357 TAS† |
| 50041 | 357 TAS† |
| 50042 | 357 TAS† |

*FY65:* **C-130H**

| Serial | Wing |
|---|---|
| 50962$ | 41 ECS |
| 50963‡ | 53 WRS |
| 50964 | 815 TAS† |
| 50966‡ | 53 WRS |
| 50967 | 815 TAS† |
| 50968‡ | 53 WRS |
| 50969 | 815 TAS† |
| 50970£ | 305 ARS† |
| 50972 | 815 TAS† |
| 50973£ | 67 SOS |
| 50974£ | 102 ARS* |
| 50975£ | 1550 CCTW |
| 50976 | 815 TAS† |
| 50977 | 815 TAS† |
| 50978£ | 102 ARS* |
| 50979 | 6514 TS |
| 50980‡ | 53 WRS |
| 50981£ | 129 ARS* |
| 50982£ | 305 ARS |
| 50983£ | 129 ARS* |
| 50984‡ | 815 TAS† |
| 50985 | 815 TAS† |
| 50986£ | |
| 50989$ | 41 ECS [DM] |
| 50993£ | 9 SOS |

*FY65:* **C-130P**

| Serial | Wing |
|---|---|
| 50971£ | 950 S |
| 50988£ | 102 ARS* |
| 50991£ | 9 SOS |
| 50992£ | 33 ARRS |
| 50993£ | 9 SOS |
| 50994£ | |

*FY85:* **C-130H**

| Serial | Wing |
|---|---|
| 51361 | 181 TAS* |
| 51362 | 181 TAS* |
| 51363 | 181 TAS* |
| 51364 | 181 TAS* |
| 51365 | 181 TAS* |
| 51366 | 181 TAS* |
| 51367 | 181 TAS* |
| 51368 | 181 TAS* |

*FY66:* **C-130P**

| Serial | Wing |
|---|---|
| 60213£ | 55 SOS |
| 60215£ | 9 SOS |
| 60216£ | |
| 60217£ | 55 SOS |
| 60219£ | 1550 CCTW |
| 60220£ | 67 SOS |
| 60221£ | 129 ARS* |
| 60222£ | 102 ARS* |
| 60223£ | 67 SOS |
| 60224£ | 129 ARS* |
| 60225£ | 1550 CCTW |

*FY86:* **C-130H**

| Serial | Wing |
|---|---|
| 60410 | 758 TAS† |
| 60411 | 758 TAS† |
| 60412 | 758 TAS† |
| 60413 | 758 TAS† |
| 60414 | 758 TAS† |
| 60415 | 758 TAS† |
| 60418 | 758 TAS† |
| 60419 | 758 TAS† |

*FY56:* **C-130A**

| Serial | Wing |
|---|---|
| 60469‡ | 711 SOS† |
| 60485 | |
| 60494 | 155 TAS* |
| 60495 | 155 TAS* |
| 60498 | 155 TAS* |
| 60503 | 155 TAS* |
| 60509‡ | 711 SOS† |
| 60511 | |
| 60517 | TAS* |
| 60522 | 711 SOS† |
| 60524 | 155 TAS* |
| 60525 | TAS† |
| 60531 | |
| 60547 | 155 TAS* |
| 60550 | TAS* |

*FY86:* **C-130H**

| Serial | Wing |
|---|---|
| 61391 | 180 TAS* |
| 61392 | 180 TAS* |
| 61393 | 180 TAS* |
| 61394 | 180 TAS* |
| 61395 | 180 TAS* |
| 61396 | 180 TAS* |
| 61397 | 180 TAS* |

| Serial | Wing |
|---|---|
| 61398 | 180 TAS* |
| 61699§ | AFFTC |

*FY87:* **C-130H**

| Serial | Wing |
|---|---|
| 70023§ | 6512 TS [ED] |
| 70024§ | AFSC |
| 70125§ | |
| 70126§ | |
| 70127§ | 6512 TS |

*FY87:* **C-130U**

| Serial | Wing |
|---|---|
| 70128‡ | |

*FY57:* **C-130A**

| Serial | Wing |
|---|---|
| 70453 | 155 TAS* |
| 70461 | 6514 TS |
| 70463 | 155 TAS* |
| 70464 | TAS* |
| 70465 | 155 TAS* |
| 70469 | 711 SOS† |
| 70474 | TAS† |
| 70476 | TAS† |
| 70480 | TAS† |
| 70481 | TAS† |
| 70497 | TAS† |
| 70513 | |
| 70515 | TAS* |
| 70516 | TAS† |
| 70519 | TAS† |
| 70521 | TAS† |

*FY57:* **C-130B**

| Serial | Wing |
|---|---|
| 70525 | 165 TAS* |
| 70526 | 6514 TS |
| 70527 | 757 TAS† |
| 70528 | 165 TAS* |
| 70529 | 152 TFTS* |

*FY67:* **C-130H**

| Serial | Wing |
|---|---|
| 77183 | 310 MAS |
| 77184 | 310 MAS |

*FY87:* **C-130H**

| Serial | Wing |
|---|---|
| 79281 | 64 TAS† |
| 79282 | 64 TAS† |
| 79283 | 64 TAS† |
| 79284 | 64 TAS† |
| 79285 | 64 TAS† |
| 79286 | 64 TAS† |
| 79287 | 64 TAS† |
| 79288 | 64 TAS† |

*FY88:* **MC-130H**

| Serial | Wing |
|---|---|
| 80191 | |
| 80192 | |
| 80193 | |
| 80194 | |
| 80195 | |
| 80264 | |

*FY58:* **C-130B**

| Serial | Wing |
|---|---|
| 80711 | 187 TAS* |
| 80713 | 731 TAS† |
| 80714 | 187 TAS* |
| 80715 | 178 FIS* |
| 80716 | 6514 TS |
| 80720 | 187 TAS* |
| 80723 | 731 TAS† |
| 80725 | 165 TAS* |
| 80726 | 164 TAS* |
| 80727 | TAS* |
| 80728 | 156 TAS* |
| 80729 | 156 TAS* |
| 80731 | 164 TAS* |
| 80732 | 165 TAS* |
| 80733 | 164 TAS* |
| 80734 | 187 TAS* |
| 80736 | 164 TAS* |
| 80738 | 731 TAS† |
| 80740 | TAS* |
| 80741 | 165 TAS* |
| 80742 | 156 TAS* |
| 80744 | 187 TAS* [I] |
| 80746 | 156 TAS* |
| 80747 | 165 TAS* |
| 80749 | 164 TAS* |
| 80750 | 186 FIS* |
| 80751 | 156 TAS* |
| 80752 | 165 TAS* |
| 80753 | 165 TAS* |
| 80754 | 187 TAS* |
| 80755 | 187 TAS* |
| 80757 | 731 TAS† |
| 80758 | 176 TFS* |

*FY78:* **C-130H**

| Serial | Wing |
|---|---|
| 80806 | 185 TAS* |
| 80807 | 185 TAS* |
| 80808 | 185 TAS* |
| 80809 | 185 TAS* |
| 80810 | 185 TAS* |
| 80811 | 185 TAS* |
| 80812 | 185 TAS* |
| 80813 | 185 TAS* |

*FY88:* **C-130H**

| Serial | Wing |
|---|---|
| 81301 | 130 TAS* |
| 81302 | 130 TAS* |
| 81303 | 130 TAS* |
| 81304 | 130 TAS* |
| 81305 | 130 TAS* |
| 81306 | 130 TAS* |
| 81307 | 130 TAS* |
| 81308 | 130 TAS* |

*FY88:* **C-130U**

| Serial | Wing |
|---|---|
| 81803 | |

*FY88:* **C-130H**

| Serial | Wing |
|---|---|
| 84401 | 95 TAS† |
| 84402 | 95 TAS† |
| 84403 | 95 TAS† |
| 84404 | 95 TAS† |
| 84405 | 95 TAS† |
| 84406 | 95 TAS† |
| 84407 | 95 TAS† |
| 84408 | 95 TAS† |

*FY79:* **C-130H**

| Serial | Wing |
|---|---|
| 90473 | 144 TAS* |
| 90474 | 160 TFS* |
| 90475 | 159 FIS* |
| 90476 | 157 TFS* |
| 90477 | 158 TAS* |
| 90478 | 199 FIS* |
| 90479 | 185 TAS* |
| 90480 | 122 TFS* |

*FY89*

| Serial | Wing |
|---|---|
| 91051 | 105 TAS* |
| 91052 | 105 TAS* |
| 91053 | 105 TAS* |
| 91054 | 105 TAS* |
| 91055 | 105 TAS* |

*FY89*

| Serial | Wing |
|---|---|
| 91181 | 105 TAS* |
| 91182 | 105 TAS* |
| 91183 | 105 TAS* |
| 91184 | 105 TAS* |
| 91185 | 105 TAS* |
| 91186 | 105 TAS* |
| 91187 | 105 TAS* |
| 91188 | 105 TAS* |

*FY59:* **C-130B**

| Serial | Wing |
|---|---|
| 91524 | 757 TAS† |
| 91525 | 164 TAS* |
| 91526 | 731 TAS† |
| 91527 | 731 TAS† |
| 91528 | 156 TAS* |
| 91529 | 165 TAS* |
| 91530 | 731 TAS† |
| 91531 | 731 TAS† |
| 91532 | 757 TAS† |
| 91533 | 156 TAS* [8] |
| 91535 | 757 TAS† |
| 91536 | TAS* |
| 91537 | 731 TAS† |

*FY69:* **C-130N**

| Serial | Wing |
|---|---|
| 95819£ | 9 SOS |
| 95820£ | 67 SOS |
| 95821£ | |
| 95822£ | 33 ARRS |
| 95823£ | 67 SOS |
| 95824£ | 301 ARS† |
| 95825£ | |
| 95826£ | 67 SOS |
| 95827£ | 67 SOS |
| 95828£ | 9 SOS |
| 95829£ | 305 ARS† |
| 95830£ | 301 ARS† |
| 95831£ | 67 SOS |
| 95832£ | 9 SOS |
| 95833£ | 305 ARS† |

FY59: **C-130B**

| Serial | Wing |
|---|---|
| 95957 | 187 TAS* |

*FY69:* **C-130H**

| Serial | Wing |
|---|---|
| 96567‡ | 16 SOS |
| 96568‡ | 16 SOS |
| 96569‡ | 16 SOS |
| 96570‡ | 16 SOS |
| 96572‡ | 16 SOS |
| 96573‡ | 16 SOS |
| 96574‡ | 16 SOS |
| 96575‡ | 16 SOS |
| 96576‡ | 16 SOS |
| 96577‡ | 16 SOS |

*FY69:* **C-130E**

| Serial | Wing |
|---|---|
| 96566 | 435 TAW |
| 96579 | 314 TAW |
| 96580 | 317 TAW |
| 96582 | 435 TAW |
| 96583 | 435 TAW |

*FY89:* **C-130H**

| Serial | Wing |
|---|---|
| 99101 | 757 TAS† |
| 99102 | 757 TAS† |
| 99103 | 757 TAS† |
| 99104 | 757 TAS† |
| 99105 | 757 TAS† |
| 99106 | 757 TAS† |
| 99107 | 757 TAS† |
| 99108 | 757 TAS† |

**Boeing C-135 Stratotanker**

* Air National Guard:
- 108 ARS Illinois ANG
- 116 ARS Washington ANG
- 117 ARS Kansas ANG
- 126 ARS Wisconsin ANG

## USAF (US based)

132 ARS Maine ANG
133 ARS New Hampshire ANG
145 ARS Ohio ANG
147 ARS Pennsylvania ANG
150 ARS New Jersey ANG
151 ARS Tennessee ANG
168 ARS Alaska ANG
191 ARS Utah ANG
197 ARS Arizona ANG
† AFRES, Air Force Reserve:
72 ARS bl Grissom AFB, In
314 ARS r Mather AFB, Ca
336 ARS y March AFB, Ca

*FY60*

| Serial | Type | Wing |
|---|---|---|
| 00313 | KC-135R | 319 BW |
| 00314 | KC-135R | 42 BW |
| 00315 | KC-135A | 2 BW |
| 00316 | KC-135A | 2 BW |
| 00318 | KC-135A | 416 BW |
| 00319 | KC-135A | 379 BW |
| 00320 | KC-135A | 379 BW |
| 00321 | KC-135R | 28 BW |
| 00322 | KC-135R | 19 ARW |
| 00323 | KC-135A | 380 BW |
| 00324 | KC-135A | 7 BW |
| 00325 | KC-135A | 379 BW |
| 00326 | KC-135A | 379 BW |
| 00327 | KC-135A | 7 BW |
| 00328 | KC-135A | 7 BW |
| 00329 | KC-135R | 93 BW |
| 00331 | KC-135R | 301 ARW |
| 00332 | KC-135A | BW |
| 00333 | KC-135R | 305 ARW |
| 00334 | KC-135R | 305 ARW |
| 00335 | KC-135Q | 376 SW |
| 00336 | KC-135Q | 380 BW |
| 00337 | KC-135Q | 380 BW |
| 00339 | KC-135Q | 380 BW |
| 00341 | KC-135R | 340 ARW |
| 00342 | KC-135Q | 9 SRW |
| 00343 | KC-135Q | 380 BW |
| 00344 | KC-135Q | 9 SRW |
| 00345 | KC-135Q | 380 BW |
| 00346 | KC-135Q | 376 BW |
| 00347 | KC-135R | 384 BW |
| 00348 | KC-135A | 410 BW |
| 00349 | KC-135A | 410 BW |
| 00350 | KC-135A | 5 BW |
| 00351 | KC-135A | 96 BW |
| 00353 | KC-135R | 93 BW |
| 00355 | KC-135A | 379 BW |
| 00356 | KC-135R (RT) | 305 ARW |
| 00357 | KC-135A (RT) | 305 ARW |
| 00358 | KC-135A | 410 BW |
| 00359 | KC-135R | 19 ARW |
| 00360 | KC-135R | 301 ARW |
| 00362 | KC-135R (RT) | 305 ARW |
| 00363 | KC-135A | 379 BW |
| 00364 | KC-135R | 305 ARW |
| 00365 | KC-135R | 28 BW |
| 00366 | KC-135R | 301 ARW |
| 00367 | KC-135R | 28 BW |
| 00371 | NC-135A | 4950 TW |
| 00372 | NC-135E | 4950 TW |
| 00374 | EC-135E | 4950 TW |
| 00375 | C-135E | 4950 TW |
| 00376 | C-135E | 8 TDCS/ 1 SpWg/ CinC CC |
| 00377 | C-135A | 4950 TW |
| 00378 | C-135E | 55 SRW |

*FY61*

| Serial | Type | Wing |
|---|---|---|
| 10261 | EC-135L | 305 ARW |
| 10262 | EC-135A | 28 BW |
| 10263 | EC-135L | 305 ARW |
| 10264 | KC-135R | 19 ARW |
| 10266 | KC-135A | 97 BW |
| 10267 | KC-135R | 319 BW |
| 10268 | KC-135E | |
| 10269 | EC-135L | 305 ARW |
| 10270 | KC-135E | 72 ARS† |
| 10271 | KC-135A | 5 BW |
| 10272 | KC-135R | 93 BW |
| 10274 | EC-135H | 6 ACCS |
| 10275 | KC-135R | |
| 10276 | KC-135R | 384 BW |
| 10277 | KC-135R | 340 ARW |
| 10278 | EC-135A | 28 BW |
| 10279 | EC-135L | 305 ARW |
| 10280 | KC-135E | 336 ARS† |
| 10281 | KC-135A | 416 BW |
| 10282 | EC-135H | 10 ACCS |
| 10283 | EC-135L | 305 ARW |
| 10284 | KC-135A | |
| 10285 | EC-135H | 10 ACCS |
| 10286 | EC-135H | 10 ACCS |
| 10287 | EC-135A | 28 BW |
| 10288 | KC-135A | 93 BW |
| 10289 | EC-135A | 4 ACCS |
| 10290 | KC-135R | 319 BW |
| 10291 | EC-135H | 10 ACCS |
| 10292 | KC-135R | 384 BW |
| 10293 | KC-135R [RT] | 305 ARW |
| 10294 | KC-135R | 42 BW |
| 10295 | KC-135R | 340 ARW |
| 10297 | EC-135A | 28 BW |
| 10298 | KC-135R | 19 ARW |
| 10299 | KC-135R | 319 BW |
| 10300 | KC-135A | 22 ARW |
| 10302 | KC-135R | 416 BW |
| 10303 | KC-135E | 336 ARS† |
| 10304 | KC-135R | 384 BW |
| 10305 | KC-135R | 305 ARW |
| 10306 | KC-135R | 384 BW |
| 10307 | KC-135R | 19 ARW |
| 10308 | KC-135R | 384 BW |
| 10309 | KC-135R | 301 ARW |
| 10310 | KC-135R | 384 BW |
| 10311 | KC-135R | 340 ARW |
| 10312 | KC-135R | 384 BW |
| 10313 | KC-135R | 340 ARW |
| 10314 | KC-135R | 340 ARW |
| 10315 | KC-135R | 28 BW |
| 10317 | KC-135R | 319 BW |
| 10318 | KC-135R | 384 BW |
| 10320 | KC-135A | 96 BW |
| 10321 | KC-135A | 410 BW |
| 10323 | KC-135R | |
| 10324 | KC-135R | 384 BW |
| 10325 | KC-135A | 42 BW |
| 10326 | EC-135E | 4950 TW |
| 10327 | EC-135Y | CinC CC |
| 10329 | EC-135E | 4950 TW |
| 10330 | EC-135E | 4950 TW |
| | | |
| 12662 | RC-135S | 6 SRW |
| 12663 | RC-135S | 6 SRW |
| 12665 | WC-135B | 55 WRS |
| 12666 | WC-135B | 55 WRS |
| 12667 | WC-135B | 10 ACCS |
| 12668 | C-135C | 89 MAW |
| 12669 | C-135C | 4950 TW |
| 12670 | WC-135B | 55 WRS |
| 12671 | C-135C | 89 MAW |
| 12672 | WC-135B | 55 WRS |
| 12673 | WC-135B | 55 WRS |
| 12674 | WC-135B | 55 WRS |

*FY64*

| Serial | Type | Wing |
|---|---|---|
| 14828 | KC-135R | 305 ARW |
| 14829 | KC-135A | 42 BW |
| 14830 | KC-135A | 5 BW |
| 14831 | KC-135A | 5 BW |
| 14832 | KC-135R | 340 ARW |
| 14833 | KC-135A | 97 BW |
| (44833) | | |
| 14834 | KC-135A | 97 BW |
| 14835 | KC-135R | 416 BW |
| 14836 | KC-135A | 2 BW |
| 14837 | KC-135A | 379 BW |
| 14838 | KC-135A | 93 BW |
| 14839 | KC-135R | |
| 14840 | KC-135A | 380 BW |
| 14841 | RC-135V | 55 SRW |
| 14842 | RC-135V | 55 SRW |
| 14843 | RC-135V | 55 SRW |
| 14844 | RC-135V | 55 SRW |
| 14845 | RC-135V | 55 SRW |
| 14846 | RC-135V | 55 SRW |
| 14847 | RC-135U | 55 SRW |
| 14848 | RC-135V | 55 SRW |
| 14849 | RC-135U | 55 SRW |

*FY62*

| Serial | Type | Wing |
|---|---|---|
| 23497 | KC-135A | 93 BW |
| 23498 | KC-135A | 97 BW |
| 23499 | KC-135R | 19 ARW |
| 23500 | KC-135R | 340 ARW |
| 23501 | KC-135A | 5 BW |
| 23502 | KC-135A | 93 BW |
| 23503 | KC-135A | 509 BW |
| 23504 | KC-135R | 93 BW |
| 23505 | KC-135A | 509 BW |
| 23506 | KC-135R | 19 ARW |
| 23507 | KC-135R | 340 ARW |
| 23508 | KC-135R | 340 ARW |
| 23509 | KC-135A | 7 BW |
| 23510 | KC-135R | 340 ARW |
| 23511 | KC-135R | 384 BW |
| 23512 | KC-135A | 379 BW |
| 23513 | KC-135R | 305 ARW |
| 23514 | KC-135R | 305 ARW |
| 23515 | KC-135R | 305 ARW |
| 23516 | KC-135R | 305 ARW |
| 23517 | KC-135A | 7 BW |
| 23518 | KC-135A | 379 BW |
| 23519 | KC-135R | 319 BW |
| 23520 | KC-135A | 379 BW |
| 23521 | KC-135A | 416 BW |
| 23523 | KC-135R | 19 ARW |
| 23524 | KC-135A | 380 BW |
| 23525 | KC-135A | 5 BW |
| 23526 | KC-135A | 2 BW |
| 23527 | KC-135A | 410 BW |
| 23528 | KC-135A | 93 BW |
| 23529 | KC-135A | 509 BW |
| 23530 | KC-135R | 19 ARW |
| 23531 | KC-135R | 340 ARW |
| 23532 | KC-135A | 509 BW |
| 23533 | KC-135R | 384 BW |
| 23534 | KC-135R | 19 ARW |
| 23537 | KC-135R | 301 ARW |
| 23538 | KC-135A | 509 BW |
| 23539 | KC-135A | 96 BW |
| 23540 | KC-135R | 28 BW |
| 23541 | KC-135R | 305 ARW |

| Serial | Type | Wing |
|---|---|---|
| 23542 | KC-135R | 301 ARW |
| 23543 | KC-135R | 19 ARW |
| 23544 | KC-135A | 2 BW |
| 23545 | KC-135R | 19 ARW |
| 23546 | KC-135R | 301 ARW |
| 23547 | KC-135R | 340 ARW |
| 23548 | KC-135R | 305 ARW |
| 23549 | KC-135R | 301 ARW |
| 23550 | KC-135R | 19 ARW |
| 23551 | KC-135A | 93 BW |
| 23552 | KC-135R | 19 ARW |
| 23553 | KC-135R | 319 BW |
| 23554 | KC-135R | 19 ARW |
| 23555 | KC-135A | 410 BW |
| 23556 | KC-135R | 340 ARW |
| 23557 | KC-135R | 19 ARW |
| 23558 | KC-135A | 380 BW |
| 23559 | KC-135A | 93 BW |
| 23560 | KC-135A | 93 BW |
| 23561 | KC-135R | 340 ARW |
| 23562 | KC-135A | 410 BW |
| 23563 | KC-135A | 93 BW |
| 23564 | KC-135R | 28 BW |
| 23565 | KC-135R | 319 BW |
| 23566 | KC-135A | |
| 23567 | KC-135A | 2 BW |
| 23568 | KC-135R | 340 ARW |
| 23569 | KC-135R | 19 ARW |
| 23570 | EC-135G | 4 ACCS |
| 23571 | KC-135R | 305 ARW |
| 23572 | KC-135A | 416 BW |
| 23573 | KC-135R | 93 BW |
| 23574 | KC-135A | 410 BW |
| 23575 | KC-135R | 305 ARW |
| 23576 | KC-135A | 2 BW |
| 23577 | KC-135R | 93 BW |
| 23578 | KC-135A | 5 BW |
| 23579 | EC-135G | 4 ACCS |
| 23580 | KC-135A | 380 BW |
| 23581 | EC-135C | 55 SRW |
| 23582 | EC-135C | 4 ACCS |
| 23583 | EC-135C | 55 SRW |
| 23584 | EC-135J | 9 ACCS |
| 23585 | EC-135C | 55 SRW |
| 24125 | C-135B | 58 MAS |
| 24126 | C-135B | 89 MAW |
| 24127 | C-135B | 89 MAW |
| 24128 | RC-135X | 6 SRW |
| 24129 | TC-135W | 55 SRW |
| 24130 | C-135B | 89 MAW |
| 24131 | RC-135W | 55 SRW |
| 24132 | RC-135W | 55 SRW |
| 24133 | TC-135S | 6 SRW |
| 24134 | RC-135W | 55 SRW |
| 24135 | RC-135W | 55 SRW |
| 24138 | RC-135W | 55 SRW |
| 24139 | RC-135W | 55 SRW |
| 26000 | C-137C | 89 MAW |
| *FY72* | | |
| 27000 | C-137C | 89 MAW |
| *FY63* | | |
| 37976 | KC-135R | 319 BW |
| 37977 | KC-135R | 19 ARW |
| 37978 | KC-135R | 305 ARW |
| 37979 | KC-135R | 340 ARW |
| 37980 | KC-135R | 305 ARW |
| 37981 | KC-135R | 340 ARW |
| 37982 | KC-135A | 2 BW |
| 37984 | KC-135R | 340 ARW |
| 37985 | KC-135R | 305 ARW |
| 37986 | KC-135A | 97 BW |
| 37987 | KC-135A | 410 BW |
| 37988 | KC-135A | 509 BW |
| 37991 | KC-135R | 28 BW |
| 37992 | KC-135R | 416 BW |
| 37993 | KC-135R | 340 ARW |
| 37994 | EC-135G | 4 ACCS |
| 37995 | KC-135R | 19 ARW |
| 37996 | KC-135R | 305 ARW |
| 37997 | KC-135R | 384 BW |
| 37998 | KC-135A | 380 BW |
| 37999 | KC-135R | 319 BW |
| 38000 | KC-135A | 92 BW |
| 38001 | EC-135G | 305 ARW |
| 38002 | KC-135R | 19 ARW |
| 38003 | KC-135R | 93 BW |
| 38004 | KC-135R | |
| 38005 | KC-135A | 2 BW |
| 38006 | KC-135R | 319 BW |
| 38007 | KC-135A | 379 BW |
| 38008 | KC-135R | 19 ARW |
| 38009 | KC-135R | 93 BW |
| 38010 | KC-135A | 93 BW |
| 38011 | KC-135R | 42 BW |
| 38012 | KC-135A | 97 BW |
| 38013 | KC-135A | 379 BW |
| 38014 | KC-135A | |
| 38015 | KC-135R | 42 BW |
| 38016 | KC-135A | 93 BW |
| 38017 | KC-135A | 93 BW |
| 38018 | KC-135A | 410 BW |
| 38019 | KC-135A | 22 ARW |
| 38020 | KC-135R | 19 ARW |
| 38021 | KC-135R | 305 ARW |
| 38022 | KC-135A | 93 BW |
| 38023 | KC-135R | 305 ARW |
| 38024 | KC-135R | 93 BW |
| 38025 | KC-135R | 306 SW |
| 38026 | KC-135R | 384 BW |
| 38027 | KC-135A | 42 BW |
| 38028 | KC-135R | 305 ARW |
| 38029 | KC-135A | 380 BW |
| 38030 | KC-135R | 319 BW |
| 38031 | KC-135A | 7 BW |
| 38032 | KC-135R | 28 BW |
| 38033 | KC-135R | 305 ARW |
| 38034 | KC-135A | 5 BW |
| 38035 | KC-135A | 379 BW |
| 38036 | KC-135R | 19 ARW |
| 38037 | KC-135R | 305 ARW |
| 38038 | KC-135R | 93 BW |
| 38039 | KC-135R | 301 ARW |
| 38040 | KC-135R | 340 ARW |
| 38041 | KC-135R | 301 ARW |
| 38043 | KC-135A | 96 BW |
| 38044 | KC-135A | 93 BW |
| 38045 | KC-135A | 93 BW |
| 38046 | EC-135C | 55 SRW |
| 38047 | EC-135C | 4 ACCS |
| 38048 | EC-135C | 55 SRW |
| 38049 | EC-135C | 55 SRW |
| 38050 | EC-135C | 55 SRW |
| 38051 | EC-135C | 4 ACCS |
| 38052 | EC-135C | 55 SRW |
| 38053 | EC-135C | 55 SRW |
| 38054 | EC-135C | 55 SRW |
| 38055 | EC-135J | 9 ACCS |
| 38056 | EC-135J | 9 ACCS |
| 38057 | EC-135J | 9 ACCS |
| 38058 | KC-135D | 305 ARW |
| 38059 | KC-135D | 305 ARW |
| 38060 | KC-135D | 305 ARW |
| 38061 | KC-135D | 305 ARW |
| 38871 | KC-135R | 305 ARW |
| 38872 | KC-135R | 42 BW |
| 38873 | KC-135A | 7 BW |
| 38874 | KC-135A | 93 BW |
| 38875 | KC-135A | 7 BW |
| 38876 | KC-135A | 7 BW |
| 38877 | KC-135A | 5 BW |
| 38878 | KC-135A | |
| 38879 | KC-135A | 93 BW |
| 38880 | KC-135R | 93 BW |
| 38881 | KC-135A | 380 BW |
| 38883 | KC-135R | 305 ARW |
| 38884 | KC-135R | 301 ARW |
| 38885 | KC-135A | 410 BW |
| 38886 | KC-135R | 416 BW |
| 38887 | KC-135A | |
| 38888 | KC-135A | 93 BW |
| 39792 | RC-135V | 55 SRW |
| *FY55* | | |
| 53118 | EC-135K | 8 TDCS |
| 53119 | NKC-135E | 555 RW |
| 53120 | NKC-135E | 4950 TW |
| 53122 | NKC-135A | 4950 TW |
| 53124 | NKC-135A | 4950 TW |
| 53125 | EC-135Y | CinC CC |
| 53127 | NKC-135A | 4950 TW |
| 53128 | NKC-135A | 6512 TS |
| 53129 | EC-135P | 6 ACCS |
| 53130 | KC-135A | 7 BW |
| 53131 | NKC-135A | 4950 TW |
| 53132 | NKC-135A | 4950 TW |
| 53134 | NKC-135A | USN/FEWSG |
| 53135 | NKC-135E | 4950 TW |
| 53136 | KC-135A | 2 BW |
| 53137 | KC-135A | 2 BW |
| 53139 | KC-135A | 92 BW |
| 53141 | KC-135E | 116 ARS* |
| 53142 | KC-135A | 93 BW |
| 53143 | KC-135E | 197 ARS* |
| 53145 | KC-135E | 314 ARS† |
| 53146 | KC-135E | 145 ARS* |
| *FY85* | | |
| 56973 | C-137C | 89 MAW |
| 56974 | C-137C | 89 MAW |
| *FY56* | | |
| 63591 | KC-135A | 380 BW |
| 63592 | KC-135A | 305 ARW |
| 63593 | KC-135E | 133 ARS* |
| 63594 | KC-135A | 5 BW |
| 63595 | KC-135A | 92 BW |
| 63596 | NKC-135A | USN/FEWSG |
| 63600 | KC-135A | 2 BW |
| 63601 | KC-135A | 93 BW |
| 63603 | KC-135A | 2 BW |
| 63604 | KC-135E | 117 ARS* |
| 63606 | KC-135E | 132 ARS* |
| 63607 | KC-135E | 151 ARS* |
| 63608 | KC-135A | 93 BW |
| 63609 | KC-135E | 151 ARS* |
| 63610 | KC-135A | 92 BW |
| 63611 | KC-135E | 145 ARS* |
| 63612 | KC-135E | 126 ARS* |
| 63614 | KC-135A | 410 BW |
| 63615 | KC-135A | 7 BW |
| 63616 | KC-135A | 96 BW |
| 63617 | KC-135A | 42 BW |
| 63619 | KC-135A | 410 BW |
| 63620 | KC-135A | 93 BW |

## USAF (US based)

| Serial | Type | Wing |
|---|---|---|
| 63621 | KC-135A | 7 BW |
| 63622 | KC-135E | 132 ARS* |
| 63623 | KC-135E | 336 ARS† |
| 63624 | KC-135A | 42 BW |
| 63625 | KC-135A | 97 BW |
| 63626 | KC-135E | 133 ARS* |
| 63627 | KC-135A | 2 BW |
| 63630 | KC-135E | 126 ARS* |
| 63631 | KC-135E | 117 ARS* |
| 63632 | KC-135A | 380 BW |
| 63633 | KC-135A | 379 BW |
| 63634 | KC-135A | 379 BW |
| 63635 | KC-135A | 96 BW |
| 63636 | KC-135A | 2 BW |
| 63637 | KC-135A | 410 BW |
| 63638 | KC-135E | 197 ARS* |
| 63639 | KC-135R | 96 BW |
| 63640 | KC-135E | 132 ARS* |
| 63641 | KC-135E | 117 ARS* |
| 63642 | KC-135A | 92 BW |
| 63643 | KC-135E | 151 ARS* |
| 63644 | KC-135A | 416 BW |
| 63645 | KC-135A | 92 BW |
| 63646 | KC-135A | 92 BW |
| 63647 | KC-135A | 410 BW |
| 63648 | KC-135E | 145 ARS* |
| 63649 | KC-135A | 2 BW |
| 63650 | KC-135E | 133 ARS* |
| 63651 | KC-135A | 92 BW |
| 63652 | KC-135A | 416 BW |
| 63653 | KC-135A | 93 BW |
| 63654 | KC-135E | 132 ARS* |
| 63656 | KC-135A | 7 BW |
| 63658 | KC-135E | 117 ARS* |
| *FY57* | | |
| 71418 | KC-135A | 96 BW |
| 71419 | KC-135A | 410 BW |
| 71420 | KC-135A | 7 BW |
| 71421 | KC-135E | 116 ARS* |
| 71422 | KC-135E | 72 ARS† |
| 71423 | KC-135A | 92 BW |
| 71425 | KC-135E | 151 ARS* |
| 71426 | KC-135E | 108 ARS* |
| 71427 | KC-135R | 319 BW |
| 71428 | KC-135E | 133 ARS* |
| 71429 | KC-135E | 117 ARS* |
| 71430 | KC-135A | 92 BW |
| 71431 | KC-135E | 126 ARS* |
| 71432 | KC-135A | 92 BW |
| 71433 | KC-135E | 197 ARS* |
| 71434 | KC-135E | 116 ARS* |
| 71435 | KC-135A | 92 BW |
| 71436 | KC-135E | 133 ARS* |
| 71437 | KC-135A | 97 BW |
| 71438 | KC-135E | 72 ARS† |
| 71439 | KC-135A | 92 BW |
| 71440 | KC-135R | 319 BW |
| 71441 | KC-135E | 108 ARS* |
| 71443 | KC-135E | 132 ARS* |
| 71445 | KC-135E | 145 ARS* |
| 71447 | KC-135A | 416 BW |
| 71448 | KC-135E | 168 ARS* |
| 71450 | KC-135E | 132 ARS* |
| 71451 | KC-135A | 2 BW |
| 71452 | KC-135E | 197 ARS* |
| 71453 | KC-135A | 7 BW |
| 71454 | KC-135R | 42 BW |
| 71455 | KC-135E | 151 ARS* |
| 71456 | KC-135A | 509 BW |
| 71458 | KC-135E | 108 ARS* |
| 71459 | KC-135A | 410 BW |
| 71460 | KC-135E | 117 ARS* |
| 71461 | KC-135A | 2 BW |
| 71462 | KC-135R | 28 BW |
| 71463 | KC-135E | 117 ARS* |
| 71464 | KC-135E | 145 ARS* |
| 71465 | KC-135E | 168 ARS* |
| 71467 | KC-135A | 2 BW |
| 71468 | KC-135E | 336 ARS† |
| 71469 | KC-135R | 42 BW |
| 71470 | KC-135A | 7 BW |
| 71471 | KC-135E | 132 ARS* |
| 71472 | KC-135R | 42 BW |
| 71473 | KC-135R | 384 BW |
| 71474 | KC-135A | 5 BW |
| 71475 | KC-135E | 197 ARS* |
| 71476 | KC-135A | 380 BW |
| 71477 | KC-135A | |
| 71478 | KC-135E | 151 ARS* |
| 71479 | KC-135E | 336 ARS† |
| 71480 | KC-135E | 108 ARS* |
| 71482 | KC-135E | 117 ARS* |
| 71483 | KC-135R | 340 ARW |
| 71484 | KC-135E | 197 ARS* |
| 71485 | KC-135E | 151 ARS* |
| 71486 | KC-135A | 93 BW |
| 71487 | KC-135R | 305 ARW |
| 71488 | KC-135R | 416 BW |
| 71490 | KC-135A | 7 BW |
| 71491 | KC-135E | 132 ARS* |
| 71492 | KC-135E | 151 ARS* |
| 71493 | KC-135A | 7 BW |
| 71494 | KC-135E | 168 ARS* |
| 71495 | KC-135E | 197 ARS* |
| 71496 | KC-135E | 197 ARS* |
| 71497 | KC-135A | 92 BW |
| 71499 | KC-135A | 380 BW |
| 71501 | KC-135E | 116 ARS* |
| 71502 | KC-135R | 319 BW |
| 71503 | KC-135E | 151 ARS* |
| 71504 | KC-135E | 72 ARS† |
| 71505 | KC-135E | 132 ARS* |
| 71506 | KC-135A | 42 BW |
| 71507 | KC-135E | 145 ARS* |
| 71508 | KC-135R | 96 BW |
| 71509 | KC-135E | 147 ARS* |
| 71510 | KC-135E | 191 ARS* |
| 71511 | KC-135E | 314 ARS† |
| 71512 | KC-135E | 336 ARS† |
| 71514 | KC-135A | 376 SW |
| 72589 | KC-135E | 55 SRW |
| 72590 | KC-135A | 5 BW |
| 72591 | KC-135A | 410 BW |
| 72592 | KC-135A | 5 BW |
| 72593 | KC-135A | 96 BW |
| 72594 | KC-135E | 108 ARS* |
| 72595 | KC-135E | 147 ARS* |
| 72596 | KC-135A | 5 BW |
| 72597 | KC-135A | 92 BW |
| 72598 | KC-135E | 336 ARS† |
| 72599 | KC-135A | 509 BW |
| 72600 | KC-135E | 116 ARS* |
| 72601 | KC-135A | 97 BW |
| 72602 | KC-135A | 7 BW |
| 72603 | KC-135E | 336 ARS† |
| 72604 | KC-135E | 126 ARS* |
| 72605 | KC-135A | 97 BW |
| 72606 | KC-135E | 150 ARS* |
| 72607 | KC-135E | 147 ARS* |
| 72608 | KC-135E | 147 ARS* |
| 72609 | KC-135A | 379 BW |
| *FY58* | | |
| 80001 | KC-135A | 7 BW |
| 80003 | KC-135E | 108 ARS* |
| 80004 | KC-135R | 301 ARW |
| 80005 | KC-135E | 117 ARS* |
| 80006 | KC-135E | 191 ARS* |
| 80008 | KC-135E | 145 ARS* |
| 80009 | KC-135A | 5 BW |
| 80010 | KC-135A | 5 BW |
| 80011 | KC-135R (RT) | 305 ARW |
| 80012 | KC-135E | 191 ARS* |
| 80013 | KC-135E | 72 ARS† |
| 80014 | KC-135E | 108 ARS* |
| 80015 | KC-135A | 380 BW |
| 80016 | KC-135A | 92 BW |
| 80017 | KC-135E | 145 ARS* |
| 80018 | KC-135R (RT) | 305 ARW |
| 80019 | EC-135P | 6 ACCS |
| 80020 | KC-135E | 116 ARS* |
| 80021 | KC-135A | 93 BW |
| 80022 | EC-135P | 6 ACCS |
| 80023 | KC-135A | 380 BW |
| 80024 | KC-135E | 126 ARS* |
| 80025 | KC-135A | 7 BW |
| 80027 | KC-135R | 416 BW |
| 80028 | KC-135A | 410 BW |
| 80029 | KC-135A | 97 BW |
| 80030 | KC-135A | 42 BW |
| 80032 | KC-135E | 150 ARS* |
| 80033 | KC-135A | 92 BW |
| 80034 | KC-135A | 410 BW |
| 80035 | KC-135R | |
| 80036 | KC-135A | 96 BW |
| 80037 | KC-135E | 147 ARS* |
| 80038 | KC-135A | 379 BW |
| 80040 | KC-135E | 150 ARS* |
| 80041 | KC-135E | 72 ARS† |
| 80042 | KC-135Q | 380 BW |
| 80043 | KC-135E | 191 ARS* |
| 80044 | KC-135A | 92 BW |
| 80045 | KC-135Q | 380 BW |
| 80046 | KC-135Q | 9 SRW |
| 80047 | KC-135Q | 380 BW |
| 80049 | KC-135Q | 380 BW |
| 80050 | KC-135Q | 380 BW |
| 80051 | KC-135R | 301 ARW |
| 80052 | KC-135E | 336 ARS† |
| 80053 | KC-135E | 314 ARS† |
| 80054 | KC-135Q | 9 SRW |
| 80055 | KC-135Q | 9 SRW |
| 80056 | KC-135A | 93 BW |
| 80057 | KC-135E | 108 ARS* |
| 80058 | KC-135E | 314 ARS† |
| 80059 | KC-135R | |
| 80060 | KC-135Q | 9 SRW |
| 80061 | KC-135Q | 380 BW |
| 80062 | KC-135Q | 380 BW |
| 80063 | KC-135A | 380 BW |
| 80064 | KC-135E | 314 ARS† |
| 80065 | KC-135Q | 380 BW |
| 80066 | KC-135A | 2 BW |
| 80067 | KC-135E | 108 ARS* |
| 80068 | KC-135E | 108 ARS* |
| 80069 | KC-135Q | 380 BW |
| 80070 | KC-135A | 410 BW |
| 80071 | KC-135Q | 9 SRW |
| 80072 | KC-135Q | 9 SRW |
| 80073 | KC-135R | 416 BW |
| 80074 | KC-135Q | 9 SRW |
| 80075 | KC-135A | 92 BW |
| 80076 | KC-135A | 96 BW |
| 80077 | KC-135Q | 9 SRW |

| Serial | Type | Wing |
|---|---|---|
| 80078 | KC-135E | 150 ARS* |
| 80079 | KC-135R | 416 BW |
| 80080 | KC-135E | 191 ARS* |
| 80081 | KC-135A | 2 BW |
| 80082 | KC-135E | 116 ARS* |
| 80083 | KC-135A | 509 BW |
| 80084 | KC-135Q | 9 SRW |
| 80085 | KC-135E | 336 ARS† |
| 80086 | KC-135Q | 9 SRW |
| 80087 | KC-135E | 150 ARS* |
| 80088 | KC-135Q | 9 SRW |
| 80089 | KC-135Q | 9 SRW |
| 80090 | KC-135E | 314 ARS† |
| 80091 | KC-135A | 5 BW |
| 80092 | KC-135A | 379 BW |
| 80093 | KC-135R | |
| 80094 | KC-135Q | 9 SRW |
| 80095 | KC-135Q | 376 SW |
| 80096 | KC-135E | 314 ARS† |
| 80097 | KC-135A | 7 BW |
| 80098 | KC-135R | 19 ARW |
| 80099 | KC-135Q | 9 SRW |
| 80100 | KC-135R | |
| 80102 | KC-135A | 96 BW |
| 80103 | KC-135Q | 9 SRW |
| 80104 | KC-135R | 416 BW |
| 80105 | KC-135A | 92 BW |
| 80106 | KC-135A | 380 BW |
| 80107 | KC-135E | 191 ARS* |
| 80108 | KC-135E | 314 ARS† |
| 80109 | KC-135A | 96 BW |
| 80110 | KC-135A | 410 BW |
| 80111 | KC-135E | 126 ARS* |
| 80112 | KC-135Q | 9 SRW |
| 80113 | KC-135A | 96 BW |
| 80114 | KC-135A | 96 BW |
| 80115 | KC-135E | 150 ARS* |
| 80116 | KC-135A | 96 BW |
| 80117 | KC-135Q | 9 SRW |
| 80118 | KC-135A | 509 BW |
| 80119 | KC-135A | 5 BW |
| 80120 | KC-135R | 319 BW |
| 80121 | KC-135A | 42 BW |
| 80122 | KC-135A | 92 BW |
| 80123 | KC-135A | 379 BW |
| 80124 | KC-135R (RT) | 305 ARW |
| 80125 | KC-135Q | 9 SRW |
| 80126 | KC-135A (RT) | 305 ARW |
| 80128 | KC-135A | 5 BW |
| 80129 | KC-135Q | 9 SRW |
| 80130 | KC-135A | 509 BW |
| 86970 | VC-137B | 89 MAW |
| 86971 | VC-137B | 89 MAW |
| 86972 | VC-137B | 89 MAW |
| *FY59* | | |
| 91444 | KC-135A | 92 BW |
| 91445 | KC-135E | 116 ARS* |
| 91446 | KC-135R | 28 BW |
| 91447 | KC-135E | 72 ARS† |
| 91448 | KC-135E | 133 ARS* |
| 91449 | KC-135A | 7 BW |
| 91450 | KC-135E | 133 ARS* |
| 91451 | KC-135E | 72 ARS† |
| 91452 | KC-135E | 116 ARS* |
| 91453 | KC-135R | 319 BW |
| 91454 | KC-135A | 410 BW |
| 91455 | KC-135R | 28 BW |
| 91456 | KC-135E | 126 ARS* |
| 91457 | KC-135E | 147 ARS* |
| 91458 | KC-135R | 340 ARW |
| 91459 | KC-135R | 28 BW |
| 91460 | KC-135Q | 9 SRW |
| 91461 | KC-135A | 92 BW |
| 91462 | KC-135Q | 380 BW |
| 91463 | KC-135R | 92 BW |
| 91464 | KC-135Q | 380 BW |
| 91466 | KC-135R | 319 BW |
| 91467 | KC-135Q | 380 BW |
| 91468 | KC-135Q | 9 SRW |
| 91469 | KC-135A | 380 BW |
| 91470 | KC-135Q | 9 SRW |
| 91471 | KC-135Q | 9 SRW |
| 91472 | KC-135R | 416 BW |
| 91473 | KC-135E | 191 ARS* |
| 91474 | KC-135Q | 9 SRW |
| 91475 | KC-135A | 42 BW |
| 91476 | KC-135R | 19 ARW |
| 91477 | KC-135E | 72 ARS† |
| 91478 | KC-135R | 19 ARW |
| 91479 | KC-135E | 126 ARS* |
| 91480 | KC-135Q | 9 SRW |
| 91482 | KC-135R | 384 BW |
| 91483 | KC-135A | 7 BW |
| 91484 | KC-135E | 147 ARS* |
| 91485 | KC-135E | 150 ARS* |
| 91486 | KC-135A | 319 BW |
| 91487 | KC-135E | 108 ARS* |
| 91488 | KC-135A | 380 BW |
| 91489 | KC-135E | 191 ARS* |
| 91490 | KC-135Q | 9 SRW |
| 91492 | KC-135R | |
| 91493 | KC-135E | 132 ARS* |
| 91495 | KC-135R | 19 ARW |
| 91496 | KC-135A | 7 BW |
| 91497 | KC-135E | 150 ARS* |
| 91498 | KC-135R | 28 BW |
| 91499 | KC-135E | 133 ARS* |
| 91500 | KC-135A | 42 BW |
| 91501 | KC-135A | 379 BW |
| 91502 | KC-135A | 96 BW |
| 91503 | KC-135E | 126 ARS* |
| 91504 | KC-135Q | 9 SRW |
| 91505 | KC-135E | 133 ARS* |
| 91506 | KC-135E | 147 ARS* |
| 91507 | KC-135R | 28 BW |
| 91508 | KC-135A | 410 BW |
| 91509 | KC-135E | 133 ARS* |
| 91510 | KC-135Q | 380 BW |
| 91511 | KC-135R | 19 ARW |
| 91512 | KC-135Q | 9 SRW |
| 91513 | KC-135Q | 9 SRW |
| 91514 | KC-135E | 55 SRW |
| 91515 | KC-135R | 384 BW |
| 91516 | KC-135E | 117 ARS* |
| 91517 | KC-135R | 28 BW |
| 91518 | EC-135K | 8 TDCS |
| 91519 | KC-135E | 126 ARS* |
| 91520 | KC-135Q | 9 SRW |
| 91521 | KC-135R | 384 BW |
| 91522 | KC-135A | 93 BW |
| 91523 | KC-135Q | 9 SRW |

**Lockheed C-141B Starlifter**
(*ANG, Air National Guard
†AFRES, Air Force Reserve)
60 MAW: Travis AFB, California
62 MAW: McChord AFB, Washington
63 MAW: Norton AFB, California
183 MAS, 172 MAG*: Jackson Field AFB, Mississippi
437 MAW: Charleston AFB, S Carolina
438 MAW: McGuire AFB, New Jersey
443 MAW: Altus AFB, Oklahoma
756 MAS, 459 MAW†: Andrews AFB, Maryland

| Serial | Type | Wing |
|---|---|---|
| *FY61* | | |
| 12778 | | 438 MAW |
| *FY63* | | |
| 38075 | | 60 MAW |
| 38076 | | 438 MAW |
| 38078 | | 437 MAW |
| 38079 | | 437 MAW |
| 38080 | | 438 MAW |
| 38081 | | 62 MAW |
| 38082 | | 62 MAW |
| 38083 | | 438 MAW |
| 38084 | | 63 MAW |
| 38085 | | 63 MAW |
| 38086 | | 62 MAW |
| 38087 | | 63 MAW |
| 38088 | | 60 MAW |
| 38089 | | 63 MAW |
| 38090 | | 438 MAW |
| *FY64* | | |
| 40609 | | 62 MAW |
| 40610 | | 437 MAW |
| 40611 | | 437 MAW |
| 40612 | | 437 MAW |
| 40613 | | 437 MAW |
| 40614 | | 172 MAG* |
| 40615 | | 437 MAW |
| 40616 | | 438 MAW |
| 40617 | | 63 MAW |
| 40618 | | 437 MAW |
| 40619 | | 437 MAW |
| 40620 | | 459 MAW† |
| 40621 | | 438 MAW |
| 40622 | | 172 MAG* |
| 40623 | | 438 MAW |
| 40625 | | 438 MAW |
| 40626 | | 438 MAW |
| 40627 | | 438 MAW |
| 40628 | | 438 MAW |
| 40629 | | 437 MAW |
| 40630 | | 437 MAW |
| 40631 | | 437 MAW |
| 40632 | | 172 MAG* |
| 40633 | | 438 MAW |
| 40634 | | 443 MAW |
| 40635 | | 62 MAW |
| 40636 | | 63 MAW |
| 40637 | | 459 MAW† |
| 40638 | | 438 MAW |
| 40639 | | 438 MAW |
| 40640 | | 172 MAG* |
| 40642 | | 443 MAW |
| 40643 | | 60 MAW |
| 40644 | | 437 MAW |
| 40645 | | 459 MAW† |
| 40646 | | 437 MAW |
| 40648 | | 60 MAW |
| 40649 | | 437 MAW |
| 40650 | | 438 MAW |
| 40651 | | 437 MAW |
| 40653 | | 63 MAW |
| *FY65* | | |
| 50216 | | 459 MAW† |
| 50217 | | 437 MAW |
| 50218 | | 437 MAW |
| 50219 | | 60 MAW |
| 50220 | | 437 MAW |
| 50221 | | 438 MAW |

## USAF (US based)

| Serial | Wing |
|---|---|
| 50222 | 438 MAW |
| 50223 | 438 MAW |
| 50224 | 438 MAW |
| 50225 | 63 MAW |
| 50226 | 459 MAW† |
| 50227 | 62 MAW |
| 50228 | 62 MAW |
| 50229 | 62 MAW |
| 50230 | 60 MAW |
| 50231 | 60 MAW |
| 50232 | 443 MAW |
| 50233 | 60 MAW |
| 50234 | 60 MAW |
| 50235 | 62 MAW |
| 50236 | 438 MAW |
| 50237 | 62 MAW |
| 50238 | 60 MAW |
| 50239 | 60 MAW |
| 50240 | 62 MAW |
| 50241 | 62 MAW |
| 50242 | 60 MAW |
| 50243 | 62 MAW |
| 50244 | 62 MAW |
| 50245 | 60 MAW |
| 50246 | 60 MAW |
| 50247 | 60 MAW |
| 50248 | 62 MAW |
| 50249 | 60 MAW |
| 50250 | 60 MAW |
| 50251 | 62 MAW |
| 50252 | 60 MAW |
| 50253 | 62 MAW |
| 50254 | 60 MAW |
| 50255 | 62 MAW |
| 50256 | 60 MAW |
| 50257 | 60 MAW |
| 50258 | 62 MAW |
| 50259 | 62 MAW |
| 50260 | 60 MAW |
| 50261 | 438 MAW |
| 50262 | 63 MAW |
| 50263 | 62 MAW |
| 50264 | 62 MAW |
| 50265 | 60 MAW |
| 50266 | 437 MAW |
| 50267 | 437 MAW |
| 50268 | 60 MAW |
| 50269 | 437 MAW |
| 50270 | 437 MAW |
| 50271 | 459 MAW† |
| 50272 | 437 MAW |
| 50273 | 437 MAW |
| 50275 | 437 MAW |
| 50276 | 437 MAW |
| 50277 | 63 MAW |
| 50278 | 443 MAW |
| 50279 | 437 MAW |
| 50280 | 438 MAW |
| | |
| 59397 | 438 MAW |
| 59398 | 63 MAW |
| 59399 | 62 MAW |
| 59400 | 443 MAW |
| 59401 | 437 MAW |
| 59402 | 443 MAW |
| 59403 | 60 MAW |
| 59404 | 63 MAW |
| 59405 | 438 MAW |
| 59406 | 63 MAW |
| 59408 | 437 MAW |
| 59409 | 438 MAW |
| 59410 | 443 MAW |
| 59411 | 438 MAW |
| 59412 | 438 MAW |
| 59413 | 438 MAW |
| 59414 | 63 MAW |
| *FY66* | |
| 60126 | 438 MAW |
| 60128 | 63 MAW |
| 60129 | 62 MAW |
| 60130 | 172 MAG* |
| 60131 | 437 MAW |
| 60132 | 438 MAW |
| 60133 | 438 MAW |
| 60134 | 63 MAW |
| 60135 | 437 MAW |
| 60136 | 63 MAW |
| 60137 | 63 MAW |
| 60138 | 63 MAW |
| 60139 | 63 MAW |
| 60140 | 438 MAW |
| 60141 | 62 MAW |
| 60142 | 62 MAW |
| 60143 | 443 MAW |
| 60144 | 437 MAW |
| 60145 | 62 MAW |
| 60146 | 443 MAW |
| 60147 | 60 MAW |
| 60148 | 60 MAW |
| 60149 | 437 MAW |
| 60151 | 60 MAW |
| 60152 | 437 MAW |
| 60153 | 459 MAW† |
| 60154 | 443 MAW |
| 60155 | 438 MAW |
| 60156 | 63 MAW |
| 60157 | 438 MAW |
| 60158 | 62 MAW |
| 60159 | 62 MAW |
| 60160 | 437 MAW |
| 60161 | 62 MAW |
| 60162 | 438 MAW |
| 60163 | 437 MAW |
| 60164 | 172 MAG* |
| 60165 | 62 MAW |
| 60166 | 438 MAW |
| 60167 | 437 MAW |
| 60168 | 437 MAW |
| 60169 | 438 MAW |
| 60170 | 62 MAW |
| 60171 | 63 MAW |
| 60172 | 63 MAW |
| 60173 | 438 MAW |
| 60174 | 459 MAW† |
| 60175 | 63 MAW |
| 60176 | 443 MAW |
| 60177 | 63 MAW |
| 60178 | 437 MAW |
| 60179 | 63 MAW |
| 60180 | 443 MAW |
| 60181 | 63 MAW |
| 60182 | 63 MAW |
| 60183 | 438 MAW |
| 60184 | 63 MAW |
| 60185 | 172 MAG* |
| 60186 | 443 MAW (VIP) |
| 60187 | 437 MAW |
| 60188 | 60 MAW |
| 60189 | 60 MAW |
| 60190 | 172 MAG* |
| 60191 | 60 MAW |
| 60192 | 62 MAW |
| 60193 | 63 MAW |
| 60194 | 437 MAW |
| 60195 | 437 MAW |
| 60196 | 437 MAW |
| 60197 | 62 MAW |
| 60198 | 63 MAW |
| 60199 | 438 MAW |
| 60200 | 63 MAW |
| 60201 | 63 MAW |
| 60202 | 437 MAW |
| 60203 | 443 MAW |
| 60204 | 438 MAW |
| 60205 | 63 MAW |
| 60206 | 62 MAW |
| 60207 | 438 MAW |
| 60208 | 63 MAW |
| 60209 | 437 MAW |
| | |
| 67944 | 60 MAW |
| 67945 | 437 MAW |
| 67946 | 63 MAW |
| 67947 | 437 MAW (70947) |
| 67948 | 438 MAW |
| 67949 | 63 MAW |
| 67950 | 438 MAW |
| 67951 | 62 MAW |
| 67952 | 63 MAW |
| 67953 | 438 MAW |
| 67954 | 438 MAW |
| 67955 | 437 MAW |
| 67956 | 437 MAW |
| 67957 | 63 MAW |
| 67958 | 63 MAW |
| 67959 | 63 MAW |
| *FY67* | |
| 70001 | 63 MAW |
| 70002 | 437 MAW |
| 70003 | 62 MAW |
| 70004 | 437 MAW |
| 70005 | 63 MAW |
| 70007 | 438 MAW |
| 70009 | 60 MAW |
| 70010 | 437 MAW |
| 70011 | 437 MAW |
| 70012 | 437 MAW |
| 70013 | 438 MAW |
| 70014 | 437 MAW |
| 70015 | 63 MAW |
| 70016 | 437 MAW |
| 70018 | 62 MAW |
| 70019 | 438 MAW |
| 70020 | 438 MAW |
| 70021 | 438 MAW |
| 70022 | 63 MAW |
| 70023 | 63 MAW |
| 70024 | 438 MAW |
| 70025 | 437 MAW |
| 70026 | 437 MAW |
| 70027 | 438 MAW |
| 70028 | 63 MAW |
| 70029 | 63 MAW |
| 70031 | 60 MAW |
| 70164 | 60 MAW |
| 70165 | 438 MAW |
| 70166 | 443 MAW (VIP) |

# US based USN/USMC Aircraft

**McDonnell Douglas**
**C-9B Skytrain II**
VR-46, Atlanta, Georgia;
VR-51, Glenview NAS, Illinois;
VR-52, Willow Grove NAS, Pennsylvania;
VR-55, Alameda NAS, California;
VR-56, Norfolk NAS, Virginia;
VR-57, North Island NAS, California;
VR-58, Jacksonville NAS, Florida;
VR-59, Dallas, Texas;
VR-60, Memphis NAS, Tennessee;
VR-61, Whidbey Island NAS, Washington;
VR-62, Detroit, Michigan;
SOES, Cherry Point MCAS, North Carolina

| | |
|---|---|
| 159113 [RU] | VR-55 |
| 159114 [RX] | VR-57 |
| 159115 [RX] | VR-57 |
| 159116 [RX] | VR-57 |
| 159117 [JU] | VR-56 |
| 159118 [JU] | VR-56 |
| 159119 [JU] | VR-56 |
| 159120 [RU] | VR-55 |
| 160046 | SOES |
| 160047 | SOES |
| 160048 [JV] | VR-58 |
| 160049 [JV] | VR-58 |
| 160050 [JV] | VR-58 |
| 160051 [RV] | VR-51 |
| 161266 [RY] | VR-59 |
| 161529 [RY] | VR-59 |
| 161530 [RY] | VR-59 |
| 162390 [RT] | VR-60 |
| 162391 [RT] | VR-60 |
| 162392 [RS] | VR-61 |
| 162393 [RS] | VR-61 |
| 162753 [RV] | VR-51 |
| 162754 [RV] | VR-51 |
| 163036 [JT] | VR-52 |
| 163037 [JT] | VR-52 |
| 163208 [JS] | VR-46 |
| 163511 [JW] | VR-62 |
| 163512 [JS] | VR-46 |
| 163513 [JW] | VR-62 |
| 164605 [RT] | VR-60 |
| 164606 [RT] | VR-60 |
| 164607 [RS] | VR-61 |

**Lockheed C-130 Hercules**
VRC-50 North Island NAS, California
VMGR-152 Futenma MCAS, Japan
VMGR-234 Glenview NAS, Illinois
VMGR-252 Cherry Point MCAS, North Carolina
VMGRT-253 Cherry Point MCAS, North Carolina
VMGR-352 El Toro MCAS, California
VMGR-452 Stewart Field, New York

| | | |
|---|---|---|
| 147572 | KC-130F | [QB] VMGR-352 |
| 147573 | KC-130F | [QD] VMGR-152 |
| 148246 | KC-130F | [GR] VMGRT-253 |
| 148247 | KC-130F | [QD] VMGR-152 |
| 148248 | KC-130F | [QD] VMGR-152 |
| 148249 | KC-130F | [GR] VMGRT-253 |
| 148890 | KC-130F | [QB] VMGR-352 |
| 148891 | KC-130F | [BH] VMGR-252 |
| 148893 | KC-130F | Blue Angels |
| 148894 | KC-130F | [GR] VMGRT-253 |
| 148896 | KC-130F | [BH] VMGR-252 |
| 148897 | KC-130F | [BH] VMGR-252 |
| 148898 | KC-130F | [BH] VMGR-252 |
| 148899 | KC-130F | [BH] VMGR-252 |
| 149787 | C-130F | [RG] VRC-50 |
| 149788 | KC-130F | [BH] VMGR-252 |
| 149789 | KC-130F | [BH] VMGR-252 |
| 149791 | KC-130F | |
| 149792 | KC-130F | [QB] VMGR-352 |
| 149793 | C-130F | [RG] VRC-50 |
| 149795 | KC-130F | [BH] VMGR-252 |
| 149796 | KC-130F | [QD] VMGR-152 |
| 149798 | KC-130F | [QD] VMGR-152 |
| 149799 | KC-130F | [BH] VMGR-252 |
| 149800 | KC-130F | [QB] VMGR-352 |
| 149803 | KC-130F | [GR] VMGRT-253 |
| 149804 | KC-130F | [GR] VMGRT-253 |
| 149805 | C-130F | [RG] VRC-50 |
| 149806 | KC-130F | NS Adak |
| 149807 | KC-130F | [QD] VMGR-152 |
| 149808 | KC-130F | [GR] VMGRT-253 |
| 149811 | KC-130F | [GR] VMGRT-253 |
| 149812 | KC-130F | [QD] VMGR-152 |
| 149815 | KC-130F | [BH] VMGR-252 |
| 149816 | KC-130F | [QB] VMGR-352 |
| 150684 | KC-130F | [GR] VMGRT-253 |
| 150686 | KC-130F | [BH] VMGR-252 |
| 150688 | KC-130F | [GR] VMGRT-253 |
| 150689 | KC-130F | [QB] VMGR-352 |
| 150690 | KC-130F | [QB] VMGR-352 |
| 151891 | TC-130G | |
| 160013 | KC-130R | [QB] VMGR-352 |
| 160014 | KC-130R | [QB] VMGR-352 |
| 160015 | KC-130R | [QB] VMGR-352 |
| 160016 | KC-130R | [QB] VMGR-352 |
| 160017 | KC-130R | [QB] VMGR-352 |
| 160018 | KC-130R | [QB] VMGR-352 |
| 160019 | KC-130R | [QB] VMGR-352 |
| 160020 | KC-130R | [QB] VMGR-352 |
| 160021 | KC-130R | [QB] VMGR-352 |
| 160022 | KC-130R | [QB] VMGR-352 |
| 160240 | KC-130R | [QB] VMGR-352 |
| 160625 | KC-130R | [BH] VMGR-252 |
| 160626 | KC-130R | [BH] VMGR-252 |
| 160627 | KC-130R | [BH] VMGR-252 |
| 160628 | KC-130R | [BH] VMGR-252 |
| 162308 | KC-130T | [QH] VMGR-234 |
| 162309 | KC-130T | [QH] VMGR-234 |
| 162310 | KC-130T | [QH] VMGR-234 |
| 162311 | KC-130T | [QH] VMGR-234 |
| 162785 | KC-130T | [QH] VMGR-234 |
| 162786 | KC-130T | [QH] VMGR-234 |
| 163022 | KC-130T | [QH] VMGR-234 |
| 163023 | KC-130T | [QH] VMGR-234 |
| 163310 | KC-130T | [NY] VMGR-452 |
| 163311 | KC-130T | [NY] VMGR-452 |
| 163591 | KC-130T | [NY] VMGR-452 |
| 163592 | KC-130T | [NY] VMGR-452 |
| 164105 | KC-130T | [NY] VMGR-452 |
| 164106 | KC-130T | [NY] VMGR-452 |
| 164180 | KC-130T | [QH] VMGR-234 |
| 164181 | KC-130T | [QH] VMGR-234 |
| 164441 | KC-130T | [NY] VMGR-452 |
| 164442 | KC-130T | [NY] VMGR-452 |

# Addendum

| Serial | Type (code/other identity) | Owner/Operator, Location or Fate | Notes |
|---|---|---|---|
| WT745 | Hawker Hunter T8C | Jet Heritage, Bournemouth | |
| XH328 | DH Vampire T11 | Jet Heritage, Bournemouth | |
| XM349 | Hunting Jet Provost T3A [T] | RAF No 2 SoTT, Cosford | |
| XM403 | Hunting Jet Provost T3A [V] | RAF No 2 SoTT, Cosford | |
| XP283 | Auster AOP9 | Privately owned, Lichfield | |
| XP532 | HS Gnat T1 | Privately owned, Colchester | |
| XV752 | HS Harrier GR3 [S] | RAF No 2 SoTT, Cosford | |
| XZ234 | WS Lynx HAS3 [412/CW] | RN No 829 Sqn, Portland | |
| XZ495 | BAe Sea Harrier FRS1 [129/N] | RN No 800 Sqn, Yeovilton | |
| XZ612 | WS Lynx HAS7 [Z] | RM3 CBAS, Yeovilton | |
| ZA392 | Panavia Tornado GR1 [EK] | *Crashed Iraq 18 Jan 1991* | |
| ZA403 | Panavia Tornado GR1 [CO] | RAF BFME, Gulf | |
| ZA446 | Panavia Tornado GR1 {EF] | RAF BFME, Gulf | |
| ZA456 | Panavia Tornado GR1 [GB] | RAF BFME, Gulf | |
| ZA475 | Panavia Tornado GR1 [FC] | RAF BFME, Gulf | |
| ZA491 | Panavia Tornado GR1 [GC] | RAF BFME, Gulf | |
| ZB648 | WS Gazelle HT2 [40/CU] | RN No 705 Sqn, Culdrose | |
| ZD375 | BAe Harrier GR5 [AO] | RAF No 3 Sqn Gutersloh | |
| ZD579 | BAe Sea Harrier FRS1 [124/N] | RN No 800 Sqn, Yeovilton | |
| ZD611 | BAe Sea Harrier FRS1 [123/N] | RN No 800 Sqn, Yeovilton | |
| ZD718 | Panavia Tornado GR1 [BH] | *Crashed Saudi Arabia 13 Jan 91* | |
| ZD791 | Panavia Tornado GR1 [BG] | *Crashed Iraq 17 Jan 91* | |
| ZD809 | Panavia Tornado GR1 [BA] | RAF BFME, Gulf | |
| ZD845 | Panavia Tornado GR1 [AF] | RAF BFME, Gulf | |
| ZD847 | Panavia Tornado GR1 [CH] | RAF BFME, Gulf | |
| ZD892 | Panavia Tornado GR1 [BJ] | RAF BFME, Gulf | |
| ZD893 | Panavia Tornado GR1 [AG] | *Crashed nr Tabuk 20 Jan 91* | |
| ZD951 | Lockheed TriStar KC1 | RAF No 216 Sqn, Bahrain | |
| ZE158 | Panavia Tornado F3 | RAF BFME, Dhahran | |
| ZE908 | Panavia Tornado F3 | RAF BFME, Dhahran | |
| ZF265 | Shorts Tucano T1 | RAF CFS, Scampton | |
| ZF266 | Shorts Tucano T1 | RAF CFS, Scampton | |
| ZF267 | Shorts Tucano T1 | RAF No 3 FTS, Cranwell | |
| ZF562 | WS Lynx HAS3CTS [345/NC] | RN No 815 Sqn, Portland | |
| ZG727 | Panavia Tornado GR1A | RAF No 13 Sqn, Honington | |
| ZH221 | WS Lynx Mk 99 | *To 90-0703 Korean Navy* | |
| ZH222 | WS Lynx Mk 99 | *To 90-0705 Korean Navy* | |
| ZH223 | WS Lynx Mk 99 | *To 90-0706 Korean Navy* | |
| ZH506 | Shorts Tucano T52 | *For Kuwait AF* | |
| ZH507 | Shorts Tucano T52 | *For Kuwait AF* | |
| ZH508 | Shorts Tucano T52 | *For Kuwait AF* | |
| ZH509 | Shorts Tucano T52 | *For Kuwait AF* | |